Rozet, Campbell County, Wyoming

and its

Homestead Families

(1880 – 1949)

by
Lorna J. Whisler
Natural Bridge, Virginia
2022

by
Lorna J, Whisler
Natural Bridge, Virginia
and
Edited by Theresa M. Flaherty
Corpus Christi, Texas

Cover photo: The home of Carroll D. 'Slim' Whisler family in 1935,
formerly the homestead of David Riley Whisler (1883-1926)
along the Adon Road seven miles north of Rozet.

Cover and print book interior design
by Theresa Marie Flaherty

Turas Publishing
4833 Saratoga Blvd., No. 129
Corpus Christi, TX 78413

www.TurasPublishing.com

ISBN: 978-0-9982215-7-1

TURAS
PUBLISHING

A brief history of Rozet, Wyoming
along with a few histories and genealogies
for some of the families
who lived along the CB&Q Railroad tracks,
north along the Cottonwood Valley to Adon,
northeast along the Little Pine Ridge to the Crook County Line,
and south to the Belle Fourche River.

"Here in these Wyoming counties (Crook, Weston, Campbell) are the once vaunted hunting and battle grounds of the Indians. As you drive through them, or fly over them, your imagination is stimulated to a point where you can see the smoke curling from the teepee tops and council fires, and hear the music of the drums and the chants of the dancers.
Can you distinguish if they are dancing for war, peace, or thanksgiving?"

(Only a Cow Country, by Dick Nelson, copyright 1951 by Mae M. Nelson)

In memory of my grandparents
Frank Herman and Laura Margarete (Young) Heptner
and
David "Riley" and Pearl "Vida" (Duvall) Whisler

Lorna J. Whisler

DEDICATED
TO OUR ANCESTORS

Our parents, grandparents, or great grandparents came to the Rozet area with their children and friends seeking a better life. Why they left their former homes to move to the Rozet area we can only speculate or rely on our own personal family histories. They came seeking new opportunities to provide a better life for themselves and their children. They worked hard in a harsh environment. Some succeeded and some failed. But those who stayed created a community that reached north to Cottonwood Creek (Adon), northeast to Little Pine Ridge (Little Iowa), south to the Belle Fouche River (Dillinger) and southwest to Timber Creek. These communities still exist to some extent today in the year 2022.

Note to Reader:

To provide updated information or additions to the material in this edition, please contact the author at ldoone@ntelos.net, the publisher at Turas.Pub@gmail.com, or the Campbell County Historical Society (Mary Kelley) @ marykelley@vcn.com.

TABLE OF CONTENTS

Alphabetical List of Family Histories

List of Illustrations

[NOTE: Photographs of families found elsewhere throughout this book are from the personal collections of my father Carroll D. "Slim" Whisler, my mother Irene Heptner Whisler, and her two younger sisters Leona and Jeanette Heptner. Other photographs were furnished by individuals who graciously sent me photos of their families who lived in the Rozet area. Other family photographs were copied (with permission) from *Campbell County, The Treasured Years* compiled in 1990 by the Campbell County Historical Society, Gillette, Wyoming. Additional family photographs were found on the internet, generally on the Ancestry.com U.S. Find A Grave website and a few selected family trees. Photographs of rural schools, Rozet Consolidated and High School are from the collections of Irene Heptner Whisler and Leona and Jeanette Heptner.]

PREFACE

The stories my mother and father, my aunts, and uncles told while I was growing up (seven miles north of Rozet along the Adon Road) and later as an adult fostered the idea of capturing as much as possible about the Rozet area and the families who lived north and south of Rozet into this book. They lived in extraordinary times, one that none of us, their children and grandchildren, will ever appreciate wholly. We are too busy living our own lives. The title of Tom Brokow's book, *The Greatest Generation,* says it all, in my opinion. I badgered them for information about their neighbors and for answers to questions such as how did they keep meat from spoiling, what games did they play as children and as adults, where did they go to school and who were their teachers, what did they do on rainy or snowy days to occupy themselves without television, video movies or video games, the internet, etc.

The Rozet community during this time was a rebellious community in many ways. Although fiercely independent and self-reliant, at the same time these people were keenly interested in doing what they thought was right for their children and their neighbors. They were hardworking, fun loving, and serious about taking care of their families and friends through the tough times and the good times. They lived through World War I, 1917-1919, the crash of 1929, the depression years in the 1930s, World War II in the early 1940s, droughts, hard winters, grasshoppers, and family tragedies. These communities have changed little from what they were during the first half of the twentieth century. Today, among the people now living in these communities, a few are descendants of those early home-steaders. They look forward into the twenty-first century with the same sense of fierce independence and expectation as their ancestors.

INTRODUCTION

In the 1700s the Staitan Indians occupied the northeastern portion of Wyoming. They were allies and forerunners of the Cheyenne. The Cheyenne were firmly established in the plains area between the Black Hills and the Big Horn Mountains when the Sioux began to make their appearance. The Sioux were poor and carried their possessions on dog driven travois. The Cheyenne took pity on them and treated them kindly. Their gifts of horses and other valuables encouraged more Sioux to come to the region. In time, the Sioux became the most powerful of the plain's tribes and the most difficult to conquer. By 1851 they had pushed the Crow northward to Montana, the Cheyenne and Arapahoe southward to southern Wyoming and northern Colorado, and the Shoshone to southwest Wyoming. In the days that the large ranchers were first establishing themselves, Indian hostilities kept them from spreading over the entire state until the end of the Indian wars. When cattle were first introduced into southeastern Wyoming, the territory north of the Platte was considered Indian country. In 1850, the area between the Belle Fourche and Little Powder Rivers in Crook County was still primarily an Indian hunting ground. After the Battle of the Little Big Horn in June 1876 it became a place where few Indians were seen. Although Indians did not heavily populate the area of Crook County, considerable evidence of their presence can still be found scattered throughout Crook County including townships 47 to 53 North, and ranges 70 and 69 West now a part of Campbell County, Wyoming.

This area was first claimed by the Spanish Conquistadors and later by the French. The area became a part of the Louisiana Purchase in 1803. The Louisiana Purchase remained unorganized until it was divided into the Nebraska and Kansas Territories under the Nebraska-Kansas Act of 1854. That was only the beginning. Eventually, these townships would fall within the Idaho, Nebraska, Dakota, and Wyoming Territories before becoming a part of the State of Wyoming in 1890. In 1854, Nebraska Territory included the present states of Idaho, Montana, North and South Dakota, Nebraska, and Wyoming. In 1861 when the Nebraska Territory was divided the northern part of Wyoming, all of Montana, and North and South Dakota became Dakota Territory and the southern part of Wyoming remained in Nebraska Territory. Also, in 1861 Wyoming's southern boundary was established with the creation of Colorado Territory. When Idaho Territory was created in 1863, it established Wyoming's present eastern boundary as it included all the present state of Wyoming except for a small portion in the southwest corner belonging to the Utah Territory. The creation of Montana Territory in 1864 established Wyoming's northern border. All of Wyoming, except for the southwest corner, became the southwestern portion of Dakota Territory. The Dakota Territorial Legislature met in Yankton, Dakota Territory, in January 1867 and approved the creation of a Dakota Territory county, Laramie County, with Fort Sanders named as its county seat. In December of that year they created a second county, Carter County, with South Pass City as its county seat. The two counties split the southwest Dakota Territory in half—Laramie County on the east and Carter County on the west. In 1868 the Dakota legislature in Yankton, Dakota Territory, moved the county seat of Laramie County from Fort Sanders to Cheyenne, which was incorporated in 1867. They also established two more counties, Albany County, with Laramie City as its county seat, and Carbon County, with Rawlins as its County Seat. This would be the last legislation the Dakota Territory legislature would enact for what would soon become the new Wyoming Territory.

Congress had begun the process of proposing the creation of the Wyoming Territory in 1865. After many discussions, they straightened the southern boundary line to include the southwestern corner previously held by Utah, and they agreed upon the name of Wyoming, which means "Great Plains." Congress created Wyoming Territory effective July 25, 1868, after holding special elections to elect a delegate to send to Congress and state representatives to their first territorial legislative assembly in September 1869. That first assembly passed the Woman's Suffrage Act on December 10, 1869, a date now celebrated as "Wyoming Day." Wyoming remained a territory until July 10, 1890, when President Harrison signed the Wyoming statehood bill, No. 2445, passed by the Fifty-first Congress of the United States after a bitter fight in the House and in the Senate.

In 1869 Crook, Campbell, and Weston Counties were in northern Albany and Laramie counties, in Wyoming Territory. In 1875 Crook and Pease Counties were created. Crook County included present day Campbell, Crook, and Weston Counties. Pease County included present day Sheridan, Johnson, and the eastern portions of Big Horn and Washakie counties. Pease County was renamed as Johnson County in 1879. Converse, Natrona, Sheridan, Big Horn, and Weston Counties were created in 1888. Campbell County was created in 1911 from the western halves of Crook and Weston Counties.

The first cattle drive was led by Nelson Story about 1866 through that area of Crook County that later would become Campbell County. The period between 1869 and 1890 was Wyoming's most colorful period of the open range—a public domain. By 1870 the owners, mostly foreign capital investors, bought cattle in Texas and trailed them north on the Chisholm trail, also called the "Texas Trail," to the open range, north of the Platte River, some as far as northeastern Wyoming. Soon these enterprising owners learned that the Wyoming plains were ideal for year-round grazing. Cattle companies were incorporated, and they turned their cattle loose to range on the tall, sweet, grass and soon built a new economic society. By the late 1870s cattle were pouring into Wyoming from every direction. The Wyoming Stock Growers Association, created in 1873, controlled the general roundups in the state from 1874 to 1884. They established laws that mostly benefited the cattlemen. At that time, no ranchers living in the western portion of Crook County belonged to the Association. Most of the cattle ranging on the tall prairie grass in the territory of the future Campbell County belonged to ranches located outside, or in other parts, of Wyoming territory.

Blizzard of 1886, *Harper's Weekly,* **Feb. 27, 1886**

By 1886 the cattle business was already showing the effects of rustling, over-stocking of the range, and fencing of water holes by homesteaders. But it was a series of bad winters that eventually drove the cattle from the open range. Previously, weather in Wyoming, despite occasional hard winters, windstorms, and blizzards, had been good to the open range ranchers. Grass grew fast and luxuriantly. Winters were mild; the cattle could forage and live through the winter. A series of bad winters from 1886 to 1889 made everyone realize that changes in the cattle business were coming. It was the winter of 1886-1887 that caused the most drastic damages. Fences were leveled, stages and trains were stalled, yet ranchers continued to believe that they would sustain no more than five per cent in losses. They were unable to determine their losses until the June and July roundups were completed. Their losses were heavier than they had hoped, but they still believed they would recoup those losses the following year. However, the next two winters in 1888 and 1889 were just as severe and harsh. Losses of those three winters ranged from thirty to ninety per cent of the stock depending upon location of the herd. The blow to the ranchers was staggering—they had continued to estimate that their losses, including rustling, would be no more than five per cent. The ranches suffering the greatest losses were in northern Wyoming. After the bad winters, many of the absentee owners of companies from the eastern United States and Europe struggled to survive, but finally were forced out of the business mostly because of heavy financial losses.

While rustlers, bad management of the open range, inaccurate cattle tallies, and severe winters were forcing the cattle from the open range; the sheep industry was steadily growing. The cattlemen fought the advance of sheep, posting lines beyond which sheep might not pass. By 1885, as the cattle kingdom reached its height, the price of wool began to increase. The winters of 1886 and 1887 did not cause as heavy losses to sheep as they did to cattle because sheep were more carefully watched and not put out upon the open range to forage for themselves. As Wyoming became a state in 1890, the cattle kingdom was making a final struggle for supremacy against rustling, sheep raising, and homesteading. Times were changing.

2

By 1890, when Wyoming became a state, several forces combined to end the open range and drive cattle from the public domain to fenced-in ranches. Families and individuals were steadily arriving and filing on homesteads near springs or rivers. They fenced the water holes and cultivated the land. Because of these actions the homesteaders were soon called "nesters" because they nested in choice locations. They were not popular with the cattlemen. However, the homestead population increased faster than the ranchers, and soon they represented the power at elections. Also, the open range policy invited rustling. For months at a time cattle foraged for themselves. Often, they were sold on book tally. Rival companies overstocked the range, and some owners instructed their cowboys to place the outfit brand on all mavericks. Many cowboys, seeing their owners' negligence, became rustlers. The Homestead Act served as a screen, for a rustler could file on a homestead and soon have a good herd of beef cattle.

Schoolteachers, mostly women, but also a few men, contributed to the growth of Campbell County. Women who became teachers were of varied backgrounds. Many came to the west from the east. Others became a teacher upon the death of a husband or a father. The atmosphere of the times provided these teachers with limited "suitable" employment and a much more desired occupation when compared to cooking, washing, or clerking. Homesteading was open to women, and many of the teachers were homesteaders needing extra funds that teaching could not provide. Teaching also gave the woman independence and a higher status than other "proper" jobs for women at that time. The impact of teachers crossed over into the tolerance of suffrage for women in Wyoming and soon resulted in greater rights for women and increased female participation in the jury and election process. Schools themselves offered a broad appeal to the growing pioneer community. They were the central producer of community education, culture, and identity. Through the schools the children became indoctrinated in the culture and were given goals to improve themselves and the future generations. Western society depended on these single and often very young women to overcome all their difficulties and teach the youth how to overcome theirs. The contribution they made is readily evident in the advances that education has provided our western society.

Cottonwood School – about 1918
in the Little Iowa Community
(From the collections of Irene Heptner Whisler)

Sources:
Wyoming Frontier State by Velma Linford, 1947, The Old West Publishing Co, Denver, CO,
Wyoming Pageant, by Virginia Cole Trenholm and Maurine Carley, Prairie Publishing Company, Casper, Wyoming, 1946.
History of Campbell County, by the 1954 Campbell County High School Senior English Class.
Atlas of Westward Expansion, by Alan Wexler and Molly Braun, copyright by Alan Wexler, 1995.
Wyoming's Teachers, by S. Houston, Cultural Resource Specialist, Wyoming State Archives (1997-1999).
Only a Cow Country, by Dick Nelson, copyright 1951 by Mae M. Nelson.

The Texas Trail

Possible site of the Texas Trail through the Cottonwood Valley

Looking north from the divide on North Heptner Road along the Frank Heptner homestead now owned by Dennis and Jenelle Miller

Looking northeast from the North Heptner Road the Adolph and Evelyn Hamm homestead. Their grandson, Don Hamm, now lives there

Photos on the page taken by Matt Avery in July 2020

The Texas Trail marks an interesting page in American history. The plains Indians held the white man at bay until the buffalo hunters killed off their main source of food. Then the U.S. Government conquered them—men cannot fight on an empty stomach. After the Indian wars were over millions of cattle were driven up this trail from Texas to not only establish cattle ranches in Wyoming, to Canada, but to feed the Indians by replacing the vanished buffalo with cattle. A new civilization was built on these high western plains. One cannot stand at the Texas Trail monument on the Belle Fourche River near Moorcroft, Wyoming, without feeling a spirit of reverence and proud admiration for the courage of those men and their horses who moved cattle along this trail.

TEXAS TRAIL
1866−1897
ALONG THIS TRAIL
PASSED HERDS OF CATTLE
FROM DISTANT TEXAS
TO REPLACE
THE FAST VANISHING BUFFALO
AND BUILD A CIVILIZATION
ON THE NORTH-WESTERN PLAINS

Edward Burnett describes the northeastern Wyoming's route in "Burnett Writes Interesting Story of Early Texas Trail," found in *The News Record,* July 20, 1935, Gillette, Wyoming, "Cattle were moved north on the Texas Trail from Texas to Wyoming, Montana, and into Canada between the late 1860s to the 1890s. Many of the herds were delivered on contract at Ogallala, Nebraska, for shipment east on the railroad. The herds heading further north continued towards Lusk, Wyoming, where they were dispensed to the various Wyoming ranges and eastern Black Hills. Herds heading for northern Wyoming, Montana, and Canada were moved north of Lusk to Rawhide Creek, then down Old Woman Creek to the Cheyenne River and up the river to the mouth of Pole Creek, up Pole Creek to the Belle Fourche divide, down Four Horse Creek to the Belle Fourche River, down the Belle Fourche River to the mouth of Donkey Creek, then the trail bent to the west over to the Little Powder River by way of Trail Creek and Cottonwood Creek and then on down Little Powder River to Powder River. This was the hardest part of the drive on the entire Texas trail—80 miles without water for horses, cattle, and hardly enough in the wagon barrel for the men. Most of movement of the cattle was done at night and was generally done without loss of cattle, but it was hard on horses, cattle, and men.

From Powder River, the herds were moved up on the Mizpah and Pumpkin Creeks divide to the Tongue River at the mouth of Wolf Creek, crossed over the divide and hit the Yellowstone River at Fort Keogh near Miles City, Montana. The herds crossed over at Fort Keogh, but the wagons were driven to Miles City to a ferry. From there the herds headed north to Fort Peck on into Canada."

Trail Creek at the mouth of Donkey Creek and Belle Fourche River, Moorcroft, Wyoming

4

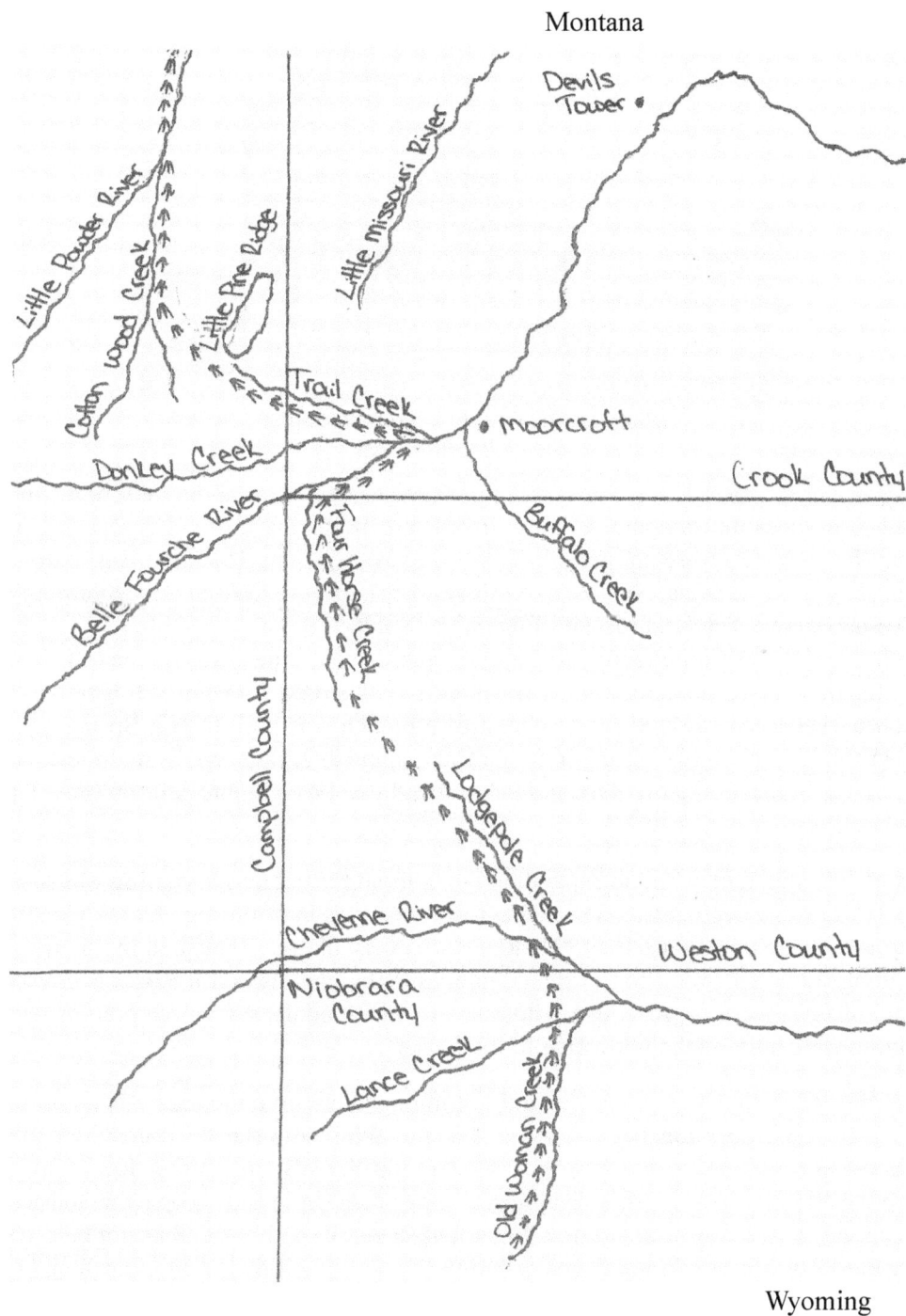

The Texas Trail
As drawn by Matt Avery, Rozet, Wyoming, from the article printed in *The News Record*, July 20, 1935 entitled
"Burnett Writes Interesting Story of Early Texas Trail," by Edward Burnett

[Author's Note: *The Texas Trail commemorative monument with a plaque can be found at the rest stop off of Interstate 90 in Moorcroft Wyoming. The rest stop in 2020 was closed due to budgetary considerations by the Wyoming State Legislature. Hopefully it will be reopened sometime in the future. Photos taken by Matt Avery, July 2020, with permission from the Wyoming State Highway Department.*]

Sources:
"Burnett Writes Interesting Story of Early Texas Trail," by Edward Burnett, <u>The News Record</u>, Gillette, Wyoming, July 20, 1935.

Railroad Station at Moorcroft, Wyoming
Late 1890s

During the 1880s and before, the Kinney Trail from Sundance to Buffalo was the mail route and the main white man's trail through what became Campbell County. In the late 1880s the railroad companies were approaching western Nebraska. The prospects were not good in 1889. However, in June 1889, the Burlington railroad decided to extend the main stem from Alliance, Nebraska, northwest across South Dakota into Wyoming—the reason was coal. Work progressed rapidly. The road reached Edgemont, South Dakota, on October 19, 1889, and Newcastle, Wyoming, a month later. A seven-mile branch to Cambria and its coal mines was opened by December. Then the CB&Q decided to tap the mineral resources of the Black Hills. Construction began at Edgemont in April 1890 and reached Deadwood by February 1891. Shortly afterwards a branch was built to Hot Springs, South Dakota, and another longer one from Englewood to Spearfish, South Dakota, in 1893. Back on the main line, work was resumed at Newcastle, Wyoming, in the spring of 1890, and the railhead was brought into Merino (now Upton), Wyoming, on August 5, 1890.

Because of a tight money situation, work on expanding the railroad further into Wyoming was suspended. Not until the summer of 1891 did work begin again. The CB&Q Railroad was built through Crook County in northeastern Wyoming arriving in Gillette on August 10, 1891. Rozet was very likely established by the railroad as a maintenance stop for loading water and wood for its steam engines. Why they named it Rozet is unknown. It may have been named for the Spanish word for rosette, a wild rose that bloomed nearby on the prairie. A section house and maintenance building were built on the north side of the tracks.

The arrival of the railroad in this high plain area did not immediately give the area a boost in population. There were several large cattle and sheep ranches in the area like the Whitcomb Bar FS Ranch along the Belle Fourche River, the Empire Sheep Company located south of Rozet, and the Wagonhammer Ranch located north to the Powder River. These cattle and sheep ranches continued to move their cattle and sheep either to Moorcroft or Gillette for shipment to markets. A stockyard was eventually built at Rozet. Exactly when has not been determined. There was one in use by the 1920s, but it did not develop into the same capabilities as Moorcroft and Gillette. With the opening of lands under various Homestead Acts, the CB&Q Railroad began advertising throughout the early 1900s in eastern newspapers about the availability of land along its western routes. They soon began creating emigrant trains to ship families, their household goods, farming machinery, and their livestock west to the end of their tracks. Many families who moved into the Rozet area got off the trains in Moorcroft and loaded their families, household goods, and farm machinery into wagons. Then with their livestock tied on behind, or driven alongside their wagons, they made their final trip to the location of their homesteads in the Rozet area and a new life.

Sources:
Burlington Route, A History of the Burlington Lines, by Richard C. Overton, 1965.
Campbell County, The Treasured Years, 1990, compiled by Campbell County Historical Society, Gillette, Wyoming.
History of Campbell County, the Senior English Class – 1954, Campbell County High School, Gillette, Wyoming.
Wyoming Place Names, by Mae Urbanek, 1988.
"First Train Arrived in Gillette 74 Years Ago," *The News Record*, Gillette, Wyoming, August 5, 1965, page 3.

1900

The turn of the century found Rozet in a desolate place alongside the CB&Q railroad with few inhabitants. Teamsters driving wagons from the ranches along the Belle Fourche would pass by on their way to Gillette to deliver wool to the railroad for shipping. Then the wagons would be loaded with supplies for the return trip home. An occasional cowboy or sheepherder would ride past after long hours of work for the established ranches in the area. The area was still considered unsuitable for farming, so it was primarily used for grazing herds of cattle and sheep.

The 1900 U.S Federal Census for Belle Fourche District, Crook County and Weston County, Wyoming, reveals 10 ranch/stockmen who owned their property and 5 who rented still living along the Belle Fourche River.

Owners			Renters		
Elias W. Whitcomb,	68, Mass.	stockman	Fred Newell,	27, Kan.	ranchman
Spencer Smith,	26, Iowa	stockman	Winfrik Marfett (?),	62, Scot	stockman
Swepson Shirley,	37, Geo.	stockman	Edward Jenner (?),	26, Ill.	stockman
Charles Tatom,	33, Miss	stockman	William Clifton,	30, Wisc.	horseman
William Mathews,	42, Texas	stockman	Alexander Milne,	31, Scot	stockman
James Graham,	74, Penn	stockman			
Frank Smith,	49, Sweden	1869, horseman			
Frank Brown,	38, Wisc.	ranchman			
George H. Amos,	42, Wisc.	stockman			
Martin Berlalette,	60, Penn.	stockman			

The following occupations, in addition to stockman, ranchman, horseman, were identified:

Cowboys:	29	Housekeepers:	1
Sheep Herders:	39	Bookkeepers:	2
Sheep Shearers:	5	Servants:	2
Ranch Laborers:	17	Cooks:	4
Foremen:	8	Butcher:	1
Teamster:	1	Iron Moulder:	1
Carpenter:	1	Quartz Miner:	2

Of these there were:

138 Males		9 Women		11 Children	
Married:	27	Married:	8	Sons:	6
Single:	110	Single/Div.:	1	Daughters:	5
Widowed:	1				

Wyoming 1910 Federal Census
Some Individuals and Families Listed

When the 1910 Federal Census was taken for Crook County, the Outside Moorcroft-School District 16, several cattle and sheep ranchers and farmers were recorded. Some of the names of numerous sheepherders, stockmen, and other laborers found living in, north of, and south of Rozet were:

Bennett, James Lee,	age 32	bro-in-law to John Brennan
Sarah	age 24	sister-in-law
James E.	age 3	nephew
Samuel D.	age 1	nephew
Campbell, Bruce M.	age 57	Well Driller – oil wells
Dinsmore, Edwin E.	age 55	farmer – homestead
Dunn, Samuel	age 45	sheepherder
Franhawk(?), Earnest	age 21	farmer – homestead
" Carl B.	age 19	farmer on brother's homestead
Garrett(?), William	age 41	farmer – homestead
Winifred	age 32	wife
Hauber, Frank	age 25	farmer – homestead
Hauber, Edward	age 23	brother

(Sec 19, T49N, R69W; --now Campbell County)

Hazzard, Herman(?) H.	age 29	farmer – homestead
(Haszard?)		

(Sec 18 and 19, T49N, R69W; --now Campbell County)

Jonason, Rasmuss	age 30	farmer – homestead (from Norway)

(Sec 28, 29, 30, T50N, R70W; now Campbell County)

Kummerfeld, Hans	age 31	farmer – stock ranch (from Germany)

(Sec 7, 18, T50N, R68W ---now Crook County)

McKinzie, John P.	age 71	oil inspector – oil wells
Wakeman, Edgar C.	age 57	owner – stock ranch
Francis H.	age 46	wife
Edgar Earl	age 25	son; farmer on homestead
Mulholland, John	age 53	bro-in-law; farmer on desert claim
Whaley, Mrs. C. J(G).	age 53	farmer – homestead
" Chas. A.	age 37	son; farmer – homestead
" Clarence	age 18	son; farmer – homestead

(Sec 29, 32, T50N, R70W; --now Campbell County)

There were sixteen section hands and trackmen working for the railroad listed. They were of various ages and their birth places were Romania, Turkey, or, Armenia.

The American Sheep Company employed about 25 individuals as horsemen, cook, and sheepherders.

The Empire Sheep Company employed about 18 individuals as cook, bookkeeper, carpenter, horse trainer, and sheepherders.

Sheep wagon, Campbell County, Wyoming – 1910
[copied from *wyomingtalesandtrails.com*]

Sources:
Bureau of Land Management, Homestead Patents Index (www.glorecords.blm.gov).
Ancestry.com, 1910 U.S. Federal Census for Outside Moorcroft-School District 16, Crook County Wyoming,
    [database online], Provo, UT.

Homesteaders

Pre-1911

1882 Whitcomb family

1900 Halverson Family
1901 Shaughnessy
Thar Family

1905 Brennan Family
Kessinger, Mary, Mrs.

1907 McClendon, Charles

1908 Jeffers, Floy
George Family
Fischer, John
Hinds, Charles
Nelson Family

1909 Clark, Alonzo
Stewart. Sarah
Stull, George
Weckwerth, Walter
Williams, Anna, Mrs.
Woolsey, Delos

1910 Cook, Winifred
Doane, Warren
Eddy, Hite
Eddy, Philo
Grunke, Paul
Marquiss, Barney
Toro, John
Raudsep, Hans
Semlek, Alex
Wells, Erastus

1911-1919

1911 Hoxsie, Roy
Lawrence, Claude
Sabatka, Joseph
Shafer, Clarence
Stewart, George
Speegle, Arthur
Wolff, Henry
Wolff, Peter

1912 Slattery, Charley
Woods, Ben
Woods, Orrin

1913 Greer, Charles
Heptner, Frank
Johnson, Thomas
Shickley, Mark
Wolfe, Jack
Woods, Charley

1914 Cain, Leslie
Cain, Nelson
Kuehne Brothers

1915 Christianson, Charley
Creach, James
Duvall, Fred
Gardner, William
Garrett. W. J.
Hamill, John
Hayes, Henry
Melton, Alonzo
Pickrel, Pick
Thompson, Faye
Ranney Family
Reed, Rueben
Shroyer, Ada
Spencer, Will
Thomas, Elmer
Thomas, Kenneth

1916 Dillinger, Jacob
Donner Brothers
Engdahl, Everett
Hamm, Fred
Jensen, George
Kottraba, Raymond
Schrand, Ben
Spencer, George
Tomingas, John
Wallace, Perry
Williams, Billy

1917 Clark, Dan
Cook, Floyd
Duvall, Jim
Garrett, Tom
Hatfield, Louis
Moon, Ora
Ridenour, Lee
Riley, Leslie
Talley, Richard
Thomas, Ray
Toland, Henry, Rev.
Weaver, Sam

1918 Mapes, Herschel
McCurdy, Otto
Moran, Bert
Moran, Julia, Mrs.
Reed, Jack
Wolff, Henry

1919 Gray, O'Neal
Pownall, Everett
Weaver, Henry

1920-1929

1920 Gilliland, Roy

1921 Burr, Ed
Burr, Andy
Johnson, Kermit
Tholson, Ted

1922 Stewart, Stanley

1923 Whisler, Riley

1924 Lubkin, William

1925 White, Cliff

1928 Prazma, John
Ware, Fred

1930-1939

1930 Reed, Paul
Whisler, Slim
Whisler, Ton

1931 Jessen, John

1932 Simpson, Jack

1933 Kennedy, Jesse

1934 Edwards, Deafy

1935 Whisler, David

1936 Brunson, C. L.

1938 Larsen, Chris
Wells, Albert

1939 Nielson, Calmer

1940-1949

1941 Baker, Ham
Cummings, Lee

1942 Whisler, Leonard
Cook, Ferris

1945 Ruff, Marion

1946 Donner, Melvin
Whisler, Dean

PART ONE

Cattle Ranchers,
Sheepman, Homesteaders, Railroaders,
School Teachers,
and
Other Individuals

An example of an early homestead
(from the collections of Carroll D. "Slim" Whisler)

Homestead Act of 1862

Signed into law by President Abraham Lincoln on May 20, 1862, the Homestead Act encouraged Western migration by providing settlers 160 acres of public land. In exchange homesteaders paid a small filing fee and were required to complete five years of continuous residence before receiving ownership of the land. In all, some 270 million acres were distributed under the act. The act remained in effect for more than a century. The last claim made under it was granted in 1988 for a parcel of land in Alaska.

ROZET (Pre-1911)
Belle Fourche District
Crook and Weston Counties, Wyoming

During the period between 1870 and the turn of the 20th Century northeastern Wyoming was sparsely settled. By the late 1860s stock grazing companies, made up mostly by Englishmen from the east, began establishing stock ranches along the Belle Fourche River, first cattle and then sheep. Several severe winters during the 1880s caused most of these companies to either fail or be sold. However, a few survived into the 20th Century.

EARLIEST RANCHES

Bartlett Richards, manager of the Shipwheel Ranch and crew (courtesy of the Campbell County Rockpile Museum, Gillette, Wyoming)

Shipwheel Ranch was established in 1879 by Bartlett Richards who was born in Waitsfield, Vermont, January 6, 1861, to Jonas De Richards, a clergyman, and Harriett Richards. When he was age 18 his parents sent him to Cheyenne to recover from a respiratory ailment. Bartlett decided he belonged in the west, and instead of returning to Vermont he borrowed enough money to buy 1,000 yearling heifers at $9 apiece. He trailed his herd 275 miles north to the Belle Fourche River. By 1881 he was managing three ranches and later had control of two large cattle companies. Shortly before his 21st birthday in 1882, he was hired to manage 6,000 head on the Upper 33 and Lower 33 ranches in Sioux County, Nebraska, which at that time bordered Converse County, Wyoming. Three years later in 1886, he sold his holdings at Shipwheel to the Standard Cattle Company. Because the 1890 Federal Census' burned there is no record as to where he was living in the last decade of the nineteenth century, but the 1900 U.S. Federal Census indicates he was married in 1897 to Inez Richards. They were living in Chadron, Dawes County, Nebraska. A family tree found on *www.trees.ancestry.com* indicates Bartlett died on September 4, 1911, in Nebraska.

After severe winters, when tens of thousands of livestock froze to death, the Standard Cattle Company began cutting its losses. In 1889, they sold the Shipwheel to Elias Whitcomb. Later Elias gave the ranch to his daughter, May, shortly after she married Ed Hume, his bookkeeper and commissary manager. Later they were divorced. In 1920 May sold the ranch to the William Schlattmann family. She and her daughter, Catherine, moved to Colorado Springs, Colorado.

Sources:
"Elias Whitcomb's Third Ranch was the Historic Shipwheel," The News Record, Gillette, Wyoming, April 4. 2011.
Ancestry.com, 1870 U.S. Federal Census for Tuscaloosa, Tuscaloosa, Alabama, [database online], Provo, UT.

Bar FS Ranch (1882) was established by Elias Whitcomb. He was one of the earliest to begin ranching in the southeast Rozet area. He developed it into one of three productive ranches. He gave the ranch to his daughter, Ida, upon her marriage to Dow Sweeney. They later divorced, and she married the family coachman, Rex Schnitger. Ida and Rex Schnitger later moved to California. The ranch was later sold to Metcalf and Neeley. In 1918 William "Bill" Bishop bought it. Today it is known as the Bishop Ranch.

Sources:
"Elias Whitcomb's Third Ranch was the Historic Shipwheel." <u>The News Record</u>, Gillette, Wyoming, April 4. 2011.

G Bar M Ranch was established by John Morton who along with his brother Jim, and Lew Jenne, a cousin, owned the John H. Morton Sheep Company, headquartered in Converse County, Wyoming Territory. It was located on the Belle Fourche River south of Rozet. In 1891, they hired a young man from Illinois as foreman named Bill Bishop.

W. O. (Bill) Bishop about 1915

William O. "Bill" Bischoff/Bishop was born December 7, 1877, at Ottawa, LaSalle County, Illinois, to John and Wilhelmina Bischoff, immigrants from Germany. They were the parents of five children. His father died when Bill was two. His mother married August Brandner, a widower with five children. They had five children making a large and noisy household. Bill, at age 14, left for Wyoming changing his name along the way to Bishop. Upon arrival in Wyoming Bill herded sheep near Lusk before a three-year stint with the Ogallala Cattle Company near Douglas. At age 21 he was hired by the John T. Morton Sheep Company. They put him to work as foreman at their G Bar M Ranch on the Belle Fourche River. Bill married Willa May Arnett, who worked at the G Bar M, on February 24, 1915, in Sheridan, Wyoming. She was born May 18, 1890. The log house on the G Bar M became their home. In 1916, John T. Morton died. Bill Bishop, having worked as foreman of the ranch for almost twenty years, acquired a major interest in the Morton Ranch Company. He used his share to purchase the G Bar M. In 1918 the Bishops sold the G Bar M and bought the old Bar FS Ranch from Metcalf and Neeley. 1921 George and Adeline Brandner, half-brother of William O. Bishop, bought the G Bar M and established a sheep business from 700 head of old ewes to several bands of sheep and later added Hereford cattle. Bill held office as Campbell County Commissioner for fourteen years and was elected to serve on the first Campbell County District School Board. In the spring of 1927 tragedy struck when their son, John Bill, died from cerebral meningitis in Sheridan, Wyoming. He was buried in Mount Pisgah Cemetery in Gillette. Bill Bishop died March 27, 1962. His wife Willa lived to celebrate both Wyoming's 100th in 1990, and her 100th birthday on May 18, 1990. She died on November 27, 1991. They were the parents of two sons:

John William "John Bill"	b: 23 Mar 1919	d: 12 May 1927	
James Oscar	b: 19 Apr 1928	d: 16 Aug 2021	m: Betty Carol Ikard

Sources:
"W. O. Bishop," pages 19, and 70-71, <u>Campbell County, The Treasured Years</u>, 1990, compiled by Campbell County Historical Society Gillette, Wyoming.
"W. O. Bishop Came West When only 14," by Mrs. Josephine McLucas, <u>The News Record</u>, Gillette, Wyoming, date of issue unknown, clipping found in scrapbook compiled by Jeannette Heptner.
Ancestry.com, Wyoming, Death Records, 1909-1969 [database online], Provo,UT.
Ancestry.com, U.S. Find-a-Grave Index, 1600s-Current, [database online], Provo, UT.
Ancestry.com, U.S. WWII Draft Cards Young Men, 1940-1947, [database online], Provo, UT.
Ancestry.com, Wyoming, Marriage Records, 1941-1966, [database online], Provo, UT.
Ancestry.com, 1880 U.S. Federal Census for Ottawa, LaSalle County, Illinois, [database online], Provo, UT.
Ancestry.com, 1920 U.S. Federal Census for Bar F S, Campbell County, Wyoming, [database online], Provo, UT.
Ancestry.com, 1930 U.S. Federal Census for Election District 20, Campbell County, Wyoming, [database online], Provo, UT.
Ancestry.com, 1940 U.S. Federal Census for Gillette, Campbell County, Wyoming, [database online], Provo, UT.
Ancestry.com, 1900 U.S. Federal Census for Chadron, Dawes County, Nebraska, [database online], Provo, UT.

The OR Ranch (1898) was established by Elias Whitcomb for his daughter Lizabeth and her husband Edward I. Rivenburg. While she was in Cheyenne, Elias drew up plans for a new ranch house. Edward was the overseer of the construction of the home. During that time he injured his thumb on a rusty nail and later died in January 1919 from blood poisoning. Lizabeth and her son-in-law, Glen Story, who married her daughter, Marjorie Badgette, in 1922, continued to live on the ranch until 1938 when, because of the drought during those depression years, they sold the ranch to William and Hazel Norman. Lizabeth moved to Colorado Springs, Colorado, near her sister May Hume. The ranch is known today as the Norman Ranch owned by Jess and Patty Norman Jessen.

Sources:
"Elias Whitcomb's Third Ranch was the Historic Shipwheel," The News Record, Gillette, Wyoming, April 4. 2011.

American Sheep Company was located north of Rozet in Township 51, Range 70 West. By 1912 it was managed by Sid Whipple. It has not been determined who owned the American Sheep Ranch. However, the 1910 Federal Census for Crook County, Wyoming, lists Dempsey A. Luton, age 21, head of the household, occupation horseman and as owner of a sheep ranch. Also listed under the household we find Eliza, his wife of one month, as cook; Charles Jensen, age 43, as foreman; and 21 sheep herders, men, ages 46 – 22. From his and his wife's obituaries we learn that Dempsey "Demps" was born on March 22, 1889, in Claremore, Rogers County, Oklahoma, to David and Rebecca (Coker) Luton. His mother was 1/16th Cherokee. About 1906 at age 17 he came to Crook County, Wyoming, bringing his horses with him. He liked the country so well he returned to Oklahoma to marry his childhood friend, Eliza Sullivan, on April 10, 1910, in Welch, Craig County, Oklahoma. Together they returned and filed on a homestead putting together a small herd of cattle and sheep. They became the parents of four children, Norman, Floyd, Lavina Jean, and Paul LeRoy. Demps always owned a good string of horses and was constantly called upon to work for the big cow outfits in the area. After a terrible infestation of grasshoppers in 1929 which wiped out all crops and grasslands in the area, Demps moved his family in the early 1930s to Jackson, Wyoming. They developed a hunting camp located on the bank of the Gros Venture River at the mouth of Slate Creek. It grew and flourished lasting for thirty-five years. Demps died July 31, 1972; Eliza died September 1978. Both are buried in the Aspen Hill Cemetery, Jackson, Wyoming.

Records indicate Charles Jensen, the foreman, was born February 29, 1866, in Piute County, Utah, to George and Marie Kristine (Thorup) Jensen, immigrants from Denmark. In 1884 he married Mettie Christina Hendricksen in Sanpete County, Utah. Seven children were born. She died in 1901. About 1916 he filed for a homestead in Township 47 N, Range 74 W, Sections 4, 5, and 6. He received patents to them in August 1921 and January 1922. The 1930 Federal Census records Charles living in Election District 27, Campbell County, as head of household, a rancher who owned property with four hired hands, married for 19 years. The name of his wife was not recorded. He died July 4, 1934, and was buried in Mount Pisgah Cemetery, Gillette, Wyoming. Cemetery records a spouse, Maude, born April 25, 1875, but no date of death.

Sources:
Sources for Dempsey Albert Luton:
Ancestry.com, U. S. Find a Grave Index, 1600s-Current, [database online], Provo, UT.
Ancestry.com, Oklahoma, U. S. County Marriage Records, 1890-1995, [database online], Provo, UT.
Ancestry.com, U. S. World War I Draft Registration Cards, 1917-1918, [database online], Provo, UT.
Ancestry.com, U. S. World War II Draft Registration Cards, 1942, [database online], Provo, UT.
Ancestry.com, (1900) Oklahoma & Indian Territory, U. S. Dawes Census Cards for Five Civilized Tribes, 1898-1914,
*   [database online], Provo, UT.*
Ancestry.com, 1900 U. S. Federal Census for Township 21, Cherokee Nation, Indian Territory, [database online], Provo, UT.
Ancestry.com, 1910 U. S. Federal Census for Moorcroft, Crook County, Wyoming, [database online], Provo, UT.
Ancestry.com, 1920 U. S. Federal Census for Election District 13, Campbell County, Wyoming, [database online], Provo, UT.
Ancestry.com, 1930 U. S. Federal Census for Election District 13, Campbell County, Wyoming, [database online], Provo, UT.
Ancestry.com, 1940 U. S. Federal Census for Jackson, Teton County, Wyoming, [database online], Provo, UT .

The Empire Sheep Company managed by Silas A. Guthrie, was located east of Rozet in Township 50 North, Range 69 and 68 West. It was a large sheep company, which ran as high as 50,000 sheep. Henry Thar went to work as a blacksmith and carpenter in 1910. He kept their sheep and trap wagons in decent shape and shoed their many horses used in operating the ranch. At the sheds on Miller Creek as many as 75,000 head of sheep were shorn in a season. At that time machine shearing was being used. Not all of these sheep were Empire sheep as other sheep ranchers in the area would bring their herds to Miller Creek for shearing. Silas A. Guthrie was born about 1847 in Marion County, Ohio, to Isaac F. and Rachel Guthrie. He and his brother William were listed as stockmen in the 1880 U.S. Federal Census in Wagon Hound and LaBonty, Albany County, Wyoming. By the 1900 Census he was recorded, twice, at age 52, living at Moorcroft, Crook County, with a wife of seven years, Isabella, age 30; and at Merino (Upton), Weston County working as a stock foreman. He died March 17, 1923, in Denver, Colorado. Isabella continued operating the ranch until her death on January 31, 1941. Both are buried in Calvary Cemetery, Clarks, Merrick County, Nebraska.
Sources:

"Dutch Henry Thar Walked to Wyoming in '91," The News Record, Gillette, Wyoming, (from a scrapbook of historical newspaper articles compiled L. J. Whisler).
Ancestry.com, 1880 U.S. Federal Census for Albany County, Wyoming, [database online], Provo, UT.
Ancestry.com, 1900 U.S. Federal Census for Moorcroft, Crook County, Wyoming, [database online], Provo, UT.
Ancestry.com, 1910 U.S. Federal Census for Moorcroft, Crook County, Wyoming, [database online], Provo, UT.

The Harris-Simpson Livestock Company (William C. "W.C." Harris and Charles H. Simpson)
Quoted in part from "Campbell County Historic Ranches: Shippy Ranch," *Gillette News Record*, January 30, 2012: ". . . Ora and W.C. Harris formed the Little Powder River Livestock Company which included the Laurel Leaf; in 1916, they bought the Wagonhammer Ranch on Big Mitchell Creek; later acquired the Koehns ranch also. 'They ran it all as a wagon outfit from the Montana line south to Donkey Creek and east to the Little Missouri,' said David (Shippy). After the 1919 death of (Ora,) Haley Harris, a former Wyoming Territorial Legislator took over. The son of a Confederate soldier from Sterling, (Logan County), Colorado, he'd amassed thousands of cattle and dozens of feedlots by 1897, and at one time had 800 employees. "His sister (Alice Ann Harris) married a Simpson (John Henry Simpson) and soon his Simpson nephews and grandnephews were managing the three ranches, now under Harris-Simpson Livestock Company. Harris (W. C.) died in 1940. His widow, Maude, sold the Koehns place to their great-nephew Jack Simpson . . . "

[Note: Regarding the Pleasant Valley Cemetery. It was Charles H. Simpson, brother to John Henry Simpson, who in Oct 1917 deeded land for the Pleasant Valley (aka Little Iowa) Cemetery.]

Sources:
"Campbell County Historic Ranches: Shippy Ranch," Gillette News Record, Gillette, Wyoming, January 30, 2012.
Pleasant Valley Cemetery Burial Book, kept by Mrs. Lucille Thompson (Xeroxed Copy-1998).
Ancestry.com, U.S. World War II Draft Registration Cards, 1942, [database online], Provo, UT.
Ancestry.com, Jane Hawley Family Tree, [database online], Provo, UT.
Ancestry.com, Colorado State Census, 1885 for Weld County, Colorado, [database online], Provo, UT.
Ancestry.com, 1910 U.S. Federal Census for Illif, Logan County, Colorado, [database online], Provo, UT.
Ancestry.com, 1920 U.S. Federal Census for Illif, Logan County, Colorado, [database online], Provo, UT.

Several other individuals came into the area prior to 1900. Some filed for homesteads while some did not; some were employed by the established cattle and sheep ranches. One such individual was:

MR. AND MRS. JOHN J. GRANT

John J. Grant employed as foreman by Elias W. Whitcomb at the Bar FS Ranch for many years. John was born in Oil City, Venango County, Pennsylvania. When he was about twelve years old his father David moved the family to Adair County, Missouri. John loved working with horses. He bought and sold horses for twenty years prior to coming west. In 1885 he went to Deadwood, South Dakota, and then in 1886 he went to work as foreman for Elias W. Whitcomb. As foreman, he was permitted to build his own spread. This was a very unusual practice among the large ranch owners. At that time Indians were roaming around the county of which he had many stories later in life. When the railroad was being built through Crook County in 1890-91, John and Mr. Whitcomb had the contract to furnish beef to the railroad contractors. After the railroad was built John moved to Gillette where he ran a livery stable, later moving it to Clearmont, and then to Sheridan.

In 1894, he returned to Crook County where he located a homestead on Hay Creek about fifteen miles north of Gillette where he established a horse ranch. He met his bride-to-be, Ellen Turner, at his brother's in Clark County, Illinois. He had shipped some horses east for sale by his brother. She was visiting her sister, his brother's wife. They were married December 10, 1905, at her parent's home in Martinsville, Clark County, Illinois. They left that evening for their home in Wyoming. They were the parents of three children; a boy who died at infancy, and two girls, Eva and Ethel. Ellen died August 17, 1933 in Newcastle, Wyoming, and was buried in Mount Pisgah Cemetery, Gillette, Wyoming. John died, age 92, on November 4, 1941, at Hot Springs, South Dakota, and was buried in Mount Pisgah Cemetery, Gillette, Campbell County, Wyoming.

Sources:
"Funeral Services for Mrs. John Grant Will be Held This Thursday," The News Record, *Gillette, Wyoming, August 17, 1933.*
"Obituary, John J. Grant," page 1, The News Record, *Gillette, Wyoming, November 13, 1941.*
Campbell County, The Treasured Years, 1990, *Pages 224-5, compiled by Campbell County Historical Society, Gillette, Wyoming.*
"John J. Grant, Rancher, Came Here in 1886," by Mrs. Henry Dennis, page S1, The News Record, *Gillette Wyoming, March 31, 1966.*
Ancestry.com, *1860 U.S. Federal Census, for Allegheny, Butler County, Pennsylvania, [data base online], Provo, UT.*
Ancestry.com, *1870 U.S. Federal Census, for Township61, Range 13, Adair County, Missouri, [data base online], Provo, UT.*
Ancestry.com, *1880 U.S. Federal Census, for Wilson, Adair County, Missouri, [data base online], Provo, UT.*
Ancestry.com, *1900 U.S. Federal Census, for Moorcroft, Crook County, Wyoming, [data base online], Provo, UT.*
Ancestry.com, *1910 U.S. Federal Census, for Gillette, Crook County, Wyoming, [data base online], Provo, UT.*
Ancestry.com, *1920 U.S. Federal Census, for, Rawhide, Campbell County, Wyoming, [data base online], Provo, UT.*
Ancestry.com, *1930 U.S. Federal Census, for Election District 11, Campbell County, Wyoming, [data base online], Provo, UT.*

EARLY HOMESTEADERS
Pre-1911

Elias W. and Katherine (Shaw) Whitcomb
(1882)

At the age of 51, Elias Whitcomb filed for homesteads located south of Rozet in Crook County, Wyoming Territory, along the Belle Fourche River, for both himself and his wife, Kate. From these beginnings, he would establish three ranches that still survive today in the 21st century. At this time, 1882, he had already spent 32 years in the western frontier.

Elias was born December 28, 1831, in Oxford, Worchester County, Massachusetts, the first born of Ansel and Phebe (Clark) Whitcomb. The 1850 Federal Census shows the family living in Windham County, Vermont.

Elias left Vermont for the west about 1852, a young man in his late teens. He signed on with the Childs' Brothers in Westport, Missouri, to drive an ox team for them on a wagon train headed for the New Mexico Territory. He worked as a trapper and as a guide for wagon trains. In 1857 in Leavenworth, Kansas, the Child's outfit, loaded supplies, including a small herd of cattle, and left for Fort Laramie, Wyoming Territory. Mr. Whitcomb related in his diary that it was unusually rainy that fall and that the going was slow. On the seventh of November they reached Fort Laramie and went into winter camp on Bear Creek. It turned bitter cold, the deepest snow and coldest weather of the winter. They lost many of their cattle. Mr. Whitcomb made one more trip with a Child's Brothers train the following spring. Then he quit and went to work for Russell, Majors, and Waddell. He passed a second winter in Fort Laramie where the following winter of 1859 he was put in charge of all work cattle they had at Fort Laramie, about twelve hundred head scattered upon the creeks of Sabile (Sybille), Chug, Horse, and Bear Creek. Mr. Whitcomb left the employ of Russell, Majors, and Waddell the following year, 1861, and started his own trading post at Horseshoe Station. The store was later burned down by the notorious outlaw, Tom Slade. There he grazed both horses and southern steers, which he sold to army posts and to emigrants who passed through on their way west.

Elias wintered over (1864-1865) on the Sybille Creek. He married Katherine "Kate" Shaw, a Sioux Indian woman, on February 15, 1865. She was the daughter of a Scottish trader and a Sioux woman. He also filed for a homestead on Crow Creek near the site of Cheyenne. However, it seems something changed his mind, and he moved himself and Kate to the Cache la Poudre area of Larimer County, Colorado Territory, sometime in 1865.

The Cache la Poudre area is located northwest of Fort Collins near the place where the Cache la Poudre River emerges from the foothills of the Rocky Mountains. Here he established another trading post and developed an interest in Texas cattle. Elias spoke about their life on the Cache la Poudre River in his diary which can be found in the *Annals of Wyoming*, Volume 57:2:21-32. The diary ends December 1868 when, because of severe Indian uprisings, he moved his family to LaPorte, Larimer County, Colorado, for the holidays, leaving three men to look after his horses. While on the Cache la Poudre, Elias and Kate became the parents of four girls and one son:

*Katya	b: 30 Jun 1863	d: 12 Mar 1867	
Elizabeth Ann	b: 17 Aug 1868	d: 22 Feb 1931	m: (1) Charles Badgette
			(2) Edward I. Rivenburg
Lily May	b: 25 Jun 1871	d: 15 Mar 1959	m: Edward P. Hume
Ida Marie	b: 12 Dec 1875	d:	m: (1) Lorenzo D. "Dow" Sweeney
			(2) Rex Gustave Schnitger
Harold Miller	b: 23 Nov 1895	d: 01 Mar 1936	(never married)

*Katya is buried in the Buckeye Ranch Cemetery, Buckeye, Larimer County, Colorado. Note found on U.S. Find-a-Grave Index for the gravesite: "INSCRIPTION Oldest child of E. W. and Kate Whitcomb AGED 3 YRS 8 MS 12 DS. Two Indians are buried beside Katya. Her mother Kate was an Indian. Grave located on Buckeye Ranch. New headstone provided by ranch owner as old headstone was badly aging."

His trading post became profitable enabling him to move his family to Cheyenne about 1874. Elias built a home on Carey Avenue and was appointed one of the city commissioners. There he established a large mercantile company, the "Whitcomb and Cowgill Dry Goods Store." He prospered and built a large magnificent home and carriage house on "cattleman's row." About 1877 he filed under the Desert Land Act of 1877, for land located along the Chugwater in Section 18, Township 14, Range 67 West, Laramie County, Wyoming, where he built a ranch and engaged largely in cattle raising. Because he believed his wife and his two oldest daughters were not being treated fairly by their Cheyenne neighbors, Mr. Whitcomb, in 1879, sent them east to a finishing school in Boston for an education. Upon their return, the social circles in Cheyenne may not have accepted Mrs. Whitcomb and the children, because for whatever reason, Mr. Whitcomb made plans to move north to Crook County, Wyoming Territory.

In 1882, he filed for a homestead south of Rozet where he bought cattle and established the Bar FS Ranch. He moved his family sometime in the late 1880s. He would later give the Bar FS Ranch to his daughter Ida Whitcomb Schnitger. Mr. Whitcomb expanded his ranch by filing under various homestead acts, for about 480 acres in:

Sections 33 and 34, Township 49 North, Range 69 West,
Sections 1 and 12, Township 47 North, Range 69 West.

In Kate Whitcomb's name, he filed for 440 acres located in:

Section 5, Township 47 North, Range 69 West,
Section 32, Township 48 North, Range 69 West,
Sections 13 and 24, Township 49 North, Range 69 West.

Mr. Whitcomb spent his time between his home in Cheyenne, Wyoming, and the ranches on the Belle Fourche River. He took an active part in the processes in obtaining statehood for Wyoming. He was a member of the Laramie County Stock Growers Association, which later became the Wyoming Stock Growers Association. Mr. Whitcomb was one of the invaders in 1892 of Johnson County during the Johnson County War. A photo, in Helena Huntington Smith's book *The War on Powder River*, taken of the invaders at Fort Russell after they were taken prisoner show him as an elderly man with a long white beard. Helena Huntington Smith on page 187, described him: "He was the oldest of the invaders, known as 'Pappy.' He was also the only genuine pioneer among them, having come west in 1857. He worked for many years for the famous freighting firm of Russell, Majors, and Waddell."

Mr. Whitcomb built a flood irrigation system with several miles of ditches and dams. He developed alfalfa meadows, which produced good hay crops until the drought years of the 1930s. He tried growing both fruit trees and grain on the ranch, but the trees could not adapt to the climate, and the soil was too sandy for the grain. He concentrated on hay production and improvements of range grass. He built spreader dams and stock dams to spread out his cattle on the grazing pastureland. Some of these dams are still in place today. Mr. Whitcomb also raised Clydesdales, Standard, and Arabian breed horses, and later Shetland ponies. He also raised Holstein milk cows and swine. In 1898, he bought the Shipwheel Ranch from the Standard Cattle Co, managed by Bartlett Richards.

Mr. Whitcomb developed ranches one for each of his three daughters: the OR Ranch for Lizabeth Whitcomb Badgette/Rivenburgh, the Shipwheel Ranch for May Whitcomb Hume, and the Bar FS Ranch for Ida Whitcomb Sweeney/Schnitger. He also, about 1915, filed on a homestead in Weston County, Wyoming, for his son, Whit Whitcomb:

Sections 1 and 12, Township 48 North, Range 69 West,
Sections 5, 6, 7, and 8, Township 47 North, Range 68 West.

Kate Whitcomb died June 27, 1912, in Cheyenne at the age of 62 and was buried in Lakeview Cemetery, Cheyenne, Wyoming. Elias Whitcomb, at age 82, was struck and instantly killed by lightning on June 15, 1915, at the Ship-wheel Ranch on the Belle Fourche River. He had been working in the corrals on horseback when struck. Under-taker W. R. Fox, of Gillette, was called and went down that evening to prepare the body for shipment to Cheyenne, Wyoming, where he was buried alongside his wife, Kate, in Lakeview Cemetery.

In 1971 Elias W. Whitcomb was posthumously inducted into the Cowboy Hall of Fame, of the National Cowboy and Western Heritage Museum, Oklahoma City, Oklahoma, nominated by his friend, Joe Watt. A sketch of Mr. Whitcomb placed near his plaque at the museum describes him as a man who possessed the traits most cherished in the men who pioneered the American West.

Sources:
Photos: from Wyoming State Archives, 2301 Central Avenue, Cheyenne, Wyoming, 82201.
Bureau of Land Management, Homestead Patents Index [www.glorecords.blm.gov].
"The Banditti of the Plains, or the Cattlemen's Invasion of Wyoming in 1892," pages 27, 71, and 112, by A. S. Mercer, copyright 1954 by The University of Oklahoma Press.
"The War on Powder River," pages 187, by Helena Huntington Smith, published 1966.
"E. W. Whitcomb," pages 550-551, Pioneers of Crook County, compiled by the Crook County Historical Society, Sundance, Wyoming 1972.
"The Whitcomb Saga," pages 44-48, The Way It Was, by Earl Dillinger, 1980.
"The Elias Whitcomb Story," pages 630-632, Campbell County, The Treasured Years, 1990, compiled by Campbell County Historical Society, Gillette, Wyoming.
"Chapter 10, The Whitcomb's," pages 55-64, 1916 Wyoming, Here We Come, by Margaret Bowden (2002).
"Death Notice of E. W. Whitcomb," page 1, Gillette News, Gillette, Wyoming, July 9, 1915.
"E.W. Whitcomb, One of First Wyoming Settlers, Killed by Lightning," obituary from the Wyoming State Archives, March 31, 2003.
Obituary E. W. Whitcomb, page 1-2, Cheyenne State Leader, Cheyenne, Wyoming, June 16, 1915.
"Mrs. Whitcomb (Kate), Friend to all, Goes to Death," page 3, Cheyenne State Leader, Cheyenne, Wyoming, June 29, 1912 .
"Badgette Funeral," page 5, Cheyenne Daily Leader, Cheyenne, Wyoming, September 26, 1903.
"Ashes to be Buried (Lizabeth Whitcomb Badgette)," page 13, Wyoming Tribune, Cheyenne, Wyoming, October 2, 1953
"Mrs. Glenn Story Dies at Gillette (Marjorie Badgette)," page 3, Wyoming State Tribune & Cheyenne State Leader, Cheyenne, Wyoming February 23, 1931.
"Story Girl is Drowned Belle Fourche River," page 3, Wyoming State Tribune, Cheyenne, Wyoming, May 23, 1927.
"Hume (May Whitcomb) Graveside Services Set," page __, Wyoming Tribune, Cheyenne, Wyoming, March __, 1959.
"Heart Ailment Takes Life of Ida (Whitcomb)Schnitger," page __, Wyoming Tribune, Cheyenne, Wyoming, April 14, 194_.
"Pioneer's Son (Harold Whitcomb) Dies in North." page 7, Wyoming State Tribune, Cheyenne, Wyoming, March 3, 1936.
Wyoming State Archives, Interments in Lakeview Cemetery, Cheyenne, Wyoming, from swalsh@cheyennecity.org March 20, 2003 www.cowboyhalloffame.org .
Annals of Wyoming, Volume 57:2:21-32, "Reminiscences of a Pioneer; An Excerpt from the Diary of Elias W. Whitcomb," as given by Mr. Whitcomb to His Daughter, Mrs. E. J. Rivenburg, Moorcroft, Wyoming, in 1906," Wyoming State Historical Society. (Note: "The above article is from a typed transcript of a portion of a diary left by Whitcomb. The transcript is in the Works Progress Administration Collection compiled in the depression of the 1930's. The total material was gathered for publishing Wyoming, A Guide to Its History, Highways and People. As indicated in the title, the original document was made available for copy in 1906 when Whitcomb was still alive. The location and final disposition of the original diary is not known. A hand written and dated note attached to the WPA transcript asks the tantalizing question, "Where is the original—2/13/39".)
Annals of Wyoming, Volume 17:1:55-56, "Stock Raising on the Plains, 1870-1871," Wyoming State Historical Society.
Annals of Wyoming, Volume 18:1:4, ". . . report on Horseshoe Station," Wyoming State Historical Society.
Annals of Wyoming, Volume 42:2:261, ". . .Horseshoe Station," Wyoming State Historical Society.
Ancestry.com, 1850 U.S. Federal Census for Townsend, Windham, Vermont, [database online], Provo, UT, USA.
Ancestry.com, 1870 U.S. Federal Census for Cache la Poudre, Larimer, Colorado Territory, [database online], Provo, UT.
Ancestry.com, 1880 U.S. Federal Census for Crow Creek, Laramie County, Wyoming Territory, [database online], Provo, UT.
Ancestry.com, 1900 U.S. Federal Census for Belle Fourche District, Weston County, Wyoming, (Elias; Charles A. Badgette), [database online], Provo, UT.
Ancestry.com, 1900 U.S. Federal Census for Ward 3, Cheyenne, Laramie County, Wyoming Territory,[database online], Provo, UT.
Ancestry.com, 1910 U.S. Federal Census for Precinct 16, Outside Moorcroft, Crook County, Wyoming, (Elias, Lorenzo and Ida Sweeney), [database online], Provo, UT, USA.
Ancestry.com, 1910 U.S. Federal Census for Cheyenne, Ward Three, Laramie County, Wyoming (Kate, Eliza, Harold Whitcomb, Marjorie and Elizabeth Badgette), [database online], Provo, UT , Lizabeth Ann (Whitcomb) Badgette/Rivenburgh.

Lizabeth Ann (Whitcomb) Badgette/Rivenburgh
OR Ranch

Lizabeth was born August 17, 1868, at Cache la Poudre, Larimore County, Colorado Territory. She married Charles A. Badgette, the Bar FS foreman, June 25, 1900. He later served in the Wyoming legislature as State Senator from Crook County. Lizabeth was well received in Cheyenne during the years her husband was a Senator. She had a beautiful singing voice and occasionally performed at the Cheyenne Opera House. Lizabeth and Charles developed the OR Ranch, the second ranch Mr. Whitcomb established along the Belle Fourche. They were the parents of one daughter:

Marjorie B.   b: 1895   d: 22 Feb 1931 m: Glenn Ellsworth Story

Charles Badgette died on September 24, 1903, at the age of 40, and was buried in Lakeview Cemetery, Cheyenne, Wyoming. Soon after Charles' death Lizabeth married the family's coachman, Edward I. (Orville) Rivenburgh in Cambridge, Massachusetts. They decided to build a new ranch house, the plans for which was developed while she was in Cheyenne. Her father sent the blueprints to a sawmill in Idaho where the lumber was cut to size and shipped to the ranch. Orville Rivenburgh was the overseer of the construction project, but Dutch Henry Thar did the carpentry work. Before the house was completed, Rivenburgh accidentally injured his thumb while trying to drive a nail, got blood poisoning and died on January 27, 1919, according to a petition of heirship posted in *The News Record*, Gillette, Wyoming, February 27, 1927.

Because of the drought and the Depression Lizabeth Rivenburgh was forced to sell the OR Ranch. She sold 280 acres of her bottomland to her neighbors the Dillingers. She placed her household goods in storage and moved to Pueblo, Colorado, to reside with her sister, Ida Schnitger. Lizabeth died in September 1953, and was buried in the Lakeview Cemetery, Cheyenne, Wyoming on October 3, 1953.

The remainder of the ranch was sold to William and Hazel Norman. Their daughter, Patty, and her husband, Jess Jessen, operated the ranch after William and Hazel retired.

2011
The original house was replaced by this New England style home in early 1900's by Lisabeth and her second husband Edward Rivenburgh. Now known as the Jessen Ranch owned by Jes and Patty Jessen.

The Jessen Ranch 2011

Marjorie Badgette Story, daughter of Lizabeth and Charles Badgette, married Glenn Ellsworth Story, a cowboy, from Sundance, Wyoming, in the Episcopal Church, Gillette, WY, June 23, 1922. They lived on the OR Ranch. They had two children:

Lizabeth Marjorie	b: 1923	d: 22 May 1927, (drowned)	
Conrad Ellsworth "Spud"	b: 1928	d: 21 Jun 1971, (Newberg, Oregon)	

Their daughter, known as Little Lizabeth, drowned in the Belle Fourche River on May 22, 1927. The river was high from the melting winter snow, and she went to play along the river with her dog. The bank was soft where she stood, it broke off, and she fell into the fast-moving water. Her body was found three days later by Elmer Thomas, a neighbor. The family held her funeral at the ranch home (OR), and she was buried in a meadow not far from the house.

On February 22, 1931, Marjorie Badgette Story, died from pneumonia. She left her infant son, Conrad, to be raised by his grandmother, Lizabeth Rivenburg, and his father Glenn Story. The family had little Lizabeth's casket taken up, and both she and her mother were taken to Cheyenne and buried in Lakeview Cemetery near Elias and Kate Whitcomb.

Glenn Story married Nellie M. Whitcher of Moorcroft, Wyoming, in Belle Fourche, Butte County, SD, on July 5, 1933. They later divorced. He served in the Army Air Corps prior to moving to Santa Maria, California, where he worked for Lockheed Missile and Space Company at Vandenberg Air Force Base. He died June 21, 1971, in Newberg, Yamhill County, Oregon, and is buried in the Valley View Memorial Park, Newberg, Oregon.

Sources:
Photos, Lizabeth Whitcomb and Marjorie Story Badgette from Wyoming State Archives, 2301 Central Avenue, Cheyenne, Wyoming, 82201.
Photos, OR Ranch house and Aerial View; "Campbell County Historic Ranches: the Jessen Ranch," The News Record, Gillette, Wyoming, April 4, 2011.
Bureau of Land Management, Homestead Patent Index, [www.glorecords.blm.gov].
"The Whitcomb Saga," pages 44-48, The Way It Was, by Earl Dillinger, 1880.
"Child Drowned Saturday in the Belle Fourche," The News Record, Gillette, Wyoming, May 26, 1927.
'Petition in Matter of the Heirship of Edward I. Rivenburg," The News Record, Gillette, Wyoming, February 27, 1927.
"Mrs. Glen Story, Rozet Resident, Claimed by Death on Last Sunday," The News Record, Gillette, Wyoming, February 26, 1931.
"Mrs. L. Rivenburgh..." Rozet, The News Record, Gillette, Wyoming, July 31, 1935.
"The Elias Whitcomb Story," pages 630-632, Campbell County, The Treasured Years, 1990, compiled by Campbell County Historical Society, Gillette, Wyoming.
"1916 Wyoming, Here We Come!" by Margaret Dillinger Bowden, 2002.
"Campbell County Historic Ranches: the Jessen Ranch," The News Record, Gillette, Wyoming, April 4, 2011.
"Badgette-Story (marriage), Moorcroft Democrat, Moorcroft, WY, June 23 about 1922 (no year given on clipping from newspaper).
Ancestry.com, Glenn Story Obit from the Find-a-Grave Index 1600s-Present, database online], Provo, UT.
Ancestry.com, South Dakota Marriages, 1905-2017, [database online], Provo, UT.

Lily May (Whitcomb) and Edward P. Hume
Shipwheel Ranch

May, as she was called throughout her life, was born June 25, 1871, at Cache La Purdre, Larimore County, Colorado Territory. She married Edward P. Hume, who was the bookkeeper and commissary manager for the Shipwheel Ranch, which Mr. Whitcomb had purchased in 1889. He was born August 31, 1877, in Marquette, Michigan. They had one daughter whom they named for her grandmother:

Katherine	b:	1901	d: 02 Apr 1994	m: Jack B. Gray

Katherine Hume graduated from Moorcroft High School, Moorcroft, Wyoming. William Schlattmann purchased the Shipwheel Ranch about 1920. Edward died in 1951 and is buried in the Kennebec Cemetery, Kennebec, Lyman County, South Dakota. May Hume died March 19, 1959, at age 88, and is buried in the Whitcomb Family lot in Lakeview Cemetery, Cheyenne, Laramie County, Wyoming.

Ida Marie (Whitcomb) Sweeney/Schnitger
Bar FS Ranch

Ida was born December 12, 1873, at Cache La Purdre, Larimore County, Colorado Territory. She married Lorenzo D. "Dow" Sweeney prior to 1900. They lived on the Shipwheel Ranch which was purchased by Mr. Whitcomb in 1889 from the Standard Cattle Company. It was located on the south bank of the Belle Fourche River. After 1916 they were divorced, and she later married Rex Gustave Schnitger, who was a silversmith and a blacksmith specializing in bits, spurs, conches, and other mountings that were heavily overlaid with silver. They lived on the Bar FS that her father had given her. It was later sold to sheepmen, Metcalf and Neeley, with J. Y. Lucas as the foreman. William O. Bishop bought the ranch in 1918.

Sources for Shipwheel Ranch:

Bureau of Land Management, Homestead Patent Index, [www.glorecords.blm.gov].
"The Whitcomb Saga," pages 44-48, The Way it Was, by Earl Dillinger, 1980.
"The Elias Whitcomb Story," pages 630-632, Campbell County, The Treasured Years, 1990, compiled by Campbell County Historical Society, Gillette, Wyoming.
Ancestry.com, 1900 U.S. Federal Census Index, Belle Fourche District, Weston County, Wyoming, page 272A.

Sources for Ida Marie (Whitcomb) Sweeney/Schnitger:

Bureau of Land Management, Homestead Patent Index, [www.glorecords.blm.gov].
"The Whitcomb Saga," pages 44-48, The Way It Was, by Earl Dillinger, 1880.
"The Elias Whitcomb Story," pages 630-632, Campbell County, The Treasured Years, 1990, compiled by Campbell County Historical Society, Gillette, Wyoming.
Ancestry.com, 1900 U.S. Federal Census Index, Belle Fourche District, Weston County, Wyoming, page 272B.
Ancestry.com, 1910 U.S. Federal Census for Precinct 16, Outside Moorcroft, Crook County, Wyoming, [database online], Provo, UT.

Harold Miller "Little Whit" Whitcomb

Elias Whitcomb with his son Harold "Little Whit" Whitcomb and granddaughter Marjorie Badgette

Whit was born November 23, 1895, the same year as his niece, Marjorie Badgette. The 1910 Wyoming Federal Census records him as age eighteen. Whit never married. He broke horses for his neighbors and became quite proficient at it. He lost his thumb and three fingers of his right hand when he was fourteen while roping a steer. Then in 1924 he was caught out in a blizzard and froze his feet and hands. His neighbors took him to Sheridan to the hospital where they amputated his feet just below the knees and the little finger of his left hand. He was fitted with artificial limbs, which did not prevent him from continuing to break horses. Whit had great fun with people who did not know he had artificial limbs. One such incident occurred when he was visiting the Bishop Ranch where they had a small Bull Terrier. The ranch cook looked out the window and said, "There's a crazy man out there, that dog's chewing on his ankles and he's just laughing at him!" Crippled as he was, Whit drew top wages wherever he worked and could ride any horse he could get on. He died of a heart attack on March 1, 1936, age 43, and was buried in Lakeview Cemetery, Cheyenne, Wyoming, alongside of his parents.

Sources:
Photo, from Wyoming State Archives, 2301 Central Avenue, Cheyenne, Wyoming, 82201.
"The Whitcomb Saga," pages 44-48, The Way it Was, by Earl Dillinger, 1980.
"The Elias Whitcomb Story," pages 630-632, Campbell County, The Treasured Years, 1990, compiled by Campbell County
*   Historical Society, Gillette, Wyoming.*
Ancestry.com, 1900 U.S. Federal Census for, Belle Fourche District, Weston County, Wyoming, [database online][, Provo, UT.
Ancestry.com, 1910 U.S. Federal Census for Precinct 16, Outside Moorcroft, Crook County, Wyoming, [database online], Provo, UT.

THE HALVERSON FAMILY
1900

The Halversons of Rozet, Jacob, Erik and their sister Anna Marie emigrated from Mora, Kopparberg, Sweden. Jacob in 1887 with their father, Halvar Persson. When Halvar returned to Sweden is not known. Jacob first came to the Rozet area in 1900 where he worked as a sheepherder. Erik and Anna Marie emigrated in 1908 from Sweden, through Canada, to Wyoming.

THE FAMILY IN SWEDEN:

Halvar Hall Persson, son of Per Pehrsson and Anna Andersdotter:

Born:	11 Oct 1850	Died: 05 Nov 1923, in Mora, Kopparberg, Sweden
Baptized:	01 Nov 1850	
Married:	Kerstan Jakobsdotter, daughter of Jacob Ersson and Kerstin Ersdr	
Born:	18 Jul 1848	Died: 23 Nov 1922, in Mora, Kopparberg, Sweden

Their children:

1. Andrew/Anders Halvarsson   b: 16 Mar 1874 in Mora, Kopparberg (Dalarna), Sverige (Sweden)
2. Jacob Halvarsson   **b: 13 Aug 1876 in Mora, Sweden ...... emigrated to US about 1887**
3. Erik Halvarsson   **b: 24 Sep 1879 in Mora, Sweden ...... emigrated to US about 1908**
4. Per Halvarsson   b: 29 Mar 1883 in Mora, Sweden ...... ?
   d: 20 Jan 1890 in Mora, Sweden ...... ?
5. Anna Marie Halvarsson   **b: 26 Oct 1886 in Mora, Sweden ...... emigrated to US about 1908**
6. Carl/Karl Halvarsson   b: 03 Dec 1892 in Mora, Sweden ...... ?

[Note: In Sweden, the children's last name is their fathers first name with son or dotter (daughter) tacked on. Hence the last name of Halvar's son Jacob becomes Halvarsson; it was shortened in America to Halverson.]

The following emigrated to the United States:

Halvar Persson	in 1887	age 37 (father)	returned to Sweden, date unknown
Jacob	in 1887	age 11	shows up in Rozet area, Crook County in 1900
Erik	in 1908	age 28	arrived in Rozet about 1908 from Sweden
Anna Marie	in 1908	age 21	arrived in Rozet about 1908 from Sweden

Jacob "Jake" Halverson
1904

Jacob "Jake" Halverson was born on August 13, 1876, in Mora, Kopparberg (Dalarna), Sverige (Sweden), to Halvar Hall Persson and Kerstan Jakobsdotter. At the age of eleven, on June 20, 1887, he and his father Halvar Persson, left Mora, Kopparberg, Sweden, for North America. The emigration record indicated he "travels with family" which would be his father. When his father returned to Sweden is not known. Jacob first came to the Rozet area in 1900 where he worked as a sheepherder. He filed in 1904 for a homestead on Section 34, Township 50 North, Range 70 West, on which the Land Office at Sundance, Crook County, Wyoming, issued him a Final Certificate dated December 6, 1906. He later filed for a homestead and was issued a patent in 1909 for a homestead on Donkey Creek in Section 13, Township 49 North, Range 70 West and Sections 26 and 35, Township 50 North, Range 70 West. He later acquired additional tracts of land in the Rozet community on which he farmed along with raising stock. He also was involved with selling lots for the "New Rozet" townsite established north of the railroad tracks in 1924. Jake died on October 27, 1951, after a lingering illness, at the age of 75. He was buried in the Rozet Cemetery, Rozet, Campbell County, Wyoming.

Erik Halverson

Erik Halverson was born September 24, 1879, in Mora, Kopparberg (Dalauna), Sverige (Sweden) to Halvar Hall Persson and Kerstin Jakobsdotter. Records indicate he left Mora, Kopparberg, Sweden, on January 31, 1908, with his sister, Anna Marie, arriving in June 1909 at Winnipeg, Manitoba Province, Canada, where they crossed the border into the United States. He was about 28 years of age. Erik filed for a homestead in Sections 35 and 26, Township 50 north, Range 70 West near his brother Jacob.

Erik lived in the Rozet area until his death on September 5, 1949, at the age of 69. He is buried in the Rozet Cemetery, Campbell County, Wyoming.

Sources for Jacob "Jake" Halverson:
"Jake Halvorsen, 75, Old-timer, Laid to Rest at Rozet," The News Record, Gillette, Wyoming, November 1, 1951.
Ancestry.com, Sweden, Indexed Birth Records, 1859-1947) (database online), Provo, UT.
Ancestry.com, Sweden, Immigrants Registered in Church Books, 1783-1991; (database online), Provo, UT.
Ancestry.com, U.S. Homestead Records, 1863-1908. (database online), Provo, UT.
Ancestry.com, U.S. Social Security Applications and Claims Index, 1936-2007; (database online), Provo, UT.
Ancestry.com, Find-a-Grave Index 1600s-Current; (database online), Provo, UT.

Sources for Erik Halverson:
Ancestry.com, Sweden, Indexed Birth Records, 1859-1947) (database online), Provo, UT, USA; Ancestry.com Operations, Inc., 2011.
Ancestry.com, Sweden, Immigrants Registered in Church Books, 1783-1991; (database online), Provo, UT.
Ancestry.com, U.S. Homestead Records, 1863-1908. (database online), Provo, UT, USA; Ancestry.com Operations, Inc., 2014.
Ancestry.com, U.S. Social Security Applications and Claims Index, 1936-2007; (database online), Provo, UT.
Ancestry.com, Find-a-Grave Index 1600s-Current; (database online), Provo, UT, USA; Ancestry.com Operations, Inc., 2012.

Anna Marie Halverson

Anna Marie Halverson was born October 26, 1886, in Mora, Kopparberg (Dalarna), Sverig (Sweden), to Halvar Persson and Kerstin Jakobsdotter. At age 21 she immigrated with her brother, Erik, to the United States via Canada arriving in Minneapolis, MN, on February 7, 1908. Later that year they arrived in Rozet, Wyoming, to locate in the Rozet community near their brother, Jacob. Anna Marie filed in Section 25, Township North, Range 70 West. She along with her brothers accumulated extensive land holdings during the early days of Rozet. She was the mother of one child:

Elvira Christina   b: 25 Oct 1926   d: 19 Feb 2006   m: Francis Joseph Thar

Anna lived on her homestead until illness caused her to move to a nursing home in Sheridan, Wyoming. Anna died on April 11, 1963, age 76, in Sheridan and was buried on April 16, 1963, in the Rozet Cemetery, Rozet, Wyoming. She was preceded in death by her four brothers, Eric and Jake of Rozet, and Carl and Andrew of Sweden.

Sources:
Bureau of Land Management, Homestead Patents Index, [www.glorecords.blm.gov].
"Service Held for A. Halverson, Rozet Resident," The News Record, Gillette, Wyoming, April 18, 1963.
Campbell County Cemetery District Burial Property Report, September 28, 1998.
Ancestry.com, 1910, U.S. Federal Census for Precinct 16, Outside Moorcroft, Crook County, Wyoming, [database online], Provo, UT.
Ancestry.com, 1920 U.S. Federal Census for Election district 5, Rozet North, Campbell County, Wyoming, [database online], Provo, UT.

The Shaughnessy Family
1901

John "Jack" Shaughnessy   **Katherine (Nestor) Shaughnessy**

The first family of Rozet was the family of John and Kate Shaughnessy. Heading for Oregon, they arrived in Gillette in June 1901 from Deadwood, South Dakota, in a covered wagon with a milk cow tied on behind. They camped for the night where the Campbell County Court House now stands. The family consisted of John Shaughnessy, his wife Katherine Agnes "Kate" (Nestor) Shaughnessy and their six children: Claire, age 12; Ellen "Nellie;" age 11; Mary, age 9; Gertrude "Toots;" age 7, were born in Crab Orchard, Johnson County, Nebraska. John, Jr., age 4, and the baby, Ruth, age 2, were born in Deadwood, Lawrence County, South Dakota.

John Shaughnessy was born in May 14, 1855, Burlington, Vermont, where his parents Lawrence and Ellen Shaughnessy lived for a short while before moving to Logan County, Illinois. His parents emigrated from County Carlow, Ireland, arriving in America on November 25, 1851, in New York City on the *Washington* from Liverpool, England, with four sons, Simon S., age 11, Michael, age 10, Patrick, age 6, Lawrence, age 1, and one daughter, Ann, age 4 (who married Matthew C. Brennan [see page: 44]). In the 1860 U.S. Federal Census we find the family living at Middletown, Logan County, Illinois, with John recorded as age five. By the 1870 Federal Census the family is living at Todd Creek, Johnson County, Nebraska.

Katherine Nestor was born on August 6, 1863, at Elkhart, Illinois, the daughter of Martin and Mary Nestor. Kate moved to Tecumseh, Johnson County, Nebraska, with her parents at an early age. There she grew to womanhood and married John Shaughnessy on September 6, 1887. They were the parents of seven children, one died in infancy:

Claire Elizabeth	b: 05 Jul 1888	d: 30 Dec 1962	m: E.A. "Tony" Littleton
Ellen "Nellie"	b: 06 Apr 1890	d: 25 Nov 1976	m: Tobias A. "Tobe" Frey
Mary G.	b: 16 Mar 1892	d: 06 Apr 1914	m: (1) John L. Thompson (div)
			(2) Clifford Chandler White
Gertrude H. "Toots"	b: 09 Nov 1894	d: 19 Aug 1974	m: Albert "Bert" Fortin
John Aloysius	b: 19 Dec 1898	d: 09 May 1950	m: (1) Dora Torbert (div)
			(2) Sheila A. Tidd
Ruth Cecelia	b: 13 Jan 1899	d: 10 Mar 1980	m: (1) Howard Freeman (div)
			(2) Earl Francis Burke,

The Shaughnessy family moved from Tecumseh, Nebraska, to Nahant, Lawrence County, South Dakota, in 1895. In 1901, they decided to move to Oregon. John and Kate may have stopped in Gillette to visit with their nephew, Lawrence Shaughnessy, who had come to this area when the railroad ended at Gillette. He worked for the Burlington Railroad as section foreman for 32 years mostly out of Arvada. He lived in Gillette for five years prior to his death in November 1934.

A man who desperately needed immediate help offered John Shaughnessy a job. The family stayed in Gillette until the job was finished. After which Mr. Shaughnessy accepted a job at Rozet with the Burlington Railroad. The family lived in the section house. There was no depot at the time. There were no neighbors, only cowboys riding through and an occasional sheepherder. The people living in Moorcroft and Gillette were considered their closest neighbors. This was before homesteaders began arriving in the area to file on homesteads.

Under the Original Homestead Entry Act of May 20, 1862, a person could only file for 160 acres. In 1903 John Shaughnessy filed for a 160-acre homestead, and Kate filed for an additional 160 acres. She was issued the final Land Patent documents on August 27, 1908, as John's widow, and on May 17, 1909 for her homestead. The homesteads were located one-half mile north of Rozet on Donkey Creek in Section 30, Township 50 North, Range 69 West. The land was one mile long and one-half mile wide. Katherine later filed on an additional homestead to bring their total to 480 acres. They did no farming, only cattle grazing. Shortly after filing on the homestead, John became ill, and Katherine took him back to Tecumseh, Nebraska, for medical treatment, where he died April 5, 1903. Katherine and the children returned to Rozet.

Determined to support her family, she cooked for the railroad workers, took in boarders, and opened a grocery store in the back of the section house—Rozet's first store. She later opened a post office in a corner of the store. They previously got their mail off the railroad's handcar. In 1911 Katherine built a larger general merchandise store. It was ten by twenty feet and built in the yard of the section house. This small store would later be used for a homestead shack. She operated the store until 1918 when she sold it to her sons-in-law, E. A. Littleton and Tobe Frey. After about a year, they built a new store on the south side of the railroad tracks. E. A. about 1920 traded Tobe his interest in the store for property on Wild Horse creek and Tobe became sole proprietor. The store burned down in 1933—arson.

Rozet's first school was established in 1903 after Mrs. Shaughnessy convinced the Crook County School Board that one was needed. On her own she attempted to attend the school board meeting in Sundance to ask for a school to be established at Rozet. There are several renditions of just how, or if, she ever got to the meeting. Whether she did or not, the school was approved after she guaranteed there would be the required five students, volunteered a room above her store in the section house to serve as the school, and promised to personally provide the desks, and chairs. She also would provide room and board, for $15.00 a month, for the teacher. She even had a teacher lined up to teach the school for $35.00 a month, her niece, Mary Shaughnessy of Tecumseh, Nebraska. Her request was approved, and that September 1903, school began with Kate's five oldest children as its first students.

Shortly afterwards John "Jack" Brennan from Tecumseh, Nebraska, filed for a homestead two miles east of Rozet in 1906, and Jacob "Jake" Halverson filed one-half mile west of Rozet in 1908. By 1911, when Campbell County was created, a good many people began arriving to take up homesteads and began to fence out the cattlemen and sheepmen.

Kate became very active in the small community of Rozet. In 1911, she served as one of three election judges for the Rozet District, Precinct #3, during the first elections held in Campbell County. The polling place was the Shaughnessy Mercantile Store. In addition to her official duties she also served a dinner meal, for thirty-five cents, and an oyster stew supper for the voters. Kate was appointed Justice of the Peace. Kate also petitioned the Bishop to allow a Catholic Church to be built in Rozet. She organized Catholics in the area to fund it and help build it. It was a mission church, and the Priest would come once a month for services. With remarkable pioneer ingenuity, she raised her six surviving children. Winter evenings at the section house were long. To pass the time the Shaughnessy girls learned telegraphy. Because of the girls' interest Kate sent Mary and Gertrude to Omaha, Nebraska, to complete their training. After school, the two girls worked as telegraph operators all along the Burlington line from Newcastle, Wyoming, to Billings, Montana. Kate's daughters also filed for homesteads.

Katherine Agnes Shaughnessy died at the age of 88 on November 17, 1951, and was buried November 20, 1951, in the Mount Pisgah Cemetery, Gillette, Wyoming.

1914
Kate Shaughnessy and her five daughters,
Claire Littleton, Nellie Frey, Ruth Burke, Toots Fortin, Mary Thompson

Nellie Frey, Kate Shaughnessy, Claire Littleton,
Ruth Burke, Toots Fortin (year unknown)

Sources:

Photos provided by Janice Day Stratman, daughter of Nellie Shaughnessy Frey.
Bureau of Land Management, Homestead Patents Index, [www.glorecords.blm.gov].
"Katherine Shaughnessy," page 532, Campbell County, The Treasured Years, 1990, compiled by the Campbell County
*   Historical Society, Gillette, Wyoming.*
"Ruth Burke and the Shaughnessy's," pages 85-88, Campbell County Profiles, by Lenora Hubbard, 1985.
"Double Wedding (Thompson-Shaughnessy and Frey-Shaughnessy)," The Gillette News, Gillette, Wyoming, June 13, 1914.
"Torbert-Shaughnessey Marriage," Campbell County Record, Gillette, Wyoming, July 29, 1920.
"Court is in Session This Week (divorce-John & Dora Shaughnessy)," The Gillette News, September 1922.
"'Rozet (marriage Gertrude Shaughnessy & Bert Fortin)," The Gillette News, Gillette, Wyoming, July 3, 1924.
"Lawrence Shaughnessy Passes Away Tuesday at Tecumseh, Nebraska," page 1, The News Record, Gillette, Wyoming,
*   November 29, 1934.*
"Funeral Services Are Held for Mrs. J. Shaughnessy," page 1, The News Record, Gillette, Wyoming, November 22, 1951.
Campbell County Cemetery District's Burial Property Report of September 8, 1998.
Ancestry.com, New York, Irish Immigrant Arrival Records, 1846-1851, [database online], Provo, UT.
Ancestry.com, 1860 U.S. Federal Census for Post Office Middleton, Logan County, Illinois, [database online] Provo, UT.
Ancestry.com, 1870 U.S. Federal Census for Todd Creek, Johnson County, Nebraska, [database online] Provo, UT.
Ancestry.com, 1880 U.S. Federal Census for Nemaha Township, Johnson County, Nebraska, [database online] Provo, UT.
Ancestry.com, 1900 U.S. Federal Census for Rapid Creek Township, Lawrence County, South Dakota, [database online] Provo, UT.
Ancestry.com, 1910 U.S. Federal Census for Precinct 16 Outside of Moorcroft, Crook County, Wyoming, [database online] Provo, UT.
Ancestry.com, 1920 U.S. Federal Census for Rozet South, Precinct 26, Campbell County, Wyoming, [database online] Provo, UT.
Ancestry.com, 1930 U.S. Federal Census for Election District 5, Rozet, Campbell County, Wyoming, [database online] Provo, UT.

Claire Elizabeth (Shaughnessy) and Earnest Anthony "Tony" Littleton

Claire Shaughnessy and Tony Littleton were married on October 15, 1913, and set up housekeeping in Gillette. Claire was born July 5, 1888, at Tecumseh, Johnson County, Nebraska. Tony was born May 27, 1888, in Rancho, Gonzales County, Texas, to Isaac Newton and Sybil Emily (Bartlett) Littleton. His mother died in 1892 and his father in 1912. After his father's death Tony's two brothers convinced him to come to Wyoming and go into the sheep business. The 1910 Federal Census shows him and his brother, Everett, living with their brother, William and his family, in Gillette. Tony went to work for the Burlington Railroad where in 1913 he lost a foot in a freight train accident. In 1910 Claire Shaughnessy filed on a homestead near her mother in Sections 29 and 30, Township 50 North, Range 69 West. In 1913 Tony filed on a homestead near Wildcat. Claire worked as an agent-operator for the CB&Q railroad from 1907 until 1913. Tony and Claire were the parents of five children:

Name	Birth	Death	Marriage
Ruth E.	b: 14 Jan 1914	d:	m: (1) Lloyd Bryant (2) _____ Dixon
Robert Thomas	b: 14 Jan 1916,	d: 27 Feb 2004	m: Helen Meade
Gail B. (son)	b: 18 Sep 1917,	d: 23 May 1999	m: Virginia Moon
Ellen Rose	b: 03 Oct 1920,	d: 24 Sep 2006	m: (1) James Ferguson (div) (2) Thomas H. Shedden
James Willis	b: 14 Sep 1921,	d: 13 Jul 1923 (from snakebite)	

They made their home on a ranch on Wild Horse Creek until 1925 when they moved to Gillette. Tony was elected Campbell County Treasurer in 1925. He served two two-year terms. Claire in turn was elected as Treasurer and served two terms. In 1929 Tony was elected to the Wyoming State Legislature and reelected in 1931. In 1933, he was appointed postmaster of the Gillette Post Office. He served for twenty-five years until his retirement in 1958, at age 70. Claire Littleton, age 74, died December 30, 1962, in Sheridan, Wyoming. She was buried on January 2, 1963, in Mount Pisgah Cemetery, Gillette, Wyoming. Tony Littleton, age 95, died June 3, 1983, in Oregon City, Clackamas County, Oregon. He was buried June 7, 1983, in Mount Pisgah Cemetery, Gillette, Wyoming.

Sources:
Bureau of Land Management, Homestead Patent Index, [www.glorecords.blm.gov].
"Little Boy Dies From Snake Bite (James)," Gillette News, Gillette, Wyoming, July 19, 1927.
"Earnest A. Littleton," pages 115-117, Campbell County Profiles, by Leora M. Hubbard, 1985.
"Requiem Mass Sung January 2 for Mrs. E. A. Littleton," The News Record, Gillette, Wyoming, January 3, 1963.
"Littleton Service Tuesday," The News Record, Gillette, Wyoming, June 5, 1983.
"Ellen Rose Shedden," obituary, The News Record, Gillette, Wyoming, Friday, September 29, 2006.
Campbell County Cemetery District Burial Property Report, September 1998.
Ancestry.com, World War I Draft Registration Cards 1917-1918, [database online] Provo, UT.
Ancestry.com, Social Security Death Index (for Claire and Tony; Robert; Gail), [database online] Provo, UT.
Ancestry.com, Oregon Death Index, 1903-989 (Tony) [database online] Provo, UT.
Ancestry.com, 1900 U.S. Federal Census, Justice Precinct 8, Gonzales, Texas, USA, [database online] Provo, UT.
Ancestry.com, 1910 U.S. Federal Census, for Gillette, Crook County, Wyoming, [database online] Provo, UT.
Ancestry.com, 1920 U.S. Federal Census, for Campbell County, Wyoming, [database online] Provo, UT.

Ellen "Nellie" (Shaughnessy) and Tobias Arnold "Tobe" Frey

1914

1949

Nellie Shaughnessy was born April 6, 1890, at Tecumseh, Johnson County, Nebraska. She came to Rozet with her mother about 1903. Nellie Shaughnessy filed in 1913 on a homestead near Wildcat, on Sections 4, 5 and 6, Township 50 North, Range 74 West, near her brother-in-law, Tony Littleton. Tobias A. Frey was born on May 11, 1881, in Switzerland. He is listed in the 1885 Nebraska State Census at age four living with his parents John and Bertha Frey and six brothers and sisters at Eight Mile Grove, Cass County, Nebraska. His birthplace was listed as Switzerland; the 1900 Federal Census for Eight Mile Grove, Cass County, Nebraska also lists his birthplace as Switzerland and that his year of immigration was 1881. He lived there until manhood where he is found in the 1910 Wyoming State Census living in Newcastle, Weston County, Wyoming. Tobe moved to Gillette in 1913 to work for the Burlington Railroad as a telephone lineman-engineer. There he met Nellie Shaughnessy who was working in Gillette as a telephone operator for the Northern Wyoming Telephone Company. They were married on June 3, 1914, in the home of her mother, Kate Shaughnessy. It was a double wedding with Nellie's sister, Mary, who married John L. Thompson, of Sheridan.

The Frey Family
Judy (holding her son David), Floyd Hoyt, Lou, Mrs. Shaughnessy, Bernice, Nellie, Tobe, Janis, and Bill Frey in front
About 1944

In 1916, Tobe and his brother-in-law, E. A. Littleton, bought two acres of land in Rozet from Claude Lawrence. On it they built a home and the Rozet Mercantile Store which they operated until the store burned down in March 1933. He sold the buildings to Jesse Kennedy and engaged in ranching until he moved to Monarch, Wyoming, in 1944. Tobe and Nellie were the parents of four children:

Bernice Elizabeth	b: 22 Apr 1915	d: 03 Dec 1991	m: Charlie Oliver Day
Louis Arnold	b: 22 Nov 1920	d: 26 Jun 1997	m: Jean M. Schoenfeld
Philip Gregory	b: 14 Oct 1924	d: 31 Aug 2013	m: Betty Waddell
Judith D. "Judy"	b: 06 Apr 1929	d: 22 Sep 2020	m: Floyd N. Hoy

Tobe died on October 30, 1950, at the Sheridan Hospital. He was buried in the Sheridan Municipal Cemetery, Sheridan, Wyoming on November 2, 1950. Nellie died on November 25, 1976, at Story, Wyoming, and was buried in the Sheridan Municipal Cemetery, Sheridan, Wyoming.

Lou Frey, U.S. Navy

Judy Frey and Janice Day
World War II -- 1942

Phil Frey, U.S. Army

Sources:
Photos provide by Janice Day Stratman, granddaughter of Nellie Shaughnessy Frey.
Bureau of Land Management, Homestead Patent Index, [www.glorecords.blm.gov].
"Ruth Burke and the Shaughnessy's," page 85-88, Campbell County Profiles, by Lenora Hubbard 1985.
"A Double Wedding," The News Record, Gillette, Wyoming, June 13, 1914.
"Rozet Rumbling-son born Nov 17," Gillette News, Gillette, Wyoming, November 19, 1920.
"Rozet-baby son born Oct 14," Gillette News, Gillette, Wyoming, October 30, 1924.
"Personals-baby daughter born," The News Record, Gillette, Wyoming, April 11, 1929.
"Society—Day-Frey Marriage," The News Record, Gillette, Wyoming, June 7, 1935.
"Final Rites Held for T. A. Frey," page 1, The News Record, Gillette, Wyoming, November 16, 1950.
"Obituary-Louis Frey," The News Record, Gillette, Wyoming, June 27, 1997.
Sheridan Municipal Cemetery Index, Sheridan, Wyoming.
Ancestry.com, World War I Draft Registration Cards, 1917-1918, [database online] Provo, UT.
Ancestry.com, Social Security Death Index (for Nellie, Tobe and Louis), [database online] Provo, UT.
Ancestry.com, U.S. Veterans Gravesites, ca. 1775-2006, [database online] Provo, UT.
Ancestry.com, 1885 Nebraska State Census Collection, 1860-1885 [database online] Provo, UT.
Ancestry.com, 1900 U.S. Federal Census, for Eight Mile Grove, Cass County, Nebraska, [database online] Provo, UT.
Ancestry.com, 1910 Wyoming Census (1860-1910) for Newcastle, Weston County, Wyoming, [database online] Provo, UT.
Ancestry.com, 1920 U.S. Federal Census for Rozet South, Precinct 26, Campbell County, Wyoming, [database online] Provo, UT.
Ancestry.com, 1930 U.S. Federal Census for Election District 5, Campbell County, Wyoming, [database online] Provo, UT.

Mary G. (Shaughnessy) Thompson and Clifford Chapman White

Mary Shaughnessy was born March 16, 1892, at Tecumseh, Johnson, Nebraska. She came to Wyoming with her mother and father in 1901. Mary was married June 3, 1914, to John L. Thompson of Sheridan, Wyoming. The wedding took place in the home of Mary's mother, Mrs. Kate Shaughnessy at Rozet. His World War I Draft Registration Card, dated June 5, 1917, filed in Casper, Wyoming, shows that he was born February 1, 1891, in Osceola, Iowa; that he had a wife, son, and mother dependent upon him; his employment was working as a conductor for the CB&Q railroad. Mary and John lived on a homestead near Wildcat. Mary also worked as an agent-telegrapher for CB&Q railroad. John and Mary Thompson were the parents of three sons:

John Anthony	b: 17 Apr 1916	d: 16 May 1991		m: Rosalee Johnson
Bernard Jeff	b: 05 Jul 1919	d: Mar 1963		m: Farrell Louise Hayden
James	b: 14 Jul 1928	d:		m: Jessie Scovel

On March 16, 1932, Mary was appointed as postmistress of the Rozet Post Office; serving for twelve years until September 30, 1944. She moved to Rozet and her sons attended school at Rozet Consolidated and graduated from Rozet High School. John and Mary were divorced in 1934. He died in June 1965 in Nevada.

On November 30, 1935, Mary married Clifford Chapman "Cliff" White in Rapid City, Laurence County, South Dakota. His World War I Draft Registration Card, dated June 5, 1917, filed in Casper, Wyoming, shows that Clifford was born July 22, 1897, in Topeka, Shawnee County, Kansas; that he was single and involved in ranching and farming west of Moorcroft. Cliff filed a homestead in Sections 12, 13, and 18, Township 52 North, Range 70 West. His father, Cassias M. "C.M.," and his brother Howard Morton White, also filed for homesteads in the Adon community. In 1920 his father leased his homestead to Henry Hayes and went back Shawnee County, Kansas. Cliff served as the Adon mail carrier out of the Moorcroft Post Office for several years. He served as the 1920 Census Taker for Iowa Precinct. He also built reservoirs for surrounding homesteaders including one for S. R. Jackson and his own, known as the "Cliff White Reservoir." Children of families living in the Rozet community have pleasant memories of attending family picnics around that reservoir. Perry Wallace bought Cliff's homestead. Clifford died in July 1963. No references have been found of where he died. Mary died on April 6, 1970, in Sheridan, Wyoming, and was buried in the Sheridan Municipal Cemetery.

Sources:
Photo taken by Matt Avery in the Rozet Post Office, Rozet, Wyoming July 2020.
Bureau of Land Management, Homestead Patent Index [www.glorecords.blm.gov].
"Double Wedding (Thompson-Shaughnessy and Frey-Shaughnessy," The Gillette News, Gillette, Wyoming, June 13, 1914.
"Assumed Postmistress (Rozet) Duties on April 1," Rozet, The News Record, Gillette, Wyoming, April 7, 1932.
"Divorce Petition Filed, January 9, 1934," The News Record, Gillette, Wyoming, January 11, 1934.
"Mrs. Mary Thompson and Clifford C. White surprise...wedding," Rozet, The News Record, Gillette, Wyoming, December 4, 1935.
"Adon Items," (Cliff White building reservoir on S. R. Jackson ranch), Gillette News, Gillette, Wyoming, December 17, 1920.
Sheridan Municipal Cemetery Index, Sheridan, Wyoming.
Ancestry.com, Social Security Death Index (John Thompson, Clifford White), [database online] Provo, UT.
Ancestry.com, Montana Death Index, 1860-2007, (John L.), database online] Provo, UT.
Ancestry.com, World War I Draft Registration Cards, 1917-1918 (John L. Thompson & Clifford C. White),
    [database on-line] Provo, UT.
Ancestry.com, South Dakota Marriages, 1905-1949, database online] Provo, UT
Ancestry.com, 1900 U.S. Federal Census, for Topeka Ward 5, Shawnee County, Kansas (Cliff White), [database online] Provo, UT.
Ancestry.com, Kansas State Census Collection, 1855-1925, Bucklin, Ford County, Kansas, Year 1915 (Cliff White), [database online]
    Provo, UT.
Ancestry.com, 1920 U.S. Federal Census, for Gillette Campbell County, Wyoming, (John A. Thompson) [database online] Provo, UT.
Ancestry.com, 1920 U.S. Federal Census, for North Gillette, Campbell County, Wyoming, (Cliff White), [database online] Provo, UT.
Ancestry.com, 1930 U.S. Federal Census, for Gillette, Campbell County, Wyoming, (John A. Thompson), [database online] Provo, UT.
Ancestry.com, 1930 U.S. Federal Census, for Election District 8, Campbell County, Wyoming, (Cliff White), [database online]
    Provo, UT.

Gertrude H. "Toots" (Shaughnessy) and Albert Addison "Bert" Fortin

Tobe and Nellie Frey, Gertrude H. "Toots" (Shaughnessy) and Bernie Mullins

Gertrude "Toots" Shaughnessy was born November 16, 1894, at Tecumseh, Johnson County, Nebraska. She came to Rozet with her mother in 1903. Gertrude Shaughnessy filed in 1916 on a homestead located in Sections 18 and 19, Township 50 North, Range 70 West near her mother. Gertrude and Bert were married June 29, 1924. Prior to their marriage Toots worked as a relief telephone operator for the Northern Wyoming Telephone Company. She also worked as a relief agent for the Burlington depot at Rozet. Toots and Bert continued to live at Rozet.

Bert was born April 7, 1897, at Shirley, Cloud County, Kansas. He served in World War I as a Private in the U. S Army. He enlisted September 3, 1918, at Newcastle, Wyoming, and was discharged on February 13, 1919, due to acute appendicitis, at Camp Stuart, Virginia. At the time of their marriage he was working as a mechanic in Upton, Wyoming. No children were born to this union.

Toots, age 79, died on August 19, 1974, in Gillette, Wyoming. She was buried on August 22, 1974, in Mount Pisgah Cemetery, Gillette, Wyoming. Bert died February 10, 1983, in Sturgis, South Dakota. He was buried in the Black Hills National Cemetery, Sturgis, South Dakota.

Sources:
Photos provide by Janice Day Stratman, granddaughter of Nellie Shaughnessy Frey.
Bureau of Land Management, Homestead Patent Index [www.glorecords.blm.gov].
"Ruth Burke and the Shaughnessy's," pages 85-88, Campbell County Profiles, by Lenora Hubbard, 1985.
"Fortin-Shaughnessy," Rozet, Gillette News, Gillette, Wyoming, July 3, 1924.
"[Gertrude] Fortin Rites Today," The News Record, Gillette, Wyoming, August 22, 1974.
Campbell County Cemetery District Burial Property Report, September 1998.
Ancestry.com, World War I Draft Registration Cards, 1917-1918 [database online] Provo, UT.
Ancestry.com, U.S. National Homes for Disabled Volunteer Soldiers, 1866-1936, [database online] Provo, UT.
Ancestry.com, U.S. Veterans Gravesites, ca. 1775-2996, [database online] Provo, UT.
Ancestry.com, Social Security Death Index, (Albert), [database online] Provo, UT.
Ancestry.com, Kansas State Census Collection, 1855-1925 (Albert), [database online] Provo, UT.
Ancestry.com, 1910 U.S. Federal Census, for Shirley, Cloud County, Kansas, (Albert), [database online] Provo, UT.
Ancestry.com, 1920 U.S. Federal Census, for Skull Creek, Weston County, Wyoming, (Albert), [database online] Provo, UT.
Ancestry.com, 1930 U.S. Federal Census, for Election District 5, Campbell County, Wyoming, (Bert and Toots), [database-online]
        Provo, UT.

John Aloysius "Jack" and Stella (Tidd) Shaughnessy

John Aloysius "Jack" Shaughnessy was born December 19, 1895, in Nyhant, Lawrence County, South Dakota. He filed, about 1916, on a homestead located in Section 19 and 30, Township 54 North, Range 69 West and Sections 24 and 25, Township 54 North, Range 70 west. He was working as a teamster on 1917 when he filled out the World War I Draft Registration Card. In June 1917, he enlisted in the army as a PVT and served during WWI in France with the 148th Field Artillry Regimnt. His unit was attached to the famed "42nd" Rainbow Division. Upon his discharge he returned in July 1919 to Campbell County where he made his homestead claim not far from where he grew up. On July 14, 1920, John married Dora Torbert in Newcastle, Wyoming. He was appointed duties as a brand inspector for Campbell County in April 1922. Jack joined the U.S. Forest Service where he would work until 1938 when he joined the US. Office of Indian Services. John and Dora were divorced in September 1922. He married Stella Tidd on October 21, 1925. They are found in the 1930 U.S. Federal Census living in Nevada Canal, Lyon County, Nevada, with two children. John and Stella were the parents of three children:

Claire F.	b: 16 Jul 1926	d: (Living?)	m:
John Burke	b: 09 Jun 1927	d: 26 Aug 1972	m:
Michael Earl	b: 12 Nov 1935	d: Living	m:

Eventually the family settled down in Carson City, Nevada, where he would retire as a city government employee. He served as a past commander of the Kit Carson Post No. 2726, Veterans of Foreign Wars (VFW), and was a member of the American Legion. He wrote a book of poetry and had a book of poems published entitled, *Songs of the Harp*. He began a tradition of dressing up as Daniel Boone for the annual Nevada Day Parade. John died May 9, 1952, possibly in Sparks, Nevada. He was buried in the Golden Gate National Cemetery, in San Bruno, California. Stella died January 16, 1980, in California or Nevada, and was buried in the Golden Gate National Cemetery alongside her husband.

Sources:
Photos; from the Rockpile Museum, Gillette, Wyoming Facebook page, June 23, 2021.
Bureau of Land Management, Homestead Patent Index [www.glorecords.blm.gov].
"Ruth Burke and the Shaughnessy's," pages 85-88, Campbell County Profiles, by Lenora Hubbard, 1985.
"Shaughnessy-Torbert Wedding," Campbell County Record, Gillette, Wyoming, July 29, 1920.
"Court is in Session This Week (divorce-John and Dora Shaughnessy)," The Gillette News, Gillette, Wyoming, September 7, 1922.
Ancestry.com, South Dakota Births, 1856-1903; [database online] Provo, UT.
Ancestry.com, World War I Draft Registration Cards 1917-1918; [database online] Provo, UT.
Ancestry.com, Social Security Death Index (for John and Stella, John Burke); [database online] Provo, UT.
Ancestry.com, U.S. Veterans Gravesites, ca. 1775-2006 (for John and Stella; John Burke); [database online] Provo, UT.
Ancestry.com, 1910 U.S. Federal Census for Moorcroft, Crook County, Wyoming, (John), [database online] Provo, UT.
Ancestry.com, 1920 U.S. Federal Census forward 2, Scottsbluff County, Nebraska, Scottsbluff County,(John), [database online] Provo, UT.
Ancestry.com, 1930 U.S. Federal Census for Canal, Lyon County, Nevada, (Jack A, Stella and 2 children), [database online] Provo, UT.

Ruth Cecelia (Shaughnessy) and Earl Francis Burke

Ruth Shaughnessy married Howard Lester Freeman, about 1918, possibly in Nebraska. No marriage record has been located. On his World War I Draft Registration Card, dated September 12, 1918, he lists as his wife, "Ruth S. Freeman" and their address as Salem, Dent County, Missouri. They are listed in the 1920 U.S. Federal Census for Nebraska, as living in Fillmore County, Exeter Township, with their eight-month-old daughter:

Marjorie Katherine   b: 29 Apr 1919   d: 25 Sep 1968   m: Kenneth DeWitt Jackson

The "Rozet" column in *The News Record* recorded several visits of this family with her mother, Kate Shaughnessy. Ruth and Howard were divorced between 1920 and 1922. He is listed in the 1930 U.S. Federal Census as living in Houston, Harris County, Texas. Howard was born April 9, 1884, in Dent County, Missouri, and died October 13, 1973, in Ellis County, Texas.

Ruth and Earl Francis Burke were married on December 22, 1922, in Minnehaha County, South Dakota. He was born January 16, 1890, in Madison, South Dakota. He enlisted in the U.S. Army on July 19, 1917, in Sioux Falls, South Dakota, and was discharged on August 11, 1919, at Camp Dodge, Iowa. Earl contacted Tuberculosis while in the service and suffered with it for the remainder of his life.

After their marriage they lived at Rozet. Earl was a carpenter and worked as the janitor for the Rozet Consolidated and High School for several years. He also served as Clerk on the District Three School Board. Marjorie attended school at Rozet School. In late 1940s due to Earl's health problems, they moved to California, where Ruth went to work. She joined the Meat Cutters union and worked at that trade in El Segundo, California, for about a year and a half. Earl died on May 3, 1950, in Orange County, California. Ruth brought him home for burial in the Custer Battlefield Cemetery, Crow Agency, Montana (now known as the Custer National Cemetery).

Ruth went to work at the Goings Hotel as the desk clerk, remaining there for fourteen years until her retirement. Ruth died in March 10, 1980, and was buried in Custer Battlefield Cemetery alongside her husband Earl. Her daughter Marjorie Jackson was also buried there upon her death on September 25, 1968; her husband Kenneth DeWitt Jackson was also buried there on September 5, 2007.

Sources:
Obituary; Mrs. Ken Jackson, The News Record, Gillette, WY, Oct 3, 1968.
Obituary: Kenneth Dewitt Jackson, The News Record, Gillette, WY, Sep 5, 2007.
Little Big Horn National Cemetery (aka: Custer National Cemetery), Crow Agency, Big Horn County, Montana (Earl, Ruth, Marjorie, and Kenneth Jackson).
"Ruth Burke and the Shaughnessy's," pages 85-88, Campbell County Profiles, by Lenora Hubbard, 1985.
Campbell County, The Treasured Years, 1990, compiled by the Campbell County Historical Society, Gillette, Wyoming.
Ancestry.com, South Dakota Births, 1856-1903, (Ruth and Earl), [data base on line] Provo, UT.
Ancestry.com, South Dakota Marriages 1905-1949 (Earl F. Burke and Ruth Freeman) [data base on line], Provo, UT.
Ancestry.com, U.S. World War I Draft Registration Cards 1917-1918(Howard Freeman and Earl Burke), [data base on line], Provo, UT.
Ancestry.com, U.S. National Homes for Disabled Volunteer Soldiers, 1866-1938 (Earl) [data base on line], Provo, UT.
Ancestry.com, Social Security Death Index (Howard Freeman and Ruth Burke), [data base on line], Provo, UT.
Ancestry.com, California Death Index, 1940-1997 (Earl Burke); [data base on line], Provo, UT.
Ancestry.com, Texas Death Index, 1903-2000 (Howard Freeman).
Ancestry.com, Social Security Death Index (Kenneth D. Jackson), [data base on line], Provo, UT .
Ancestry.com, 1920 U.S. Federal Census for Exeter, Fillmore County, Nebraska, (Howard, Ruth and Marjorie Freeman), [database online] Provo, UT.
Ancestry.com, 1930 U.S. Federal Census for Election District 5, Campbell County, Wyoming, (Earl, Ruth and Marjorie Burke) [database online], Provo, UT.

THE THAR FAMILY
Henry "Dutch" Henry and Mary Agnes (Thomas)Thar
1901

Page 6   The News-Record, Gillette, Wyoming, March 7, 1968

MR. AND MRS. HENRY THAR (1951)

Henry Thar, age 24, filed for a homestead in 1902 located south of Rozet along Timber Creek. He was born January 28, 1878, in An Den Hausen, Germany, to Ernest and Elizabeth (Heisenhahn) Thar. He attended school there until he was ten years old. His mother died when Henry was eight and due to his father's poor health, at age ten he was sent to his mother's brother at Columbus, Nebraska, in 1888. The ship he came on was powered by both steam and sail and took twenty-one days to make the crossing. The fare was $50.00. His father died a year later, and young Henry made the trip back to Germany where he remained for a year and then returned to his uncle in Columbus, Nebraska. In the spring of 1891, at age 13, he went to Chadron, Nebraska, with a freighter named *Arkansas John* driving an ox team. In 1892 he drifted west, walking from Chadron to Cheyenne, Wyoming

While in Cheyenne he took any job offered from selling newspapers to making bicycles for the Granger Wagon Works. He later learned that the wagons made at this shop were used for the "invaders" of the Johnson County War. Having only completed the fourth grade when living in Germany he started back to school. His teacher was Mrs. Parry Organ, and realizing this boy needed a home, she opened her home to him. Her husband was depot superintendent at Camp Carlin in the early days of Cheyenne history. Henry worked for him for a time and later for George D. Rainsford, a wealthy easterner who had owned the famous Diamond ranch north of Cheyenne. Later he worked at the railroad shops, for Italian well drillers, and as a horse wrangler for the Durbin's ranch on the Sweetwater. Earnest Logan of Cheyenne taught him to make bits and spurs during these years in Cheyenne, and he learned carpentry. He made effective use of both trades in his later years. He also was a paid driver for the Cheyenne Volunteer Fire Department. While in Cheyenne, Henry made the acquaintance of Elias W. Whitcomb, who owned the Bar FS southeast of Rozet on the Belle Fourche River. In 1899, Henry came north to the Bar FS to work for Mr. Whitcomb.

In 1902 he filed on a homestead eight miles south of Rozet. The place had been the headquarters for the CQ horse outfit in the early days. There had been buildings and corrals constructed of logs, but they were burned as the ranchers of the area felt the place was being used by cattle and horse thieves. Henry built a nice four room house, and he called his place "the meadows." When Mr. Whitcomb sold the Bar FS to Metcalf and Neeley, and Jay Lucas came to manage it, Henry was hired to build and repair buildings on the Bar FS and the Shipwheel ranches. In 1910 he went to work for the Empire Sheep Company as a carpenter and blacksmith.

Henry married Mary Agnes Thomas, on July 22, 1914, at Newcastle, Wyoming, the daughter of Theodore M. and Elizabeth (Cotter) Thomas. She was born on March 8, 1886, in Council Bluffs, Pottawattamie County, Iowa. Mary spent her early years there. Her family moved to California twice during her childhood. She attended both parochial and public schools in Iowa and California. As a young girl she worked in a bank at Neola, Iowa. In 1913 her parents moved to Wyoming and homesteaded southwest of Moorcroft. Mary worked for a brief time at the Moorcroft Post Office. Henry Thar was issued land patents on March 25, 1913, November 20, 1914, and January 11, 1916, for about 640 acres in Section 30, Township 49 North, Range 69 West. Mary was issued her land patent on February 23, 1922, for about 320 acres in Sections 25, 30, and 31. Henry and Mary were the parents of five children:

John Henry, Jr.	b: 17 Feb 1916	d: 21 Apr 1977	m: Anna Louise Uhl
Elizabeth Florence	b: 29 Mar 1918	d: 25 May 1987	m: (1) Everett G. Achen
			(2) Calvin Clark Horger
Francis Joseph	b: 04 Oct 1920	d: 10 Oct 2014	m: Elvira Halverson
Vincent Robert	b: 03 May 1921	d: 06 Jul 2010	m: Leola Kottraba
Mary Ella	b: 22 May 1922	d:	m: (1) Bernard C. "Fuzz" Scott
			(2) Clinton Shannon Bartlett

In 1916 Henry built a blacksmith shop at his place where he built a thriving business doing blacksmith work for neighbors. Henry became renowned as a blacksmith, carpenter, and silversmith (his spurs were sought after far and wide). He made a pair of spurs for the Cheyenne Elks Club to present to President Theodore Roosevelt on his visit to Cheyenne. He built many houses and ranch or farm buildings for people south of Rozet before and after his marriage. Many are still standing today. They also farmed the place. In the early 1920s Mary's father Theodore Thomas became ill, and he died in 1925. Her mother, Elizabeth Thomas, came to live with Mary and Henry until she died in 1928. Mary Thar died on March 7, 1955, and was buried March 10, 1955, in Mount Pisgah Cemetery, Gillette, Wyoming. Henry Thar continued to live on the ranch until his death on April 15, 1958. He was buried on April 19, 1958, beside his wife in the Mount Pisgah Cemetery, Gillette, Wyoming.

Homestead of Dutch Henry Thar
(photo taken in 2010 by Shellie Thar Clark)

Barn he built on the Bar FS Ranch about 1910
(photo taken by Shellie Thar Clark)

Sources:
Photo of Dutch and March Thar from "Henry 'Dutch' Thar Walked to Wyoming in '91,'" by Mrs. Josephine McLucas, The News Record,
*   Gillette, Wyoming, date of issue unknown; from a scrapbook compiled by Jeanette Heptner, inherited by L. J. Whisler.*
Photos of Henry "Dutch" Thar's homestead courtesy of Shelle Thar Clark, June 2021.
Bureau of Land Management, Homestead Patents Index [www.glorecords.blm.gov].
"Requiem Mass Said Thursday for Mrs. Henry Thar," page 1, The News Record, Gillette, Wyoming, March 17, 1955.
"Requiem Mass Sung Saturday for Henry Thar, 80," The News Record, Gillette, Wyoming, April 24, 1958.
"Funeral Services Held Monday for B. C. Scott," page 1, The News Record, Gillette, Wyoming, July 1, 1958.
"Henry 'Dutch' Thar Walked to Wyoming in '91'," by Mrs. Josephine McLucas, The News Record, Gillette, Wyoming,
*   date of issue unknown; from a scrapbook compiled by Jeanette Heptner, inherited by L. J. Whisler.*
"Dutch Henry and Mary Thar," pages 590-591, Campbell County, The Treasured Years, 1990, compiled by Campbell County
*   Historical Society, Gillette, Wyoming.*
The Campbell County Cemetery District Burial Report of September 8, 1998.
Ancestry.com, U.S. Find-a-Grave Index, 1600s-Current, [database online], Provo. UT.
Ancestry.com, Laramie County, Wyoming, Naturalization Records, 1867-1920, [database online], Provo. UT.
Ancestry.com, U.S. World War I Draft Registration Cards, 1917-1918, [database online], Provo. UT.
Ancestry.com, 1910 Wyoming, Compiled Census Index, 1860-1919, [database online], Provo. UT.
Ancestry.com, 1910 U.S. Federal Census for Outside Moorcroft, school district 16, Crook County, Wyoming,
*   [database online], Provo. UT.*
Ancestry.com, 1920 U.S. Federal Census for Rozet South, Precinct 26, Campbell County, Wyoming, [database online], Provo, UT.
Ancestry.com, 1940 U.S. Federal Census for Campbell County, Wyoming, [database online], Provo. UT.

John Henry, Jr. and Anna Louise "Annie" (Uhl) Thar

John Henry, Jr. was born February 17, 1916, at home near Rozet, Campbell County, Wyoming, to John Henry "Dutch" and Mary Agnes (Thomas) Thar, Sr. He grew up on the ranch and attended rural schools and then the Rozet Consolidated school. John married Anna Louise Uhl about 1940. Anna was born September 21, 1910, in Sundance, Crook County, Wyoming. She was the daughter of Augustus and Christine (Hanson) Uhl. Anna was raised and educated in Moorcroft, Wyoming. John and Anna were divorced on October 1, 1942. Two children were born:

Joanna Uhl	b: 1939	d:		
Wilma Louise Thar	b: 1940	d:	m:	(1) Monte Leach
				(2) _____ Hanson

John was working for Charley Slattery when he registered in 1940 for the World War II draft. He served in the U.S. Army and was discharged with the rank of Corporal. Upon his return from the war he and Anna took up ranching in the Moorcroft and Rozet areas. John died on April 21, 1977, at Denver, Colorado, and was buried in Mount Pisgah Cemetery, Gillette, Wyoming. Annie died January 20, 2003 in Gillette, Wyoming. No record as to where she was buried.

Anna Louise was born September 21, 1910, in Sundance, Crook County, Wyoming. She was a daughter of August and Christine (Hanson) Uhl, immigrants from Germany to Douglas County, Nebraska, he in 1885, she in 1887. August and Christine were married October 26, 1891, in Douglas County, Nebraska. They came to Crook County, Wyoming in 1904 and settled near Sundance. In 1916 they homesteaded seven miles northeast of Moorcroft where they lived until they moved to Moorcroft, Wyoming. August died October 7, 1953; Christine May 7, 1956. Both are buried in the Moorcroft Cemetery, Moorcroft, Wyoming.

[Note from Moorcroft Burial Book #4: August Uhl was taken into custody April 24, 1918, by a deputy U.S. Marshall and taken to Cheyenne. He was an alien enemy never having been naturalized, and according to affidavits filed with the Federal authorities had made pro-German remarks. He was taken to an internment camp at Fort Douglas, Utah, and confined there until the end of the war. He returned May 12, 1918, and was granted a hearing and returned home. On June 12, 1920 he was made a citizen of the United States at Sundance by Judge I. P. Ilsley.]

Sources:
"Henry 'Dutch' Thar Walked to Wyoming in '91," The News Record, Gillette, Wyoming, 1985 (from scrapbook of historical articles compiled by L. J. Whisler.
Moorcroft Cemetery Burial Book #4, pages 354-5 and page 384 (August and Christine Uhl).
"Obituary-John Henry, Jr.," page 14, The News Record, Gillette, Wyoming, April 25, 1977.
"Obituary-Anna Louise Thar," page 15, Casper Star-Tribune, Casper, Wyoming, January 22, 2003.
Ancestry.com, Wyoming, U.S. Divorce Records, 1941-1969, [database online], Provo, UT.
Ancestry.com, U.S. Find-a-Grave, 1600s-Current, [database online], Provo, UT.
Ancestry.com, U. S WWII Draft Cards Young Men 1940-1947, [database online], Provo, UT.
Ancestry.com, U.S. Social Security Applications and Claims Index, 1936-2007, [database online], Provo, UT.
Ancestry.com, Newspapers.com Obituary Index, 1800s-current, [database online], Provo, UT.
Ancestry.com, Nebraska, Marriage Records, 1855-1908 (August and Christine Uhl), [database online], Provo, UT.
Ancestry.com, 1900 U.S. Federal Census, for Jefferson, Douglas County, Nebraska, [database online], Provo, UT.
Ancestry.com, 1930 U.S. Federal Census for Moorcroft, Crook County, Wyoming, [database online], Provo, UT.
Ancestry.com, 1940 U.S. Federal Census for Moorcroft, Crook County, Wyoming, [database online], Provo, UT.

Calvin and Elizabeth Florence (Thar) Horger

Elizabeth Thar was born March 29, 1918, in Council Bluffs, Pottawattamie, Iowa, at the home of her grandparents, Theodore and Elizabeth Thomas. Her parents were John "Dutch" Henry and Mary Agnes (Thomas) Thar. Elizabeth grew up on the homestead going to school at home and then in Rozet Consolidated School. On April 28, 1936, she married Everett G. Achen in Terry, Prairie County, Montana. They moved to Portland, Multnomah, Oregon. They divorced.

Elizabeth was a lady barber and worked in a barber shop in Portland. She married Calvin C. Horger on September 28, 1940, in Payette, Payette County, Idaho. They lived in Sandy, Clackamas County, Oregon. No children were born to this union. Elizabeth died in May 1987, in Sandy, Oregon. Calvin died November 23, 1999, in Sandy, Oregon.

Francis Joseph and Elvira Christina (Halverson) Thar

Francis was born on October 4, 1919, on the ranch to John "Dutch" Henry and Mary Agnes (Thomas) Thar. He grew up on the ranch and attended school at Rozet. After graduating from the Rozet High School, Francis served in the Army Air Corps during World War II from 1943 until honorably discharged in 1945. After returning home from the war he worked for various ranchers and eventually purchased his parents homestead near the Belle Fourche River, south of Rozet.

On June 16, 1963, Francis married Elvira Christina Halverson, daughter of Anna Marie Halverson. They lived most of their lives on their ranch north of Weston on the Little Powder River. Francis' life was centered around ranching and farming his land. He was especially proud of his wheat farming on the "South Ranch," In 2000 they moved to the Pioneer Manor in Gillette, Wyoming, Elvira died February 19, 2006; Francis on October 10, 2014. Both were buried in the Rozet Cemetery, Rozet, Wyoming.

Sources for Calvin and Elizabeth Florence (Thar) Horger
"Henry 'Dutch' Thar Walked to Wyoming in '91'," The News Record, Gillette, Wyoming, date of issue unknown, article found
    in scrapbook compiled by Jeanette Heptner.
Ancestry.com, U.S. Social Security Death Index, 1935-2014, [database online], Provo, UT.
Ancestry.com, Iowa, Births and Christenings Index, 1800-1999, [database online], Provo, UT.
Ancestry.com, Montana, County Marriages, 1865-1987, [database online], Provo, UT.
Ancestry.com, Idaho, County Marriage Records, 1864-1967, [database online], Provo, UT.
Ancestry.com, 1940 U. S Federal Census, for Portland, Multnomah County, Oregon, (Elizabeth), [database online], Provo, UT.
Ancestry.com, 1940 U.S. Federal Census for Portland, Multnomah, Oregon (E. G. Achen), [database online], Provo, UT.
Ancestry.com, U.S. Find-a-Grave Index, 1600s-Current, [database online], Provo, UT.
Ancestry.com, U.S. World War Draft Cards Young Men, 19401947, [database online], Provo, UT.

Sources for Francis and Elvira Christina (Halverson) Thar:
"Henry 'Dutch' Thar Walks to Wyoming in '91'," The News Record, Gillette, Wyoming, date of issue unknown, from a scrapbook
    compiled by Jeanette Heptner.
Obituary for Francis Thar from Ancestry.com, U.S. Find-a-Grave Index, 1600s-current, [database online], Provo, UT.
"Elvira Christina Thar, obituary," The News Record, Gillette, Wyoming, February 22, 2006.
Obituary for Elvira Halverson Thar, from Ancestry.com, U.S. Find-a-Grave Index, 1500s-current, [database online], Provo, UT.
Ancestry.com, U.S. World War II Draft Cards Young Men, 1940-1947, [database online], Provo, UT.
Ancestry.com, U.S. Social Security Applications and Claims Index, 1936-2007, [database online], Provo, UT.

Vincent Robert and Leola (Kottraba) Thar

Vince Thar was born May 3, 1921, Wyoming, to John "Dutch" Henry and Mary Agnes (Thomas) Thar at the ranch south of Rozet, Campbell County. He attended school in Rozet and graduated from Rozet High School in 1939. He worked for many area ranches as a working cowboy before enlisting in the U.S. Army Air Corps on February 16, 1942. Ten days before he was shipped off for World war II, on September 16, 1942, he married Leola Kottraba in Broadus, Powder River County, Montana. She was a daughter of Raymond and Kathryn (Lowery) Kottraba. Upon returning from the war in February 1946, Vince and Leola settled down to make a living and to raise a family. They became the parents of four children:

Rebecca "Becky"	b: 20 Jun 1943	d: Living	m: Robert Trigg
Gary	b: 09 Jun 1948	d: Living	m: Susan Taylor
Sherryl	b: 13 Jul 1960	d: Living	m: Greg Lindblom
Rochelle "Shelly"	b: 28 May 1963	d: Living	m: Kent Clark

After the war, Vince was a mechanic for various garages in Gillette and Moorcroft area working towards purchasing his own ranch on the Timber Creek Road where he raised Black Angus cattle and sold many black bulls. He planted crops in the spring and put up hay in the summer. He had a great love of the land and the ranching life. Vince was a strong supporter of the local 4-H and FFA programs and enjoyed watching his kids and grandkids participate in the events.

Leola grew up on her family's homestead south of Rozet. She attended Owens School in her early years and completed the remainder of her school years at Rozet Consolidated school graduating from high school in 1941. Their first daughter was born while Vince was away in the war. Leola raised her along with her two sisters Hazel and Helen Kottraba. Knowing she needed to provide for her young family, she applied for and was appointed postmistress of the Rozet Post Office before she was twenty-one years old, a position she held for thirty-seven years, retiring in 1980. She and Vince lived in the post office building while she served as postmistress. They remodeled it to accommodate the raising of four children there. Eventually they were able to move their family back to the ranch on Timber Creek Road where they raised Black Angus cattle and watched their family grow. After Leola retired in 1980 she began developing her love of art. She painted beautiful flowers and scenery and did incredible work with leather. She submitted her work to the County Fair and came home with many "Best in Show" ribbons.

Vince died July 16, 2010. Leola died February 2, 2020. Both are buried in Mount Pisgah Cemetery, Gillette, Wyoming.

Sources:
Email June 26, 2021 from Shellie Thar, Re: Henry Thar Families.
Photos copied from obituaries on Ancestry.com, U.S. Find-a-Grave Index, 1600s-Current, [database online}, Provo, UT.
Correspondence (email) from Shellie Thar Clark, June 26, 2021.
"Henry 'Dutch' Thar Walked to Wyoming in '91', The News Record, Gillette, Wyoming, 1985 (from scrapbook compiled by Jeanette Heptner inherited by L. J. Whisler.
"Dutch Henry and Mary Thar," pages 590-591, Campbell County, The Treasured Years, 1990, compiled by Campbell County Historical Society, Gillette, Wyoming.
"In Rozet it's a Tradition the Postmaster is a Mrs.," The News Record, Gillette, Wyoming, April 12, 1979.
Obituary for Vince Thar, from Ancestry.com, U.S. Find-a-Grave Index 1600s-Current, [database online], Provo, UT.
Obituary for Leola Kottraba Thar, from Ancestry.com, U.S. Find-a-Grave Index 1600s-Current, [database online], Provo, UT.
Ancestry.com, U.S. Appointments of U.S. Postmasters, 1832-1971, [database online], Provo, UT.
Ancestry.com, Montana, County Marriages, 1865-1987, [database online], Provo, UT.
Ancestry.com, U.S. WWII Draft Cards for Young Men, 1940-1947, [database online], Provo, UT.
Ancestry.com, U.S. Department of Veterans Affairs BRILS Death File, 1850-2020, [database online], Provo, UT.
Ancestry.com, Newspapers.com Obituary Index, 1800s-current, [database online], Provo, UT.
Ancestry.com, 1940 U.S. Federal Census for Campbell County, Wyoming, [database online], Provo, UT.

Bernard C. "Fuzz" and Mary (Thar) Scott

Bernard C. "Fuzz" was born on March 5, 1901, at Cainsville, Harrison County, Missouri, to Cortes S. and Delilah Jane (Bain) Scott. Fuzz grew to young manhood on the family farm in Cainsville, Missouri. In their later years his parents engaged in the restaurant business for twelve years before they came to Wyoming in 1917. Fuzz was sixteen years old when the family homesteaded in the Dillinger area. He returned to Cainsville, Missouri, in 1930 where he married Verene Vista Wright. They immediately left for Rozet, Wyoming. Two children were born to this union:

Peggy Ruth	b: 12 Mar 1931	d: 16 Mar 1933	
Donald	b: 30 Aug 1934	d: 30 Dec 2008	m: Ruth Marie Kahle

Verene died on August 14, 1942, of burns suffered from a gasoline stove fire in her home.

Fuzz married Mary Thar on August 12, 1942, at Broadus, Powder River County, Montana. They were parents of two children:

Mary Lyle	b: 17 Sep 1944	d:	m: William Browning
Jim	b: 8 Apr 1950	d:	m: Shellie

Fuzz and Mary lived on a ranch south of Rozet where he also served as a rural mail carrier for that area. They later moved to Gillette where he operated the Gillette Motor Company for a number of years, having the Hudson and Rambler dealerships. Fuzz died on June 26, 1958, and was buried on June 30, 1958, in Mount Pisgah Cemetery, Gillette, Wyoming.

Mary later married Clinton Shannon Bartlett. They lived in Gillette, Wyoming, until his death on January 19, 1991. He was buried in Mount Pisgah Cemetery, Gillette, Wyoming. Shortly after Mary moved to Albuquerque, New Mexico.

Sources:
Email dated June 26, 2021, from Mary Lye Scott Browning.
"Funeral Services Held Monday for B. C. Scott, 57," page 1, The News Record, Gillette, Wyoming, July 1, 1958.
"Dutch Henry Thar Walked to Wyoming in '91'," The News Record, Gillette, Wyoming, 1965 (from scrapbook of historical
        articles compiled by L. J. Whisler).
"Henry Thar," Campbell County, The Treasured Years, 1990, compiled by Campbell County Historical Society, Gillette, Wyoming.
Obituary for Cortes S. Scott, The News Record, Gillette, Wyoming, November 23, 1933.
Obituary for Delilah Jane Johnson Scott, The News Record, Gillette, Wyoming, February 22, 1938.
"Mrs. B. C. Scott dies Wednesday," The News Record, Gillette, Wyoming, January 15, 1942
"Funeral Services Held Monday for B. C. Scott," The News Record, Gillette, Wyoming, July 3, 1958.
Campbell County Cemetery District Burial Property Report, September 28, 1998.
Ancestry.com, Montana, County Marriage Records, 1865-1993, [database online], Provo, UT.
Ancestry.com, U.S. Find-a-Grave Index, 1600s-Current, [database online], Provo, UT.
Ancestry.com, 1940 U.S. Federal Census, Campbell County, Wyoming, [database online], Provo, UT.

THE BRENNAN FAMILY
1905
Matthew C. and Anna (Shaughnessy) Brennan
and their son
Matthew Simon Brennan

Matthew C. Brennan was born in 1846 in County Carlow, Ireland. It is not known what year he immigrated to the United States, but it was by 1870 as he married Anna Shaughnessy in Logan County, Illinois, on April 24, 1870. She was born in 1846 in County Carlow, Ireland, daughter of Lawrence and Ellen (McNamara) Shaughnessy and sister of John "Jack" Shaughnessy who arrived at Rozet with his wife Katherine "Kate" about 1901. Matthew and Anna left Illinois shortly after their marriage for Johnson County, Nebraska where their first child was born in 1871. They were the parents of 10 children; one died young.

Patrick Henry	b: 22 Feb 1871	d: 1958	m: Catherine Marron
Nellie Catherine	b: 1872	d: 05 Oct 1962	m: Joseph F. Landrigan
Thomas Addis	b: 31 Dec 1873.	d: 22 Nov 1925	m: Adeline Mary Howey
Lawrence David "Dot"	b: 07 Jun 1875	d: 1936	m: Claire Weckwerth
John Edward "Jack"	b: 27 Jun 1877	d: 03 May 1920	m: Daisy Celia Bennett
Margaret Ann "Maggie"	b: 16 Jan 1880	d: 16 Dec 1966	m: William J. Vasey
Matthew Simon	b: 02 Feb 1885	d: 03 Dec 1963	(never married)
Marion "Mamie"	b: 1888	d:	m: William A. Kelley
Cora Agnus	b: 19 Feb 1890	d: Aug 1973	m: Frank T. Vasey

When Matthew and Anna came to Rozet is not known but in reviewing Rozet News items in the newspapers it appears they were here before 1910. Matthew filed for a homestead located in Sections 8, 18, and 17, Township 49 North, Range 69W in February 1910. He and Anna appear in the1910 U.S. Federal Census for Gillette, Crook County, Wyoming. He became ill and they returned to Tecumseh, Nebraska, where he died April 28, 1910. He was buried in the St. Andrews Catholic Cemetery, Tecumseh, Johnson County, Nebraska.

Matthew Simon, their youngest son continued proving up on the homestead with his mother. He supplemented his farming income as a salesman in a mercantile company in Moorcroft. On June 3, 1912, he was issued final papers on the homestead. In 1912 he was served as an election judge at Rozet. However by 1919 the homestead was foreclosed on for nonpayment of taxes. His mother died February 3, 1919, in Tecumseh, Nebraska. She was buried next to her husband in St. Andrews Catholic Cemetery. During the depression Matthew worked for the railroad and farmed with his brother, Dot Brennan. At the time he registered for the World War II draft he was living in Hulett working at the sawmill owned by A. C. Nieman. Matthew died December 3, 1963, in Hulett, Crook County, Wyoming, and is buried in the Hulett Cemetery.

Sources for for Matthew C. Brennan:
Bureau of Land Management, Homestead Patent Index, [www.glorecords.blm.gov].
Campbell County Commissioners Proceeding, Gillette News, Gillette, Wyoming, Fri, May 9, 1912.
"Mrs. M. Brennan died Feb 3, 1919, Tecumseh, Nebraska," Local News, Gillette News, Gillette, Wyoming, Fri Feb 14, 1919.
"Mamie Brennan & William Kelly Wedding", Rozet News, Gillette News, Gillette, Wyoming, November 12, 1919.
"Obituary-J.E. 'Jack Brennan," Campbell County Record, May 13, 1920.
"T.A. Brennan Dies at Hardin, Montana," The News Record, Gillette, Wyoming, November 26, 1925.
Ancestry.com, U.S. Find-a-Grave Index, 1600s-Current, [database online], Provo, UT.
Ancestry.com, Illinois, Marriage Index, 1860-1920, [database online], Provo, UT.
Ancestry.com, 1860 U.S. Federal Census for Middletown, Logan County, Illinois, [database online], Provo, UT.
Ancestry.com, 1880 U.S. Federal Census, for Sterling, Johnson County, Nebraska, [database online], Provo, UT.
Ancestry.com, 1889 U.S. Selected Federal Census (Agriculture) Non-Population Schedules, 1850-1880, [database online], Provo, UT.
Ancestry.com, 1910 U.S. Federal Census for Gillette, Crook County, Wyoming, [database online], Provo, UT.
Sources for Matthew Simon Brennan:
Ancestry.com, U.S. Find-a-Grave Index, 1600s-Current, [database online], Provo, UT.
Ancestry.com, U.S. General Land Office Records, 1776-2015, [database online], Provo, UT
Ancestry.com, U.S. Social Security Applications and Claims Index, 1936-2007, [database online], Provo, UT.
Ancestry.com, U.S. World War I Draft Registration Cards, 1917-1918, [database online], Provo, UT.
Ancestry.com, U.S. World War II Draft Registration Cards, 1942, [database online], Provo, UT.
Ancestry.com, 1910 U.S. Federal Census for Moorcroft, Crook County, Wyoming, [database online], Provo, UT.

Lawrence and Clare (Weckwerth) Brennan

Lawrence D. "Dot" Brennan was born June 7, 1875, in Smartsville, Johnson County, Nebraska, to Matthew C. and Anna (Shaughnessy) Brennan. He came to Cambria, Crook County, prior to 1900 to work. In the spring of 1900, he married Clare Weckwerth, sister of Walter Weckwerth who homesteaded near Rozet in late 1900s. About 1903 he began working for the Chicago, Burlington, and Quincy (CB&Q). He was transferred to Rozet in 1916 where he was the railroad Section Forman. Dot filed for a homestead in Sections 29 and 32, Township 50 North, Range 69 West. Dot and Clare were the parents of seven children:

Leo Edward	b:	27 Jun 1900	d:	24 May 1962	m: Edith Mildred "Billee" Emperor
Ruth Elizabeth	b:	1903	d:	1949	m: Earl F. Carr
Irene Bertha	b:	15 Apr 1905	d:	18 Sep 1989	m: Jessie A. Scott
Fred Matthew	b:	01 Sep 1907	d:	22 Oct 2001	m: Neta Moran
Mary Agnes	b:	15 Feb 1910	d:	Nov 1973	m: Leo A. Carr
Helen Clara	b:	02 Aug 1912	d:	21 Nov 1956	m: Harry Robert Elliott
Evelyn Pearl	b:	06 Jul 1921	d:	25 Oct 2018	m: Myron Carr

Dot Brennan was accidentally killed on October 22, 1936, age 61, when a train at Rozet ran over him. At the time of his death four sisters survived him: Mrs. W. J. Vasey of Gillette, Mrs. J. E. Landrigan and Mrs. Frank Vasey of Newcastle, Wyoming, Mrs. W. A. Kelley of Tecumseh, Nebraska; and two brothers, P. H. Brennan of Casper, Wyoming, and Matthew of Tecumseh, Nebraska. Clare died in 1961 and was buried beside her husband in Greenwood Cemetery, Newcastle, Weston County, Wyoming.

Sources:
Bureau of Land Management, Homestead Patent Index [www.glorecords.blm.gov].
"L. D. Brennan Steps in Front of Slow Train," The News Record, Gillette, Wyoming, October __, 1936.
"Brennan Services at Rozet Sunday," page 1, The News Record, Gillette, Wyoming, October 23, 1936.
"Married-Earl Carr-Ruth Brennan," Campbell County Record, Gillette, Wyoming, August 16, 192__.
"Carr-Brennan," Gillette News, Gillette, Wyoming, August 30, 1923.
"Carr-Brennan Nuptials," The News Record, Gillette, Wyoming, August 8, 1929.
"Elliott-Brennan," Society Page, The News Record, Gillette, Wyoming, February 2, 1933.
"Moran-Brennan," Society Page 6, The News Record, Gillette, Wyoming, June 25, 1935.
"Obituaries-Irene (Brennan) Scott," The News Record, Gillette, Wyoming, September 19, 1989.
"Mary (Brennan) Carr Services Slated," The News Record, Gillette, Wyoming, date of issue unknown 1973.
"Fred Brennan, obituary," The News Record, Gillette, Wyoming, October 25, 2001.
Ancestry.com, U.S. Find-a-Grave Index, 1600s-Current, [database online], Provo, UT.
Ancestry.com, U.S. World War I Draft Registration Cards, 1917-1918, [database online], Provo, UT.
Ancestry.com, 1880 U.S. Federal Census (Clara Weckwerth) Shirley, Cloud County, Kansas, [database online], Provo, UT.
Ancestry.com, 1900 U.S. Federal Census for Cambria, Weston County, Wyoming, [database online], Provo, UT.
Ancestry.com, 1910 U.S. Federal Census for Precinct 16-Outside Moorcroft, Crook County, Wyoming, [database online], Provo, UT.
Ancestry.com, 1920 U.S. Federal Census for Election District 5, Rozet North, Campbell County, Wyoming, [database online], Provo, UT
Ancestry.com, 1930 U.S. Federal Census for Election District 5, Campbell County, Wyoming, [database online], Provo, UT.
Ancestry.com, 1940 U.S. Federal Census (Clara Brennan, widow) for Newcastle, Weston County, Wyoming, [database online], Provo, UT.

John Edward "Jack" and Daisy Celia (Bennett) Brennan

John Edward "Jack" Brennan was born June 27, 1877, at Smartsville, Johnson County, Nebraska, to Matthew C. and Anna (Shaughnessy) Brennan. As a young man he came to Cambria, Wyoming, to work for the Cambria Fuel Company. He married Daisy Celia Bennett, daughter of Edward Bennett, on September 18, 1902. In 1906 Jack filed for an Original Homestead Entry in Sections 28 and 29, Township 50 North, Range 69 West. Later Daisy filed for a homestead located in Sections 28, 29, 32, and 33. Their land was located east of the CB&Q Railroad's section house on the north side of the tracks. Jack and Daisy were the parents of four children:

Margaret Anne	b: 03 Dec 1904	d: 16 Aug 1969	m: Richard Lawrence Daniel
Daniel Matthew	b: 25 Apr 1906	d: 24 Aug 1984	m: Alma Mae Day
Richard Lawrence	b: 27 Nov 1908	d: 27 Jan 1985	(never married)
Eileen Gertrude	b: 04 Sep 1912	d: 24 May 1999	m: Richard York Hiles

Jack Brennan was elected in 1912 as the first County Assessor for Campbell County He served three terms until 1918. During the first term he covered the entire county by horseback, the second he was allotted one deputy, and he bought a Model T Ford which he drove when weather and roads permitted. During this time the family lived in Gillette. In 1918 the family moved back to the homestead. Then in 1919, the family moved to the Kessinger place (later known as the Kuehne place) one mile north of Rozet so Margaret could begin high school at Rozet. Jack died suddenly on May 2, 1920, from acute appendicitis at the age of 42. He was buried on May 6, 1920, in Mount Pisgah Cemetery, Gillette, Wyoming.

Daisy and her children moved into Rozet, where she worked for T. A. Frey in his Rozet Mercantile Store. She worked there until the store burned to the ground in March 1933. After that she worked for School District Three as a custodian at the Rozet Consolidated School, and she provided room and board to numerous schoolteachers. On November 10, 1934, she married William P. "Bill" McDermott. In 1935 she and Bill, along with her son, Richard, moved to Winter, Wisconsin. After the death of Bill, she and Richard moved in 1944 to Roseville, California, where she lived until her death on May 25, 1976, at the age of 93 years. She was buried on June 1, 1976, in Mount Pisgah Cemetery, Gillette, Wyoming.

Sources:
Photo: copied from Ancestry.com, U.S. Find-a-Grave Index, [database online}, Provo, UT.
Bureau of Land Management, Homestead Patent Index [www.glorecords.blm.gov].
" John E. Brennan Family," pages 81-82, Campbell County, The Treasured Years, 1990; compiled by Campbell County Historical Society.
"Jack Brennan is Called to Reward," Campbell County Record, Gillette, Wyoming, May 6, 1920.
"At Rest-Obituary," Campbell County Record, Gillette, Wyoming, May 13, 1920, page 1.
"Obituary," The Gillette News, Gillette, Wyoming, May 14, 1920.
"Popular Rozet Couple United in Marriage," The News Record, Gillette, Wyoming, October 21, 1926.
"Brennan-McDermott marriage," Rozet News, The News Record, Gillette, Wyoming, November 15, 1934.
"Final Rites Held Aug 22 (Margaret Brennan Lawrence)," The News Record, Gillette, Wyoming, August 28, 1969.
"McDermott Dies," The News Record, Gillette, Wyoming, June 1, 1976.
"Brennan (Richard) Funeral Wednesday," The News Record, Gillette, Wyoming, January 28, 1985.
"Hiles (Richard) Service to be Monday," The News Record, Gillette, Wyoming, November 15, 1987.
"Alma Mae Brennan Obituary," The News Record, Gillette, Wyoming, June 20, 1988.
"Obituary-Eileen (Brennan) Hiles," The News Record, Gillette, Wyoming, May 26, 1999.
Ancestry.com, U.S. Find-a-Grave Index, 1600s-Current, [database online], Provo, UT.
Ancestry.com, U.S. Social Security Death Index, 1935-2014, [database online], Provo, UT.
Ancestry.com, 1910 U.S. Federal Census for Outside Moorcroft-School district 16, Crook County, Wyoming, [database online] Provo, UT .
Ancestry.com, 1920 U.S. Federal Census for Election District 5, Campbell County, Wyoming.

Mrs. Mary Kessinger's Family
1905

Mrs. Mary Kessinger was born November 3, 1848, at Wrights, Greene County, Illinois. She was married in Wrights, Illinois, to Woodward Kessinger in 1868 and to this union three children were born:

Francis Elmer	b: 29 May 1869	d: 22 Jun 1870	
Edward Johnson	b: 19 Dec 1873	d: 19 Mar 1959	m: Delania J. Wellinger
William Lee	b: 08 Apr 1881	d: 24 Mar 1943	m: Edith V. Charlton

Woodward Kessinger died in October 1899 and a few years later Mrs. Kessinger moved to Wyoming about 1905 with her two sons, Edward and William. She filed on a homestead located one mile north of Rozet on Sections 19 and 30, Township 50 North, Range 69 West. She was known locally as "Aunt Mary." Her son Edward J. Kessinger filed on Sections 7 and 18, Township 50 North, Range 69 West, but he later returned to Wrights, Greene County, Illinois, to live. Mary resided on her homestead for the remainder of her life. She died December 28, 1924, age 76, and was buried in Wrights, Illinois.

William Lee Kessinger, youngest son of Mary Kessinger, was born April 8, 1881, in Wrights, Green County, Illinois. Enlisting in the U.S. Army on January 8, 1901 he served as a PFC until he was honorably discharged January 16, 1904.

He came to Wyoming with his mother Mrs. Mary Kessinger and his brother, Edward, about 1905. He filed on a homestead located in Sections 20, 29, and 30, Township 50 North, Range 69 West. In 1906 he married Edith V. Charlton in Moorcroft, Wyoming. They were the parents of two daughters and an adopted son, all born in Wyoming:

Ruby Elouise	b: 02 Nov 1907	d: 05 Dec 1975	m: William George Pomrenke
Mary Lee.	b: 1922	d:	m: Raymond A. Speetzen
William Robert	b: 18 Dec 1925	d: 03 Jul 1995	m: _____

Sometime after 1925 and before 1930 he moved his family to Oakland, Alameda County, California, where he lived until his death in March 24, 1943. William worked most of his life for the CB&Q Railroad as a Burlington agent and telegrapher. He was buried in the Golden Gate National Cemetery, San Bruno, San Mateo County, California. Edith Charlton Kessinger died August 27, 1967, San Francisco, California, and was buried next to her husband in the Golden Gate National Cemetery, San Bruno, California.

Ruby Kessinger, Tobe Frey about 1920

Sources for Mary Kessinger:
Bureau of Land Management, Homestead Patents Index, [www.glorecords.blm.gov].
"Mrs. Mary Kessinger Died Sunday," The Gillette News, Gillette, Wyoming, January 1, 1925.
"Obituary (Mary Kessinger)," The Gillette News, Gillette Wyoming, January 8, 1925.
Ancestry.com, 1910 U.S. Federal Census for Precinct 16, Outside Moorcroft—School District 16, Crook County, Wyoming, [database online], Provo, UT.
Ancestry.com, 1920 U.S. Federal Census for Election District 5, Rozet North, Campbell County, Wyoming, [database online], Provo, UT.
Sources for William Lee Kessinger:
Ancestry.com, U.S. Find-a-Grave Index, 1600s-Current, [database online], Provo, UT
Ancestry.com, Newspapers.com Obituary Index, 1800-curret, [database online], Provo, UT
Ancestry.com, U.S. Veterans' Gravesites, ca.1775-2019, [database online], Provo, UT
Ancestry.com, National Cemetery Interment Control Forms, 1928-1962, [database online], Provo, UT
Ancestry.com, U.S. World War I Draft Registration Cards, 1917-1918, [database online], Provo, UT
Ancestry.com, U.S. World War II Draft Registration Cards, 1942, [database online], Provo, UT
Ancestry.com, 1900 U.S. Federal Census for Wrights, Greene County, Illinois, [database online], Provo, UT
Ancestry.com, 1910 U.S. Federal Census for Moorcroft, Crook County, Wyoming, [database online], Provo, UT
Ancestry.com, 1920 U.S. Federal Census for Rozet North, Campbell County, Wyoming, [database online], Provo, UT

Charles Joseph "JoJo" and Ella Louise (Damrow) McClendon
1907

Charles "JoJo" was born in Platteville, Weld County, Colorado, on July 1, 1878, son of James Francis and Mary (Cook) McClendon. The family moved to Spearfish, Lawrence County, South Dakota, when JoJo was young. The children grew up and attended school. JoJo attended the Spearfish Normal, now the Black Hills State College. He left school to enlist in the Army during the Spanish American War. He joined Company L, 1st South Dakota Volunteers regiment on April 25, 1898, and was discharged on April 5, 1899, with a medical discharge from the Battle Mountain Sanitarium, Hot Springs, South Dakota. After returning home he worked for various ranches. Later he came to Gillette to work for the Burlington Railroad. He was express messenger on the passenger train when Lincoln, Nebraska, was the end of the run.

On one of his lay-overs in Lincoln, he met Miss Ella Damrow at his brother's home. She was a daughter of Fred and Minnie Damrow natives of Germany. She was born April 16, 1881, in Pickrell, Gage County, Nebraska. JoJo and Ella were married March 10, 1904, in Firth, Lancaster County, Nebraska. They were the parents of five children:

Edith Wilhelmina "Toots"	b: 12 Jun 1905	d: 19 Dec 1999	m: Wally Hendricks
Mae	b: 17 Feb 1912	d:	m: Ben Board/Brown?
Robert Francis	b: 13 Aug 1913	d: 13 Mar 1973	m: Toni I Sullivan
Tom John	b: 04 Sep 1916	d: 04 Jan 2009	m:
Olly Josephine "Jody"	b: 10 Feb 1919	d: 14 Dec 2004	m: Anton J. Chelewski

JoJo and Ella lived for a few years in Beatrice, Nebraska, and in Firth, Nebraska, where their first two daughters were born. In 1906, JoJo moved his family to Moorcroft, Wyoming. He worked for several big ranches in the area prior to filing for a homestead in Section 19, Township 49 North, Range 69 West. JoJo and Ella's neighbors were Frank Hauber, Henry Thar, and Mike Hazzard. During these years, JoJo had built up the ranch and had tried many new methods of farming. He grew some wheat and corn and was one of the first to grow dry-land potatoes commercially in the county. But after several years of severe losses, in 1922 he sold his homestead to Mrs. Mae Talley and went to the booming oilfield of Midwest. His family joined him in 1923. They resided in Midwest until early in 1927 when they moved to Casper where they lived for the remainder of their lives.

Ella died June 30, 1967; JoJo died July 31, 1968. They were buried in Highland Cemetery, Casper, Natrona County, Wyoming.

Sources:
Bureau of Land Management, Homestead Patents Index [www.glorecords.blm.go.
"The McClendon Family," pages 395-396, Campbell County, The Treasured Years, 1990, compiled by Campbell County
     Historical Society.
"Early Rozet Homesteader Is Now Living in Casper," by Josephine McLucas, The News Record, date of issue unknown, article
     found in a scrapbook kept by Jeanette Heptner.
Ancestry.com, U.S. Find-a-Grave Index, 1600s-Current, [database online], Provo, UT.
Ancestry.com, Nebraska Marriage Records, 1855-1908, [database online], Provo, UT.
Ancestry.com, U.S. Evangelical Lutheran Church in America Church Records, 1781-1969, [database online], Provo, UT.
Ancestry.com, Newspapers.com Obituary Index, 1800s-current, [database online], Provo, UT.
Ancestry.com, U.S. World War II Draft Registration Cards, 1941, [database online], Provo, UT.
Ancestry.com, U.S. World War I Draft Registration Cards, 1917-1918, [database online], Provo, UT.
Ancestry.com, U.S. National Homes for Disabled Volunteer Soldiers, 1866-1938, [database online], Provo, UT.
Ancestry.com, 1880 U.S. Federal Census for Weld County, Colorado, [database online], Provo, UT.
Ancestry.com, 1910 U.S. Federal Census for Outside Moorcroft-School District 16, Crook County, [database online], Provo, UT.
Ancestry.com, 1930 U.S. Federal Census for Casper, Natrona County, Wyoming, [database online], Provo, UT.
Ancestry.com, 1940 U.S. Federal Census for Casper, Natrona County, Wyoming, [database online], Provo, UT.

THE GEORGE FAMILY
1908

Frank and Lucinda J. (Ely) George

Edith, Frank, Raymond (back), Doro, and Lucinda George

Frank and Lucinda George homesteaded about five miles northeast of Rozet near Well Creek on Sections 8 and 17, Township 50 North, Range 69 West, and Section 11, Township 50 North, Range 70 West. Frank was born October 2, 1856, to Pete and Amy (Green) George, in Green County, Wisconsin. His father moved the family in the early 1870s to Grafton, Nebraska. In the spring of 1877, when Frank was age 20, he got the urge to come West. He arrived in Cheyenne on March 12, 1877, and went to his uncle Stephen George who had ranching interests on Chugwater Creek to work as a cowboy. Late that fall Frank went to Fort Fetterman, which was fully garrisoned with several hundred soldiers for the wars with the Cheyenne, as well as many civilians who made their home at the Fort. In 1878 his parents Pete and Amy George and his younger brother, Charlie, stopped at Fort Fetterman on their way to California. Frank's mother was very sick, and they were advised not to continue with their wagon train. His father Peter George bought a dugout house six miles from the fort on the north-flowing LaPrele creek near where the Orgon Trail crossed. It became a stage stop on the route to Rock Creek which flowed south towards the Medicine Bow River. They remained in Wyoming for the rest of their lives.

Frank lived with his parents and worked at Fort Fetterman. During the next two or three years Frank worked for a Swedish wagon maker named Charles Hogsen and a Norwegian blacksmith Fred Erickson. It was here that he would learn a trade that he would use for the rest of his life. When he was not working in the wagon/blacksmith shop he worked with a freight outfit owned by George Powell. Frank would drive a team of oxen (nine yoked oxen and three wagons). One of the routes he drove was to Rock Creek and back to Fort Fetterman, eighty-two miles. Rock Creek was about 50 miles from Laramie. The winters were long at Fort Fetterman. Frank played the violin and played for the dances at the fort. He played for the officers until midnight and then played for the enlisted men and their wives until sunrise, when the stage would be pulling out for Rock Creek. He would send his violin home on the stage while he rode horseback.

In 1883, at age 27, Frank went back to Wisconsin and married Lucinda J. Ely on December 20, 1883. She was born August 23, 1852, in Green County, Wisconsin. In late 1884 Frank and Lucinda moved to Grafton, Fillmore County, Nebraska, where he opened a wagon and blacksmith shop. His only son, Raymond, was born there March 12, 1886. Shortly after his son was born Frank decided to move back to Wyoming near his parents on La Prele creek. He worked again at the fort, which was no longer garrisoned. For months after the U.S. Army abandoned Fort Fetterman many people occupied it. The wagon shops became repair depots for wagon trains from Fort Reno, Fort Laramie, and other places. Frank worked in these shops as a blacksmith and a wagon maker and operated his own freight outfit from Cheyenne and Rock River, whenever freight was available to be moved.

After the railroad came into Douglas, the fort began losing residents. They were moving to Douglas, including Frank when he decided to move there and opened his own wagon shop. There he built what is believed to be the first sheep wagon ever built for the Florence Hardware Company. It was named the Florence wagon, after Florence Kittle, wife of one of the owners. These were busy years; Frank played his violin in the town band. His two daughters were born in Douglas, Dora on August 17, 1889, and Edith on October 27, 1894. His parents gave up the ranch on LaPrele creek and moved into Douglas where they lived until they died; Peter in October 1911 and Grandma Amy as she was then known, in April 1919. Frank maintained his wagon and blacksmith shop in Douglas until 1902 when he decided to move his family to Sheridan, Wyoming. There he again operated a wagon shop where he made more sheep wagons. Some that he made were shipped to Gillette for W. P. Parks, W. R. Wright, W. O. Bishop, Paxton "Pax" Irvine and other sheep men.

In 1908 Frank filed on a homestead about five miles northeast of Rozet, Wyoming along the current South Heptner Road. His three children also filed on nearby homesteads. In 1921 or 1922 after a tornado went through the John Daly ranch Frank George's daughter, Edith, recalls that he built five new wagons for the Daly business to replenish those that were damaged by the tornado. About 1923 he rented his place to Riley Whisler and moved into Gillette where he once more established a wagon and blacksmith shop on Second Street and Kendrick Avenue. The last sheep wagon Frank built was for Pax Irvine. Frank's last visit with Pax was to tell him to be sure to drive the truck pulling the new sheep wagon very slowly, so as not burn out the axles. In 1928, new sheep wagons were as nice as new trailer houses in that day. Frank retired from the sheep wagon business in 1930. He had built a residence at 302 Richards Avenue where he lived the rest of his life. Lucinda George died on August 2, 1933, at her home on Richards Avenue, Gillette, Wyoming. She was buried in Mount Pisgah Cemetery, Gillette, Wyoming. Frank died in 1941, age 84, while visiting his son Raymond in Casper, Wyoming. He was buried May 10, 1941, in Mount Pisgah Cemetery, Gillette, Wyoming.

The George Place - 1924

Sources:
Photos: the family page 218, <u>Campbell County, The Treasured Years</u>, 1990, compiled by Campbell County Historical Society.
The George Place, from the collections of Carroll D. "Slim" Whisler.
Bureau of Land Management, Homestead Patents Index [<u>www.glorecords.blm.gov</u>]
"Mrs. F. George is Claimed by Death," <u>The News Record</u>, August 3, 1933, page 1.
"Frank George Came to State Early in 1877," <u>The News Record</u>, Gillette, Wyoming, August 20, 1935.
"Story of Edith George's Family Back to Civil War Days," by Mrs. Josephine Lucas, <u>The News Record</u>, Gillette, Wyoming, about 1965.
*"Frank George," page 218, and "Peter and Amy George," page 215-216, <u>Campbell County, The Treasured Years, 1990</u>, compiled
        by Campbell County Historical Society.*
*"A Letter from Edith George Blatchford to Jack Nisselius, editor of the News Record in 1975," courtesy of the Campbell County Rockpile
        Museum, Gillette, Wyoming, July 2001.*
Campbell County District Burial Report of September 8, 1998.
<u>Ancestry.com</u>, 1910 U.S. Federal Census for Precinct 16, Outside Moorcroft, Wyoming, [database online], Provo, UT.

Raymond and Zelia (Holman) George

Raymond George, Frank and Lucinda's only son, was born on March 12, 1886, in Grafton Fillmore County, Nebraska. Shortly after he was born his father decided to move back to Wyoming near his parents, Pete and Amy George, on La Prele creek. Settling in, at Fort Fetterman, Raymond and his younger sisters grew up in various wagon repair shops along the Oregon trail from Fort Fetterman, Fort Reno, Fort Laramie, and other places where-ever his dad had set up his blacksmith and wagon maker shops. After the railroad came into Douglas, Fort Fetterman began losing residents, including Raymond's father, who moved to Douglas, where he opened his own wagon shop. In 1908 Raymond's father filed on a homestead about five miles northeast of (today's South Heptner Road) Rozet, Wyoming. Raymond also filed on a nearby homestead.

On December 25, 1917, Raymond married Zelia Holman at the home of his father. The ceremony was performed by the Rev. H. A. Toland. Zelia had come to Wyoming from Missouri to teach school the previous year. They lived on his homestead located in Section 9, Township 50 North, Range 69 West. She also filed on a homestead in Sections 7 and 18, Township 51, range 69 West. Raymond and Zelia were the parents of three daughters:

Martha Jean	b: 17 Nov 1918	d: 02 Feb 2009	m: Bradford William Byron
Mildred Irene	b: 30 May 1920,	d: 30 Aug 1988	m: James Harry Thompson
Ramona Hope	b: 02 April 1922	d: 04 Mar 1962	m: Thomas Keith Sizeman

Raymond left the ranch during the 1920s and engaged in roadwork. He built the road from Recluse to Gillette. It was about 30 miles of gravel and at that time it was classified as a highway. He later moved to Sheridan, Wyoming, and then to Casper, Wyoming, where he died in 1954. His daughter Martha Jean also lived in Casper.

Dora M. (George) and Mark B. Shickley

Dora George was born August 17, 1889, in Douglas, Converse County, Wyoming, to Frank and Lucinda George. She attended school in Douglas and Sheridan, Wyoming. She became a schoolteacher after completing her own schooling. She taught in the local rural schools, including the George School. She filed on a homestead in Section 9, Township 50 North, Range 69 West, where Mark and Dora lived after their marriage. They were married in October 1913. He was born July 6, 1885, at Geneva, Nebraska. Mark was an electrician and served as city electrician for the city of Gillette for many years before they moved to Clearmont, Wyoming, in the early 1930s. Mark and Dora were the parents of one son:

Theodore Marcus	b: 16 Nov 1921	d: 19 May 2005

Mark died on August 4, 1964, and was buried on August 7, 1964, in the New Hope Cemetery, now the Sheridan Municipal Cemetery, Sheridan, Wyoming. Dora continued to live in Clearmont, Wyoming, until her death on November 27, 1969, at Sheridan, Wyoming. She was buried on December 2, 1969, in the Sheridan Municipal Cemetery, Sheridan, Wyoming.

Sources for Raymond and Zelia (Holman) George:
Bureau of Land Management, Homestead Patents Index [www.glorecords.blm.gov].
"Marriage George-Holman." The Gillette News, Gillette, Wyoming, January 4, 1918.
"George-Toland marriage," Rozet Rumblings, Gillette News, Gillette, Wyoming, December 1917.
"Story of Edith George's Family Back to Civil War Days," by Mrs. Josephine Lucas, The News Record, Gillette, Wyoming, about 1965.
Casper Star-Tribune, Casper, Wyoming, December 20, 1954.
Ancstry.com, 1920 U.S. Federal Census for Election District #5, Rozet-North, Campbell County, Wyoming [database online].
    Provo, UT.
Sources for Dora M. (George) and Mark B. Shickley:
Bureau of Land Management, Homestead Patents Index [www.glorecords.blm.gov].
Local Items: "marriage license was issued to Mark B. Shickley and Miss Dora M. George," The Gillette News, October 13, 1913.
Sheridan Municipal Cemetery Records, Sheridan, Wyoming.
Ancstry.com, U.S. Social Security Applications and Claims Index, 1936-2007, [on line], Provo, UT.

Edith B. George

Edith George was born October 27, 1894, at Douglas, Converse County, Wyoming, to Frank and Lucinda George. She began school in Douglas but finished through the eighth grade in Sheridan when in 1908 her parents moved to the homestead about four miles north of Rozet on Well Creek. There was no school close enough for her to attend so she rode horseback to attend school at Rozet in the red schoolhouse by the railroad depot. There were five students, Gertrude Shaughnessy, Ruth Shaughnessy, Ruth Brennan, Edith George, and one small boy. Edith believed he was the son of the section boss who was living there then. During the late summer of 1910 she went to "town" school in Gillette to attend high school. There were thirteen students in high school. Alonzo M. Clark, of Rozet, was the superintendent of Gillette schools that year. She stayed with the W. D. June family who lived where the Catholic Church was located (in 1965). The Gillette School at that time was a white frame building with green trimming at the corner of Kendrick Avenue and Fourth Street. About 1911/1912 a new brick school was built across the road with an assembly room and a gymnasium. All grades were taught in the new building except the primary grades which were put in across the street in what later would house the Presbyterian Church. The old schoolhouse became the first courthouse for the newly created Campbell County.

After completing high school in the spring of 1915, she attended a two-day state teacher's examination. That fall she began teaching five pupils in a school on her sister's homestead. Before long more homesteaders moved in and she had 15 pupils in eight grades. About 1915 she filed for a homestead located in Sections 17 and 20, Township 50 North, Range 69 West. Edith continued to teach and further her own education, attending school at Spearfish and at Laramie and soon became qualified to teach in the Gillette Grade School. Teachers worked long, hard hours and the days were never long enough. The school year was divided into two terms, April through July and September through December. Salaries were low, $50.00 a month, at first, but by 1922 when she was teaching at the Rozet Consolidated School, she was receiving $125 per month.

In 1919 Edith was appointed to fill out the term of the county superintendent of schools who had resigned. There were over eighty schools in Campbell County, and with poor roads it was quite a task to visit all the schools. She drove her own car or took the train and then a stage, or some school board members would take her to the schools in their districts. After three years as Superintendent and low pay, $1,000 per year, she decided she wanted to teach again, accepting a position at the Rozet Consolidated School. After that term she taught in the Gillette Grade School until 1930. That year she was chosen as the librarian for the newly established library. In 1937 she married John T. Blatchford and moved to Hot Springs, South Dakota to live. Mr. Blatchford died 1960 and Edith continued to live with her stepson, Norman Blatchford, until her death in May 1979 at Custer, South Dakota. She was buried in the Evergreen Cemetery, Hot Springs, South Dakota, alongside her husband.

Sources:
Photo copied from "Story of Edith George's Family Back to Civil War Days," by Mrs. Josephine Lucas, The News Record, Gillette, Wyoming, about 1966.
Bureau of Land Management, Homestead Patents Index [www.glorecords.blm.gov].
"Story of Edith George's Family Back to Civil War Days," by Mrs. Josephine Lucas, The News Record, Gillette, Wyoming about 1966.
"Edith George," page 217, Campbell County, The Treasured Years, 1990, compiled by Campbell County Historical Society.
"Letter from Edith George Blatchford to Jack Nisselius," editor of The News Record in 1975, courtesy of the Campbell County, Rockpile Museum, 2001.
"Edith Blatchford's Obituary," page 16, The News Record, Gillette, Wyoming, May 14, 1979.

John C. and Jessie Belle (Wells) Fischer
1908

John Fischer was born October 26, 1877, Liberty, Grant County, Wisconsin, to Henry L. and Kate (Wenzel) Fischer. He married Jessie Bell Wells, on June 2, 1902, in Clarion County, Iowa, daughter of Erastus and Lorinda Wells and a sister to Miss Carrie Wells and Mrs. D. D. Woolsey. In 1908 John Fischer filed for a homestead and additional stock raising entry northeast of Rozet in Sections 5 and 8, Township 50 North, Range 69 West, and Section 32, Township 51 North; Range 69 West. John worked for the railroad as an engineer while he was proving up on his homestead. In the summer of 1924, the family moved to Los Angeles, California. That fall Frank Heptner moved his family to their homestead so that their oldest daughter, Irene, could begin attending Rozet High School. John and Jessie were the parents of three children:

Gertrude Gwendolyn	b: 20 Apr 1903	d: 20 Jan 1971	m: _____
Lynn Charles	b: 05 Jun 1906	d: 01 Sep 1925	
Carolyn Lorinda	b: 17 Apr 1908	d: 02 Jan 1995	m: (1) Leslie A. Lane
			(2) Melbourne W. Raybourn

In September 1925 they suffered the loss of their only son, Lynn Charles, who died at age 19. Jessie Fischer died in 1956 and was buried in the Hollywood Forever Cemetery, Hollywood, Los Angeles County, California, next to her son.

John Fisher lived another eleven years until his death on April 1, 1964. He was buried in the Hollywood Forever Cemetery, alongside his wife. Their youngest daughter, Carolyn Fischer Raybourn, returned to Rozet in December 1965. She and her husband built a house on the old homestead along the North Heptner Road. She lived there until her death on June 2, 1995.

Sources:
Bureau of Land Management, Homestead Patent Index, [www.glorecords.blm.gov].
"Carolyn Raybourn's Obituary," page 2, *The News Record*, Gillette, Wyoming, January 3, 1995.
Ancestry.com, U.S. Find-a-Grave Index, 1600s-Current, [database online], Provo, UT.
Ancestry.com, California, Death Index, 1940-1997, [database online], Provo, UT.
Ancestry.com, U.S. Social Security Death Index, 1935-2014, [database online], Provo, UT.
Ancestry.com, Wisconsin, Birth Index, 1820-1907, [database online], Provo, UT.
Ancestry.com, Iowa, Marriage Records, 1880-1951, [database online], Provo, UT.
Ancestry.com, U.S. World War II Draft Registration Cards, 1942, [database online], Provo, UT.
Ancestry.com, 1880 U.S. Federal Census for Liberty, Grant County, Wisconsin, [database online], Provo, UT.
Ancestry.com, 1910 U.S. Federal Census for Clarion, Wright County, Iowa, [database online], Provo, UT.
Ancestry.com, 1920 U.S. Federal Census for Election District #5, Rozet-North Campbell County, Wyoming, [database online], Provo, UT.
Ancestry.com, 1930 U.S. Federal Census for Los Angeles, Los Angeles County, California, [database online], Provo, UT.
Ancestry.com, 1940 U.S. Federal Census for Los Angeles, Los Angeles County, California, [database online], Provo, UT.

Charles Alexander "Charlie" and Nora (Gove) Hinds
1908

Charlie Hinds was born May 20, 1876, in Louisburg, Miami County, Kansas, to Samuel S. and Anna Matilda Hinds. On February 26, 1905, he married Nora Gove, in Glenwood, Mills County, Iowa, daughter of Alice (Owens) Gove Spencer. Nora was born October 22, 1874, at Glenwood, Mills County, Iowa. They left shortly after their marriage for Parkman, Sheridan County, Wyoming to work on a ranch. Later he moved to Riverton, Fremont County, Wyoming, where he served as its first sheriff before he homesteaded north of Rozet, Campbell County, Wyoming in 1908. He filed on Sections 6, 7, and 8, Township 50 North, Range 69 West and Section 1, Township 50 North, Range 70 West.

Charlie was active in serving his community in many ways. He assisted incoming persons looking for land in the Rozet area on which they could file for homesteads. He assisted Thomas Johnson and Frank Heptner to their homestead locations, among others. He also was appointed from time to time as a deputy assessor for Campbell County. In 1922 he was a candidate for County Sheriff. Charlie and Nora moved to Sheridan, Wyoming in 1925. The Wyoming State Game and Fish Commission in 1930 appointed him as game warden for Campbell County. He made his headquarters in Gillette, making frequent trips to Sheridan to take care of his family there. He was appointed by Governor Alonzo

The Charlie Hinds place; riders Dorothy Whisler and Belle Gardner

M. Clark in May 1932 as Wyoming's first "Highway Patrolman," which included duties as the Motor Vehicle License Inspector for Campbell, Crook, and Weston Counties, a position he would be appointed to many times before he retired. He would own and operate a motel and service station in Dayton, Wyoming, for many years before retiring to Sheridan, Wyoming. Nora Gove Hinds died October 13, 1964, and was buried in the Sheridan Municipal Cemetery, Sheridan, Wyoming. Charlie died on October 15, 1973, and was buried in the Sheridan Municipal Cemetery, Sheridan County, Wyoming.

Mrs. George Spencer, Mrs. Nora (Gove) Hinds (daughter of Mrs. George Spencer), Leona Heptner, Irene Heptner, on the Charlie Hinds Place

Sources:
Photos: from the collections of Leona and Jeanette Heptner.
       https://www.facebook.com/RockpileMuseum (John as a young man in Kansas).
Ancestry.com, U.S. General Land Office Records, 1776-2015, [database online], Provo, UT.
"Charles Hinds is a Game Warden in This District", the News Record, Gillette, Wyoming, August 14, 1930.
"Gets Berth in Enforcement Department", News Record, Gillette Wyoming, May 5, 1932.
Sheridan Municipal Cemetery Records, Sheridan, Wyoming.
Ancestry.com, Newspapers by Ancestry, Obituary for Charles Hinds (Billings Gazette, Billings. MT, page 10, 17 Oct 1973).
Ancestry.com, U.S. Find-a-Grave Index, 1600s-Current, [database online], Provo, UT.
Ancestry.com, Iowa, Marriage Records 1880-1945, [database online], Provo, UT.
Ancestry.com, U.S. World War I Draft Registration Cards, 1917-1918, [database online], Provo, UT.
Ancestry.com, 1885 Kansas State Census Collection, 1855-1925, [database online], Provo, UT.
Ancestry.com, 1905 Iowa State Census Collection, 1836-1925, [database online], Provo, UT.
Ancestry.com, 1910 U.S. Federal Census for Horse Creek, Crook County, Wyoming, [database online], Provo, UT.
Ancestry.com, 1940 U. S. Federal Census for Dayton, Sheridan County, Wyoming, [database online], Provo, UT.

Floy Beverly and Rufina May (Moore) Jeffers
1908

Floy B. Jeffers was born April 2, 1864, at Osceola, Iowa. He left Iowa when a boy of 13, going first to Kansas and later to Wyoming where he rode the range as a cowboy. He settled in Nebraska in 1885 when he began working for the Burlington Railroad. On November 8, 1887, in Taylor, Loop County, Nebraska, he married Ella Dressback, daughter of Mr. and Mrs. B. M. Dressback. Ella was born August 19, 1873, in Stockham, Hamilton County, Nebraska. They moved to Sergeant, Nebraska. Floy continued working with the Burlington Railroad. He worked in various assignments for the railroad working up through successive grades starting as an engine wiper until he became a passenger engineer. By the time he left the railroad in 1915, he had been working for the railroad company over 37 years, many of them on the Lincoln Division. Ella Dressback Jeffers died on February 22, 1902, in Sergeant, Custer County, Nebraska. She was buried in Mount Hope Cemetery, Sergeant, Nebraska. Floy and Ella were the parents of eight children:

Roy Gordon	b: 20 May 1887	d: 21 Aug 1964	m: Lana Alvina Kunz
Frank Victor	b: 27 Mar 1893	d: 15 Mar 1977	m: Elsie Nyquist
Olive Louise "Ollie"	b: 09 May 1894	d: 09 Apr 1962	m: Bert R. Moyer
William Webster	b: 10 Aug 1896	d: 03 Sep 1966	m: Leona J. Morgan
Lester Floy	b: 01 Aug 1898	d: 03 Jul 1977	m: Freda Ann Rehfeldt
Marie Lucille	b: 13 Aug 1900	d: 29 Mar 1920	m: Charles Edgar Evans
Leone Margaret "Mary"	b: 13 Aug 1900	d: 28 Mar 1995	m: Floyd Miguel
Christian Verne	b: 05 Nov 1901	d: 25 Aug 1997	m: Frances Lucy Curtis

Floy returned to Osceola, Clarke County, Iowa, where he married Rufina May Moore on November 15, 1903, daughter of John M. and Elizabeth (Webster) Moore. She was born in Osceola, Iowa, on May 9, 1866. She grew up and attended schools there. Shortly after their marriage, they moved to Sargent, Custer County, Nebraska, where they made their home, and Floy continued working for the Burlington Railroad. It is not clear whether Floy retired from the railroad while in Nebraska or whether he transferred to Crook County, Wyoming, where in 1909 he filed on a homestead in Section 35, Township 51 North, Range 69 West, in the Little Iowa community. Three sons, Frank, Lester, and Verne, and two daughters, Marie Lucille and Leone Margaret "Mary" came with their father to Crook County, Wyoming. Floy and Rufina were the parents of two children:

May	b: 1905	d: in infancy	
John Moore	b: 25 Feb 1909	d: 10 Sep 1975	m: Mary Margaret Turk

Floy B. Jeffers was known as an untiring and extremely conscientious worker. At the time of his death he was serving his second two-year term as a trustee to the Campbell County High School Board, and he had filed for re-election shortly before his death. He also served for a number of years as a member of the District Four School Board. Floy B. Jeffers died on June 14, 1932. He was buried in the Pleasant Valley Cemetery on June 17, 1932. His gravestone reads "He Rode the Texas Trail." Rufina, his wife, died on August 24, 1933, and was buried next to her husband on August 26, 1933.

[Note re: Frank, Lester, Verne, and John Jeffers:

Frank Jeffers enlisted in the Marine Corps in 1917, served during World War I and returned home. He worked for the Burlington Railroad. He moved about 1923 to Lincoln, Nebraska, where his brother Roy was then living. By 1923 his brother William was living in Pine River, Minnesota.

Lester Jeffers enlisted in World War I and was still living at the Jeffers ranch in 1923

Verne Jeffers also enlisted in 1917 in the army and served in World War I. He returned to the Rozet homestead in 1919 before being stationed in Coblenz, Germany, after World War I.

John Jeffers was still living at home northeast of Rozet in 1923.]

Rufina and Floy Jeffers out in their garden with a field of shocked wheat waiting to be threshed

Floy B. Jeffers on his homestead

Marie Lucille (Jeffers) Evans

(Photos this page from the collections of Leona and Jeanette Heptner)

Sources:
Photo: Ancestry.com, U.S. Find-a-/Grave Index, 1600s-Current, [database online], Provo, UT.
Bureau of Land Management, Homestead Patents Index [www.glorecords.blm.gov].
Pleasant Valley Cemetery Burial Book, kept by Mrs. Lucille Thompson (Xeroxed Copy-1998).
"Obituary for Marie Lucille Jeffers Evans," Campbell County Record, Gillette, Wyoming, April 8, 1920.
"F. B. Jeffers is Called by Death," The News Record, Gillette, Wyoming, June 16, 1932, page 1.
"Mrs. F. B. Jeffers Passes Away Last Week; Hold Services Last Saturday," The News Record, August 13, 1933.
Ancestry.com, Iowa, Marriage Records, 1880-1937, [database online], Provo, UT.
Ancestry.com, 1900 U.S. Federal Census for Sargent, Custer County, Nebraska, [database online], Provo, UT.
Ancestry.com, 1910 U.S. Federal Census for Crook County, Wyoming, Precinct 16, Outside Moorcroft-School District 16;
    [database online], Provo, UT.
Ancestry.com, 1920 U.S. Federal Census for Election District #8, Iowa Precinct, Campbell County, Wyoming, [database online],
    Provo, UT.

THE NELSON FAMILY

Oscar B. and Sarah Ann (Marshall) Nelson
1908

Oscar B. Nelson was born July 14, 1855, at Eslof, Sweden. He immigrated to the United States at the age of fifteen years. When or where Oscar entered the United States is unknown, but it may have been Minnesota as the Kansas State Census taken March 1, 1895, indicates that he came from Minnesota to Union, Washington County, Kansas. According to the *Minnesota Naturalization Index* he received his naturalization papers while living in Washington County, Minnesota. Oscar married Sarah Ann Marshall in November 1889, in Mahaska, Washington County, Kansas. She was born January 1, 1860, in Iowa, the daughter of William Fletcher and Landora (Larne) Marshall. (See Note below.) Oscar and Sarah were the parents of ten children, but only six lived to adulthood:

Belinda	(date of birth/death unknown, buried at Mahaska Cemetery, Mahaska, Kansas)		
Pearl Ray	b: 04 Nov 1894	d: 13 May 1965	m: Esther H. _____
Francis "Lee"	b: 07 Jan 1891	d: 22 Jan 1954	(never married)
Oscar Lloyd	b: 23 Jun 1896	d: 12 Aug 1970	m: Maude M. Kornman
George Obel	b: 23 Jan 1898	d: 05 Jul 1949	m: Mary Estelle Weaver
Marian Marna	b: 21 Apr 1899	d: 21 May 1997	m: Frank Kuehne
Margarete Mateen "Maggie"	b: 10 Jan 1904	d: 05 May 1996	m: Ralph R. Wall
Nellie			

About 1908 Oscar and Sarah moved the family to Crook County, Wyoming, and filed for homesteads in Sections 13, 14, and 24, Township 50 North, Range 60 West, and in Section 18, Township 50 North, Range 69 west, about two and one-half miles northwest of Rozet. The children attended the Well Creek School and Rozet Consolidated School The family was opposed to the consolidation of schools in School District Three. Oscar served as a Justice of the Peace in 1914-1915. Sarah died November 30, 1919, and Oscar died November 9, 1922. Both were buried in the Mahaska Cemetery, Mahaska, Kansas, next to their daughter Belinda.

[Note: Sarah Nelson's father, after her mother's death in 1914, came to Wyoming to live with them. William F. Marshall, Sarah Ann's father, also filed for a homestead located in Sections 14 and 23, Township 50 North, Range 70 West. He died February 22, 1922, age 86 years, in the Nelson home at Rozet. He was buried in Mount Pisgah Cemetery, Gillette, Wyoming.]

Sources:
Bureau of Land Management, Homestead Patents Index [www.glorecords.blm.gov].
"Local News (William F. Marshall died at Rozet)," The Gillette News, Gillette, Wyoming, February 26, 1915.
"Nelson-Kuehne," The Gillette News, Gillette, Wyoming, February 13, 1920.
"O. B. Nelson Died at Rozet," page 1, Campbell County Record, Gillette, Wyoming, November 9, 1922.
"Married (Nelson-Weaver)," The News Record, Gillette, Wyoming, July 1, 1926.
"Mrs. Nelson, Rozet Resident, Passes on," The News Record, Gillette, Wyoming, December 5, 1929.
"Military Honors Held Tuesday for F. Lee Nelson, 63," The News Record, Gillette, Wyoming, January 25, 1954.
Campbell County District Burial Report of September 8, 1998.
Ancestry.com, Web: Minnesota, Naturalization Index, 1849-1985), [database online], Provo, UT.
Ancestry.com, 1875, (Lakeland, Washington County) Minnesota Territorial and State Censuses, 1849-1905, [database online], Provo, UT.
Ancestry.com, 1895 Kansas State Census Collection, (Union, Washington County), 1855-1925, [database online], Provo, UT.
Ancestry.com, 1900 U.S. Federal Census for Union, Washington County, Kansas, [database online], Provo, UT.
Ancestry.com, 1905 (Union, Washington County) Kansas, [database online], Provo, UT.
Ancestry.com, 1910 U.S. Federal Census for Moorcroft, Crook County, Wyoming, [database online], Provo, UT.
Ancestry.com, 1920 U.S. Federal Census for Rozet North, Campbell County, Wyoming, [database online], Provo, UT.

Pearl Ray "Ray" Nelson was born November 4, 1894, in Washington County, Kansas. He came to Rozet with his parents in the spring of 1910. He was drafted in July 1918 into the U.S. Army for service during World War I with the I. C. S. Battalion as a Private. Upon returning home in May 1919, he filed on a homestead located in Sections 9 and 10, Township 50 North, Range 70 West. He eventually moved to Sheridan, Wyoming. No record of his marriage was found other than of their burial at the Custer National cemetery. He died May 13, 1965; his wife, Esther H. Nelson, died August 2, 1966.

Sources:
Ancestry.com, *U.S. Find-a-Grave Index, 1600s-Current*, [database online], Provo, UT.
Ancestry.com, *U.S. Veterans' Gravesites, ca. 1775-2019*, [database online], Provo, UT.
Ancestry.com, *U.S. Social Security Death Index (Esther H. Nelson), 1935-2014* [database online], Provo, UT.
Ancestry.com, *U.S. World War I Draft Registration Cards, 1917-1918*, [database online], Provo, UT.
Ancestry.com, *U.S. World War II Draft Registration Cards, 1942*, [database online], Provo, UT.
Ancestry.com, *U.S. Army Transport Service, Passenger Lists, 1910-1939*, [database online], Provo, UT.

Francis Lee "Lee" Nelson was born January 7, 1891, at Hollenburg, Kansas. At an early age he moved with his parents to Mahaska, Kansas. In the spring of 1910, the Nelson family came to the Rozet area where he lived the remainder of his life. He filed on a homestead located in Sections 21 and 22, Township 50 North, Range 70 West. Lee enlisted in the army on July 4, 1918, and served during WWI in Germany and France. He was honorably discharged on October 12, 1919, and returned home to Rozet, Wyoming. He was a member of the Gillette American Legion Post. Lee never married. He died on January 22, 1954, at the home of his sister Marna Kuehne and was buried on January 26, 1954, in Mount Pisgah Cemetery, Gillette, Wyoming, with final military honors by Campbell County Post 42, of the American Legion.

Sources:
Bureau of Land Management, Homestead Patent Index, [www.glorecords.blm.gov].
"Military Honors Held Tuesday for F. Lee Nelson, 63," *The News Record*, Gillette, Wyoming, January 28, 1954.
Ancestry.com, *U.S. Headstone Applications for Military Veterans, 1925-1963*, [database online], Provo, UT.
Ancestry.com, *U.S. World War I Draft Registration Cards, 1917-1919*, [database online], Provo, UT.
Ancestry.com, *U.S. World War II Draft Registration Cards, 1942*, [database online], Provo, UT.

Oscar Lloyd Nelson was born June 23, 1896, in Mahaska, Washington County, Kansas, to Oscar and Sarah (Marshall) Nelson. In the spring of 1910, he came to Rozet with his parents, brothers and sisters. He was educated in the Well Creek school and Rozet Consolidated School. Oscar was drafted into the Army and served in World War I. He filed for a homestead located in Sections 3, 10 11, 14, and 15, Township 50 North, Range 70 West. His draft registration indicates he was married at that time, but no name was given. He lived in the Rozet area until the mid-1930s when he moved to Delta County, Colorado. Oscar married Maude M.(Shiflet) Kornman on July 21, 1934, in Lamar, Prowers County, Colorado. They had two sons:

Oscar Lloyd, Jr.,	b:	1935	d:	16 Dec 1952
Harley Vern	b:	17 Jul 1942	d:	05 Jul 1995

Oscar died August 1, 1970, in Grand Junction, Mesa County, Colorado and was buried in the Delta Cemetery, Delta County, Colorado. Maude lived for twenty-six years until her death Mary 24, 1996. She was buried in the Delta Cemetery, Delta County, Colorado near her husband and son.

Sources:
Ancestry.com, *U.S. Find-a-Grave Index, 1600s-Current*, [database online], Provo, UT.
Ancestry.com, *Colorado, County Marriage Records and State Index, 1862-2006*, [database online], Provo, UT.
Ancestry.com, *Newspapers.com Obituary Index, 1800s-current*, [database online], Provo, UT.
Ancestry.com, *U.S. World War I Draft Registration Cards, 1917-1918*, [database online], Provo, UT.
Ancestry.com, *U.S. World War II Draft Registration Cards, 1942*, [database online], Provo, UT.
Ancestry.com, *1930 U.S. Federal Census for Election District 5, Campbell County, Wyoming*, [database online], Provo, UT.

George Obel "Obe" Nelson was born January 23, 1898, to Oscar and Sarah (Marshall) Nelson in Union, Washington County, Kansas. In the spring of 1910, he came to Rozet with his parents, brothers and sisters. He was educated in the Well Creek school and Rozet Consolidated School. On June 16, 1926, he married Mary Estelle Weaver, daughter of Sam and Hattie Weaver. They were the parents of one son:

Billy Lee   b: 05 Sep 1931   d: 05 May 1984   m: Faye Packett

In spring of 1927 Obe and Mary moved to the Charles Hinds place. On September 17, 1935, he was issued deeds to the homestead he filed for in 1929 on Sections 2, 3, and 11 in Township 50 North, Range 70 W, and Section 34 in Township 51 North, Range 70 W. At the age of 44 he registered for the World War II draft on February 16, 1942, but was not called up. George died July 5, 1949, and was buried in Mount Pisgah cemetery, Gillette, Wyoming. Their son Billy Lee would be buried next to him in 1984.

On December 2, 1953, Mary married Gordon LeRoy Crabill in Gillette Wyoming. They moved to Norcatur, Norton County, Kansas. After the death of her second husband in 1984 she returned to Gillette to be nearer to her family. Mary died January 24, 1996, at the age of 90, in the Pioneer Manor Nursing Home in Gillette. Her body was returned to Kansas and buried in the Norcatur Cemetery, Norton County, Kansas beside her husband Gordon LeRoy Crabill.

Marian Marna Nelson was born April 21, 1899, in Mahaska, Washington County, Kansas, to Oscar and Sarah (Marshall) Nelson. In the spring of 1910, she came to Rozet, at the age of seven, with her parents and older brothers. She attended the Well Creek school and Rozet Consolidated School. She married Frank Kuehne on February 11, 1920. See page 110 for the history of Frank and Marna Kuehne.

Source for George Obel "Obe" Nelson:
Bureau of Land Management, Homestead patent Index [www.glorecords.blm.gov].
"Married, Obe," The News Record, Gillette, Wyoming, July 1, 1926 (Obe and Mary Weaver).
"Obituary for Mary Estella Crabill," The News Record, Gillette, Wyoming, January 26, 1996.
Ancestry.com, U.S. Find-a-Grave Index, 1600s-Current (for Obe Nelson), [database online], Provo, UT.
Ancestry.com, U.S. Find-a-Grave Index, 1600s-Current (for Mary E Crabill), [database online], Provo, UT.
Ancestry.com, U.S. General Land Office Records, 1776-2015, [database online], Provo, UT.
Ancestry.com, U.S. WWII Draft Cards Young Men, 1940-1947, [database online], Provo, UT.
Ancestry.com, 1930, U.S. Federal Census for Election District 5, Campbell County, Wyoming, [database online], Provo, UT.
Ancestry.com, 1940 U.S. Federal Census for Campbell County, Wyoming, [database online], Provo, UT.

Margarete Maxine "Maggie" Nelson was born January 10, 1904, in Mahaska, Washington County, Kansas, to Oscar and Sarah (Marshall) Nelson. She was six years old when she came to Wyoming with her parents, brothers and sister. Maggie attended the Well Creek school and Rozet Consolidated School. In 1924 Maggie married Ralph Reginald Wall, brother of Frank Wall, who was one of the high school teachers at the Rozet School and the first superintendent at Rozet Consolidated School established in 1921, and sister to Edna Wall, a rural school teacher in Campbell County. Ralph was born June 21, 1899, in Burdette, Franklin County, Iowa. He served in World War I. His service began on July 1, 1917 and ended on March 5, 1919. After returning home he came to the Rozet area and settled near his brother Frank and sister Edna.

Ralph and Margarete Wall

After their marriage Maggie and Ralph settled on a farm a few miles northeast of Rozet; they became the parents of four children:

Dora Mae	b: 31 Dec 1925	d: 25 Mya 1929	m: Ernst George Murray
John Ernest	b 10 Jan 1929	d: 04 Dec 1983	m: Evelyn M. Strand
Nellie Joan	b: 14 Jun 1930	d:	m: William Asher Heaton
Nila Edna	b: 06 Sep 1933	d: 13 Jun 1997	m: _____ LeComte

In the spring of 1935 Ralph and Maggie moved to Ashmont, Alberta, Canada to start a ranch. They crossed the border into Canada on May 3, 1935, at Coutts, Alberta, on the Montana border. Nothing can be established how long they remained in Ashmont. They returned to the United States in the summer of 1944, settling in Spokane, Washington, where they are found in the City Directory from 1947-1957. Ralph's occupation was salesman. Ralph died December 9, 1982; Maggie May 5, 1996. Their place of death was Ritzville, Adams County, Washington. They were buried in the Willamette National Cemetery, Portland, Oregon.

Sources:
Photo: Campbell County; The Treasured Years,1990, Campbell County Historical Society, Gillette, WY.
Ancestry.com, U.S. Find-a-Grave, 1600s-Current, [database online], Provo, UT.
Ancestry.com, U.S. Veterans' Gravesites, ca. 1775-2019, [database online], Provo, UT.
Ancestry.com, U.S. Department of Veterans Affairs BIRLS Death file, 1850-2010, (for WWI service), [database online], Provo, UT.
Ancestry.com, Newspapers.com Obituary Index, 1800s-current, [database online], Provo, UT.
Ancestry.com, U.S. WWII Draft Cards Young Men, 1940-1947 (living in Canada at the time), [database online], Provo, UT.
Ancestry.com, U.S. Border Crossings: From U.S. to Canada, 1908-1935, [database online], Provo, UT.
Ancestry.com, U.S. Border Crossings from Canada to U.S. 1895-1960, [database online], Provo, UT.
Ancestry.com, U.S. City Directories, 1822-1995 (Spokane, Washington), [database online], Provo, UT.
Ancestry.com, 1900 U.S. Federal Census for Lee, Franklin County, Iowa, [database online], Provo, UT.
Ancestry.com, 1920 U.S. Federal Census for Election District 18, Park County, Wyoming, [database online], Provo, UT.
Ancestry.com, 1930 U.S. Federal Census for Election District 5, Campbell County, Wyoming, [database online], Provo, UT.

Ernest E. and Eliza (McDonough) French
1908

The French Place
Taken from the George Place looking west along the present South Heptner Road
1925

Ernest E. and Eliza (McDonough) French came to Wyoming in the late 1890s. They settled in the Sheridan area about 1896. Ernest was born July 8, 1861, near Monroe, Wisconsin. Eliza McDonough was born March 31, 1861, at Monroe, Wisconsin, the daughter of Mr. and Mrs. Fred McDonough. They were the parents of one son:

Ray Eugene   b: 1887   d: 23 Oct 1943   m: Rhoda Newman

About 1908 Ernest filed for a homestead located in Sections 8 and 17, Township50North, Range 69 West about seven miles northeast of Rozet. About 1920 Ernest and Eliza moved back to Sheridan, Wyoming. Ernest French died on October 23, 1943, and was buried in the Sheridan Municipal Cemetery, Sheridan, Wyoming. Eliza French died June 4, 1947, and was buried in the Sheridan Municipal Cemetery, Sheridan, Wyoming.

Ray Eugene and Rhoda (Newman) French, age 21, filed for a homestead on December 4, 1908, located northeast of Rozet near Well Creek in Section 7, Township 50 North, Range 69 West. They left the Rozet area by the end of 1920, moving first to Sims, Montana, and later to Sheridan, Wyoming, where he died December 7, 1922, at the age of 35. His wife and a two-year-old baby son survived him. He was buried in the Sheridan Municipal Cemetery, Sheridan, Wyoming.

Sources:
Photo: from the collections of Carroll D. "Slim" Whisler.
Bureau of Land Management, Homestead Patent Index [www.glorecords.blm.gov].
"Ray French is Dead," quoted from the Sheridan Enterprise, The Gillette News, Gillette, Wyoming, page 1, December 14, 1922.
"Rozet News." The Gillette News, Gillette, Wyoming, July 10, 1924.
Sheridan Municipal Cemetery Records, Sheridan, Wyoming.
Ancestry.com, 1910 U.S. Federal Census for Precinct 16, Outside Moorcroft-School District 16, Crook County, Wyoming,
    [database Online], Provo, UT .
Ancestry.com, 1920 U.S. Federal Census for Election district 5, Rozet North, Campbell County, Wyoming,
    [database online], Provo, UT.

Alonzo Monroe and Lucy Myra (Smith) Clark
1909

Alonzo Clark, and J. Brennen behind the counter
Other two gentlemen names unknown
County Clerk's Office, Gillette, Wyoming

Alonzo was born August 13, 1868, in Flint, Steuben County, Indiana. His mother was related to President Grover Cleveland. His father was a veteran of the Civil War and served as County Judge of Thayer County, Nebraska, where the family had moved from Indiana. Alonzo attended Chadron Academy, Chadron, Nebraska. His first teaching assignment was in Thayer County, Nebraska. On November 28, 1896, he married Lucy Smith of Carleton, Nebraska. They were the parents of one child:

> Donald Curtis   b: 1898   d: Feb 1924 while attending Stanford university

Alonzo served as the County superintendent of Schools in Dawes County, Nebraska and later Deputy County Clerk. About 1909 the family moved to Wyoming where both taught schools. In 1909 Alonzo filed for a homestead in Sections 26 and 27, Township 50 North, Range 70 West. His sister Emily E. Clark also filed in 1910 for a homestead located in Sections 27 and 28, Township 50 North, Range 70 West. She was a schoolteacher at the Rozet School in 1914. He became the superintendent of Gillette schools in 1910.

Alonzo was elected the first County Clerk of Campbell County in November 1912 serving several terms with Lucy as his deputy. He served until 1920 when his wife, Lucy M. Clark, succeeded him as County Clerk. Alonzo ran for, and won, the office of Wyoming's Secretary of State in 1926. In his second term upon the death of Governor Emerson on February 18, 1931, he became the Governor of Wyoming to fill out the term until the next general election two years away. After retiring from public life, he returned to his first profession of teaching, but was compelled to resign on account of illness. Lucy Clark died January 1, 1944. He married Mrs. Florence Clark, the widow of his nephew. At this time, he was working in the workmen's Compensation Department of the State Treasurer's Office. He died October 12, 1952, at Thermopolis, Hot Springs County, Wyoming. Alonzo and Lucy are buried in Carleton Cemetery, Carleton, Thayer County, Nebraska.

Sources:
Photo: courtesy of the Campbell County Rockpile Museum, 2012.
Bureau of Land Management, Homestead Patents Index [www.glorecords.blm.gov].
"Donald Clark Expires in California," Campbell County Record, Gillette, Wyoming, February 21, 1924.
"Death Claims Mother Sec'y of State Clerk; Mrs. Emily Clark," The News Record, Gillette, Wyoming, January 1, 1931.
Bruning Banner, Carleton, Nebraska, October 23, 1952.

Sarah Elizabeth (Thurston) Stewart
1909

Sarah Elizabeth Thurston was born on May 23, 1848, in New Hampshire to Nathaniel Kimbell and Sarah Ann Thurston. Sarah married Rev. William Charles Stewart on February 9, 1865 in Exeter, Rockingham County, New Hampshire. He served and was wounded in the Civil War. He was ordained in 1869 as a minister of the Advent Christian Church, traveling as evangelist and pastor. He held pastorates in Kennebunkport and Biddeford, Maine; Concord, New Hampshire; Hinesburg, Vermont; Sommerville and Westfield, Massachusetts; Winsted, Connecticut; and Lafayette, Rhode Island. In the spring of 1883 they came west to Anoka county, Minnesota Territory where he settled as pastor in a little church in Anoka then in its infancy. Later they moved to Lexington, Sanilac County, Michigan, where he divided the majority of his time between the Lexington and county churches; also serving the Shore and Ridge Churches. Their next move was to Sparta, Ohio, where they stayed two years before moving further west to Black Hawk County, Iowa, settling in Waterloo.

After several years of receiving less and less support from the Advent Christian Church, he began seeking another church. In 1897 he was received into the Baptist church as an ordained minister. They continued to live in Waterloo until his death on April 18, 1906. His funeral was held at their home; afterward his body was taken to Lake Mills, Winnebago County, Iowa, the home of his mother (see note below). William and Sarah became the parents of ten children; only five lived to adulthood (see 1900 U.S. Federal Census for Allamakee County, Iowa):

Sarah Abbie	b: 24 Jul 1866	d: 17 Nov 1868	
Charles Kimball	b: 19 Nov 1868	d: 12 Sep 1945	m: Mertie Iva Shane
George Albian	b: 06 Dec 1873	d:	m: Cora Etta Taylor
Annie Mae	b: 30 Dec 1878	d: 07 Feb 1923	m: (1) George H. Ensign; (div)
			(2) Warren L. Doane
Alice Elizabeth	b: __ Jun 1871	d: 10 May 1938	m: George E. Stull
Dwight Thurston	b: 11 Mar 1884	d: 05 Jan 1973	m: Bessie Mae Ford

In 1909, at age 61, Sarah E. Stewart continued her westward journey. She filed for a homestead on Sections 27, 34, and 35, Township 51 North, Range 69 West, in the Little Iowa community north of Rozet, Campbell County, Wyoming. Here she would live until her death on January 4, 1925, attended by her son, Dr. Charles. K. Stewart of Moorcroft. Her body was shipped to Waterloo, Iowa, for burial alongside of her husband. Her daughters Annie Mae Doane and Alice Elizabeth Stull are both buried in Pleasant Valley Cemetery on the Grey Road, northeast of Rozet, Wyoming.

(Note: Majority of the information about her husband, William, was taken from a statement she wrote for a Vermont paper and was retained by the Archives of the Advent Christian Church. A transcribed copy was posted on U.S. Find-a-Grave Index for William Stewart. In it she states, "The funeral was held at our home in Waterloo, ... Then we took the dear one to Lake Mills, Iowa, the home of his aged mother." *Ancestry.com*, U.S. Find-a-Grave Index indicates both she and her husband are buried in Fairview Cemetery, Waterloo, Iowa.)

Sources:

Photos: Courtesy of Cindy Stewart, Rozet, Wyoming.
Record of Funeral, Fox Mortuary, Gillette, Wyoming, June 6, 1925.
Pleasant Valley Cemetery Burial Book, kept by Mrs. Lucille Thompson (Xeroxed Copy-1998).
Ancestry.com, New Hampshire Marriage Records Index, 1637-1947, [database online], Provo, UT.
Ancestry.com, U.S. Find-A-Grave Index 1600's to Current, [database online], Provo, UT.
Ancestry.com, 1860 U.S. Federal Census for Exeter, Rockingham County, New Hampshire, [database online], Provo, UT.
Ancestry.com, 1870 U.S. Federal Census for Brentwood, Rockingham County, New Hampshire, [database online], Provo, UT.
Ancestry.com, 1880 U.S. Federal Census for Exeter, Rockingham County, New Hampshire, [database online], Provo, UT.
Ancestry.com, 1885 Minnesota, Territorial and State Censuses, 1849-1905, [database online], Provo, UT.
Ancestry.com, 1900 U.S. Federal Census for Makee, Allamakee County, Iowa, [database online], Provo, UT.
Ancestry.com, 1910 U.S. Federal Census for Waterloo Ward 4, Black Hawk County, Iowa, [database online], Provo, UT
Ancestry.com, 1920 U.S. Federal Census for Iowa, Campbell County, Wyoming, [database online], Provo, UT.

George E. and Alice Elizabeth (Stewart) Stull
1909

George Stull   Taken 1903   Alice Elizabeth Stewart   Wedding Day 1903

George Stull was born about 1875 in Benton County, Iowa, to James and Decedent "Dell" (Delorme) Stull. His father was a Laborite farmer (see note below). He married Alice Elizabeth Stewart on September 9, 1903, in Hancock, Pottawattamie County, Iowa. She was born in June 1871 in Litchfield County, Connecticut to the Reverend William C. and Sarah E. (Thurston) Stewart. At an early age Alice's parents moved their family to Ohio before settling in Waterloo, Blackhawk County, Iowa. George and Alice were the parents of one daughter:

     Miriam Marjorie   b: 24 Dec 1904   d: 07 Apr 1966   m: Albert B. Wells

In 1910 George and Alice came to Crook County, Wyoming with their five-year old daughter. They filed for homesteads located northeast of Rozet; he in Sections 26, 27, and 34, Township 51 North, Range 69 West, and she in Section 26, Township 51 North, Range 69 West. They worked to improve their homestead as their daughter went to school. She attended the Little Iowa School for all eight grades. The school began in the home of her aunt, Mrs. May Stewart Doane. George was very involved with the community. He served as Road Director for District Eight on the Good Roads Committee in 1921. Alice Stull died May 10, 1938; George died August 4, 1940, and was buried August 4, 1940. beside his wife in the Pleasant Valley Cemetery on Grey Road, Rozet, Wyoming.

Note: A member of the Farmer-Labor party which was a minor political party in the U. S. in those times.

Sources:
Photos courtesy of Cindy Stewart, Rozet, Wyoming.
Bureau of Land Management, Homestead Patent Index [www.glorecords.blm.gov].
Pleasant Valley Cemetery Burial Book, kept by Mrs. Lucille Thompson (Xeroxed Copy-1998).
"Good Roads Day," The Gillette News, Gillette, Wyoming, July 30, 1921
"Let Your Light Shine," Volume III, Pioneer Women Educators of Wyoming, 1994, edited by Sheryl Lain, published by Alpha Xi State, Delta Kappa Gamma, page 218.
Ancestry.com, Iowa, Marriage Records, 1880-1937, [database online]. Provo, UT.
Ancestry.com, 1880 U.S. Federal Census for Bruce, Benton County, Iowa, [database online], Provo, UT.
Ancestry.com, 1885 Iowa State Census Collection, 1836-1925, [database online], Provo, UT.
Ancestry.com, 1900 U.S. Federal Census for Makee, Allamakee County, Iowa, [database online], Provo, UT.
Ancestry.com, 1910 U.S. Federal census for Waterloo Ward 4, Blackhawk County, Iowa, [database online], Provo, UT.
Ancestry.com, 1920 U.S. Federal Census for Iowa, Campbell County, Wyoming, [database online], Provo, UT.
Ancestry.com, 1930 U.S. Federal Census for Moorcroft, Crook County, Wyoming, [database online], Provo, UT.
Ancestry.com, 1940 U.S. Federal Census for Campbell County, Wyoming, [database online], Provo, UT.

Walter M. and Mary Louise (Verboncoeur) Weckwerth
1909

Walter Weckwerth was born June 24, 1884, in Ames, Cloud County, Kansas, to John F. and Alvina (Rinka) Weckwerth. By 1900 Walter's sister, Claire had married Lawrence Brennan and moved to Cambria, Weston County, Wyoming. Walter followed them. There on February 15, 1904, he married Mary Loise Verboncoeur. They moved to Rozet, Crook County, before 1910 with their three oldest children. He worked for the CB&Q Railroad as a Section Boss. Walter also filed on a homestead located in Sections 7, and 8, Township 49 North, Range 69 West and Section 13, Township 49 North, Range 70 West. They were the parents of four children:

Charles Henry	b: 25 Nov 1904	d: 31 Jul 1978	m: Helen D. _____
Dorothy Kathryn	b: 08 Mar 1906	d: 23 Nov 1993	m: Roy L. Pearson
Walter Willard	b: 25 Sep 1909	d: 31 Mar 2004	m: _____
Donald Lee	b: 21 Nov 1913	d: 19 Jun 1976	m: Frances J. Bowell
Geraldine Louise	b: after 1913	d: _____	

The family left Rozet before 1920 as the Federal Census for that year finds the family living in Platte County, Wyoming. Walter is working as a section foreman for the railroad. Later in that decade the family moved to Nemaha, Johnson County, Nebraska. He was working as a road master for the CB&Q Railroad. The 1940 Federal Census shows the family living at Fort Laramie, Goshen, Wyoming, where he was working as a foreman for the railroad. Eventually he and Louise moved to Edgemont, Fall River County, South Dakota, where Walter died on November 27, 1948. Louise died there on March 22, 1963, and both are buried in the Edgemont Cemetery, Edgemont, Fall River County, South Dakota.

Sources:
Bureau of Land Management, Homestead Patents Index [www.glorecords.blm.gov].
Ancestry.com, U.S. Find-a-Grave Index. 1600s-current, [database online], Provo, UT.
Ancestry.com, Newspapers.com Obituary Index, 1800s-current, [database online], Provo, UT.
Ancestry.com, U.S. Social Security Applications and Claims index, 1936-2007, [database online], Provo, UT.
Ancestry.com, Web: Western States Marriage Index, 1809-2011, [database online], Provo, UT.
Ancestry.com, U.S. World War I Draft Registration Cards, 1917-1918.
Ancestry.com, U. World War II Draft Registration Cards, 1942, [database online], Provo, UT.
Ancestry.com, 1900 U.S. Federal Census, Shirley, Cloud County, Kansas, [database online], Provo, UT.
Ancestry.com, 1910 U.S. Federal Census Precinct 16, Outside Moorcroft, Crook County, WY, [database online], Provo, UT.
Ancestry.com, 1920 U.S. Federal Census Election District 2, Platte County, WY, [database online], Provo, UT.
Ancestry.com, 1930 U.S. Federal Census for Nemaha, Johnson County, Nebraska, [database online], Provo, UT.
Ancestry.com, 1940 U.S. Federal Census for Fort Laramie, Goshen County, Wyoming, [database online], Provo, UT.

Mrs. Anna Williams
and Sons
Louis "Happy" and Charlie Williams
1909

Anna and her husband August both immigrated from Germany in 1879 to Donley County, Texas. There they met and were married in 1881. They became the parents of seven children, one died young:

Louis "Happy"	b: 04 Sep 1882	d: 04 May 1963	m: Agnes Gehet
Dora Louise	b: 24 Jun 1885	d: 04 Jun 1951	m: Robert M. Richardson
Charles James	b: 05 Jun 1890	d: 28 Aug 1955	m: Mable Lucille Morse
Augustus	b: Jun 1893	d:	m: Mary L. Goedde
Annie L.	b: Feb 1897	d: before 1909	m:
Carrie Agnes	b: 12 Nov 1899	d: 27 Jan 1953	m: Frank J. Dunlap

August deserted the family shortly after the turn of the century. Anna's oldest son, Louis "Happy" Williams came to the Rozet area shortly after his father's desertion on a trail drive from Texas heading for Montana and beyond. Locating a homestead southeast of Rozet in Section 24, Township 49 North, Range 70 West, he sent for his mother, his brothers, Charles and Gus (Augustus), and his sister, Carrie. In 1909 Mrs. Anna Williams and her son Charlie filed for homesteads located next to Louis in Sections 24 (Charlie) and 25 (Anna), Township 49 North, Range 70. On October 30, 1923, Louis married Agnes Gehet, in Fort Smith, Sebastian County, Arkansas. Louis worked in the oil fields and by 1930 he had moved to Thermopolis where his mother and brother, Charles had moved before 1920. His wife, Agnes, returned to Arkansas during the depression, about 1934, with their son. Louis moved to Sheridan, Wyoming where he lived until his death May 4, 1963, He is buried in Sheridan Municipal Cemetery.

Charles was a blacksmith and a farrier, a trade he learned in Fort Smith, Arkansas, as a fifteen-year-old boy after the disappearance of his father. He had a blacksmith shop first in Moorcroft, Wyoming, then for a brief time in Gillette before moving with his mother to Thermopolis, Hot Springs, Wyoming. He married Mable L. (Morse) Thomas. Later, in 1936, he moved his shop to Sheridan, Wyoming. Charles and Mable divorced after 1940 and she remarried. Charles continued with his blacksmith shop in Sheridan until he died August 28, 1955. He was buried in the Sheridan Municipal Cemetery, Sheridan, Wyoming.

Augustus left Wyoming before 1920 for Oklahoma where he married and raised a family in Durant, Bryan County, Oklahoma.

Sources:
Bureau of Land Management, Homestead Patents Index [www.glorecords.blm.gov].
"Charles James Williams," page 641, *Campbell County the Treasured Years*, 1990, compiled by Campbell County Historical
        Society, Gillette, Wyoming.
Sheridan Municipal Cemetery Records, Sheridan, Wyoming.
"Infant Daughter of Williams Family Dies," *The News Record*, Gillette, Wyoming, February 18, 1936.
"Funeral Services for Mrs. Williams Friday," *The News Record*, Gillette, Wyoming, February 26, 1936.
Ancestry.com, U.S. Find-a-Grave Index, 1600s-Current, [database online], Provo, UT.
Ancestry.com, U.S. World War I Draft Registration Cards, 1917-1918, [database online], Provo, UT.
Ancestry.com, U.S. World War II Draft Registration Cards, 1942, [database online], Provo, UT.
Ancestry.com, 1900 U.S. Federal Census for Justice Precinct 2, Donley County, Texas, [database online], Provo, UT.
Ancestry.com, 1910 U.S. Federal Census for Precinct 16, Outside Moorcroft-School District 16, Crook County, Wyoming,
        [database online], Provo (for Anna, Louis, Charlie, Gus and Carrie).
Ancestry.com, 1920 U.S. Federal for Thermopolis, Hot Springs County, Wyoming, [database online], Provo, UT (Anna and Charlie).
Ancestry.com, 1930 U.S. Federal Census for Thermopolis, Hot Springs County, Wyoming, [database online], Provo, UT.
Ancestry.com, 1940 U.S. Federal Census for Sheridan, Sheridan County, Wyoming, [database online], Provo, UT.

Durward "Delos" and Gertrude (Wells) Woolsey
1909

Delos and Gertrude were married June 12, 1906, in Fort Dodge, Webster County, Iowa. In 1909 he filed on a homestead located in Section 6, Township 50 North, Range 69 West. Gertrude Woolsey was a daughter of Erastus Wells, a sister to Mrs. Jessie Fischer, Carrie, and Charles Wells, and a half-sister to George Wells. Durward and Gertrude were the parents of one daughter:

Genevieve Lorinda "Jenny"   b: 10 Jun 1907   d: 26 Jan 1990 m: Ferdinand Kennett Rule

They moved to Billings, Montana, about 1918, where he worked as a traveling salesman for the National Biscuit Company out of Helena, Montana. By 1940 they were living in Los Angeles, Los Angeles County, California, living near their daughter Genevieve and husband Ferdinand Rule. Durward died in 1948 in Los Angeles and was buried in Hollywood Forever Cemetery, Hollywood, Los Angeles County, California. Gertrude died on July 31, 1968, and was buried in Tulocay Cemetery, Napa, Napa County, California.

Sources:
Bureau of Land Management, Homestead Patent Index, [www.glorecords.blm.gov].
"Rozet Postmistress Succumbs...," The News Record, Gillette, Wyoming, October 15, 1931.
Ancestry.com, U.S. Find-a-Grave Index, 1600s-Current, [database online], Provo, UT.
Ancestry.com, California, Death Index, 1940-1997, [database online], Provo, UT.
Ancestry.com, Newspapers.com Obituary Index, 1800s-current, [database online], Provo, UT.
Ancestry.com, Iowa, Delayed Birth Records, 1856-1940, [database online], Provo, UT.
Ancestry.com, Iowa, Marriage Records, 1880-1951, [database online], Provo, UT.
Ancestry.com, U.S. General Land Office Records, 19776-2015, [database online], Provo, UT (for Crook County, Wyoming).
Ancestry.com, U.S. World War I Draft Registration Cards, 1917-1918, [database online], Provo, UT.
Ancestry.com, U.S. World War II Draft Cards Young Men, 1940-1947 (Ferdinand Rule), [database online], Provo, UT.
Ancestry.com, 1880 U.S. Federal Census for Washington, Webster County, Iowa, [database online], Provo, UT.
Ancestry.com, 1900 U.S. Federal Census for Newark, Webster County, Iowa, [database online], Provo, UT.
Ancestry.com, 1910 U.S. Federal Census for Clarion, Wright County, Iowa, [database online], Provo, UT.
Ancestry.com, 1920 U.S. Federal Census for Billings Ward 1, Yellowstone County, Montana, [database online], Provo, UT.
Ancestry.com, 1930 U.S. Federal Census for Los Angeles, Los Angeles County, California, [database online], Provo, UT.
Ancestry.com, 1940 U.S. Federal Census for Los Angeles, Los Angeles County, California, [database online], Provo, UT.

Winifred Scott and Sophia Kit (Groce) Cook
1910

Winfield Scott Cook was born in June 1851 in Clarion County, Pennsylvania, to Philip John and Susan Cook. In the 1870 U.S. Federal Census Schedule we find the family living in Pittsburg Ward 12, Allegheny County Pennsylvania. Winifred, age 18, was working as a laborer. He married Sophia Kit Groce, daughter of John Henry and Catherine (Gates) Groce, about 1873. She was born about 1853 in Clarion County, Pennsylvania. The 1880 Federal Census find them and three children living in Richland, Venango County, Pennsylvania. They were the parents of nine children:

Grace	b:	Apr 1875	d:	m:	Josiah Oliver
Carrie Cecil	b:	11 Mar 1876	d: 02 Oct 1923	m:	Perry Thompson
John Wesley	b:	17 Apr 1878	d: 01 Dec 1963	m:	Margaret A. Neilson
James A.	b:	Jul 1881	d: before 1920?	m:	Ida Hefland
Maude Eleanor	b:	07 Jan 1884	d: Aug 1974	m:	Frank Gifford Davis
Floyd Elmo	b:	21 Apr 1885	d: 06 Sep 1971	m:	Myrtle Agnes Allen
Blanche Elsie	b:	07 Dec 1887	d: 26 Jul 1975	m:	Bert James Moran
Clifford	b:	__ Jun 1890	d: after 1929	m:	_____
Ray (Raoul)	b:	__ Jul 1892	d: after 1929	m:	_____

It has not been established when the family moved to Nebraska. Nebraska marriage records show they were living in Sheridan County, Nebraska when his daughter Carrie married Perry Thompson on August 15, 1892, in the home of her father. One of the witnesses was her sister, Grace Cook.

About 1894 the family moved to Hot Springs, Fall River County, South Dakota. Sophia Groce Cook died there on May 5, 1896. She is buried in the Evergreen Cemetery, Hot Springs, South Dakota.

1900 U.S. Federal Census find Winifred, widowed, working as a carpenter in Rapid River, Idaho County, Idaho and his son Floyd, age 15, and daughter Blanche, age 12, living with their sister, Carrie Thompson, in Sheridan County, Nebraska. And, we find Clifford, age 9, and Raoul (Ray), age 7, Cook living with their older sister Grace and her husband Josiah Oliver in Lead City, Lawrence County, South Dakota.

November 12, 1906, daughter Maude E. Cook married Frank Gifford Davis, in Lead, Lawrence County, South Dakota.

In 1910 Winifred Cook filed on a Section in Township 51 North, Range 69 West in the Little Iowa community, north of Rozet, Campbell County, Wyoming.

March 18, 1912, son James A. Cook married Ada Hefland in Butte, Silver Bow County, Montana.

Winfred Cook, age 76, died on February 29, 1929 and was buried in the Moorcroft Cemetery, Moorcroft, Wyoming. Notation made in the Moorcroft Cemetery Book indicated he was survived by four sons—John, Ray, and Clifford all of Seattle, Washington, Floyd (of Rozet), and three daughters—Mrs. Frank Davis of Sundance, Wyoming, Mrs. Bert Moran of Rozet, Wyoming, and Mrs. G. Cusson (Grace?) of San Francisco, California.

Sources:
Bureau of Land Management, Homestead Patent Index (www.glrecords.blm.gov).
Moorcroft Cemetery Book #2, page 161, (April 1922 – November 1934).
Ancestry.com, U.S. Find-a-Grave Index, 1600s-Current, [database online], Provo UT.
Ancestry.com, 1860 U.S. Federal Census for Farmington, Clarion County, PA, [database online], Provo, UT.
Ancestry.com, 1870 U.S. Federal Census for Pittsburg Ward 12, Allegheny County, PA, [database online], Provo, UT.
Ancestry.com, 1880 U.S. Federal Census for Richland, Venango, PA, [database online], Provo, UT.
Ancestry.com, 1900 U.S. Federal Census for Rapid River County, Idaho, [database online], Provo, UT.
Ancestry.com, Nebraska, U.S, Select County Marriage Records 1855-1908 (Carrie Thompson), [database online], Provo, UT.
Ancestry.com, Washington, U.S. Marriage Records 1854-2013 (John Wesley Cook), [database online], Provo, UT.
Ancestry.com, Montana, U.S, County Marriages, 1865-1987), (James A. Cook), [database online], Provo, UT.
Ancestry.com, South Dakota, U.S. Marriages 1905-2017), (Maude E. Cook), [database online], Provo, UT.
Ancestry.com, 1900 U.S. Federal Census for Lead City, Lawrence County, SD (Grace Oliver), [database online], Provo, UT.
Ancestry.com, 1900 U.S. Federal Census, Lead City, Lawrence County, SD, (Clifford), [database online], Provo, UT.
Ancestry.com, 1900 U.S. Federal Census, Lead City, Lawrence County, SD, (Raoul), [database online], Provo, UT.

Warren Leonard and Annie May (Stewart) Doane
1910

Annie May was born on December 30, 1878, to Rev. William and Sarah E. (Thurston) Stewart in Westfield, Hampden County, Massachusetts. She married George H. Ensign on April 16, 1899, in Waukon, Allamakee County, Iowa. They had one son:

Stewart Ellery	b: 13 Mar 1900	d: 26 Dec 1985	m. Verna J. Wall

They were divorced before 1910. After the death of her father on April 14, 1906, in Waterloo, Blackhawk County, Iowa, Annie May and her mother came west to Moorcroft. Her mother filed on a homestead located in Sections 27, 34, and 35, Township 51 North, Range 69 West, in the Little Iowa community. Sarah Stewart's son, Dr. Charles Kimball Stewart, had filed on a homestead near Moorcroft, Crook County, Wyoming. He was one of the early doctors in the area. In 1910 Charles moved to Moorcroft., Wyoming, where he and his family lived until they died. Annie May filed for two homesteads near her mother in Township 50 North, Range 69 West, the first under the name of May S. Ensign; later the second under the name of May S. Doane. Annie began teaching the winter of 1910 at what was then called the Rozet School. In 1913 Annie May established the Little Iowa School, first as a summer school held in her house for fourteen students. Annie May had moved out of her house to live in a tent during the summer. A school meeting was called and, with the aid of the children's parents and neighbors, native lumber was hauled in, and they built a schoolhouse across the road north of the Fayette Thompson homestead. The Pleasant Valley Cemetery was established in 1917 across the road, west of the school house. In her later years Annie May taught school in Moorcroft.

Annie May and Warren L. Doane were married in 1911 in Crook County, Wyoming. They became the parents of two children:

Leonard Nelson	b: 30 Sep 1914	d: 30 Mar 2006	m: Jean E. Cunningham
Mary Elizabeth	b: 20 Jan 1917	d: 14 Nov 2004	m: Harold Lenz

Warren was born September 29, 1873, in Richland, Jasper County, Iowa, to Charles Nelson and Mary Freelove (Dean) Doane. Warren died March 21, 1919, in Gillette, Campbell County, Wyoming, and was buried in Pleasant Valley Cemetery. Annie May died on February 7, 1943, in Hastings, Adams County, Nebraska, and was buried in Pleasant Valley Cemetery alongside her husband Warren.

Sources:
Photo of Annie May Courtesy of Cindy Stewart, Rozet, Wyoming.
Photos from Ancestry.com, U.S. Family Tree Find-A-Grave, Index, (data base on-line), Provo, UT.
Pleasant Valley Cemetery Burial Book, kept by Mrs. Lucille Thompson (Xeroxed Copy-1998).
Notes from "The Doane Family & Their Descendants" provided by Sandy Stewart Holyoak, August 2017.
"Ensign funeral to be Monday," The News Record, Gillette, Wyoming, December 29, 1985.
"Obituary, W. L. Doane," page 1, The Gillette News, Gillette, Wyoming, April 4, 1919.
Ancestry.com, U.S., World War I Draft Registration Cards, 1917-1918, (data base on-line), Provo, UT.
Ancestry.com Record of Funeral, Fox Mortuary, Gillette, Wyoming, June 6, 1925.

Ulysses "Hite" and Mary Josephine "Josie" (Bozer) Eddy
1910

Wedding picture – 1886

Ulysses "Hite" was born on September 28, 1865, in Rome City, Noble County, Indiana, to Ithmer and Elizabeth (Hite) Eddy. He married Mary Josephine "Josie" Bozer on December 27, 1886, daughter of John Francis and Mary Elizabeth (Read) Bozer.

Her sister Samantha married Hite's brother, Rollin Eddy, in 1879. Hite and Mary were the parents of four children:

Philo Bell	b: 16 Mar 1888	d: 28 May 1959	m: Evalene Maria Hester
Mary Fern	b: 26 Dec 1889	d: 07 May 1953	m: (1) John F. Rensch
			m: (2) Ivan Ellsworth Newman
Vera Grace	b: Oct 1892	d: 17 Feb 1961	m: Arthur Malcomb Speegle
Forrest Read	b: 25 Dec 1894	d: 16 Jan 1957	m: Vera Faye Dilgard

Hite and Josie arrived in the Rozet area about 1913. Their daughter Vera Speegle was already living in the Rozet area. He filed for a homestead in Section 5, Township 49 North, Range 69 West, and Section 32, Township 50 North, Range 69. He served as a Primary Judge in the Rozet Precinct for the county and state elections in October 1914. He served on the Executive Committee of the newly organized (1921) Rozet Protestant Community Church. In 1922 they placed a bid for one of the rural school houses that had been closed when the schools in District three were consolidated. A school building was purchased in February 1923, and volunteers from the community worked all that year to convert the school house into a community church. Hite Eddy died at Rozet on March 31, 1928, age 62, and was buried in Mount Pisgah Cemetery, Gillette, Wyoming. Mary continued to live on their homestead until at some point during the depression years she sold the land and moved to California. She died at the age of 75, on January 2, 1943, in Los Angeles County, California.

Back row: Vera Grace Eddy, Myrtle, Josie Eddy, and Minnie
Middle Row: Philo & Forrest Eddy, Uncle R___, Hite Eddy
Front Row: Jennie, Aunt Emma, Dolly, Mary Eddy

Sources:
Photo: Ancestry.com, Jenkins Family Tree, [database online], Provo, UT.
Bureau of Land Management, Homestead Patent Index, [www.glorecords.blm.gov].
"Proceedings of the Board of County Commissioners," The Gillette News, Gillette, Wyoming, October 23, 1914.
"Wedding Bells – Rensch-Eddy (Mary)," The Gillette News, Gillette, Wyoming, November 7, 1919.
"Funeral Services Held for U. H. Eddy, Well Known Resident of County," The News Record, Gillette, Wyoming, February 2, 1928.
"Society-Eddy –Hester Marriage," The News Record, Gillette, Wyoming, July 3, 1930.
Campbell County Cemetery District Burial Report of September 8, 1998.
Ancestry.com, U.S. General Land Office Records, 1776-2015, [database online], Provo, UT.
Ancestry.com, U.S. Find-a-Grave Index, 1600s-Current, [database online], Provo, UT.
Ancestry.com, California, Death Index, 1940-1997, [database online], Provo, UT.
Ancestry.com, Indiana, Marriages, 1810-2001, [database online], Provo, UT.
Ancestry.com, 1870 U.S. Federal Census for Elkhart, Noble County, Indiana, [database online], Provo, UT.
Ancestry.com, 1880 U.S. Federal Census for Elkhart, Noble County, Indiana, [database online], Provo, UT.
Ancestry.com, 1900 U.S. Federal Census for Elkhart, Noble County, Indiana, [database online], Provo, UT.
Ancestry.com, 1910 U.S. Federal Census for North Elkhart, Noble County, Indiana, [database online], Provo, UT.
Ancestry.com, 1920 U.S. Federal Census for Rozet, Campbell County, Wyoming, [database online], Provo, UT.
Ancestry.com, 1930 U.S. Federal Census for Election District 5, Campbell County, Wyoming, [database online], Provo, UT.

Philo B. and Evalene Marie (Hester) Eddy

Philo B. Eddy was born March 16, 1888, in Wolcottville, Noble County, Indiana, to Ulysses and Mary (Bozer) Eddy. Philo came to Rozet with his parents in 1910. He filed for an Entry-Stock Raising Homestead in Sections 4, 5, 8, and 9. Township 51 North, Range 69 West, and was issued a land patent in June 1926. He married Evalene Marie Hester in 1931 in Gillette, Wyoming. She was born March 26, 1892, in Quaker, Vermillion County, Indiana to Cassius Mills and Rosella Hester. Evalene was teaching once again at the Rozet High School for one term 1931-1932. She had previously taught there beginning in the fall of 1927 through to spring 1929. That fall she was teaching at a high school in Leoti, Wichita County, Kansas. After school ended in May 1931, she returned to teach high school at Rozet for one year, 1931-1932. After 1935 and before 1940, Philo and Hester moved to Tillamook County, Oregon. Philo died on May 28, 1959; Evalene died on November 1, 1980. They are both buried in the Friends Cemetery, Newberg, Yamhill County, Oregon.

Mr. Wagner, Alma Day, Miss Cameron, Ann Brenna
and Miss Evalene Hester – 1928, Rozet Consolidated school teachers
(Photo from the collection of Irene Heptner Whisler)

Sources:
Bureau of Land Management, Homestead Patent Index, [www.glorecords.blm.gov].
"Hester-Eddy Wedding," Society Page, The News Record, Gillette, Wyoming, July 3, 1930.
Ancestry.com, U.S. General Land Office Records, 1776-2015, [database online], Provo, UT.
Ancestry.com, U.S. Find-a-Grave Index, 1600s-Current, [database online], Provo, UT.
Ancestry.com, Oregon, Select Births and Christenings, 1868-1929, [database online], Provo, UT.
Ancestry.com, North America, Family Histories, 1500-2000 (Evalene Hester), [database online], Provo, UT.
Ancestry.com, U.S. World War I Draft Registration Cards, 1917-1918, [database online], Provo, UT.
Ancestry.com, U.S. World War II Draft Registration Cards, 1042, [database online], Provo, UT.
Ancestry.com, 1900 U.S. Federal Census for Elkhart, Noble County, Indiana, [database online], Provo, UT.
Ancestry.com, 1910 U.S. Federal Census for North Elkhart, Noble County, Indiana, [database online], Provo, UT.
Ancestry.com, 1920 U.S. Federal Census for Rozet, Campbell County, Wyoming, [database online], Provo, UT.
Ancestry.com, 1930 U.S. Federal Census for Election district 5, Campbell County, Wyoming, [database online], Provo, UT.
Ancestry.com, 1930 U.S. Federal Census for Leoti, Wichita County, Kansas (Evalene Hester), [database online], Provo, UT.
Ancestry.com, 1940 U.S. Federal Census for Fairview, Tillamook County, Oregon, [database online], Provo, UT.

Paul Max Grunke
1910

Paul wrote on his World War I Registration Card he was born on October 12, 1872. The 1920 Census records indicates he was born in Germany. We find him at age 2 years and 2 months along with presumably his mother, Rosalie Grunke, listed as passengers on board the *USS Rhein*. The ship left the port of Bremen, Germany, and arrived in the port of New York on December 31, 1872. Where they first immigrated to in America is not known. According to his obituary, Paul Grunke came to northeast Wyoming at the age of 21 (about 1894). However, the 1900 Census Records for Gage County, Nebraska, show him at age 27 working as a hired hand for Charly D. Mathews in Island Grove. He is in Wyoming by 1910 as the 1910 Census Records show him working as a hired hand for Charley Baker in Belle Fourche, Weston County, Wyoming. He probably worked as a sheepherder for the sheep ranches in northeast Wyoming. About 1914 Paul filed on a homestead located in Section 4, Township 50 North, Range 69 West and Sections 33 and 34, Township 51 North, Range 69 West. He raised cattle, hogs, and corn. Grunke was well known in the Little Iowa community. He played the violin/fiddle for community dances. Josephine Weaver Bryant, in her written account in the *Campbell County, The Treasured Years*, 1990, page 89, remembered him coming to her parent's homestead (Sam and Hattie Weaver) in his buggy pulled by a team of white horses ready to visit awhile before playing a few tunes on his violin for his neighbors.

Due to ill health he gave up working his homestead about 1933 and moved into Rozet where he lived until his death, at age 64, on August 3, 1937. He committed suicide in the coalhouse at the back of Ida E. Wells' home in Rozet where he was boarding at that time. He left a note citing financial problems. There were no known relatives. Services were held at the Rozet Community Church on August 12, 1937, and he was buried in the Rozet Cemetery.

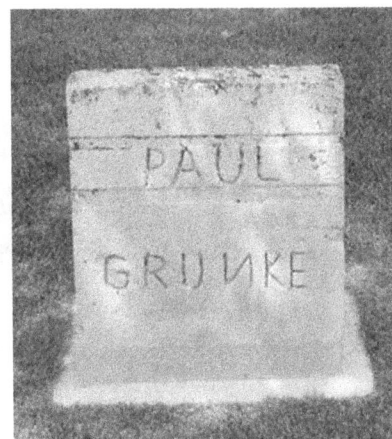

Sources:
Bureau of Land Management, Homestead Patent Index, [www.glorecords.blm.gov].
Ancestry.com, U. S. General Land Office Records, 1776-2015, [database online]. Provo, UT.
Ancestry.com, New York, U.S., Arriving Passenger and Crew Lists (including Castle Garden and Ellis Island), 1820-1958,
    [database online], Provo, UT.
"Self-Inflicted Rifle Bullet Kills P. Grunke, The News Record, Gillette, Wyoming, August __, 1937."
"Man Shoots Himself in Rozet", The News Record, Gillette, Wyoming, August 1937, page 1.
Ancestry.com, U. S. Find a Grave Index, 1600s-Current, [database online], Provo, UT.
Ancestry.com, U. S. World War I Draft Registration Cards, 1917-1918, [database online], Provo, UT.
Ancestry.com, 1900 U. S. Federal Census for Island Grove, Gage County, Nebraska, [database online], Provo, UT.
Ancestry.com, 1910 U. S. Federal Census for Belle Fourche, Weston County, Wyoming, [database online], Provo, UT.
Ancestry.com, 1920 U. S. Federal Census for Campbell County, Wyoming, Election District #5, Rozet-North;
    [database online], Provo, UT.
Ancestry.com, 1930 U. S. Federal Census for Election District 5, Campbell County, Wyoming, [database online], Provo, UT.

Harry Milton "Barney" and Nora Zeretta (Simms) Marquiss
1910

Barney Marquiss was born December 31, 1869, in Pulaski, Giles County, Tennessee, to Earl Douglas and Mary (Cokayne) Marquiss. His parents moved him and his brothers Roy Bynn "Ted" and Frank Clifford and his sister Ollie Mae, to Broken Bow, Nebraska, about 1884; later about 1910 they all moved to Rozet, . In 1898 he married Nora Zeretta Simms. They were the parents of:

Gladys	b: 28 Nov 1898	d: 23 Dec 1990	m: James Otis Wright
Gerald	b: 01 Jan 1900	d: 21 Jul 1914	
Juanita "Polly"	b: 24 Apr 1903	d: 15 Dec 1989	m: Lester R. Page
Gordon	b: 12 Jan 1901	d: 29 May 1960	m: Elta Wheeler

About 1910 the families moved again to Rozet, Crook County, Wyoming. Two years later Earl, Barney's father, died on July 15, 1912; his mother, Mary, died on September 9, 1914. They were buried in Mount Pisgah Cemetery, Gillette, Wyoming. His brother Roy B. "Ted" and his sister Ollie remained in Campbell County, but his brother Clifford left and eventually moved to California. Barney filed for a homestead located in Section 24, Township 50 North, Range 70 West, and Sections 18 and 19, Township 50 North, Range 69 West, about 2 miles north of Rozet. His wife, Nora Z. Marquiss, filed in 1919 for a desert land entry homestead in Section 24, Township 50 North, Range 70 West. Barney proved upon his claim in October 1919 and then sold the place and moved his family to Ogden, Utah. Barney Marquiss died in May 11, 1927, age 58, in Ogden, Utah. He was buried in Mount Pisgah Cemetery, Gillette, Wyoming on May 16, 1927 alongside his son Gerald. Nora Zeretta died in 1959 in Yerington, Lyon County, Nevada, and was buried in the Valley View Cemetery, Yerington, Lyon County, Nevada.

The hill over which the Adon Road passed was still called the Marquiss Hill into the 1940s and 1950s. It was always a challenge to drive up and over in the winter and in the summers after a rain. Later, in the 1960s when the Adon Road was paved the hill was flattened out. The Marquiss Hill is now only a memory.

Thomas Johnson and Barney Marquiss Families
1913

Sources:
Photo: Leona Heptner collections.
Bureau of Land Management, Homestead Patent Index, [www.glorecords.blm.gov].
"Gerald Marquiss Dead," The Gillette News, Gillette, Wyoming, July 24, 1914.
For Sale," The Gillette News, Gillette, Wyoming, September 26, 1919.
"Rozet Items," Campbell County Record, Gillette, Wyoming, August 30, 1923.
"H. M. Marquiss Dies in Utah, Will be Buried Here," The News Record, Gillette, Wyoming, May 12, 1927 .
Campbell County Cemetery District Burial Report of September 8, 1998.

Hans and Emilie (Saskin) Raudsep
1910

Hans was born in Estonia, Russia. He married Ann Kotkas and they became the parents of two children:

John	b:	1899	d:	
Selma	b: 5 Oct 1902		d: 07 Apr 1986	(never married)

Ann died sometime between 1902 and 1906. Hans married Emilie Saskin about 1907, in Samara, Estonia, Russia. Emilie was born June 4, 1885, to Nikolas and Lisa Saskin, in Samara, Estonia. She grew to womanhood there. On November 25, 1907, Hans, Emilie, John and Selma left Kubyshev, Samara, Estonia, Russia, and boarded the *S.S. Cherson* sailing from Lilase, Germany. Their destination listed on the passenger list was Fort Pierre, South Dakota. They lived there about three years. Their son, Hugo, was born at Fort Pierre, South Dakota. They arrived in Moorcroft, Crook County, Wyoming in 1908. In 1910 Hans filed on a homestead, on Miller Creek, in Section 12, Township 51 North, Range 69 West and Section 7, Township 51 North, Range 68 West. Six additional children were born to them in Crook/Campbell County, Wyoming:

Hugo	b: 13 May 1908	d: 17 Sep 1912	
Alexander	b: 12 Aug 1910	d: 11 Jul 1911	
Hilda	b: 23 Mar 1914	d: 21 Dec 1986	m: John H. "Jack" Simpson
Ella	b: 19 Aug 1915	d: 25 Jul 2012	m: Harold G. "Jack" Rawhouser
Arnold	b: 19 Dec 1919	d: 10 Jun 1990	m: Margaret C. McIntyre
Albert Robyn	b: 08 Oct 1922	d: 01 Jul 1996	m: Anna "Ann" Mae White
Leida Emilie	b: 15 Dec 1924	d: 10 Dec 2004	m: (1) Emory V. Hatfield
			(2) Robert "Bob" Hubing

Hugo and Alexander were buried in the Raudsep Family Cemetery. The five youngest children attended West End (formerly Kohns) school on Miller Creek to which they walked four miles. Hans Raudsep died in July 1925, and was buried July 19, 1925, in Pleasant Valley Cemetery, on Miller Creek Road, (currently known as Gray Road) northeast of Rozet, Wyoming. Emilie Raudsep died on April 12, 1956, and was buried in Pleasant Valley Cemetery.

John, Hans, Selma, and Emilie on board ship

Sources:
Photos: Courtesy of Diann Larsen Avery, Rozet, Wyoming, 2019, and of Lois Simpson Schlup August 1, 2017.
Family Info provided by Lois Simpson Schlup, August 1, 2017.
Bureau of Land Management, Homestead Patent Index, [www.glorecords.blm.gov].
"Funeral Services Held Sunday for Mrs. E. Raudsep," The News Record, Gillette, Wyoming, April 26, 1956.
"Albert R. Raudsep obituary," The News Record, Gillette, Wyoming, July 3, 1996.
Pleasant Valley Cemetery Burial Book, kept by Mrs. Lucille Thompson (Xeroxed Copy-1998).
Ancestry.com, New York, Passenger List, 1820-1957 [database on-line], Provo, UT.
Ancestry.com, 1910 U.S. Federal Census, (Hous Rovorsup) Crook County, Wyoming, [database on-line], Provo, UT.
Ancestry.com, 1940 U.S. Federal Census, (Emilie Raudsep), Campbell County, Wyoming, [database on-line], Provo, UT.

Selma Raudsep

Selma was born October 25, 1902, in Baltika, Samara, Estonia (now part of Russia), to Hans and Ann (Kotkas) Raudsep. She was five years old when she immigrated to the United States in 1907, with her father and stepmother, Emilie, and older brother, John. Their destination per the New York passenger list for the *S.S. Cherson* sailing from Lilase, Germany, on November 25, 1907, was Fort Pierre, South Dakota. The family arrived in Moorcroft in 1908. Selma's early schooling did not begin until she was eight years old because of the distances to travel to the nearest country school. Selma graduated from Moorcroft High School in 1924, taking normal training during her last year, which qualified her to teach. Beginning in 1924, until her retirement from teaching in 1970, she taught only in country schools in Crook, Campbell, and Weston counties, teaching all eight grades. During the summer she attended summer school classes and extension courses from the University of Wyoming and Black Hills State College to keep up her teaching certificate. In 1951 the Wyoming State Education Department required that teachers have a four-year degree, so she set about acquiring her BA degree in elementary education from the University of Wyoming. By attending summer sessions at the university she received her degree in August of 1960. Selma's last school, where she taught only six grades, was at the Black Thunder School in Weston County from 1965 to 1970. She lived in Newcastle, Wyoming, until in 1985 she moved to Joliet, Montana, where she lived with her sister, Leida Hubing, until her death on April 7, 1986, in the Deaconess Medical Center, Billings, Montana. Selma was buried near her parents in Pleasant Valley Cemetery, Rozet, Campbell County, Wyoming.

1918 John Raudsep, Selma Raudsep, Julia Toro Trembath

Sources:
Photos: Top photo copied from "Let Your Light Shine, Volume II, Pioneer Women Educators of Wyoming," Published by Alpha Xi State, Delta Kappa Gamma, 1985; bottom photo courtesy of Diann Larsen Avery, 2020.
Pleasant Valley Cemetery Burial Book, kept by Mrs. Lucille Thompson (Xeroxed Copy-1998).
Ancestry.com, New York, Passenger List, 1820-1957 (database online), Provo, UT.
"Let Your Light Shine, Volume II, Pioneer Women Educators of Wyoming," Published by Alpha Xi State, Delta Kappa Gamma, 1985.
"Selma Raudsep Dies," page 16, The News Record, Gillette, Wyoming, April 13, 1986.

Alexander "Alex" and Anna Wilhelmina (Saar) Semlek
1910

Alex Semlek was born January 22, 1878, in Estonia. As a young man he learned the blacksmith trade and, at the age of 19, he moved to Tallian, Estonia, where he worked for ten years before immigrating to the United States in 1907. After arriving in this country, he went to Ft. Pierre, South Dakota, where he was employed by the railroad. In the spring of 1910, at the age of 32, he moved to Crook County where he filed on a homestead about 30 miles northwest of Moorcroft and where he made his home until his death. According to BLM records his homestead was in Section 1, Township 51 North, Range 69 West, and Section 6, Township 51 North, Range 68 West, in Crook County. Later a portion of his homestead became located in Campbell County when Campbell County was created in 1911. Alex married Anna Wilhelmina Saar on June 14, 1913, in Moorcroft, Crook County, Wyoming. Anna was born January 12, 1885, in Tallian, Estonia. She immigrated to the United States in 1913 at age 23. Alex and Anna became the parents of three sons and two daughters:

Hertha	b: 08 May 1914	d: 23 May 2011	m: George Larsen
Erna	b: 12 Dec 1917	d: 29 Dec 2005	m: Wm. Kenneth McCaughin
William August	b: 24 Sep 1919	d: 21 Oct 2011	m: Louise Pauline Glotzbac
Valdemar Frank	b: 25 Jun 1923	d: 16 Aug 1960	(never married)
Robert	b: 02 Feb 1916	d: 18 Feb 1971	m: (1) Nellie Frances Neville
			(2) Becky Hawkins

Their son William entered the U.S. Army in February 1942 as a member of the 35th Division. He served in the European theatre where he fought in France and then was held in a German prisoner of war camp for eight months before being liberated. He returned to Rozet after the war with his wife, Louise, and he helped his dad on the ranch until his father died. They continued to live on the ranch until William's death. He and his wife Louise are buried in the Black Hills National Cemetery, Sturgis, Meade County, South Dakota. Erna graduated from Campbell County High School in 1936 and went to work at the Gillette hospital until the fall of 1939 when she entered the Sheridan County Memorial Hospital School of Nursing, graduating in 1942. She married William McCaughin on March 20, 1943. They lived almost all their married life in Montana. Robert graduated from Moorcroft High School and volunteered for the army in 1939. He retired as a major, and he is buried in the Custer National Cemetery, Crow Agency, Big Horn County, Montana. Anna Semlek died December 28, 1948; Alex died on October 12, 1960. They are both buried in Pleasant Valley Cemetery, Rozet, Wyoming.

Sources:
Photos: Courtesy of Diann Larsen Avery, April 2017.
Bureau of Land Management, Homestead Patent Index [www.glorecords.blm.gov].
Obituaries, The News Record, Gillette, Wyoming, copies provided by Diann Avery, April 2017.
Pleasant Valley Cemetery Burial Book, kept by Mrs. Lucille Thompson (Xeroxed Copy-1998).
Ancestry.com, U.S. Find-a-Grave Index, 1600s-Current, [database online], Provo, UT.
Ancestry.com, U.S. World War I Draft Registration Cards, 1917-1918 [database online], Provo, UT.
Ancestry.com, U.S. World War II Draft Registration Cards, 1942 [database online], Provo, UT.
Ancestry.com, 1910 U.S. Federal Census for Crook County, Wyoming, [database online], Provo, UT.

John and Alvina (Wassil) Toro
1910

Jaan "John" was born on 12 December 1872, in Liftlandka, Petropowlaski, Russia to Hans and Julia (Susi) Toro. He served in the Russian Imperial Army as the inscription on the back of his photo tells us. Jaan Toro and Alvina Wassil were married on December 9, 1900, in Ufa, Russia. Alvina was born December 24, 1879, in Samaras, Russia, (now Denmark). Three children were born:

Julia   b: 08 Oct 1901, Siberia   d: 14 Jul 1975

Maria   b: 25 May 1903, Siberia   d: 07 Mar 1904   m: Charles Trembath

August   b: 26 Mar 1905, Siberia   d: 26 Aug 1977   m: Joyce E. Glover

In 1907 John and Alvina with their two surviving children and John's father Hans immigrated to the United States settling in Meers, Stanley County, South Dakota. Hans died there in 1908. A son was born:

Edward   b: 19 Sep 1907   d: 16 Oct 1975   m: Marjorie May Henderson

By 1910 the family had moved to Crook County, Wyoming, where John Toro filed on a homestead in Township 51 North, Range 70 West, northwest of Moorcroft in the Little Iowa community. 1920 he filed on another homestead located in Township 52 North, Range 70 West. John and Alvina's family grew to include:

Andrew	b 12 Jan 1911	d: 25 Oct 2002	m: Llena Kennedy (div)
Carl	b: 02 May 1913	d: 11 Aug 1996	(never married?)
Helmi "Alma"	b: 11 May 1915	d: 03 May 1998	m: Harold Elkins
Linda	b: 05 Dec 1917	d: 01 Mar 1984	m: Arvil Ashment
John, Jr	b: 28 Jul 1920	d: 18 May 2000	m: 1) Pearl Evelyn Nelson
			2) Beulah Reid
Elsie	b: 02 Feb 1924	d: 20 Jul 2006	m: Harold E. Dempsey

Andrew and John served in the U. S. Army during World War II and Edward served in the Air Force after WWII and during the Korean War. Alma Toro taught in the Cottonwood School in the Little Iowa community.

By 1930 the four oldest children had left home. In the 1930 U.S. Federal Census we find John, Alvina, Carl Helen, Linda, John, Jr., and Elsie, living in on their ranch in Election District 8, Campbell County, Wyoming.

By 1940, Alvina & their youngest daughter, Elsie, had moved to Colorado. They were found living with her son-in-law and daughter, Charles and Julia Trembath, in the 1940 U.S. Federal Census for Weld County, Colorado. John remained in Wyoming and was listed in 1940 census living alone on his homestead. It appears he did not move to Greeley until 1950 as his obituary found on page 11 of the June 16, 1950 Greeley Daily Tribune, states: ". . . a newcomer to Greeley from Moorcroft, Wyo., ... was admitted to Weld County Public Hospital on arrival here. He died Tuesday,(June 13, 1950) after an illness of 11 days.". He was buried in the Evans Cemetery, Greeley, Weld County, Colorado. Nine years later Alvina died on December 26, 1959 and was buried alongside of her husband.

Alma Toro

Sources:

Photo: (John) U.S. Find-a-Grave Index, 1600s-Current, [database online], Provo. UT.

Photo: (Alvina) from her funeral leaflet that was written by her son John, compliments of Diann Avery, Rozet, Wyoming.

Xeroxed copy of Toro Children sent to Diann Avery by a son of John Toro, Jr. listing names, birthdates and places of birth.

Newspaper.com by Ancestry, Obit for John Toro, Greeley Daily Tribune, Greeley, Colorado, June 16, 1950, page 11.

Newspaper.com by Ancestry, Obit for Mrs. Alvina Toro, Greeley Daily Tribune, Greeley, Colorado, Dec 26, 1959, page 12.

Ancestry.com, U.S. Find-A-Grave Index, 1500s to current, [database online], Provo, UT.

Ancestry.com, 1910 U.S. Federal Census for Gillette, Crook County, Wyoming, [database online], Provo, UT.

Ancestry.com, 1920 U.S. Federal Census for Iowa, Campbell County, Wyoming, [database online], Provo, UT.

Ancestry.com, 1930 U.S. Federal Census for Election District 8, Campbell County, Wyoming, [database online], Provo, UT.

Ancestry.com, 1940 U.S. Federal Census for Campbell County, Wyoming (John, Sr. living in Adon area), [database online], Provo, UT

Ancestry.com, 1940 U.S. Federal Census for Greeley, Weld County, Colorado (Alvina Toro living with daughter Julia), [database online], Provo, UT.

Erastus E. and Lorinda A. (Shafer) Wells
1910

Erastus E. Wells was born February 27, 1835, in Merrimac County, New Hampshire, to Benjamin and Calista Wells. Erastus grew up there until 1856, two years after his mother died, when his father left New Hampshire and headed west to Iowa. Benjamin settled in Dubuque County, Iowa. He was a stone cutter by trade, but he took up farming in Iowa. Erastus married Elizabeth Sorber in 1859, and they had two children:

George Wells	b: Sep 1859	d: 1919	m: Ida Ellen Belvail
Elizabeth	b: 1862	d: 1862	

Elizabeth Wells died in 1860. Soon after he and his son George, moved to Jackson County, Iowa, where he married Lorinda Shafer, daughter of Daniel and Mary (Jones) Shafer a native of Mercer County, Pennsylvania, on November 11, 1863. In 1866 Erastus moved his family to Webster County, Iowa and settled in Washington Township on Section 8, being one of the first settlers in Washington County. Many were the hardships and privations experienced in the early days of the county but assisted by his frugal wife he was successful. He sold the farm in 1878 and bought eighty acres in Newark Township on section 14, to which he added acreage until he owned 160 acres all under cultivation. Erastus and Lorinda became the parents of six children:

Addie	b: 06 Feb 1865	d: 30 Mar 1925	m: James W. Haiden
Carrie M.	b: 17 Feb 1868	d: 15 Nov 1931	never married
Viola	b: 10 May 1870	d: 21 Jan 1946	m: Richard S. "Dick" Ashpole
Charles	b: 12 Feb 1873	d: 22 Jun 1944	m: Sabella Mae Norton Campbell
Jessie Belle	b: 20 Aug 1877	d: 1956	m: John Charles Fischer
Gertrude	b: 26 Oct 1883	d: 31 Jul 1968	m: Durward. D. Woolsey

In 1910, at age 75, Erastus and Lorinda moved to Rozet, Wyoming. Lorinda Wells, age 69, died March 22, 1913, at her home in Rozet. She was buried in the Moorcroft Cemetery, Moorcroft, Wyoming. Erastus Wells died, age 83, on November 8, 1918, at the home of his son Charles in Rozet, Wyoming. He was buried beside his wife in the Moorcroft Cemetery, Moorcroft, Wyoming.

**Lorinda and Erastus
Gillette, Wyoming, 1911**

Sources:
Photo: Ancestry.com, Family tree
Personal Column, "Mrs. Wells, aged 69 years, Died at her home ...," The Gillette News,
Gillette, Wyoming, March 28, 1913.
Moorcroft Cemetery Burial Book #1, page 21, 62.
"Obituary for Erastes Wells," Campbell County Record, Gillette, Wyoming, November 14, 1918.
"Local news item," The Gillette News, Gillette, Wyoming, November 22, 1918.
Webster and Hamilton Counties, Iowa, Biographical Record and Portrait Album 1888, Page 14, 1918.
Ancestry.com, U.S. Find-a-Grave Index, 1600s-Current, [database online], Provo, UT.
Ancestry.com, Iowa, Select Marriages Index, 1758-1996, [database online], Provo, UT.
Ancestry.com, 1860 U.S. Federal Census for Farmers Creek, Jackson County, Iowa, [database online], Provo, UT.
Ancestry.com, 1870 U.S. Federal Census for Washington, Webster County, Iowa, [database online], Provo, UT.
Ancestry.com, 1880 U.S. Federal Census for Fremont, Hamilton County, Iowa, [database online], Provo, UT .
Ancestry.com, 1895 Iowa, State Census Collection, 1836-1925, [database online], Provo, UT.
Ancestry.com, 1900 U.S. Federal Census for Newark, Webster County, Iowa, [database online], Provo, UT.
Ancestry.com, 1910 U.S. Federal Census for Newark, Webster County, Iowa, [database online], Provo, UT.

Carrie M. Wells

Carrie M. Wells was born February 17, 1863, in Duncombe, Webster County, Iowa. She moved with her parents to Vincent, Iowa, in 1882 and grew up in that community. In 1909, at age 46, she located on a homestead in Carpenter, Laramie County, Wyoming. In 1912 she came to Rozet to join her parents and brother Charles. She filed on a homestead alongside her brother in Section 10, Township 50 North, Range 69 West. Carrie was active in the Rozet community. In 1914 she was elected by the Campbell County Board of Commissioners to serve as the Rozet Polling Clerk in the 1914 elections and as the Republican State Representative. In 1920 she moved into the Shaughnessy house in Rozet so her niece, from Vincent, Iowa, Lyla Ashpole, could attend school in Rozet. She later adopted Lyla. Carrie also served as Clerk on the District Three School Board for several years. In 1924 she announced her candidacy for Campbell County Treasurer. She was appointed postmistress of the Rozet Post Office in November 1928 and held that position until her death, at age 62, on October 15, 1931. She was buried in the Moorcroft Cemetery, Moorcroft, Wyoming alongside her parents. One adopted daughter (Lyla) Mrs. Rich Weaver of Rozet, and three sisters survived her, Mrs. Viola Ashpole, Mrs. Gertrude Woolsey, and Mrs. Jessie Fischer, all residing in California, and one brother, Charles of Rozet.

Charles Wells

Charles Wells, the youngest son of Erastus and Lorinda (Shafer) Wells, filed for a homestead about five miles northeast of Rozet in the Well Creek community located in Section 10, Township 50 North, Range 69 West. He served as Rozet bus driver on the northeast route for 1922-1923 school term and may have been for other years that was unrecorded in the newspapers. Just when he left Wyoming is not known. The 1940 Federal Census for Phillips County, Kansas records him, at age 62, living in Greenwood, with a wife, Sabella, age 54. She was the widow of David D. Campbell who died in 1931. Charles Wells died June 22, 1944, in Phillipsburg, Kansas; Sabella died February 7, 1976. Both are buried in Iowa Union Cemetery, Phillipsburg, Phillips County, Kansas, on the Campbell lot. Her stone reads "Sabella Mae Norton Campbell Wells" and she rests between her husbands.

Sources for Carrie M. Wells:
Photo: taken by Matt Avery at the Rozet Post Office, July 2020.
"Proceedings of the Board of County Commissioners," The Gillette News, Gillette, Wyoming, July 10, 1914.
"Rozet Postmistress Succumbs; Services Held on Wednesday," page 1, The News Record, Gillette, Wyoming, October 15, 1931.
Moorcroft Cemetery Burial Book #2, (April 1923-Nov 1934), page 186, Moorcroft, Wyoming.
Ancestry.com, U.S. Find-a-Grave Index, 1600s-Current, [database online], Provo, UT.
Ancestry.com, 1920 U.S. Federal Census for, Election District #5, Rozet-North; [database online], Provo, UT.
Ancestry.com, 1930 U.S. Federal Census for Election District #5, Campbell County, Wyoming, [database online], Provo, UT.

Sources for Charles Well:
Ancestry.com, U.S. Find-a-Grave Index, 1600s-Current, [database online], Provo, UT.
Ancestry.com, U.S. World War I Draft Registration Cards, 1917-1919, [database online], Provo, UT.
Ancestry.com, 1920 U.S. Federal Census for Rozet North, Campbell County, Wyoming, , [database online], Provo, UT.
Ancestry.com, 1930 U.S. Federal Census for Election district 5, Campbell County, Wyoming, [database online, , Provo, UT.
Ancestry.com, 1940 U.S. Federal Census for Greenwood, Phillips County, Kansas, [database online], Provo, UT.

George and Ida (Belvail) Wells

George Wells was born in September 1859, in Dubuque County, Iowa, to Erastus and his first wife, Elizabeth (Sorber) Wells. Soon after the death of his mother in 1962 George's father moved them to Jackson County, Iowa, and married Lorinda Shafer. George married Ida Ellen Belvail on June 24, 1883, in Sac County, Iowa. They became the parents of two daughters:

Edith Mae b: Jan 1884 d: 03 Aug 1930 m: John Hoiten
Fern Izora b: 11 Dec 1889 d: 14 Mar 1963 m: Joe Kearns

George and Ida came to the Rozet area about 1916 via Meade County, South Dakota where they lived for a short time. George Wells died October 20, 1919, at Rozet and his body was returned to Sac County, Iowa, for burial in Wall Lake Cemetery Wall Lake, Iowa. His wife, Ida, moved to Sheridan, Wyoming, but returned to Rozet in the summer of 1923 to keep house for Robert Preston. She remained in the Rozet area taking a new position of managing the Rozet School dining hall. In 1928 she was placed in charge of children boarding with her while going to school at Rozet. By 1940 her daughter, Fern, and her husband Joe Kerns had moved in with her. They continued to live in Ida's house in Rozet until her death in 1952. Her body was taken to Wall Lake, Sac County, Iowa where she was buried alongside of her husband George in the Wall Lake Cemetery.

Mrs. Ida Wells and daughter Fern Kearns

**Ida (Belvail) Wells
at her home in Rozet, Wyoming**

Sources:
Photos: from the collections of Leona Heptner.
  From Ancestry.com, family tree.
"George Wells Passes Away," The Gillette News, Gillette, Wyoming, October 24, 1919.
"Local News Item, George Wells," Campbell County Record, Gillette, Wyoming, October 23, 1919.
"Rozet," The Gillette News, Gillette, Wyoming, July 10, 1924.
Ancestry.com, U.S. Find-a-Grave Index, 1600s-Current, [database online], Provo, UT.
Ancestry.com, Iowa, Marriage Records, 1880-1940, [database online], Provo, UT.
Ancestry.com, 1860 U.S. Federal Census for Farmers Creek, Jackson County, Iowa, [database online], Provo, UT.
Ancestry.com, 1880 U.S. Federal Census for Fremont, Hamilton, Iowa, [database online], Provo, UT.
Ancestry.com, 1900 U.S. Federal Census for Levey, Sac County, Iowa, [database online], Provo, UT.
Ancestry.com, 1910 U.S. Federal Census for North, Meade County, South Dakota, [database online], Provo, UT.
Ancestry.com, 1920 U.S. Federal Census for Rozet North, Campbell County, Wyoming, [database online], Provo, UT.
Ancestry.com, 1930 U.S. Federal Census for Election District 5, Campbell County, Wyoming, [database online], Provo, UT.
Ancestry.com, 1940 U.S. Federal Census for Campbell County, Wyoming, (Ida), [database online], Provo, UT

1911 – 1919
Rozet, Campbell County Wyoming

Frank Heptner Homestead with Local Art - about 1918.
Neighboring children came to visit. Frank Heptner standing in the back.
Standing on the porch: Laura Heptner holding Wallace, unknown, unknown.
Last four standing on the ground: Leona Heptner, Irene Heptner, Eugene Heptner, Oscar Heptner.
Front: All three unknown. The unknown children most likely are from the
Charley Woods and Fred Hamm families who were the Heptner's closest neighbors.
(photo from the Leona and Jeanette Heptner collections)

ROZET, CAMPBELL COUNTY, WYOMING
1911-1919
(Campbell County was created May 4, 1911)

Introduction

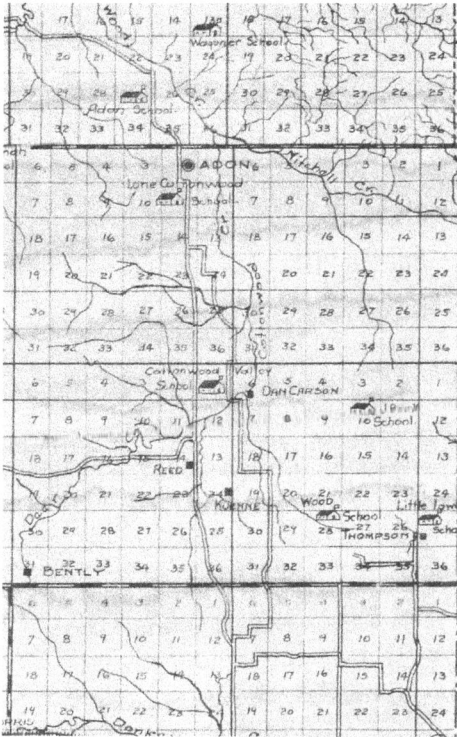

The creation of Campbell County from the western regions of Crook and Weston Counties began with the signing by Governor Joseph M. Carey, on May 4, 1911, of a petition signed by 300 qualified taxpayers and electors in the territory of the unorganized county of Campbell. This petition asked for the authority to establish a provisional board of commissioners to put into motion the machinery needed to hold elections to determine the organization and boundaries of Campbell County and the location of its county seat. The population of the unorganized territory in question exceeded 1,500. At the Provisional Board of Commissioners' third meeting on July 11, 1911, they organized the territory into the following election districts, precinct numbers and polling places:

District	Precinct	Polling Place
Trail Creek District	Precinct #1	Parks Ranch
Bertha District	Precinct #2	Pool and Carpenter Ranch
Rozet District	Precinct #3	Shaughnessy Mercantile
Sunnyside District	Precinct #4	W. P. Rickets Ranch
Keystone District	Precinct #5	F. M. Whitten Ranch
Echeta District	Precinct #6	Echeta School House
Gillette Outside	North Precinct #7	W. D. Townsend Residence
Gillette Outside	South Precinct #8	S. D. Perry Residence
Gillette Inside District	Precinct #9	City Hall
4J District	Precinct #10	4J Ranch
G-M District	Precinct #11	John Morton Sheep Ranch
O-K District	Precinct #12	O-K Ranch
21 District	Precinct #13	21 Ranch
Bar FS District	Precinct #14	Bar FS Ranch

The provisional board of commissioners also appointed the following Judges and Clerks to oversee in the special election in the Rozet and Bar FS voting districts:

DISTRICT	JUDGES	CLERKS
Rozet	Jacob Halverson	Edyth T. Kessinger
Rozet	Mrs. J. Shaughnessy	H. M. Marquiss
	J. Y. Lucas	
Bar FS	Elizabeth Whitcomb Badgette	C. A. Westover
	Jess Myers	
	Drew Smith	

At their next meeting J. Y. Lucas was replaced with O. B. Nelson in the Rozet District. During the special election the voters voted on whether or not to establish a new county. When the votes were counted it was found that 398 voters favored the new county and 36 opposed. They also voted on where the county seat would be located--381 voters voted for Gillette and 15 voted for Rozet. Thus, the citizens of this territory voiced their desire to create the new County of Campbell.

83

Primary elections to fill the various Campbell County offices were to be held on August 20, 1912. To oversee these elections the following judges and clerks for Rozet and Bar FS Districts were appointed:

DISTRICT	JUDGES	CLERKS
Rozet	Frank George	Raymond George
	Mrs. J. Shaughnessy	Mrs. W. L. Kessinger
	C. J. McClendon	
Bar FS	Mrs. C. A. Badgette	Drew Smith
	J. Y. Lucas	George Trowbridge
	Jesse Myers	

At Rozet, on Election Day, for the moderate price of 35 cents, Mrs. Shaughnessy served a good old fashion dinner (noon), consisting of roast chicken and roast pork, with apple and cranberry sauce, and the choicest vegetables of the season. Apple and pumpkin pie were served for dessert. In the evening she served an oyster supper, which "will supply the wants of the inner man while waiting for election results." All kinds of fresh fruits were available for sale at the store, also fresh cider. (*The Gillette News*, Friday, November 1, 1912, page ___?). Later as more homesteaders moved into the area the polling place was moved to the Rozet Schoolhouse. Mrs. Shaughnessy also served as the election judge that first election and continued to be appointed to serve as an election judge or clerk for several election years afterwards.

The Provisional Board of Commissioners of the unorganized county of Campbell met on January 6, 1913, to examine the bonds of the new Board of Commissioners and to administer their oaths of office. The first county officers elected in the primary election included two from Rozet; Alonzo M. Clark as County Clerk and Clerk of Court, and John E. Brennan as County Assessor.

Gillette Railroad Depot – 1912
Standing on platform: George Keeline, Harry Sands, Ida Farmer, Cora Brennan
Beulah Barnett, Bell Arnett, Helen Erd;
Sitting: Roy Hackett;
Standing on the ground: Lawrence "Dot" Brennan
(Photo courtesy of The Rockpile Museum, Gillette, Wyoming)

WORLD WAR ONE VETERANS
(1917-1919)

Andrew Albert "Andy" Burr
Edgar H. "Ham" Baker
Russell Best
Jay Brown

W. G. Cady

Sy Cain
Leslie W. Cain
Alfred Carson
Ralph Harry Czpanisky

Hawley D. Drumm

Roy V. Gilliland
Harvey Graves

O'Neal Gray

Louis Hatfield
L. R. Hipple

Stephan R. Ilff

Frank Jeffers
Lester Jeffers
Vernon Jeffers

George Jensen
Herman Jensen

Carl Jones

Henry Kearns
Ray Kottraba
Lester L. Kyle/Kile

John Lavender

Bill McDermott
Joseph McDermott
Herschel Mapes

Lee Nelson
Lloyd Nelson
Ray Nelson
Charley F. Peterson
Clarence Willard Piper

John William Reed
Edward D. Rhaney
Lee Ridenour
Albert C. Reinsch
John "Jack" Reinsch
Harry Herman Roesken

John Shaughnessy
Stanley V. Stewart
J. H. Smith
Vern Smith
Ben Sprague

Fay Thompson

John Wolfe
Roy B. Woods

Edward LeRoy "Roy" and Irean/Irene (Cain) Hoxsie
1911

Roy was born on February 6, 1889, in O'Neill, Holt County Nebraska, to Wilson and June Hoxsie. He attended schools in O'Neill and married Irean Helen Cain on April 15, 1909 near O'Neill, Holt County, Nebraska. She was the daughter of Nelson E. and Frances (Thompson) Cain. Deciding they wanted to homestead in Wyoming. Roy came to the Rozet area and staked out a homestead located seven miles south and east of Rozet in Sections 15, 21, and 22, Township 49 North, Range 69 West. He returned to Nebraska until after the birth of their second child when they moved to the homestead in Wyoming. The family came by train, and the family belongings, livestock, and what machinery they had, come by emigrant car. Roy worked on the railroad at Rozet and for the OR Ranch until he accumulated a herd of about six cows that someone later stole. Roy and Irene became the parents of five children:

Thelma Ellen	b: 12 Oct 1910	d: 02 Sep 1999	m: Joe Weaver
Lester Edward	b: 18 Sep 1912	d: 03 Jan 1913	
Roycie May	b: 02 Jan 1915	d: 03 Oct 2006	m: Otto Stok
Ethel Louise	b: 16 May 1917	d: 16 Jan 2003	m: Melvin Clark
Mary Jane	b: 28 Sep 1919	d: 14 Oct 2008	m: Lester Lee Fonner

The children attended school at Rozet. Thelma, Lester, and Mary Jane graduated from Rozet High School. In 1937 after their daughters were married Roy sold the homestead and moved to Whitefish, Montana, with his son Lester. They ranched and raised Angus cattle until 1969 when they retired. Roy and Irene moved to Somers, a place south of Kalispell, Montana. They celebrated their sixty-second wedding anniversary in 1970. Irean died in January 1971, at age 78. Roy died on March 22, 1979, at Bigfork Convalescent Center in Kalispel, Montana, at the age of 90. They are buried in the Whitefish Cemetery, Whitefish, Montana.

Sources:
Bureau of Land Management, Homestead Patent Index [www.glorecords.blm.gov].
"Homestead Life of Edward Roy and Irene Cain Hoxsie 1910 to 1979," Campbell County, The Treasured Years, 1990, page 288, compiled by Campbell County Historical Society, Gillette, Wyoming.
"Society—Weaver-Hoxsie Marriage," The News Record, Gillette, Wyoming, December 27, 1934.
"Clark-Hoxsie Marriage," Rozet, The News Record, Gillette, Wyoming, March 29, 1935.
"Obituary-Edward LeRoy Hoxsie," page 20, The News Record, Gillette, Wyoming, April 6, 1979.
"Ethel L. Clark," obituary, The News Record, Gillette, Wyoming, January 19, 2003.
"Obituary for Edward Hoxsie," Newspaper.com, The Missoulian, Missoula, MT, Sat. 24 March 1979, Page 15.

Claude and Ruby (Hamill) Lawrence
1911

Claude W. Lawrence was born January 6, 1879, in Grimes County, Texas, to Alfred M. and Catherine Lawrence. The 1900 Federal Census showed the family living in Portales, Chaves County, New Mexico. On January 5, 1902, Claude married Rubeigna Virginia "Ruby" Hamill in Portales, Chavez County, New Mexico. She was born July 28, 1881, in Callahan County, Texas, the daughter of Robert G. and Mary M. Hamill. At some point after their first son was born, Claude and Ruby moved to Ardmore, Oklahoma, where their next two sons were born. In 1911 Claude moved his family to Rozet, Campbell County, Wyoming. Ruby's brother, John Newton Hamill, would follow them in 1915 filing for a homestead south of Rozet. In 1912, Claude and Ruby Lawrence filed on a homestead located in Section 31, Township 50 North, Range 69 West, which is where the town of Rozet is now located. He built a house and a blacksmith shop and moved the family into their home that fall. They became the parents of eight children:

Richard Oscar	b: 10 Mar 1903	d: 08 Apr 1984	m: Margaret Ann Brennan
Russell Claud	b: 02 Nov 1907	d: 25 Feb 1988	m: Marian Kauffman
Paul	b: 24 May 1910	d: 05 Dec 1997	m: Marion Virginia Asmus
Pat	b: 17 Nov 1912	d: 29 Apr 1994	m: Irene Bailey
Arnetta Ruth	b: 29 Jul 1915	d: 21 May 2010	m: Wayne Leonard Evans
Katherine	b: 03 Nov 1917	d: 22 Jun 2008	m: Bert A. Johnson
Hallie Marselete	b: 22 Aug 1920	d: 03 Mar 2002	m: (1) Wilbur Larson
			(2) _____ Henrie
Ned	b: 22 May 1924	d: 20 Jul 1946	m:

Claude was a water well driller, and he drilled many water wells for the homestead families north and south of Rozet. He donated land for the Rozet school which stood where the Rozet Store was located in 1972. He was hired in 1923 by the Rozet Oil and Gas Company to drill the first oil well in Campbell county located on his homestead about a mile east of Rozet. The people around Rozet were very enthusiastic and hoping to have the first well in the county. Because of this new possibility Claude along with the Halverson brothers, established town site lots for sale in "New Rozet." However, by 1924 when lots were being offered for sale, the well was down 2,600 feet the company ran out of money. Claude and his family continued to live on the homestead until 1926 when he moved the family to Moorcroft then to Hot Springs, South Dakota, and Sheridan, Wyoming. By the 1940 Federal Census the family was living in Cedaredge, Delta County, Colorado, where they lived until their deaths; Claude died in July 1958; Ruby died in 1966.

Winter of '24-25
Claude Lawrence, son Ned, Rich Lawrence, and Dick Talley

Sources:
Photo: *Ancestry.com*, *Kathy Wood Family Tree*, [database online], Provo, UT.
Ancestry.com, U.S. General Land Office Records, 1876-2015, [database online], Provo, UT.
"Richard Lawrence Obituary," *The News Record*, Gillette, Wyoming, April 27, 1984.
"Lawrence Family," page 330, *Campbell County, the Treasured Years*, 1990, compiled by Campbell County Historical Society, Gillette, Wyoming.
"First oil attempt at Rozet 50 years ago never succeeded," by Josephine Lucas, page 4, *The News Record*, Gillette, Wyoming, Thursday, Sept. 7, 1972.
Ancestry.com, Newspapers.com Obituary Index, 1800s-current, [database online], Provo, UT.
Ancestry.com, U.S. World War I Draft Registration Cards, 1917-1918, [database online], Provo, UT.
Ancestry.com, U.S. World War II Draft Registration Cards, 1942, [database online], Provo, UT.
Ancestry.com, 1900 U.S. Census Federal Census for Ozark, Polk County, Arkansas (Ruby), [database online], Provo, UT.
Ancestry.com, 1900 U.S. Census Federal Census for Portales, Chaves County, New Mexico (Claude), [database online], Provo, UT.
Ancestry.com, 1910 U.S. Census Federal Census for Ardmore Ward 1, Carter County, Oklahoma, [database online], Provo, UT.
Ancestry.com, 1920 U.S. Federal Census for Rozet-South, Precinct #26, Campbell County, Wyoming, [database online], Provo, UT.
Ancestry.com, 1930 U.S. Census Federal Census for Sheridan, Sheridan County, Wyoming, [database online], Provo, UT.
Ancestry.com, 1940 U.S. Census Federal Census for Cedaredge, Delta County, Colorado, [database online], Provo, UT.

Joseph and Anna (Proser) Sabatka Family
of Stroner, WY
1911

Joseph Sabatka was born on March 19, 1880, in Prague, Czechoslovakia, to James and Katherine Sabatka. He came to the United States with his parents in 1888. The family settled in Chicago, Illinois, where he attended school. Following school, he operated a tailor shop. Joseph married Anna Proser on September 21, 1907. She was born on July 26, 1882, in Czechoslovakia. She came to the United States when a young woman. Joseph and Anna lived in Chicago for three years after their marriage. In 1911 they came to Wyoming with Joseph's mother, two brothers, and one sister. They homesteaded in the Stroner, Wyoming, community where they made their home for 39 years. During 1949 Joseph and Anna moved to Gillette, Wyoming. They were the parents of seven children:

Anna	b: 10 Aug 1908	d: 03 May 2002	m: James Prazma
Josephine	b: 31 Jul 1909	d: 18 Aug 2000	m: Mitchell Batinovich
Elizabeth "Bessie"	b: 22 Mar 1920	d: 16 Aug 1989	m: (1) John Prazma
			(2) Christian Huber, Jr.
Rose	b: 13 Jul 1915	d: 29 May 2001	m: (a) Americo Onisto
			(2) _____ Knebel
Mary	b: 15 Aug 1916	d: 21 Aug 1991	m: Leland George Turner
Agnes	b: 04 Jun 1921	d: 03 Aug 2014	m: (1) John Z. Ganef
			(2) Fred Lassie
Joseph James	b: 22 Aug 1923	d: 04 May 2008	m: Hazel Goerke

Anna, age 74, died on October 8, 1956; Joseph, age 80, died January 5, 1961; both were buried in Mount Pisgah Cemetery, Gillette, Wyoming.

Sources:
Moorcroft Cemetery Book #2 (April 1923-Nov 1934), page 173.
"Sabatka-Prazma" News Items, The News Record, Gillette, Wyoming, November 15, 1928.
"Requiem Mass on Wednesday for Mrs. J. Sabatka," The News Record, Gillette, Wyoming, October 11, 1956.
"Requiem Mass Sung Monday for Joseph Sabatka," The News Record, Gillette, Wyoming, January 12, 1961.
"Obituary-Josephine Batinovich," page 2, The News Record, Gillette, Wyoming, August 20, 2000.
Campbell County Cemetery District Burial Property Report, September 28, 1998.
Ancestry.com, U.S. Find-a-Grave Index, 1600s-Current, [database online], Provo, UT.
Ancestry.com, U.S. and Canada, Passenger and Immigration Lists Index, 1500s-1900, [database online], Provo, UT.
Ancestry.com, Illinois, Federal Naturalization Records, 1856-1991, [database online], Provo, UT.
Ancestry.com, U.S. Naturalization Record Indexes, 1791-1992 (Indexed in World Archives Project), [database online], Provo, UT.
Ancestry.com, U.S. World War I Draft Registration Cards, 1917-1918, [database online], Provo, UT.
Ancestry.com, 1900 U.S. Federal Census for Chicago Ward 8, Cook County, Illinois, [database online], Provo, UT.
Ancestry.com, 1910 U.S. Federal Census for Chicago Ward 10, Cook County, Illinois, [database online], Provo, UT.
Ancestry.com, 1920 U.S. Federal Census for New Haven, Crook County, Wyoming, [database online], Provo, UT.
Ancestry.com, 1930 U.S. Federal Census for Stroner, Crook County, Wyoming, [database online], Provo, UT.
Ancestry.com, 1940 U.S. Federal Census for New Haven, Crook County, Wyoming, [database online], Provo, UT.

Clarence Joseph and Myrtle Elizabeth (Thompson) Shafer
1911

Clarence Shafer was born August 21, 1888, in Carroll County, Illinois, to Joseph and Elizabeth (Dambman) Shafer. It is not known whether his father died, or they divorced, as we find Clarence, age 11, in the 1900 and 1910 U.S. Federal Censuses for East Waterloo, Black Hawk County, Iowa, living with Henry Appel, his wife Elizabeth, and two younger step-brothers. Clarence came to Campbell County, Wyoming, about 1911; filed for a homestead on Section 1, Township 50 W, Range 69 W, northeast of Rozet. He was issued his deed on April 12, 1916. Clarence married Myrtle Elizabeth Thompson, on December 22, 1915, in Gillette, Wyoming. She was a daughter of Fayette and Mary (Holbrook) Thompson. They were the parents of four children:

Ruth Elizabeth	b: 11 Oct 1916	d: 22 Jun 1987	m: Albert Russell "Russ" Moon
Ralph Joseph	b: 03 Nov 1918	d: 19 Sep 1998	m: Lorraine Ruth Garwood
Richard Fayette	b: 25 Dec 1920	d: 20 Nov 2005	m: Louise Curl
Carol Ida "Kay"	b: 16 Mar 1925	d: 16 Oct 2009	m: (1) Howard Garner
			(2) Chester Vern Shinn
Clara Pearl	b: 16 Mar 1925	d: 16 Mar 2022	m: James B. Gothard

In 1936 Clarence and Myrtle left Campbell County and moved to Albany, Linn County, Oregon. Clarence earned his living in a variety of ways, by buying and selling houses. For a few years they ran an auto court and a small café. At the time, 1942, when he registered for the WWII draft he was employed by the Oregon Shipbuilding Corporation, in Portland, Oregon. Myrtle worked at the front desk of several of the finer hotels in Portland, Oregon. In 1956 they moved once more to Willamina, a city in Polk and Yamhill Counties. Clarence died in February 10, 1979, and Myrtle died in February 4, 1980, in Yamhill County, Oregon. Both are buried the Buck Hollow Cemetery, Willamina, Yamhill County, Oregon.

Sources:
Photos: Courtesy of Gayle Moon Parish, email (Wed October 16, 2019), granddaughter.
Obituary for Clarence Joseph Shafer, copied from a family tree on Ancestry.com.
Ancestry.com, U.S. Find-a-Grave Index, 1600s-Current, [database online], Provo, UT.
Ancestry.com, Oregon, Death Index, 1898-2008, [database online], Provo, UT.
Ancestry.com, Newspaper.com Obituary Index, 1800s-current, [database online], Provo, UT.
Ancestry.com, U.S. General Land Office Records, 1776-2015, [database online], Provo, UT.
Ancestry.com, U.S. World War I Draft Registration Cards, 1917, [database online], Provo, UT.
Ancestry.com, U.S. World War II Draft Registration Cards, 1942, [database online], Provo, UT.
Ancestry.com, 1900 U.S. Federal Census for East Waterloo, Black Hawk County, Iowa,
    [database online], Provo, UT.
Ancestry.com, 1910 U.S. Federal Census for Waterloo Ward 3, Black Hawk County, Iowa,
    [database online], Provo, UT.
Ancestry.com, 1920 U.S. Federal Census for Rozet North, Campbell County, Wyoming.
Ancestry.com, 1930 U.S. Federal Census for Election District 5, Campbell County, Wyoming
    [database online]. Provo, UT.
Ancestry.com, 1940 U.S. Federal Census for Albany, Linn County, Oregon, [database online], Provo, UT.

Clara Shafer
WWII Navy WAVE

Arthur Malcom and Vera G. (Eddy) Speegle
1911

**Viola Woods, Mrs. Laura Heptner, Leona and Jeanette Heptner,
Lillie Woods, Marna (Nelson) Kuehne, Mrs. Vera Speegle and son David
about 1923**

Arthur Malcom Speegle was born October 7, 1883, in Austin, Travis County, Texas. Arthur and Vera filed on homesteads located north of Rozet along Deer Creek in Cottonwood Valley community. Arthur filed for a homestead located in Section 1, Township 51 North, Range 70 West, and Section 6, Township 51 North, Range 69 West. Vera was the daughter of Mr. and Mrs. Ulysses Height "Hite" Eddy. Arthur and Vera were the parents of four children:

David Arthur	b: 28 Apr 1917	d: Aug 1986	m: Betty Jane Hamilton
Robert Hite	b: 17 Aug 1919	d: 17 Aug 1991	m: Evelyn Alice Serier (div)
Marian Fern	b: 02 Apr 1923,	d: 19 Apr 1923 (see note below)*	
Virginia Isobel	b: 25 Jun 1925,	d: 25 Jun 1925 (see note below)*	

The family moved by 1930 from the farm into Moorcroft, Crook County, where he worked as a manager of an implement house. The 1940 U.S. Federal Census records the family living at New Haven, Crook County, where his occupation was ranch hand. Soon after 1940 the family moved to Compton, Los Angeles County, California, as indicated as his address on his U.S. World War II Draft Registration Card in 1942. When Arthur and Vera moved to Oregon is unknown. They probably moved to be closer to their son Robert who settled near Jackson County, Oregon. Arthur died November 8, 1956, in Lane County, Oregon; Vera died on February 17, 1961. Both are buried in the Hillcrest Memorial Park Cemetery, Grants Pass, Josephine County, Oregon.

[Note: *Both infant daughters are buried in the Pleasant Valley Cemetery northeast of Rozet.]

Sources:
Photo: from the collections of Leona and Jeanette Heptner.
Bureau of Land Management, Homestead Patents Index [www.glorecords.blm.gov].
"Obituary (Marian Fern Speegle)," The Gillette News, Gillette, Wyoming , May 3, 1923.
"Infant Daughter of A. M. Speegle Dies at Rozet," Campbell County Record, Gillette, Wyoming, May 3, 1925.
Pleasant Valley Cemetery Burial Book, kept by Mrs. Lucille Thompson (Xeroxed Copy-1998).
"Speegle-Eddy," (wedding), The Topeka-Journal, Topeka, Indiana, May 25, 2016, page 1.
Ancestry.com, U.S. Find-a-Grave Index, 1600s-Current, [database online], Provo, UT.
Ancestry.com, U.S. World War I Draft Registration Cards, 1917-1919, [database online], Provo, UT.
Ancestry.com, U.S. World War II Draft Registration Cards, 1942, [database online], Provo, UT.
Ancestry.com, Washington, U.S. Death Index, 1940-2017, [database online], Provo, UT.
*Ancestry.com, 1910 U.S. Federal Census for Crook County, Wyoming, Outside Moorcroft—School District 16,
       [database online], Provo, UT.*
Ancestry.com, 1920, U.S. Federal Census for Iowa, Campbell County, Wyoming, [database online], Provo, UT.
Ancestry.com, 1930, U.S. Federal Census for Moorcroft, Crook County, Wyoming, [database online], Provo, UT.
Ancestry.com, 1940, U.S. Federal Census for New Haven, Crook County, Wyoming, [database online], Provo, UT.

George M. and Martha J. (Milton) Stewart
1911

George Stewart was born May. 18, 1859, in Stewartville, Vermont, to Charles May and Abigail (Wadsworth) Stewart. Before 1880 his father moved the family to Lake Mills, Winnebago County, Iowa. George married Martha J. Milton, daughter of Edward and Mary Milton on June 29, 1884, in Anoka County, Minnesota. The 1900 and 1910 U.S. Federal Census tells us the family lived in Bristol, Worth County, Iowa, and Waterloo, Black Hawk County, Iowa, before coming to Rozet, Wyoming, in 1910. He filed for a homestead located in Sections 2, 3, 11, 13, and 14, Township 50 North, Range 69 West, and Sections 34 and 35, Township 51 North, Range 69 West, in the "Little Iowa" community northeast of Rozet. They built a dug-out house with three sides tented. George went back to Iowa to work, while Martha and their children remained in the dug-out. The next year George returned. He was a building contractor by profession and a farmer. George built the Rozet School and the Clearmont School. He fell off the roof of the Clearmont School and limped from then on. George and Martha were the parents of nine children:

Mary Abigail	b: 25 April 1885	d: 23 Feb 1974	m: (1) Al Grimm (2) William McGaffey
Ethel Gertrude	b: 06 May 1886	d: 20 Dec 1972	m: (1) William Allen (2) John Miller (3) Herbert Penfold-Blake
Emma L.	b: 03 Jun 1889	d: 30 Nov 1955	m Fred H. Ware
George M., Jr.	b: 25 Jun 1891	d: 12 Dec 1973	m: Blanche Marie Gossard
Frank Royal	b: 15 Aug 1893	d: 28 Mar 1969	m: Della Maud Torbert
Edna Grace	b: 25 Aug 1895	d: 05 Oct 1947	m: (1) Joseph Stone (2) Floyd Vaughn
Stanley Vern	b: 07 Jun 1898	d: 09 Jun 1947	m: Myrtle Agnes Johnson
Gladys Lucille	b: 15 Jul 1901	d: 02 Sep 1975	m: James Francis Quinn
Curtis Earl	b: 25 Nov 1905	d: 17 Feb 1927	(never married)

George died June 23, 1928, and was buried in the Moorcroft Cemetery, Moorcroft, Wyoming. Martha continued living on their farm for a few years, as her daughter Edna and her husband moved in with her to help work the farm. Later Martha moved over on the Adon road to live with her daughter Emma and husband Fred Ware. She then moved to Moorcroft to live with her son Frank and his wife Della, where she lived until her death on October 25, 1957 in Gillette. She was buried alongside her husband in the Moorcroft Cemetery. Moorcroft, Wyoming.

___, George Milton is in the buggy, Curtis, George Martin Martha Jane in the back, ___, ___, ___, Mary Abigail, Frank Royal Edna Grace, Stanley. Joe Stone, Emma Stewart were cut off at the left of the photo. The other folks remain unknown.

Frank Royal, Martha Jane, Ethel, Mary Abigail

Frank Royal, George Milton, Martha Jane, Stanley Stewart

Sources:

Photos: courtesy of Cindy Stewart, Rozet, Wyoming, 2019.
Bureau of Land Management, Homestead Patent Index, [www.glorecords.blm.gov].
"Stewart-Stone," <u>The Gillette News</u>, Gillette, Wyoming, February 16, 1917.
"Zimmerschied-Stewart," <u>The Gillette News</u>, Gillette, Wyoming, September 24, 1920.
<u>*Moorcroft Cemetery Book #2*</u> *(April 1922-November 1934), page 140, 152.*
<u>*Moorcroft Cemetery Book #4*</u> *(April 1946-April 1958), page 397.*
<u>*Ancestry.com*</u>*, U.S. Find-a-Grave Index, 1600s-Current, [database online], Provo, UT.*
<u>*Ancestry.com*</u>*, WEB: Minnesota, Marriages from the Minnesota Official Marriage System, 1850-2019, [database online], Provo, UT.*
<u>*Ancestry.com*</u>*, 1870 U.S. Federal Census for Canaan, Essex County, Vermont, [database online], Provo, UT.*
<u>*Ancestry.com*</u>*, 1880 U.S. Federal Census for Lake Mills, Winnebago County, Iowa, [database online], Provo, UT.*
<u>*Ancestry.com*</u>*, 1900 U.S. Federal Census for Bristol, Worth County, Iowa, [database online], Provo, UT.*
Ancestry.com, 1910 U.S. Federal Census for Waterloo Ward 4, Black Hawk County, Iowa, [database online], Provo, UT.
<u>*Ancestry.com*</u>*, 1920 U S. Federal Census for Campbell County, Election District #5, Rozet-North, Wyoming, [database online], Provo, UT.*
<u>*Ancestry.com*</u>*, 1930 U.S. Federal Census for Election District 5, Campbell County, Wyoming, [database online], Provo, UT.*
<u>*Ancestry.com*</u>*, 1940 U.S. Federal Census for Campbell County, Wyoming, [database online], Provo, UT.*

Frank Royal and Della (Torbert) Stewart

Frank Royal Stewart and Della Torbert were married in Sheridan, Wyoming, on July 3, 1916. Frank was born August 15, 1893, at Lake Mills, Iowa, where he lived until he moved to Wyoming in 1910 with his parents. Della was born April 24, 1896, at Andover, South Dakota, to Elmer and Savilla (Cunningham) Torbert. As a young girl she moved with her parents from South Dakota to a homestead in Crook County. She graduated from Moorcroft High School in 1914. After her graduation she taught in the Torbert Rural School near Carlisle. After her marriage to Frank they lived in Moorcroft where he worked at various jobs for several years. In 1923 he purchased a ranch north of Rozet where he raised registered Hereford cattle. Frank and Della were the parents of five children:

Marlys Anita	b: 12 Apr 1919	d: 22 Feb 2005	m: Woodrow W. Petersen
Rex Royal	b: 26 Oct 1919	d: 13 Mar 1992	m: Shirley Tunst_____
Donna Belle	b: 27 Oct 1925	d: 15 Nov 2012	m: Earl Robert Johnson
Beryl Jean	b: 21 Jul 1927	d: 28 Feb 1941	
Doris Marie	b: 03 Jan 1930	d: 27 Oct 2007	m: Roy Wilber Carlson

Frank continued to purchase portions of the ranch until they developed it into a full-sized ranch. He retired from ranching in 1947, and they moved to Moorcroft, Wyoming. Frank died March 28, 1969, and was buried in the Moorcroft Cemetery, Moorcroft, Wyoming. Della was active in many civic organizations and in the First Presbyterian Church, in Moorcroft. She died April 18, 1984, in the Johnson County Memorial Hospital, Buffalo, Wyoming. She was buried next to her husband in the Moorcroft Cemetery, Moorcroft, Wyoming.

Frank and one of his prize Herefords

Doris, Della, Rex, Frank, Marlys, and Donna

Sources:
Photos: Courtesy of Cindy Stewart, Rozet, Wyoming 2019
Moorcroft Cemetery Burial Book #3, (1935-Nov 1945), page 267, and Book #7 (1982-1992), page 628
"Funeral Service Held April 2 for Frank R. Stewart," The News Record, Gillette, Wyoming, April 3, 1969
"Della Stewart, 87, dies," page 14, The News Record, Gillette, Wyoming, Friday, April 20, 1984Littleton
"Marlys A. Petersen obituary," The News Record, Gillette, Wyoming, February 24, 2005
"Doris Carlson, obituary," The News Record, Gillette, Wyoming, October 30, 2007

Peter and Louisa (Boehm) Wolff
1911

Peter immigrated to America in 1885 from Eschweiler, Rhineland, Prussia, Germany. He settled in Franklin County, Missouri. The following year, 1886, he married Louisa Boehm at St. Joseph, Buchanan County, Missouri. In the spring of 1911 Peter and Louisa with their family of 1 girl and four boys, came to Campbell County, Wyoming. He filed on a homestead about 12 miles southeast of Gillette. They lived on their homestead only a few years until Peter's health began to fail so they moved to California. Later they moved back to the home place in Sullivan, Missouri, where he died on July 3, 1932. She died May 22, 1948. Both are buried in the Holy Martyrs of Japan Cemetery, Japan, Franklin County, Missouri. Their children:

John	b: 06 Mar 1887	d: 19 Dec 1957	m: Helen Skrinjar
Henry Peter	b: 22 Jan 1890	d: 29 Sep 1973	m: Catherine L. O'Hara
George	b: Aug 1893	d: 17 Aug 1961	never married
Anna C.	b: 05 Feb 1896	d: 20 Jul 1963	
Edward James	b: 08 Sep 1900	d: Sep 1966	m: Madge Daugherty
Albert	b: 16 May 1908	d: 28 Jan 1968	

John and Helen (Skrinjar) Wolff   **Henry Peter and Catherine (O'Hara) Wolff**

Sources:
Photos: Courtesy of Judy Whisler Kehn, Gillette, Wyoming - 2019.
Bureau of Land Management, Homestead Patent Index, [www.glorecords.blm.gov].
"Henry Wolff," page 654-656, Campbell County, The Treasured Years, 1990, compiled by Campbell County Historical Society, Gillette, Wyoming.
Correspondence from Mrs. Judy Whisler Kehn, January 2020.
Ancestry.com, U.S. Find-a-Grave Index, 1600s-Current, [database online], Provo, UT.
Ancestry.com, Germany, Select Births and Baptisms, 1558-1898, [database online], Provo, UT.
Ancestry.com, Web: Missouri, Death Certificates, 1910-1962, [database online], Provo, UT.
Ancestry.com, U.S. Indexed County Land Ownership Maps, 1860-1918, [database online], Provo, UT.
Ancestry.com, 1900 U.S. Federal Census for Boone County, Missouri, [database online], Provo, UT.
Ancestry.com, 1910 U.S. Federal Census for Boone, Franklin County, Missouri, [database online], Provo, UT.
Ancestry.com, 1920 U.S. Federal Census for Laney, Campbell County, Wyoming, [database online], Provo, UT.
Ancestry.com, 1930 U.S. Federal Census for Boone, Franklin County, Missouri, [database online], Provo, UT.
Ancestry.com, 1940 U.S. Federal Census for Boone, Franklin County, Missouri, [database online], Provo, UT.

Charles J. "Charley" and Bridget Susan "Bea" (Boyle) Slattery
1912

1947
Charles and Bea Slattery
35th Wedding Anniversary

1925
Bea in front of homestead with a pig and chickens

Charley Slattery, born June 17, 1888, in Holt County, Nebraska, to Michael and Sarah (McGowan) Slattery, natives of Ireland, whose parents settled in Allegheny County, Pennsylvania. Charley's father, Michael Slattery enlisted in the Civil War on July 5, 1861. He served as a Corporal with Company F, 6th Cavalry Regiment. He was discharged on July 5, 1869. He received an Invalid Pension in July 1879. Michael married Sarah McGowan about 1867. They lived in Pittsburgh, Pennsylvania, until after 1880 when they moved to O'Neill, Holt County, Nebraska, and later to Grattan where they lived for the remainder of their lives.

Charles and Bridget Susan "Bea" Boyle were married on June 17, 1912, at O'Neill, Holt County, Nebraska. She was born December 16, 1888, O'Neill, Holt County, Nebraska, to Edward and Bridget Boyle. She graduated from St. Mary's Academy at O'Neill after which she taught school in the O'Neill area. They became the parents of one son:

Joseph Ambrose   b: 21 Mar 1913   d: 19 Feb 1996   m: Caroline Hicks

In 1912 Charley went to Wyoming to look for land to homestead. They purchased a homestead southeast of Rozet. Returning to Nebraska he and Bea began the process of leaving Nebraska and moving to Wyoming. Charley arrived in Rozet on March 7, 1916, in an emigrant railroad car full of all his family's possessions, horses, cows, machinery, and household goods. He set about building a two-room house and a four-stall barn with the help of Fred Duvall. Bea and their three year old son, Joe, arrived in May 1916. They built two more rooms on the house in 1928, the year before the big crash of the economy. Most of Charley's time was spent wrangling his horses and hauling water, until he got some fences built and a well dug. Life was hard but Charley and Bea prevailed in spite of harsh environment. Charley and Bea bought out other homesteaders who decided to go elsewhere which increased the size of their land that would become the Sunny Slope Ranch.

There were no schools near their homestead so Bea taught Joe for his first two years. Charley and Bea helped folks to promote the Rozet Consolidated Elementary and High School. Their first school term was 1921-1922. Joe attended that school until he graduated in 1930. Charley served on the school board for eighteen years.

The Depression years brought grasshoppers and drought. Charley and Bea hung on raising hogs, chickens, sheep and gradually beef cattle. Crops of potatoes were sold in town; hay, oats, wheat, barley, and rye were grown to feed their own livestock. Charley died in October 1949 leaving Bea and Joe to carry on. Bea remained on the ranch until she died November 22, 1976, at the age of 87. Both were buried in Mount Pisgah Cemetery, Gillette, Wyoming.

Charley and Bea Slattery and neighbors – 1949

Charley, Joe and Leo (hired man) cutting and binding wheat 1925

Preparing sheep for shearing – 1940s

Sources:
Photos: Courtesy of Dorothy Slattery, Rozet, Wyoming, 2019.
Bureau of Land Management, Homestead Patent Index, [www.glorecords.blm.gov].
"Pioneer Resident Dies in Gillette (Bea)," The News Record, Gillette, Wyoming, November 19, 1976.
"Obituaries-Joseph A. Slattery," The News Record, Gillette, Wyoming, February 20, 1996.
"Charles Joseph and Bridget Susan Slattery Family," pages 538-539, Campbell County, The Treasured Years, 1990,
    compiled by Campbell County Historical Society, Gillette, Wyoming.
"Sunny Slope Ranch, 1916, The Michael & Dorothy Slattery Family," pages 77-82, 2016 Wyoming Centennial Farm
    and Ranch Yearbook.
Ancestry.com, U.S. Find-a-Grave Index, 1600s-Current, [database online]. Provo, UT.
Ancestry.com, South Dakota, Death Index, 1879-1955, [database online]. Provo, UT.
Ancestry.com, U.S. World War II Draft Registration Cards, 1943, [database online]. Provo, UT.
Ancestry.com, U.S. Civil War Pension Index: General Index to Pension Files, 1861-1934, [database online]. Provo, UT.
Ancestry.com, Michael Slattery in the 1890 Veterans Schedules (Holt County, Nebraska); [database online]. Provo, UT.
Ancestry.com, 1870 U.S. Federal Census for Pittsburgh Ward 12, Allegheny County, Pennsylvania, (Michael), [database online],
    Provo, UT.
Ancestry.com, 1880 U.S. Federal Census for Pittsburgh, Allegheny County, Pennsylvania, [database online]. Provo, UT.
Ancestry.com, 1885 Nebraska State Census for O'Neill, Holt County, Nebraska (Michael), [database online]. Provo, UT.
Ancestry.com, 1900 U.S. Federal Census for Grattan, Holt County, Nebraska (Michael), [database online]. Provo, UT.
Ancestry.com, 1900 U.S. Federal Census for Grattan, Holt County, Nebraska (E "C".J. Slattery), [database online]. Provo, UT.
Ancestry.com, 1910 U.S. Federal Census for Grattan, Holt County, Nebraska (Mrs. Sarah Slattery), [database online]. Provo, UT.
Ancestry.com, 1910 U.S. Federal Census for Grattan, Holt County, Nebraska (Charlie Slattery), [database online]. Provo, UT.
Ancestry.com, 1910 U.S. Federal Census for Inman, Holt County, Nebraska (Susan Boyl), [database online]. Provo, UT.
Ancestry.com, 1920 U.S. Federal Census for Rozet South, Precinct 26, Campbell County, Wyoming, [database online]. Provo, UT.
Ancestry.com, 1930 U.S. Federal Census for Election District 5, Campbell County, Wyoming, [database online]. Provo, UT.
Ancestry.com, 1940, U.S. Federal Census for Campbell County, Wyoming, [database online]. Provo, UT.

Joseph Ambrose "Joe" and Caroline "Callie" (Hicks) Slattery

Joseph Ambrose Slattery was born March 21, 1913, in O'Neill, Holt County, Nebraska, the only child of Charles and Bea Slattery. He was three years old when he arrived in Rozet, Campbell County with his parents to live on the homestead his father filed on southeast of Rozet, Wyoming. He attended country school and then after the consolidation of schools in School District Three he attended Rozet Elementary and High School. He graduated from Rozet High School in 1930. On September 23, 1936, in Idaho Falls, he married Caroline Hicks, daughter of Will Arthur and Anna Mae (Myrick) Hicks. Joe and Caroline were the parents of nine children:

Joseph Ambrose, Jr.	b: 20 Apr 1938	d: 18 Oct 2020	m: Martha Davidson
Susan Marie	b: 14 Mar 1940	d: Living	m: Jack Zimmerschied
Caroline May	b: 07 Oct 1941	d: Living	m: Willis Burke
Catherine Joan	b: 14 Jul 1943	d: 22 Apr 2017	m: Larry Beck
James Robert	b: 07 Apr 1945	d: Living	m: (1) Deann Fortin (deceased)
			(2) Nancy Cates Cummings
Charles William	b: 18 Apr 1946	d: 23 Sep 1999	m: Linda Hackney
Mary Ruth	b: 27 Mar 1947	d: Living	m: Earl Joseph Wandler
Ann Frances	b: 01 Sep 1950	d: Living	m: Richard Wandler
Michael John	b: 14 Jul 1952	d: Living	m: Dorothy Dorothy Funk

After the death of his father in 1949 his mother and his family continued operating the ranch. Joe and Caroline had purchased the Fred Duvall place two miles to the north from his parents. There they raised their children. Joe died February 19, 1996. Callie on December 26, 1997. Both are buried in Mount Pisgah Cemetery, Gillette, Wyoming.

Back row: Jim, Bill, Mike, Joe Sr., Mary, Joe Jr.
Front Row: Ann, Caroline, Callie, Catherine, Sue

Sources:
Photos: Courtesy of Dorothy Slattery, Rozet, Wyoming - 2019.
"Joseph A. Slattery, obituary," The News Record, Gillette, Wyoming, February 20, 1996.
"Sunny Slope Ranch, 1916, The Michael & Dorothy Slattery Family," pages 77-82, 2016 Wyoming Centennial Farm
*   and Ranch Yearbook.*
Ancestry.com, U.S. Find-a-Grave Index, 1600s-Current, [database online]. Provo, UT.
Ancestry.com, U.S. Social Security Death Index, 1635-2014, [database online]. Provo, UT.
Ancestry.com, Newspapers.com Obituary Index, 1800s-current, [database online]. Provo, UT.
Ancestry.com, Idaho Select Marriages, 1878-1898; 1903-1942. [database online]. Provo, UT.
Ancestry.com, 1930 U.S. Federal Census for Election District 5, Campbell County, Wyoming, [database online]. Provo, UT.
Ancestry.com, 1940 U.S. Federal Census for Rock Springs, Sweetwater County, Wyoming, [database online]. Provo, UT

Roy Benjamin Woods
1912

Roy Benjamin was born October 2, 1888, in Allison, Butler County, Iowa, to Orrin and Mary (Jungkunz) Woods. He came to about 1912 Rozet with his parents Orrin and Mary Woods. He filed on a homestead located next to his father located in Township 51 North, Range 69 West, Sections 22, 27, 28, 33 and 34. Roy was drafted into the army in July 1917, and served in the Wyoming Corp., 377th Field Hospital, 95th Division during World War I.

On July 10, 1918, he married Ida Irene Thompson, daughter of Fayette and Susan Thompson. While at a training camp near Cincinnati, Ohio, he became critically ill with the Spanish influenza. Ida came from Wyoming to nurse her husband back to health. Shortly after returning to Wyoming she contacted the flu herself and died on November 17, 1918, the day after her sister Esther died from the flu. She was buried at Pleasant Valley Cemetery. Roy, age 46, died on July 14, 1934, at the Fort Mackenzie hospital near Sheridan, Wyoming, and was buried July 17, 1934, in Pleasant Valley Cemetery, northeast of Rozet, Wyoming.

Sources:
Bureau of Land Management, Homestead Patent Index, [www.glorecords.blm.gov].
"Woods-Thompson Marriage," The Gillette News, Gillette, Wyoming, August 23, 1918.
"Mrs. Ida Woods Dies," The Gillette News, November 22, 1918.
"Final Rites Are Held for Rozet Resident," The News Record, Gillette, Wyoming, July 19, 1934.
Pleasant Valley Cemetery Burial Book, kept by Mrs. Lucille Thompson, (Xeroxed copy-1998).
Ancestry.com, World War I Draft Registration Cards, 1917-1918, [database online], Provo, UT.
Ancestry.com, U.S. Find-a-Grave Index, 1600-Current, [database online],Provo, UT.

Orrin Alfred and Mary (Jungkunz) Woods
1912

Orrin Woods was born in Jun 1861 in Butler County, Iowa, to James R. and Mercie Lucinda (Ballver) Woods. He married Mary Ann Jungkunz about 1887 in Butler County, Iowa. She was the daughter of Joe and Mary Jungkunz. Sometime in the early 1890s they moved to Columbia County, Oregon, where he worked as a logger. The 1900 U.S. Federal Census finds Orrin living in Lavinia, Fergus County, Montana, working for a sheep rancher. Mary and the children were living in Allison, Butler County, Iowa. By 1910 the family is living on a farm in Washington, McPherson County, South Dakota. In 1912 Orrin filed on a homestead in Campbell County, Wyoming. It was located in Sections 22, 27, 28, and 33, Township 51 North, Range 69 West, in the Little Iowa community. They were the parents of eight children:

Name	b:	d:	m:
Roy Benjamin	02 Oct 1888	14 Jul 1934	Ida Thompson
Mable Ethel	06 Nov 1890	08 Jan 1986	Arthur H. Reinecke
James Grover	28 Oct 1892	17 Jul 1966	Anna R. Romanowski (div)
Franklin R	Sep 1894	before 1910	
Ruth JoAnna	Nov 1899	04 Jul 1989	(1) Christian Jensen
			(2) Elwyn L. Lee
Lyle Alfred	01 Mar 1900	__ Jul 1977	(1) Gladys Mae Hamm
			(2) Florence M. Agerup
Verne Orrin	23 May 1902	10 Oct 1917	
Bertha Irene	_____ 1904	1986	Arthur B. Hermansen

Their son, Verne Orrin, at age 15, was accidentally killed on October 10, 1917, while helping to dehorn cattle at the Forney ranch near Moorcroft, Wyoming. A frightened steer lunged under a corral pole leading to the loading chute thrusting upwards, striking Orrin in the neck. In October 1924 Orrin filed for a divorce and moved to Everett, Snohomish County, Washington, near his children, Lyle and Mabel, and their families. Mary married Harvey J. Curtis. She died April 25, 1927, near Lake Stevens, Snohomish County, Washington, and was buried in Evergreen Cemetery, Everett, Washington. Orrin died on February 2, 1946, at Everett, Snohomish County, Washington. He was cremated and his ashes were returned to Rozet, Wyoming, where they were buried at Pleasant Valley Cemetery, northeast of Rozet, Wyoming, on March 21, 1946.

[Note: Orrin's name was found spelled several ways. Orrin was chosen as that is how he signed a form on April 8, 1945, when his son Lyle Alfred Woods requested an Iowa Delayed Birth Record. It listed his full name as Orrin Alfred Woods and was signed "Orrin A. Woods, father".]

Sources:
Photos: *Ancestry.com*, (Photo chopped from group picture found in Rupinski/Mushynski/Sargalski/ Szaroletta Tree, 12.19.2016), [database online], Provo, UT.
Ancestry.com, Iowa, Delayed Birth Records, 1856-1940 for Orrin Alfred Woods, [database online], Provo, UT.
Bureau of Land Management, Homestead Patent Index, [www.glorecords.blm.gov].
"Obituary, Vern Oscar Woods," *The News Record*, Gillette, Wyoming, October 12, 1917.
"Woods-Jensen (Marriage)," *Campbell County Record*, Gillette, Wyoming, Jan 15, 1920.
"Funeral of Mrs. (Lyle) Woods Held Last Monday," *The News Record*, Gillette, Wyoming September 13, 1928.
"Rites Held for Former Rozet Man (Grover Woods)," *The News Record*, Gillette, Wyoming, Aug 18, 1966.
District Court 7th Judicial District, *Gillette News*, Gillette, Wyoming, Friday October 23, 1924.
Pleasant Valley Cemetery Burial Book, kept by Mrs. Lucille Thompson (Xeroxed Copy-1998).
Ancestry.com, Washington, Select death Certificates, 1907-1960, [database online], Provo, UT.
Ancestry.com, U.S. Find-a-Grave Index, 1600s-Current, [database online], Provo, UT.
Ancestry.com, 1900 U.S. Federal Census for Lavinia, Fergus County Montana, [database online], Provo, UT.
Ancestry.com, 1910 U.S. Federal Census for Washington, McPherson County, South Dakota, [database online], Provo, UT.
Ancestry.com, 1920 U. S Federal Census for Campbell County, Wyoming, Election District #8, Iowa Precinct, [database online], Provo, UT.
Ancestry.com, 1930 U.S. Federal Census for Everett, Snohomish County, Washington, [database online]. Provo, UT.
Ancestry.com, 1940 U.S. Federal Census for Port Susan, Snohomish County, Washington, [database online]. Provo, UT

Charles Cleveland and Eva May (Ketchem) Greer
1913

Charles Cleveland Greer was born March 27, 1888, in DeKalb County, Missouri; to Madison and Eliza (Patton) Greer. Charles married Eva May Ketchem on June 20, 1908, in Maysville, DeKalb County, Missouri. Eva May Ketchem was born October 3, 1888, in Rochester, Andrew County, Missouri. Madison Greer, Charlie's father, had traveled to Gillette in 1910, liking the looks of the country, returned to Missouri, and encouraged his sons and sons-in-law to consider moving to Wyoming. In 1911 his son John moved to Wyoming and filed on a homestead southeast of Gillette. Two years later in 1913 Charles Greer filed on Sections 6 and 7, Township 48 North, Range 70 West, southwest of Rozet, adjoining another brother, Liburn. Madison, their father, also filed on a homestead southeast of Gillette. However, he overlooked the water question when persuading his family to move to Crook County. The only source of drinkable water was from a spring on Madison's homestead. This spring furnished water for the families who lived nearby. They would fill their wooden barrels from the spring and haul it home. Over a period of years, discouraged by hard stock-killing winters and drought and hailstorms in summer, Madison and his sons, John and Liburn, moved back to Missouri. Charlie and Eva stayed. They became the parents of six children. The three eldest were born in DeKalb County, Missouri.

Dorothy Frances	b: 07 Feb 1909	d: 26 Oct 1992	m: (1) Russell F. Addison
			(2) Gerald L. Jasper
Herma Lucille	b: 10 Jun 1910,	d; 25 Oct 1991	m: Theodore W. Czapla
Olen Clyde	b: 19 Apr 1913	d: 08 Mar 2002	m: Clara Ellen Mulder

And, three children were born in Campbell County, Wyoming:

Orville Clayton	b: 22 Aug 1915	d Sep 1974	m: Shirley Ruth Ogden
Charles Junior "C.J."	b: 04 Jul 1921,	d: 24 Apr 2013	m: Carrie E. Neiman
Jack Dale	b: 27 Jun 1929	d: 09 Apr 1991	m: Elsie Spielman

The children attended country schools. The two girls and the older boys attended high school in Gillette. They "batched" in Gillette and walked the 12 miles home on Friday and walked back on Sunday. Olen, Orville, and C.J. quit school, but Dorothy and Herma graduated from Campbell County High School. They became rural schoolteachers. Jack graduated from Rozet High School in 1948. Charlie Greer died on April 18, 1955, age 67, and was buried in Mount Pisgah Cemetery, Gillette, Wyoming, on April 23, 1955. Eva Greer died in December 1974, age 86, and was buried in Mount Pisgah Cemetery.

Charlie and Eva Greer

Jack and Elsie Greer by the wash house
1951

Jack Greer and his father on the ranch

Standing: Jack Greer, C. J. Greer, Orville Greer, Olen Greer
Sitting: Herma Greer Czapla, Eva May Greer, Dorothy Greer Addison Jasper
1972

Sources:

Photos: Courtesy of Elsie Spielman Greer Sicks, Gillette, Wyoming - 2020.
Bureau of Land Management, Homestead Patent Index [www.glorecords.blm.gov].
"Addison-Greer Wedding," The News Record, Gillette, Wyoming, October 25, 1928.
"Society—Greer-Mulder Marriage," The News Record, Gillette, Wyoming, August 9, 1934.
"Large Crowd at Funeral Services of C. C. Greer," The News Record, Gillette, Wyoming, Apr 24, 1955 .
"Obituary-Jack Greer," The News Record, Gillette, Wyoming, April 11, 1991.
"Obituary-Herma L. Czapla," The News Record, Gillette, Wyoming, October 27, 1991.
"Dorothy Jasper-Pioneer and Teacher," The News Record, Gillette, Wyoming, October 8, 1992.
Campbell County, The Treasured Years, 1990, compiled by Campbell County Historical Society.
Correspondence, Elsie Spielman, Greer Sicks, Gillette, Wyoming,- 2020.
Ancestry.com, Missouri, U.S. Marriage Records, 1895-2002 [database online], Provo, UT.
Ancestry.com, 1900 U.S. Federal Census for Sherman, DeKalb County, Missouri, [database online], Provo, UT.
Ancestry.com, 1910 U.S. Federal Census for Sherman, DeKalb County, Missouri, [database online], Provo, UT.
Ancestry.com, 1920 U. S Federal Census for Bar F S, Campbell County, Wyoming, [database online], Provo, UT.
Ancestry.com, 1930 U.S. Federal Census for Election District 30, Campbell County, Wyoming, [database online], Provo, UT.
Ancestry.com, 1940 U.S. Federal Census for Campbell County, Wyoming, [database online], Provo, UT .

Frank Herman and Laura (Young) Heptner
1913

back: Frank, Oscar, Eugene, Laura, Irene
front: Jeanette, Leona

Frank Herman was born December 6, 1876, in Russellville, Cole County, Missouri. About 1902 he moved to Mills County, Iowa, where on April 14, 1904, he married Laura Margarete Young, daughter of Jacob and Fredericka (Reinert) Young. She was born October 29, 1883, in Glenwood, Mills County, Iowa. Frank rented a farm near Laura's parents outside Glenwood, Mills County, Iowa. Five children were born in Iowa: Olive May, who died at the age of three, Irene Lydia, Eugene John, Oscar Herman, and Leona Sophia. In 1913 Frank left Iowa on an emigrant train for Rozet to look for land. On September 13, 1913, at the U.S. Land Office in Sundance, Wyoming, he filed for a homestead located in Sections 30, 31, and 32, Township 51 North, Range 69 West, in the Little Iowa community. His family arrived May 31, 1914, in Moorcroft on an emigrant car with household items and a trunk full of family memorabilia. Frank met them with a team and wagon to bring them to the homestead. Frank and Laura were the parents of eight children:

Olive May	b: 04 May 1904	d: 21 Dec1907, (buried in Iowa)	
Irene Lydia	b: 31 May 1905	d: 09 Nov 1983	m: Carroll D. Whisler
Eugene John	b: 29 Feb 1908	d: 06 Jan 1979	(never married)
Oscar Herman	b: 28 Jul 1910	d: 05 May 1977	m: Dorothy C. Whisler
Leona Sophia	b: 02 Aug 1912	d: 13 Jan 2001	(never married)
Wallace Edwin	b: 19 Jan 1918	d: 29 Mar 1919	
Jeanette Louise	b: 01 Mar 1920	d: 02 Dec 2002	(never married)
Walter (nmn)	b: 08 Aug 1922	d: 09 Aug 1922	

Their two infant sons, Wallace Edwin and Walter, died from influenza and were buried in the Pleasant Valley Cemetery, Rozet, Wyoming. The children attended the Cottonwood/Woods School, two miles east of the Heptner homestead. Irene and Leona graduated from the Rozet High School—Irene in 1928 and Leona in 1930. Frank died March 3, 1928 and was buried beside his two infant sons in Pleasant Valley Cemetery. Laura continued living on the homestead and with the help of her sons, Eugene and Oscar, they survived the depression and a World War. She was quick to lend a hand to any in need and was known throughout the community as "Grandma Heptner". Irene married Carroll Duvall "Slim" Whisler on July 2, 1930; Oscar married Dorothy Catherine Whisler on June 5, 1929. Laura died on October 10, 1950 at the Mayo Clinic, Rochester, Olmstead County, Minnesota. She was buried at Pleasant Valley Cemetery. Eugene, Leona and Jeanette never married. Eugene continued ranching while Leona and Jeanette became schoolteachers, spending their summers at the ranch when they were not attending summer classes at universities working towards their degrees in education.

Branding Time - 1917
Frank Heptner, Charlie Hinds, George Spencer

Irene Heptner, age 14, keeping the long horns
out of the garden patches 1920

The Heptner Homestead - 1919

Heptner Homestead - 1927
Leona is on rake, Eugene and Oscar working the buck rake, Frank Heptner on the hay stack.

Heptner Homestead - 1927
Stacking straw after the threshing is finished.

Summer 1933 - A gathering of Heptner and Whisler families and visiting cousins from either Colorado or Iowa.
On horseback: Ellen Whisler, Pauline Whisler
Adults standing: Jeanette Heptner, Grandma Laura Heptner, Mildred Whisler, unknown holding unknown, Dorothy Heptner, Irene Whisler, unknown, unknown holding unknown, Leonard Whisler, Elmer Whisler, unknown, Eugene Heptner
Children standing: unknown, Eurith Whisler, Phil Whisler, unknown in front of unknown, Charles Whisler, Joan (Joanne) Whisler, Dean Whisler, Evelyn Whisler
Sitting on the ground: Slim Whisler, Oscar Heptner holding Darleen, Ton Whisler holding Alberta.

The Heptner Homestead about 1945
The old Ben Schrand place at far right where David and Marge Whisler lived during the 1940's

Sources:
Photos: from the collections of Leona and Jeanette Heptner.
Bureau of Land Management, Homestead Patent Index, [www.glorecords.blm.gov].
Pleasant Valley Burial Book, kept by Mrs. Lucille Thompson (Xeroxed copy 1998).
"Rozet Items," "Obit for Wallace Edwin," *Campbell County Record*, Gillette, Wyoming, April 3, 1919 and
    The Gillette News, Gillette, Wyoming, April 3, 1919.
"Frank Heptner of Rozet Passes Away Last Week," *The News Record*, Gillette, Wyoming, March 8, 1928.
"Rozet Couple (Oscar & Dorothy) Married," *The News Record*, Gillette, Wyoming, June 13, 1929.
" Society-Whisler-Heptner (Irene) Marriage," *The News Record*, Gillette, Wyoming, July 10, 1930.
"Funeral Services Held Sunday for Mrs. F. Heptner," *The News Record*, Gillette, Wyoming, October 19, 1950.
"Funeral Service for Oscar Heptner," *The News Record*, Gillette, Wyoming, May 12, 1975.
"Eugene Heptner Passes Away," *The News Record*, Gillette, Wyoming, January 11, 1979.
"Mrs. Carroll Whisler Passes," *The News Record*, Gillette, Wyoming, November 17, 1983.
"Obituary-Leona S. Heptner," *The News Record*, Gillette, Wyoming, January 15, 2001.
"Heptner-Young Family History," compiled by L. J. Whisler, 1998.
Ancestry.com, 1920 Federal Census for Campbell County, Wyoming, Election District #8, Iowa Precinct,
    [database online], Provo, UT

Thomas Judson and Isabelle (Kite) Johnson
1913

Ruth, Belle, Kermit, Edna, Myrtle, Faye, Thomas and Fred

Thomas was born about 1857 in Ohio. Drucilla Isabelle "Belle" Kite was born January 22, 1873, in Coles County, Illinois. She was the daughter of Benjamin and Elizabeth (Strole) Kite. Thomas and Belle were married in 1900 in Indian Territory, Oklahoma. They moved to Sharp County, Arkansas, then later to Kansas where their youngest daughter was born. Thomas came to Wyoming first to look for and then to file on a homestead. Thomas filed about 1913 on a homestead five and one-half miles northeast of Rozet on Section 15, Township 50 North, Range 69 West. His family arrived at Moorcroft, Campbell County, Wyoming, on April 1, 1914. Thomas met them and brought them all to the homestead with a team and wagon. After a brief time, he built a house, plowed twenty-eight acres and put in grebe corn, put up some fence, and went out freighting wool for cash money. He took his team of mules and left the family with one horse, Thomas spent his last seven years on the homestead. He bought some milk cows from a neighbor, H. E. "Barney" Marquiss, and he acquired enough workhorses for the work to be done. A good wheat crop was harvested in 1918 bringing a good price. That winter Thomas was pleased to be able to treat his children with new winter coats. He bought a grain binder the next year and went about cutting grain for some of his neighbors making additional cash money. Thomas and Belle Johnson were the parents of six children:

Edna May	b: 07 Aug 1896	d: __ Jul 1978	m: (1) James H. Cady
			(2) Watson Cady
Myrtle Agnes	b: 02 Mar 1902	d: 26 Dec 1999	m: Stanley Stewart
Ruth Belle	b: 30 May 1904	d: 05 Apr 2006	m: Elmer Whisler
Fred Judson	b: 10 Oct 1905	d: 23 Mar 1989	m: Lottie Weaver
Kermit Raymond	b: 20 Dec 1908	d: 28 Oct 1987	m: Jessie Lee Gray
Faye Marie	b: 11 Sep 1911	d: 17 Jan 2011	m: (1) Nyle Weaver
			(2) ____ McLeod
			(3) Leslie Wolfe

Thomas's health began to fail and by the winter of 1920-1921 he was bedridden until his death on June 4, 1921. Belle Johnson continued living on the homestead after her husband's death, and with the help of her sons continued to improve it. The Johnson children attended the Well Creek School before consolidation of School District Three rural schools. They attended the Rozet Consolidated School when it opened in the fall of 1921. Ruth and Faye graduated from Rozet High School, Ruth in 1924 and Faye in 1929. Belle Johnson died February 5, 1943, and was buried in the Pleasant Valley Cemetery beside her husband. Kermit Johnson, their youngest son, purchased his parents homestead.

Thomas Judson Johnson Homestead – 1925

Sources:

Photos: Courtesy of Ruth Johnson Whisler - 2001.
Bureau of Land Management, Homestead Patent Index, [www.glorecords.blm.gov].
Pleasant Valley Cemetery Burial Book, kept by Mrs. Lucille Thompson, (Xeroxed Copy-1998).
Ancestry.com, 1920 U.S. Federal Census, Election District #5, Rozet-North, Campbell County, Wyoming, [database online], Provo, UT.
"Stewart-Johnson," The Gillette News, Gillette, Wyoming, October 12, 1922.
"Whisler-Johnson marriage," Personal Column, The News Record, Gillette Wyoming, May 6, 1926.
"Johnson-Weaver Marriage," The News Record, Gillette, Wyoming, July 5,1924(?).
"Weaver-Johnson Marriage," The News Record, Gillette, Wyoming, January 26, 1933.
"The Johnson Family," pages 301-303, Campbell County, The Treasured Years, 1900, compiled by the Campbell County
*   Historical Society, Gillette, Wyoming.*

Mark B. and Dora (George) Shickley
1913

Dora George was born on August 17, 1889, in Douglas, Natrona County, Wyoming. She moved to the Rozet area from Sheridan, Wyoming, with her parents Frank and Lucinda George. Dora became a rural schoolteacher after graduation from Campbell County High School in 1913. She filed for a homestead located in Section 9, Township 50 North, Range 69W. Dora married Mark Benjamin Shickley in September 1913, in the Moorcroft Presbyterian Church, Moorcroft, Wyoming. He was born July 6, 1885, at Geneva, Nebraska, to Vinton C. and Maude Luella (Neeves) Shickley. They lived on Dora's homestead located near her father and brother's homesteads about seven miles north of Rozet until they moved to Gillette where Mark worked as an electrician and as Gillette city electrician for some years before they moved to Clearmont, Sheridan County, Wyoming, in the early 1930s. They were the parents of one son:

Theodore Marcus "Teddie"   b: 16 Nov 1921   d: 19 May 2005   m. Phyllis Arlene Snider

Their son Teddie was a veteran of World War II. He enlisted June 22, 1942, and was discharged December 4, 1943. Mark died on August 4, 1964, and was buried in the Sheridan Municipal Cemetery, Sheridan, Wyoming. Dora Shickley died November 27, 1969, and was buried in the Sheridan Municipal Cemetery, Sheridan, Wyoming.

Sources:
Bureau of Land Management, Homestead Patent Index, [www.glorecords.blm.gov].
Local Items: "Marriage license was issued to Mark B. Shickley and Miss Dora M. George," The Gillette News, Gillette, Wyoming, October 3, 1913.
Ancestry.com, U.S. Find a Grave Index, 1600s-Current, [database online], Provo, UT.
Ancestry.com, U.S. World War II Draft Registration Cards, 1942, [database online], Provo, UT.
Ancestry.com, 1900 U.S. Federal Census for Geneva, Fillmore County, Nebraska, (Mark), [database online], Provo, UT.
Ancestry.com, 1910 U.S. Federal Census for Moorcroft, Crook County, Wyoming, (Dora), [database online], Provo, UT.
Ancestry.com, 1920 U.S. Federal Census for Antioch, Sheridan County, Nebraska, [database online], Provo, UT.
Ancestry.com, 1930 U.S. Federal Census for Gillette, Campbell County, Wyoming, [database online], Provo, UT.
Ancestry.com, 1940 U.S. Federal Census for Clearmont, Sheridan County, Wyoming, [database online], Provo, UT.

John Eligh "Jack" and Catherine E. "Kit" (Boyle) Wolfe
1913

John Eligh "Jack" Wolfe was born September 14, 1888, at O'Neill, Holt County, Nebraska, to Samuel E. and Sarah (Thompson) Wolfe. He was one of a large family. He struck out on his own at an early age and came to Wyoming in 1911 and filed on a homestead south of Rozet in Sections 22, 23, and 27, Township 49 North, Range 69 West. He worked for the Whitcomb Ranch while proving up on his homestead. Jack served in WWI. He was a bachelor until 1927 when he returned to O'Neill, Holt Couty, Nebraska, and married Catherine Elizabeth "Kit" Boyle on November 10, 1926. She was born on May 11, 1889, at O'Neill, Holt County, Nebraska, to Edward and Bridgette Boyle. Jack and Kit were the parents of two sons:

John Eligh Jr.	b: 28 Jan 1928	d: 13 Apr 1983	m: Candace Sullivan
Samuel Edward	b: 01 Jun 1930	d: 31 Jul 2019	m: Betty Ruff

Both sons attended the Rozet Consolidated School and graduated from the Rozet High School. John and Sam both learned the craft of sheep shearing from their neighbor John Fox. Jack drove a school bus for the Rozet Consolidated School for many years. He died on March 31, 1969/70. Kit died March 4, 1982. Their son, John Eligh Jr., died in April 13, 1983. All three are all buried in the Mount Pisgah Cemetery, Gillette, Wyoming.

Sources:
Bureau of Land Management, Homestead Patents Index [www.glorecords.blm.gov].
"Requiem Mass Held Apr 4 for John E. Wolfe, Sr.," The News Record, Gillette, Wyoming, April 7, 1970.
"Funeral Tuesday for Local Pioneer (Kit Wolfe)," The News Record, Gillette, Wyoming, March 8, 1982.
"Wolfe Service Held (John Wolfe, Jr.)," The News Record, Gillette, Wyoming, April 15, 1983.
Campbell County Cemetery District," Burial Property Report of September 8, 1998.
"John Eligh and Catherine Wolfe Family," pages 669-670, Campbell County, The Treasured Years, 1990, compiled by
      Campbell County Historical Society, Gillette, Wyoming .
Ancestry.com, U.S. Find-a-Grave Index, 1600s-current. [database online], Provo. UT.

Charley and Minnie (Reed) Woods
1913

Charley Woods was born September 1878, in Minnesota, the son of Edward R. and Mary F. Woods. The family appears in the 1900 U.S. Federal Census as living in Franklin, O'Brien County, Iowa. He married, date unknown, Minnie Reed daughter of John L. and Lillie Caroline Reed of Cheyenne County, Nebraska. She was born August 12, 1880, in Nebraska. They were the parents of six children. Their first four were born in Nebraska; the two youngest were born in Wyoming.

Viola Matilda	b: 04 Jan1902	d: 03 Sep 1982	m: (1) William Gillian
			(2) Lester Kanzleiter
Gerald "Jed"	b: 25 Feb 1904	d: Dec 1986	
Lillian Caroline	b: 12 May 1906	d: 24 May 1990	m: Manuel Matthews
Clarence	b: 1908	d:	
Harold Frank	b: 01 Mar 1916	d: 30 Jan 1982	m: Nannette J. Scott (div)
June Eileen	b: 12 Jun 1919	d: 16 Oct 2004	m: Theodore R. Olsen

Charley and Minnie lived in Deuel, Merrick, and Garden Counties, Nebraska, before they set forth by covered wagon from Dalton, Cheyenne County, for Wyoming. While at Dalton they lived with George and Lillie Reed.

In 1913, Charley and Minnie (Reed) Woods filed on a homestead about 9 miles northeast of Rozet near John Cook, for Section 29, Township 51, Range 69 West, in the Little Iowa community. The children attended the Cottonwood School and high school in Rozet until 1930 when Charley and Minnie lost their homestead, like so many others, to the Federal Land Bank. The family moved to Chelan County, Washington. Lillian Woods Matthews wrote, "I remember special times when all the neighbors got together at one of the neighbors' houses for picnics or when we gathered at Eunice and Harley Ranney's for old fashioned square dances, etc. Everyone took a cake or sandwiches for a midnight lunch. We had local musicians who played their violins or guitars. Some winters were very snowy, and all went out in homemade sleighs. Children were never left at home. The hardest times were during the depression in the 30s."

Charley died in 1957; Minnie died August 4, 1965. Both were buried in the Hillside Cemetery, Issaquah, King County, Washington. Later two of their children, Lillian Matthews and Harold were buried near them.

The Charlie and Minnie Woods homestead

Sources:
Photos: Charley and Minnie Homestead from Leona and Jeanette Heptner collections.
Bureau of Land Management, Homestead Patent Index, [www.glorecords.blm.gov].
Correspondence with Lillian Mathews, Redmond, Washington, 1988.
Ancestry.com, U.S. Find-a-Grave Index 1600s-Current, [database online], Provo, UT.
Ancestry.com, U. W. World War I Draft Registration Cards, 1917-1918.
Ancestry.com, 1900 U.S. Federal Census for Franklin, O'Brien County, Iowa, [database online], Provo, UT.
Ancestry.com, 1910 U.S. Federal Census for Park, Garden County, Nebraska, [database online], Provo, UT.
Ancestry.com, 1920 U.S. Federal Census for Iowa, Campbell County, Wyoming, [database online], Provo, UT.
Ancestry.com, 1930 U.S. Federal Census for Campbell County, Wyoming, Election District #8, [database online], Provo, UT.
Ancestry.com, 1940 U.S. Federal Census for Monitor, Chelan, Washington, [database online], Provo, UT.

Nelson and Frances (Thompson) Cain
1914

Nelson Cain was born March 17, 1861, in Fayette County, Iowa. He married Frances T. Thompson on Christmas day 1886 in O'Neill, Holt County, Nebraska. They were the parents of:

Leslie William	b: 03 Nov 1890	d: 17 Mar 1980	m: Bertha Irene Osborne
Irene Helen	b: 18 Apr 1892	d: 14 Jan 1971	m: Arthur LeRoy Hoxsie
Edna Mae	b: 06 May 1894	d: 17 Feb 1980	m: William J. C. Lubkin
Hazel Ethel	b: 17 Sep 1896	d: 19 Oct 1916	m:
Glen Norval	b: 11 Jul 1898	d: Jul 1976	m: Neta M. Jones
Ivan Henry	b: 16 Jan 1901	d: 11 Apr 1988	m: Cora Ruth Hewett
Esther Sarah	b: 14 May 1904	d: 10 Nov 1993	m: Thomas Goodykoontz
Helen Francis	b: 23 Jan 1906	d: 24 Nov 2006	m: (1) Niles DeLand
			(2) _____ Scott
			(3) Isaac C. Palmer

Frances died on February 14, 1906, and was buried in the O'Neill Cemetery, O'Neill, Holt County, Nebraska. One year later Nelson married Eliza E. "Maggie" (Sanford) Palmer on February 28, 1907.

About 1914 Nelson and Maggie with his son Leslie came to Campbell County, Wyoming, from O'Neill, Holt County, Nebraska. Nelson and Leslie filed for homesteads located southeast of Rozet. Nelson and Maggie were divorced by 1940 according to the 1940 Federal Census for Campbell County. Nelson died October 29, 1947, in Sundance, Wyoming. He was buried in Mount Pisgah Cemetery, Gillette, Wyoming. Maggie died July 26, 1956, in Meade County, South Dakota.

Sources:
Bureau of Land Management, Homestead Patent Index, [www.glorecords.blm.gov].
Campbell County, The Treasured Years, page 94-95, 1990, compiled by Campbell County Historical Society, Gillette, Wyoming.
"Goodykoontz-Cain Wedding," The Gillette News, Gillette, Wyoming, November 6, 1924.
"Obituary-Edna Mae Lubkin," page 16, The News Record, Gillette, Wyoming, February 21, 1980.
Moorcroft Cemetery Burial Book #6, (1972-June 1982), page 578.
Ancestry.com, Nebraska, U.S. Select County Marriage Records, 1855-1908, (Francis T. Thompson), [database online], Provo, UT.
Ancestry.com, Nebraska, U.S. Select County Marriage Records, 1855-1908, (Eliza E. Palmer), [database online], Provo, UT.
Ancestry.com, U.S. Find a Grave Index, 1600s-Current (Francis T. Cain), [database online], Provo, UT.
Ancestry.com, 1900 U.S. Federal Census for Grattan, Holt County, Nebraska, [database online], Provo, UT.
Ancestry.com, 1910 U.S. Federal Census for Grattan, Holt County, Nebraska, [database online], Provo, UT.
Ancestry.com, 1930 U.S. Federal Census for Election District 5, Campbell County, Wyoming, [database online], Provo, UT.

Leslie William and Bertha (Osbourne) Cain
1914

Leslie W. Cain was born November 3, 1890, in O'Neill, Holt County, Nebraska. He married Bertha Irene Osborne, a schoolteacher at Rozet School, on June 3, 1918, in Gillette, Wyoming. Leslie served in WWI, reporting on July 5, 1918, to the U.S. Army and sailed for Europe in August. He served in France until August 1919 and returned to Rozet in September to resume farming his homestead. Bertha was born and raised in Red Cloud, Nebraska. After she attended Normal Training she taught one year in Harrison, Sioux County, Nebraska. The next year she came to Rozet to teach. Bertha taught while Leslie served in WWI and upon his return, she returned to be a wife and mother. Her sister Flora Osborne arrived to teach in Rozet also. Because it was difficult to make a living on the homestead, Leslie went to work for the railroad. Leslie and Bertha were the parents of:

Pauline Edna	b: 23 Dec 1920	d: 13 Jul 2003	m: Oscar Annis
Phyllis Irene	b: 14 Jul 1924	d: 01 Apr 2015	m: (1) Joseph A. Snyder
			(2) Larry Schroeder
Robert Leslie	b: 19 Dec 1928	d:	m: Donna Rae McElwain
Margaret Anne	b: Jan 1931	d:	m: Ron Weenig

The family eventually moved into Rozet and then later into Gillette, later about 1935 moving to Midwest and on to Casper. Leslie and Bertha spent the remainder of their years in Casper, Wyoming. Leslie died in March 17, 1980, Bertha died July 30, 1974, both in Casper, Wyoming. Both are buried in Natrona Memorial Gardens, Casper, Wyoming.

Sources:

Bureau of Land Management, Homestead Patent Index [www.glorecords.blm.gov].
Campbell County, The Treasured Years, 1990, compiled by Campbell County Historical Society, Gillette, Wyoming.
Campbell County Cemetery District, Burial Property Report, September 1998.
Obituary, "Bertha Cain Rites Pending," page 2, Casper Star-Tribune, Casper, Wyoming, August 1, 1974.
Ancestry.com, Vital Records: Social Security Death Index, 1937-1998, [database online], Provo, UT.
Ancestry.com, U.S. Department of Veterans Affairs BIRLS Death File, 1850-2010, [database online], Provo, UT.

The Kuehne Brothers
1914

The Kuehne brothers, Frank, Carl, and William came to Wyoming from Big Springs, Nebraska. They were the sons of Herman and Wilhelmina Kuehne who immigrated from Germany in 1884. They located on homesteads about nine miles north of Rozet along the Adon Road and Cottonwood Creek,

Frank and Marna Mary (Nelson) Kuehne
1914

Frank Kuehne, born October 14, 1889, in Big Springs, Deuel County, Nebraska, to Herman and Wilhelmina Kuehne who immigrated to the United States in 1884. Frank grew up with his three brothers and three sisters. He came to Campbell County in 1913; filed for a homestead on September 8, 1913, about nine miles north of Rozet along Cottonwood Creek in Sections 17 and 19, Township 51 North, Range 69 West, and Sections 13 and 24, Township 51 North, Range 70 West. He was drafted into the army in July 1918 and served in world War I After the war he married Marian Marna known as "Marna" Nelson, daughter of Oscar B. and Sarah (Marshall) Nelson, on February 11, 1920. They were the parents of one daughter:

Alberta Marie   b: 17 Jan 1925   d: 18 Jan 1925

They buried their infant daughter in Pleasant Valley Cemetery, Rozet, Wyoming. Frank died, on March 27, 1948, age 48, and Marna died, on May 21, 1997, at the Pioneer Manor Nursing Home, Gillette, Wyoming, age 98. They are both buried in Pleasant Valley Cemetery.

Sources:
Photos: from the collections of Leona and Jeanette Heptner.
Bureau of Land Management, Homestead Patent Index, [www.glorecords.blm.gov].
Pleasant Valley Cemetery Burial Book, kept by Mrs. Lucille Thompson (Xeroxed Copy-1998).
"Nelson-Kuehne," The Gillette News, Gillette, Wyoming, February 13, 1920.
"Obituaries: Marna M. Kuehne," The News Record, Gillette, Wyoming, May 25, 1997.
Ancestry.com, U.S. Find-a-Grave Index, 1600s-Current, [database online], Provo, UT.
Ancestry.com, U.S. World War II Draft Registration Cards, 1942, [database online], Provo, UT.
Ancestry.com, 1900 U.S. Federal Census for Park, Deuel County, Nebraska, [database online], Provo, UT.
Ancestry.com, 1910 U.S. Federal Census for Big Spring, Deuel County, Nebraska, [database online], Provo, UT.
Ancestry.com, 1920 U.S. Federal Census for Iowa, Campbell County, Wyoming, [database online], Provo, UT.
Ancestry.com, 1930 U.S. Federal Census for Election District 8, Campbell County, Wyoming, [database online], Provo, UT.
Ancestry.com, 1940 U.S. Federal Census for Campbell County, Wyoming, [database online], Provo, UT.

Carl and Esther (Spencer) Kuehne
1914

Carl Kuehne, born August 18, 1891, at Big Springs, Nebraska, in Big Springs, Deuel County, Nebraska, the third son of Herman and Wilhelmina Kuehne. He filed on a homestead located in Sections 19 and 30, Township 51 North, Range 69 West, and Section 24, Township 51 North, Range 70 West, in Campbell County, Wyoming. On January 1, 1918, he married Esther Spencer, daughter of Will and Myrtle Spencer at the home of Rev. H. A. Toland, near Rozet. Rev. Toland performed the ceremony. No children were born to this union. Carl died February 7, 1925, from pneumonia, and was buried in Pleasant Valley Cemetery, Rozet, Wyoming. He was survived by his father and mother, Mr. and Mrs. Herman Kuehne, of Big Springs, Nebraska; four brothers, Frank and William of Rozet, Wyoming, Fred and Herman, Jr., of Big Springs, Nebraska; and three sisters, Mrs. Wallie Leder and Mrs. Marie Oberstein of Big Springs, Nebraska, and Mrs. Hattie Leff of Peety, Colorado.

On May 4, 1927, in Julesburg, Sedgwick County, Colorado, Esther married Carl's brother Herman James Kuehne, Jr., of Big Springs, Nebraska. They lived on their farm outside of Big Springs for the remainder of their lives. Herman died on October 5, 1990; Esther died May 15, 2001. Both are buried in Big Springs Cemetery, Big Springs, Nebraska.

Sources:
Photos: from the collections of Leona and Jeanette Heptner.
Bureau of Land Management, Homestead Patent Index [www.glorecords.blm.gov].
Pleasant Valley Cemetery Burial Book, kept by Mrs. Lucille Thompson (Xeroxed Copy-1998).
"Kuehne-Spencer Wedding," Rozet Rumblings, The Gillette News, Gillette, Wyoming, January ___, 1918.
"Obituary for Carl Kuehne," The Gillette News, Gillette, Wyoming, February 19 and 12, 1925.
Ancestry.com, Colorado, County Marriage Records and state Index, 1862-2006, [database online}, Provo. UT.
Ancestry.com, U.S. Find-a-Grave Index, 1600s-Current, [database online}, Provo. UT.
Ancestry.com, U.S. Federal Census for Big Springs, Deuel County, Nebraska, [database online}, Provo. UT.
Ancestry.com, U.S. Federal Census for Big Springs, Deuel County, Nebraska, [database online}, Provo. UT.

William D. "Bill" Kuehne, born March 24, 1895, at Big Springs, Nebraska, filed on a homestead located in Sections 23, 24, and 24, Township 50 North, Range 69 West, in Campbell County, Wyoming. He also bought forty acres from the American Sheep Company across the railroad tracks north of Rozet. He died on July 13, 1929, from injuries due to a car accident on July 4th near Beulah in Crook County. He was buried in Pleasant Valley Cemetery on July 10, 1929. Bill served during World War I. He was survived by his father, Herman Kuehne, brothers, Frank Kuehne, Fred Kuehne, Herman Kuehne, and sisters, Mrs. William C. Leder, and Mrs. Ernest Koberstein.

Sources:
Bureau of Land Management, Homestead Patent Index, [www.glorecords.blm.gov].
Pleasant Valley Cemetery Burial Book, kept by Mrs. Lucille Thompson (Xeroxed Copy-1998).
"Rozet Man Near Death as Result of Auto Accident," The News Record, Gillette, Wyoming, July 11, 1929.
"Victim of Car Crash Succumbs to Injuries," The News Record, Gillette, Wyoming, July 18, 1929.
Ancestry.com, U.S. Find-a-Grave Index, 1600s-Current, [database online}, Provo. UT.
Ancestry.com, 1910 U.S. Federal Census for Big Spring, Deuel County, Nebraska, [database online], Provo, UT.
Ancestry.com, 1920 U.S. Federal Census for Iowa Precinct, Campbell County, Wyoming, [database online], Provo, UT.

Kharstan Karl "Charley" and Jennie (Pearson) Christianson
1915

Charley Christianson was born on April 1, 1882, in Elvrum, Innlandet County, region of Osterdalen, Norway. About 1899, at the age of seventeen, he immigrated to the United States settling in Deer River, Itasca County, Minnesota. There he met a pretty Swedish girl named Jennie Louise, the daughter of Anton Persson and Lotta Olsdotter. She was born as Jennie Lovisa Antonsdotter on September 6, 1883, in Langscrud, Varmland, Sweden. On November 14, 1900, at the age of 17, she immigrated to the United States from Goteborg, Sweden. Jennie changed her surname to Jennie Louise Persson when she became naturalized. Charley and Jennie married on April 5, 1907. They became the parents of eight children:

Arthur Forest	b: 13 Apr 1908	d: 1964	m: Vida Faye Goodrich
Bertha Margaret	b: 15 Nov 1909	d: 07 Sep 1971	m: Charles Hamilton
Alvin Clifford	b: 1915	d: 1943 (U.S. Army, WWII; Prisoner of War in Japan)	
Helen Agnes	b: 27 Jun 1917	d: 10 Sep 1983	m: Harry Douglas Turner
Roy Karson	b: 08 Jul 1920	d: 23 Jun 1979	m: Lorraine _____
Donald Wyoming" Bud"	b: 24 Aug 1922	d: 15 Jan 1998	m: Alice Irene Lorah
Charles Theodore "Ted"	b: 08 Apr 1924	d: 21 Jul 1946	m: _____
Allen H. "Chub"	b: _____	d:	m: _____

About 1915 Charlie and Jennie with their two children came to Campbell County, Wyoming, where Karl filed for a homestead in the Adon community located on Sections 22, 26, and 27, Township 53 North, Range 69 West.

The children attended school in the Adon community. Charley served on the School District 12 School Board and as a county commissioner of Campbell County. Karl died July 17, 1961, and was buried in Mount Pisgah Cemetery, Gillette, Wyoming, on July 20, 1961. Jennie died in January 1969 and was buried on January 15, 1969, in Mount Pisgah Cemetery alongside her husband and two sons, Charles and Donald.

Sources:
Photo: _Ancestry.com, U.S. Find-a-Grave Index, 1600s-Current, [data base online], Provo, UT._
Bureau of Land Management, Homestead Patent Index, [www.glorecords.blm.gov].
"Society—Hamilton-Christensen Marriage," _The News Record_, Gillette, Wyoming, June 14, 1934.
"Pioneer Rancher Passes Away in Gillette Hospital," _The News Record_, Gillette, Wyoming, July 25, 1961.
"Turner Funeral Tuesday," _The News Record_, Gillette, Wyoming, September 12, 1983.
Ancestry.com, Sweden, Indexed birth Record, 1859-1947, [data base online], Provo, UT.
Ancestry.com, Sweden Selected Indexed Household Clerical Surveys, 1880-1983, [data base online], Provo, UT.
Ancestry.com, Sweden, Emigrants Registered in Church Books, 1783-1991, [data base online], Provo, UT.
Ancestry.com, U.S. World War II Draft Registration Cards, 1942, [data base online], Provo, UT.
Ancestry.com, U.S. World War II Army Enlistment Records, 1938-1946, [data base online], Provo, UT.
Ancestry.com, U.S. World War II Draft Cards Young Men, 1940-1947, [data base online], Provo, UT.
Ancestry.com, World War II Prisoners of War, 1941-1946, [data base online], Provo, UT.
Ancestry.com, World war II Prisoners of the Japanese, 1941-1945, [data base online], Provo, UT.
Ancestry.com, U.S. Department of Veterans Affairs BIRLS Death File, 1850-2010, [data base online], Provo, UT.
Ancestry.com, Newspapers.com Obituary Index, 1800-current, [data base online], Provo, UT.
Ancestry.com, 1910 U.S. Federal Census for Deer River, Itasca, Minnesota, [data base online], Provo, UT.
Ancestry.com, 1930 U.S. Federal Census for Election District 9, Campbell County, Wyoming, [data base online], Provo, UT.
Ancestry.com, 1940 U.S. Federal Census for Campbell County, Wyoming, [data base online], Provo, UT.

James Lafayette and Florence May (Brode) Creach
1915

James Lafayette Creach was born June 29, 1892, in Beloit, Lyon County, Mitchell County, Kansas, to Lafayette Mills and Ida Mae (Keim) Creach (see note below). By 1905 his parents had moved the family to Jewell County, Kansas. James Creach married Florence Mae Brode, on February12, 1913, in Waterloo, Black Hawk County, Iowa. She was born on March 7, 1984, to John and Elsie (Mitchelltree) Brode. James and May were the parents of three children:

Juanita Elsie	b: 12 Aug 1913	d: 22 Dec 1993	m: Paul Ashmore Folt	
Jack Mills	b: 23 Jan 1921	d: 09 Dec 1985	m: Elizabeth L. Pieper	
Lorraine	b: _____ 1924	d:	m: _____ Roundtree	

By 1915 they were living in Abilene, Dickinson County, Kansas before moving further west to Campbell County, Wyoming. James filed on a homestead in Sections 30 and 31, Township 51 North, Range 69 West. He was a carpenter by trade. The homestead was located west of the Frank Heptner homestead. They moved to the Christ Kinas farm about seven miles north of Gillette in March 1929. In August 1929, May Creach, at age 35, met with a terrible accident, causing her death on August 21 from a twelve-gauge shot gun wound to her left leg on the family's way home from the corn field where they had been picking corn. The gun standing in the car tipped over as she was getting out to open a gate. The gun was loaded and exploded sending a charge into the left leg between the ankle and the knee. She died in Dr. Sayles office in Gillette, Wyoming, from shock and loss of blood. She left three children ages 16, 8, and 5. May was buried in the Moorcroft Cemetery, Moorcroft, Wyoming.

It is not known when Jim moved his family to Helena, Montana. He was not found in the 1920, 1930, or 1940 federal census. He married Marian (Castle) Wright on December 25, 1942, in Helena, Lewis and Clark County, Montana. One child was born:

James Castle	b: 05 Feb 1949	d: _____	m: _____

James died September 8, 1957, in Helena, Lewis and Clark County, Montana. He was buried in the Forestvale Cemetery, Helena, Montana. Marian died in Ontario, Malheur County, Oregon, on December 6, 1991, and was buried in the Cambridge Cemetery, Cambridge, Washington County, Idaho.

[Note: James's parents, Lafayette and Ida Creach homesteaded near Plum Creek, Osage in Weston County, Wyoming, after 1910 and before 1920. He died in 1922, and his wife Ida died in 1953; both are buried in the Moorcroft Cemetery, Moorcroft, Wyoming.]

Sources:
Photos: Ancestry.com, U.S. Find-a-Grave Index, 1600s-Current, [database online], Provo, UT.
Bureau of Land Management, Homestead Patent Index [www.glorecords.blm.gov].
"Funeral Service for Lafayette Creach in Osage," Personal Column, Gillette News, Gillette, Wyoming, Jun 8, 1922.
"Woman Dies from Injury Sustained When Loaded Gun Falls from Car," page 1, Gillette News, Gillette, Wyoming, August 22, 1922.
Moorcroft Cemetery Book #1, (1902-April 1923), page 93.
Moorcroft Cemetery Book #2, (April 1923-Nov 1934, page 165.
Moorcroft Cemetery Book #4, (April 1946-April 1958), page 363.
Ancestry.com, Montana, State Deaths, 1907-2016, [database online], Provo, UT.
Ancestry.com, Newspapeers.com Obituary Index, 1800s-current, [database online], Provo, UT.
Ancestry.com, U.S. Social Security Applications and Claims Index, 1936-2007, [database online], Provo, UT.
Ancestry.com. U.S. Family Photo Collections, c. 1850-2000 [database online], Provo, UT.
Ancestry.com, Iowa, Select Marriages Index, 1758-1996, [database online], Provo, UT.
Ancestry.com, Montana, County Marriage Records, 1865-1993, [database online], Provo, UT.
Ancestry.com, U.S. World War I Draft Registration Cards, 1917-1918 (living in Rozet, WY), [database online], Provo, UT.
Ancestry.com, U.S. World Wat II Draft Registration Cards, 1942, [database online], Provo, UT.
Ancestry.com, Montana, County Births and Deaths, 1830-2011, [database online], Provo, UT.
Ancestry.com, 1900 U.S. Federal Census for Beloit, Mitchell County Kansas, [database online], Provo, UT.
Ancestry.com, 1905 Kansas State Census Collection, Ionia, Jewell County, Kansas, [database online], Provo, UT.
Ancestry.com, 1915 Kansas State Census Collection, Abilene, Dickinson County, Kansas, [database online], Provo, UT.

Frederick Louis "Fred" and Letha (Gaffney) Duvall
1915

Fred Duvall was born May 22, 1881, in Ozark, Monroe County, Ohio, to Jephthah Powell and Matilda Ann (Chaddock) Duvall. The family moved to Lafayette, Bremer County, Iowa, prior to 1900. On August 29, 1906, in Waverly, Bremer County, Iowa, Fred married Letha L. Gaffney, daughter of Joseph Nelson and Margaret (Boyle) Gaffney. Letha was born November 18, 1881, in Greene, Butler County, Iowa. Fred and Letha came to the Rozet area from Waverly, Iowa, about 1915. He filed on a homestead located in Sections 14, 15, and 22, Township 49 North, Range 69 West, east of Rozet. They were the parents of two daughters:

Helen Margaret	b:	30 Jul 1915	d:	09 Dec 2003	m: Virgil Jerome Gilson
Jean Maxine	b:	1922	d:	02 Mar 2013	m: (1) Edward L. Schoenfield
					(2) Louis Frey

Fred farmed and raised hogs through the depression. The children went to school at Rozet. Fred served on the District Three School Board for several years. About 1935 Fred and Letha divorced. She moved into Gillette with their two daughters; Fred remained at Rozet. The 1940 census records him as boarding with the Leo Ridenour family; his occupation was noted as Supervisor with the Soil Conservation Program. He also worked part time with the Agricultural Adjustment Administration in the early 1940's.

Letha Duvall died on January 27, 1972, age 89, in Sheridan, Sheridan County, Wyoming, and was buried in the Sheridan Municipal Cemetery. Fred Duvall died on August 25, 1977, and was buried in the Rozet Cemetery, Rozet, Wyoming.

Helen Margret Duvall 1935
Teacher at the Woods
School

Sources:
Bureau of Land Management, Homestead Patent Index, [www.glorecords.blm.gov].
Campbell County Cemetery District Burial Property Report for Rozet Cemetery, September 1998.
Sheridan Municipal Cemetery Records, Sheridan, Wyoming.
Ancestry.com, Iowa, U.S. Marriage Records, 1880-1951, [database online]. Provo, UT.
Ancestry.com, Iowa, Select Marriages Index, 1758-1996, [database online], Provo, UT.
Ancestry.com, U.S. World War I Draft Registration Cards, 1917-1918, [database online], Provo, UT.
Ancestry.com,, U.S. World War II Draft Registration Cards, 1942, [database online], Provo, UT.
Ancestry.com, U.S. Find-s-Grave Index, 1600s-Current, [database online]. Provo, UT.
Ancestry.com, Social Security Death Index, 1935-1998, [database online], Provo, UT.
Ancestry.com, U.S. Obituary Collection, 1930-Current. [database online], Provo, UT.
Ancestry.com, Newspapers.com Obituary Index, 1800s-current, [database online], Provo, UT.
Ancestry.com, 1900 U.S. Federal Census for Lafayette, Bremer County, Iowa,(Fred), [database online], Provo, UT.
Ancestry.com, 1900 U.S. Federal Census for Shell Rock, Butler County, Iowa, (Letha), [database online], Provo, UT.
Ancestry.com, 1920 U.S. Federal Census for Rozet, Campbell County, Wyoming, [database online], Provo, UT.
Ancestry.com, 1930 U.S. Federal Census for Election District 5, Campbell County, Wyoming, [database online], Provo, UT.
Ancestry.com, 1940 U.S. Federal Census for Campbell County, Wyoming, (Fred), [database online], Provo, UT.
Ancestry.com, 1940 U.S. Federal Census for Campbell County, Wyoming, (Letha), [database online], Provo, UT.

William Allen and Hattie Bell (Baker) Gardner
1915

William Gardner was born June 23, 1868, in White Oak, Harrison County, Missouri, to Thomas and Mary Gardner. At some point before 1896 William had relocated to Custer County, Nebraska, where he married Hattie Bell Baker on December 4, 1896. Hattie was born on March 31, 1878, at York, Nebraska, to Thompson and Sara Baker. At the age of four her parents moved their family to Custer County, Nebraska. About 1915 William and Hattie moved their growing family to Rozet, Campbell County, Wyoming. Shortly after their arrival William filed on a homestead located in Sections 28, 29, 32, and 33, Township 49 North, Range 69 West. Their last two children were born at Rozet, Campbell County, Wyoming. They were the parents of twelve children:

Clarence Allen	b: 27 Nov 1897	d: ?? (1920 census shows him in the Army at Ft. Bliss TX)	
Ralph Lloyd	b: 11 Apr 1899	d: 10 Jan 1958	m:
Thomas "Tommy"	b: 28 Sep 1900	d: 04 Mar 1975	m: (1) Anna Wataznauer
			(2) Lucille M. (Welch) Hurd
Walter H.	b: 28 Mar 1902	d: 25 Dec 1977	(never married)
Leo Michael	b: 18 Apr 1904	d: 09 Apr 1959	m: _____
John B.	b: 10 Jun 1906	d: 02 Jun 1970	m: Etna G. Darlington
Rexie Glenn	b: 14 Apr 1907	d: 22 Dec 1966	m: Alma Mabel Landingham
Mary Elizabeth	b: 02 Dec 1909	d: 25 Jan 1951	m: Albert Schlattmann
Laine L.	b: 22 May 1910	d:	m: Emmett Clark
William B.	b: 08 Jul 1913,	d:	m: Florence Thacker
Hattie Belle	b: 04 Aug 1917,	d: 23 Apr 2003	m: (1) William Still
			(2) Harold Shipley
Catherine Lucille	b: 29 July 1923	d: 18 Mar 1999	m: (1) James Bennick, II
			(2) Clifford Massie

The children attended Rozet School. William drove the school bus on the south route for 1922-1923 school term. William died in December 1945 and was buried in Mount Pisgah Cemetery, Gillette, Wyoming. Hattie died on May 23, 1955 and was buried on May 26, 1955, alongside her husband in Mount Pisgah Cemetery.

Sources:
Bureau of Land Management, Homestead Patent Index, [www.glorecords.blm.gov].
"Rozet Rumblings: daughter born," Gillette News, Gillette, Wyoming, August 28, 1917.
"Rozet Items: baby daughter is born," Gillette News, Gillette, Wyoming, August 2, 1923.
"Society—Double Wedding: Gardner-Thacker and Still-Gardner," The News Record, Gillette, Wyoming, August 30, 1934.
"Funeral Services Held Thursday for Mrs. H. Gardner," page 1, The News Record, Gillette, Wyoming, June 2, 1955.
"Hattie Belle Shipley, obituary," The News Record, Gillette, Wyoming, April 25, 2003.
Campbell County Cemetery District Burial Property Report, September 1998.
Ancestry.com, U.S. Find a Grave Index, 1600s-Current, [database online], Provo, UT.
Ancestry.com, 1870 U.S. Federal Census for White Oak, Harrison County, Missouri (William), [database online], Provo, UT.
Ancestry.com, 1880 U.S. Federal Census for Precinct 7, Custer County, Nebraska (Hattie), [database online], Provo, UT.
Ancestry.com, 1900 U.S. Federal Census for Westerville, Custer County, Nebraska, [database online], Provo, UT.
Ancestry.com, 1910 U.S. Federal Census for Westerville, Custer County, Nebraska, [database online], Provo, UT.
Ancestry.com, 1920 U.S. Federal Census for Rozet, Campbell County, Wyoming, [database online], Provo, UT.
Ancestry.com, 1930 U.S. Federal Census for Election District 5, Campbell County, Wyoming, [database online], Provo, UT.
Ancestry.com, 1940 U.S. Federal Census for Gillette, Campbell County, Wyoming, [database online], Provo, UT.

Winslow James and Susie Belle (Kelly) Garrett
1915

Winslow James Garrett was born on March 6, 1869, in Douglas County, Missouri, the son of Robert and Nancy Garrett. He married Susie Belle Kelly/Kelley in 1894. She was born in Boone County, Kentucky, in 1876. Prior to arriving in Rozet they lived in Mountain Grove, Missouri, and in Oklahoma until 1915 when they moved to Rozet where he filed on a homestead south of Rozet in Section 8, Township 48, range 69 West. They were the parents of six children of which three died in infancy:

Irene G.	b: 19 Feb 1902	d: Apr 1986	m: William "Billy" Williams
Tessie	b: 16 Feb 1904	d: 19 Dec 1983	m: Andrew Burr
Wayne Kelly	b: 28 Dec 1906	d: 27 Jan 1987	m: Janetta Marie Satter

Susie Garrett died in February 18, 1927, and was buried on February 19, 1927, in Mount Pisgah Cemetery, Gillette, Wyoming. Winslow died on November 9, 1950, and was buried on November 12, 1950, in Mount Pisgah Cemetery, Gillette, Wyoming.

Sources:
Photos: copied from Ancestry.com Find-a-Grave Index, 1600s-Current, [database online], Provo, UT.
Bureau of Land Management, Homestead Patent Index, [www.glorecords.blm.gov].
"Burr-Garrett," The Gillette News, Gillette, Wyoming, April 27, 1922 .
"Mrs. Winslow Garrett Answers the Final Call," The News Record, Gillette, Wyoming, March 3, 1927.
"Final Rites for W. J. Garrett," The News Record, Gillette, Wyoming, November 16, 1950.
"Obituary Wayne K. Garrett," The News Record, Gillette, Wyoming, February 18, 1987.
Campbell County Cemetery District Burial Property Report for Mount Pisgah Cemetery, page 14,
*   dated September 8, 1998, Gillette, Wyoming.*
Ancestry.com, U.S. Find-a-Grave Index, 1600s-Current, [database online], Provo, UT.
Ancestry.com, Kentucky, Birth Records, 1847-1911, [database online], Provo, UT.
Ancestry.com, U.S. Social Security Death Index, 1935-2014, [database online], Provo, UT.
Ancestry.com, 1880 U.S. Federal Census for Clinton, Douglas County, Missouri, [database online], Provo, UT.
Ancestry.com, 1910 U.S. Federal Census for Center, Dade County, Missouri, [database online], Provo, UT.
Ancestry.com, 1930 U.S. Federal Census for Election District 20, Campbell County, Wyoming, [database online], Provo, UT.

John Newton and Mary E. (Lyons-Williams) Hamill
1915

John Newton Hamill was born December 28, 1869, in Callahan County, Texas. On March 8, 1891, he married Maggy E. Culver of Montague, Texas. They were the parents of two children:

Mae	b: 01 May 1897	d: 29 Dec 1982	m: Richard V. Talley
John Robert	b: _____ 1904	d: at birth	

Maggy Hamill died in childbirth in 1904. In 1907 John Hamill married Mary Emma (Lyons) Williams, a widow with two young children.

Mary Emma Elizabeth Lyons was born near Jackson, Tennessee, on April 1, 1868, the daughter of James Americus and Amelia June (Wilson) Lyons. Her mother died when she was five years old. Mary and her two sisters and a brother went to live with their maternal grandmother until their father moved them to northeast Texas when she was seven. In 1885 she married Henry K. Williams. They were the parents of five children, three died in infancy:

Etta Frances	b: 13 Oct 1889	d: 16 Aug 1963	m: Edwin C. Moore
William James	b: 04 Apr 1898	d: 27 Oct 1967	m: Irene C. Garrett

Mary Emma Elizabeth Lyon-Hamill
John Newton Hamill (no photo date)

In midwinter of 1895 the Williams family moved to Old Indian Territory just north of Texas, where, after a year on already cultivated land, they built their pioneer home on the edge of a beautiful valley on the Wildcat in Chickasaw Indian reservation. The family lived there until January 1901, when they moved about 75 miles west to a new location about two miles east of Magee, Oklahoma, along the South Canadian River. Here they entered their daughter, Etta, in one of the few good schools in that frontier country. A short four months later tragedy struck the Williams family with the death of her husband, Henry Williams. Mary Williams moved her family to Purdy, Oklahoma, six miles from their farm. To support herself and children she became a photographer.

On January 19, 1907, in Ada, Oklahoma, Mary Williams married John Hamill. They lived there until 1915 during which they saw the Indian Territory and Oklahoma Territory become the state of Oklahoma. In 1915 they moved to the Rozet area where they filed on a homestead located in Sections 4, 5, 8, and 9, Township 48 North, Range 69 West, about six miles south of Rozet and a few miles west of the old Shipwheel ranch. This was their home until 1938 when they moved to Gillette. They had no children. John Hamill, age 80, died on March 26, 1950, and was buried March 28, 1950, in Mount Pisgah Cemetery, Gillette, Wyoming. Mary died May 20, 1950, and was buried alongside her husband in Mount Pisgah Cemetery.

Sources:
Photo: James D. Hitt website: www.hitt_genealogy.homestead.com/files/WILLIAMS.htm.
Bureau of Land Management, Homestead Patent Index, [www.glorecords.blm.gov].
"Funeral Services Held Thursday for J. N. Hamill, 80," The News Record, Gillette, Wyoming, April 1, 1950.
"Mrs. Hamill Passes Away After Long Pioneer Life," page 1, The News Record, Gillette, Wyoming, May 25, 1950.
"Final Rites Held for 'Billy' Williams," The News Record, Gillette, Wyoming, November 2, 1967.
"Williams (Irene) funeral Thursday," The News Record, Gillette, Wyoming, April __, 1986.
Campbell County Cemetery District Burial Property Report, September 8, 1998.
Campbell County, The Treasured Years, 1990, compiled by Campbell County Historical Society.
Marriage Records, Chickasaw Nation-1907, 'Hamill-Williams,' Book K, page 12.
Moorcroft Cemetery Burial Book #5, (1958-1972), page 437, 446.

Henry Kearns and Anna (Reinsch) Hays
1915

Henry Kearns Hayes was born March 9, 1894, in Mexico, Audrain County, Missouri, to Richard Thomas Henry and Clara Anne (Logsden) Hayes. Henry came to Campbell County in 1915 from Oxford, Nebraska, and immediately filed for a homestead in Sections 14, 23, and 24, Township 52 North, Range 70 West. In June 1917 he enlisted in the medical department of the U.S. Army at Sheridan, Wyoming, and was assigned to duty at Fort Riley, Kansas. He went overseas with Hospital Train No. 60, remaining in foreign service for sixteen months. Henry was honorably discharged in August 1919.

Anna Reinsch was born August 13, 1895, at Shickley, Nebraska, to Pius/Frank and Anna (Gehrke) Reinsch. At an early age the family moved to Denver, Colorado, where she received her education. She graduated from Denver High School and attended the University of Wyoming at Laramie. After graduating from college she taught school in Colorado for two years before coming to Campbell County, Wyoming, in 1917 and filed for a homestead in the Adon community near her brothers, Albert and John F. Reinsch, on Sections 10, 11, and 24, Township 52 North, Range 70 West. Anna taught at the Adon School one mile from her homestead for three years until her marriage to Henry Hayes. They were married on November 23, 1920, in Newcastle, Weston County, Wyoming. After a short wedding trip they returned to Adon where they lived until 1938 when they moved to Gillette. They were the parents of five children:

Mary Katherine *	b: 26 Sep 1921	d: 16 Dec 2011	
Robert H.	b: 15 Nov 1922	d: 15 Oct 1998	m: (1) Betty Jean Biddle (div)
			(2) Donna Jean (Laramore) Schmidt
William R.	b: 19 Feb 1925	d: 27 Mar 2020	m: Verna May Fox
James Thomas	b: 30 Dec 1932	d: 15 Jul 1994	m: Karle R. Church
Joyce	b: about 1933	d: after 1998	m _____ Burrell

*Mary Katherine entered the Sisters of St. Francis of Penance and Christian Charity at Marycrest, Denver, Colorado where she was professed as Sister Mary Anne on August 20, 1940.

Henry Kearns Hays died January 17, 1972 and was buried at the Black Hills National Cemetery, Sturgis, South Dakota. Anna Hays died July 19, 1986 and was buried alongside her husband at Black Hills National Cemetery.

Sources:
Bureau of Land Management, Homestead Patent Index, [www.glorecords.blm.gov].
"Hays-Reinsch," The Gillette News, Gillette, Wyoming, November 26, 1920 .
"Hays-Reinsch marriage," Campbell County Record, Gillette, Wyoming, November 25, 1920.
"Hays burial Thursday--Anna Hays," The News Record, Gillette, Wyoming, July 22, 1986, page 12.
"Obituary-Robert H. Hays," The News Record, Gillette, Wyoming, October 19, 1998.
"Obituary Sister Mary Anne Hays," copied from U.S. Find-a-Grave Index, 1600s-current on www.Ancestry.com.
Ancestry.com, U. S, Find-a-Grave Index, 1600s-Current, [database online], Provo, UT.
Ancestry.com, U.S. Veterans' Gravesites, ca.1775-2019, [database online], Provo, UT.
Ancestry.com, U.S. Department of Veterans Affairs BIRLS Death Files, 1850-2010, [database online], Provo, UT.
Ancestry.com, U.S. World War I Draft Registration Cards, 1917-1918, [database online], Provo, UT.
Ancestry.com, U.S. World War II Draft Registration Cards, 1942, [database online], Provo, UT.
Ancestry.com, 1900 U.S. Federal Census for Linn, Audrain County, Missouri, [database online], Provo, UT.
Ancestry.com, 1910 U.S. Federal Census for Indian Creek, Monroe County, Missouri, [database online], Provo, UT.
Ancestry.com, 1930 U.S. Federal Census for Election District 5, Campbell County, Wyoming.

Lorenzo Albert and Margaret Emeline "Maggie" (Reed) Melton
1915

Margaret "Maggie" Reed was born June 20, 1884, in Hardin County, Iowa, to Rueben and Sarah (Emerson) Reed who homesteaded north of Rozet along the Adon Road. Maggie married Lorenzo Albert Melton on October 11, 1906, in Tekamah, Burt County, Nebraska. He was born January 16, 1882, at Litchfield, Illinois. They moved to Wyoming and homesteaded in the Adon community on Sections 22, 23, and 27, Township 51 North, Range 70 West. They were the parents of two children:

Helen Elizabeth	b: 22 Apr 1906	d: 17 May 2001	m: John Alfred Wilson
Carl Whitley	b: 12 Apr 1908	d: 28 Jan 1988	m: Vera Christine Sealock

And they were foster parents for five nieces and nephews, children of Edyth Cordelia (Reed) Hanslip, Maggie's sister:

Earl Reed Hanslip	b: 23 Mar 1914	d: 09 Jan 1995	m: Mary Pauline Marshall
John Rueben Hanslip	b: 26 Aug 1915	d: 11 Dec 1981	m: Lola Agnes
Marjorie Elizabeth Hanslip	b: 05 Feb 1917	d: 15 Dec 2012	m: Bert Irving VanderHaydin
Ruby Gladys Hanslip	b: 19 Mar 1919	d: 01 Dec 2005	m: Ralph Marion McCoy
Mary Darlene Hanslip	b: 06 Jun 1925	d:	m: (1) Leonard Lavell Bentz
			(2) _____ Griffith
			(3) Oscar Charles Coltrin

Maggie and Lorenzo lived in the Adon community until about 1935, when they moved to Oakland, Douglas County; Oregon, where Lorenzo worked for Martin Brothers Box Company until his retirement. Lorenzo Melton died May 15, 1959 and was buried May 22, 1959, in Mount Pisgah Cemetery, Gillette, Wyoming. Maggie died September 15, 1976, at Oakland, Oregon. She was buried on September 21, 1976, in Mount Pisgah Cemetery, Gillette, Wyoming.

Sources:
Bureau of Land Management, Homestead Patent Index, [www.glorecords.blm.gov].
Ancestry.com, U.S. General Land Office Records, 1776-2015, [database online], Provo, UT.
"Miss Helen Melton A Bride," The News Record, Gillette, Wyoming, November 8, 1928.
"Funeral Services Held for L. A. Melton, '77,'" The News Record, Gillette, Wyoming, May 28, 1959.
"Melton {Maggie} Funeral here Tuesday," The News Record, Gillette, Wyoming, September 22, 1976.
"Obituary-Helen Wilson," The News Record, Gillette, Wyoming, May 20, 2001.
Ancestry.com, U.S. Find-a-Grave Index, 1600s-Current, [database online], Provo, UT.
Ancestry.com, Newspapers.com Obituary Index, 1800s-current, [database online], Provo, UT.
Ancestry.com, Nebraska, Marriage Records, 1855-1908, [database online], Provo, UT.
Ancestry.com, U.S. World War I Draft Registration Cards, 1917-1918, [database online], Provo, UT.
Ancestry.com, U.S. World War II Draft Registration Cards 1942, [database online], Provo, UT.

Irvin Arthur "Pick" and Nora Mae (Bagent) Pickrel
1915

Pick Pickrel was born June 2, 1907, in Omaha, Douglas County, Nebraska, the only child to George Arthur and Hazel Dell (Gray) Pickrel. His father died when he was six years old. After that he and his mother lived with his paternal grandparents, George and Lottie Pickrel, in Omaha, Nebraska. In 1916, Pick came to Rozet with his mother and uncle, Ralph E. Pickrel. Ralph and Hazel filed on homesteads located between Four Horse Creek and the Belle Fourche River; he in Sections 33 and 34, Township 48 North, Range 69 West, and Section 3, Township 47 North, Range 69 West, and Hazel in Sections 26, 27, and 34, Township 48 North, Range 69 West. They worked the land during the summer and returned to Omaha, Nebraska, for the winter so Pick could continue attending school there. When spring arrived they would return to Wyoming. After they proved up on the homesteads, they returned to Omaha until Pick finished his education. Hazel married Sam Stover in 1920. During those years, Pick would return to Wyoming for the summers and worked at many things including gathering wild horses. About 1925, Pick, his mother, and stepfather moved to Midwest, Wyoming, to work in the oil fields. In February of 1927, Pick married Nora Mae Bagent in Casper. They lived in Midwest for about four years. Pick and Nora were the parents of three daughters and one adopted son:

Shirley Dell	b: 09 Aug 1928	d: 20 Feb 2006	m: Howard Thobro Christensen
Mary Lynn	b: 17 Oct 1934	d: 27 Mar 1969	m: (1) Glen Darlington
			(2) Lester Vern Lang
George Ann	b: 15 Mar 1946	d:	m: Max Burch
Clinton Irvin	b: 23 Dec 1956	d:	m: Rebecca Remington

Pick's mother and stepfather returned to the homestead south of Rozet followed by Pick, Nora, and their 3-year- old daughter in 1931. They eventually acquired the land, which his mother and his uncle had originally homesteaded where Pick ranched. Over the years they accumulated 1080 acres from original homesteaders who moved on further west. Two more daughters were born. All three daughters were active in the work of the ranch. Pick and Nora began the first of many acquisitions in 1959 when they bought and moved onto the Spaeth ranch near Gillette. They lived there while raising their youngest daughter and their adopted son Clinton. They had adopted their grandson Clinton Darlington, age 12, in 1969 after the death of his mother Mary Lynn Lang. Five years later Pick died on May 8, 1974. Nora continued operating the ranch while establishing her own oil leasing company, NOREX Inc. and managing property in Sheridan, Wyoming. In 1978 she moved to Moorcroft, Wyoming, where she lived until her death at age 94, on April 1, 2005. Both are buried in Mount Pisgah Cemetery, Gillette, Wyoming.

Sources:
Bureau of Land Management, Homestead Patent Index, [www.glorecords.blm.gov].
"Irvin Arthur Pickrel Family," pages 456-457, Campbell County, The Treasured Years, 1990, compiled by Campbell County
        Historical Society, Gillette, Wyoming.
"Center honors early residents," page 6, The News Record, Gillette, Wyoming, Thursday, February 14, 1980.
"Land and Lifeblood," by Julie Mankin, for the Gillette News Record, Gillette, Wyoming, February 7, 2011.
"Pioneer Gillette Rancher Dies," Casper Star-Tribune, Casper, Wyoming, May 13, 1974, Page 2.
"Nora Mae Pickrel obituary," The News Record, Gillette, Wyoming, April 4, 2005.
Ancestry.com, U.S. Find-a-Grave Index, 1600s-Current, [database online], Provo, UT.
Ancestry.com, Newspapers.com Obituary Index, [database online], Provo, UT.
Ancestry.com, U.S. Social Security Death Index, 1935-2014, [database online], Provo, UT.
Ancestry.com, Montana, Marriage Records, 1943-1988, [database online], Provo, UT.
Ancestry.com, 1910 U.S. Federal Census for Omaha Ward 11, Douglas County, Nebraska, [database online], Provo, UT.
Ancestry.com, 1920 U.S. Federal Census for Omaha Ward 10, Douglas County, Nebraska, [database online], Provo, UT.
Ancestry.com, 1930 U.S. Federal Census for Election District 2, Natrona County, Wyoming, [database online], Provo, UT.
Ancestry.com, 1940 U.S. Federal Census for Campbell County, Wyoming, [database online], Provo, UT.

The Ranney Family
1915

Harley C. Ranney filed for a homestead in the Little Iowa community about nine miles northeast of Rozet in Sections 15, 21, 22, and 28, Township 51 North, Range 69 West. Harley was born December 10, 1893, in Spencer, Iowa, to Amos D. and Flora (Barber) Ranney. He was a cripple since he was fourteen years old but had been able to work until two years before his death when he met with an accident, which made him an invalid. Harley died October 27, 1940, and was buried in the Pleasant Valley (Little Iowa) Cemetery. At the time of his death he was survived by two nieces, Mrs. C. P. Christensen of Everett, Washington, Mrs. T. G. Bol, of Sibley, Iowa, and one nephew, David Earnest, of Marshalltown, Iowa.

Flora E. Ranney, Harley's mother, was born April 1, 1854, in Peoria County, Illinois. She married Amos D. Ranney at Central City, Iowa, on March 31, 1869. They were the parents of eight children. The deaths of her husband and five children preceded her moving to Wyoming with her son in 1915. She made her home with her daughter and son in the Little Iowa community for seventeen years. When their mother died, she raised her grandchildren: Lois, Blanche, Clarence, David, and Genevieve Ernest. Flora died in April 1934. She was buried in the Pleasant Valley (Little Iowa) Cemetery on April 10, 1934.

Eunice Ranney, Harley's sister, was born July 4, 1888, at Spencer, Jackson County, Iowa. She was educated at Milford, Iowa, and moved to Campbell County in 1918. She never married but she made friends easily within the Little Iowa community. She was Laura Heptner's closest friend. She helped her brother and mother on the homestead. Shortly before her brother's death they bought a small lot on the corner of Fifth Street and U.S. Highway 59 in Gillette, Wyoming. They were in the process of building a small house when Harley passed away. The house was completed, and she made a living for herself by taking in ironings for several Gillette families, including the Barlows, Hannums, Lanes, and Tantums. She was a member of the First Presbyterian Church and sang in its choir for many years. Eunice enjoyed playing old hymns on her pump organ (now in the Rockpile Museum, Gillette, Wyoming). She was an avid card player and played every opportunity she got. She was an excellent cook and members of the Heptner and Whisler families never turned away an invitation to dinner at her home. Eunice Ranney died on September 6, 1973, at the Pioneer Manor Nursing home, age 85. She was buried September 10, 1973, in the Pleasant Valley Cemetery alongside her mother and her brother.

Sources:
Photos: from the collections of Leona and Jeanette Heptner.
Pleasant Valley Cemetery Burial Book, kept by Mrs. Lucille Thompson (Xeroxed Copy-1998)
"Rites for Eunice E. Ranney," The News Record, Gillette, Wyoming, September 6, 1973.
"Miss (Lois) Earnest Weds Clayton Roberts," The Gillette News, Gillette, Wyoming, July 31, 1924.
"Final Rites Held for Mrs. Flora Ranney on Tuesday at Little Iowa," The News Record, Gillette, Wyoming, April 12, 1934.
"Funeral Rites are Held for Harley Ranney," The News Record, Gillette, Wyoming, October 27, 1940.
Ancestry.com, 1920 Federal Census Schedule for Election District #8, Iowa Precinct, Campbell County, Wyoming, [database online], Provo, UT.

Rueben Whitney and Sarah Elizabeth (Emerson) Reed
1915

Rueben Whitney "Rube" was born February 4, 1857, in Hardin County, Iowa, near Steamboat Rock, to Benjamin Franklin and Harriet Emeline (Whitney) Reed. He grew to manhood there and received his education in that community. He was the last surviving nephew of Eli Whitney, the inventor of the cotton gin. He married Sarah Elizabeth Emerson on January 25, 1881, daughter of George and Margaret (Finlayson) Emerson, in a Presbyterian parsonage in Eldora Township, Hardin County, Iowa. Sarah Elizabeth "Lizzie" was born May 17, 1861, in Richland, Rice County, Minnesota. Her father moved their family in 1869 to Eldora, Hardin County, Iowa, where she grew up and graduated from high school. Reuben and Sarah became the parents of eight children:

Margaret Emeline	b: 20 Jun 1884	d: 15 Sep 1976	m: Lorenzo A. Melton
Jessie Edna	b: 31 Oct 1886	d: 15 Mar 1973	m: Steven Smith Sears
Rueben Whitney, Jr.	b: 27 Dec 1888	d: 07 Jan 1889	
Everette	b: 12 Sep 1890	d: 07 Mar 1891	
Ruth Charlotte	b: 06 Mar 1893	d: 24 Jun 1957	m: James Harvey Bray
Edith Cordelia	b: 28 Jul 1895	d: 07 Nov 1926	m: William H. Hanslip
John William "Jack"	b: 28 Aug 1897	d: 16 Apr 1972	m: Mary Jane Houser
Gladys Olive	b: 21 Jul 1900	d: 05 Dec 1985	m: Roy Virgil Gilliland

The early years of their marriage Reuben and Sarah lived near Ashton, Osceola County, Iowa, where they ran the B. F. Reed farm. In October 1888 they moved to Decatur, Burt County, Nebraska. In 1915 they moved the family to Campbell County, Wyoming, and filed on a homestead located nine miles north of Rozet on Sections 13 and 14, Township 51 North, Range 70 West, along the Adon Road near Deer Creek. Sarah was almost six feet tall and walked very straight and tall. Her hair was black and her eyes dark brown. Like her brothers and sisters, she was a good singer. She and her husband played violins and called for dances in the Adon and Little Iowa communities. Sarah died at age 57 at home on January 14, 1919, and was buried in Pleasant Valley Cemetery, Rozet, Wyoming. Reuben continued to work the homestead until about 1938 when his daughter, Gladys, her husband Roy Gilliland and their son, Orie, moved onto the home farm. Reuben returned to Nebraska, and from 1938-1945, he lived with his daughters, Ruth and Jessie. Later he lived in a private home until his death, at age 99, on March 17, 1956, in Tekamah, Nebraska. His body was returned to Rozet where he was buried next to his wife in the Pleasant Valley Cemetery.

Sources:
Photos: Copied from the Ancestry.com, Eikenbary-Wilson/McGinley Family Tree.
Bureau of Land Management, Homestead Patent Index, [www.glorecords.blm.gov].
"Obituary—Sarah Elizabeth Emerson Reed," Campbell County Record, Gillette, Wyoming, January 23, 1919.
Obituary, "Drums of Death' Funeral Services Held Friday for R. W. Reed," The News Record, March ___, 1956.
"Melton Funeral here Tuesday," The News Record, Gillette, Wyoming, September 22, 1976.
Pleasant Valley Cemetery Burial Book, kept by Mrs. Lucille Thompson (Xeroxed Copy-1998).
Ancestry.com, 1920 U.S. Federal Census for Election District #8, Iowa Precinct, Campbell County, [database online], Provo, UT.

Mrs. Ada Florence Shroyer
1915

Ada Florence was born on August 24, 1877, at Maryville, Nodaway County, Missouri, to Joseph and Louisa (Nash) Chamberlain. She grew up with her five sisters on her father's farm. On Christmas eve December 1895, Ada married Charles Wesley Shroyer, in Pickering, Nodeaway County, Missouri. Shortly after the birth of their first child, Gladys, they migrated to Wray, Yuma County, Colorado. Joseph filed on a homestead and they worked to prove it up. They became parents of six children:

Gladys Gwendolyn	b:26 Apr 1897	d: Jan 1984	m: Robert Verle Hawks
Joe Preston	b: 26 Mar 1900	d: 19 May 1951	m: Ruth Nottingham
Lou Elda	b: _____ 1902	d: _____	m: Carl. J. Kuhl
Mary Blanche	b: 11 Feb 1905	d: 26 Mar 1998	m: Robert Nelson
Anna Wynona	b: 03 Nov 1910	d: 27 Jul 1992	m: (1) Benjamin M Cunningham
			(2) Eugene R, Cornell (div)
			(3) Leland E "Red" Benner (div)
			(4) Harold Wolfe (div)
Donald David	b: 13 Nov 1915	d: 16 Jul 1982	m: LaVonne Lula Copple

About 1915 Mrs. Shroyer came to the Rozet area with her four youngest children from Wray, Colorado. She filed on a homestead located in Sections 20, 28, and 29, Township 49 North, Range 69 West. She received her homestead patent on May 29, 1920, from the U.S. Land Office at Sundance. Charles Shroyer remained in Colorado until his death on October 10, 1923; he was buried in the Las Animas Cemetery, Las Animas, Bent County, Colorado.

Louella, Blanche, Wynonna, and Donald attended school at Rozet. In 1920 she built a new home in Rozet and moved the post office from the Shaughnessy building into her home. Ada was appointed as the Postmistress at the Rozet Post Office on November 25, 1918, succeeding Katherine Shaughnessy. She served until she resigned in November 1927. On November 28, 1927, she sold her farm at an auction sale and moved to Niles, Ohio, where she married W. J. Hatfield in December 1927. This marriage ended in divorce, and by 1930 she was living at Basin, Big Horn County, Wyoming, and working as a cook at the Wyoming State Tubercular Sanitarium. She remarried on January 12, 1932, to Augustus T. Allen, at Billings, Yellowstone County, Montana. According to the 1940 Federal Census she was widowed and living in Gillette, Campbell County, Wyoming; her occupation was listed as poultry raiser. Ada died on October 5, 1958, where is unknown at this time; she was buried in Monument Hill Cemetery, Thermopolis, Hot Springs County, Wyoming.

Sources:
Photo: taken by Matt Avery at the Rozet Post Office, Rozet, Wyoming – July 2020.
Bureau of Land Management, Homestead Patent Index [www.glorecords.blm.gov].
Ancestry.com, U.S. General Land Office Records, 1776-2015, [database online], Provo, UT.
"Marriages; Kuhl-Shroyer," Campbell County Record, Gillette, Wyoming, December 23, 1920.
"Rozet Rumblings: new house/P.O.," Gillette News, Gillette, Wyoming, August 13, 1920.
"Postmaster at Rozet Resigns," The News Record, Gillette, Wyoming, November 17, 1927.
"Auction Sale," The News Record, Gillette, Wyoming, November 24, 1927.
"Shroyer-Hatfield Marriage," The News Record, Gillette, Wyoming, December 15, 1927.
Ancestry.com, Missouri, Marriage Records, 1805-2002, [database online], Provo, UT.
Ancestry.com, Montana, County Marriages, 1865-1950, [database online], Provo, UT.
Ancestry.com, U.S. Find-a-Grave Index, 1600s-Current, [database online], Provo, UT.
Ancestry.com, U.S. Appointments of U.S. Postmasters, 1832-1971, [database online], Provo, UT.
Ancestry.com, 1880 U.S. Federal Census for Union, Nodaway County, Missouri, [database online], Provo, UT.
Ancestry.com, 1900 U.S. Federal Census for Wray, Yuma County, Colorado, [database online], Provo, UT.
Ancestry.com 1910 U.S. Federal Census for West Wray, Yuma County, Colorado, [database online], Provo, UT.
Ancestry.com 1920 U.S. Federal Census for Rozet South Precinct #26, Campbell County, Wyoming, [database online], Provo, UT.
Ancestry.com, 1930 U.S. Federal Census for Basin, Big Horn County, Wyoming, [database online], Provo, UT.
Ancestry.com, 1940 U.S. Federal Census for Campbell County, Wyoming, [database online], Provo, UT.

Will and Myrtle (Ribble) Spencer
1915

The Spencer Homestead

Willie and Myrtle Spencer with their daughter Esther and son Emery came to Rozet from Estherville, Emmet County, Iowa, about 1915. He filed for original homestead entry on January 28, 1916, for land located in Section 18, Township 51 North, Range 69 West, located in the Little Iowa community. The homestead was located about 3 miles east of the Frank Heptner homestead. Willie Spencer was born on July 28, 1868, in Covington, Linn County, Iowa, to Theodore and Cordelia (Eaton) Spencer. On June 29, 1892, he married Myrtle Ribble, daughter of Nelson and Helena (Usher) Ribble, in Cedar Rapids, Linn County, Iowa. They raised three children of their own, plus two grandchildren:

Ora Leone	b: 12 Jan 1893	d: 15 Jun 1920	m. Edward Anton McCune
Esther	b: 29 Apr 1904	d: 15 May 2001	m: (1) Carl Kuehne
			(2) Herman Kuehne
Emory	b: 09 Feb 1903	d: 10 Mar 1981	

Shortly after the death of their daughter, Ora, they adopted her two youngest children Donald W., age 3 and Lester L. McCune, age 1. Her oldest son, James Leroy, age 6, stayed with his father Edward McCune. The children attended Cottonwood School nearby for a few years. Myrtle's mother, Helena Ribble, is buried in Pleasant Valley Cemetery. Later when the family moved to Minnesota her remains were removed and reburied in Palo Cemetery, Pala, Linn County, Iowa, alongside of her husband Nelson Riddle.

By the middle of the depression, 1935, the family was unable to keep up their land, so they left Wyoming and moved to Akeley, Hubbard County, Minnesota, to live. Will died on April 17, 1954; Myrtle died February 25, 1962. Both were buried in the White Oak Cemetery, Chamberlain, Hubbard County, Minnesota.

Emory, Lester and Donny McCune, Will and Myrtle

Lester and Esther Spencer

Sources:
Photos: from the collections of Leona and Jeanette Heptner.
Bureau of Land Management, Homestead Patent Index, [www.glorecords.blm.gov].
"Aged Lady Dies," Gillette News, Gillette, Wyoming, April 16, 1925.
Pleasant Valley Cemetery Burial Book, kept by Mrs. Lucille Thompson (Xeroxed Copy-1998).
Ancestry.com, U.S. Find-a-Grave Index, 1600s-Current, [database online], Provo, UT.
Ancestry.com, Iowa, Select Marriages Index, 1758-1996, [database online], Provo, UT.
Ancestry.com, 1910 U.S. Federal Census for Estherville, Emmett County, Iowa, [database online], Provo, UT.
Ancestry.com, 1930 U.S. Federal Census for Election District 5, Campbell County, Wyoming, [database online], Provo, UT.
Ancestry.com, 1940 U.S. Federal Census for Badoura, Hubbard County, Minnesota, [database online], Provo, UT.

Elmer and Bertha (Webb) Thomas
1915

Elmer was born January 19, 1889, at Mifflin, Iowa County, Wisconsin, to John and Mary (Hart) Thomas. By 1900 the family had moved to Union County, Iowa, where they appear in the 1900 Federal Census. Elmer married Bertha Lutesia Webb on December 21, 1910, at Creston, Union County, Iowa. She was born October 30, 1892, in Jefferson County, Iowa, to James W. and Lucy Jane Webb.

By 1915 Elmer and his brother George both had secured land approximately eight miles south of Rozet to the west of the Bishop Road, in Sections 7 and 8, Township 48 North, Range 69 West, and Section 12, Township 48, Range 70 West. They returned to Union County, Iowa. In 1917 Elmer, his wife, Bertha, with their five-year-old daughter, Mildred, moved to the Rozet community. They became the parents of five children:

Mildred L.	b: 31 Mar 1912	d: 02 Aug 2008	m: (1) Kenneth L. Chace
			(2) Parke Fox
Elmer Gale	b: 14 Nov 1921	d: 24 Jun 1999	m: Marjorie Mae Stok
Gerald	b: 03 Dec 1923	d: 07 Dec 1923	
Marion Eugene "Curly"	b: 12 Dec 1925	d: 25 Nov 2007	m: Patricia Wade
Carol Lee	b: 24 Dec 1927	d: 12 Mar 2018	m: (1) Delbert Weese
			(2) Harry Turner
			(3) Kenneth Irish

Bertha died from scarlet fever on December 29, 1927, five days after the birth of her daughter Carol Lee. She was buried in Mount Pisgah Cemetery, Gillette, Wyoming. Ray and Lucille Thomas, Elmer's brother, now living in Gillette, took his youngest daughter, Carol Lee, to care for.

In December 1932 Elmer married Emma Elva (Eskew) Day, daughter of Harry and Chloe Eskew. She was born June 4, 1912, in McCook, Nebraska. Elmer and Emma were the parents of a daughter:

Betty Rae	b: 11 Jan 1936	d:	m: (1) _____ Ross (div)
			(2) Dennis W. King (div)
			(3) Wayne Dygert

In the summer of 1941 Elmer sold the livestock and equipment and moved the family to Hillcrest just north of Moorcroft. Later they moved to Gillette and again later in 1955 they moved to Buffalo, Wyoming, where they owned and operated the Lariat Café for three years. Emma continued to work as a waitress until retiring in 1975. Elmer died on February 22, 1965, in Sheridan, Wyoming, and was buried on February 25, 1965, in Mount Pisgah Cemetery, Gillette, Wyoming. Emma continued to live in their home until she moved into the Amie Holt Care Center in Buffalo, Wyoming, until her death on January 26, 1988. She was buried in the Willow Grove Cemetery, Buffalo, Wyoming.

Sources:
Bureau of Land Management, Homestead Patent Index [www.glorecords.blm.gov].
Campbell County Historical Society, Gillette, Wyoming.
"Society--Chace-Thomas Wedding," The News Record, Gillette, Wyoming, March 30, 1933.
"Funeral Services Held Thursday for Elmer Thomas, 76," The News Record, Gillette, Wyoming, February 25, 1965.
"Mildred L. Fox, obituary," Gillette News Record, Gillette, Wyoming, August 7, 2008.
Ancestry.com, U.S. Find a Grave Index, 1600s-Current, [database online], Provo, UT.
Ancestry.com, U.S. Newspapers.com Obituary Index, 1800s-current, (Emma), [database online], Provo, UT.
Ancestry.com, Iowa, U.S., Select Marriages Index, 1758-1996 (Elmer and Bertha, [database online], Provo, UT.
Ancestry.com, 1900 U.S. Federal Census for Pleasant, Union County, Iowa, [database online], Provo, UT.
Ancestry.com, 1920 U.S. Federal Census for Bar F S, Campbell County, Wyoming, [database online], Provo, UT.
Ancestry.com, 1930 U.S. Federal Census for Election District 20, Campbell County, Wyoming, [database online], Provo, UT.
Ancestry.com, 1940 U.S. Federal Census for Campbell County, Wyoming, [database online], Provo, UT.

Fayette Rush and Mary Susan (Holbrook) Thompson
1915

Fayette was born February 13, 1860, in Marshall County, Indiana, to William Edward, Jr. and Martha E. (McDonald) Thompson. The family moved to Lancaster County about 1885, settling on a farm near Yankee Hill. Fayette married Mary Susan Holbrook on July 7, 1888, in Lincoln Nebraska. Mary was born May 3, 1870, in Northfield, Summit County, Ohio, to O. G. and Mary E. (Jorden) Holbrook. About 1890 they moved to Yankee Hill where Fayette rented a farm. Fayette and Mary's twelve children were all born in Yankee Hill, Lancaster County, Nebraska.

Cecil Martha	b: 15 Feb 1889	d: 24 Oct 1918	m: Herbert L. McGowan
Maud Ellen	b: 18 Jul 1890	d: 27 Jul 1908	
George Edward	b: 31 Oct 1891	d: 17 Jul 1893	
Ida Irene	b: 20 Jun 1894	d: 17 Nov 1918	m: Roy B. Woods
Myrtle Elizabeth	b: 08 Jan 1896	d: 04 Feb 1980	m: Clarence J. Shafer
Fayette Ossian	b: 18 Jul 1897	d: 10 Aug 1976	m: Faye Irene Hamm
Clara May	b: 08 Dec 1899	d: 15 Sep 1991	m: George Jensen
Esther Sarah	b: 01 Mar 1902	d: 16 Nov 1918	
Katherine Gertrude	b: 16 Apr 1905	d: 27 Sep 1994	m: Earl Odessa Melotte
Paul Rush	b: 01 Oct 1907	d: 07 Dec 1973	m: Elsie Margaret Rush
Richard William	b: 08 Sep 1909	d: 25 Aug 1999	m: Anne B. Prazma
Wilbur Ernest "Bill"	b: 03 Jul 1911	d: 20 Mar 1988	m: Mary Lucille Williams Hill

In 1911, Herb McGowan, their son-in-law, after losing his lease on his farm learned of some land in Wyoming that was open for homesteading went to Wyoming and filed on it and returned to Lancaster County. In May 1912 he, Cecil, and their children boarded an immigrant train along with a team of horses, six cows, chickens, and a hog and headed for Campbell County, Wyoming. In the early fall of 1914, at the age of 54, Fayette made a trip to Wyoming to visit his son, and while there he bought a relinquishment of a homestead located 1½ miles north of the McGowan's homestead. According to BLM records, Fayette filed on Sections 8 and 17, Township 50 North, Range 68 West (Crook County) and Section 23 and 25, Township 51 North, Range 69 West. Mary Thompson went to Wyoming that December to be with her daughter, Cecil, when she had her second baby. Mary stayed a month during which she had a good look at the countryside and decided she liked the looks of the country there. Hence, in the spring of 1915, the Thompson family were packing up to move to Wyoming. Fayette would remain on the farm for the next two years. He had a good business going loading clay from a pit on the farm to the brickyard in Lincoln. The family would use this income to get started on the homestead in Wyoming. In late April 1915 Faye Thompson, his Uncle Perry Thompson and a family friend boarded an immigrant train after loading a few of pieces of machinery, household goods, horses, some chickens, and feed for the horses and chickens in a boxcar and headed for Wyoming.

When they departed the train at Wessex, Wyoming, which consisted of a side track, several wooden corrals, and a telephone booth, no one was there to meet them. Herb McGowan was to meet them there. Faye took one of the horses and started out to find the McGowan homestead, six miles north of Wessex. After taking several wrong directions he finally found the homestead of his sister and brother-in-law only to find that Herb had left to meet the train. After a quick lunch he went back to the train to find them all waiting for him to come back as they needed the horse he was riding to help pull the wagon. While at his sister's homestead word was brought from their mother that she and the rest of the family would be leaving on the train May 3, 1915, and would be getting off in Moorcroft, Wyoming. Faye, Herb, and their Uncle Perry got busy and set up the tent they had brought to live in while they were building a house. There was a 10'x12' shack on the place that the sheep herder Fayette had bought the relinquishment from used to live in.. Moving it to a level place near the trail, they set up the tent in front of it. They set the bed up in the tent and the kitchen range in the shack; placed some boards down to walk on in the tent. Monday morning Faye and his sister Cecil drove a wagon to Moorcroft to meet their mother and siblings when they arrived on the train.

As quoted from page 3 of the booklet entitled *Yesteryear* written by Faye Thompson and Myrtle Thompson Shafer, Myrtle wrote: "We left Lincoln Nebraska on May 3, 1915 (mother's birthday); there were nine of us, Dad (Fayette) remaining behind to fulfill a contract he had with a brickyard to load clay from a pit on his farm. The money which he would earn was badly needed. There would be no income from the new home for the first year and a large family to feed besides a house to build, a well to drill, et. cetera."

Mary and her children worked hard at building up their homestead home in this growing community named Little Iowa. In January 1917, Fayette returned to Wyoming after fulfilling his contract in Nebraska. The family was now once again complete. Here Fayette farmed and raised cattle for the remainder of his life. The Thompson home was located south across the road from the Little Iowa schoolhouse where the children attended school.

That fall (1917) a young boy, Vern Woods, was killed in an accident while helping a neighbor dip cattle. The community did not have a cemetery. One of the ranchers offered a plot of ground for a cemetery near the schoolhouse. After the funeral was over, a few of the men got together and decided a meeting should be held at the schoolhouse ,and the word was passed around. All of the neighbors near and far were there. Each man gave a donation to help build a fence and whatever else needed to be done. Fayette Thompson was voted chairman, and for those who donated monies towards establishing a neighborhood cemetery, a plot was designated for them. The neighbors worked hard at clearing sage brush, setting fenceposts, and stringing wire until the fence was completed. The women came along bringing food to feed the working men. Dinner was served at the Thompson home. The cemetery was named Little Iowa Cemetery. Later its name was changed to Pleasant Valley Cemetery.

In 1918 during the Spanish Flu within three weeks Fayette and Mary lost three of their children; Cecil who, after she and her husband Herb proved up on their homestead in 1917 sold it and moved back to Lancaster County, died there on October 24, 1918; Ida, who had married Roy Woods that year, died on November 17, one day after her sister Esther died on November 16, 1918. Ida and Esther are both buried in Pleasant Valley Cemetery. Fayette Rush Thompson died June 5, 1944, age 84, and Mary died November 20, 1955, age 85. They are buried in the Pleasant Valley Cemetery

About 1943

Sources:
Photos copied from the Battin Family Tree, Ancestry.com.
Photo 1943 from the Leona and Jeanette Heptner collection.
Bureau of Land Management, Homestead Patent Index www.glorecords.blm.gov.
Ancestry.com, 1900 U.S. Federal Census for Yankee Hill, Lancaster County, Nebraska, [database on line], Provo, UT.
Ancestry.com, 1910 U.S. Federal Census for Yankee Hill, Lancaster County, Nebraska, [database on line], Provo, UT.
Ancestry.com, 1920 U.S. Federal Census for Campbell County, T51N, R69W, District 8, Iowa Precinct.
Ancestry.com, Nebraska, U.S. Select County Marriage Records, 1855-1908 for Fayette Thompson and Mary Holbrook.
Ancestry.com, Copy of a handwritten list of birth dates and some death dates from the Battin Family Tree.
"Yesteryear," a 14-page booklet written by Faye O. Thompson and Myrtle Thompson Shafer; complement of Gayle Moon Parish Buhl, Idaho, 2021.
"Woods-Thompson Marriage," The Gillette News, Gillette, Wyoming, August 23, 1918.
"Little Iowa Vicinity News," The Gillette News, November 18, 1918.
"Katherine Thompson Weds Earl Melotte," The News Record, Gillette, Wyoming, December 17, 1925.
Wyoming 1920 Federal Census Schedule for Campbell County, T51N, R69W, Election District #8, Iowa Precinct.
"Obituary-Wilbur E. 'Bill' Thompson," The News Record, Gillette, Wyoming, March 22, 1988, page 12.
"Obituary-Katherine (Thompson) Mellott," Pleasant Valley Cemetery Burial Book (Xeroxed Copy-1998).

Jacob and Della (Coffey) Dillinger
1916

Jacob Dillinger was born October 12, 1883, in Trade, Tennessee. Della Coffey was born October 9, 1889. They met at the Appalachian Training School at Boone, North Carolina, where they both took teacher's training. After their marriage they farmed near Wilmore, Kansas, for seven years but were not able to obtain any land. After reading literature put out by the Chicago, Burlington and Quincy Railroad urging people to "go West," the young couple and their three children went west. Jacob filed on a homestead located in Sections 34 and 35, Township 48 North, Range 69 West, and Section 4, Township 47 North, Range 69 West. They arrived in Moorcroft by passenger train late 1916. After collecting their household goods and necessary machinery from the railroad's emigrant car and loading them on to a wagon hitched to team of black horses, they continued to their homestead located about sixteen miles southwest of Moorcroft. Because winter was coming on, they built a dugout to live in through that first winter. They built a log cabin the next summer. Jacob made

Jacob and Della Dillinger in 1909

extra money by helping people locate on land already filed on or showing them pieces of land still available for homesteading. A school was needed so the parents of this new community named Dillinger built a small log schoolhouse. Later a frame building was built. It served as a community center for church services, dances, school activities, and other community activities. It soon became apparent that they needed a post office. One was established and named "Dillinger" with Della appointed as postmistress. Jacob and Della were the parents of seven children:

Clarence Earl	b: 11 Apr 1911	d: 03 Jul 1982	m: Marie Louise Scott
Margaret Mabel	b: 30 Oct 1912	d: 23 Oct 2003	m: Hugh Bowden
Infant daughter	b: 12 Oct 1883	d: 12 Oct 1883	
Inez Irene	b: 16 Sep 1915	d: 19 Aug 1991	m: Rex Niswender
Jay Martin	b: 26 Aug 1917	d: 05 Dec 1987	m: Jeanne Rhoads
William Raymond	b: 01 Oct 1920	d: 17 Sep 1998	m: Ruby Thomas
Robert Lee	b: 19 May 1931	d: 11 May 2019	m: Claralee Fox

On April 14, 1945, Jacob was run over by his team of horses and the disc they were pulling. The whole community felt his death at age 62 years. He was buried on April 20, 1945, in the Mount Pisgah Cemetery, Gillette, Wyoming.

After fourteen years of widowhood, Della married Robert Bratton on February 22, 1959. Their marriage was cut short by his sudden death on September 25, 1961. Della continued to live in the house she and Bob bought in Gillette, until her death, at age 84, on November 10, 1973. Both Robert and Della were buried in Mount Pisgah Cemetery, Gillette, Wyoming.

Sources:
Photo: "1916 Wyoming Here We Come!" by Margaret Bowden, 2002.
Bureau of Land Management [www.glorecords.blm.gov].
"Society—double wedding: Niswender-Dillinger and Dillinger-Scott", The News Record, Gillette, Wyoming, January 10, 1935.
"Obituary-Jay M. Dillinger," The News Record, Gillette, Wyoming, December 11, 1987.
"Obituary-Marie Dillinger," The News Record, Gillette, Wyoming, March 19, 1994.
"Obituaries-William 'Bill' Dillinger," The News Record, Gillette, Wyoming, September 20, 1998.
"The Jacob and Della Dillinger Story," pages 164-168, Campbell County, The Treasured Years, 1990, compiled by
    Campbell County Historical Society.

Charlie Melvin and Dora Pauline (Harvey) Donner
1916

Charlie Melvin was born November 16, 1893 at Burwell, Garfield County Nebraska, to John and Emma (Jenks) Donner. He spent his childhood in Nebraska and Iowa. A son, Daryle Milton, was born 12 September 12, 1918, to Charlie and a Florence Mae Slater.

Charlie came to the Adon community by 1916 with his brother, George. Later in the mid-twenties their younger brother, John Anseley "Jack" came to Wyoming to help his brothers farm. He would marry Paula Tomingas, daughter of one of their neighbors, John and Anna Tomingas. George and Charlie settled on homesteads in the Adon community. Charlie filed on a homestead located in Sections 8, 9, 34, and 35, Township 53 North, Range 70 West. On March 4, 1922, he married Dora Pauline Harvey, at Newcastle, Weston County, Wyoming. Dora was born September 30, 1906, in Moorcroft, Wyoming, to Weston and Flossie (Fox) Harvey. She spent her childhood in the Weston Community in northern Campbell County. Charlie and Dora were the parents of eight children:

Daryle Milton	b: 12 Sep 1918	d: 18 Dec 2004	m: Mary Elizabeth Pierce
Melvin Harvey	b: 12 Apr 1923	d: 23 Apr 2008	m: Evelyn Whisler
Dorothy Lucille	b: 14 Jul 1924	d: 14 Jan 2008	m: J. D. Brown
Joyce Deane	b: 30 Nov 1925	d: 19 Dec 1925	
Dale Lorraine	b: 24 Apr 1927	d: 18 Sep 1976	m: Alice Mae Bloomer (div)
Evelyn Jean	b: 07 Oct 1928	d: 21 Nov 2015	m: Bernard Evans
Gary Harold	b: 12 Mar 1933	living	m: Cloma Hazel Evans
Bob Lee	b: 10 Feb 1935	d: 12 Nov 2009	m: Deloris DeWitt

The children attended the Christensen, Deer Creek and Adon Schools. Charlie and Dora lived at Adon until 1948 when they moved to Hollister, Idaho, for three years. In 1951 they returned to Moorcroft, Wyoming. Charlie was a carpenter by trade. Charlie was the U.S. Postal Service Mail Carrier on the Adon Route out of Moorcroft for many years. Charlie Donner died on September 5, 1963, of complication from injuries from a car accident with a deer in 1962. He was buried in the Pleasant Valley Cemetery, Rozet, Wyoming. In 1975 Dora moved to Ten Sleep. Dora died on December 29, 1983, in the Washakie Memorial Hospital in Worland, Wyoming. She was buried January 2, 1983 in Pleasant Valley Cemetery alongside her husband.

Back: Evelyn, Dorothy, Melvin
Front: Gary, Bob, Dale

Sources:
Photos: Courtesy of Vida Donner McCollam.
Bureau of Land Management, Homestead Patent Index, [www.glorecords.blm.gov].
Pleasant Valley Cemetery Burial Book, kept by Mrs. Lucille Thompson (Xeroxed Copy-1998).
Newspaper.com, obit for Dale L. Donner, page 2, The Times-News, Twin Falls, Idaho, September 19, 1976
"Donner-Harvey," The Gillette News, Gillette, Wyoming, April 6, 1922.
"Final Services for Charlie M. Donner At Moorcroft," The News Record, Front: Gary, Bob, Dale, Gillette, Wyoming, September 12, 1963.
"Former Moorcroft resident (Dora) Dies," The News Record, Gillette, Wyoming, December 30, 1983.

George O. and Merle (Greathouse) Donner
1916

George O. Donner was born October 21, 1883, Taylor County, Iowa, the first born child of John and Emma (Jenks) Donner. About 1890 the family moved to Burwell, Garfield County, Nebraska. About 1916 he and his brother Charlie arrived in Campbell County, Wyoming. George filed for a homestead on May 18, 1916 in Sections 11 and 12, Township 51 North, Range 70 West, and Sections 28 and 33, Township 52 North, Range 69 West, in the Adon community, Campbell County, Wyoming. On April 12, 1918, George married Merle Alice Greathouse, daughter of Hiram and Amanda Greathouse, in Glenwood, Mills County, Iowa. George and Merle were the parents of five children:

Virgil	b: 07 Jan 1922	d: 07 Jan 1922		
Mildred Ione	b: 20 Jun 1919	d: 22 Mar 1926		
George, Jr.	b: _____ 1923(?)	d: 1923?		
Leone Avis	b: 08 May 1924	d:		m: Harry Adolph Williams
Iris June	b: 09 Jun 1926	d: 16 Jun 2019		m: Floyd Arthur Cuthbert

George died on February 12, 1962, in Modesto, Stanislaus County, California. Merle died in Sheridan, Sheridan County, Wyoming in November 1977.

The Donner Brothers

The Donner Brothers
Back row: Jack, Loren, George, Walter and Charlie Donner
Front row: Cousins of the Donner brothers (names unknown)
(*Photo courtesy of Vida Donner McCollum*)

Sources:
Photos: Courtesy of Vida Donner McCollam.
Bureau of Land Management, Homestead Patent Index, [www.glorecords.blm.gov].
"Little George Donner," Adon Items, Gillette News, Gillette, Wyoming, July 26, 1923.
"Little George & Big George," Adon Items, Gillette News, Gillette, Wyoming, Aug 2, 1913.
"Obituary-Mildred Ione Donner," The News Record, Gillette, Wyoming, March 25, 1926.
Campbell County Cemetery District Burial Property Report of September 8, 1998.
Ancestry.com, 1920 U.S. Federal Census for Election District #8, Iowa Precinct, Campbell County, Wyoming, [database online], Provo, UT.

Merle Stanley and Leota Viola (Huffaker) Engdahl
1916

Merle was born June 20, 1895, in Ong, Clay County, Nebraska, to Sanford and Esther Engdahl. By 1910 his parents moved the family to Hopdale, Yakima County, Washington. Merle served in the Army during World War I in Europe with the Battery D 148th Field Artillery. Soon after his return in 1919 he married Leota Viola Huffaker on September 24, 1919. They left family and friends in Nebraska to come to the Adon area of Campbell County, Wyoming. He filed on a homestead located in Sections 30 and 31, Township 53 North, Range 69 West, located about a mile and a half northeast of the Adon Post Office. There they built their house and ranch buildings close to a flowing artesian well that was soft and very cold, a luxury in dry northeastern Wyoming. Merle later filed an additional stock-raising homestead located in Sections 23 and 26, Township 53 North, Range 69 West. Merle and Leota moved to Gillette where he worked as a contractor. They were the parents of:

James Richard	b: 11 Nov 1922	d: 20 Aug 1992	m: Aileen Mary Evans
Dorothy Elaine	b: 20 Apr 1924	d: 17 Jun 2004	m: Oren Odell Smith
Bertha Mildred	b: _____ 1926	d: 04 Dec 2017	m: Robert L. Parnell

Leota died in July 1957 and was buried on July 26, 1957, in Mount Pisgah Cemetery, Wyoming. In 1959, Merle married a widow, Ioris May (Winland) Baker. They lived in Gillette until his death in August 1980, at age 85. He was buried on August 20, 1980, in Mount Pisgah Cemetery, Gillette, Wyoming, alongside of Leota. Ioris Engdahl died September 16, 1991, and was buried alongside her first husband Ham Baker in Mount Pisgah Cemetery, Gillette, Wyoming.

Sources:

Bureau of Land Management, Homestead Patent Index, [www.glorecords.blm.gov].

Ancestry.com, U.S. General Land Office Records, 1776-2016, [database online], Provo, UT.

"Obituary-Merle S. 'Pete' Engdahl," page 13, The News Record, Gillette, Wyoming, August 18, 1980. "Ioris May Engdahl-Obituary," The News Record, Gillette, Wyoming, September 18, 1991.

Manuscript (typed) entitled "School Trials and Triumphs by Betty (Hughes) Tilson Morrish," 1990.

Ancestry.com, U.S. Obituary Collection 1930-Current, [database online], Provo, UT.

Ancestry.com, Colorado, County Marriage Records and State Index, 1862-2006, [database online], Provo, UT.

Ancestry.com, U.S. Social Security Death Index, 1935-2014, [database online], Provo, UT.

Ancestry.com, U.S. Obituary Collection, 1930-current, [database online], Provo, UT.

Ancestry.com, U.S. Social Security Applications and Claims Index 1936-2007, [database online], Provo, UT.

Ancestry.com, Utah, Select Marriage Index (James Richard), 1887-1985, [database online], Provo, UT.

Ancestry.com, Arizona, Select Marriages, (Elaine) 1888-1908, [database online], Provo, UT.

Ancestry.com, U.S. Department of Veterans Affairs BIRLS Death File, 1850-2010, [database online], Provo, UT.

Ancestry.com, U.S. Army Transport Service, Passenger Lists, 1910-1939, [database online], Provo, UT.

Ancestry.com, U.S. World War I Draft Registration Cards, 1917-1918, [database online], Provo, UT.

Ancestry.com, U.S. World War II Draft Registration Cards, 1942, [database online], Provo, UT.

Ancestry.com, 1900 U.S. Federal Census for Mead, Merrick, Nebraska, [database online], Provo, UT.

Ancestry.com, 1910 U.S. Federal Census for (Merle) Hopdale, Yakima, Washington, [database online], Provo, UT.

Ancestry.com, 1910 U.S. Federal Census for (Leota) Custer, Custer County, Nebraska, [database online], Provo, UT.

Ancestry.com, 1920 U.S. Federal Census for Tow, Campbell County, Wyoming (near Adon) [database online], Provo, UT.

Ancestry.com, 1930 U.S. Federal Census for Election District 9, Campbell County, Wyoming, [database online], Provo, UT.

Ancestry.com, 1940 U.S. Federal Census for Gillette, Campbell County, Wyoming, [database online], Provo, UT.

Fred Leland and Matilda Jane "Tillie" (Cline) Hamm
1916

Fred L. Hamm was born May 26, 1872, at Cambridge, Story County, Iowa. On October 6, 1896, he married Matilda Jane Cline at Story, Iowa. Matilda Jane was born on December 21, 1871. He spent the next seventeen years as a R.F.D. mail carrier in Iowa. In the spring of 1916, he moved his family to Wyoming where he filed for a homestead ten miles north of Rozet in the Little Iowa community. He filed on Sections 21 and 28, Township 51 North, Range 69 West. Fred and Matilda were the parents of ten children.

Eva Elnora	b: 29 Apr 1897	d: 22 Jun 1960	m: Floyd Arley Huff
Faye Irene	b: 12 Dec 1898	d: 03 Dec 1990	m: Faye O. Thompson
Adolph Sabin	b: 27 Jan 1902	d: 17 May 1965	m: (1) Florence Fair
			(2) Evelyn M. (Jones) Barnes
Gladys Mae	b: 08 Sep 1903	d: 09 Sep 1928	m: Lyle Alfred Woods
Jack Wilson	b: 29 Jan 1905	d: 07 Feb 1971	m: Beulah Pearl Plemmons
Bessie Cloe	b: 20 Jun 1907	d: 12 Dec 1996	m: Cecil Raymond Crayne
Mildred	b: 15 Sep 1908	d: 28 Jan 1965	m: Charles W. Graham
Winifred	b: 13 Oct 1909	d: 24 Mar 2013	m: Dee Jasper Hux
Dorothy Ileene	b: 21 Sep 1911	d: 01 May 2010	m: Edward Sidney Hays
Beulah Beatrice	b: 22 Mar 1916	d: 06 Nov 1987	m: Vernon R. Kissell

The children attended the Cottonwood School. Adolph's first wife was a teacher there from fall 1920 - spring 1922.

Matilda Jane Hamm died on April 21, 1948, and was buried in Mount Pisgah Cemetery, Gillette, Wyoming. Fred L. Hamm died on October 30, 1950, in Lander, Fremont County, Wyoming. He was buried in Mount Pisgah Cemetery, Gillette, Wyoming on November 1, 1950.

Sources:
Photos: Ancestry.com, Hamm Family Tree; Fred and Tillie from the collections of Leona and Jeanette Heptner.
Bureau of Land Management, Homestead Patent Index, [www.glorecords.blm.gov].
"Rozet Couple Wed at Fort Collins," The News Record, Gillette, Wyoming, July 2, 1925.
"Funeral of Mrs. (Lyle) Woods," The News Record, Gillette, Wyoming, September 13, 1928, page 1.
"Society 'Hayes-Hamm Marriage'," The News Record, November 21, 1929.
"Final Rites Held Wednesday for Fred L. Hamm," page 1, The News Record, Gillette, Wyoming, November 2, 1950,
"Funeral Service Held Friday for Adolph S. Hamm," The News Record, Gillette, Wyoming, May 27, 1965.
Campbell County Cemetery District, Burial Property Report, September 8, 1998.
Ancestry.com, 1920 U.S. Federal Census for Election District #8, Iowa Precinct, Campbell County, Wyoming, [database online],
*   Provo, UT.*

George and Clara (Thompson) Jensen
1916

WWI

George was born on July 27, 1889, in Crawford County, Iowa, to Hans Christian and Christina Jensen, immigrants from Germany. In the spring of 1909 the family moved to Dickinson County, Iowa. About 1916 George came west looking for land. He filed for a homestead in Section 26, Township 51 North, Range 70 West, located on the Cottonwood Valley about eight miles north of Rozet, Campbell County, Wyoming. He served in World War I. He enlisted on June 27, 1918, in the U.S. Army. George served as a Private First Class with the 38th Field Artillery Regiment statoned at Camp Lewis, Washington. He was discharged on January 21, 1919. Shortly after his return to Rozet he married Clara Thompson, daughter of Fayette R. and Mary Thompson. They became the parents of eight children. The first five children were born at Rozet, Wyoming:

Frederick Leslie	b: 10 Feb 1920	d: 04 Feb 2010	
Virgil George	b: 19 Oct 1921	d: 17 Aug 2007	
Alfred Maurice	b: 13 Aug 1923	d: 09 Aug 2013	m: Donna Ruth Potter
Thelma Louise	b: 29 Jun 1925	d: 12 Aug 1946	
Fayette Hans	b: 26 Apr 1928	d: 30 Mar 1994	m: Betty Ingeborg
Irma Mae	b: 1930	d: after 1940	m. Elvern H. Olson
Esther Ellen	b: 10 Jul 1932	d: 11 Jun 2013	m. Curtis Hanson
Mary Jane	b: 14 Nov 1938	d: 14 Nov 1938	

By 1930 George and Clara returned to Iowa, settled on a farm in Superior, Dickinson County, Iowa, where their last three children were born. By 1938 they had moved once again to Yellow Medicine County, Minnesota, settling in Clarkfield where they lived until George's death on November 14, 1968, in Yellow Medicine County, Minnesota. Clara died on September 15, 1991, in Clarkfield, Minnesota, and was buried alongside her husband in the Clarkfield Cemetery.

Sources:
Photos: Middle – from the Irene Heptner Whisler collection;
        Others from U.S. Find-a-Grave Index 1600s-Current [database online], Provo, UT.
Bureau of Land Management, Homestead Patent Index, [www.glorecords.blm.gov].
Ancestry.com, U.S., General Land Office Records, 1776-2015, [database online], Provo, UT.
Ancestry.com, U.S. Department of Veterans Affairs (BIRLS Death File, 1850-2010, [database online], Provo, UT.
Ancestry.com,, Obituary, "Farmer at Superior Dies (Hans Jensen)," Estherville Daily News (Estherville, Iowa) 17 Oct 1939, page 1,
        [database online], Provo, UT.
Ancestry.com, U.S. Find a Grave Index, 1600s-Current, [database online], Provo, UT.
Ancestry.com, 1900 U.S. Federal Census, for Nishnabotny, Crawford County, Iowa, [database online], Provo, UT.
Ancestry.com, 1910 U.S. Federal Census, for Okoboji, Dickinson County, Iowa, [database online], Provo, UT.
Ancestry.com, 1930 U.S. Federal Census, for Superior, Dickinson County, Iowa, [database online], Provo, UT.
Ancestry.com, 1940 U.S. Federal Census for Superior, Dickinson County, Iowa, [database online], Provo, UT.

Raymond W. and Kathryn M. (Lowery) Kottraba
1916

Raymond W. "Ray" Kottraba was born August 16, 1893, in Jamestown, Mercer County, Pennsylvania, to Amos and Jenny Kottraba. He was the eldest of three children. His parents moved to Gustavus, Trumbull County, Ohio, where the family lived until 1919 when his father moved the family to Rozet, Wyoming. Ray filed for a homestead south of Rozet in Section 29, Township 48 North, Range 69 West. Ray was a veteran of WWI and served in the cavalry. He married Kathryn Lowery on June 1, 1920, at Gillette, Wyoming. She was born November 25, 1891, in Lorton, Nebraska. She came to Wyoming in 1918 and taught at the Weckwerth School, south of Rozet for two years. They were the parents of six children:

Annie Willa Cortell	b: 07 Apr 1922	d: 23 Oct 2001	m: William Russell Irwin
Leola Rebecca	b: 20 Sep 1923	d: 02 Feb 2020	m: Vince Robert Thar
Charles Wilford	b: 15 Jul 1925	d: 05 May 2007	m: Alta Mae Mellott
James Leland	b: 03 Aug 1927	d: 14 Nov 1986	m: Edith Middaugh
Helen Mae	b: 30 Jan 1929	d: 25 Nov 2017	m: Dean Robert Whisler
Hazel Lucille	b: 01 Aug 1930	d: 17 Oct 2013	m: Neil Reisland

Ray's parents, Amos and Jennie Kottraba moved to Moorcroft, and Ray and Kathryn lived on the homestead about seven years. Times were hard. They raised cattle, chickens, and a garden. In 1927 the family moved to Erve Owens' place so their oldest child, Willa, could start school in the Owens School. Ray ran a mail route out of Rozet Post Office to the Piney Post Office, located at the Thomas place, and to Dillinger Post Office at the Dillinger ranch.

In 1928 Ray moved his family moved to Davenport, Thayer County, Nebraska, where Ray worked for a blacksmith shop. Ray moved his family to Morrill, Scotts Bluff County, Nebraska, where he worked on a sugar beet farm. In the early 1930s they moved back to Rozet, Wyoming. The years that followed were the depression years, which brought drought, grasshoppers, and dust storms. The children attended school at the Rozet Consolidated School—all graduated from Rozet High School. Ray and Kathryn bought a ranch north of Moorcroft in 1946. They lived there until 1964 when they sold the ranch to their son, Charles, and moved to Buffalo, Johnson County, Wyoming. Ray died on August 10, 1974, and Kathryn on February 10, 1975. They are both buried in Mount Pisgah Cemetery, Gillette, Wyoming.

Mr. and Mrs. Ray Kottraba on their 52nd Wedding Anniversary

Sources:
Bureau of Land Management, Homestead Patent Index, [www.glorecords.blm.gov].
"The Raymond W. Kottraba Family", pages 321-322, Campbell County, The Treasured Years, 1990; compiled by Campbell County Historical Society, Gillette, Wyoming.
"Anniversary (52nd) Noted," The News Record, Gillette, WY, June 21, 1973, page 1.
Campbell County Cemetery District Burial Report, September 8, 1998.
"Kottraba (Leland) Service Tuesday," The News Record, Gillette, Wyoming, November 12/13, 1986.
"Willa (Kottraba) Irwin obituary," The News Record, Gillette, Wyoming, October 25, 2001.
"Charles 'Chuck' Kottraba, obituary," The News Record, Gillette, Wyoming May 7, 2007.
Ancestry.com, Newspapers.com Obituary Index, 1899s-current, [database online], Provo, UT.
Ancestry.com, U.S. Cemetery and Funeral Home Collection, 1847-Current, [database online], Provo, UT.
Ancestry.com, U.S. Obituary Collection,1930-Current, [database online], Provo, UT.
Ancestry.com, U.S. Find-a-Grave Index, 1600s-Current, [database online], Provo, UT.
Ancestry.com, U.S. Department of Veterans Affairs BIRLS Death File, 1850-2010, [database online], Provo, UT.
Ancestry.com, U.S. World War I Draft Registration Cards 1917-1918, [database online], Provo, UT.
Ancestry.com, U.S. World War II Draft Registration Cards, 1942, [database online], Provo, UT.
Ancestry.com,1900 U.S. Federal Census for Gustavus, Trumbull County, Ohio, [database online], Provo, UT.
Ancestry.com, 1910 U.S. Federal Census for Gustavus, Trumbull County, Ohio, [database online], Provo, UT.
Ancestry.com, 1920 U.S. Federal Census for Moorcroft, Crook County, Wyoming, [database online], Provo, UT.
Ancestry.com, 1930 U.S. Federal Census for Davenport, Thayer County, Nebraska, [database online], Provo, UT.
Ancestry.com, 1940 U.S. Federal Census for Campbell County, Wyoming, [database online], Provo, UT.

Herman Ben Schrand
1916

Ben Schrand, born September 2, 1872, filed for a homestead about nine miles northeast of Rozet in Section 29, Township 51 North, Range 69 West, bordering the Frank Heptner homestead just to the west of him. Nothing is known about when he left his homestead. In the 1930s Oscar and Dorothy Heptner lived there for a few years, followed by her brother, Ton Whisler, and his family. Later, David and Marge Whisler lived there during the 1940s until they bought the Potter place about 1950.

Ben Schrand died in March 1948 in Gillette and was buried March 6, 1948, in Mount Pisgah Cemetery, Gillette, Campbell County, Wyoming.

**The Heptner Place, on left; the old Ben Schrand Place on the right
where David and Marge Whisler lived during the 1940s**

Sources:
Photo: from the collections of Leona and Jeanette Heptner.
Bureau of Land Management, Homestead Patent Index, [www.glorecords.blm.gov].
Campbell County Cemetery District Burial Report, September 8, 1998.
Ancestry.com, U.S. Find-a-Grave Index, 1600s-Current, [database online], Provo, UT.
Ancestry.com, U.S. General Land Office Records, 1776-2015,(Issue date 22 Oct 1915); [database online], Provo, UT.
Ancestry.com, U.S. World War I Draft Registration Cards, 1917-1918, [database online], Provo, UT.
Ancestry.com, 1900 U.S. Federal Census for Gillett Grove, Clay County, Iowa (farm laborer); [database online], Provo, UT.

George B. and Alice (Owens) Gove Spencer
1916

George Spencer filed for a homestead on July 31, 1916, located in Sections 6 and 7, Township 50 North, Range 69 West, and Section 1 and 12, Township 50 North, Range 70 West. George Spencer was born June 7, 1858, in Vermont. His parents moved to the state of Wisconsin when he was five years old. At the age of 12 he was left an orphan, and at the age of 21 he moved to Iowa. Soon afterwards he moved on to Montana and spent the next sixteen years in the mines of Montana. He married Alice Gove on December 3, 1916. Alice was born October 21, 1854. She was the mother three children from a previous marriage:

Flora Mae Gove	b: 13 Nov 1873	d: 21 Sep 1959	m: Nicholas Peter Kuhl
Nora Gove	b: 22 Oct 1875	d: 13 Oct 1964	m: Charles A. Hinds
Carlos "Carl" Elmer Gove	b: 26 Sep 1877	d: Nov 1963	m: Amy Leota

George Spencer died in March 31, 1920, at the age of 62. He was buried in the Gillette Cemetery (Mount Pisgah), Gillette, Wyoming. Alice Spencer then spent her time between her two daughters, Mrs. Nora Hinds in Rozet, Wyoming, and Mrs. N. P. Kuhl in Sheridan, Wyoming. Alice Spencer died in October 1932, and was buried in Mount. Pisgah Cemetery, Gillette, Wyoming, on October 21, 1932.

Alice Spencer, Mrs. Charlie Hinds, Jeanette and Leona Heptner
1922

Sources:
Photo: from the collections of Leona and Jeanette Heptner.
Bureau of Land Management, Homestead Patent Index, [www.glorecords.blm.gov].
"Rozet Rumblings—George Spencer's Obituary," The Gillette News, Gillette, Wyoming, April 9, 1920.
"George Spencer Deceased," Campbell County Record, Gillette, Wyoming, April 15/22, 1920.
Campbell County Cemetery District Burial Property Report, September 1998.
Sheridan Municipal Cemetery Records, Sheridan, Wyoming.
Ancestry.com, U.S. Find-a-Grave Index, 1600s-Current, [database online], Provo, UT.
Ancestry.com, Iowa, Marriage Records, 1880-1945, [database online], Provo, UT.
Ancestry.com, 1880 U.S. Federal Census (Alice Gove) for Oak, Mills County, Iowa, [database online], Provo, UT.
Ancestry.com, 1900 U.S. Federal Census (Alice Gove) for Oak, Mills County, Iowa, [database online], Provo, UT.
Ancestry.com, 1905 Iowa State Census (Alice Gove) for Mills County, Iowa, [database online], Provo, UT.
Ancestry.com, 1910 U.S. Federal Census (George and Alice) for Oak, Mills County, Iowa, [database online], Provo, UT.
Ancestry.com, 1920 U.S. Federal Census for Rozet North, Campbell County, Wyoming, [database online], Provo, UT.
Ancestry.com 1930 U.S. Federal Census (Alice; widow) for Sheridan, Sheridan County, Wyoming, [database online], Provo, UT.

John and Emma (Kinna) Tomingas
1916

John (Jaan) Tomingas was born June 27, 1883, in Tallina, Estonia, Russia, to Denis and May (Anderson) Tomingas. The family had a farm on the outskirts of town. Shortly after the turn of the century, 1900, the country was in turmoil. John finally had to flee, and he immigrated to the United States through the port at Sault Ste Marie, Michigan, arriving there on November 10, 1906. He declared for Naturalization on January 25, 1907 in the District Court, Butte, Silver Bow County, Montana. In his declaration he states: "I now reside at 415 Kemper Avenue, Butte, Montana. I emigrated to the United States of America from Coppercliffe, [Ontario] Canada on the Canadian Pacific R. R.; my last foreign residence was Coppercliffe, Canada. It is my bona fide intention to renounce forever all allegiance and fidelity to my foreign prince, potentate, state, or sovereignty, and particularly to Nicholas II Emperor of Russia, of which I am now a subject; I arrived at the port of Duluth, in state of Minnesota on or about the 12th of November 1906." From this statement, we can speculate that he may have went to work in the copper mines at Coppercliffe prior to entering the United States at Sault Ste Marie, Michigan.

Working the ground
John and Emma with the help of youngest daughter Donna

In 1908 John married Emma Kinna in Lacombe, Alberta, Canada. John applied for a homestead on April 21, 1908, on SW Township 40 North, Range 4, Section 2, Meridian WS near Red Deer, Alberta, Canada. He was granted the homestead on September 14, 1911. Four of John and Emma's children were born at Eckville, Alberta, Canada. In March 1916 John, Emma, and their four children crossed the border into Sweet Grass, Montana. They traveled on to Campbell County, Wyoming, where John filed for a homestead on Township 53 North, Range 70 West and again in 1917 on Township 53 North, Range 70 West, located north of Rozet in the Adon community. Their four youngest children were born in Adon. When they first started farming there "anything grew if you added water" as the soil had not grown anything except grass in centuries. Many adventures were experienced by the Tomingas family, some fun. Emma was an accomplished musician having been taught music at school in Saint Petersburg. She would play her pump organ with her feet and sing "Dark Eyes," an old Ukranian Gypsy tune. Her children remember listening to her songs drifting out over the Wyoming prairie. Other periods were more difficult, such as the drought, the depression. About 1935, after all of their children had left the home, John and Emma moved back to Red Deer, near Edmonton, their Alberta, Canada, homestead where they lived for the rest of their lives.

138

Children:

Paula Emma	b: 25 May 1909	d: 21 Feb 2003	m: John Ansley "Jack" Donner
Arthur Denis	b: 29 May 1910	d: 20 Dec 1996	
Anna Elizabeth	b: 07 Dec 1911	d: 13 Sep 2005	m: (1) Ray Morehouse
			(2) Wendall Raymond Griffin
			(3) _____ Barone
Sadie Lily	b: 05 Feb 1915	d: 05 Mar 1999	m: Robert J. Gourley
Robert John "Bob"	b: 11 Jun 1916	d: 28 Oct 1999	m: Hallowese Morrison (div)
Arnold Raymond	b: 04 Sep 1920	d: 14 Sep 2012	m: Marjorie Little
Henry Roy	b: 07 Dec 1921	d: 07 Aug 2006	m: Patsy Pringle
Donna B.	b: 08 Scp 1931	d: 14 Jan 2020	m: Ed Reznicek

Sons Arthur, Arnold and Henry served in World War II with the U.S. Army Air Corps.

John Tomingas died on September 27, 1951, in Red Deer, near Edmonton, Alberta, Canada. He was buried in the Gilby Kalm Cemetery, Eckville, Red Deer Census Division, Alberta, Canada. Emma Tomingas died February 12, 1963, and was buried in the Gilby Kalm Cemetery next to her husband.

The Tomingas Family – Adon, Wyoming
Back row: John, Paula, Arthur, Anna, Emma
Front row: Arnold, Henry, Sadie, Robert

Sources:
Photos: Courtesy of Diann Larsen Avery, 2019.
Bureau of Land Management [www.glorecords.blm.gov].
Ancestry.com, Canada, Find-a-Grave Index, 1600s-Current. [database online]. Provo, UT.
Ancestry.com, U.S. Social Security Applications and Claims Index, 1936-2007, [database online]. Provo, UT.
Ancestry.com, Swedish Emigration Records, 1873-1951, [database online]. Provo, UT.
Ancestry.com, U.S. Border Crossings from Canada to U.S., 1895-1960, [database online]. Provo, UT.
Ancestry.com, Montana, County Naturalization Records, 1867-1970, [database online]. Provo, UT.
Ancestry.com, Alberta, Canada, Marriages Index, 1898-1942, [database online]. Provo, UT.
Ancestry.com, Manitoba Saskatchewan and Alberta, Canada, Homestead Grand Registers, 1872-1930, [database online]. Provo, UT.
Ancestry.com, U.S. World War I Draft Registration Cards 1917-1918, [database online]. Provo, UT.
Ancestry.com, 1930 U.S. Federal Census for Election District 9, Campbell County, Wyoming, [database online]. Provo, UT.
Ancestry.com, Canada, Voters Lists, 1935-1980, [database online]. Provo, UT.

Thomas Perry and Ollie May (Vincent) Wallace
1916

Thomas Perry Wallace was born May 16, 1896, Halfway, Polk County, Missouri, to James and Georgia Wallace. About 1916 Perry and two brothers, John and Otis came to Campbell County, Wyoming, and filed on homesteads. Perry and Otis in sections 2, 3, and 11 in Township 51 North, Range 70 West, about eleven miles north of Rozet. The land was located on the west side of the Adon Road in the Cottonwood Valley community. Their brother John filed further west in Township 52 North, Range 71 and 70 West, on Cow Creek. Otis, aged 24, died in Greybull Wyoming, on February 24, 1919. John and his family moved to Humboldt County, California, after 1935.

Perry Wallace married Ollie May Vincent on October 17, 1915, in Bolivar, Polk County, Missouri. She was born April 7, 1900, to Thomas and Sarah (Bridges) Vincent. Ollie came with Perry from Bolivar, Missouri, to northeastern Wyoming as a fifteen-year-old bride with their four-month-old daughter, Jewell. They dug into a hillside and built a dugout, which served as a temporary residence until a suitable house could be built. Food was not plentiful. Perry obtained most of the meat (jackrabbits and sage hens) with aid of his trusty .22 rifle. Perry carried what few store-bought supplies they could get that first winter on his back from Rozet.

Perry and Ollie with children: Jewell, Ted, Lee, Ruth

As most homesteaders did through the years, the Wallace's tried farming their claim. "In those days, we figured if we weren't in the fields by seven," said Mrs. Wallace, "there wasn't any use going." She learned to fix breakfast, clean the house by seven o-clock, and then take the children to the field to play all day around the wagon. There she worked one team of horses while Perry worked another. The Wallace's raised sheep and cattle, in addition to their years of farming. But cattle won out. Their homestead eventually grew to a 4,200 acre ranch called the Slash Open Box. In 1964 the Wallaces were one of four original homesteaders remaining in the Cottonwood Valley. They were the parents of four children:

Jewell Myree	b: 23 Jul 1916	d: 23 Jul 1984	m: Carl O. Carlson
Alberta Ruth	b: 16 Jan 1919	d: 15 Jan 2009	m: Eugene Fuller
Otis Lee	b: 25 Jul 1921	d: 09 Apr 1969	m: Naomi F. "Katy" Porter
Ted Raymond	b: 16 Aug 1924	d: 04 Dec 2001	m: Frances Audrey Barrett

The children attended the Cottonwood Valley School about a quarter mile from the homestead. Perry Wallace died October 30, 1976, and was buried in Mount Pisgah Cemetery, Gillette, Wyoming. Ollie Wallace died July 9, 1985, in Big Horn, Wyoming, and was buried alongside her husband in Mount Pisgah Cemetery.

Sources:
Photo: Ancestry.com, Wallace Family Tree, [Wallace Porter Connection].
Bureau of Land Management, Homestead Patent Index, [www.glorecords.blm.gov].
"Last of the Cottonwood Valley Homesteaders," The International Harvester Farm Magazine, Winter, 1964, pages 4-7.
"Rancher Held in Gunshot Death of Lee Wallace, 47," The News Record, Gillette, Wyoming, April 24, 1970.
"Rancher Dies from Gunshot," The News Record, Gillette, Wyoming, November 1, 1976.
"Jewell M. (Wallace) Carlson Obituary," The News Record, Gillette, Wyoming, July 13, 1984.
"Ollie Wallace Funeral Friday", The News Record, Gillette, Wyoming, July 11, 1985.
"Ted R. Wallace obituary," The News Record, Gillette, Wyoming, December 7, 2001.
"Ruth A (Wallace) Fuller, obituary," Gillette News Record, Gillette, Wyoming, January 18, 2009.
"Perry Wallace," page ___, The Historical Encyclopedia of Wyoming, published by the Wyoming Historical Society, Cheyenne, WY, 1970.
Campbell County, The Treasured Years, 1990, page 619-620, compiled by Campbell County Historical Society.
Ancestry.com, U.S. Find-a-Grave Index, [database online], Provo, UT.
Ancestry.com, U.S. World War I Draft Registration Cards, 1917-1918, [database online], Provo, UT.
Ancestry.com, U.S. World War II Draft Registration Cards, 1942, [database online], Provo, UT.
Ancestry.com, 1930 U.S. Federal Census for Election District 8, Campbell County, Wyoming, [database online], Provo, UT

Clarence Clay and Cora Ellen Margaret "Maggie" (Barrett) Weaver
1916

Clay Weaver was born January 26, 1875 in Knox County, Ohio, to William Price and Mary Jane (Bottenfield) Weaver. About 1878 the family moved to Jewell County, Kansas. Maggie (Cora Ellen Margaret Barret) was born on May 14, 1878, in Smith Center, Smith County, Kansas, to William and Hannah (Snowden) Barrett. Her youth was spent in eastern Kansas. Margaret and Clay were married on May 12, 1896. After their marriage they spent a few years in Kansas and then moved to Red Cloud, Webster County, Nebraska. Clay came to Wyoming in 1916 where on December 18, 1916, he filed a contest on the homestead filed by Mr. W. H. Brown for Sections 21, 27, 28, and 33, in Township

Clay and Maggie Weaver – 1946
on their 50th Wedding Anniversary

50 North, Range 69 West. It was located three miles east of Rozet along the Custer Battlefield Highway now known as S/S 14-16 near his daughter and son-in-law, Elsie and James Duvall. Clay returned to Red Cloud until September 26, 1917, when he and his sons, Ritchie and Wardie, left Red Cloud, Nebraska, on an emigrant train. They brought with them farm equipment, livestock, and household furniture. Margaret and the remaining family members arrived by passenger train on February 2, 1918. Shortly upon arriving Clay and Margaret inquired about establishing a school nearby. That fall the children attended the Happy Hollow School and continued to do so until the Rozet Consolidated School was established in 1921. Clay worked on the railroad to help support the family along with establishing his homestead. He, along with Dot Brennan, worked to establish the Rozet Cemetery. They were the parents of eleven children:

Elsie May	b: 04 Mar 1897	d: 03 Aug 1959	m: James Dewey Duvall
Miles Clay	b: 12 Feb 1899	d: 21 Feb 1984	m: Imogene Laverne Dales
Mina Margarette	b: 18 Jul 1900	d: 08 Sep 1982	m: Leo Vigil Sweem
Charles Barrett	b: 25 Nov 1901	d: 22 Jan 1987	m: Leona Craley
Zelma	b: 24 Nov 1903	d: 10 Nov 1987	m: Ed Fitch
Craig Ritchie	b: 17 Jul 1905	d: 04 Apr 1977	m: Lyla Wells
Hannah M.	b: 25 Aug 1907	d: 20 Aug 1949	m: Leslie R. Harrod
Wardie Earl	b: 09 Aug 1909	d: 09 Apr 1967	(never married)
Lois Marie	b: 31 Jul 1911	d: 27 Feb 1997	m: Oscar Clyde Gormley
Gladys Lavonne	b: 28 Feb 1913	d: 11 Feb 2001	(never married)
Clair Bud	b: 26 Sep 1916	d: 23 Nov 2004	m: Doris Dickey

Clay Weaver died in 1949 and was buried March 1, 1949, in Mount Pisgah Cemetery, Gillette, Wyoming. Margaret died June 29, 1962, at Gillette, Wyoming, and was buried in Mount Pisgah Cemetery alongside her husband.

Sources:
Photo: from Ancestry.com, U.S. Find-a-Grave Index, 1600s-Current, [database online], Provo, UT.
Bureau of Land Management, Homestead Patent Index, [www.glorecords.blm.gov].
"The Clay Weaver Family," Campbell County, The Treasured Years, 1990, pages 622-623, compiled by Campbell County
Historical Society.
"Eddy Fitch and Zelma Weaver Wed," The News Record, Gillette, Wyoming, September 17, 1925.
"Popular Young Couple Married Harrod-Weaver," The News Record, Gillette, Wyoming, September 2, 1926.
"Final Rites Held Monday for Mrs. M. Weaver," page 1, The News Record, Gillette, Wyoming, July 5, 1962.
"Funeral Services Held Thursday for Wardie Weaver," page 1, The News Record, Gillette, Wyoming, April 20, 1967.
"Obituary-Zelma Z. Fitch," The News Record, Gillette, Wyoming, November 12, 1987.
"Obituary-Gladys Weaver," The News Record, Gillette, Wyoming, February 17, 2001.
"Clair Bud Weaver obituary," The News Record, Gillette, Wyoming, November 26, 2004.
Ancestry.com, Wyoming Death Records, 1909-1969, [database online], Provo, UT.
Ancestry.com, 1900 U.S. Federal Census for Logan, Smith County, Kansas, [database online], Provo, UT.
Ancestry.com, 1910 U.S. Federal Census for Garfield, Webster County, Nebraska, [database online],Provo, UT.
Ancestry.com, 1920 U.S. Federal Census for Rozet-South, Precinct #26, Campbell County, Wyoming, [database online], Provo, UT.
Ancestry.com, 1930 U.S. Federal Census for Election District 5, Campbell County, Wyoming, [database online],Provo, UT.
Ancestry.com, 1940 U.S. Federal Census for Campbell County, Wyoming, [database online],Provo, UT.

William James "Billy" and Irene C. (Garrett) Williams
1916

William James "Billy" Williams was born April 4, 1898, in Indian Territory near Ardmore, Oklahoma, to Henry K. and Mary Emma (Lyons) Williams. He came to Campbell County with his mother and stepfather, John Newton Hamill, as a young man. He filed for a homestead in 1916 south of Rozet in Sections 5 and 6, Township 48 North, Range 69 West, near his mother and stepsister, Mae Hamill Talley. Irene Celeste Garrett was born February 19, 1902, at Mountain Grove, Wright County, Missouri, to Winslow J. and Susie Bell (Kelly) Garrett. She attended school in both Mountain Grove and in Wright County, Missouri. In 1916 at the age of fourteen she moved with her parents to a homestead south of Rozet. Billy and Irene were married on August 28, 1918 and lived on his homestead. They were the parents of four children:

Kenneth Warren	b: 26 Nov 1919	d: 02 May 1973	m: (1) Bessie Hunt (2) Mildred Burns
James Leon	b: 03 Mar 1922	d: 26 Aug 2003	m: Helen M. Schnieder
Sylvia Irene	b: 10 Dec 1923	d: 11 Aug 1983	m: Herschel S. Crosby
Robert E. "Buck	b: 25 Sep 1931	d: 07 Jun 1988	m: (1) Ruby Mae Ruff (2) Charlotte Ford

Up until his death, Billy and Irene maintained the ranch where they raised their family. Billy also was a water well driller and drilled many water wells in the Rozet area and elsewhere. Billy Williams died in October 27, 1967, and was buried in Mount Pisgah Cemetery, Gillette, Wyoming. Irene continued to operate the ranch until the mid-1970s when she moved to Gillette. She died April 7, 1986, and was buried alongside her husband in Mount Pisgah Cemetery.

Sources:
Bureau of Land Management, Homestead Patent Index, [www.glorecords.blm.gov].
"Final Rites Held for 'Billy' Williams," The News Record, Gillette, Wyoming, November 2, 1967.
"Williams Service Held in City," The News Record, Gillette, Wyoming, May 10, 1973.
"Crosby Funeral Monday," page 12, The News Record, Gillette, Wyoming, August 14, 1983.
"Williams (Irene) Funeral Thursday," The News Record, Gillette, Wyoming, April 1986.
"R. E. 'Buck' Williams," The News Record, Gillette, Wyoming, June 8, 1988.
"James Williams, obituary," The News Record, Gillette, Wyoming August 29, 2003.
Campbell County Cemetery District Burial Report of September 8, 1999.
James D. Hitt website: www.hitt_genealogy.homestead.com/files/WILLIAms.htm - read 6/24/2001-ljw.
Ancestry.com, U.S. Find-a-Grave Index, 1600s-Current, [database online], Provo, UT.
Ancestry.com, U.S. Find-a-Grave Index, 1600s-Current (obituary for Ed Moore [married Etta Williams]),
    [database online}, Provo, UT.
Ancestry.com, 1900 U.S. Federal Census for Township 2, Chickasaw Nation, Indian Territory, [database online], Provo, UT.
Ancestry.com, 1900 U.S. Federal Census for Township 2, Chickasaw Nation, Indian Territory, (for Henry Williams),
    [database online], Provo, UT

Daniel W. and Catherine (Slade) Duvall Clark
1917

Dan W. Clark

Catherine (Slade) Duvall Clark "Grandma Clark" with her
great grandchildren: Darleen Heptner, Joanne Whisler,
Phil Whisler and Eurith Whisler

Dan Clark was born on September 15, 1860, to Franklin and Mary Clark in Sangamon, Illinois. By 1870 the family moved to Camp Branch, Cass County, Missouri, where they stayed for about fifteen years before they packed up once more and moved to Vesta, Johnson County, Nebraska. On October 14, 1883, Dan married Emma Louisa Noyce at The Wolfords, Nebraska. Seven children were born at their farm in Vesta, Nebraska:

Charles V.	b: 23 Aug 1884	d: 18 Feb 1949,	m: Loretta Adeline Taylor
Julia Edna	b: 16 Jul 1888	d: 29 Nov 1966	m: John Henry Mommens
Ellen M.	b: 1889	d: 1889	(she lived less than a day)
Beatrice Sarah	b: 01 Aug 1891	d: 19 Feb 1980	m: Harman C. Holtmeyer
Daniel W. J.	b: 1895	d: 1895	(he lived less than a year)
Lulu	b: 1899	d: 1899	(he lived less than a year)
Vernon N.	b: 1901	d: 1906	

Emma Louisa died in 1908 and was buried in the Vesta Cemetery, Vesta, Nebraska. No record of Dan's marriage to Catherine (Slade) Duvall Pearson has been found. They may have married in 1915, the time Dan's youngest living child, Beatrice, married and moved to Iowa.

By 1920 Dan and Catherine had moved to Wray, Yuma County, Colorado, where we find them listed in the 1920 Federal Census with two of her grandchildren, Irene and Ivan Cain. After the death of Catherine's daughter, Goldie (Duvall) Cain in February 1920, they became the guardians of her three children, Irene age 17, Ruth age 15, and Ivan, age 9. In 1922 when Dan and Catherine moved to Campbell County, Wyoming, Ivan, now ten years old, came to live with them. Dan filed on a homestead southeast of Rozet near Catherine's son James Duvall.

Their household grew by one when her daughter Vida Whisler, died in June 1928 leaving ten children from ages 23 to 1½ without parents. Catherine took in the youngest Evelyn to live with her and her husband Dan Clark. Daniel W. Clark died on November 30, 1931. After a funeral service held in the Rozet Community Church his son Charles accompanied his body on the train to Vesta, Johnson County, Nebraska for burial alongside of his first wife, Emma Louisa, in the Vesta Cemetery. Catherine (Slade) Duvall Clark died July 16, 1936. After which Evelyn went to live with her sister and brother-in-law, Dorothy and Oscar Heptner. She was buried in the Rozet Cemetery.

Grandma Clark as she was known by her family and friends in the Rozet Community was born on April 16, 1866, in Tatamagouche, Colchester County, Nova Scotia. By 1885 her parents, Ephraim and Ellen (Dunphy) Slade, had immigrated to Butler County, Nebraska, from Tatamagouche, Colchester County, Nova Scotia. On April 22, 1886,

Catherine married Richard Duvall in David City, Butler County, Nebraska, whose father Andrew Duvall had immigrated about 1845 from Quebec Provence, Canada. Richard and Catherine became the parents of seven children all born in David City, Butler County, Nebraska:

Goldie Mae	b: 15 Jul 1885	d: 02 Feb 1920	m: William A. Cain
Pearl Vida	b: 07 Oct 1887	d: 06 Jun 1928	m: David Riley Whisler
Infant twins	b: 24 Sep 1889	d: 24 Sep 1889	
Carroll William	b: 24 Sep 1889	d: 25 Jul 1961	m: Sylvia B. Helmer
Helen Fay	b: 08 Aug 1894	d: 08 Aug 1894	
James Dewey	b: 30 Oct 1897	d: 03 May 1990	m: Elsie Mae Weaver

Richard Duvall
Born: 02 Apr 1846, Clinton County, NY
Died: 06 Apr 1924, Highland County, KS

Goldie Mae, Catherine (Slade) Duvall
Pearl Vida, Carroll William, and James Dewey
1898

Ivan Cain

Catherine and Richard later divorced. On December 15, 1904, she married Clarence Pearson in Tecumseh, Johnson County, Nebraska. They were found in the 1910 Federal Census living in Vesta, Johnson County, Nebraska, with two of her sons, Carroll and J. D. When they divorced in the 1920s is not known. No records have been found for her marriage to Daniel Willian Clark. However, in the 1920 Federal Census, we find them living on a farm in Wray, Yuma County, Colorado, with two of Catherine's grandchildren, Irene and Ivan Cain, living with them. Their mother Goldie Mae Cain had died suddenly in February 1920.

Catherine (Slade) Duvall Clark "Grandma Clark" and her children
Carroll Duvall, Grandma Clark, Vida (Duvall) Whisler, Jim Duvall
Taken after Goldie (Duvall) Cain's funeral, February 2, 1920, in
Wray, Yuma County, Colorado

Sources:
Photos: from the collections of Carroll Duvall "Slim" Whisler.
"Services for Rozet Man to be Held 2:30 Today," page 1, The News Record, Gillette, Wyoming, December 3, 1931.
Ancestry.com, U.S. Find a Grave Index, 1600s-Current (Dan Clark), [database online], Provo, UT.
Ancestry.com, Nebraska, , Marriage Records, 1885-1908 (Dan's first), [database online], Provo, UT.
Ancestry.com, Nebraska, U.S. Select County Marriage Records, 1855-1908 (Richard Duvall), [database online], Provo, UT.
Ancestry.com, Nebraska, U.S. Select County Marriage Records, 1855-1908 (Clarence Pearson), [database online], Provo, UT.
Ancestry.com, 1900 U.S. Federal Census for Todd Creek, Johnson Co., Nebraska (Dan and Emma Clark), [database online], Provo, UT.
Ancestry.com, 1900 U.S. Federal Census for David City, Butler County, Nebraska, (Richard Duvall), [database online], Provo, UT.
Ancestry.com, 1910 U.S. Federal Census for Vesta, Johnson County, Nebraska, (Clarence Pearson) [database online], Provo, UT.
Ancestry.com, 1920 U.S. Federal Census for Wray, Yuma County, Colorado, (Dan Clark), [database online], Provo, UT.
Ancestry.com, 1930 U.S. Federal Census for Election District 5, Campbell Co., Wyoming, (Dan Clark) [database online], Provo,

Floyd Elmo and Myrtle Agnes (Allen) Cook
1917

Floyd Cook was born April 21, 1885, in Harrisburg, Clarion County, Pennsylvania, to Winfred Scott and Sophia Kit (Croce) Cook. In 1886, when Floyd was but one year old, his parents moved their family by covered wagon to South Dakota. His mother died on May 5, 1896, when he was 11 years old. He and his sister Blanche lived for some time with their sister, Carrie Thompson, in Minnetonka, Sheridan County, Nebraska. He attended school in Minnetonka, Nebraska and in Hot Springs, South Dakota. Upon completion of school he went to work at Lead, South Dakota, to help support his family. While at Lead, he met Myrtle Agnus Allen, and they were married at Deadwood, Lawrence County, South Dakota, on June 22, 1909. Myrtle was born October 26, 1891, at Selby, Shelby County, Iowa. She attended school in Lead, South Dakota. Floyd and Myrtle lived in Lead for a while before moving to Sheridan County, Nebraska, and to Butte, Silver Bow County, Montana, where he worked in the copper mines. After the death of their daughter, May, Floyd moved his family to Campbell County, Wyoming. On December 17, 1917, Floyd Cook acquired a relinquished homestead located about ten miles southwest of Rozet in Sections 7, 8, 17, and 18, Township 49 North, Range 70 West, on Timber Creek Road. They were the parents of four children:

May Olivia	b: 29 Mar 1910	d: 24 Feb 1915	
Cleo C.	b: 02 Jan 1914	d: 12 Aug 2001	m: 1) James Harvey
			2) Loren Hellman
Hazel Irene	b: 19 Feb 1917	d: 24 Jun 1993	m: 1) _____Jones
			2) Merrill Johnson
			3) _____ Langley
Ferris Edwin	b: 23 May 1922	d: 02 Feb 1995	m: Pauline Louise Whisler

Floyd made some additions to the property, including a barn, garage, and workshop and of course a house. According to family history the family did not move into the house until around 1921. The only thing left (2021) is the house. Floyd retired from ranching in 1963, and they moved to Gillette. Myrtle Cook died May 23, 1970, in Gillette, Wyoming, and Floyd died September 6, 1971. They are both buried in Mount Pisgah Cemetery, Gillette, Wyoming.

Today the ranch is owned by his grandson, Gilbert Cook. The ranch was recognized in 2020 as a Wyoming Centennial Farm and Ranch because it has been family owned and operated for more than a century.

The original Cook Ranch house still stands on the homestead along Timber Creek Road in Campbell County.

Photo by Gregory Hasman used with permission from the *Gillette News Record*, December 15, 2020.

Sources:
Bureau of Land Management, Homestead Patent Index, [www.glorecords.blm.gov].
Ancestry.com, U.S. General Land Office Records 1776-2015, [data base online], Provo, UT.
Ancestry.com, U.S. Find a Grave Index, 1600s-Curret, [data base online], Provo, UT.
Ancestry.com, Montana, U.S., County Births and Deaths, 1830-2011, [data base online], Provo, UT.
Ancestry.com. 1900 U.S. Federal Census for Minnetonka Precinct, Sheridan County, NB [data base online], Provo, UT.
Ancestry.com, 1910 U.S. Federal Census for Butte Ward 5, Silver Bow County, Montana, [data base online], Provo, UT.
Ancestry.com, 1920 U.S. Federal Census for Rozet-South, Campbell County, WY, [data base online], Provo, UT.
Ancestry.com, 1930 U.S. Federal Census for Election District 5, Campbell County, WY, [data base online], Provo, UT.
Ancestry.com, South Dakota, U.S., Marriages, 1905-2017, [data base online], Provo, UT.
"Harvey-Cook Marriage," *The News Record*, Gillette, Wyoming, _____
"Pioneer Resident Dies May 23," *The News Record*, Gillette, Wyoming, May -25, 1970.
"Pioneer Resident Dies Monday," *The News Record*, Gillette, Wyoming, September 9, 1971.
"A Legacy Brand, After a Century, Gilbert Cook Recalls Family's Ranching History," by Gregory Hasman, <u>Gillette News Record</u>,
     Tuesday, December 15, 2020, page 1 and 9.

James Dewey "Jim" and Elsie (Weaver) Duvall
1917

Jim Duvall filed for a homestead located Section 35, Township 50 North, Range 69 West and Sections 1, 2, 11, 12, Township 49 North, Range 69 West. He was born October 30, 1897, at David City, Butler County, Nebraska, the youngest child of Richard and Catherine (Slade) Duvall. Elsie was born March 4, 1897, in Smith County, Kansas, to Marguerite and Clay Weaver. At the age of three she moved with her parents to Red Cloud, Webster County, Nebraska where she spent her youth attending grade and high school, graduating in 1915. She taught school in Wray, Yuma County, Colorado. Jim and Elsie Weaver were married on April 4, 1916, in Wray, Colorado. They moved to Rozet in July 1916, where they filed on a homestead east of Rozet. Jim and Elsie were the parents of eight children:

Carroll Weaver	b: 04 Jul 1917	d: 14 Jun 1975	m: Jessie M. Johnson
Kathryn Marguerite	b: 11 Aug 1918	d: 09 Nov 2017	m: John Kummerfeld
Merle Miles	b: 01 Dec 1921	d: 05 Dec 2003	m: Pauline Gabera
James Clark	b: 09 Feb 1920	d: 05 Mar 1920	m;
Kenneth Richard	b: 14 Aug 1926	d:	m: Norma L. Hayden,
Norma Lee	b: 1928	d: 02 Apr 1938	m:
Verlin Gwyn	b: 16 Jan 1932	d:	m: Judith A. Kimball
Nadine Louise	b: 02 Sep 1933	d: 23 Mar 2015	m: James L. Tayler

Back Row: Carroll, Merle, Katheryn, Elsie and Jim, Kenneth
Front: Verlyn and Nadine

146

In September 1923 he went to Wray, Colorado, to help his step-father Daniel W. Clark, his mother Catherine (Slade) Duvall Clark, and his brother Carroll William "Toad" Duvall move to the to the Rozet area. Toad Duvall relieved Mr. H. P. James as Section Foreman for the railroad. Jim Duvall drove a school bus for the Rozet Consolidated School for many years. Elsie Duvall died July 31, 1959, and was buried in the Rozet Cemetery. He died May 3, 1990, and was buried in the Rozet Cemetery, Rozet, Wyoming.

1986
Marguerite Kummerfeld, Merle, Kenneth, Jim, Nadine Taylor, Verlin
Duvall

Sources:
Photos: courtesy of Nadine Duvall Taylor - 2012.
Bureau of Land Management, Homestead Patent Index, [www.glorecords.blm.gov].
Whisler-Duvall Family Records, compiled by Lorna J. Whisler, 1995.
"Funeral Services Held Monday for Mrs. James Duvall," page 1, The News Record, Gillette, Wyoming, August 6, 1959.
Ancestry.com, 1920 U.S. Federal Census for Rozet-South, Precinct #26, Campbell County, Wyoming, [database online], Provo, UT.
Obituary of Merle Duvall www.stevensonandsons.com/2003/200bits.%20Duvall.htm.

Thomas B. and Mary (Boehm) Garrett
1917

Thomas Garrett was born March 11, 1851, in Keokuk County, Iowa, to Jeremiah Vardeman Garrett, Sr. His father moved the family numerous times to Nebraska, Iowa, Arkansas, and Holt County, Missouri, where Thomas met and married Kesiah Elizabeth Lawrence on December 21, 1873. They were the parents of three children:

Olive May	b: 23 Jan 1877	d: 28 May 1899	
Albert Leslie	b: 15 Oct 1876	d: 28 Jan 1967	m: Margaret Ellen "Maggie" Reed
Nellie Jane	b: 06 Oct 1879	d: 1972	m: Christian Lee Fender

Kesiah Garrett died in December 1881. On November 11, 1884, he married Mary Boehm in Fargo, Cass County, North Dakota,. They were the parents of one daughter:

Arvilla	b: 8 Sep 1884	d:18 Feb 1909	m: Charles Newton

Arvilla and Charles Newton had two children:

Alta Josephine	b: 29 Nov 1906	d:	m: Walter L. Shell
Thomas C.	b: 29 Dec 1908	d: 1975	m: Violet Eastwood

Their daughter Arvilla died in 1909. Soon afterwards Tom and Mary adopted their grandchildren, Alta and Thomas Garrett and raised them through high school. Thomas moved his family to Wyoming about 1917 and filed for a homestead on Section 3, Township 50N, Range 69W. In 1921 he filed for additional land in sections 4, 5, 8, and 9, Township 50N, Range 70W. Their grandchildren attended school at Rozet. He died March 4, 1931, age 80, at Hot Springs, South Dakota, and was buried in Hot Springs, South Dakota. Mary Garrett was born December 11, 1852, in Cook County, Illinois. She died April 3, 1932, at her home northeast of Wyodak. She was survived by two grandchildren: Tommy Garrett, of Rozet, and Mrs. Alta Shell, of Belle Fourche, South Dakota.

Sources:
Photo: From the collections of Leona and Jeanette Heptner.
Bureau of Land Management, Homestead Patents Index [www.glorecords.blm.gov].
"Aged Rozet Resident Dies at Hot Springs," The News Record, Gillette, Wyoming, March 12, 1931, page 1.
"Funeral Services Held for Mrs. Mary Garrett," page 1, The News Record, Gillette, Wyoming, April 7, 1932.
Ancestry.com, U.S. General Land Office Records, 1776-2015, [database online], Provo, UT.
Ancestry.com, U.S. National Homes for Disabled Volunteer Soldiers, 1866-1938, [database online], Provo, UT.
Ancestry.com, 1860 U.S. Federal Census for Mills County, Iowa, [database online], Provo, UT.
Ancestry.com, 1870 U.S. Federal Census for Holt County, Missouri, [database online], Provo, UT.
Ancestry.com, 1880 U.S. Federal Census for Holt County, Missouri, [database online], Provo, UT.
Ancestry.com, 1900 U.S. Federal Census for Hay Creek, Butte County, South Dakota, [database online], Provo, UT.
Ancestry.com, 1910 U.S. Federal Census for Precinct 16, Outside Moorcroft, Crook County, Wyoming, [database online], Provo, UT.
Ancestry.com, 1920 U.S. Federal Census for Election District #5, Rozet-North, Campbell County, Wyoming, [database online], Provo, UT.

Louis Hiram and Eva Blanche (Schofield) Hatfield
1917

Louis Hiram and Eva Blanche (Schofield) Hatfield arrived in Adon about 1917 from Burwell, Nebraska. Louis was born July 28, 1890, near Burwell, Nebraska, to Hiram L. and Sarah (Lewis) Hatfield. He and Eva were married on December 25, 1912, in Burwell, Nebraska. She was born September 17, 1894, the daughter of Marion E. and Sarah (Weatherby) Schofield. They continued to farm near Burwell until September 1919 when he decided to look for land in Campbell County, Wyoming. He filed on a homestead in the Adon community on what is now known as Cow Creek, located in Sections 21, 28, and 29, Township 53 North, Range 69 West. They returned to Burwell and in 1920 they came back to Adon with their three young sons and a newborn daughter. Louis and Eva became the parents of six children:

Garland Wilbur	b: 03 Jan 1914	d: 26 Sep 1943 *	
Douglas Everett	b: 25 Jul 1915	d: 26 Jan 1979	m: Alma Georgia Strausser
Emory V.	b: 14 May 1918	d: 14 Aug 1981	m: Leida Raudsep
Alta Emeline	b: 08 May 1920	d: 10 Apr 1980	m: John J. Means
Margaret L.	b: 06 May 1924	d: 07 Dec 2012	m: Dayton E. Allen
Ivan Leonard	b: 18 Jan 1928	d: 06 Jan 2000	m: Lillian Verna Clark

All four of their sons served in WWII. Louis and Eva lived on the ranch until 1979 when they moved to Gillette. Eva died in June 1981 and was buried in Mount Pisgah Cemetery on June 5, 1981. Louis moved into the Pioneer Manor Nursing Home in 1982. Louis died September 20, 1990, age 100. He was buried on September 24, 1990 in Mount Pisgah Cemetery, Gillette, Wyoming.

*died from an explosion at Naval Air Station, Norfolk, Virginia, serving in U.S. Navy.

Sources:
Photo: Ancestry.com, U.S. Find-a-Grave Index, 1600s-Current, [database online], Provo, UT.
Bureau of Land Management, Homestead Patent Index, [www.glorecords.blm.gov].
"Louis Hiram and Eva Blanche Hatfield," page 265, Campbell County, The Treasured Years, 1990, compiled by Campbell County Historical Society.
"Hatfield Funeral Friday," The News Record, Gillette, Wyoming, June 3, 1981.
Obituaries-Louis H. Hatfield," The News Record, Gillette, Wyoming, September 23, 1990.
Ancestry.com, Virginia, Death Records, 1912-2014, [database online], Provo, UT.
Ancestry.com, Newspapers.com Obituary Index, 1800s-current, [database online], Provo, UT.
Ancestry.com, U.S. Department of Veterans Affairs BIRLS Death File, 1850-2020, [database online], Provo, UT.
Ancestry.com, U.S. WWII Draft Cards Young Men 1940-1947, [database online], Provo, UT.
Ancestry.com, U.S. World /war II Army Enlistment Records, 1938-1946, [database online], Provo, UT.
Ancestry.com, Montana, County Marriage Records, 1865-1993, [database online], Provo, UT.

Ora Elvin and Sabitha Ellen (Burch) Moon
1917

Ora was born February 28, 1881, in Pickering, Missouri. Sabitha was born on March 23, 1879, at Wilcox, Missouri, to John and Martha Burch. She moved with her parents by covered wagon to Fort Collins, Colorado, when she was a small girl. She made three trips by covered wagon with her parents between Marysville, Missouri, and Fort Collins, Colorado. Ora and Sabitha Ellen Burch were married on October 15, 1904, at Marysville, Missouri. They were the parents of four children:

Clara B.   b: 29 Apr 1905 d: 01 Nov 1998 m: (1) Frank H. Granger
                                                    (2) Lee Silvester

Albert Russell b: 16 Nov 1906 d: 07 Apr 1986 m: Ruth Shafer
Addie Marie   b: 01 Aug 1908 d: 1997 m: Earl Jacob Rush
George Vonley b: 10 Jun 1910 d: 18 May 1991 m: Zina Verzella Owens

Before coming to the Rozet area in 1913, the family made their home at Braddyville, Iowa. Soon after their arrival Ora filed for a homestead south of Rozet on Sections 10 and 15, Township 49 North, Range 70 West. Ora E. died in June 10, 1933, from tick fever complications. He was buried at Mount Pisgah Cemetery. Sabitha made her home with her daughter, Mrs. Clara Silvester, at Imperial, Nebraska, and later moved to Sidney, Nebraska. Sabitha died March 3, 1958, at Sidney, Nebraska. She was buried on March 4, 1958, next to her husband in Mount Pisgah Cemetery, Gillette, Wyoming.

Top to Bottom
Clara B., Sabitha, Marie, Ora,
Russ, and George Moon about 1917

Sources:
Photo: Courtesy of Gayle Moon Parish, Buhl, Idaho.
Bureau of Land Management, Homestead Patent Index, [www.glorecords.blm.gov].
"Moon-Granger Marriage," The News Record, Gillette, Wyoming, April 12, 1928.
"Rush-Moon Nuptials on Sunday," The News Record, Gillette, Wyoming, June 6, 1929.
"O. E. Moon, First Victim of Tick Fever this Season, Passes Away Sat," The News Record, Gillette, Wyoming, June 15, 1933.
"Funeral Services Held Tuesday for Mrs. O. E. Moon, 79," page 1, The News Record, Gillette, Wyoming, March 6, 1958.
"Albert (Russell) Moon Service Held," The News Record, Gillette, Wyoming, April 20, 1986, page 14.
Ancestry.com, U.S. Find-a-Grave Index, 1600s-Current, [database online], Provo, UT.
Ancestry.com, Iowa Delayed Birth Records, 1856-1940, [database online], Provo, UT.
Ancestry.com, 1920 U.S. Federal Census for Rozet-South, Precinct #26, Campbell County, Wyoming, [database online], Provo, UT.

Leo Otto "Lee" and Gladys (Fear) Ridenour
1917

Lee Ridenour was born October 26, 1892, in Broken Bow, Custer County, Nebraska, to Oliver Ambrose and Margaret (Armada) Ridenour. He and his brother, Clinton, came to Campbell County, Wyoming, from Holdrege, Phillips County, Nebraska, in 1914. He filed for a homestead in Sections 8, 9, and 17, Township 49 North, Range 69 West, south of Rozet, Wyoming. Lee served in WWI. He enlisted in the U.S. Army on July 12, 1918, in Gillette, Wyoming and received his discharge in Kansas on November 15, 1918. On April 16, 1919, he married Gladys Fear at North Platte, Lincoln County, Nebraska. Gladys was born December 6, 1901, in Fremont, Dodge County, Nebraska, to William E. and Anna M. (Brittendall) Fear. She graduated from high school in Schuyler, Colfax County, Nebraska. When Lee and Gladys came to Wyoming they worked on the Stevenson Ranch near Moorcroft. Later they moved to the homestead. About 1925 they sold their homestead and purchased a ranch one mile south of Rozet which became the family home. Lee was employed by the C. B&Q Railroad until 1927. Their baby daughter, Carolyn who was born and died on December 11, 1926, was buried in Pleasant Valley Cemetery, nine miles northeast of Rozet, Wyoming. Lee both farmed and raised cattle with the help of his two oldest sons. Through the years Lee served as a member of the District Three School Board and was active in the Farmers Union and the American Legion. Lee and Gladys Ridenour were the parents of nine children:

Fern Opal	b: 03 Apr 1920	d: 01 Dec 1999	m: (1) John D. Fittro
			(2) Bud Hoffman
Kathryn Mildred	b: 10 Oct 1922	d: 07 Jul 2014	m: (1) Charles Vergith
			(2) Edwin Moran
Alta Pauline	b: 30 Oct 1924	d: 2010	m: Bruce Baker Welch
Carolyn	b: 11 Dec 1926	d: 11 Dec 1926	
Ruth Frances	b: 12 Dec 1928	d: 20 May 2017	m: James Richard Mankin
Gerald Allen "Jerry"	b: 25 Mar 1930	d: 20 Mar 1963	m: Audrey Jean Robing
Harold Alvin	b: 03 Dec 1931	d: 16 Jul 1981	m:: (1) Helen Dewey
			(2) Annette Bird
Rosa	b: 1933	d:	m: (1) Donald Patton
			(2) _____ Benallo
Michael Franklin "Mickey"	b: 05 Aug 1946	d:	m: (1) Linda Thompson
			(2) Louise Beverly Wilke

Gladys with Fern and Kay in 1923.

They lived on the family home until Lee's death on April 24, 1961. Gladys moved to Gillette in 1964 where she lived until she moved to Malta, Montana in 1974. In 1986 Gladys moved to the Cascade County Nursing Home in Great Falls, Montana, where she died on October 28, 1989. Both Lee and Gladys are buried in Mount Pisgah Cemetery, Gillette, Wyoming, near their son Jerry Ridenour who died March 20, 1963, when a farm hay stacker he was driving went off a bridge on the Bishop Road six miles south of Rozet. In 1981 their son Harold and his stepson, Chris Bird, were shot while on a fishing trip to the Big Horn Mountains above Buffalo, Wyoming. Harold and Chris were buried in the Rozet Cemetery, Rozet, Wyoming.

Ridenour Ranch - 1940

Sources:
Photos: Courtesy of Corina Heptner Allen, Gillette, Wyoming, 2018; Jannelle Mankin, Gillette, Wyoming, 2020; Mickey Ridenour, 2020.
Bureau of Land Management, Homestead Patent Index, [www.glorecords.blm.gov].
"Farm Accident Claims Life of Leo O. Ridenour," The News Record, Gillette, Wyoming, April 7, 1961.
"Final Rites for Accident Victim, Jerry Ridenour," The News Record, Gillette, Wyoming, March 28, 1963.
"Obituary-Helen Dewing Ridenour," page 12, The News Record, Gillette, Wyoming, March 1, 1977.
"Obituary-Harold Ridenour," page 16, The News Record, Gillette, Wyoming, July 21, 1981.
"Obituary-Gladys Ridenour,", The News Record, Gillette, Wyoming, November 1, 1989.
Pleasant Valley Cemetery Burial Book, kept by Mrs. Lucille Thompson (Xeroxed 1998).
Campbell County Cemetery District, Burial Report for Mount Pisgah Cemetery, Gillette, Wyoming, and Rozet Cemetery, 1998.
Ancestry.com, U.S. Find-a-Grave Index, 1600s-Current, [database online], Provo, UT.
Ancestry.com, U.S. Social Security Death Index, 1935-2014, [database online], Provo, UT.
Ancestry.com, U.S. World War I Draft Registration Cards, 1917-1918, [database online], Provo, UT.
Ancestry.com, U.S. World War II Draft Registration Cards, 1942, [database online], Provo, UT.
Ancestry.com, U.S. Veterans' Gravesites, ca.1775-2019, [database online], Provo, UT.
Ancestry.com, 1900 U.S. Federal Census for Custer, Custer County, Nebraska, [database online], Provo, UT.
Ancestry.com, 1920 U.S. Federal Census for Election District 16, Crook County, Wyoming, [database online], Provo, UT.
Ancestry.com, 1930 U.S. Federal Census for Election District 5, Campbell County, Wyoming, [database online], Provo, UT.
Ancestry.com, 1940 U.S. Federal Census for Campbell County, Wyoming, [database online], Provo, UT.

Leslie Burton and Sarah Elizabeth (Benesh) Riley
1917

Leslie Riley was born June 1, 1885, near Cedar Rapids, Linn County, Iowa, to Andrew Jackson and Clara (Williams) Riley. He spent his early years there. Sarah Elizabeth Benesh, born December 13, 1888, in Iowa County, Iowa, to Frank and Sara Jane Benesh. She grew up near Shellsburg, Iowa. Leslie and Sarah were married in February 1909 in Superior, Iowa. They lived at several different locations in South Dakota and northern Iowa before Leslie came to Rozet in March 1917 from Superior, Iowa, on an emigrant train with household furniture, farm machinery, four cows, and two horses. Upon arriving at Rozet he filed on a homestead in Sections 26 and 35, Township 51 North, Range 70 West located about eight miles north of Rozet on the Adon Road. Sarah and four children traveled by passenger train to Moorcroft, Wyoming, where they transferred to the local train and rode to Rozet in the caboose, arriving on May 28,

Leslie Riley in front of his homestead house with his children.

1917. Their first house was a dugout in the side of a hill. It was one room with a cement floor. The second year they built a new house with two rooms, one up and one down. There was no source of water on the place, so they hauled water in barrels on the lumber wagon from the Heptner place three miles east. Leslie and Sarah were the parents of five children:

Doris Evelyn	b: 28 May 1910	d: 13 Jun 1994	m: Edgar "Brick" Goodykoontz
Ione Elizabeth	b: 05 Jan 1912	d: 16 Apr 1935	m: Raymond Schlattmann
Marvel Edris	b: 24 Dec 1913	d: 24 Jul 2007	m: Arvid "Harvey" Schlattmann
Thaine Gilbert	b: 12 Nov 1915	d: 10 Mar 2009	m:
Sylvia	b: 29 Jun 1924	d :	m: John M. Spangler

Doris and Ione went to the Deer Creek School three miles northwest of their homestead when weather permitted. After living on the homestead the required three years for "proving up," Leslie sold it to William Kuehne whose land joined them on the east. For the next five years they lived on rented places north of Rozet. It was while they were living in the Little Iowa community that their youngest child was born, Sylvia Jane, in June 1924. Leslie and Sarah were divorced in 1933. She married Alfred Glassley in 1947, and they lived in Edgemont, South Dakota, for several years until she returned to live in Gillette, Wyoming. Sarah Glassley sold her home in Gillette in 1972 and moved to Worland, Wyoming, to live near her daughter Sylvia Spangler. In 1980 she moved once again to the Pioneer Home in Thermopolis, Wyoming, where she remained alert and in good health until her death.

Leslie died in April 1956, age 70, and was buried in the Pleasant Valley Cemetery alongside his daughter Ione Riley Schlattmann who had died April 18, 1935, age 23, of pneumonia. She was buried with her baby son, Gary Lee, who was born and died in March 1935. Sarah Glassley died on June 21, 1986, at age 97, in Basin, Wyoming. She was buried in Pleasant Valley Cemetery alongside her first husband, Leslie Riley, and her daughter Ione.

Riley Homestead Barn

1946
Eugene Heptner on the binder, Leslie Riley on the John Deere
binding wheat on the Riley place north of Rozet

Sources:

Photos: From the Leona and Jeanette Heptner collections.

Campbell County, The Treasured Years, 1990, Page 487, compiled by Campbell County Historical Society, Gillette, Wyoming.

Bureau of Land Management, Homestead Patent Index, [www.glorecords.blm.gov].

"The Rileys of Rozet," page 487, Campbell County, The Treasured Years, 1991, compiled by Campbell County Historical Society, Gillette, Wyoming.

Pleasant Valley Cemetery Burial Book, kept by Mrs. Lucille Thompson (Xeroxed Copy-1998).

"Doris Riley-Goodykoontz," Society, The News Record, Gillette, Wyoming, Aug 25, 1932.

"Riley-Schlattmann marriage," The News Record, Gillette Wyoming, December 27, 1934.

"Mrs. Schlattmann of Rozet Succumbs to Pneumonia Attack," The News Record, Gillette, Wyoming, April 17, 1935.

"Glassley Service Held Tuesday," The Campbell County Record, Gillette, Wyoming, June 27, 1986.

"Riley's Rozet History," compiled by Marvel (Riley) Schlattmann, Spring 1988.

Ancestry.com, Iowa, Select Marriages Index, 1758-1996, [database online], Provo, UT.

Ancestry.com, 1920 U.S. Federal Census for Election District #8, Iowa Precinct, Campbell County, Wyoming; [database online] Provo, UT.

Ancestry.com, 1930 U.S. Federal Census for Election District 5, Campbell County, Wyoming, [database online]. Provo, UT.

Ancestry.com, Iowa, Select Marriages, 1758-1996, [database online]. Provo, UT.

Richard Virgil "Dick and Mae (Hamill) Talley
1917

World War I Veteran

Mae Talley

Richard Talley was born October 22, 1893 in Butte County, South Dakota, to Joseph C. and Emma Talley. He grew up in and worked for various ranches in the South Dakota area. When he came to Wyoming is not known, but he was here by 1917 when he entered his occupation as cowpuncher on his World War I Draft registration card. He also stated he was currently working for the Whitcomb estate on the Whitcomb ranch south east of Rozet. He had also filed for a homestead about 1915 located on Sections 25 and 32, in Township 49 North, Range 69 West, and Section 5, in Township 48 North, Range 69 West.

Richard and Mae Hamill were married about 1920 in Gillette, Campbell County, Wyoming. Mae was born on May 1, 1900, in Oklahoma Territory to John Newton and Maggie E. (Culver) Hamill. Her mother and baby brother John Robert died at his birth in 1904. In 1907 her father married Mary E. (Lyons) Williams, a widow with two young children. Mae came to Wyoming with her father and stepmother in 1915. Richard and Mae were the parents of two children:

John Vernon	b: 04 Dec 1922	d: 16 Sep 2016	m: Ruth (DeWolf) Gauthier
Phyllis Evelyn	b: 24 Jan 1925	d: 24 Apr 1994	m: (1) Carl Bechtold
			(2) John E. Walsh

The children attended Rozet Consolidated School and graduated from Rozet High School. Richard Talley died in July 22, 1972, in Gillette, Wyoming. He was buried in the Black Hills National Cemetery, Sturgis, Meade County, South Dakota. Mae Talley died in December 29, 1982. She was buried in the Mount Pisgah Cemetery, Gillette, Wyoming.

Dick Talley, about 1923

Sources:
Photos: Ancestry.com, Hobson Family Tree; Ancestry.com, James Arthur Murphy Family Tree.
Bureau of Land Management, Homestead Patent Index, [www.glorecords.blm.gov].
Ancestry.com, U.S. General Land Office Records, 1776-2015, [database online], Provo, UT.
"Funeral Services Held Thursday for J. N. Hamill, 80," The News Record, Gillette, Wyoming, April 1, 1950.
"Phyllis E. Walsh obituary," The News Record, Gillette, Wyoming, May 11, 1994.
Ancestry.com, U.S. Social Security Death Index 1935-1998, [database online], Provo, UT.
Ancestry.com, U.S. Find-a-Grave Index, 1600s-Current, [database online], Provo, UT.
Ancestry.com, U.S. Veterans' Gravesites, ca. 1775-2019, [database online], Provo, UT.
Ancestry.com, U.S. Army Transport Service, Passenger Lists, 1910-1939, [database online], Provo, UT.
Ancestry.com, U.S. World War I Draft Registration Cards, 1917-1918, [database online], Provo, UT.
Ancestry.com, U.S. World War II Draft Registration Cards, 1942, [database online], Provo, UT.
Ancestry.com, 1900 U.S. Federal Census for Empire, Butte County, South Dakota, [database online], Provo, UT.
Ancestry.com, 1930 U.S. Federal Census for Election District 5, Campbell County, Wyoming, [database online], Provo, UT.
Ancestry.com, 1940 U.S. Federal Census for Campbell County, Wyoming, [database online], Provo, UT.

Raymond "Ray" and Etha Lucille (Moffitt) Thomas
1917

Ray and Etha Lucille came to Wyoming to join his brothers Elmer and George and their families living southeast of Rozet in 1917. He filed for a homestead in Sections 2, 3, and 4, Township 47 North, Range 70 North, and Section 34, Township 48 North, Range 70 West. They built their house on a knoll against a bank, approximately one-fourth mile north of the county road (now called the Bishop Road) and a mile from the Belle Fourche River near Piney Creek. A post office was established there, with Lucille Thomas as the postmistress. Ray was born January 17, 1891, at Mifflin, Wisconsin, to John F. and Mary (Hart) Thomas. As a child the family moved to Afton, Iowa, where he received his education. He married Etha Lucille Moffitt, the daughter of Edwin and Margaret Moffitt, on October 7, 1917, in Afton, Union County, Iowa. Lucille was born September 4, 1893, in Afton, Iowa. Ray and Lucille were the parents of four children:

Kenneth Cam	b: 19 Oct 1919	d: 26 Dec 1990	m: Dorothy Middaugh
Shirley Jane	b: 1920s	d: 1920s (buried on the homestead)	
*Carol Lee Thomas	b: 24 Dec 1927	d: 12 Mar 2018	m: 1) Delbert Weese
			2) Harry Turner
			3) Kenneth Irish
Donna Roberta	b: 13 Jan 1931	d: 09 Jun 2002	m: Richard "Dick" Blakeman

The children attended the Piney School until it and the post office were closed. Then they went to the Enterprise School, 12 miles away for grades 1-8, to Rozet or Gillette for high school. Ray and Lucille decided to sell their home in the early 1940s and moved to Gillette, Wyoming. Lucille died July 3, 1965, in Sheridan, Wyoming. She was buried in Mount Pisgah Cemetery, Gillette, Wyoming. Ray died February 22, 1970, and was buried in Mount Pisgah Cemetery.

* Ray and Lucille's niece. Her mother Bertha Thomas died from scarlet fever on December 29, 1927, five days after Carol's birth. See page 126.

Sources:
Bureau of Land Management, Homestead Patent Index, [www.glorecords.blm.gov].
Ancestry.com, U.S. General Land Office Records, 1776-2015, [database online] Provo, UT.
"Ray and Lucille Thomas," page 595, Campbell County, The Treasured Years, 1990, compiled by Campbell County Historical Society, Gillette, Wyoming.
"Funeral Service Held Tuesday for Mrs. Ray Thomas," The News Record, Gillette, Wyoming, July 8, 1965.
"Thomas Dies February 22," The News Record, Gillette, Wyoming, February 25, 1970.
Carol Lee Turner-Irish of Gillette, Wyoming 1927-2018, www.walkerfuneralgillette.com.
Ancestry.com, Iowa, U.S. Select Marriages Index, 1758-1996, [database online] Provo, UT.
Ancestry.com, 1900 U.S. Federal Census for Pleasant, Union County, Iowa, [database online] Provo, UT.
Ancestry.com, 1910 U.S. Federal Census for Union, Union County, Iowa, [database online] Provo, UT.
Ancestry.com, 1920 U.S. Federal Census for Bar F. S. Campbell County, Wyoming (Ray), [database online] Provo, UT.
Ancestry.com, 1920 U.S. Federal Census for Afton, Union, Iowa, (Lucille), [database online] Provo, UT.
Ancestry.com, 1930 U.S. Federal Census for Election District 20, Campbell County, Wyoming, [database online] Provo, UT.
Ancestry.com, 1940 U.S. Federal Census for Campbell County, Wyoming, [database online] Provo, UT.

Rev. Henry A. and Emma (Correll) Toland
1917

Reverend and Mrs. Henry Toland

Henry was a missionary pastor of the Methodist Church. He was born on February 18, 1852, in Clebourne, Texas, to Dr. John M. and Mary Toland who had moved to Texas for their health. Shortly after his birth his parents died leaving him an orphan. At the age of 18 he entered Lewis College at Glasco, Missouri, and was ordained to the ministry in 1873. His first pastorage was at High Point, Missouri. On September 14, 1882 Henry married Emma C. Correll at Wooster, Wayne County, Ohio. Two children were born:

Joseph E. b: 24 Sep 1883 in Missouri   d: 29 Sep 1967   m: Lenor "Lena" Lendoll
Ona D.   b: 23 Apr 1893 in Nebraska   d: 08 Jan 1992   m: Laurence Gunstrum

A year after their marriage they returned to Missouri where their son Joseph was born on September 24, 1883. They came to Wyoming in 1892. Their daughter, Ona was born April 23, 1892, in Marshland, Nebraska, on their way to Clearmont, Wyoming, that then marked the end of the Burlington rails into Wyoming. At Clearmont they traveled by wagon to Buffalo, Wyoming. The 1900 U.S. Federal Census finds them living in St. Anthony, Fremont County, Idaho. By 1910 they were back in Wyoming living in Sheridan, Wyoming. Rev. Toland served as a missionary pastor traveling over almost impossible trails, driving or traveling horseback through snow drifts and zero weather to reach the communities which he served. He served at Buffalo, Casper, and Big Horn. Later as a supply pastor he served Evanston, Upton, and Hyattville where he built a church, and he spent several years in the mining community of Dietz. Rev. Toland was the pastor in the Rozet community during the years of 1917-1920. Services were held in homes or possibly the Rozet schoolhouse. Rev Toland retired from the ministry in 1920 and with the exception of three winters spent in Florida the Toland's made their home in Sheridan, Wyoming. In 1921 the Rozet Protestant Community Church was organized. (See page 241 for a brief history of this church.)

Rev Toland's son, Joseph, was issued a homestead on Township 50 North, Range 70 West, Section 35 S1/2 on April 14, 1919. His daughter Ona was issued a homestead on August 26, 1921, for SE ¼ SW ¼, of Section 2, Range 70 West, Township 49 North, and again on February 3, 1922, for SE ¼ NE ¼, E ½ NW ¼, W ½NE ¼ , in Section 11.

Emma Correll Toland died on October 14, 1933, at the age of 81; Rev Toland died seven years later on May 16, 1940. Both are buried in the Sheridan Municipal Cemetery, Sheridan, Sheridan County, Wyoming.

Sources:
Photo: *Ancestry.com, U.S Find A Grave Index, 1600s-Current, [database online], Provo, UT.*
Ancestry.com, Ohio, County Marriage Records, 1774-1993, [database online], Provo, UT.
Ancestry.com, 1900 U.S. Federal Census for Fremont County, Idaho, [database online], Provo, UT.
Ancestry.com,, U.S. General Land Office Records, 1776-2015, [database online], Provo, UT.

Samuel K. and Hattie (Black) Weaver
1917

Sam Weaver was born August 25, 1877, in Hardin County, Iowa, to Joseph and Mary Weaver. On March 26, 1902, he married Hattie Jeannette Black in Palo Alto, Iowa. She was born April 12, 1884, in Oshkosh, Winnebago County, Wisconsin. They made their home in Richland, Keokuk County, Iowa. They were the parents of seven children:

Hattie Josephine	b: 02 May 1903	d: 05 Dec 1997	m: Ray Chester Bryant (div)
Nyle Samuel	b: 07 Oct 1904	d: 22 Oct 1952	m: Faye Johnson
Mary Estella	b: 13 Dec 1905	d: 24 Jan 1996	m: (1) George Obe Nelson
			(2) Gordon LeRoy Crabill
LeRoy Eugene	b:17 Oct 1907	d: 14 Jun 1954	m: Opal _____
Lottie Augusta	b:13 Feb 1909	d: 01 Aug 2001	m: (1)
			(2) Max E. Elder
Joseph Black	b: 10 Feb 1912	d: 16 Aug 1993	m: Thelma Ellen Hoxsie
Allen Lynn Garland	b: 21 Apr 1913	d: 28 Oct 1918	

Sam came to Wyoming in the spring of 1917 to look the state over. Returning to Lake Okabogee, Iowa, he moved his wife Hattie and their seven children to Rozet in July 1917. They followed the Black and Yellow Trail with two covered wagons carrying the family and their belongings. The milk cows followed their wagons which were milked three times a day for fresh milk. When the Weavers arrived at Sundance, Mr. Weaver paid for his filing fees, after which they had $1.35 left. Sam Weaver filed for a homestead in 1916 located in Section 32, Township 51 North, Range 69 West, eight miles north of Rozet in the Little Iowa community. Their home on the homestead was partly dug in the bank with rocks along the sides and a roof. There was a floor in the kitchen, which was larger than the rest of the house. The Spanish influenza epidemic of 1918-1919 took the life of their youngest son, Allen Lynn. He was buried in Pleasant Valley Cemetery, Rozet, Campbell County, Wyoming. Sam and Hattie Weaver sold their homestead after 1935 and moved to Washington County, Oregon, for a short time before moving to Whitefish, Flathead County, Montana. Sam died on January 10, 1950, in Whitefish, Montana; Hattie died March 10, 1959. Both are buried in the Whitefish Cemetery, Whitefish, Montana.

Sources:
Photos: from the collections of Leona and Jeanette Heptner.
Bureau of Land Management, Homestead Patent Index, [www.glorecords.blm.gov].
"Departed (Allen Linn Weaver)," Campbell County Record, Gillette, Wyoming, November 14, 1918.
"Bryant-Weaver Nuptials," Campbell County Record, Gillette, Wyoming, December 16, 1920.
"Married (Nelson-Weaver)," The News Record, Gillette, Wyoming, July 1, 1926.
"Johnson-Weaver Marriage," The News Record, Gillette, Wyoming, July 5, 1928.
"Weaver-Hoxsie marriage," The News Record, Gillette, Wyoming, December 27, 1934.
"The Clay Weaver Family," page 622-623, Campbell County, The Treasured Years, 1990, compiled by Campbell County Historical Society.
"Josephine Bryant," The News Record, Gillette, Wyoming, Dec 14, 1997.
Pleasant Valley Cemetery Burial Book, (Allen Lynn Weaver) kept by Mrs. Lucille Thompson (Xeroxed Copy-1998).
Ancestry.com, U.S. Find-a-Grave Index, 1600s-Current, (Linn Garland Weaver) [database online], Provo, UT.
Ancestry.com, Iowa, Marriage Records, 1880-1940, [database online], Provo, UT.
Ancestry.com, U.S. World War II Draft Registration Cards, 1942, [database online], Provo, UT.
Ancestry.com, 1900 U.S. Federal Census for Eldora, Hardin County, Iowa, [database online], Provo, UT.
Ancestry.com, 1910 U.S. Federal Census for Richland, Dickinson, Iowa, [database online], Provo, UT.
Ancestry.com, (1915) Iowa, U.S. Federal Census Collections, 1836-1925, [database-online], Provo, UT.
Ancestry.com, 1920 Federal Census for Campbell County, Election District #8, Iowa Precinct, Wyoming, [database online], Provo, UT.
Ancestry.com, 1930 U.S. Federal Census for Election District 5, Campbell County, Wyoming, [database online], Provo, UT.

Herschel Coventry Mapes
1918

Herschel Coventry Mapes was born on February 1, 1893, Rogers, Colfax County, Nebraska, to Lewis Sherman and Mary Christina (Coventry) Mapes. At the age of 25 he came to Campbell County, Wyoming where he filed for a homestead on May 8, 1918, located about eight miles north of Rozet on Sections 14, 15, 22, and 23, Township 52 North, Range 70 West. That fall he was drafted into the U.S. Army. Herschel served in World War I from October 2, 1918, to December 20, 1918, with 9th Recruit, Co. GLI, in Fort Logan, Colorado. He was honorably discharged.

Herschel returned to Rozet where he remained until his death. The 1940 Federal Census records him as owning a ranch and working for himself. He never married. Herschel died March 23, 1961, Gillette, Wyoming. His body was taken to Fremont, Nebraska, where he was buried near his parents in the Memorial Cemetery, Fremont, Dodge County, Nebraska.

[Note from the author: I remember him as a good neighbor who always came to help my father when it was time to thrash grain. I can still see him coming up the road with his team of horses pulling a hay wagon to pick up the bundles of grain in the fields to take them to the thrashing machine. – ljw]

Sources:
Bureau of Land Management, Homestead Patent Index, [www.glorecords.blm.gov].
Ancestry.com, Vital Records: Social Security Death Index, 1937-1998, [database online], Provo, UT.
Ancestry.com, U.S. Find-a-Grave Index, 1600s-Current, [database online], Provo, UT.
Ancestry.com, Newspapers.com Obituary Index, 1800-current, [database online], Provo, UT.
Ancestry.com, U.S. Social Security Applications and Claims Index, 1936-2007, [database online], Provo, UT.
Ancestry.com, U.S. Headstone Applications for Military Veterans, 1925-1963, [database online], Provo, UT.
Ancestry.com, U.S. World War I Draft Registration Cards, 1817-1918, [database online], Provo, UT.
Ancestry.com, U.S. World War II Draft Registration Cards, 1942, [database online], Provo, UT.
Ancestry.com, 1900 U.S. Federal Census for Inman, Holt County, Nebraska, [database online], Provo, UT.
Ancestry.com, 1910 U.S. Federal Census for Rogers, Colfax County, Nebraska, [database online], Provo, UT.
Ancestry.com, 1920 U.S. Federal Census for Iowa, Campbell County, Wyoming, [database online],Provo, UT.
Ancestry.com, 1930 U.S. Federal Census for Lincoln, Lancaster County, Nebraska (as a lodger), [database online], Provo, UT.
Ancestry.com, 1940 U.S. Federal census for Campbell County, Wyoming, [database online], Provo, UT.

Gaston Otto and Sarah (Scrivens) McCurdy
1918

"Otto" McCurdy was born on May 21, 1883, in Kansas City, Wyandotte County, Kansas, to Charles and Eliza Jane (Foster) McCurdy. On May 21, 1910, he married Sarah Belle Scrivens, in Jackson county, Missouri. Four children were born prior to their decision to go to Wyoming to homestead. They arrived in Rozet about 1918 where he filed on a homestead located in Sections 21, 11, 27, and 28 of Township 51 North, Range 70 West. Four more children were born:

Mary Bell	b: 04 Sep 1911	d: 29 Apr 2008	m: Edgar Nichols
Tessie E.	b: 29 Dec 1912	d: 03 Aug 2002	m: Herman Jenkins
Genevieve	b: 29 Apr 1914	d: 23 Jul 1996	m: Elgin Martin Baston
Helen Louise	b: 27 Sep 1916	d: 05 Nov 1992	m: James Howard Dowdy
Dorothy	b: 21 Feb 1918	d: 1984	m: Foster Weaver
Irvin Otto	b: 07 Feb 1925	d: 15 Jul 1989	
Virl O.	b: Sep 1919	d: Nov 1920 (after accidentally being scalded with hot water)	
Pauline E.	b: 07 Mar 1928	d: 09 Mar 1929	

Irvin, Sarah and Pauline

Newspaper records indicate that Otto moved his family in 1923 to Deaver, Big Horn County, Wyoming, where he worked in a hardware and lumber company. Their last child, Pauline, was born on March 7, 1928, but only lived a year. She was taken back to Campbell County, Wyoming, where she was buried next to her brother Virl in Pleasant Valley Cemetery, Rozet, Wyoming.

Although her gravestone reads otherwise, it has been concluded (see note below) that Pauline Evelyn was born March 7, 1928, possibly in Deaver, Big Horn County, Wyoming, and died March 9, 1929. Both Virl and Pauline were buried at Pleasant Valley Cemetery. Campbell County, Wyoming. The 1940 Census records indicate their parents and five sisters, Mary, Jessie, Genevieve, Helen, and Dorothy, and their youngest son Irvin were living in Cody, Park County, Wyoming, where Otto worked as a manager and a bookkeeper in a hardware and lumber Company. Later the family moved to King County, Washington, where Gaston died in 1963; wife Sarah in 1974. Both were buried in the Mount Pleasant Cemetery, Seattle, King County, Washington.

[Note: Pauline's gravestone in Pleasant Valley Cemetery reads: "Pauline McCurdy Mar 7, 1929 – Mar 9, 1929." Description of photo of Pauline Evelyn McCurdy, her brother, Irvin, and her mother, Sarah, on Ancestry.com, Find-a-Grave, 1600s –Current stated: "Sarah (Scrivens) McCurdy holding her youngest daughter, Pauline Evelyn McCurdy, and holding the hand of her youngest son, Irvin Alfred McCurdy, late summer or early fall 1928". Email received 9/18/2017 from the person who had posted the photos on the Find-a-Grave Index of Virl and Pauline states Pauline was born Mar 7, 1928 and died Mar 9, 1929. Unfortunately, the statement did not include where the photo was taken. Death records indicate Irvin was born in 1925, in Deaver, Big Horn County. Wyoming. Photo of Pauline for this book has been cropped from that photo.]

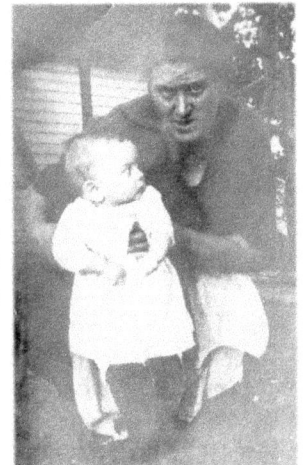

Virl O. McCurdy

Sources:
Photos: Ancestry.com, U.S. Find-a-Grave Index, 1600s-Current, (photos), [database online], Provo, UT.
Bureau of Land Management, Homestead Patent Index, [www.glorecords.blm.gov].
Email Message received 9/18/2017 re: birth/death dates for Pauline.
"Local News Column 'death of Virl McCurdy,'" Campbell County Record, Gillette, Wyoming, November 25, 1920.
Pleasant Valley Cemetery Burial Book, kept by Mrs. Lucille Thompson (Xeroxed Copy-1998).
Ancestry.com, Missouri, Marriage Records, 1805-2002, [database online], Provo, UT.
Ancestry.com, U.S. Social Security Applications and Claims Index, 1936-2007, [database online], Provo, UT.
Ancestry.com, U.S. Find-a-Grave Index,, 1600s-Current (Photos,), [database online], Provo, UT.
Ancestry.com, 1920 U.S. Federal Census for Campbell County, Wyoming, Rozet-South Precinct #26, taken February 1920.
  [handwriting almost illegible], [database online], Provo, UT.
Ancestry.com, 1940 U.S. Federal Census for Cody, Park County, Wyoming, [database online], Provo, UT.

Julia (Gilsenan/Gilson) Moran
1918

Julia Gilsenan Moran was born about 1835 in Ireland. On March 22, 1852, at the age of 17, she stepped off the ship Niagara into the port of New York, New York city. Her occupation was listed as servant. In the 1860 U.S. Federal Census we find her living in the household of W. T. Moak in Watertown, Jefferson County, Wisconsin, working as a servant. Julia married Patrick Moran about 1866. Patrick was born March 1842 in Blanchardstown. Dublin County, Ireland, to Joseph and Mary (Creagin) Moran. In 1851, at the age of 9 years he immigrated to America from Ireland to Walworth County, Wisconsin where we find him, age 18, in the 1860 U. Federal Census working as a farm laborer. Patrick and Julia became the parents of eight children:

Laura Margaret	b: 10 Feb 1868	d: 22 Oct 1959	m: Edwin Thomas Reid
Joseph T.	b: 1869	d: 1895	
Katherine Elizabeth	b: Dec 1870	d: 01 Jan 1969	m: Albert T. Hunt
Hugh William	b: 20 Oct 1873	d: 27 Oct 1948	m: _____
Henry	b: 1875	d: 03 Jan 1876	
Frances Julia	b: 16 May 1876	d: 15 Feb 1950	m: Charles B. Keplinger
Mary Ida	b: 1880	d: 04 Feb 1901	
Albert James "Bert"	b: 07 Jul 1881	d: 13 May 1958	m: Blanche Elsie Cook

After their second child, Joseph, was born Patrick and Julia left Wisconsin for Cerro Gordo County, Iowa, where they lived until the late 1890's when they moved to Butte, Silver Bow County, Montana. Patrick worked as a teamster with the copper mines. Patrick died August 8, 1906, from a runaway wagon accident. He was buried in the Saint Patrick's Cemetery, Butte, Montana. It appears that Julia left Montana about 1908 for Rushville, Sheridan County, Nebraska, along with Bert, her youngest child, and his wife Blanche Cook. They married in February 1907, in Lead, Lawrence County, South Dakota, and according to a local Lawrence County news item were returning to Butte, Montana, to live. However for whatever reasons, their plans changed. Bert and Blanche's first child, Neta, was born in 1909 in Rushville, Sheridan County, Nebraska.

Julia Moran and her son Bert moved to Rozet from Rushville, Nebraska, about 1918. Julia filed for a homestead March 5, 1918, located southwest of Rozet in Sections 10, 11, and 12, Township 49 North, Range 70 West. Her son, Bert, filed on Sections 13 and 14, Township 49 North, Range 70 West. She sold her homestead in October 1922 and moved to Omaha, Douglas County, Nebraska, to live near her daughter Margaret and her family. Julia died July 25, 1930, in Omaha. She was buried in the Holy Sepulcher Cemetery, Omaha, Douglas County, Nebraska.

Sources:
Bureau of Land Management, Homestead Patent Index, [www.glorecords.blm.gov].
Ancestry.com, U.S. General Land Office Records, 1776-2015, [database online], Provo, UT.
Ancestry.com, U.S. General Land Office Records, 1776-2015), [database online]. Provo, UT.
Ancestry.com, Ireland, Catholic Parish Registers, 1655-1915, (Patrick baptism), [database online]. Provo, UT.
Ancestry.com, State of Montana, Bureau of vital Statistics Certificate of death (Patrick), [database online]. Provo, UT.
Ancestry.com, U.S. Find a Grave Index, 1600s-Current, [database online]. Provo, UT.
Ancestry.com, U.S. Find a Grave Index, 1600a-Current, ,[database online], Provo, UT, (Mary Ida Moran, age 21).
Ancestry.com, New York, U.S. Arriving Passenger and Crew Lists (including Castle Garden and Ellis Island), 1820-1957,
        [database online]. Provo, UT (Julia Gilsenan).
Ancestry.com, 1860 U.S. Federal Census for Watertown, Jefferson County, WI, [database online].Provo, UT, (Julia).
Ancestry.com, 1860 U.S. Federal Census for Darien, Walworth County, WI, [database online], Provo, UT, (Patrick).
Ancestry.com, 1870 U.S. Federal Census for Geneseo, Cerro Gordo County, Iowa, [database online]. Provo, UT.
Ancestry.com,,1880 U.S. Federal Census for Dougherty, Cerro Gordo County, Iowa, [database online]. Provo, UT.
Ancestry.com, 1900 U.S. Federal Census for Butte Ward 8, Silver Bow County, MT, [database online]. Provo, UT.
Ancestry.com, 1930 U.S. Federal Census for Omaha, Douglas County, NB, [database online]. Provo, UT, (Julia).
Rozet Items, Campbell County Record, October 19, 1922.

Albert James 'Bert' and Blanche Elsie (Cook) Moran
1918

Albert James "Bert" Moran was born July 7, 1881, at Mason City, Cerro Gordo County, Iowa, to Patrick and Julia (Gilshen) Moran. In the late 1890's his parents moved to Butte, Silver Bow County, Montana, where his father worked as a teamster for the copper mines. Their children, except Bert, were married and raising their own families. It is not clear whether Bert went with his parents to Butte or not. In any case records show he married Blanche Elsie Cook on December 7, 1907, in Lead, Lawrence County, South Dakota. She was youngest child of Winifred Scott and Sophia (Groce) Cook. Local news item indicated they planned to go to Butte, Montana to live near his mother. His father, Patrick Moran, died the previous year from injuries obtained in a wagon accident on August 8, 1906. However plans change as he and Blanche along with his mother moved to Rushville, Sheridan County, Nebraska about 1908. Their four children were all born in Rushville, Nebraska:

Juaneta	b: 07 Jul 1909	d: 09 Oct 2008	m: Fred M. Brennan
Gilbert	b: 17 Apr 1911	d: 30 Jun 1935	
Edwin N.	b: 18 Sep 1916	d: 15 Jul 2001	m: Kathryn Ridenour Vergith
Thelma	b: 01 Jan 1917	d: 09 Aug 1921	

In 1918 Bert and his mother filed for a homesteads located west of Rozet where he and Blanche would live for the remainder of their lives raising cattle and farming. Bert Moran died on May 11, 1958, and Blanche died July 26, 1975. They were buried alongside of their son Gilbert, and daughter Thelma, in Mount Pisgah Cemetery, Gillette, Wyoming.

Sources:
Bureau of Land Management, Homestead Patent Index, [www.glorecords.blm.gov].
Ancestry.com, U.S. General Land Office Records, 1776-2015, [database online], Provo, UT.
"Rozet Resident (Gilbert) Dies Yesterday", The News Record, Gillette, Wyoming, June 29, 1935; "Requiem Mass Held Tuesday for Bert Moran, 76," The News Record, Gillette, Wyoming, May 15, 1958.
"Obituary-Edward N. Moran," The News Record, Gillette, Wyoming, July 20, 2001.
Ancestry.com, U.S. Find-a-Grave Index, 1600s-present, [database online], Provo, UT.
Ancestry.com, South Dakota, U.S. Marriages, 1905-2017, [database online], Provo, UT.
Ancestry.com, Iowa, U.S., Iowa Delayed Birth Records, 1856-940, [database online], Provo, UT.
Ancestry.com, U.S. Social Security Applications and Claims Index, 1936-2007, [database online], Provo, UT.
Ancestry.com, U.S. World War II Draft Registration Cards, 1942, [database online], Provo, UT.
Ancestry.com, 1900 U.S. Federal Census for Minnetonka, Sheridan County, NB, (Blanche), [database online], Provo, UT.
Ancestry.com, 1910, U.S. Federal Census for Minnetonka, Sheridan County, NB, [database online], Provo, UT.
Ancestry.com, 1920 U.S. Federal Census for Rozet, Campbell County, WY, [database online], Provo, UT.
Ancestry.com, 1930 U.S. Federal Census for Election District 5, Campbell County, WY, [database online], Provo, UT.
Ancestry.com, 1940 U.S. Federal Census for Campbell County, WY, [database online], Provo, UT.

John William "Jack" and Mary Jane "Mayme" (Houser) Reed
1918

John William "Jack" Reed, filed on a homestead across the Adon Road from his father Rueben in Sections 4, 5, 9, 12, and 13, Township 51 North, Range 70 West. He was born August 28, 1897, in Monona County, Iowa. At an early age his parents took him to Burt County, Nebraska, where he received his formal education. Jack served in WWI, receiving his army discharge in July 1918 at Ft. Lewis, Washington. He married Mary Jane "Mayme" Houser on March 30, 1918, in Gillette. She was born March 21, 1898, in Dubois, Nebraska, to Charles Franklin and Marietta (Howard) Houser. Mayme received her education in Dubois, and in 1913 her family moved to Campbell County. She kept house for her father until she was married. Their first son was born in Gillette, Wyoming. John and Mayme had rented a house so Mayme could be in town close to a doctor. The birth of two more sons followed:

Ernest Clifton	b: 28 May 1919	d: 14 Jul 2011	m: Mary Marvel
John William, Jr.	b: 22 Dec 1920	d: 18 Sep 1999	m: Billie Louise Scott
Charles Francis	b: 17 Dec 1922	d: 17 Oct 1997	m: Jacquelyn J. Marvel

The family returned to the homestead in 1926. The children attended the Deer Creek School. John Reed went to work in 1933 for Roy Montgomery on his ranch south of Gillette on the 4J Road. In 1936 he moved his family to Ellensburg, Washington, where he worked in the timber industry. By 1939 they were back in Gillette. Jack died on April 16, 1973, age 74, and Mayme died July 1975, age 77. They are both buried in Pleasant Valley Cemetery, northeast of Rozet Wyoming.

Gladys Reed Gilliland, Jack Reed, Ruth Reed Bray and Margaret Reed Melton

Sources:
Photo: from the collections of Leona and Jeanette Heptner.
"Obituary—John W. Reed," The News Record, Gillette, Wyoming, April 20, 1972.
"Reed (Mayme) Funeral Held Today," The News Record, Gillette, Wyoming, July 22, 1975.
"Obituary for Ernest Clifton Reed," https://www.gillettememorialchapel.com/obituary/4336644.
"Obituary-John W. Reed, Jr.," The News Record, Gillette, Wyoming, September 20, 1999.
"Mary (Marvel) Reed obituary," The News Record, Gillette, Wyoming, February 3, 2003.
Pleasant Valley Cemetery Burial Book, kept by Mrs. Lucille Thompson (Xeroxed Copy-1998.
Bureau of Land Management, Homestead Patent Index, [www.glorecords.blm.gov].
Campbell County, The Treasured Years, 1990, page 475, compiled by Campbell County Historical Society.
Ancestry.com, U.S. Find a Grave Index, 1600s-Current, [database online], Provo, UT.
Ancestry.com, 1920 U.S. Federal Census for Iowa, Campbell County, Wyoming, [database online], Provo, UT.
Ancestry.com, 1930 U.S. Federal Census for Election District 8, Campbell County, Wyoming, [database online], Provo, UT.
Ancestry.com, 1940 U.S. Federal Census for Gillette, Campbell County, Wyoming, [database online], Provo, UT.

Henry Wolff and Catherine Loretta (O'Hara) Wolff
1918

Standing: Mary, Gertrude, front: Vincent, Henry holding Ruth, Catherine, Louis, Donald and Catherine

Back: Thomas, William Edward, Raymond Front: James, Joanne, Harry Lee

Henry Wolff was born January 22, 1890, in Japan, Missouri, to Peter and Louisa (Boehm) Wolff. In the spring of 1911 at the age of 21 he came to Crook County, Wyoming, with his parents, Peter and Louisa Wolff, one sister and four brothers. His father filed on a homestead about 12 miles southeast of Gillette. The family lived on their homestead only a few years until his father's health began to fail. His mother and father moved to California for a number of years before they returned to Franklin County, Missouri. Henry remained in Wyoming, filing on Section 11, Township 70 North, Range 48 North, and Sections 22, 34, 26, and 27, Township 71 North, Range 69 West. He returned to Sullivan, Missouri, in the fall of 1913 where he met and married Catherine Loretta O'Hara, daughter of William Francis and Mary Elizabeth (Stinson) O'Hara, on January 7, 1914. She was born on September 26, 1893, in Bourbon, Missouri. Henry and Katie became the parents of thirteen children:

Gertrude Ann	b: 28 Apr 1915	d: 22 Dec 1932	
Louis Francis	b: 27 Sep 1916	d: 28 Feb 2010	m: Loveretta Boccia
Mary Elizabeth	b: 13 Jun 1918	d: 24 Feb 1993	m: Lawrence W. Shippy
Catherine Margaret	b: 06 Aug 1919	d: 13 Aug 1954	m: Leonard P. Whisler
Vincent Henry	b: 04 Jan 1921	d: 10 Jan 2008	m: Hazel Handran
Donald Lawrence	b: 25 Feb 1922	d: 30 Jul 2007	m: Dorothy Felde
Ruth Agnes	b: 08 Sep 1923	d: 14 Sep 1985	m: Warren J. Handran
Thomas Anthony	b: 15 May 1926	d: 18 Dec 1944 (at sea on USS Hull, typhoon in the Pacific)	
William Edward	b: 18 Sep 1928	d: 11 Jun 1983	m: Nancy K. Whisler
Raymond Richard	b: 29 Mar 1930	d: 23 Dec 2018	m: Phyllis Badger
James Albert	b: 20 Dec 1931	d: 21 Oct 2013	m: Martha Joan Groves
Joanne Ellen	b: 20 Dec 1931	d:	m: Donald R. Brent
Harry Lee	b: 21 Aug 1933	d:	m: Ruth Marie Japp

Katie died October 6, 1939 from appendicitis surgery complications. Henry continued farming and ranching raising his children. He died on September 29, 1973. They are both buried in Mount Pisgah Cemetery, Gillette, Wyoming, alongside their two children Gertrude Anne and Thomas Anthony.

Sources:
Photos: courtesy of Judy Whisler Kehn, Gillette, Wyoming, 2019, granddaughter.
Bureau of Land Management, Homestead Patent Index, [www.glorecords.blm.gov].
"Henry Wolff," page 654-656, Campbell County, The Treasured Years, 1990, compiled by Campbell County Historical Society.
"Death Claims Gertrude Wolff," The News Record, Gillette, Wyoming, December 22, 1932.
"Mary E. Shippy obituary," The News Record, Gillette, Wyoming, February 26, 2003.
"Vincent Henry Wolff obituary," The News Record, Gillette, Wyoming, January 14, 2008.
Ancestry.com, Find-a-Grave Index 1600s-Current, [database online], Provo, UT.
Ancestry.com, Missouri, Marriage Records, 1805-2002, [database online], Provo, UT.
Ancestry.com, U. S, World War I Draft Registration Cards, 1917-1918, [database online], Provo, UT.
Ancestry.com, 1900 U.S. Federal Census for Boone, Franklin County, Missouri, [database online], Provo, UT.
Ancestry.com, 1910 U.S. Federal Census for Boone, Franklin County, Missouri, [database online], Provo, UT.
Ancestry.com, 1920 U.S. Federal Census for Laney, Campbell County, Wyoming, [database online], Provo, UT.
Ancestry.com, 1930 U.S. Federal Census for Election district 30, Campbell County, Wyoming, [database online], Provo, UT.
Ancestry.com, 1940 U.S. Federal Census for Campbell County, Wyoming, [database online], Provo, UT.

O'Neal "Neal" and Louise "Lula" (Hancock) Gray
1919

Neal Gray was born January 5, 1896, at Iva, Pike County, Indiana, to Ellis and Jessie (Glossbrenner) Gray. He enlisted in the U.S. Army in 1917 and served in WWI with the Army Infantry in France. He was discharged July 19, 1919. In March 1920 Neal arrived in Moorcroft, Wyoming, and went to work herding sheep for Dow Sweeney. He filed on a homestead near the T7 Ranch in southern Campbell County. He built a shack, but someone stole the stove, so he left and never went back. That fall he worked with a team and fresno on the original highway between Moorcroft and Sundance. In the late fall of 1920 and spring of 1921 Neal herded sheep for Ed Stevenson; in the summer he built fence for Louis Stok where he spied a nice house on the neighbor's place and wished he could buy it. In the fall of 1921, O'Neal Gray purchased a homestead (located in Section 13, 14, and 24, Township 50 North, Range 69 West) from Jerry Nemick for $1,000.00. It was located six miles northeast of Rozet near Wessex (the first railroad siding east of Rozet). It had 320 acres, all fenced and 30 acres of plowed fields. That winter and spring of 1922 he herded sheep for Cy Guthrie. In the spring of 1922, he bought the homestead with the nice house on it from Shorty Faught for $100.00 and taking over a $1800.00 debt.

Louise "Lulu" Hancock was born February 26, 1899, at Otwell, Pike County, Indiana, to William and Mabel (Abbott) Hancock. In September 1922, Lulu Hancock left Otwell, by train for Wyoming. She and Neal were married September 5, 1922, in Gillette, Wyoming. For the rest of their lives, they lived on and developed their ranch. They farmed, hayed, and milked cows and in the fall. Neal would build reservoirs with a team and fresno to supplement their income. Neal was known for his hard work and keen interest in ranching and horses. Times were hard but neighbors worked together to harvest crops and then stopped to play cards and to dance during the long winter evenings. They were the parents of three children:

Dorothy "Dottie"	b: 22 Jun 1924	d: 08 Oct 2015	m: Jack Mobley
Richard Lee	b: 13 Aug 1925	d: 03 July 2021	m: Betty Macy
Alvin	b: 11 Sep 1927	d: 13 May 1985	m: Charleen Felds

The children received their twelve years of schooling at Rozet Consolidated School and graduating from Rozet High School. Their fondest memories of their youth centered around the Rozet School and its planned and unplanned extracurricular activities. They celebrated their 60th Wedding Anniversary with a family gathering at their ranch home east of Rozet in September 1962. Lula Gray died August 29, 1986 at her home. Neal died February 17, 1988, in the Pioneer Manor Nursing Home, Gillette, Wyoming. They are both buried in the Moorcroft Cemetery, Moorcroft, Wyoming.

Sources:
Photo: copied from the Gray's "60th Wedding Anniversary Program," September 1982.
Bureau of Land Management, Homestead Patent Index, [www.glorecords.blm.gov].
Local Notes: "O'Neill Gray & Miss Louise Bell Hancock marriage," Campbell County Record, September 7, 1922.
"60th Wedding Anniversary Program," September 1982.
"Alvin Gray Funeral Today," The News Record, Gillette, Wyoming, May 17, 1985.
Gray (Lulu) Service Tuesday," The News Record, Gillette, Wyoming, August 31, 1986, page 14.
"O'Neal Gray Funeral Saturday," The News Record, Gillette, Wyoming, February 18, 1988.
"Obituary-Charleen Gray," The News Record, Gillette, Wyoming, September 11, 1998.
Ancestry.com, U.S. Find A Grave Index, 1600s-Present, [database online], Provo, UT.

Everett L. and Ruth (Jackson) Pownall
1919

Everett Pownall was born November 20, 1889 in Mountain Grove, Texas County, Missouri, to Warren M. and Elizabeth Pownall. He married Ruth Jackson on November 17, 1915, in Holyoke, Phillips County, Colorado. Elizabeth was born on January 25, 1899, at Drexel, Bates County, Missouri, to George and Florence Jackson. At the time he registered for the draft for World War I, on Jun 5, 1917, they were living in Sterling, Logan County, Colorado, where he was working for the Harris Livestock Company. They first arrived at the Laurel Leaf Ranch in the spring of 1916. Ruth cooked for the cowboys and any additional men who were there from time to time. That fall they returned to Sterling, Colorado. In the spring of 1918 they came back to Wyoming to work for Harris and Simpson. They lived in the Wade house, located just down the creek west of the Wagonhammer ranch, until late that summer when it burned to the ground with everything they owned with it. The family moved to the Wagonhammer ranch where Everett worked. In 1922 Everett filed on a homestead located in Section 14, Township 53 North, Range 70 West, but did not move his family to it until 1924. Everett and Ruth were the parents of four children:

Veva June	b: 19 Jun 1919	d: 10 Jun 2003	m: (1) Christy Doyle, Jr.
			(2) Leslie T. Wilson
Everett Jackson "Jack"	b: 22 Apr 1922	d: 10 Mar 2001	m: Ruth Marie Hord
Douglas W.	b: 13 Feb 1927	d: 19 Feb 2008	m: Irene C. Reel
Stanley C.	b: 09 Oct 1938	d:	m: _____

The children attended school at the Adon, Christianson, or Engdahl Schools, whichever had enough students to hire a teacher. They lived on their ranch all of their lives. Everett died November 1, 1962, at home in his sleep. Ruth died in July 1969. She was buried July 5, 1969, in Mount Pisgah Cemetery, Gillette, Wyoming.

Sources:
Bureau of Land Management, Homestead Patent Index, [www.glorecords.blm.gov].
Campbell County, The Treasured Years, page 463-4, compiled by the Campbell County Historical Society, 1990.
"Funeral Services Held Saturday for Everett Pownall," The News Record, Gillette, Wyoming, November 5, 1962.
"Funeral Services for Mrs. Ruth Pownall," The News Record, Gillette, Wyoming, July 10, 1969.
"Douglas W. Pownall, obituary," Gillette News Record, Gillette, Wyoming, February 28, 2008.
"June (Pownall) Wilson obituary," The News Record, Gillette, Wyoming, June 12, 2003.
Manuscript "School Days Trials and Triumphs," by Betty Hughes Morrish, 1990.
Ancestry.com, U.S. Find-a-Grave Index, 1600s-Current, [database online]. Provo, UT.
Ancestry.com, U.S. Social Security Death Index, 1936-2014, [database online]. Provo, UT.
Ancestry.com, U.S. Social Security Applications and Claims Index, 1936-2007, [database online]. Provo, UT.
Ancestry.com, U.S. Public Records Index, 1950-1993, Volume 1, [database online]. Provo, UT.
Ancestry.com, Montana, County Marriage Records, 1865-1993, [database online]. Provo, UT.
Ancestry.com, South Dakota, Marriages, 1905-2017, [database online]. Provo, UT.
Ancestry.com, Wyoming, Marriage Records, 1941-1966, [database online]. Provo, UT.
Ancestry.com, Colorado, County Marriage Records and State Index, 1862-2006, [database online]. Provo, UT.
Ancestry.com, U.S. World War I Draft Registration Cards, 1917-1918, [database online]. Provo, UT.
Ancestry.com, U.S. World War II Draft Registration Cards, 1942, [database online]. Provo, UT.
Ancestry.com, 1900 U.S. Federal Census for Roubidoux, Texas County, Missouri, [database online]. Provo, UT.
Ancestry.com, 1920 U.S. Federal Census for Northeast Sterling, Logan County, Colorado, [database online]. Provo, UT.
Ancestry.com, 1930 U.S. Federal Census for Election District 9, Campbell County, Wyoming, [database online]. Provo, UT.
Ancestry.com, 1940 U.S. Federal Census for Campbell County, Wyoming, [database online]. Provo, UT.

Henry Cleveland and Nellie (Ebben) Weaver
1919

Henry was born on November 9, 1884, in Ashland, Saunders County, Nebraska, to Solomon and Minnie Weaver. He married Nellie Ebben on December 5, 1906, in Lincoln, Lancaster County, Nebraska. Henry and Nellie Weaver came to Rozet area about 1918 from Ashland, Nebraska, with two boys, Arthur and Clarence. Henry filed for a homestead located along Deer Creek, off the Adon Road about nine miles north of Rozet on Sections 15, 21, and 22, Township 51 North, Range 70 West. Two more children were born:

Arthur Louis	b: 25 Aug 1907	d: 14 Sep 1997	m: Loretta Bailey Ward
Clarence	b: 14 Apr 1911	d: 1936	
John William	b: 19 Sep 1925	d: 15 Oct 1961	m: Ruby Harper Ward
Alvina C.	b: 11 May 1921	d: 29 Oct 2005	m: George Sunderland

Johnny and Alvina attended school at the Deer Creek school. The family left Rozet at some point in the late 1930s and moved to Casper, Wyoming.

Joint End of Year Picnic in 1934

[Note: A combined end-of-the-year picnic in the spring of 1934 of the Deer Creek and Cottonwood Valley schools. The teachers were Leona Heptner and Elsie Weaver. Children in the picture are from left to right: Lee Wallace, June and Leona Donner, Ted Wallace, Dean Whisler, Mary Hanslip and Alvina Weaver. The adults in the back row are Leona Heptner and Elsie Weaver. Johnny Weaver and Leonard Whisler also attended Deer Creek School throughout the years.

Sources:
Photos: Photo from the collections of Leona Heptner.
Bureau of Land Management, Homestead Patent Index, [www/glorecords.blm.gov].
Campbell County Cemetery District Burial Report of September 8, 1998.
Campbell County, The Treasured Years, 1990, page 253, compiled by Campbell County Historical Society.
Ancestry.com, Nebraska, Marriage Records, 1855-1908, [database online], Provo, UT.
Ancestry.com, U.S. World War II Draft Registration Cards, 1942, [database online], Provo, UT.
Ancestry.com, U.S. Social Security Applications and Claims Index, 1936-2007, [database online], Provo, UT.
Ancestry.com, Vital Records: Social Security Death Index 1937-1998, [database online], Provo, UT.
Ancestry.com, U.S. Find-a-Grave Index, 1600s-Current, [database online], Provo, UT.
Ancestry.com, 1900 U.S. Federal Census for Ashland, Saunders County ,Nebraska, [database online], Provo, UT.
Ancestry.com, 1920 U.S. Federal Census for Campbell County, Election District #8, Iowa Precinct, Wyoming, [database online], Provo, UT
Ancestry.com, 1930 U.S. Federal Census for Iowa, Campbell County, Wyoming, [database online], Provo, UT.

1920 – 1929
Rozet, Campbell County Wyoming

Charlie and Bea Slattery Homestead
1925
(Photo courtesy of Dorothy Slattery 2020)

Introduction

By 1920 the population of Campbell County was growing at such a rate that the Board of Commissioners voted to realign the voting districts. They revised boundary lines to establish new districts and renamed previous districts to reflect their communities. These revised or new districts located north and south of Rozet were assigned polling places as follows:

District #5	Rozet, North Precinct	Polling Place: George School
District #8	Iowa Precinct	Polling Place: Woods School
District #10	Rozet, South Precinct	Polling Place: Rozet School
District #20	Bar FS Precinct	Polling Place: Brower School

(Campbell County Record, July 15, 1920; Proceedings of the Board of Commissioners)

Again, in 1924, to accommodate additional families now living in the Adon area north of Rozet a new precinct was created, others renamed, and the polling places revised as follows:

District #5	Rozet Precinct	Polling Place: Rozet School
District #8	Iowa Precinct	Polling Place: Speegle Ranch
District #9	Bertha South Precinct	Polling Place: Christianson School
District #10	Bar FS Precinct	Polling Place: Brower School

Whitcomb County?

In 1922 city fathers of Moorcroft and others within the area worked on a petition to present at the Wyoming legislature in January 1923 asking for the creation of a new county to be named Whitcomb after Elias W. Whitcomb, with Moorcroft as it's county seat. The total area would be twenty-four miles wide and eighty-four miles long. It would consist of the east row of townships in Campbell County and three rows each from Crook and Weston Counties. The Rozet, Adon and Dillinger communities opposed the petition. Petitions opposing the action were placed in the Rozet Mercantile Company Store at Rozet and at the post offices in Adon and Dillinger for citizens to sign. The Whitcomb County Petition did not make it out of the lower house of the legislature. A new proposal was drawn up for the January 1927 session. The proposed area this time would consist of eleven and a half townships south from the Montana line, and would only be four townships wide, with twenty-eight and a half townships from Crook County, eleven and a half townships from Campbell County, and six townships from Weston County. The Whitcomb County Committee, chaired by J. A. Stewart, the mayor of Moorcroft, presented a pamphlet to the legislatures setting forth full data on the proposal. Moorcroft was designated as the county seat. It was estimated that the new county would have a population of 3,500 and a property valuation of $5,122,548. Petitions signed by more than 550 resident taxpayers of the district asking for the establishment of the new county were submitted to the legislature. State Senator Frank O. Horton, of Johnson County, introduced the bill, Number H-52 to the senate. This revised bill, like the first in 1923, was defeated.

Sources:
"Propose a New County", page 1, The Gillette News, Gillette, Wyoming, December 14, 1922.
"ROZET-Petitions of Protest," Gillette News, December 14, 1922.
Whitcomb County Talked to Death in Wyoming House," The Cheyenne Tribune, page 1, Campbell County Record, Gillette, Wyoming, February 8, 1923.
"County Division Bill Killed in the Legislature," page 1, Gillette News, Gillette, Wyoming, February 8, 1923.
"Moorcroft to Make Bid for a New County," page 1, The News Record, Gillette, Wyoming, December 16, 1926.
"Bill to Create the New County of Whitcomb Presented to Senate Monday—Opposition is Expected," The News Record, February 3, 1927.

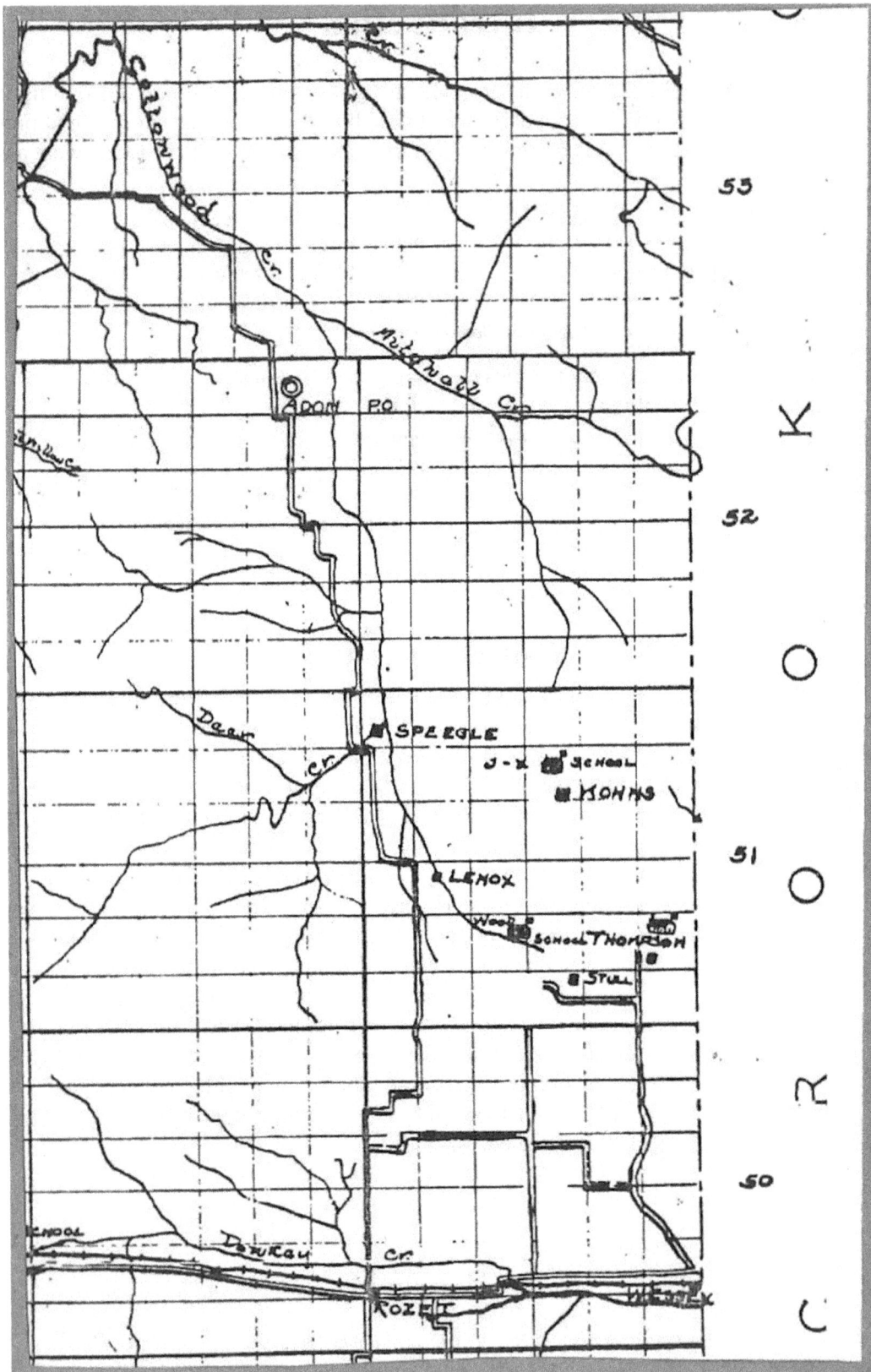

Townships 50-53, Ranges 69-70, Campbell County, Wyoming
Showing J Bar X, Woods and Little Iowa Schools
Copied from the 1922 Map
By J. E. Spielman, Civil Engineer, January 10, 1922

172

FAMILIES (1920-1929)
The Burr Brothers, Ed and Andy Burr
1921

Edward Eckdahl "Ed" Burr was born November 1, 1890, near Davenport, Thayer County, Nebraska, to Alwyn E. and Hilda (Eckdahl) Burr. He married Marguerite Lowrey on October 20, 1915, at Edgar, Clay County, Nebraska. Marguerite was born November 29, 1893, in Norton, Norton County, Nebraska, to Charles Oscar and Annie May (West) Lowrey. After their marriage they lived near Davenport, Nebraska, for about three years until in 1918. Ed and Marguerite moved to Wyoming, locating on a ranch near Rozet. They lived there until 1943 when they moved to Gillette. They were the parents of seven children:

Mildred Alvera	b: 11 Nov 1917	d: 11 Dec 2003	m: Gordon Byron Mooney
Charles Edward	b: 18 Mar 1920	d: 09 May 2012	m: Florence Eileen Eads
Evelyn Verle	b: 1922	d: 01 Jun 2016	m: Henry Leroy Fisher
Leslie Alwyn	b: 14 Oct 1924	d: 15 Jun 2016	m: Arthena Herbage
Walter Eugene	b: 06 Jun 1927	d: 20 Jul 2014	m: Edrie Jean Harle
Kenneth Wilson	b: 30 Sep 1930	d: 13 Nov 2020	m: Darlene Roberts
Curtis Joy	b: 05 Jul 1933	d: 08 Apr 2014	m. Doris E. Drown

After moving to Gillette, Ed became active in the Farm Bureau, Farmers Co-op and the Farmers Union. He also worked at the carpenter trade. Ed died on November 9, 1958. He was buried in Mount Pisgah Cemetery, Gillette, Wyoming. Marguerite Burr died in April 1989 and is also buried in Mount Pisgah Cemetery, Gillette, Wyoming.

Sources:
Photo: Ancestry.com (Ryan Burr Family Tree) https://www.ancestry.com/family-tree/person/tree/67662739/person 48172705246/facts.
"Society—Mooney-Burr Wedding," The News Record, Gillette, Wyoming, June 27, 1935.
"Services Held for E. E. Burr, 69, After Short Illness," The News Record, Gillette, Wyoming, November 13, 1958.
"Marguerite Burr Obituary," The News Record, Gillette, Wyoming, Wednesday, April 5, 1989.
"Mildred Mooney, obituary," The News Record, Gillette, Wyoming, December 15, 2003

Andrew Albert "Andy" Burr was born November 1, 1894, to Alwyn Ellicot and Hilda (Ekdahl) Burr, in Upland, Franklin County, Nebraska. Andy was drafted into the army during WWI. After his discharge from the army he settled at Rozet where he filed on a homestead in Sections 15, 21, and 22, Township 49 North, Range 70 West, southwest of Rozet. Andy married Tessie P. Garrett, daughter of Winslow and Susie Belle (Kelly) Garrett, on April 20, 1922. They became the parents of four children:

Wayne Deane	b: 30 May 1923	d: 20 Dec 2015	m: Mary Lou Ellis
Clifford Garrett	b: 18 Apr 1927	d: 07 Jul 1968	
Elsie Josephine	b: 20 Dec 1930	d: 19 Mar 2018	m: Ronald P. Germann
Pauline Alberta	b: 28 Oct 1934	d:	m: Thomas H. Green

Andy and Tessie operated a farm and raised cattle and later he drove a school bus for the Rozet School. In 1946, they sold the farm and moved to Sheridan, Wyoming, where they raised a vegetable garden and sold its produce. Andy died January 16, 1972, at the V.A. Hospital in Sheridan. Tessie died December 19, 1983, in Buffalo, Wyoming. They are both buried at Custer Battlefield National Cemetery in Montana.

Sources:
Photos: Courtesy of the Campbell County Rockpile Museum, Gillette, Wyoming - 2022.
Bureau of Land Management, Homestead Patent Index, [www.glorecords.blm.gov].
"Burr-Garrett," The Gillette News, Gillette, Wyoming, April 27, 1922.
"Andrew and Tessie Burr," Campbell County, The Treasured Years, 1990, page 91-2.

Gladys Olive (Reed) and Roy Virgil Gilliland
1920

Orie, Gladys, and Roy Gilliland about 1946

Gladys Olive Reed was born July 21, 1900, in Decatur, Burt County, Nebraska, to Rueben W. and Sarah E. Reed. Roy Virgil Gilliland was born September 23, 1894, Blair, Washington County, Nebraska, to John Edward and Dorothy "Dolly" (Nye) Gilliland. By 1910 the family was living on a farm in Burton, Fall River County, South Dakota. Roy served in WWI. Gladys and Roy were married on September 8, 1920, in Tekamah, Burt County, Nebraska. According to the 1930 Federal Census Gladys and Roy were living in Herman, Washington County, Nebraska, where Roy worked as a manager of a garage. They were the parents of one son:

Orie Virgil   b: 16 Jun 1922   d: 01 Dec 1970

Before 1935 they moved to Wyoming to live on a ranch ten miles north of Rozet homesteaded by her father Rueben Reed. Gladys spent most of her time on the ranch and was an active member of the Veterans of Foreign Wars for many years. Her son Orie graduated from Campbell County High School, Gillette, Wyoming, in 1942 and entered the army. He served in WWII with the Merrill Marauders and was with the group of first American soldiers under American Command to fight on Asiatic soil. In 1945 he returned to the ranch and lived there until his death at age 48 on December 1, 1970. His father, Roy Gilliland died ten days later on December 11, 1970. They were both buried at the Custer Battlefield National Cemetery, Crow Agency, Montana, with military graveside services conducted by the VFW and American Legion. Gladys continued to live on the ranch until her death on December 5, 1986, age 86. She was buried alongside her husband and son at the National Battlefield, Crow Agency, Montana.

[Note: This family brings wonderful memories to me. On hot summer evenings after supper my dad would take us for a ride a few miles north to the Gilliland's to visit. My sister and I would patiently wait for Mr. Gilliland to ask the question, "would you like some ice cream?" We always said yes with the biggest grins. Then Mrs. Gilliland would stir up the eggs, milk, and sugar with a drop of vanilla while Mr. Gilliland filled the hand-cranked ice cream maker with ice from his ice house. Then the serious visiting began. The guys on the porch taking turns turning the handle and we gals in the kitchen while Mrs. Gilliland prepared shortcake to go with the ice cream when it was ready to eat. I have not tasted any ice cream as good as what we ate those long, hot, summer evenings so long ago.ljw]

Sources:
Photo: from the collections of Carroll D. "Slim" Whisler.
"Rites Held Monday for O. Gilliland," The News Record, Gillette, Wyoming, December 10, 1970.
"Gilliland (Roy)," The News Record, Gillette, Wyoming, December 17, 1970.
"Graveside Service in Montana (Gladys Gilliland)," The News Record, Gillette, Wyoming, December 8, 1986.
Ancestry.com, U.S. Find a Grave Index, 1600s-Current, [database online], Provo, UT.
Ancestry.com, U.S. Veterans' Gravesites, ca. 1775-2019, [database online], Provo, UT.
Ancestry.com, U.S. World War I Draft Registration Cards, 1917-1918, [database online], Provo, UT.
Ancestry.com, U.S. World War II Draft Cards Young Men 1940-1947, [database online], Provo, UT.
Ancestry.com, 1910 U.S. Federal Census for Burton, Fall River, South Dakota, [database online], Provo, UT.
Ancestry.com, 1920 U.S. Federal Census for Riverside, Burt County, Nebraska, [database online], Provo, UT.
Ancestry.com, 1930 U.S. Federal Census for Herman, Washington County, Nebraska, [database online], Provo, UT.
Ancestry.com, 1940 U.S. Federal Census for Campbell County, Wyoming, [database online], Provo, UT.

Kermit Raymond and Jessie Lee (Gray) Johnson
1921

Kermit Raymond was born December 20, 1908, in Mammoth Springs, Fulton County, Arkansas. When he was five years old, he came to Rozet, Campbell County, Wyoming, in 1914 with his mother, four sisters, and one brother. They were met in Moorcroft by his father who brought them all to the homestead with a team and wagon. He and his brother, Fred, grew up on the homestead, operating it together with their mother's guidance, after their father died in 1921. They filed on homesteads north of Rozet about eight miles. They lived on them enough to prove up on them and then sold them. He married Jessie Lee Gray on April 10, 1936, in Otwell, Pike County, Indiana. She was born July 7, 1915, in Otwell, Pike County, Indiana, daughter of Oliver Ellis W. and Jessie (Glossbrenner) Gray. She grew up there and graduated from Otwell Senior High School. As a young woman, she traveled to Wyoming to visit her brother, O'Neal Gray, who ranched northeast of Rozet. In 1936 Kermit, Jessie and his mother, Belle, moved to Peoria, Linn County, Oregon, where they spent several years. In late 1942 they came back to Wyoming with their two daughters and one son. They were the parents of four children:

Phyliss	b: 03 Mar 1937	d: 29 Jul 2018	m: Raymond "Red" Record
Joyce	b: 18 Dec 1940	Living	m: Larry "Butch" Ruff
Marvin	b: 02 Oct 1942	Living	m: Walline Drake
Roger	b: 27 Mar 1947	Living	m: Jane Burke

After the death of his mother in 1943 Kermit bought the homestead from his sisters and brother and spent the rest of his life there farming, raising cattle and sheep. From about 1948 Kermit raised his four children alone, as his wife, Jessie, was hospitalized and in nursing homes for the rest of her life. In addition to his ranching activities, Kermit worked at the former Gillette Livestock Exchange, which was located in northwest Gillette, during all the years of its operation. He remained active in ranching until his death. Kermit died in his sleep on October 28, 1987; Jessie Lee died April 14, 1989, following a lengthy illness. They are both buried in Pleasant Valley Cemetery, Rozet, Wyoming.

Johnson Homestead about 1925
Ruth Johnson, mother Belle Johnson, Kermit Johnson

Sources:
Photos: Photo of Kermit courtesy of Joan Whisler Miller, June 2017.
Photo of Jessie courtesy of Joyce Johnson Ruff, July 26, 2017.
Campbell County, the Cherished Years, 1991, pages 301-303, Campbell County Historical Society.
Pleasant Valley Cemetery Burial Book, kept by Mrs. Lucille Thompson (Xeroxed Copy-1998).
"Johnson Funeral scheduled (Kermit)," The News Record, Gillette, Wyoming, October 30, 1987.
"Obituary for Jessie Lee Johnson," page A5, The Press-Dispatch, Otwell, IN, dated May 4, 1989.
Ancestry.com, U.S. Social Security Applications and Claims Index, 1936-2007[database on-line], Provo, UT.
Ancestry.com, Find-A-Grave Index, 1600s – Current [database on-line], Provo, UT.
Ancestry.com, U.S. Obituary Collection, 1930-Current, (Phyllis Record), [database online], Provo, UT.
Ancestry.com, 1940 U.S. Federal Census for Peoria, Linn County, Oregon, District 22-40. [database online], Provo, UT.

Theodore Emanuel "Ted" and Kittie (Preston) Tholson
1921

Ted Tholson was born February 13, 1889, in Dakota Territory, near Black Hawk in Meade County, South Dakota, to Swedish immigrants Thol and Kerstin Tholson. The Tholson homestead was located about 12 miles east of Rapid City. By the time he was 12 years old he was riding as a cowboy, for cow outfits; one of the first being the Spanish Five, Jim Cox was the owner. In 1915 Ted helped trail horses to Gillette, Wyoming. He liked the area so well that he decided to return in 1916. He worked for the Lee and Spaeth ranch for the next ten years. On December 22, 1920, Ted married Kittie Preston, daughter of John Chester and Sara Jane (McIntosh) Preston and a sister of Tom Preston who homesteaded south of the Belle Fourche River. She was born March 24, 1899, in Lucas County, Iowa. Kittie was educated in Western Kansas and came to Wyoming in 1908 at the age of 19. Ted and Kittie were the parents of three sons:

Infant son	b:	1921	d: 23 Oct 1921	
Calvin Eugene	b:	21 Dec 1923	d: 14 Apr 2006	m: Sophia Danilewicz Egloff
John Lawrence	b:	13 Jun 1929	d: 08 Feb 2008	m: JoAnn Young

Ted and Kittie Tholson homesteaded on Sections 8 and 9, Township 47 North, Range 70 West, south of Rozet on Caballo Creek. Upon the death of Kittie's father, on July 19, 1923, her mother Sara Jane Preston came to live with them until her death in 1938. An article "Ted Tholson Honored with S.D. Certificate," published in the _News Record_ on May 10, 1973, states, "While building up his homestead Ted continued to work for the Lee and Spaeth Ranch. However, when their two sons, Calvin and John, were ready for high school. Ted and Kittie sold their homestead to W. O. Bishop and moved to Rozet. They bought a ranch from Ona Toland, who was an early schoolteacher at Rozet. Ted didn't farm on a very large scale but continued to build up his cattle herd. Some years were good, some bad through drought and blizzards but life was good, and they prospered."

They retired from ranching in 1959 and moved to Gillette, Wyoming. where they lived until 1970 when they moved to Douglas, Wyoming. Ted and Kittie were married for fifty-two years. Ted died on April 14, 1973, at the Michael Manor Nursing Home, Douglas, Wyoming, and Kittie died on May 3, 1973, also at the home. They are both buried in Mount Pisgah Cemetery, Gillette, Wyoming.

Sources:
Bureau of Land Management, Homestead Patent Index, [www.glorecords.blm.gov].
"Theodore Tholson and Kittie Preston Tholson," Campbell County, The Treasured Years, 1990, pages 592-693, compiled by
    Campbell County Historical Society, Gillette, Wyoming
"Tholson Baby Dies," Gillette News, Gillette, Wyoming October 27, 1921.
"Former Resident (Ted) Succumbs," The News Record, Gillette, Wyoming, April 19, 1973.
"Former Resident (Kittie) Dies," The News Record, Gillette, Wyoming, May 10, 1973.
"Ted Tholson Honored with S.D. Certificate," The News Record, Gillette, Wyoming, February 19, 1970.
"Sophie Danilewicz Tholson obituary," The News Record, Gillette, Wyoming, December 22, 2005.
"Calvin Tholson obituary," The News Record, Gillette, Wyoming, April 17, 2006.
"John Lawrence Tholson paid obituary," Gillette News Record, Gillette, Wyoming, February 11, 2008.
Ancestry.com, California, Marriage Index, 1949-1959, [database online]. Provo, UT.
Ancestry.com, U.S. Find-a-Grave Index, 1600s-Current, [database online]. Provo, UT.
Ancestry.com, U.S. World War I Draft Registration Cards, 1917-1918, [database online]. Provo, UT.
Ancestry.com, U.S. World War II Draft Registration Cards, 1942, [database online]. Provo, UT.
Ancestry.com, U.S. Department of Veterans Affairs BITLS Death File, 1850-2010, [database online]. Provo, UT.
Ancestry.com, 1900 U.S. Federal Census for Township 5, Meade County, South Dakota, [database online]. Provo, UT.
Ancestry.com, South Dakota, State of Census, 1905, [database online]. Provo, UT.
Ancestry.com, 1920 U.S. Federal Census, for Laney, Campbell County, Wyoming, [database online]. Provo, UT.
Ancestry.com, 1930 U.S. Federal Census for Election District 20, Campbell County, Wyoming, [database online]. Provo, UT

Stanley and Myrtle (Johnson) Stewart
1922

Stanley Vern Stewart was born June 7, 1898, in Lake Mills, Iowa, to George and Martha (Milton) Stewart. Stanley was twelve years old when he arrived in Rozet with his parents. He grew up attending rural schools. He served in World War I in the U.S. Army. On October 7, 1922, in Gillette, Wyoming, Stanley married Myrtle Johnson. Myrtle was born March 2, 1902, in Oklahoma Territory, to Thomas and Isabell "Belle" (Kite) Johnson, who came to Rozet in 1913 from Oklahoma. Myrtle attended grade school at Well Creek School and three years at Rozet High School. She later received her high school diploma from Moorcroft High School, Moorcroft, Wyoming. They were the parents of four children:

Elaine Marie	b: 12 Aug 1924	d: 17 Jan 2015	m: (1) Laurence E. Nadeau
			(2) Henry L. Hanscom, Sr.
Corinne Leigh	b: 23 Jul 1926	d: 09 Dec 2013	m: Juel Kermit Lone
Clyde Earl	b: 09 Apr 1927	d: 26 Oct 1977	m: Olive Jerrine Nicholson
Stanley James "Jim"	b: 06 Nov 1941	Living	m: (1) Julianne _____
			(2) Linda Miotke
			(3) Paula Matheson

Myrtle and Stanley ranched in the Rozet area for many years until Stanley died in June 9, 1947. He was buried in the Moorcroft Cemetery, Moorcroft, Wyoming; later he was exhumed and reburied in the Sheridan Cemetery, Sheridan, Wyoming, after Myrtle and her son, Jim, relocated to Sheridan, Wyoming. Myrtle was married to Milton Baker for about five years before divorcing and eventually moving to Riverside, California, where she lived for the remainder of her life. She died December 26, 1998, at the Community Rehabilitation Center, Riverside, California, age 96. At her request she was cremated and her ashes scattered at the Stewart homestead in the spring of 1999. A memorial stone was placed in the Pleasant Valley Cemetery, Rozet, Wyoming.

Stanley, Corinne, Myrtle, Clyde, Elaine, Jim – about 1942

World War I Veteran

Sources:
Photos: Courtesy of Cindy Stewart, Rozet, Wyoming, August 2017, and Jim Stewart, May 2017.
"Stewart-Johnson," News Item, The Gillette News, Gillette, Wyoming, October 12, 1922.
"Obituary—Myrtle Stewart," The News Record, Gillette, Wyoming, December 29, 1998.
Family data furnished by Cindy Stewart and Sandy (Stewart) Holyoak via email in August 2017.
Email from Jim Stewart May 20, 2017, with pictures.
Pleasant Valley Cemetery Burial Book, kept by Mrs. Lucille Thompson (Xeroxed Copy-1998).
Ancestry.com, U.S. Find-a-Grave Index, 1600s-Current;[database online], Provo, UT.
Ancestry.com, 1940, U.S. Federal Census for Enumeration District3-6, Campbell County, Wyoming, , [database online], Provo, UT.

David Riley and Pearl Vida (Duvall) Whisler
1923

David Riley "Riley" Whisler was born June 14, 1882, in Smartsville, Johnson County, Nebraska, to Henry and Adell (Crandall) Whisler. Riley married Pearl Vida "Vida" Duvall, daughter of Richard and Catherine (Slade) Duvall, on October 4, 1904 in Tecumseh, Johnson County, Nebraska. He rented farms in Johnson and Pawnee Counties until 1920 when the family moved to Wray, Yuma County, Colorado. Dry weather caused Riley, in 1923, to drive north in his Model T truck with his three older sons, Carroll, Elmer, and Ashton, to look for land to homestead. He filed on a homestead in Section 2, Township 50 North, Range 70 West and Section 35, Township 51 North, Range 70 West located seven miles north of Rozet on the Adon Road. However, he needed a house large enough for Vida and their eight children to live in until the homestead was ready to accommodate the family. He rented the Frank George place until he could build an adequate house on his homestead. Their two youngest children were born at Rozet. Riley and Vida were the parents of sixteen children—ten lived to adulthood:

Carroll Duvall "Slim"	b: 02 Oct 1905	d: 09 Jun 1983	m: Irene Lydia Heptner
Elmer Dewey	b: 05 Aug 1907	d: 13 Nov 1968	m: Ruth Belle Johnson
Ashton Alfred "Ton"	b: 21 Jan 1909	d: 24 Feb 1994	m: Mildred Maurine Day
Dorothy Catherine	b: 28 Nov 1910	d: 02 Jul 2001	m: Oscar Herman Heptner
Laura May	b: 28 Sep 1912	d: 17 Dec 1915 (in Johnson County, Nebraska)	
David R.	b: 11 Oct 1914	d: 27 Apr 1992	m: Margorie Adell Mayden
Ross Jennings	b: 17 May 1916	d: 24 Dec 1916 (in Pawnee County, Nebraska)	
Jess Willard	b: 25 Nov 1917	d: 26 Nov 1917 (in Pawnee County, Nebraska)	
Leonard Pershing	b: 13 Oct 1918	d: 06 May 2003	m: (1) Catherine M. Wolff (2) Mary Jean Woods Brownlee
Joseph Adrian	b: 16 Aug 1919	d: 13 Jan 1920 (in Pawnee County, Nebraska	
Josephine Adell	b: 16 Aug 1919	d: 1920 (in Yuma County, Colorado)	
Ellen Joan	b: 14 Mar 1921	d: 31 Oct 2007	m: Lee Cummings
Helen Irene	b: 18 Jan 1922	d: 18 Jan 1922 (in Yuma, County, Colorado)	
Pauline Louise	b: 29 Oct 1922	d: 15 May 1992	m: Ferris Edwin Cook
Dean Robert	b: 11 Apr 1924	d: 28 Jul 2005	m: Helen Mae Kottraba
Evelyn Lillie	b: 22 May 1926	d: 29 Apr 2011	m: Melvin Harvey Donner

The family was still living at the George place when Riley suddenly died on November 15, 1926, at the age of 43. When Riley died, his son, Slim Whisler, who had been living and working in Nebraska, came home to help his mother with the homestead. Elmer Whisler married Ruth Johnson in 1927.

Vida Whisler died June 6, 1928, age 40, leaving the care and welfare of the younger children to the older children, primarily Slim and Dorothy. The youngest, Evelyn, at age 1 1/2, was taken in by their "Grandma Clark," Catherine (Slade) Duvall Clark;

The Whisler Homestead 1925

Pauline went to live with their Uncle Carroll Duvall until he decided to move his family to Republic, Kansas, and Ellen went to live with their Uncle Jim and Aunt Elsie Duvall. The oldest brothers and sister remained living at and working from the George Place. Dorothy took care of her two youngest brothers, Leonard age 10 and Dean age 4. After June 5, 1929, when Dorothy married Oscar Heptner, Pauline came to live them, followed later by Ellen. After the death of their grandmother Catherine Clark in July 1936, Evelyn came to live with Dorothy and Oscar. When Slim marrid Irene Heptner in July 1930, Leonard and Dean came to live with them on the Riley Whisler homestead seven miles north of Rozet along the Adon Road. They went to Deer Creek school about two miles north of the homestead.

Pawnee County, Nebraska - 1919

Yuma County, Colorado - 1922

Elmer, Dorothy, Riley holding Leonard, David,
Vida, Slim, and Ton

Joseph and Josephine
"The Twins"

Back: Slim, Riley, Vida, Elmer, Ton
Front: David, Dorothy, Leonard, Ellen

At the George Place, Rozet, Campbell County, Wyoming
(1923-1928)

The George Place
(The French Place in far distance on the left)

Vida and Riley Whisler - 1924

Leonard, David, Ellen, Pauline
1924

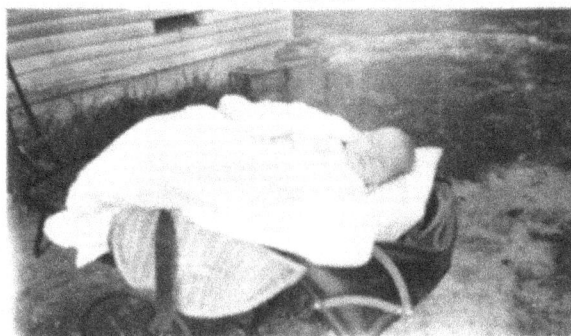

Dean Robert Whisler
1924

Evelyn Lillie - 1926

179

Right: The Whisler siblings in their brother Slim's little red convertible at the George Place. In the car, Leonard and David; on the running board Ellen, Dean, Pauline

The Whisler brothers and sisters, 1928
Back Row: Carroll "Slim," Ton, Dorothy, Elmer
Front Row: Leonard, Ellen, Evelyn, Dean, Pauline
David is missing from picture

Summer 1944 when Dean was home on leave from the Navy
Back Row: Carroll Duvall, Elmer Dewey, Ashton Alfred
David R., Leonard Pershing, Dean Robert
Front Row: Dorothy Catherine Heptner, Ellen Joan Cummings,
Pauline Louise Cook, Evelyn Lillie Donner

Sources:
Photos: from the collections of Carroll D. "Slim" Whisler.
Bureau of Land Management, Homestead Patent Index, [www.glorecords.blm.gov].
"Campbell County, The Treasured Years, 1991, Campbell County Historical Society, Gillette, WY.
"Personals 'Whisler-Johnson Marriage,'" The News Record, Gillette, Wyoming, May 6, 1926.
"Rozet Couple (Heptner-Whisler) Married," The News Record, Gillette, Wyoming, June 13, 1929.
"Society-Whisler-Day Marriage," The News Record, Gillette, Wyoming, April 3, 1930.
"Society-'Whisler-Heptner Marriage", The News Record, Gillette, Wyoming, July 10, 1930.
"Rozet Resident Dies-David Riley Whisler," The News Record, Gillette, Wyoming, November 18, 1926.
"Mother of Ten Passes Away at Rozet," The News Record, Gillette, Wyoming, June 14, 1928.
Ancestry.com, 1920 U.S. Federal Census for Vesta, Pawnee County, Nebraska, [data-base], Provo, UT.
Ancestry.com, 1930 U.S. Federal Census for Election District 5, Campbell County, Wyoming, [data-base online], Provo, UT.
Ancestry.com, 1940 U.S. Federal Census for Campbell County, Wyoming, [data-base online], Provo, UT.

William J. C. and Edna Mae (Cain) Lubkin
1924

William John Carl "Bill" Lubkin was born January 16, 1890, at O'Neill, Holt County, Nebraska. He married Edna Mae Cain, daughter of Nelson and Frances (Thompson) Cain, also of O'Neill, Nebraska. She was born May 6, 1894. Bill and Edna lived on a farm near Neligh, Antelope County, Nebraska, until they moved to Rozet in March of 1924. They drove an Allis Chalmers car from Nehigh to the Lester Cain (her brother) homestead south of Rozet. They lived there for two years. They moved to the Jack Wolfe homestead for about two years. Then they moved to the Elmer Gelish farm which Bill had bought in 1922 while still living in Nebraska. Bill and Edna were the parents of nine children:

Name	Birth	Death	Marriage
Wilma Irean	b: 18 Nov 1914	d: 21 Nov 1995	m: Henry H. Wright
Verna	b: 10 Sep 1916	d: 19 Mar 2002	(never married)
William Edmond "Willie"	b: 11 Sep 1918	d: 20 May 2001	m: Rita Mary Schlattmann
Cleston Derold	b: 06 Jun 1920	d: 12 Apr 2003	m: Coralie Minnich
Wayne	b: 01 Feb 1922	d: (as an infant)	
Ruth	b: 18 Jun 1923	d:	m: Ed Prazma
Jean	b: 14 Sep 1925	d: 27 Jan 1974	m: Elmer Groves
Robert	b: 02 May 1927	d:	m: Shirley Glocher
Patricia	b: 03 Oct 1928	d:	m: Garth Hardee

In 1935, Bill moved the family to Gillette where he worked on WPA (Work Progress Administration) jobs and Saunders Lumber Company. Later he worked for the Underwood Lumber Company for about 15 years. Bill died on November 14, 1954. He was buried in the Moorcroft Cemetery, Moorcroft, Wyoming. Edna died on February 17, 1980, in Sundance, Wyoming, and was buried in the Moorcroft Cemetery, next to her husband.

Sources:
"Obituary-Edna Mae Lubkin," page 16, The News Record, Gillette, Wyoming, February 21, 1980.
Moorcroft Cemetery Burial Book #4 (April 1946-April 1958), page 373.
Moorcroft Cemetery Book #6 (1972-June 1982), page 578.
"Lubkin Family of Rozet," page 340, Campbell County, The Treasured Years, 1990, compiled by Campbell County Historical Society, Gillette, Wyoming.
"Obituary for Cleston Derold Lubkin," The News Record, Gillette, Wyoming, April 15, 2003.
Ancestry.com, U.S. Find A Grave Index, 1600s-Current, [database online], Provo, UT.

Clifford Chapman and Mary (Shaughnessy) Thompson White
1925

Cliff Chapman White was born on July 22, 1898 in Shawnee County, Kansas, to Cassias and Emma Elvira (Chapman) White. His mother died when he was four years old. About 1915 Cliff came to Wyoming with his father Cassias M. "C.M.," his sister Nellie and his brother, Howard. His father filed for a homestead in the Adon community on May 31, 1916, in Sections 27, 28, and 33, Township 52 North, Range 70 West. He named his homestead the White Hall Ranch. His brother, H. Morton White, filed for a homestead located in Sections 33 and 34, Township 52 North, Range 70 West. In 1920 Cliff's father leased his land to Henry K. Hays and returned to Topeka, Shawnee County, Kansas, with his sister Nellie. After proving up on his homestead in 1923 Cliff's brother also returned to Topeka, Shawnee County, Kansas.

Cliff remained in Campbell County, and in 1925 he filed for a homestead in Sections 12, 13, and 18, Township 52 North, Range 70 West. He served as the Adon mail carrier out of Moorcroft, Wyoming for several years; served as the 1920 Census Taker for Iowa Precinct. On November 30, 1935, he married Mary (Shaughnessy)Thompson on November 30, 1935, in Pennington County, South Dakota. She was the postmistress at the Rozet Post Office since her appointment on March 16, 1932. He also built reservoirs for surrounding homesteaders including one for S. R. Jackson and his own, known as the "Cliff White Reservoir." Children of families living in the Rozet community have pleasant memories of attending family picnics around that reservoir. Perry Wallace bought Cliff's homestead. About 1940 they moved to Rozet. Clifford died in July 1963. No references found of where he died or where he is buried. Mary died on April 6, 1970, in Sheridan, Wyoming, and was buried in the Sheridan Municipal Cemetery.

Commemorative Envelope, 100th Year Anniversary
April 1, 2004

Sources:
Photo: taken by Matt Avery in the Rozet Post Office, Rozet, Wyoming, July 2020
Bureau of Land Management, Homestead Patent Index, [www.glorecords.blm.gov].
Ancestry.com, South Dakota Marriages, 1905-2017, [data base online], Provo, UT.
Ancestry.com, U.S. WWII Draft Cards Young Men, 1940-1947 [database online], Provo, UT.
Ancestry.com, 1920 U.S. Federal Census for Election District #8, Iowa Precinct. Campbell County, Wyoming, [database online], Provo, UT.

Elmer Dewey and Ruth Belle (Johnson) Whisler
1926

Elmer Whisler was born on August 5, 1907, in Tecumseh, Johnson County, Nebraska. He grew up in Tecumseh and Mayberry, Nebraska until 1920 when his parents moved to Wray, Weld County, Colorado. In 1922, at age fourteen, he came to Wyoming with his parents. He attended school at the Rozet School. His first job was as a section hand on the railroad. After his marriage to Ruth Belle Johnson on April 28, 1926, in Gillette, Wyoming, at the Presbyterian manse, he drove a school bus and farmed a little. In 1932 he filed on a homestead seven miles north of Rozet. He spent several years there farming and working for road construction crews, the railroad, etc. In 1935 he moved his family, first to Idaho, and then to Oregon and Washington where he followed the seasonal work harvesting fruit and vegetable crops. In 1940 he went to welding school and learned the electric welding process. He worked for the Kaiser Shipbuilding Company in Portland, Oregon, building Liberty ships. He moved the family back to Wyoming in late 1942. He bought a small farm southeast of Rozet where he got a start in cattle and acquired a few head of sheep. In 1947 Elmer sold this place and bought the Stanley and Myrtle Stewart place northeast of Rozet. He spent the rest of his life there. Elmer's favorite pastimes were hunting and fishing. On November 13, 1968, while on an elk hunting trip in the Big Horn Mountains, Elmer died of a heart attack while putting chains on his pickup. He was 61 years old. He was buried in Pleasant Valley Cemetery, Rozet, Campbell County, Wyoming. Ruth Belle Johnson was born May 30, 1904, in Hardy, Sharpe County, Arkansas, to Thomas Judson and Drusilla (Kite) Johnson. In April 1914, at age 9, Ruth and her mother and brothers and sisters were met in Moorcroft by their father who brought them to their homestead northeast of Rozet in Campbell County with a team and wagon. She and her brothers and sisters attended school at the Well Creek School, a rural school, near by the homestead. She graduated from Rozet High School in 1924 as the salutatorian of her class. Three children were born to Elmer and Ruth:

Eurith Arlene	b: 02 Apr 1927	Living:	m: Ralph Romel
Philip Raymond	b: 11 Apr 1928	Living	m: Joyce Ann Norris (div)
Joan Barbara	b: 03 Jan 1939	Living	m: (1) Edward John Kuntz (div)
			(2) Ronald John "Ron" Miller

Soon after returning from Oregon in1943 she began teaching school. Ruth attended summer school most every summer, took extension classes and did correspondence work to earn her B.S. degree from the Black Hills State Teachers College in Spearfish, South Dakota. She taught in mostly rural schools throughout her teaching years. She retired from teaching in May 1969 after her husband, Elmer, died in November 1968. Ruth continued to live on the home place. She kept sheep for a few years and cattle until 1986. Her brother, Kermit Johnson, helped her for years until he retired in 1975. Ruth continued to do the work alone. She was a member of the First Presbyterian Church, in Gillette, Wyoming, where she taught Sunday school and served as a Deacon for nine years. Ruth continued to live at home on the ranch until she was 100 years old. When her health no longer allowed her to live at home she moved to Rapid

Ruth, Phil, Elmer and Eurith picking apples in Oregon - 1936

City, South Dakota, to live with her daughter Eurith Romel. Ruth died just two months before her 102nd birthday on April 05, 2006, in Rapid City, Pennington County, South Dakota. She was buried in Pleasant Valley Cemetery, north east of Rozet alongside her husband and parents.

Sources:
"The History of the David Riley and Pearl Vida (Duvall) Whisler Family, the First three Generations," by L. J. Whisler for the first Whisler Family Reunion, June 18-20, 1993.

John and Jenny (Slechta) Prazma
1928

John was born December 26, 1871, in Czechoslovakia. Jenny Slechta was born May 25, 1876, in Czechoslovakia. She grew to become a young woman there, coming to the United States at the age of eighteen. She and John Prazma were married on October 15, 1898, in Chicago, Cook County, Illinois. They later moved to Indiana, Wisconsin, Minnesota, and then to Bolivar, Missouri, for a brief time before they settled, in 1928, on a place about six or seven miles east of Rozet. They were the parents of eleven children:

James	b: 09 Sep 1900	d: 09 May 1970	m: Anna Sabatka
Frank W.	b: 07 Oct 1901	d: 14 Jan 1989	m: Avis Dobbs
Rose	b: 09 Feb 1903	d: 09 Jul 1990	m: Ernest Marion Stillion
Joseph	b: 11 Mar 1904	d: (in infancy)	
John Robert "John Bob"	b: 11 Mar 1904	d: 16 Sep 1971	m: Elizabeth "Bessie" Sabatka
Jennie "Jean"	b: 22 Apr 1906	d: 05 Sep 1995	m: Vincent William Bittner
Charles	b: 9 May 1908	d: 26 Jan 1986	m: Ailene May Jones
Anna Belle	b: 20 Apr 1909	d: 25 Oct 1997	m: Richard W. Thompson
George Louis	b: 01 Sep 1916	d: 29 Nov 2006	m: Nina L. Amende
Edward Reid	b: 30 May 1917	d: 25 Apr 1996	m: (1) Ruth Lubkin
			(2) Mary Houston
Alice Mae	b: 28 Nov 1915	d: 14 Jun 2016	m: Clarence W. Elder

Jennie Prazma died on May 3, 1956, and was buried May 5, 1956, in Mount Pisgah Cemetery, Gillette, Wyoming. John Prazma died almost two years later in December 1957, and is buried in Mount Pisgah Cemetery, Gillette, Wyoming. Their son Edward owned and lived on their place until 1989.

Sources:
"Thompson-Comer," page 126-127, Campbell County, The Treasured Years, *1990, compiled by Campbell County Historical Society.*
"Funeral Services Held Saturday for Mrs. John Prazma," The News Record, *Gillette, Wyoming, May 10, 1956.*
"Obituary-Charles Prazma," Casper Star Tribune, *Casper, Wyoming, February 1, 1986.*
"Obituary-Edward Prazma," The News Record, *Gillette, Wyoming, April 25, 1996.*
"Obituary-George Prazma," The News Record, *Gillette, Wyoming, December 1, 2006.*
Campbell County Cemetery District Burial Property Report, September 1998.
Moorcroft Cemetery Burial Book #5 *(1958-1972), page 498.*
Ancestry.com, *Cook County, Illinois, Marriages Index 1871-1929 (for John Prazma and Jenny Slechta), [database online], Provo, UT.*
Ancestry.com, *South Dakota Marriages, 1905-2017) (John B and Bessie Sabatka).*
Ancestry.com, *Iowa Marriage Record, 1880-1951 (Jennie and Vincent W. Bittner), [database online], Provo, UT.*
Ancestry.com, *Montana, Marriage Records, 1943-1988 (for George and Nina Amende), [database online], Provo, UT.*
Ancestry.com, *Vital Records: Social Security Death Index, 1937-1998; [database online], Provo, UT.*
Ancestry.com, *U.S. Find-a-Grave, Index, 1600s-Current, [database online], Provo, UT.*
Ancestry.com, *1910 U. S, Federal Census for Adams, Adams County, Wisconsin, [database online], Provo, UT.*
Ancestry.com, *1920 U.S. Federal Census for Marion, Polk County, Missouri, [database online], Provo, UT.*
Ancestry.com, *1930 U.S. Federal Census for Moorcroft, Crook County, Wyoming, [database online], Provo, UT.*
Ancestry.com, *1940 U.S. Federal Census for Moorcroft, Crook County, Wyoming, [database online], Provo, UT.*

Fred H. and Emma L. (Stewart) Ware
1928

Emma Stewart Ware
1889~1955

Fred Ware
1888~1973

Fred Ware was born September 10, 1888, in Nebraska, son of Henry E. and Harriet A. (Powers) Ware. Emma L. Stewart was born May 3, 1889, in Lake Mills, Iowa, to George and Martha Stewart. Emma came to Wyoming with her parents in 1911. Fred and Emma were married on January 17, 1914, in Newcastle, Weston County, Wyoming. They were the parents of four children:

Bonnie Eileen	b: 04 Feb 1917	d: 22 Apr 1917	
Merle Jean	b: 05 Jun 1918	d: 24 Jun 1918	
Shirley Ann	b: 26 Jan 1930	d: 25 Aug 1980	m: William Eisele
Keith Frederick	b: 15 Nov 1920	d: 28 Apr 2011	m: Patricia Ann Mohan

Fred and Emma lived near Rozet for several years, the children attended Rozet High School. They moved to Sheridan in 1946. Emma died on November 30, 1955, and was buried in the Sheridan Municipal Cemetery, Sheridan, Wyoming. Fred died on February 12, 1973, and was buried in the Sheridan Municipal Cemetery, Sheridan, Wyoming.

Sources:
Photo: courtesy of Cindy Stewart, Rozet, Wyoming, 2017.
"Funeral Services Held Saturday for Mrs. Fred Ware," page 1, The News Record, Gillette, Wyoming, December 8, 1955.
Moorcroft Cemetery Burial Book #1, (1902-Apr 1923), pages 26, 42, 55, Book #3 (1935-Nov 1945), page 225.

Oscar Herman and Dorothy Catherine (Whisler) Heptner
1929

Oscar Herman was born July 31, 1910, at Glenwood, Mills County, Iowa. He came to Wyoming when his parents Frank and Laura Heptner homesteaded about nine miles northeast of Rozet in 1914. He went to the Cottonwood School and when he grew older he began helping his father and older brother in the fields. He attended school at Rozet High School until his marriage to Dorothy Catherine Whisler on June 5, 1929. Three children were born:

Darleen Lavonne	b: 06 Oct 1930	d: 14 Nov 2013	m: Gerald Marvin McGraw
Darrell Lelan	b: 22 May 1933	d: 01 Aug 2014	m: (1) Barbara Joy Edmison (div)
			(2) Audrey (Robing) Ridenour
Shirley Joyce	b: 04 Aug 1935	Living	m: Robert Prazma

During the Depression years, work was hard to find. Oscar entered the Civilian Construction Corps (CCC) in 1934-1935 along with his brothers-in-laws, Slim and Ton Whisler. They worked on building a road between Moorcroft and the Devils Tower. In 1937 Oscar and Dorothy moved their family, Darleen, Darrell, Shirley, and her sisters, Pauline and Evelyn Whisler, to Idaho Falls, Idaho, where they found work picking fruit and potatoes; and then moved to Oregon to find work in the vegetable fields and fruit orchards. They stayed there for about two years before returning to Rozet in 1939 where Oscar rented the former Miller place. Oscar farmed his own acreage and raised cattle and also helped his brother, Eugene, farm their mother's homestead. Dorothy Catherine was born November 28, 1910, in Tecumseh, Johnson County, Nebraska. She arrived in Rozet, via Heartstrong, Yuma County, Colorado, with her parents Riley and Vida (Duvall) Whisler. She went to school at the Rozet Consolidated School for her 7th and 8th grade. After her father died, just before her 16th birthday, she left high school to help her mother with her younger sisters and brothers. Her mother died in 1928. After she and Oscar were married they took her sister, Pauline, to live with them. Later they also took in her sister, Ellen. In 1936 after the death of Dorothy's grandmother, Catherine (Slade) Duvall Clark, her youngest sister, Evelyn, came to live with them. Occasionally her two youngest brothers, Leonard and Dean Whisler, would also live with them especially during their high school years.

In 1953, they moved to their new ranch and a new house that Oscar built for her, located a few hundred feet from the Frank George place where Dorothy's parents lived after they arrived in Rozet. Oscar died May 5, 1977, and Dorothy continued to live on the ranch, raising cattle and sheep with the help of her son Darrell, and assisted by her daughter and son-in-law, Shirley and Robert Prazma. She lived at the ranch, until health issues forced her to move to a retirement apartment in Gillette about 1997. Dorothy died July 2, 2001. Both Oscar and Dorothy were buried in Pleasant Valley Cemetery, Rozet, Wyoming..

Sources:
"The History of the David Riley and Pearl Vida (Duvall) Whisler Family, the First three Generations," by L. J. Whisler for the first Whisler Family Reunion, June 18-20, 1993.
Pleasant Valley Cemetery Burial Book, kept by Mrs. Lucille Thompson (Xeroxed Copy-1998).
"Heptner-Whisler marriage," The News Record, Gillette, Wyoming, June 13, 1929.
"Dorothy Heptner, obituary," The News Record, Gillette, Wyoming, July 3, 2001.

1930 – 1939
Rozet, Campbell County
Wyoming

Thomas Johnson Homestead
Well Creek- about 1929
(Photo courtesy of Ruth Johnson Whisler – 2001)

Introduction

This decade brought on the "Great Depression." After the 1929 Wall Street crash several original homestead families soon quit, sold their farms and moved on to other points, either back east to their previous homes, or westward to make new homes in California, Oregon, or Washington states. Others, bit down on the bit and stayed, or as my Uncle Eugene Heptner said, "We didn't have any money to move, so we stayed!" Consequently a few new families moved in buying these abandoned homesteads and becoming a part of the Rozet community. They spent their energies at keeping "the wolf from the door" throughout most of the decade. Weather did not help. Several years of drought forced many families to abandon their homes temporarily and driving to the west coast to find jobs in vegetable and fruit orchards. Several families from the Rozet community were among them. The Civilian Conservation Corps created by President Roosevelt provided job opportunities for many without jobs. A severe winter in the 1934-1935 was devastating. Livestock were lost that the families could ill afford to lose. Men hunted small animals for their skins. Slim Whisler hunted badgers and rabbits to sell their skins to Sears & Roebuck for cash money. By the end of the decade things were beginning to ease.

Slim Whisler hunted badgers and rabbits to sell to Sears & Roebuck, Co. during the 1930's

The Whisler homestead in winter of 1934-35

During this decade farming methods changed to planting crops in strips in the fields and to alternate the type of crop planted every other year. Threshing machines began appearing in the neighborhoods. One individual with a threshing machine would go from farm to farm to thrash their grains for his neighbors. Other neighbors would come with their hay racks and teams of horses to haul the bundles of grain out of the fields to the threshing machine. Noon dinners and evening suppers were cooked by the wives for the men helping her husband each day. Sometimes she would also have a few for breakfast. With fresh produce from the garden and a few chicken fryers running around in the yards, those dinners were always filling and enough for several refills.

Civilian Conservation Corps
1933-1934

The Civilian Conservation Corps (CCC) was a voluntary public work relief program that operated from 1933 to 1942 in the United States for unemployed, unmarried men. The legislation and mobilization of the program occurred quite rapidly. President Roosevelt made his request to Congress on March 21, 1933; the legislation was submitted to Congress the same day; Congress passed it by voice vote on March 31; Roosevelt signed it the same day, then issued an executive order on April 5, 1933 creating the agency. CCC enrollees will clear underbrush in forests, help in historic excavations, stabilize buildings and ruins, build roads and trails, park buildings, campgrounds, picnic areas, picnic tables, fireplaces, signs and exhibits, and other public structures, erect telephone poles and install electric lights, They also did some reforestation in the parks, although less than in the Forest Service, and organized eradication campaigns against harmful insects and tree diseases. The enrollees also fought fires and helped in natural disasters.

Beginning in June 1933 the first CCC camp in Campbell County was established. The enrollment included:
> John A. Thompson, Donald Osbourne, Wayne K. Garrett, William B. Gardner, Arthur L. Weaver
> Oscar Heptner, Otto Stok, Ashton Whisler, Carroll D. Whisler, Thaine G. Riley, Carl Toro

All were from Rozet. (Gillette News, July 13, 1933 and Gillette News, May 17, 1934) One of its primary assignments was in the extinguishing of burning coal mines near Gillette and southeast of Gillette.

They also worked on improving the entrance road to the Devils Tower. During the initial phase of President Roosevelt's "New Deal" legislation aimed at relief and recovery funds were provided for maintenance or improvement of park roads. Some portions of the road were reconstructed on new grades and alignment during 1933 and 1934 by the CCC. Some roads in the national park system have been listed on the National Register as significant examples of engineering or due to their exceptional architectural features. The Devil's Tower entrance road is an example of how road designers sought to integrate a transportation route with its natural surroundings. President Roosevelt wrote: *"I propose to create a Civilian Conservation Corps to be used in simple work more important, however, than the material gains will be the moral and spiritual value of such work."*

The following photographs were taken by Carroll D. "Slim" Whisler. The years he noted on some of the photographs are off a year when he tried to remember the years he took the photos 50 years later.

Rozet Encampment at Felix - 1933

Lunch break. Oscar Heptner 3rd from left
Ton Whisler on the right

Site Unknown - 1934

Working on the road to Devil's Tower – 1933

Devil's Tower Road

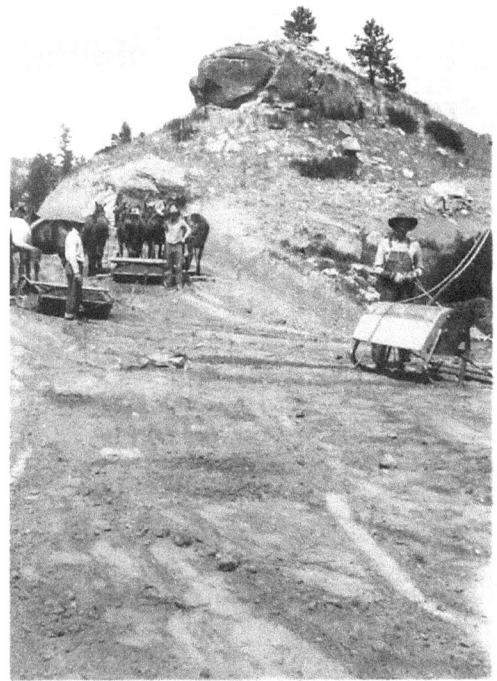

1932

1 932

Slim Whisler with his team and slip

Construction of Wessex underpass east of Rozet about 1934

1934 C.C.C.

Oscar Heptner on caterpillar

"WYOMING'S 1936 LICENSE PLATE UNIQUE"

Lester C. Hunt, Secretary of State, has originated and produced a unique and attractive idea in the 1926 Wyoming automobile license plate. Prior to the 1935 Legislature, the makeup of the plates was always the same, since specifications were definitely set out by statutes, allowing only a change in color from year to year. This made it possible for wide-spread counterfeiting of plates which was very difficult to detect; and with the thought in mind of overcoming this counterfeiting, together with the idea of producing the present plate, Secretary Hunt has introduced in the Legislature a bill to allow any changes in the makeup and design of the license plate the Secretary of State deemed necessary.

The art work in connection with the plates was done by Alvin True, brother of State Highway Engineer James B. True, in the form of a drawing 20x26 inches, which was reduced by photostatic machines in State Engineer Burritt's office to the dimensions for use on the plates. The plate has been made up in black and white, the two colors which hold their identity at the greatest distance, and has the approval of Governor Miller, Highway Engineer True and Captain George R. Smith of the Highway Patrol. The plate is slightly larger in size. The contract for the manufacture of the 1936 license plate has been granted to the Gopher Stamp and Die Company of St. Paul, Minnesota, at approximately the same figure as in 1935.

Secretary of State Hunt is of the opinion that the new plate not only is symbolic of our State, but also carries with it a definite advertising value for Wyoming. That he is correct in this assumption is evidenced by the extraordinary amount of interest that the new "Cowboy Plate" is already attracting.

FAMILIES (1930-1939)

Carroll Duvall "Slim" and Irene Lydia (Heptner) Whisler
1930

Slim was born October 2, 1905, northeast of Tecumseh, Johnson County, Nebraska, the first child of Riley and Vida Whisler. The family moved in 1910 to Mayberry, Pawnee County. Here Slim grew up with his brothers and sister. About 1920 the family moved again to Heartstrong, Yuma County, Colorado. He attended school only three months out of the year for two years. Slim never got his eighth grade diploma, as his father kept him busy in the fields during the summers and shucking corn in the winters. Due to no rain in two years, his father in 1923 brought the family to Rozet where his mother-in-law, Mrs. Catherine Clark was living. The family stayed with her until his father rented the George Place,

northeast of Rozet. Riley Whisler bought a relinquishment homestead claim from Frank George about seven miles north along the road to Adon. The family stayed at the George place while Slim and his older brothers helped their father improve the homestead. Slim left for Nebraska where he worked for a family in Custer County. Upon the death of his father in 1926 he returned to help his mother work the homestead. After his mother died in 1928 he continued to prove up the homestead. When he married Irene Heptner on July 2, 1930, in Gillette, Wyoming, they took his two younger brothers, Leonard and Dean, into their home. Irene was born May 31, 1906, in Glenwood, Mills County, Iowa. She was eight years old when she came with her parents Frank and Laura Heptner, who filed on a homestead nine miles north of Rozet in the Little Iowa community. She attended Cottonwood School and graduated from Rozet High School in 1928. They were the parents of four daughters:

ArLou Leona	b: 27 Sep 1933	d: 30 Sep 1936
Pearl Margaret	b: 11 Nov 1934	d: 18 Sep 1936
Lorna Jean	b: 07 Mar 1936	Living
Olive Carroll	b: 16 Dec 1940	Living

Slim Cutting telephone lines

Slim, Ton and Leonard shucking corn

In late September 1936 the two oldest daughters, ArLou and Pearl, died two weeks apart from complications of the influenza. They were buried in the Rozet Cemetery. During the 1930s Slim worked with the Civilian Conservation Corps (CCC) building roads between Moorcroft and the Devil's Tower. To supplement his income during the depression era he hunted coyotes, rabbits, and badgers which he would stretch and dry their skins and sell them to Sears and Roebuck. In 1943-45 he bought the

George "Obe" Nelson homestead south of them. In 1947, when his parents' estate was finalized, Slim bought out his sisters and brothers' share of the homestead. Slim worked in Gillette during the winter as a mechanic for Smith Implements Company to supplement their income. The only luxury he allowed himself was learning how to fly in the late 1940s and becoming a member of the Wyoming Flying Farmers. During the terrible winter of 1949 when he was working in town, he flew over the farm dropping the Sunday newspapers (*The Denver Post*) and mail to Irene and the girls; cigarettes to his brother-in-law, Eugene Heptner. He also flew over his neighbors to make sure they were out and about. Slim and Irene lived there until they moved to Gillette in 1950 when their oldest daughter was ready to enter high school. At that time, he went to work for the County maintaining roads and later on in the 1970s he worked for Paul's Tractor & Trucking in the oil fields building oil rig sites. In June 1971, they sold the farm to Raymond "Red" and Phyllis (Johnson) Record. Slim died June 9, 1983 and Irene died November 7, 1983. They are both buried in Pleasant Valley Cemetery.

Whisler Homestead - 1933
Slim Whisler on the binder; Eugene Heptner on the tractor

fall harvest of pumpkin and squash -1935
Slim, Leonard and Dean Whisler

January 1, 1936
Arlou Leona died 30 Sep 1936 and Pearl Margaret died 18 Sep 1936

Slim was a member of the
Wyoming Flying Farmers

Slim, Irene, Dean, Olive and Lorna
1944

Sources:
Photos from the collections of Carroll D. "Slim" Whisler.
 "The History of the David Riley and Pearl Vida (Duvall) Whisler Family, the First three Generations," by L. J. Whisler for the first
   Whisler Family Reunion, June 18-20, 1993.
 Pleasant Valley Cemetery Burial Book, kept by Mrs. Lucille Thompson (Xeroxed Copy-1998).
 "Whisler-Heptner marriage," News items, The News Record, Gillette, Wyoming, July 10, 1930.

Ashton Alfred "Ton" and Mildred Maurine (Day) Whisler
1930

Ton was born January 21, 1909, in Johnson County, Nebraska, a few miles northeast of Tecumseh. The family moved in 1910 to Mayberry, Pawnee County. Here Ton grew up with his brothers and sister. About 1920 the family moved again to Heartstrong, Yuma County, Colorado, where they stayed for about three years when his father moved the family north to Rozet, Wyoming in 1923. Ton's father died suddenly in fall of 1926; his mother in the late spring of 1928. He was nineteen years old, so to make ends meet and to help support his younger brothers and sisters he began working with neighbors and on the railroad.

Ton met and married Mildred Maurine Day, daughter of Mrs. Jennie Day. Mildred's father, Charles Otto Day, had died when she was four years old. Soon after her mother moved Mildred, her sister Alma, and her brother Charles to Moscow, Idaho, to take care of her father, Willard David Morgaeidge. Two years later she moved them back to Gillette where she began teaching at the Gillette Grade School. Mildred grew up in Gillette attending grade school and high school. She played girls basketball and played against two of her future sisters-in-law, Irene Heptner and Dorothy Whisler. Her mother died one month before she graduated from high school in May 1928. That fall she entered the Spearfish Teachers College, Spearfish, South Dakota. Mildred began teaching school in the fall of 1929 at the Barnes School located about fifteen miles south of Gillette. She married Ton Whisler on March 28, 1930, in the First Presbyterian Church manse, Gillette, Wyoming. They became the parents of ten children:

Joan Mae	b: 31 Jan 1930	d: 28 Jun 1936	
Charles Allen	b: 20 Nov 1932	d: 23 Jul 1941	
Alberta Maurine	b: 25 Nov 1934	d: 23 Jul 1941	
Sally Ella	b: 03 Nov 1936	d: 15 Sep 1987	m: Rolland Mellinger
Nancy Kay	b: 28 Jul 1938	d: 05 Dec 2019	m: (1) John Hugh Hallman
			m: (2) Edward Wolff
Virginia Phyllis	b: 10 Aug 1940	d: Living	m: Lloyd Bolton
Merle Robert "Buster"	b: 24 Dec 1942	d: Living	m: (1) Diane Smallwood
			(2) Kathy McManamen
			(3) Dianne Brodie
			m: (4) Joella Anne Robinson
Gary Alfred	b: 10 Jun 1946	d: 30 Oct 2021	Never Married
Steven Raymond	b: 11 Aug 1948	d: Living	m: Jill Suzanne Soltesz
Gary Allen (adopted)	b: 30 Dec 1961	d: Living	

Following their marriage on March 28, 1930, Ton continued working with the railroad while Mildred continued teaching at the Barnes School east of Dunlap's. After school was out in 1930 Mildred joined Ton at the Ray Nelson place and then shortly after they moved into a boxcar in Rozet where their first child Joan Mae was born on New Year's Eve, 1930. Their next move would be to a small white house in Rozet where Charles and Alberta were born. During this time they welcomed their brothers, Leonard Whisler and Charlie Day, to live with them while they attended school in Rozet. Soon they moved into another box car in Rozet where their first child, Joan, died from rheumatic fever on June 28, 1936, and they welcomed their third daughter, Sally, in November 1936.

Whisler Family Christmas -December 1930, Rozet, Wyoming
Back: Leonard, Ton, Mildred, Ruth, Elmer holding Phil, Dorothy holding Darleen, Oscar, and Irene
Front: Pauline, Ellen, Eurith and Dean

195

Shortly they moved again into a house just south of the school house in Rozet where their fourth daughter Nancy was born in July 1938. Ton was working for Charlie Sorenson as a ranch hand making the grand sum of $30.00 a month. About 1939 they left the "big" city of Rozet for the country moving north of Rozet about nine miles to the old Ben Schrand place. It was located across the road east of the Heptner place. Here their fifth and last daughter Virginia was born in August 1940. In 1941 during the first part of June this family was packing once again and settling a few miles south on the Lee Nelson farm where Ton became a farmer. A month later the family suffered a tragedy, Charles and Alberta drowned in a reservoir near their home. Ton and Mildred remained at that place for the next thirteen years. During that time three sons were born, Merle Robert, Gary Alfred, and Steven Raymond. Ton went to work for the Wyodak Coal Mine in 1954, and the family moved into one of the company's houses there. Years later he worked at the Underwood Lumber Company in Gillette until he retired in 1975. In 1953 Mildred began her twenty-year career as a nurse's aide at the Campbell County Memorial Hospital. She tended newborns and their mothers. She retired in 1973.

In 1962 they moved to Gillette, bought a trailer court on Laramie Street in Northside, named it the Whisler Trailer Court, and lived there for the remainder of their lives. About 1966 they adopted their grandson, Gary Allen, and raised him through his graduation from Campbell County High School after which he joined the U.S. Navy.

Ton died on February 24, 1994; Mildred died on May 31, 1999. Both are buried in the Rozet Cemetery beside Joan, Charles, and Alberta.

Joan Mae

Alberta and Charles

45th Wedding Anniversary 1975
Sitting: Ton and Mildred; Standing: Gary
Allen, Steve, Nancy Wolff, Gary Alfred,
Sally Mellinger, Virginia Bolton

Sources:
Photos: from the collections of Carroll D. "Slim" Whisler.
Script from a play about their lives written and performed by their grandchildren for their 50th wedding anniversary,
*   March 28, 1980.*
The History of the David Riley and Pearl Vida (Duvall) Whisler Family, the First three Generations, for the first Whisler Family,
*   Reunion June 18-20, 1993.*
"Whisler-Day marriage," The News Record, Gillette, Wyoming, April 3, 1930.
Mrs. Jennie Day Taken by Death on Last Tuesday (Mildred's mother), The News Record, Gillette, Wyoming, 1928.

Paul Madison Reed
1930

Paul Reed, the youngest brother of Rueben Reed, was the last child born of Benjamin Franklin and Harriet Emeline (Whitney) Reed. He was born August 28, 1867, near Steamboat Rock in Hardin County, Iowa. He never married. Paul lived between the Whisler homestead and his brother's homestead along the Adon Road, north of Rozet, Wyoming. Census records tell us Paul was a bit of a wanderlust. In the 1910 census we find him living in Garfield County, Colorado; in the 1920 census, in Hall County, Nebraska, living with his older brother, John. In May 1921 he crossed the border into Canada bound for Smithers, British Columbia, to farm. When he returned to the states is not known, but in the 1930 census he is found in Rozet, Wyoming, living near his older brother Rueben Reed. He was a good neighbor helping his neighbors harvest their fields. Paul died on December 21, 1946, and was buried in the Dayton Cemetery, Dayton, Sheridan County, Wyoming.

Paul Madison Reed

May 1936, at the home of Slim and Irene Whisler
Paul Reed (sitting down with a pipe and hat on) was a good friend of the Whisler and Heptner families. They included him often in their family gatherings.
Standing: Laura Heptner, holding Pearl Whisler, Arlou Whisler and Darleen Heptner standing in front of her, Irene Whisler, Marge Whisler, Pauline Whisler
Sitting: David Whisler, Allan Whisler, Ton Whisler with Alberta Whisler, Jeanette Heptner peeking over his shoulder, Mildred Whisler holding Joan Whisler, Dorothy Heptner holding Shirley Heptner, Ellen Whisler behind her, and Slim Whisler
On the ground: Dean Whisler, Eugene Heptner, Darrell Heptner, and Oscar Heptner

Sources:
Photos: from the collections of Carroll Duvall "Slim" Whisler.
Ancestry.com, 1870 U.S. Federal Census for Clay, Hardin County, Iowa, [database online], Provo, UT.
Ancestry.com, 1880 U.S. Federal Census for Clay, Hardin County, Iowa, [database online], Provo, UT.
Ancestry.com, 1910 U. S Federal Census for West Rifle, Garfield County, Colorado, [database online], Provo, UT.
Ancestry.com, 1920 U.S. Federal Census for Doniphan, Hall County, Nebraska, [database online], Provo, UT.
Ancestry.com, 1930 U.S. Federal Census for Election district 8 (Rozet), Campbell County, Wyoming, [database online], Provo, UT.
Ancestry.com, 1940 U.S. Federal Census for Campbell County, Wyoming, [database online], Provo, UT.
Ancestry.com, Border Crossings: From U.S. to Canada, 1908 – 1935 (May 11, 1923), [database online], Provo, UT.
Ancestry.com, U.S. Find A Grave Index, 1600s – Current, [database online], Provo, UT.

Johannes Nicolai "John" and Marie (Christensen) Jessen
1931

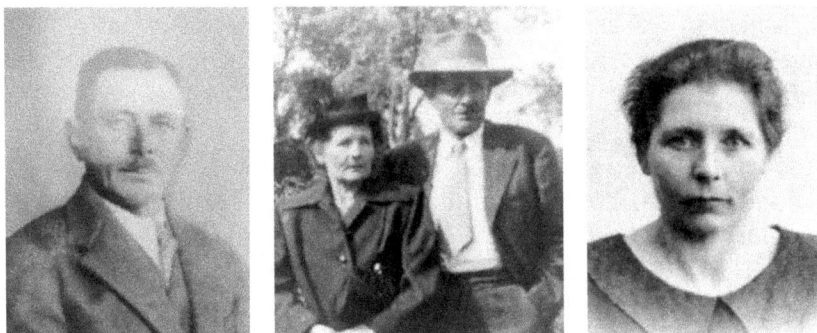

Johannes Nicolai "John" was born August 16, 1893, in Stoltelund, Germany. John spent most of his life in Germany and was a veteran of World War I, serving in the German army. On April 24, 1919, he married Marie Christensen. Marie was born January 27, 1894, in Terkelsbel, Sonderjylland, Denmark. John and Marie were the parents of six children who were born before they immigrated to the United States in 1931 from Tinglev, Germany, (now Denmark).

Unnamed	b: 27 Jan 1921 in Germany	d: 27 Jan 1921 in Germany	
Anna Marie	b: 27 Jan 1921 in Germany	d: __ Dec 1945 in Germany	
Jes Ratenburg	b: 29 Sep 1927 in Germany	d: 05 May 2011	m: Patty Norman
Jacob Walter	b: 29 Jul 1924 in Germany	d: 13 Nov 1934	
Crystal	b: 22 Dec 1927 in Germany	d: 21 May 2000	m: (1) Lon Cain Camp
			(2) Douglas G. Booren
Gertrude	b: 07 Apr 1929 in Germany	d: 25 Sep 1927	m: Hank Barlow

John arrived in the United States on May 24, 1930, and settled on a ranch northeast of Rozet. Marie arrived in 1931 with Jess, Walter, Crystal and Gertrude; leaving their oldest daughter, Anna Marie, with a family in Germany because she had become ill with tuberculosis. They planned to bring her when she had recovered but she died in December 1945. Their son, Jacob Walter, died from a terrible accident on November 13, 1934. He was ten years old leading a colt to water. The colt became frightened and bolted toward the corral, dragging the boy, who had tied the rope about his waist, behind him. He died instantly of a broken neck. Jacob was in the fourth grade at Rozet Consolidated School. Funeral services were held at Little Iowa Cemetery where he was buried.

John and Marie lived on their ranch for the rest of their lives. John made his livelihood by farming. Their son, Jess, served in the U.S. Navy on board a submarine during World War II. John was a member of the Buffalo-Belle soil conservation district. The children attended Rozet schools. John Jessen died on April 26, 1955, and was buried on April 26, 1955, in the Pleasant Valley Cemetery, northeast of Rozet. Marie died August 28, 1988, at age 94 and was buried on August 31, 1988, at the Pleasant Valley Cemetery beside her husband and son, Jacob.

Sources:
Photos: courtesy of Gertrude Jessen Barlow, Buffalo, Wyoming, July 5, 2017.
Correspondence from Gertrude Barlow, Buffalo, Wyoming, July 5, 2017.
"Rozet Lad Dies of Broken Neck; dragged by a Colt," The Gillette News, Gillette, Wyoming, November 15, 1934.
"Funeral Services Held Friday for John Jessen, 61," The News Record, Gillette, Wyoming, May 5, 1955.
Pleasant Valley Cemetery Burial Book, kept by Mrs. Lucille Thompson (Xeroxed Copy-1998.
Photo (John)s copied from Jessen Family Tree on Ancestry.com.
Ancestry.com, New York Passenger Lists, 1820-1957, [database online], Provo, UT.
Ancestry.com, List or Manifest of Alien Passengers for the United States, [database online], Provo, UT.
Ancestry.com, U.S. World War II Draft Registration Cards, 1942, [database online], Provo, UT.
Ancestry.com. U.S. Find-a-Grave Index, 1600s-Current, [database online], Provo, UT.
Ancestry.com, 1940 U.S. Federal Census for Campbell County, Wyoming, [database online], Provo, UT.

John Harris "Jack" and Hilda (Raudsep) Simpson
1932

Jack Simpson was born August 20, 1911, at Illif, Logan County Colorado, to Howard Harris and Bertha A. (Wirsig) Simpson. He spent his childhood in Illif where he delivered milk with horse and wagon to help his family with living expenses. Upon graduation from Illif High School in 1929 he worked on the Logan ranch in southern Montana with his father. That fall he attended the University of Colorado at Boulder. While attending college he worked for the Hines Pickle Company of LaSalle, Colorado. In 1932 Jack packed up his Model A Ford and his milk cow and headed to Wyoming, where he homesteaded north of Wyodak on Deer Creek. In 1933 he went to work for the Harris-Simpson Livestock Company, managing the Laurel Leaf, the Wagonhammer, and the Kohns ranches in northeast Campbell County. On November 15, 1941, he married Hilda Raudsep in Miles City, Montana. Hilda Raudsep was born March 23, 1914, in Crook County, Wyoming, to Hans and Emilie (Saskin) Raudsep. She spent her childhood on the family homestead and attended West End School in Crook County, graduating from Moorcroft High School in 1932. After receiving her normal training in Moorcroft, Hilda taught rural schools during the winter months and attended the University of Wyoming Summer Schools. She continued teaching in Crook and Weston county schools until her marriage. Jack and Hilda lived on the Wagonhammer ranch until 1947 when they moved to the Kohns ranch. In 1951, the couple bought this ranch, which became their family home. They were the parents of five children:

Loren	b: 07 Oct 1942	d: 05 Sep 2016	m: June Marguerite Smith
Hilda Ann	b: 09 Apr 1945	Living	m: Leland Brimmer
Kay Rene	b: 29 Oct 1947	Living	m: Leroy Jones
Cheri Rae	b: 25 Jul 1953	Living	m: George Eldon Faris
Lois	b: 11 Dec 1955	Living	m: Marlon Schlup

Throughout his life, Jack was active in agriculture and in his early life enjoyed 4-H. He had a keen knowledge of different soils and the ability of soils to produce crops. Jack was a member of the Agriculture Advisory Board, the Farmers Co-op Association Board, Agriculture Stabilization and Conservation Service Board, Conservation District and the National Association of Conservation Districts. He was a member of the Powder River Basin Resources Council, of which he served as a board member and chairman of the board. Jack loved to read and enjoyed writing homespun poetry. Jack was inducted into the Wyoming Cowboy Hall of Fame posthumously on September 25, 2016, in Casper, Wyoming. Hilda was a member of Pythian Sisters, Gloria Temple #6 of Moorcroft, Wyoming, where she held numerous offices and was Past Grand Chief for the State of Wyoming. She was also a member of Campbell County Woolgrowers Auxiliary.

Jack and Hilda were members of the University of Wyoming Agricultural Scholarship Foundation. Their legacy lives on in that capacity with the scholarship that still helps University of Wyoming students in the College of Agriculture. Hilda died December 21, 1986, in Campbell County Memorial Hospital, Gillette, Wyoming. Jack died at his ranch home on July 8, 1988, of a massive heart attack. They are both buried in the Pleasant Valley Cemetery, northeast of Rozet, Wyoming, on the south edge of the ranch where they raised their family and always worked so hard together. This plot of land was deeded for the cemetery by Jack's uncle Charles Simpson.

Sources:
Photos: courtesy of Lois Simpson Schlup by email on July 31, 2017.
"Simpson Funeral Scheduled Friday (Hilda)," The News Record, Gillette, Wyoming, Dec 23, 1986.
"Jack Simpson, obituary," The News Record, Gillette, Wyoming, July 10, 1988.
Simpson, Faris wed in Moorcroft," The News Record, _____, Gillette, Wyoming.
"Campbell County Historic Ranches: Shippy Ranch," Gillette News Record, Jan 30, 2012.
Pleasant Valley Cemetery Burial Book, kept by Mrs. Lucille Thompson (Xeroxed Copy-1998).
Wyoming Cowboy Hall of Fame Recipients www.wyomingcowboyhalloffame.com.
Ancestry.com. U.S. Find-a-Grave Index 1600s-Current; Obituary [database online], Provo, UT.
Ancestry.com, 1920 U.S. Federal Census for Illif, Logan County, County, CO, [database online], Provo, UT.

Jesse R. and Nancy "Maye" (McClure) Kennedy
1933

Jesse Kennedy was born May 17, 1885, in Cedarville, Kansas, to John and Alice Kennedy. He spent his boyhood near Cedarville and Cloverdale, Kansas. On April 6, 1910, he married Nancy "Maye" McClure, at Winfield, Kansas. She was born on May 11, 1892, the daughter of Ulysses S. Grant and Mary Eliza (Huse) McClure. Jesse and Maye were the parents of one son:

Doyle	b: 21 Jan 1911	d: 09 Jun 1978	m: (1) Opal Swartz
			(2) Odell Jewell Shaw

Jesse and Maye made their home at Winfield, Kansas, until 1918 when he moved his family to Otto, Kansas, and later to Towner, Kansas. In 1920, he moved with his family to Wyoming and settled on a homestead north of Gillette in the Recluse area. Later they sold the place and bought the Weston Harvey place in Weston on Little Powder River. In 1933 he moved with his wife to Rozet, where he owned and operated the Rozet Store until he retired in 1943 and moved to Sheridan, Wyoming. Jesse died February 8, 1963, in Sheridan and was buried February 12, 1963 in Mount Pisgah Cemetery, Gillette, Wyoming. Maye died in November 1953 and was buried November 21, 1952, in Mount Pisgah Cemetery, Gillette, Wyoming.

Sources:
"Society-Kennedy-Swartz Wedding," The News Record, Gillette, Wyoming, October 18, 1934.
"Kennedy [Odell Jewell] Services Saturday," The News Record, Gillette, Wyoming, October29, 1976.
"Obituary-Doyle Kennedy," page 12, The News Record, Gillette, Wyoming, June 12, 1978.
Campbell County, The Treasured Years, 1990, compiled by Campbell County Historical Society. Gillette, Wyoming.

Henry M. "Deafy" and Daphne E. (Goerke) Edwards
1934

Deafy Edwards was born June 7, 1895, at Topeka, Shawnee County, Kansas. His family moved to Buffalo, Wyoming when he was a small child. While he was working for the FJ Ranch, he was struck by lightning in 1913. He suffered severe burns and burst eardrums, leaving him with a nearly total loss of hearing. In 1918 He was again struck by lightning without further disability, but in 1957 he was struck again by lightning, resulting in the loss of the remainder of his hearing. On April 4, 1918 he married Daphene Goerke. She was born October 4, 1899, at Topeka, Kansas, to Lewis and Anna May Goerke. She spent her childhood in Topeka and Wakarusa, Kansas, where she received her education. In 1916, she moved to Wyoming with her parents where they established a homestead near Oriva, on the Echeta Road west of Gillette. Deafy also had established a homestead near Oriva where they lived until he sold it in 1925 and moved to a farm fourteen miles south of Gillette. Deafy and Daphene remained there until 1933 when they purchased the former Charlie Hinds place north of Rozet. Deafy and Daphene were the parents of seven children;

Melvin Russell "Smokey"	b: 11 Feb 1920	d: 20 Jun 2013	m: Bernadine May Heckathorn
Irene Isabelle	b: 19 Oct 1921	d: 30 Jul 2012	m: Howard E. Hladkey
Clyde Remely	b: 24 Feb 1924	d: 02 Jun 2014	m: Nancy Josephine Southern
Clara May	born: 15 Jul 1925	d: 13 Jan 2006	m: (1) Edgar M. Homers
			(2) Wesley Leroy VanBuskirk
Charles Leo	b: 26 May 1928	d:	m: Anna L. Ketcham
Myrtle Marie	b: 12 Mar 1933	d: 12 Mar 1933	
Verna Mae	b: about 1942	d:	m: Charles Martin

Daphne died on January 2, 1978, age 78, at her home, the result of injuries received when she fell down a flight of stairs. She was buried in the Mount Pisgah, Cemetery, Gillette, Wyoming. Deafy then moved to Casper to live near his daughter, Clara May. He died in Casper, Wyoming, in March 1980, age 84, and was buried in the Mount Pisgah Cemetery alongside his wife.

Sources:
Photo: _Ancestry.com_, U.S. Find-a-Grave Index, 1600s-Current, [database online]. Provo, UT.
"Funeral Services Held for Baby Who Dies on Sunday [parents Mr. and Mrs. Henry Edwards]," _The News Record_, March 16, 1933.
"Fall Results in Death of Rozet Ranch wife," _The News Record_, Gillette, Wyoming, January 3, 1978.
"Funeral Set Thursday for Area Homesteader," _The News Record_, Gillette, Wyoming, March 11, 1980.
Ancestry.com, U.S. Cemetery and Funeral Home Collection, 1847-Current, [database online], Provo, UT.
Ancestry.com, Montana, County Marriage Records, 1865-1993, [database online], Provo, UT.
Ancestry.com, California, Marriage Index, 1949-1959, [database online], Provo, UT.
Ancestry.com Newspapers.com Obituary Index, 1800s-current, [database online], Provo, UT.
Ancestry.com, U.S. Veterans' Gravesites, ca. 1775-2019, [database online], Provo, UT.
Ancestry.com, U.S. World War I Draft Registration Cards, 1917-1918, [database online], Provo, UT.
Ancestry.com, U.S. World War II Draft Registration Cards, 1942, [database online], Provo, UT.
Ancestry.com, U.S. World War II Draft Cards Young Men, 1940-1947, [database online], Provo, UT.
Ancestry.com U.S. World War II Cadet Nursing Corps Card Files, 1942-1948, [database online], Provo, UT.
Ancestry.com, 1900 U.S. Federal Census (for Daphne) for Topeka, Shawnee County, Kansas, [database online], Provo, UT.
Ancestry.com, 1900 U.S. Federal Census (for Deafy) for St. Joseph Ward 7, Buchanan County, Missouri, [database online], Provo, UT.
Ancestry.com, 1920 U.S. Federal Census for Felix, Campbell County, Wyoming, [database online], Provo, UT.
Ancestry.com, 1930 U.S. Federal Census for Election District 19, Campbell County, Wyoming, [database online], Provo, UT.
Ancestry.com, 1940 U.S. Federal Census for Campbell County, Wyoming, [database online], Provo, UT.

David R. and Marjorie Adelle (Mayden) Whisler
1935

David Whisler was born October 11, 1911, at May-berry, Pawnee County, Nebraska, the third son of David Riley and Pearl Vida (Duvall) Whisler. David was twelve years old when he came to Rozet, via Yuma County, Colorado, with his parents. His father bought a homestead reclamation claim; rented the George place for his family to live while he and his older sons worked on improving the homestead. He attended the Well creek school and later Rozet High School. David's father died suddenly in November 1926; his mother two years later in June 1928. He quit school and began working for neighbors and later on the railroad. David was working in Nebraska when he met and married Marjorie Adella Mayden in Ogallala, Nebraska on June 22, 1935. He was twenty and she was seventeen. They were the parents of three children:

Barbara, Marge, Don, David, Deloris

Donald Lewis	b: 25 May 1936	d: 28 Nov 2014	m: Patricia Fitzgerald
Deloris Rose "Dee"	b: 03 Jun 1937	Living	m: Bernard "Red" McGillis
Barbara Jean "Bobbie"	b: 12 Oct 1938	Living	

The children attended the Whisler School until the fall of 1949 when they renrolled in Rozet Consolidated School. All three graduated from Rozet high school. They farmed and ranched in the Rozet area from the time they were married until 1965. They first lived on the old Schrand place, across the road east of Grandma Heptner at the north end of present day North Heptner Road. Here the children attended the Whisler School. In the early 1950s they bought the Potter Place across the road from Oscar and Dorothy Heptner on the South Heptner Road where they lived until he sold it to Claude Kissick in 1965 and moved to Moorefield, Nebraska. Later because he had wandering feet, he bought and sold and moved to Oshkosh, Nebraska. They lived in various places in Nebraska including Kearney and Morrill, until the early 1980s when they moved back to Wyoming, living in various places including Lusk and Torrington. Their children called them "gypsies." In March of 1992 he suffered a stroke and returned to Gillette until his death April 27, 1992.

Marge was born April 15, 1918, in Stoneham, Well county, Colorado, to Lewis Joshua and Bertha Adeline (Thomson) Mayden. She grew up in Northport, Nebraska, where she attended grade school and two years of high school. The family moved to Ogallala, Nebraska, in 1932 where she attended high school until her marriage to David Whisler in June 1935. Twelve years later she returned to high school at Rozet and received her diploma in May 1947. While living in Kearney, Nebraska, she went to the Central Nebraska Technical College, School of Practical Nursing. She graduated in 1971 and began her nursing career with the Gothenburg Hospital and always found work wherever they lived until David died. After his death she lived in Gillette and Sheridan, Wyoming, until her death on July 22, 1999. Both were buried in the Rozet Cemetery, Rozet, Wyoming.

Source:
"The History of the David Riley and Pearl Vida (Duvall) Whisler Family, the First Three Generations," by L. J. Whisler for the first Whisler Family Reunion, June 18-20, 1993.

Clarence Lavedia "C.L." and Esther O. (Howe) Brunson
1936

C. L. Brunson was born April 20, 1901, in Olathe, Johnson County, Kansas, to John Orville and Emma May (Demmick) Brunson. He attended country school in Olathe. After school, he was a mail carrier out of Walsh, Colorado, and he also had a job selling Maytag washing machines. On August 20, 1934, he married Esther Howe in Syracuse, Kansas. Esther was born October 10, 1914, in Knowles, Oklahoma, to Henry Joseph and Mary Iola (Lonberg) Howe. At the age of eleven, after her mother died of cancer, she kept house and cooked for her father and brothers. She attended various schools in Kansas and Colorado and quit in her senior year of high school in Holly, Colorado, where she worked as a housekeeper and babysitter for her room and board. C. L. and Esther made their home near Holly, Colorado. However, after they lost everything they owned in a fire and then again in a flood, he decided in the spring of 1936, with $2.00 in his pocket, to move his wife and child to Gillette, Wyoming. They farmed the old Brownlee Ranch southwest of Rozet for approximately nineteen years. In the early 1940s, they bought the Ben Kelly homestead. C. L. and Esther were the parents of two children:

Emma Iola	b: 05 Apr 1935	d: 12 Dec 2012	m: Paul Edward Cooper
Winfred L.	b: 03 Nov 1937	d: 14 May 2021	m:

C. L. drove a Rozet School bus route for approximately fourteen years starting in 1940, using a homemade school bus. He designed the bus by building a wood topper over the bed of a pickup truck, like modern camper toppers. He lined the sides of the truck bed with bench-type seats for the children. After seeing Brunson's bus, many other rural residents built similar buses. C. L. supported the World War II effort by collecting scrap iron and hauling it to the Gillette depot to be shipped for defense use. Esther helped with the ranch work; sold butter, eggs, milk, and cream in Gillette; and at one time furnished the frying chickens for Demos Restaurant, later known as the Stockman's Cafe. After World War II, Esther went back to school and graduated with her son from Campbell County High School in 1955. In the late 1950s to the early 1970s C. L. worked as a bartender at the Stockman's bar. Poor health and the discovery of oil on his land prompted the Brunson's to move into Gillette and go into semi-retirement.

C. L. died June 6, 1989, at home, after an extended illness. Esther died eight months after her husband on February 13, 1990. They are both buried in the Mount Pisgah, Cemetery, Gillette, Wyoming.

Sources:
"Obituary—C. L Brunson," *The News Record*, Gillette, Wyoming, June 6, 1989 .
"Obituary—Esther Brunson," *The News Record*, Gillette, Wyoming, February 18, 1990.
"Obituary—W. L 'Fred' Brunson," *Gillette News Record*, Gillette, Wyoming, __ May 2021.
Ancestry.com, U.S. Find-a-Grave Index, 1600s-Current, [database online], Provo, UT.
Ancestry.com, U.S. World War II Draft Cards Young Men, 1940-1947, [database online], Provo, UT.
Ancestry.com, 1920 U.S. Federal Census for Eagle, Sedgwick, Kansas, [database online], Provo, UT.
Ancestry.com, 1930 U.S. Federal Census for Fort Collins, Larimer County, Colorado, [database online], Provo, UT.
Ancestry.com, 1940 U.S. Federal Census for Campbell County, Wyoming, [database online], Provo, UT.

Kristian Emil "Chris" and Marie (Spirup) Larsen
1938

Chris Larsen was born on November 5, 1888, in Damholds, Denmark. He attended school there and was employed on farms until 1907 when he came to the United States and went to Hamlin, Iowa. He married Marie Spirup, on January 13, 1911, in Hamlin, Iowa. She was the daughter of George and Caroline (Rasmussen) Spirup. She was born January 31, 1891, in Hamlin, Iowa. She grew up and attended schools in Hamlin. Chris and Marie became the parents of two sons:

Marion Emil	b: 25 Jun 1911	d: 30 Apr 1998	m: Margaret Federer
George Louis	b: 08 Aug 1914	d: 09 Dec 2011	m: Hertha Semlek

Chris and Marie owned a farm in Iowa, and they lived there until 1920, when he sold his farm and they moved to a homestead in the Thunder Basin community south of Gillette. They lived there until 1926 when they decided to move to Oregon. But they returned to Wyoming in 1929 to their farm at Thunder Basin. Almost ten years later in 1938 they sold their farm in the Thunder Basin community and moved to the Little Iowa community northeast of Rozet. Here they farmed the land taking the good years and the not so good years that brought grasshoppers, hail storms, snow storms, and droughts. Life was not easy on the high plains. but there they made their home until Chris' death on March 4, 1966. He was buried in the Mount Pisgah Cemetery, Gillette, Wyoming. That fall Marie moved to Gillette, Wyoming, where she lived the rest of her life. She died July 2, 1989, and was buried alongside her husband in Mount Pisgah Cemetery. Both of their sons served in World War II; both returned home; George to work the ranch with his father while Marion settled Cheyenne, Wyoming.

Winter 1949

Marie getting some sun on a sunny
February day

The grove of trees did its job keeping snow in the trees
February day

Sources:
Photos: of Marie and Chris from the collections of Leona and Jeanette Heptner from the Winter of 1949, courtesy of Diann Larsen Avery, 2020.
"Funeral Services Held Tuesday for C. E. Larsen, 77," The News Record, Gillette, Wyoming, March 10, 1966.
"Obituary—Marie Larsen," The News Record, Gillette, Wyoming, July 5, 1989.

George and Hertha (Semlek) Larsen

George Louis was born August 8, 1914, to Chris and Marie (Spirup) Larsen, in Iowa. His parents sold their farm in 1920 and moved to a homestead in the Thunder Basin community south of Gillette. They lived there until 1926 when they moved to Oregon. In 1929, they returned to the ranch at Thunder Basin. Chris and Marie lived there until 1938 when they sold the ranch and moved to the Little Iowa community northeast of Rozet.

George was inducted into the Army in February 1941. He served the duration of World War II, first in Fort Lewis, Washington, then camps in Oregon, California, and Texas. In 1944 he was sent overseas where he served in France, Germany and Austria. He spent all of his time in the service as a cook for officers and enlisted men. He was discharged from active duty in August 1945, and he returned to the family ranch.

On June 3, 1951, George married Hertha Semlek, daughter of Alex and Anna Semlek. She was born May 8, 1914. They became the parents of four children (two sets of twins):

Ann	b: 26 Apr 1952	Living:	m: John Shellhart
Diann	b: 26 Apr 1952	Living	m: Matt Avery
Don	b: 23 Feb 1955	Living	m: (1) Shirley Morgan
			(2) Sheila Parks
Dan	b: 23 Feb 1955	Living	

George continued to farm his parents' place. Hertha taught school for many years in various country schools and eventually for the Gillette Elementary School District. Upon their respective retirements they continued to live on the farm. At the age of 97 they both died in 2011, Hertha on May 23rd and George on December 9th. They were both buried at Pleasant Valley Cemetery, Rozet, Wyoming.

Sources:
Photos: courtesy of Diann Larsen Avery May 2017.
Pleasant Valley Cemetery Burial Book, kept by Mrs. Lucille Thompson (Xeroxed Copy-1998).
Ancestry.com, U.S. Find-a-Grave Index, 1850-2012, [database on-line], Provo, UT.

Albert B. and Miriam Marjorie (Stull) Wells
1938

Albert was born July 19, 1904, in Lamar, Chase County, Nebraska, to John and Mattie E. (Dawson) Wells. His father was killed in an accident in 1914. Mattie Wells and her son moved to northeast Wyoming in 1919 from Kimball, Kimball County, Nebraska. She filed on a homestead located seven miles north of Gillette. Albert found work in the area ranches, breaking horses as well as working to improve the family homestead. Albert filed on a homestead northeast of Rozet and east of Adon in Sections 27 and 28, Township 53 North, Range 69 West in 1938.

Miriam Marjorie Stull also filed on a homestead in Sections 33, 34, and 35, Township 53 North, Range 69 West, in 1930. Miriam was born December 24, 1904, in Waterloo, Iowa, daughter of George and Alice (Stewart) Stull. She was five years old when her parents moved to Wyoming to settle on a homestead. Her first school was in her aunt's home (Mrs. May Stewart Doane) which was a tent in her back yard. Her aunt had moved out of her house in the summer to live in a tent, and she held summer school in her house for fourteen children. This school later evolved into the Little Iowa School where Miriam attended through the 8th grade. In the fall of 1921, she attended Moorcroft High School through her sophomore year when she transferred to Campbell County High School. Upon graduation in 1924 she was given a two-year normal training certificate. This allowed her to teach in rural elementary schools for two years without additional credits. She and Albert were married in her log house on May 1, 1927. The Reverend Samuel Ryland officiated. They were the parents of five children:

Elmer Levi	b: 09 Jun 1929	d: 22 Jun 1952	killed in Korean War
Merle Albert	b: 02 May 1931	d: 18 Jan 1932	age 8 months
Shirley A.	b: 22 Apr 1935	d: 08 Oct 2021	m: Edwin N. Dillinger (div)
Cecil Thurston	b: 23 Aug 1940	d: 30 Oct 1985	m: (1) Rita Reynolds (div)
			(2) Joyce _____
James Dwaine	b: 28 Mar 1947	d: 1965, age 17	

While Albert worked on developing their ranch Miriam taught rural schools and attended summer schools through the University of Wyoming to keep her teaching certificates current. She graduated from the University of Wyoming in 1959 with a BA degree in education. Miriam taught school in the area northwest of Moorcroft and in other rural schools for twenty-one years. In 1959 she started teaching the first grade at Sundance. Miriam died at her home, age 63, of a sudden illness on April 7, 1966. She was buried in the Pleasant Valley Cemetery, northeast of Rozet, Wyoming. Albert died June 19, 1981, and was buried alongside his wife and three sons.

PFC Elmer Levi Wells

Sources:
Bureau of Land Management, Homestead Patent Index, [www.glorecords.blm.gov].
"Personals-'Wells-Stull Marriage,'" the *News Record*, May 5, 1927.
"Funeral Services Held for Wells Child Sunday," *the News Record*, Gillette, Wyoming, January 28, 1932.
"Services Held for Mrs. Albert Wells Area Teacher," page 5, *The News Record*, Gillette, Wyoming, April 21, 1966.
"Funeral Wednesday for Albert Wells," *The News Record*, Gillette, Wyoming, June 30, 1981.
Campbell County, The Treasured Years, 1990, pages 623-624, compiled by Campbell County Historical Society.
Pleasant Valley Cemetery Burial Book, kept by Mrs. Lucille Thompson (Xeroxed Copy-1998).
"Let Your Life Shine," Volume III, *Pioneer Women Educators of Wyoming*, edited by Sheryl Lain, published by Alpha Xi,
    State Delta Kappa Gamma, 1994.

Calmer Christian and Hazel Irene (Perkins) Nielsen
1939

Calmer Christian Nielson was born on April 21, 1905, at Wisner, Nebraska, to Niels Peter and Karen Marie Nielson. In 1911 he moved with his parents to O'Neill, Holt County Nebraska. They moved in 1913 to Chambers where Calmer grew to young manhood. Hazel was born December 12, 1907, at Ewing, Nebraska, to Howard and Myrtle Perkins. She grew up there attending school and graduating from high school in Ewing, Nebraska. On June 2, 1926, Calmer and Hazel were married in Lake Andes, South Dakota, Nebraska. They were the parents of one daughter:

Bonnie Jean   b: 1930   d: 06 Apr 2017   m: Clarence William "Bill" Switzer

In 1930 Calmer and Hazel moved the family to Wyoming where they homesteaded at Dull Center, 60 miles northeast of Douglas, Wyoming. They lived there until 1939 when they moved to Rozet, Wyoming. Their daughter Bonnie Jean graduated from Rozet High School in 1947. Calmer died on August 1, 1959, and was buried in the Mount Pisgah Cemetery, Gillette, Wyoming. Hazel moved to Sheridan, Wyoming, where she worked as a nurse's aide in Sheridan County Memorial Hospital until her retirement in 1969. She then moved to Dayton, Wyoming. Hazel, age 85, died on April 18, 1993, in Sheridan, Wyoming, and was buried in Mount Pisgah Cemetery, Gillette, Wyoming.

Sources:
Photo: *from the collections of Leona and Jeanette Heptner.*
"Services Held Wednesday for Calmer C. Nielsen," The News Record, Gillette, Wyoming, August 6, 1959.
"Obituary-Hazel Nielsen," The News Record, Gillette, Wyoming, April 21, 1993.
"Obituary-Herbert Nielson," page 18, The News Record, Gillette, Wyoming, June 1, 1978.
Ancestry.com, Newspapers.com Obituary Index, [database line], Provo, UT.
Ancestry.com, U.S. Find-a-Grave Index, 1600s-Current, [database line], Provo, UT.
Ancestry.com, South Dakota, Marriages, 1905-2017, [database line], Provo, UT.
Ancestry.com, U.S. Social Security Applications and Claims Index, 1936-2007, [database line], Provo, UT.
Ancestry.com, 1900 U.S. Federal Census for Wisner, Cuming County, Nebraska (for Niels Nelson-immigrant), [database line], Provo, UT.
Ancestry.com, 1910 U.S. Federal Census for Beemer, Cuming County, Nebraska, [database line], Provo, UT.
Ancestry.com, 1920 U.S. Federal Census for Conley, Holt County, Nebraska, [database line], Provo, UT.
Ancestry.com, 1930 U.S. Federal Census for Cheyenne River, Converse County, Wyoming, [database line], Provo, UT.
Ancestry.com, 1940 U.S. Federal Census for Campbell County, Wyoming, [database line], Provo, UT.

1940 – 1949

Rozet, Campbell County Wyoming

Grandma (Laura) Heptner in her Victory Garden
1943
(Photo from collections of Leona and Jeanette Heptner)

Introduction

This decade started expectantly of a brighter future. The families of Rozet, Adon, and Dillinger were beginning to feel they could stay on in this land in spite of personal hardships, dry summers, cold winters. Fields were beginning to take shape and producing better crops, livestock herds were building up; new families were moving into the area purchasing abandoned homesteads. They quickly became a part of the community, bringing their own special contributions to the area. However, many plans were put on hold when Japan attacked Pearl Harbor, Hawaii, on Sunday, December 7, 1941. Europe was already at war with Germany and this attack brought the United States into another World War. Rationing became a way of life for every family —gas, sugar, oil. Cast off iron from obsolete machinery was cut up and hauled to Gillette for shipment to factories to help build ships. Victory gardens were planted and tended. Sons, husbands and brothers enlisted into the armed forces. Some would not return to their families. From 1942-1945 the families looked forward to rare letters from their loved ones. Some censored to the point the only comfort for the families was to hold the letter close to their hearts. They listened to the radio for news on the war. The death of President Franklin D. Roosevelt was felt around the world. He is the only president to be elected to four consecutive terms of office. His influence throughout the previous decade, the "depression years" and through World War II was felt in every community in the nation. With the surrender of the Germans in May 1945 followed by the Japanese in September the Rozet community felt both relief and a determination to put the war behind them. Returning veterans took advantage of the G. I. Bill and completed their college education. Some to build up the family farms and ranches. Some to be married and start raising a family.

Veterans of World War II

Standing: Leland Ewing, Bob Hamm, George Larsen, Warren Williams, Clyde Stewart, Charlie Howell, Don Osborne, Richard Grey, Lee Wallace, David Bryant, James Bryant, Vince Thar
Sitting: Melvin Donner, Calvin Tholsen, Fred Kummerfeld, Phil Frey, Merle Duvall, Keith Ware, Johnny Talley, Jes Jessen, Ron Osborne, Neil Riesland, Charles Kottraba
1945/46

Jesse Lee Cummings   **Clara Mae Edwards**   **Phil Frey**   **Louis Frey**

Orie Gilliland   **Bob Hamm and Dean Whisler**   **Jess Jessen**

Clara Shafer   **Dean Whisler**   **Leonard Whisler**   **Leonard Whisler**

Photos from the collections of Leona and Jeanette Heptner, and Carroll D. "Slim" Whisler.
Photo of Clara Shafer courtesy of Gayle Moon Parish, Idaho, 2020.
Photos of Louis and Phil Frey courtesy of Janice Day Stratman.
Photos of Lee Cummings, Dean and Leonard Whisler from the collections of Carroll D. "Slim" Whisler.
Photo of Jess Jessen from a family tree on Ancestry.com.

WORLD WAR TWO (1941-1945)
VETERANS

Veteran	from	Parents
Charles E. Alexander		
David R. Bryant	Rozet	Ray & Josephine Weaver Bryant
James E. Bryant	Rozet	Ray & Josephine Weaver Bryant
Nyles S. Bryant	Rozet	Ray & Josephine Weaver Bryant
Walter D. Burr	Rozet	Ed & Marguerite Burr
Wayne Burr	Rozet	Andy & Tessie Burr
Arthur Christenson	Adon	Charley & Jenny Christianson
Alvin Christenson (died as a POW in Bataan, Japan)	Adon	Charley & Jenny Christianson
Roy Christenson	Adon	Charley & Jenny Christianson
Donald "Bud" Christenson	Adon	Charley & Jenny Christianson
Charles "Ted" Christenson	Adon	Charley & Jenny Christianson
Charles Cullivan	Miller Creek	
Lee Cummings	Rozet (Basin)	Myrtle Cummings, Basin, WY (married: Ellen Whisler)
P. A. Davis		
John R. Davis		
Melvin Donner	Adon	Charley & Dora Donner
Kenneth R. Duvall	Rozet	Jim & Elsie Duvall
Merle Duvall	Rozet	Jim & Elsie Duvall
Clyde R. Edwards	Rozet	Deafy & Daphne Edwards
Clara Mae Edwards	Rozet	Deafy & Daphne Edwards
Melvin R. Edwards	Rozet	Deafy & Daphne Edwards
Richard Engdahl	Adon	Merle & Leota Engdahl
Louis A. Frey	Rozet	Tobe & Nellie Frey
Phillip G. Frey	Rozet	Tobe & Nellie Frey
Orie V. Gilliland	Adon Road	Roy & Gladys Gilliland
Raymond Ghramm	Rozet	George & Nellie Ghramm
Billy W. Ghramm	Rozet	
Richard Lee Gray	Rozet	O'Neal & Lulu Gray
Hugh R. "Bob" Hamm	Rozet	Adolph & Evelyn Hamm

Veteran	from	Parents
Garfield Hatfield	Adon	Louis & Eva Hatfield
Douglas Hatfield	Adon	Louis & Eva Hatfield
Emory Hatfield	Adon	Louis & Eva Hatfield
Ivan Hatfield	Adon	Louis & Eva Hatfield
Robert Hayes	Adon	Henry K Hayes
Maynard High	Adon	
Richard L. Hiles	Rozet	Eileen Brennan Hiles (wife)
C. E. Howe		
Jes Jessen	Miller Creek	John & Marie Jessen
Earl B. Johnson	Rozet	Lee & Emma Johnson (Weston)
Louis Johnson	Rozet	Lee & Emma Johnson (Weston)
Darrell D. Jones		
Charles W. Kottraba	Piney Creek	Ray & Kathryn Kottraba
George L. Larsen	Miller Creek	Chris & Marie Larsen
Wilbur J. Lairmore		
Ernest R. Lairmore		
Willie Lubkin	Rozet	William & Edna Lubkin
John C. Matthews	Rozet	
W. L. Mayden		
Ernest McSparren		
Albert R. Moon	Rozet	Ora & Sabitha Moon
Edwin N. Moran	Rozet	Mrs. Julia Moran
Thomas Noe		
Ronald J. Osbourne	Rozet	Francis & Elizabeth Osborne
Donald E. Osbourne	Rozet	of Whitefish, Montana; (step-brothers of Richard, Charles, Dorothy & Betty Gray)
Edward J. Poll		
Everett Pownall	Adon	

Veteran	from	Parents
Lewis Preston	Timber Creek	John & Bertha Preston
Rodney Ellis Reel	Rozet	Virgil & Agnes Reel
Neal R. Riesland	Rozet	
Thaine Riley	Rozet	Leslie & Sarah Riley
Omar Ruff	Rozet	Marion & Effie Ruff
Velmer Ruff	Rozet	Younger brother of Marion Ruff
William A. "Bill" Semlek (POW; liberated June 28, 1945)	Miller Creek	Alex & Anna Semlek
Ralph J. Shafer	Miller Creek	Clarence & Myrtle Shafer
Richard Shafer	Miller Creek	Clarence & Myrtle Shafer
Clara Pearl Shafer	Miller Creek	Clarence & Myrtle Shafer
Eugene I. Simpson	Miller Creek	_____
Clyde E. Stewart	Rozet	George & Martha Stewart
Edward L. Stok		
John V. Talley	Rozet	Mrs. Mae Talley
Francis J. Thar	Rozet	Henry & Mary Thar
John H. Thar	Rozet	Henry & Mary Thar
Vincent Thar	Rozet	Henry & Mary Thar
Calvin E. Tholson	Rozet	John & Kitty Tholson
John Lawrence Tholson	Rozet	John & Kitty Tholson
Eldon Tholson	Rozet	Oscar & Bernice Tholson
Marion E. Thomas		
Bernard J. Thompson	Rozet	Mary (Shaughnessy) Thompson White
Arnold Tomingas	Adon	John & Emma Tomingas
Arthur Tomingas	Adon	John & Emma Tomingas
Henry Tomingas	Adon	John & Emma Tomingas
Andrew Toro	Miller Creek	John & Alvina Toro
John Toro, Jr	Miller Creek	John & Alvina Toro
Otis Lee Wallace	Adon Road	Perry & Ollie Wallace
Keith F. Ware	Rozet	Fred & Emma Ware
Arthur L. Weaver		
Miles Weaver	Rozet	Sam & Hatttie Weaver
Robert Weaver	Rozet	Sam & Hattie Weaver

Veteran	from	Parents
Joe Weaver		Henry Weaver
Dean Robert Whisler	Rozet	Riley & Vida Whisler, decd
Leonard Pershing Whisler	Rozet	Riley & Vida Whisler, decd
Robyn E. Whitcher		
James Leon Williams	Rozet	Billy & Irene Williams
Kenneth Warren Williams	Rozet	Billy & Irene Williams
Charles Williams, Jr.	Rozet	Anna Williams
Wade Williams		(Anna Williams family?)
James Wolff	Timber Creek	Henry & Catherine Wolff
Donald Wolff	Timber Creek	Henry & Catherine Wolff
Francis Wolff	Timber Creek	Henry & Catherine Wolff
Louis Wolff	Timber Creek	Henry & Catherine Wolff
Thomas Wolff (MIA, KIA Feb 1945)	Timber Creek	Henry & Catherine Wolff
Ross J. Wright		

Sources:
"Complete List of Service Men's Names Corrected to Nov 1st, 1944;" a Zeroxed copy received from Phil Frey, Sheridan, WY, in April 2003.

Map of Rozet, Wyoming (1942-1943)
(Map is not to scale.)

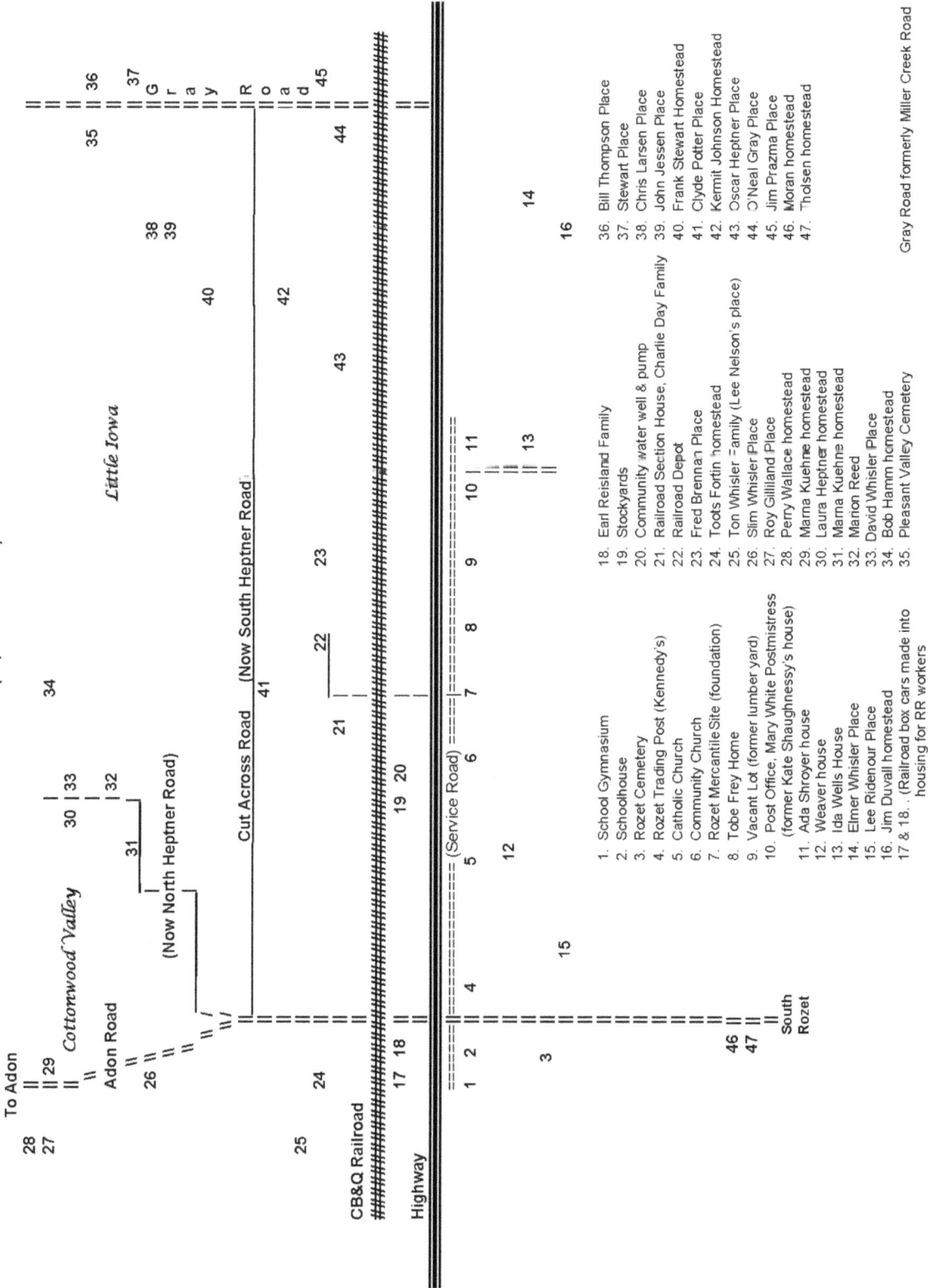

Little Iowa

Cottonwood Valley

To Adon

Adon Road

(Now North Heptner Road)

Cut Across Road   (Now South Heptner Road)

(Service Road)

CB&Q Railroad

Highway

South Rozet

Gray
r
a
y

R
o
a
d

1. School Gymnasium
2. Schoolhouse
3. Rozet Cemetery
4. Rozet Trading Post (Kennedy's)
5. Catholic Church
6. Community Church
7. Rozet Mercantile Site (foundation)
8. Tobe Frey Home
9. Vacant Lot (former lumber yard)
10. Post Office, Mary White Postmistress (former Kate Shaughnessy's house)
11. Ada Shroyer house
12. Weaver house
13. Ida Wells House
14. Elmer Whisler Place
15. Lee Ridenour Place
16. Jim Duvall homestead
17 & 18. (Railroad box cars made into housing for RR workers

18. Earl Reisland Family
19. Stockyards
20. Community water well & pump
21. Railroad Section House, Charlie Day Family
22. Railroad Depot
23. Fred Brennan Place
24. Toots Fortin homestead
25. Ton Whisler Family (Lee Nelson's place)
26. Slim Whisler Place
27. Roy Gilliland Place
28. Perry Wallace homestead
29. Marna Kuehne homestead
30. Laura Heptner homestead
31. Marna Kuehne homestead
32. Marion Reed
33. David Whisler Place
34. Bob Hamm homestead
35. Pleasant Valley Cemetery

36. Bill Thompson Place
37. Stewart Place
38. Chris Larsen Place
39. John Jessen Place
40. Frank Stewart Homestead
41. Clyde Potter Place
42. Kermit Johnson Homestead
43. Oscar Heptner Place
44. O'Neal Gray Place
45. Jim Prazma Place
46. Moran homestead
47. Tholsen homestead

Gray Road formerly Miller Creek Road

Map of Rozet, Wyoming (1942-1943)
Revised by Lorna Whisler, 2021
As recalled by Janice (Day) Stratman; additions by Lorna Whisler, April 2011
(Janice is the daughter of Charlie Day, brother of Mildred Day Whisler)

217

The Winter of '49

The decade ended with a super blizzard that was actually a series of blizzards that completely shut down the county for almost two months from January 1st through mid-February 1949. The Blizzard of '49 as it became known impacted not only people but wildlife and livestock. People became isolated in their homes, stranded in their cars or on trains. Livestock froze to death or were suffocated by the snow. By February the snow caused rail service to be stopped for several days delaying delivery of feed for livestock. By January the American Legion Post 42 in Gillette sent a plane to check on county ranchers. The ranchers made crosses on the ground to indicate they needed food, fuel, or feed for their livestock. Other community members joined in this relief effort, forming convoys that followed the snowplows.

During this blizzard the President ordered military personnel to begin Operation Snowbound, the largest bulldozer operation in American History. On February 2, 1949, the Army began plowing county roads which began with 11 dozers and were guided by local ranchers. Snowdrifts were estimated to 20 to 30 feet high in places. The continuing snow and wind quickly covered newly plowed roads making progress very slow.

Operation Snowbound Jan-Feb 1949.
Convoy to Bishops, Normans, Pickrels, Dillingers, and
Williams, southeast of Rozet

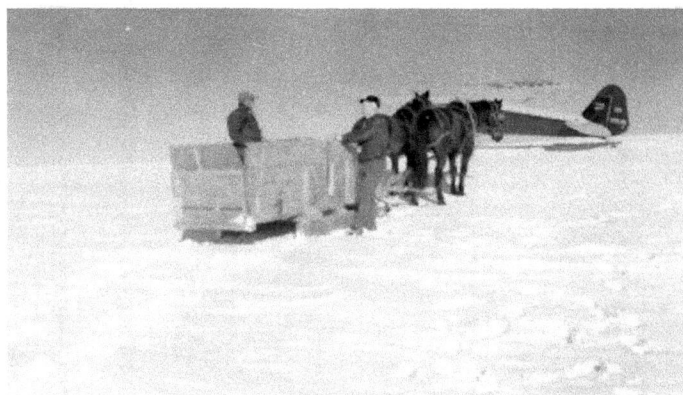

Chris Larsen, northeast of Rozet, talking with County Agent
Ben Kohrs who flew out to check on them one sunny day,
after the storms

Slim Whisler, who worked in Gillette during the winters, with
his two-seater Taylorcraft delivered mail, newspapers and
cigarettes to snowbound neighbors along the Adon and
North Heptner Road

Oscar and Dorothy Heptner's home on Miller road
after the winds quit and the sun came out
North Heptner Road

Slim Whisler putting chains on the car.

**Dean and Helen Whisler
came visiting by sleigh**

**Irene Whisler hauling pails of water from the well
for the family's personal needs and laundry**

*Photos: from the collections of Carroll D. "Slim" Whisler,
       courtesy of Diann Larsen Avery, and the Rockpile Museum, Gillette, Wyoming.*

FAMILIES and INDIVIDUALS
(1940-1949)
Edgar Hamilton "Ham" and Ioris M. (Winland) Baker
1941

Edgar Hamilton "Ham" Baker was born on March 2, 1891, to Norvel and Alice Baker, at Grafton, Taylor County, West Virginia. He was one of nine children. At the age of three weeks his family moved to Sundance, Crook County, Wyoming, where his father was a practicing physician. It was there that Ham spent his childhood and school days. He began work on ranches in Campbell County as a young man. He rode for years for the Harry Keeline and T7 ranches. On July 23, 1918, he enlisted in the United States Army. He served in World War I and was honorably discharged with the grade of sergeant on February 10, 1919. He was a member of the Campbell County American Legion Post No. 42. On August 29, 1928, he married Ioris M. Winland. She was born May 8, 1910, at Humphreys, Missouri, to Clifford R. and Vivian E. (Wright) Winland. At age six she moved with her parents to Lawver, Wyoming, where her father homesteaded. She attended rural schools and attended high school in Gillette, Wyoming. Ham and Ioris were the parents of six children:

Clifford Hamilton	b: 24 Mar 1930	d: 07 Aug 2007	m: Rose Ella Shroyer
Vivian Irene	b: 17 Feb 1932	d: 15 Mar 1988	m: Melburn W. Moser
John Henry	b: 15 Feb 1934	d: 18 Dec 1968	m: Vivian Morrison
William Hugh	b: 02 Jul 1935	d: 20 Aug 2010	m: Michael Holbert
Anna Louise	b: 25 May 1937	d: 07 Sep 2004	m: William C. Rodgers
Ethel Marie	b: 29 May 1939	d: 19 Apr 1951	

The family moved to Rozet in 1941 and lived in the Four Corners area south of Rozet. The children attended school at Rozet. Due to failing health, Ham and Ioris moved to Gillette in 1954. Ioris worked for Gibson's Snack Bar Cafe and the City Lunch Cafe. Ham entered the Veterans Hospital in Denver, Colorado on August 11, 1957, where he was a patient until his death on October 22, 1958. He was buried on October 27, 1958, in Mount Pisgah Cemetery, Gillette, Wyoming, with military honors presented by the American Legion Post No. 42. In 1959, Ioris married Merle S. "Pete" Engdahl, a Gillette contractor, in Gillette, Wyoming. Pete died in 1980. Ioris died on Sepember 16, 1991, at Gillette. She was buried on September 20, 1991, in Mount Pisgah Cemetery, Gillette, Wyoming.

Sources:
"Rites Held Monday for Ethel Baker," The News Record, Gillette, Wyoming, April 24, 1951.
"Military Honors Held Monday for E. H. Baker, 67," page 1, The News Record, Gillette, Wyoming, October 30, 1958.
"Obituary-Ioris May Engdahl," The News Record, Gillette, Wyoming, September 18, 1991.
"Clifford H. Baker," The News Record, Gillette, Wyoming, Aug 23, 2007.
Ancestry.com, U.S. Find-a-Grave Index, 1600s to Current, [database online], Provo, UT.
Ancestry.com, Iowa, Births and Christenings Index, 1800-1999, [database online], Provo, UT.
Ancestry.com, U.S. Social Security Applications and Claims Index, 1936-2007, [database online], Provo, UT.
Ancestry.com, U.S. World War I Draft Registration Cards, 1917-1918, [database online], Provo, UT.
Ancestry.com, U.S. Headstone Applications for Military Veterans, 1925-1963, [database online], Provo, UT.
Ancestry.com, 1900 U.S. Federal Census for Gillette, Campbell County, Wyoming, [database online], Provo, UT.
Ancestry.com, 1910 U.S. Federal Census for Sheridan Ward 2, Sheridan County, Wyoming.
Ancestry.com, 1920 U.S. Federal Census for G Bar M, Campbell County, Wyoming, [database online], Provo, UT.
Ancestry.com, 1930 U.S. Federal Census for Election District 10, Campbell County, Wyoming, [database online], Provo, UT.
Ancestry.com, 1940 U.S. Federal Census for Lawver, Campbell County, Wyoming, [database online], Provo, UT.

Jesse Lee and Ellen Joan (Whisler) Cummings
1941

Ellen Whisler was born March 14, 1921, at Wray, Yuma County, Colorado to David Riley and Vida Fern (Duvall) Whisler. In 1923 her father moved the family to Rozet, Campbell County, Wyoming, where his mother-in-law Catherine (Slade) Duvall Clark was living with her husband Dan Clark. Riley Whisler rented the George place for his large family to live while he worked the homestead. He died from a sudden heart attack while he and Ellen were visiting a neighbor. Ellen's mother died in June 1928 leaving ten children ages 21 to 1 1/2 years old. She was taken in by her uncle, Carrol Duvall, until he moved his family to Republic, Kansas. She went to live with her grandmother, Catherine Clark, where her sister Evelyn was living. After her sister Dorothy married Oscar Heptner in 1929 she went to live with them. She attended four years at a country school and four years at Rozet Consolidated School. She went to Campbell County High School graduating in 1939. After attending Normal Training she taught two terms at a school located on the Crook/Campbell county line until her marriage to Jesse Lee Cummings on June 18, 1941. They became the parents of two sons:

June 1941

Douglas Oscar Riley	b: 20 Aug 1942	d: 09 Dec 2011	m: Sara Lu Schuster
Jeffrey Lee	b: 08 Mar 1948	Living	m: (1) Inese Lilija Verzemnieks
			(2) Kate Zhung

Soon after the war was declared Lee enlisted in the U.S. Army Air Corps and served as a transportation driver with the 8th Air Force in England. He was discharged in November 1945 at Fort Leavenworth, Kansas. Upon returning home Ellen and Lee made their home in Basin, Wyoming. Lee worked for an oil company until 1960 when he went to work for the Wyoming Highway Department until he became seriously ill. He died April 1, 1962, in Billings, Montana at the age of forty-two.

Ellen raised her two sons alone. She worked for twenty-four years at the Town and Country Department Store until her retirement in 1985. She was an active member of the United Methodist Church and Choir, the American Legion Auxiliary, and the community choir. She died October 31, 2007, at the age of 86 after a long illness. She was buried next to her husband in in Mount View Cemetery, Basin, Wyoming.

Ellen, Doug, Jeff, and Lee

Sources:
Photos from the collection of Carroll D. "Slim" Whisler.
Correspondence with Ellen Cummings, 2005.
Obituaries for Lee and Ellen.
"The History of the David Riley and Pearl Vida (Duvall) Whisler Family, the First three Generations," by L. J. Whisler for the first Whisler Family Reunion, June 18-20, 1993.

Ferris Edwin and Pauline Louise (Whisler) Cook
1942

Pauline Whisler was born October 29, 1922, at Heartstrong, Yuma County, Colorado, to David Riley and Pearl Vida (Duvall) Whisler. In 1923 her father moved the family to Rozet, Campbell County, Wyoming, where his mother-in-law Catherine (Slade) Duvall Clark was living with her husband Dan Clark. Riley Whisler rented the George place for his large family to live while he worked the homestead. He died from a sudden heart attack in November 1926. Pauline's mother died in June 1928 leaving ten children ages 21 to 1 1/2 years old. Her Uncle Jim and Aunt Elsie Duvall took her to live with them until her older sister Dorothy married Oscar Heptner in 1929 when Pauline went to live with them. Pauline attended school at Rozet. About 1937 she moved to Idaho Falls, Idaho with Dorothy and Oscar. She attended school there. Oscar and

Guy, Ferris, Gib, Pauline

Dorothy decided to try Oregon for work. Pauline remained in Idaho Falls living with Oscar's aunt and uncle. In the fall of 1941 Dorothy and Oscar left Oregon to return to Wyoming by way of Idaho Falls to pick up Pauline. They all returned to Rozet. She attended Rozet High School until she married Ferris Edwin Cook on September 26, 1942, in Rapid City, Pennington County, South Dakota. They became the parents of two sons:

Guy Elmo	b: 13 Apr 1946	d: Living	m: Jeana Louise Davis (div)
Gilbert Ray "Gib"	b: 10 Nov 1951	d: Living	m: Yvonne Schwab

Ferris Cook was born May 23, 1922, in Billings, Yellowstone County, Montana, the only son of Floyd Elmo and Myrtle Agnes (Allen) Cook. Before moving into the Rozet community his parents lived in Lead, South Dakota, where his father worked in the Homestake Gold Mine. In 1920 they came to Wyoming filing on a homestead southwest of Rozet. Ferris and his two older sisters attended grade school in Rozet. He graduated from Rozet High School in May 1942.

They lived in Gillette all their lives. Ferris worked at Wyodak for about eleven years between 1946 and 1957. He then took up ranching on his folk's homestead. Later he began pumping for oil companies, which he did until he retired. Pauline died May 15, 1992, two weeks after her brother, David Whisler died. Ferris died on February 2, 1995. Both are buried in Mount Pisgah Cemetery, Gillette, Wyoming.

Sources:
Photo from the collection of Carroll D. "Slim" Whisler.
Obituaries for Pauline and Ferris.
"The History of the David Riley and Pearl Vida (Duvall) Whisler Family, the First three Generations," by L. J. Whisler for the first Whisler Family Reunion, June 18-20, 1993.
Ancestry.com, 1930 U. S Federal Census for Election District 5, Campbell County, Wyoming, [database online], Provo, UT.

Leonard Pershing and Catherine Margaret "Kitty" (Wolff) Whisler
1942

Leonard was born October 13, 1918, in Mayberry, Pawnee County, Nebraska, to Riley and Vida Whisler. He was five years old in 1923 when his parents moved into the Frank George Place northeast of Rozet. His father died in 1926 and his mother in 1928. He lived with his older brother and his wife, Carroll Duvall "Slim" and Irene Whisler. He attended Deer Creek School with his brother Dean. Later he lived with his older brother Ashton Alfred "Ton" and Mildred Whisler so he could go to school at Rozet. He graduated from Rozet High School in 1939. He enlisted in the Army 1942 and was assigned to a Calvary Unit in Fort Lewis, Washington. Later when the Army disbanded Calvary units he was discharged from active duty. On August 17, 1942, he married Catherine Margaret "Kitty" Wolff. They became the parents of three daughters:

Elizabeth Ruth "Betty Ruth"	b: 19 Feb 1943	d: Living	m: Walt Kanode
Dorothy Ellen	b: 02 May 1944	d: Living	m: (1) Kokie Fortin (div)
			(2) Joe Wondercheck
Judith Ann "Judy"	b: 12 Aug 1945	d: Living	m: Ken Kehn

In the spring of 1948 they moved to a place south of Gillette where he farmed and raised cattle. He served as a special sheriff's deputy in Campbell County from 1952 to 1956. Kitty died on August 30, 1954, from complications of polio. She was buried in Mount Pisgah Cemetery, Gillette, Wyoming. Leonard served with the Gillette Police Department from 1956 until he and his three daughters moved to Upton, where he was offered the job as City Marshall. For the next fifteen years he was the only law enforcement officer in Upton. Besides being the only policeman, he was also the city maintenance man and did most of the street grading and snow removal.

On March 2, 1964 Leonard married Mary Jean (Woods) Brownlee. She had a son, Kevin Lee Brownlee, whom Leonard later adopted. Mary Jean was born October 1, 1935, in Upton, Weston County, Wyoming, to Maurice Gaylord "Jack" and Mary Frances (Schmitt) Woods. She attended Upton public schools, graduating from Upton High School in 1953. She began working for the Upton Bank after graduation. After a brief move to California she returned to Upton in 1962 and resumed working for the bank. Leonard and Mary Jean were the parents of:

Kevin Lee	b: 26 Feb 1960	Living	m: Linda Kay Lynch
David Leonard	b: 24 Jun 1964	d: 04 Sep 2011	m: (1) Lynette Ewing (div)
			(2) Jenise Cathleen Wallace
Mary Pauline "Polly"	b: 19 Jan 1967	Living	m: (1) Hank Alexander (div)
			(2) Adam Charles Miller

Leonard retired in 1984 as City Marshall of Upton. He spent his retirement years watching his grandchildren and great grandchildren grow from his and Mary Jean's large home along the highway east of Upton. Mary Jean died November 10, 2000; Leonard died May 6, 2003. Both are buried at Pleasant Valley Cemetery, Rozet, Wyoming.

Sources:
Photos from the collection of Carroll D. "Slim" Whisler.
"The History of the David Riley and Pearl Vida (Duvall) Whisler Family, the First three Generations," by L. J. Whisler for the first Whisler Family Reunion, June 18-20, 1993.
Pleasant Valley Cemetery Burial Book, kept by Mrs. Lucille Thompson (Xeroxed Copy-1998).
Correspondence with Judy Kehn and Betty Kanode; Mary Jean Whisler.

Marion and Effie (Eisele) Ruff
1945

Marion Ruff was born December 16, 1888, at Point Peter, Searcy County, Arkansas, to John M. and Minnie (Bell) Ruff. He married Effie Eisele, daughter of John and Rosa Garrison Eisele, on January 1, 1910, in Waurika, Jefferson County, Oklahoma. She was born January 1, 1906, in Brook, Indiana. Marion and Effie became the parents of two children before they came to Campbell County, Wyoming to homestead. On his World War I Draft Registration Card he stated Soukup as his residence. The 1920 Federal Census shows them living at Recluse. Marion and Effie were the parents of six children:

Omar Albert	b: 19 Jan 1911	d: 30 Aug 1994	m: Eleanor S. Gould
Alfred Dennis "Pug"	b: 14 May 1915	d: Jan 1986	m: Emma Mae Morris
Mildred R.	b: 02 Aug 1923	d: 11 Feb 2006	m: Delbert Henry Hoblit
John Marion	b: 06 Jul 1926	d: 24 Dec 2009	m: (1) Lois K. Winn (div)
			(2) Phyllis (Peterson) Hensley
Ruby Mae	b: 09 May 1929	d: 05 Nov 1999	m: (1) Bucky Williams
			(2) Dean Cox
Betty	b: 1933	d:	m: Sam Wolfe

Marion and Effie divorced in the early 1940s. He died November 27, 1950, and was buried in the Waurika Cemetery, Waurika, Jefferson County, Oklahoma.

Effie married Eddie E. Schlattmann on March 24, 1945, in Hardin, Big Horn, Montana. Eddie was born September 8, 1902, at Deshler, Nebraska, to Mr. and Mrs. William Schlattmann. The family moved to Kearney, Nebraska, in 1905, and in 1920 they moved to Campbell County, Wyoming, settling near Weston. Eddie and Effie made their home on the ranch north of Rozet. Eddie died, age 58, on September 14, 1960, in Gillette, Wyoming. He was buried in Mount Pisgah Cemetery, Gillette, Wyoming. Effie married Caesar Flori on June 12, 1962, in Gillette, Wyoming. She died September 18, 1976, at Sheridan County Memorial Hospital, Sheridan, Wyoming. Effie was buried in the Mount Pisgah Cemetery, Gillette, Wyoming.

Sources:
"Society—Ruff-Morris Marriage," The News Record, Gillette, Wyoming, April 30, 1935.
"Funeral Services Held Monday for Eddie Schlattmann," The News Record, Gillette, Wyoming, September 22, 1960.
"Flori services held Today," The News Record, Gillette, Wyoming, September 22, 1976.
"Mildred R. (Ruff) Hoblit obituary," The News Record, Gillette, Wyoming, February 13, 2006.
Ancestry.com, U.S. Find-a-Grave Index, 1600s-Current, [database online], Provo, UT.
Ancestry.com, Oklahoma, County Marriage Records, 1890-1995, [database online], Provo, UT.
Ancestry.com, Montana, County Marriage Records, 1865-1993, [database online], Provo, UT.
Ancestry.com, Newspapers.com Obituary Index, 1800s-current, [database online], Provo, UT.
Ancestry.com, U.S. Social Security Death Index (Caesar Flori), [database online], Provo, UT.
Ancestry.com, U.S. Social Security Applications and Claims Index, 1936-2007, [database online], Provo, UT.
Ancestry.com, Montana, County Marriage Records, 1865-1987), [database online], Provo, UT.
Ancestry.com,, U.S. WWI Draft Registration Cards, 1917-1918, [database online], Provo, UT.
Ancestry.com, U.S. WWII Draft Cards Young Men, 1940-1947, [database online], Provo, UT.
Ancestry.com, South Dakota, Marriages, 1905-2017, [database online], Provo, UT.
Ancestry.com, 1910 U.S. Federal Census, for Bourland, Jefferson County, Oklahoma, [database online], Provo, UT.
Ancestry.com, 1920 U.S. Federal Census for Recluse, Campbell County, Wyoming, [database online], Provo, UT.
Ancestry.com, 1930 U.S. Federal Census for Election District 12, Campbell County, Wyoming, [database online], Provo, UT.
Ancestry.com, 1940 U.S. Federal Census for Campbell County, Wyoming, [database online], Provo, UT.

Melvin Harvey and Evelyn Lillie (Whisler) Donner
1946

Melvin Harvey was born on April 12, 1923, in Gillette, Campbell County, Wyoming. His parents were Charlie and Dora Donner who homesteaded in the Adon community in 1919. Melvin grew up with his seven brothers and sisters. He attended 1st through 6th grades at the Christiansen School, 7th grade at Deer Creek School, 8th grade at the Adon School. He attended Campbell County High School through the 10th grade. Melvin helped his family on the ranch until he enlisted in the U.S. Navy on December 18, 1943. He served in the Asiatic, Pacific and Philippine theaters. Melvin was honorably discharged April 16, 1946.

Evelyn Lillie was born on May 22, 1926, at Rozet, Campbell County, Wyoming, the last child of Riley and Vida Whisler. She was six months old when her father died suddenly in November 1926. After her mother died in 1928 she lived with her grandmother Catherine (Slade) Duvall Clark until her grandmother's death in 1936. Evelyn then lived with her sister and brother-in-law, Dorothy and Oscar Heptner. Evelyn began the 1st grade at Rozet Consolidated School until Dorothy and Oscar moved their family to Idaho, and later Oregon to pick vegetables and fruit. Upon their return to Rozet she attended the Cottonwood School through the 8th grade. Evelyn graduated from Rozet High School in 1944. After graduation, she went to work for the Campbell County School District until she accepted a call to teach in the fall of 1945 at the West End School in Crook County. On December 25, 1946, Evelyn and Melvin were married at the home of her sister and brother-in-law, Dorothy and Oscar Heptner, at Rozet, Wyoming. Evelyn and Melvin were the parents of:

Harvey Melvin	b: 23 Jul 1948	Living	m: Jennifer June Jeter
Vida Fern	b: 30 Oct 1956	Living	m: Paul David McCollam

Melvin and Evelyn lived in Moorcroft, Wyoming. He worked for several ranches in the area until in 1960 he began working for the Belle Fourche Pipeline Company as an assistant supervisor, retiring on January 5, 1989. Upon Melvin's retirement they moved to Powell, Wyoming. Several years later they returned to Moorcroft, Wyoming, where they lived until they moved to the Pioneer Apartments in Gillette, Wyoming. Melvin died April 23, 2008, at Sturgis, Meade County, South Dakota. Evelyn died April 11, 2011. Both are buried at Pleasant Valley Cemetery, Rozet, Wyoming.

Melvin, Evelyn, Vida, Harvey

Sources:
Photos: from the collections of Carroll D. "Slim" Whisler.
Obituaries for Melvin and Evelyn Donner.
Pleasant Valley Cemetery Burial Book, kept by Mrs. Lucille Thompson (Xeroxed Copy-1998).
"The History of the David Riley and Pearl Vida (Duvall) Whisler Family, the First three Generations," by L. J. Whisler for the first Whisler Family Reunion, June 18-20, 1993.
Ancestry.com, 1930 U.S. Federal Census for Election District 5, Campbell County, Wyoming, [database online].

Dean Robert and Helen May (Kottraba) Whisler
1946

Dean Whisler was born on April 11, 1924, at Rozet, Campbell County, Wyoming, to David Riley and Pearl Vida (Duvall) Whisler. He was two and a half years old when his father suddenly died in November 1926. His mother died two years later in June 1928. He and his brother Leonard lived with their brother Carroll Duvall "Slim" Whisler and went to the Deer Creek rural school north of the Whisler homestead. He moved into Gillette to attend Campbell County High School for his freshman and sophomore years, staying with Grandma Heptner. He returned to Rozet and started his junior year but quit to work for Virgil Reel before finishing high school. After the United States declared war with Japan, Dean enlisted, at age 18, in the U.S. Navy on August 13, 1942. Dean sailed from San Francisco, California, on September 23, 1942, arriving at American Samoa on October 8, 1942. He served one year with Mobil #3 at American Samoa when he was reassigned to the USS ATTALA (APA-130) as Ship's Cook 2nd Class. All the time he served in Samoa he would send packages and letters home to his brothers and sisters. The letters were censored and sometimes were nothing but a shredded letter upon its arrival in Rozet. His location was not made known to his family, so for two years they did not know where he was located. In the summer of 1944 he was given a 60-day leave. Upon his returning to duty he served another year and a half before he was discharged on January 3, 1946.

Dean and Helen were married on September 14, 1946, in Lincoln, Nebraska. She was born on January 30, 1919, at Davenport, Thayer County, Nebraska, to Raymond and Kathryn (Lowrey) Kottraba. They became the parents of:

Rusty Dean,	b: 28 Apr 1957	d: Living	m: Tina Michele Knapp
Deana May	b: 28 May 1963	d: Living	m: (1) Charlie T. George
			(2) Michael L. "Mike" Orona

They lived north of Rozet until 1951 or 1952. Dean began working with a seismograph company which moved them to work in Lander, Rawlins, and Douglas, Wyoming, then in 1953 to East Glacier Park, Montana. They moved back to Gillette in March 1954. Dean began drilling water wells. At that time Helen began working at the Campbell County Hospital as a nurse's aide. In September 1965 they moved to Kaycee, Wyoming, where Dean continued to drill water wells for a few years until he began contracting out to put up hay. He did this for a number of years before he went to work for the Black Hills Bentonite Company. Later he worked for the Campbell Oil Field Service until he retired in 1986. Dean worked summers at the Beckton Stock Farm west of Sheridan irrigating their pastures and hayfields. They eventually sold their home in Kaycee and moved to Sheridan, Wyoming, to be closer to needed medical facilities.

Dean died on July 28, 2005, and is buried in Sheridan Municipal Cemetery, Sheridan, Wyoming. Helen continued to live in Sheridan for a few years and then she moved to Worland, Wyoming, to live near her daughter. She died on November 27, 2017, in Worland, Wyoming. She was buried next to her husband in Sheridan Municipal Cemetery, Sheridan, Wyoming.

Sources:
Photos from the collections of Carroll D. "Slim" Whisler.
"The History of the David Riley and Pearl Vida (Duvall) Whisler Family, the First three Generations," by L. J. Whisler for the first Whisler Family Reunion, June 18-20, 1993.

PART TWO

A
Brief History
of
The Communities

Rozet,
Adon, Little Iowa,
Dillinger, Timber Creek

Introduction

Within the area of Townships 47-53 North, and Ranges 69-70 West, the people living in certain areas named their communities based on where they came from, or the names of creeks, or a valley, on or in which they lived. Some of these communities had their own post offices, some did not. As transportation became easier all the post offices, except for Rozet, were closed. After proving up on their homestead's, houses were built so the family could move from the homestead shack and in a few instances from caves built into creek banks, into a larger and cleaner residence. In areas where trees were available the houses were made from logs. However, in most areas of northeastern Wyoming, trees were not readily available so parts of these new houses were made in other places. The material for the houses and most of the things that went in them were brought to Wyoming on trains. The houses were heated by "potbelly" wood stoves. Cooking was done on wood cook stoves. Refrigeration was non-existent, except for a few iceboxes in some homes. Ice was cut into blocks from reservoirs during the winter and, placed into an icehouse using sawdust for insulation. These buildings became children's favorite cool place to play during hot summer days. Barns, granaries, and other sheds were built for sheltering livestock, storing grains and machinery. Trees became available through the Agriculture Department of the University of Wyoming for planting windbreaks around the prairie homes, barns and other outside buildings. Reservoirs were built damming up creeks so that when it did rain, water could be saved to provide water for livestock out on their pastures. Gardens were put in and enlarged year after year to provide fresh vegetables and some fruit during the summer. Wild plums and chokeberry bushes abundant along some creeks provided additional fruit for canning, making jams, or syrup. The excess produce was canned and stored in cellars for consumption during the winter months. Meat, beef and pork, were butchered in the fall; chickens, ducks and geese were raised during the summer. The meat was canned, cured, or dried. In some households the pork sausage patties were fried and stored in large crock jars in rendered lard. Link sausages were made by inserting the ground sausage into cleaned pork intestines with a sausage machine, then it was canned or fried and stored same as the sausage patties.

Besides working hard to clear the land, establish fields and pastures for crops and livestock, tend to gardens and store food for the winter, what did these ancestors of ours do? Holidays were observed much as they are today. School Christmas programs were presented in the schoolhouse by the students and their teacher for families and friends in the neighborhood. Special Christmas church services were held again in the local schoolhouse or in Rozet at the two churches located there. Exchanging of gifts between families and friends, and holiday dinners were all a part of their Christmas. Halloween and Valentine parties were held with much anticipation of games and hilarity. Sleigh and bob sled rides were enjoyed during the winters.

The Fourth of July was the biggest summertime celebration. The neighborhoods provided fireworks, picnics, and in an election year, speeches from their local candidates for local, state, and federal offices. Baseball games were played between teams from Adon, Dillinger, Rozet, Cottonwood Valley, and others. Other games played were foot, wheelbarrow, or sack races. Horseshoes was a popular pastime during Fourth of July celebrations or at home. Card parties were popular and usually went far into the wee hours of the next day's morning. A midnight supper was usually served by the host and hostess. People attended "Old Settlers" picnics at the Laurel Leaf Ranch, Cottonwood Creek, the Devil's Tower, or other suitable locations every year. Many people participated in the Campbell County Iowans picnics, the first one being held at Rozet in 1920 (Page 1, *Gillette News*, August 20, 1920)

The most popular means of entertainment within these rural communities were dances. Word would spread from ranch to ranch, homestead to homestead, that a dance was to be held at someone's home on a certain day. Whole families would pack up wagons and drive to that home. They would bring food to share for the evening meal—the supper meal. After eating, a pick-up band would assemble and start to play. The adults and children would dance through the night. At midnight they would stop for a snack. The children were put to bed wherever there was a place for them to sleep—the wagons, the barn, the back bedroom. Dances often went on all night long. After breakfast the people would pack up and return to their own homes. At these dances the tricksters would try to outdo each other much like the one Owen Wister wrote about in his "The Virginian" in which he had cowboys switch all the babies around in other baby's blankets. When the people left the dance, they took the wrong baby home with them.

At this time there were more men than women. So, at these dances women were in great demand. Sometimes there were not enough women around to dance with, so the men would tie ribbons on their arms and take the part of the women in the dance. Dances were held for all to have fun and to forget the demanding work that awaited them at home. *The Rozet News* columns records dances were held at the following homes or places: Raymond George, the Christianson School House at Adon, Rozet School, L. D. Brennan, the new post office (1920), the Adon School House, Mitchell Creek, railroad section house, S. R. Jackson, Fred Johnson, F. L. Jones, Sam Weaver, Halverson's, South Rozet School House, Shipwheel, Cady and Irvin Owens, Bailey School, Kohn Ranch, Ray Thomas, JoJo McClendon, the Johnson barn, and others that were not mentioned in the newspapers.

Shivaree's were another popular means of entertainment. When a young man and woman were married their friends and neighbors would "shivaree" them. The people would sneak up to the young couple's home and ring bells, blew horns, beat drums or anything else that made noise until the couple would come out and treat the crowd with refreshments and drinks. Baby showers were given the new mother to help provide her and the baby with extra clothing, blankets, diapers and other items that would cause a great hardship on the new family if they had to purchase all these items themselves. It became another social event enjoyed by the women of the community.

Literary Societies were formed in several communities. The people would develop a program on some social issue to debate upon. There would be two sides given and much debate on the pros and cons of the issue. In this manner the people kept themselves informed of what was happening outside their immediate community. They also discussed literature, from Shakespeare plays to locally written poetry and stories, sang songs, played musical instruments, or other material of common interests that they decided to learn more about. Again, light lunches or suppers were provided by the host and hostess.

Organizations began to develop that provided education and information about what the people in the Adon, Rozet, and Dillinger areas were interested in because it affected how they could improve their lives. The Farm Bureau was organized and most of the ranchers and homesteaders joined. It became a co-operative, and they could buy feed for their livestock, and other supplies needed to operate their ranches and farms.

In the 1930's homebuilding clubs were organized through the agriculture department of the University of Wyoming. A home demonstration agent and the county agent were sometimes invited to give a program of interest during these meetings. Other times, a member of the club would volunteer to provide a program for the ladies. It was through these clubs that the women of the community were kept informed about new methods of cooking, preserving food, sewing, gardening, etc. and learn of new health issues and home medical treatments. The readers of this book must keep in mind that these ladies kept households with no electricity or running water in the early years.

Rozet Women's Club 1923
(photo from the collections of Leona and Jeanette Heptner)

By 1930's rural electricity was available in some areas, but not in most homes. In some homes, inside running water was now available. Many homes however were still without electricity or inside running water. At a few farms or ranches a wind charger was built that charged batteries to provide power for electric lights, but not for the appliances we enjoy using today. Through these clubs the women shared how they managed different or common situations while caring for their families and home. As they shared their individual accomplishments and their failures with each other these women built friendships that would last for a lifetime.

Also, in the 1930's the first 4-H clubs were organized. Rozet's was called the Happy Sewers and it was for young ladies to help them learn how to sew their own clothes and other household necessities. Later the boys would become involved with livestock and farming methods.

These organizations, clubs, groups, celebrations and dances were enjoyed by all, men, women and children. They helped the people to relax from their daily work. The ways these folks had fun were based on the things they enjoyed back where they came from, but they also added other ways and traditions which in time built their communities. Families living in these communities today still enjoy some of these same things, but as times change, they have also added other ways to enjoy their lives. Thus, the traditions of the area continue to live.

Other Communities

Several other areas were located north and south of Rozet. They were given names based on the location where the families settled:

North of Rozet: Adon, Cottonwood Valley, Little Iowa, Miller Creek, Well Creek
South of Rozet: Dillinger, Enterprise, Piney Creek, Timber Creek

1934
Slim Whisler "dragging the road" on the Adon Road between his
turn off and Rozet after a lengthy rain.

ROZET

Early history of Rozet is scarce, if not non-existent. When the CB&Q railroad was built through northeastern Wyoming in 1891, the railroad developed section maintenance and service stops, or depots, every so many miles along the railroad tracks. Hence the possibility of why the buildings placed alongside the tracks were called the Section House. It is fair to guess that they named this depot/section house Rozet. Why they chose the name of Rozet is unknown. They may have named it after the Spanish word "rosette" for the wild roses blooming nearby. An 1895 map of northeastern Wyoming shows Rozet on the railroad line but not Moorcroft nor Upton.

It is well documented that the Shaughnessys were the first family to live at the section house. There Mrs. Shaughnessy established the first store and "post office." She set up a store in the railroad section house and later built a larger (20 feet by 10 feet) store in the section yard. It is very likely she also cooked meals for men working on the railroad. There were not many people living nearby, and her nearest neighbors were living in Gillette or Moorcroft. Several cowboys or sheepherders would ride through from the "big cities" back to their respective places of employment. Just when the stockyards were built is unknown, they were there in the 1920s as references were made in the local Rozet news columns of people trailing cattle, sheep, and hogs to Rozet for shipping to eastern markets.

Some of the family names who lived in the Rozet area were Shaughnessy, Brennan, Halverson, Kessinger, Lawrence, Weaver, Duvall, Clark, Ridenour, Nelson, Marquiss, Miller, Shroyer, Gray, Moran, Toland, McClendon,

In the 1920s there were attempts build a "New Rozet." Lots were for sale located south and north of the railroad tracks for $50-150.00 a lot. There were only a few takers, and the dreams of the residents of Rozet were short lived. However, over the years several business establishments were constructed in Rozet, also two churches were eventually built, and a cemetery developed about a half-mile south of Rozet. Mercantile stores, warehouses, rooming houses, lumber yards, blacksmith shops, etc., were established. Some were short lived, but several remained throughout the years. And some remain there today.

First Oil Attempt at Rozet 50 Years Ago Never Succeeded
(Quoted from article found on page 4, *The News-Record*, Gillette, Wyoming, Thursday, September 7, 1972, by Josephine Lucas)

"The Rozet Oil and Gas Company was having a derrick erected about a mile east of Rozet and as soon as it is complete the well will spud in reads the newspaper article. .... To the writers knowledge (Arthur Nisselius) this well will be the first well spudded in Campbell County. The people around Rozet are very enthusiastic and are hoping to have the first well in the County. The Rozet Oil Co was formed by O. M. Turk, D. B. Ott and Harry Larson and Larson was left in charge of the operation. Claude Lawrence, who had homesteaded the site in 1911, was a water well driller and was hired as the driller....For the next nine to ten months the company struggled in the drilling and money problems were encountered. Continuous cave-ins made the drilling very slow and about the only thing that could be done was to case the well before going down farther. Though the news items kept reporting progress, there were money problems.

"The well was on Claude Lawrence's homestead and in a newspaper dated April 1924, a full-page advertisement offered lots for sale in Rozet. By this time Tony Littleton and Tobe Frey had a small store on the south side of the railroad track, and Lawrence had donated land for the school which stood where the present Rozet store is now located. Parcels called "trackage lots" were $150, corner lots $75 and others, $50. Streets were named bearing the names of Campbell, Weston, Sheridan, Nebraska, and Montana. The advertisement noted that drillers struck a light seepage of heavy oil in their well one-half mile east of Rozet in mid-February (1924) and 75 percent of the oil and gas rights went with the lots. When the lots were offered for sale, the well was down 2,600 feet but the company was out of money. It is believed the lot sales were an attempt to raise more, but this proved unsuccessful and drilling was

This was the area's very first oil drilling rig, constructed near Rozet about 1922.
The first drilling crew posed for this photo near the cook shack; they are from
left Paul, Russ and Rick Lawrence, Edgar Beck, D. B. Ott, and Claude Lawrence.
The operation was money-plagued from the start and finally it was abandoned.
(Page 4, the _News Record_, Gillette, Wyo., Thursday, Sept. 7, 1972)

not resumed. It was not until 1947 before attempts were made to drill another oil well on land owned by Mrs. Bea Slattery, but she reported it was only five barrels a day. The first well that was considered good is believed to have been on land owned by the late Pete Svalina, but this was in the late 1950's.

According to Preston Gilstrap, the first producing well in the county was "born" in October 1947 on the Walter Monnett Ranch.

Source:
"First Oil Attempt at Rozet 50 Years ago Never Succeeded," page 4, The News Record, Gillette, Wyoming, September 7, 1972.

Rozet Townsite

Is a tract of level ground lying just south of the Burlington Depot at Rozet, Wyoming, 14 miles east of Gillette on the Custer Battlefield Hiway. Rozet is the logical trading point for a large Territory, which includes some of the best dry-farming land in Wyoming. It is located about half way between Moorcroft and Gillette and is bound to make a good business town.

The territory around Rozet is now attracting the attention of large oil companies. Thousands of acres have been leased with a provision that drilling operations be started within from three to six months. If they get oil——

Rozet lots now present an unusual opportunity for profitable investment. Some lines of business are now represented but more are needed. Get in on the ground floor. Buy a lot and start a business. Let us tell you about the business opportunities now open. If you do not want to go into business buy one or more lots as an investment.

For prices and other information write or see us today.

Ben C. Binns or J. E. Walters

Moorcroft, Wyoming

Gillette News, April 23, 1920

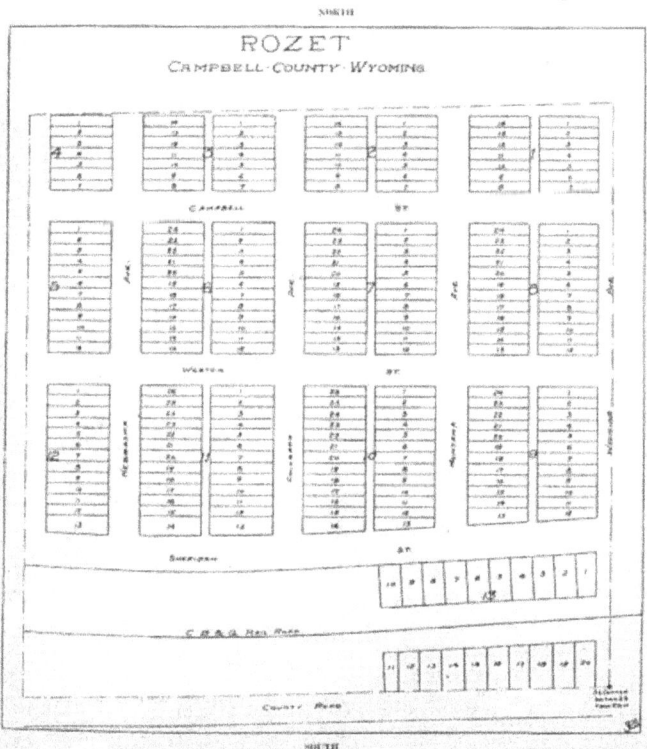

Campbell County Record, April 3, 1924

235

The Rozet Store(s)

The Rozet store was very likely the first business at Rozet. About 1904, Kate Shaughnessy opened a small grocery store in the back of the Railroad Section House. Later she opened a post office in the corner of the store. During the period of 1900-1949 the following stores were doing business in and for the Rozet community.

Rozet Store owned by Mrs Kate Shaughnessy

Shaughnessy Mercantile Company Store (1904 – 1916): Kate Shaughnessy's store in the railroad section yard was probably the first "business" in Rozet. This store expanded into the Shaughnessy Mercantile Company Store when she built a larger general merchandise store, ten by twenty feet in the yard of the section home. This store served as Rozet's first polling place in Campbell County's first elections in 1912. The always enterprising Mrs. Shaughnessy served dinner and supper, for .35 cents, for the voters on election days. Kate operated the store until 1918.

Shaughnessy Mercantile Company Store (1904 – 1916)
(photo courtesy of Campbell County Rockpile Museum)

Rozet Mercantile (1916-1934): On On December 7, 1916, Claude Lawrence sold E. A. Littleton and Tobe Frey two acres of land at $900.00 an acre, on the south side of the railroad tracks on which they built a store and the Frey's home. About 1918 they bought Katherine Shaugnessy's store (business and inventory only). The building her store was located in was later used as a homestead shack. About 1920 Tony Littleton traded Tobe his interest in the store for property on Wild Horse Creek.

After the sudden death of her husband Jack in May 1920, Daisy Brennan bought property in Rozet from Claude Lawrence where she built a house for herself and her children. She worked in the store until March 1933 when the store burned down (see page 46). The fire was of unknown origin, and it destroyed the store and warehouses. When discovered, the fire had made such headway that it was impossible to save anything. About 500 bushels of wheat was destroyed in one warehouse. The loss was partially covered by insurance.

Rozet Mercantile Company (1916-1934)

Sources:
Photo courtesy of Janice Day Strattman (Tobe Frey's granddaughter).
Rozet, The News Record*, Gillette, Wyoming, March 16, 1933.*
Campbell County, The Treasured Years*, 1990, compiled by the Campbell County Historical Society.*
Warranty Deed dated September 1920 from Claude Lawrence to Daisy Brennan, Campbell County Court House, Gillette, Wyoming.

Aerial Photo about 1957
(Courtesy of Shellie Thar Clark 2021)

The Rozet Trading Post (1934-1953): After the Frey store burned down in March 1933, Jesse and Maye Kennedy bought the business, and in 1936 when the new Rozet Consolidated & High School was completed, they bought the old school. They moved to Rozet from Wildcat where they had a homestead (former Weston Harvey place on the Powder River) having purchased the home of Daisy Brennan McDermott in 1935. Jesse built a new store attached to the old school and renamed it the Rozet Trading Post. The store opened in 1937. They operated the store until he retired in 1943 and moved to Sheridan, Wyoming (see page 199). Maye Kennedy died in November 1953. Jesse died on February 8, 1963. Both were buried in Mount Pisgah Cemetery, Gillette, Wyoming.

From 1943 to 1947 the store was operated by George "Obe" and Mary Weaver Nelson (see page 59). The Kennedy's leased the store to C. L. Faulkner in July 1948 and then to Alfred Matheson in September 1949. The store was leased once again in March 1953 to C. N. Bray and his son Claude who operated the store until 1956. According to warranty deed records in the court house the Kennedy's sold the property in May 1953 to John A. Blakeman.

In August 1956 the property was sold to Buck and Ruby Williams.

Source:
Photo courtesy of Shellie Thar Clark, Gillette, Wyoming, 2021.
Campbell County, The Treasured Years, 1990, compiled by the Campbell County Historical Society.
Warranty Deed dated March 22, 1935, from Daisy Brennan McDermott to J. R. Kennedy, Campbell County Court House, Gillette, Wyoming.
"George 'Obe' Nelson of Rozet Dies Here Tuesday," page 1, The News record, Gillette, Wyoming, July 7, 1949.
"A. E. Matheson Buys Rozet Store," page 1, The News Record, Gillette, Wyoming, September 29, 1949.
"Rozet Trading Post Bought by Brays," page 1, The News Record, Gillette, Wyoming, Thursday, March 12, 1953.
Warranty Deed dated May 10, 1953 from Jesse Kennedy to John A. Blakeman, Campbell County Court House, Gillette, Wyoming.
Warranty Deed dated August 21, 1956 from John A. Blakeman to Buck and Ruby Williams, Campbell County Court House, Gillette, Wyoming.
Ancestry.com, U S. Find a Grave Index, 1600s-Current, [database online], Provo, UT (re: Obituary for Marie Matheson)

The Rozet Bar(s)

History shows us that as soon as a small town or camp was established, one of the first business establishments to open was the saloon. When the first bar, or saloon, was set up at Rozet is unknown. The original building was first used as a schoolhouse. From time to time more buildings were added and it was remodeled into a store. The bar was added and remodeled with a back bar originally used in the American Legion at Gillette and JB Blues near Gillette. Lunches were later prepared for men customers, and oilfield hands frequented the cozy, warm rooms in winter and the cool air conditioner in summer.

That the Rozet Bar and Grill is the only business still in existence at Rozet, says much about the durability and role saloons/bars plays in the community. In the very early days when there were no building materials readily available, they were first set up in tents. They served as a place the men working on the railroads and ranches could come to "relax" in the company of fellow laborers and the occasional cowboy or sheepmen who stopped in on their way home from the "big city." Saloons and bars became very numerous in the young frontier towns. Depending on which side of the issue of "drinking spirits" a person was on, the argument for and or against these bars were both strong and vigorous.

During 1969-1972 Mr. and Mrs. Buck Ruff leased the business. Bill Norman and Dennis Johnston had recently (1979) purchased the building from Mrs. Ruby Cox. In January 1980 the Rozet Bar was destroyed by a fire starting about 8:30pm of an unknown origin. Firefighters fought the blaze most of the night to keep it from spreading.

Source:
"Tavern Terminated by Fire," page 16, Moorcroft Leader, January 17, 1980

The Rozet Post Offices

Seeing a need Katherine Shaughnessy sent petitions in 1903 to the Postmaster General spelling out the difficulties of receiving or sending mail to or from Rozet. Her persistence paid off as Rozet's first post office was created on April 1, 1904. It was in the Shaughnessy Store located in the section yard north of the railroad tracks. Previously they had gotten their mail from the handcar. The post office department paid Kate $48.00 a year. In 1913 she bought a half-acre from Claude Lawrence. It was located south across from the railroad depot. She built a building, which housed a hotel, her private residence, and space for the post office. In May 1914, the U.S. Post Office Department officially appointed her as Postmistress. Kate served as Postmistress for twelve years, officially and unofficially. She resigned in 1918.

On November 25, 1918, Mrs. Ada F. Shroyer became the second Postmistress. She had built a new house and moved the post office into her home, which was located east of Mrs. Shaughnessy's hotel. It also served as a cream station. In 1920 a new post office was being built with a dance held to celebrate its opening in July. Ada served as Postmistress for a little over ten years when she resigned in November 1927. She sold her place and moved to Niles, Ohio, where she married Mr. W. J. Hatfield.

On December 3, 1927, Miss Carrie Wells, sister-in-law of Mrs. Ida Wells, became Acting Postmistress, until April 9, 1928, when she was appointed as Postmistress. She served in that position until her death on October 11, 1931. Mrs. Lyla Wells Weaver, Carrie Wells' niece/adopted daughter, assumed the duties as Acting Postmistress on October 12, 1931, during the time the Post Office Department considered applications for the vacated position. She served five months.

Mrs. Mary Thompson, Kate Shaughnessy's daughter, was appointed Acting Postmistress on March 16, 1932. She was appointed Postmistress on April 1, 1932. The post office then was moved back to her mother's hotel, which at that time was Mary Thompson's home. Mary married Clifford C. White in 1935. She served as Postmistress for twelve years.

In August 1, 1944, two years after her marriage to Vincent Thar, Leola Kottraba Thar, age 20, went to work as the postmaster's assistant. Two days later when the postmaster left, she became the acting postmaster. But at the age of 20 Leola could not officially become the postmaster until she turned 21. She was finally appointed on a permanent basis on July 1, 1945. The office was still located in the Shaughnessy Hotel. Leola rented the Building at first and later purchased it.

At the time she was first appointed the post office was classified as a Fourth-Class Post Office, the wages were $472.00 per year, and the postage was three cents for a letter. The office was open eight hours per day except Sundays and holidays. The mail came by trains, which ran twice a day, one east bound and one west bound. There were two rural delivery routes served from the Rozet Post Office. One route was south down the Bishop Road to Piney along the Belle Fourche River and back to Rozet; the other was north of Rozet. One of the mail carriers was Ray Kottraba, Leola's father. Included in the duties of the postmistress was serving as Central Operator for the Rozet Mutual telephone switchboard. Rural telephone lines, built by Fred Duvall, ran north and south of Rozet fed into the switchboard installed at the post office. The lines were maintained by the ranchers and farmers. Additionally Leola ran the community emergency center; fires were reported to her, telegrams came in, and she delivered them when there was no phone at a ranch or farm.

The post office was classified as fourth class until October 1978 when it was designated as a third Class post office. Which mean the Thar's had to furnish the building when she took over the duties as mail manager. So, they bought the present building which was then a motel. Making the remodeled hotel her home as well as her place of employment, Leola found she was working more hours than was required, because people came for their mail at different times of the day and night. Leola would say "when people drive 20 miles, you just can't say we're closed."

By the time of Leola's retirement on June 13, 1980, she and Vince had been living on their ranch seven miles east of Gillette which they had owned for thirty years. Susan Thar, Leola's daughter, was appointed Acting postmistress on June 13, 1980, and was appointed Postmistress on November 1, 1980. She served until May 19, 1981, when Gayle Brunsvoid was appointed as Officer in Charge.

On September 5, 1981, the first man, Ralph J. Wrightson, was appointed as Postmaster. He transferred from Newcastle, Wyoming. The post office was moved to a trailer east of Rozet. Then in 1987, after eighty-four years of makeshift accommodations and lots of challenging work by its former postmistresses, a new official United States Post Office building was built about five hundred feet west of its former location of so many years. The former post office building was sold and bought by John and Mary K. Jones.

Sources:
Photos of Postmistress's taken by Matt Avery at the Rozet Post Office, Rozet, Wyoming, July 2020.
Rozet Rumblings, Gillette News, May 17, 1918.
"Postmaster at Rozet Resigns," The News Record, Gillette Wyoming, November 17, 1927.
"Shroyer-Hatfield Marriage," The News Record, Gillette, Wyoming, December 15, 1927.
Rozet Items, The News Record, Gillette, Wyoming, December 29, 1927.
"Rozet Postmistress Succumbs," The News Record, Gillette, Wyoming, October 15, 1931.
"Exam for Post Office at Rozet Announced," The News Record, Gillette, Wyoming, October 29, 1931.
"Rozet-White-Thompson marriage," The News Record, Gillette, Wyoming, April 7, 1932.
"Rozet Post Office," Campbell County, The Treasured Years, 1990, page 30, compiled by Campbell County Historical Society.
"Neighbors," (re: Leola's Thar's retirement), page 6, The News Record, Gillette, Wyo., Tuesday, June 3, 1980.
"In Rozet it's a Tradition, The Postmaster is a Mrs.," The News Record, Gillette, Wyo., (_____ 1979), by Ethel Gillette.
"Rozet Post Office Centennial Celebration," April 1, 2004, brochure.
Ancestry.com, U.S. Postmasters Assignments, [database online], Provo, UT.

The Catholic Church of Rozet

Father/Reverend Brady came from Newcastle beginning in 1919 through 1924 when he was transferred to the Buffalo Parish (Assorted items from the Gillette News and Campbell County Record's Rozet Items column through those years.)

In January 1924 a Father/Reverend E. Schneider, of Newcastle, held his first service at the Rozet Catholic Church.

Sources:
Rozet Items, <u>Gillette News</u>, January 24, 1924.

The Rozet Protestant Community Church

In January 1921 the Rozet Protestant Community Church was organized. (*Gillette News*, January 28, 1921; Rozet Rumblings) and the following officers were elected: Deaconesses: Mrs. Robert Peterson and Miss Carrie Wells; Treasurers: Mrs. M. B. Shickley and Mrs. W. L. Kessinger; Executive Committee: Mrs. U. H. Eddy, Mrs. Bertha Miller, Mrs. Mary Kessinger, Mr. U. H. Eddy, Mr. M. B. Shickley and Mr. W. L. Kessinger. Services were most likely held in homes or possibly the Rozet School house. (*Gillette News*, February 4, 1921; Rozet Rumblings)

In July 1922 a bid was placed for one of the rural schoolhouses that had been closed due to the consolidation of School District Three schools into one schoolhouse in Rozet. A school building was purchased in February 1923 and moved to Rozet. (Campbell County Record, February 22, 1923; Rozet Items) The remainder of that year volunteers worked to convert the school building into a community church. They held bake sales and other events to raise money to build a basement to place the school building upon. Because it was a volunteer effort the basement was not ready until February 1924. It took an additional year to complete modifications by George Stewart, Sr., and other helpers—such as Riley Whisler and Earn French who hauled gravel and Philo Eddy and Mr. Willie Lubkin who painted the church.

The Rozet Protestant Community Church was dedicated on July 12, 1925, with the Reverend T. A. Toland, of Sheridan, Wyoming, officiating.

Ministers rotated throughout the years both before the Community Church was dedicated and afterwards. The following Ministers have been identified:

1917-1920	Rev. H. A. Toland *
1919	Dr. Rev. Kendall (a Methodist minister of Sheridan)
1920-1921	Rev. Gamble (of Gillette)
1921-1922	Rev. Clarke
June 1924	a Rev. Davidson, an Episcopal minister from Newcastle made calls to Rozet **
1922-1940	Rev. Samuel C. Ryland (a Presbyterian minister of Gillette)
	Rev. Ray Cornwall

Rev Toland's son Joseph filed a homestead in Section 35, Township 50 North, Range 70 West; and his daughter Ona L. Toland filed a homestead in November 1914 in Section 2, Township 49 North, Range 70 West. Rev. Toland later moved to Sheridan, Wyoming.

**Rozet Items, <u>Gillette News</u>, June 12, 1924.*

Summer Bible School - 1946
Standing rear: Rosa Ridenour, Lorna Whisler, _____, _____, ____, Norma Jean Duvall,
Eurith Whisler, Shirley Heptner
Standing middle: Mrs. Cornwell with _____, Barbara Whisler, Doug Cummings, _____, Joan Whisler, _____, _____,
Alice Cornwell, Verna Mae Edwards, Joyce Johnson, Deloris Whisler, _____
Sitting rear: Forrest Cornwell, Darrell Heptner, Verlin Duvall
Sitting front: Johnny Duvall, Damon Reel, Harold Ridenour
(photo from the collections of Leona and Jeanette Heptner)

Summer Bible School was conducted by the Rev. Ray Cornwell, a Presbyterian Minister, who was assigned to the First Presbyterian Church in Gillette to do missionary work in the rural communities throughout Campbell County. He and his wife traveled around to the various communities to preach on Sundays and provided Bible school during the summers.

Rev. Ray Cornwell was born in Ellsworth, Pierce County, Wisconsin, on June 2, 1902, to William Albert and Ella A. (White) Cornwell. The family moved to Cold Spring, Stearns County, Minnesota, at some point as his mother died there in 1928; his father in 1930. He attended Yankton College in Yankton, South Dakota, Moody Bible Institute in Chicago, Illinois, and the Omaha Theological Seminary in Omaha, Nebraska. On August 29, 1933, Ray married Rosy Etha Hink in Raymond, Clark County, South Dakota. She was the daughter of Fredrich W. and Mayme (Fegmeter) Hink. Rosy was born October 21, 1903, in Arthur, Ida County, Iowa. Shortly after their marriage they were living in Nodeway, Iowa, where their son Forest William was born on November 27, 1934. Shortly after his birth they moved to Bayfield, Colorado. Their daughter Alice Rae was born November 9, 1937.

Rev. Cornwell held pastorates in Wisconsin, Iowa, Colorado, and Wyoming. The 1940 U.S. Federal Census shows the family living at Lingle, Goshen County, Wyoming. In 1943 they moved to Gillette, Campbell County, where he was installed at the First Presbyterian Church as a mobile minister for the Presbyterian Board of National Missions. He, with Rosy beside him, served the rural communities of Campbell County until his retirement in 1967 at which time he was appointed assistant pastor of the First Presbyterian Church in Gillette. He held this position until his death. Rosy died November 3, 1953, in Gillette. Ray continued living and preaching until his death on January 27, 1973. Rev Cornwell and his wife Rosy are buried in Mount Pisgah Cemetery, Gillette, Campbell County, Wyoming.

Sources:
"Obit for Rev Ray W. Cornwell," Newspapers.com, Casper Star Tribune, Casper, Wyoming, 31 Jan 1973, Page 2.
Ancestry.com, 1910 U.S. Federal Census for Pierce County, Wisconsin, [database online], Provo, UT.
Ancestry.com, 1920, U.S. Federal Census for Stearns County, Minnesota, [database online] Provo, UT.
Ancestry.com, 1940 U.S. Federal Census for Goshen County, Wyoming, [database online], Provo, UT.
Ancestry.com, U.S. Find A Grave Index, 1600s-Current, [database online], Provo, UT.
Ancestry.com, Newspapers.com Obituary Index, 1800s-current, [database online], Provo, UT.

1965
Dedication of the refurnished Rozet Community Church
Rev. Ray Cornwell, Daphne Edwards, Oscar Heptner, Eugene Heptner
(photo from *The News Record,* Gillette, Wyoming, 1965, date of issue unknown)

The Rozet Cemetery

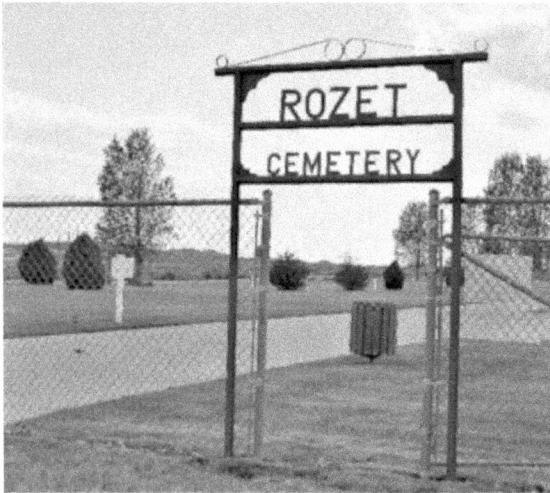

In 1920 the Rozet community realized the need for a cemetery. Several families came together to decide what needed to be done towards establishing a Rozet Cemetery. In December 1920 a cemetery was established. In January 1921 the cemetery was surveyed, and Mr. L. D. "Dot" Brennan purchased the land in May 1921. It is located about one half mile south of Rozet on the right side of the road. A meeting was called to form the Rozet Cemetery Association. Officers and committees were appointed as follows: President, Mr. L. D. Brennan, Treasurer, Mr. Frank Wall, Secretary, Mrs. W. L. Kessinger, Finance Committee: Mr. C. A. Hinds, Mr. W. L. Kissinger, and Mr. C. J. McClendon. (Rozet Rumblings item Gillette News, Thursday, December 17, 1920). Afterwards several benefit dances were held to raise money towards purchasing a fence and work to clear the land of sagebrush and cactus began.

The location of the original burial book is unknown. It became lost sometime in the earlier years. If burials occurred between 1921 and 1936 there is no record of them. According to the burial records currently held by the Campbell County Cemetery District, the first person buried in the Rozet cemetery was Catherine (Slade) Duvall Clark who died July 19, 1936, followed by three of her great granddaughters. Joan Whisler, age 11, daughter of Ashton and Mildred Whisler, died July 30, 1936, Pearl Whisler, age 2, died September 18, 1936, and two weeks later her sister Arlou, age 3, died on September 30, 1936. They were the daughters of Carroll D. "Slim" and Irene Whisler.

One of the deaths in 1920 that lead to the community's action for a cemetery was that of James Clark Duvall, baby son of James and Elsie Duvall. He was born on February 9, 1920, and died March 5, 1920. He was buried on their ranch. In 2010 the family moved his body from the ranch to the Rozet Cemetery and buried it beside his memorial stone.

Mrs. Clark with four of her great grandchildren: Darleen Heptner, Joan (Joanne) Whisler, Phil, and Eurith Whisler 1933

Sources:
Photo of cemetery gate taken by Matt Avery, July 2020.
Photo of Grandma Clark from the collection of Carroll D. "Slim" Whisler.
Photos of baby James stones courtesy of Nadine Duvall Taylor, 2012.

ROOMING HOUSES, HOTELS, AND RESIDENCES

Mrs. Shaughnessy bought one-half acre south of the railroad tracks from her sons-in-law to build a hotel in which she moved the Rozet Post office into. She also moved in and made it her private residence. Schoolteachers were her main boarders.

Mrs. Ida Wells, after the consolidation of schools in School District Three, boarded children in her home at Rozet through the school term due to the lack of transportation to and from the Rozet Consolidated and High Schools from where they lived. She also took in adult boarders such as schoolteachers.

Several people built homes in Rozet in which they lived during the school terms over the winters.

Other Businesses/Shops

Lumber Companies: The Logan Lumber and Hardware Company was begun sometime prior to 1919 (*Gillette News*, June 27, 1919, Advertisement). The Saunders Brothers bought the yard in 1921. In 1921 W. B. Saunders bought one-half acre from Tobe Frey and E. A. Littleton to build a lumberyard. They opened the Saunders Lumberyard in June 1922 (*Gillette News*, June 22, 1922, Rozet Rumblings,). With the steady influx of homesteaders into the Rozet area they felt that the immediate availability of lumber would be both beneficial to them and the new Rozet families arriving daily. However by December 1923 they were making plans to move their inventory to their lumberyard in Gillette (Rozet Items, *Gillette News*, December 3, 1923).

Blacksmith Shops: Claude Lawrence opened a blacksmith shop probably about 1913.

The Telephone Lines/Companies

In 1917 a telephone line was put in from Rozet towards northeast of Rozet, Mark B. Shickley, was the manager. The switchboard was at the Rozet Post Office.

In 1920 the Rozet-Adon Telephone Line was established after a meeting at the A. M. Speegle ranch. In 1921, Rozet buys the phone line (Page 1, Gillette News, March 11, 1921) and organizes the Rozet Mutual Telephone Company with the following lines: Adon, Burr, East, North, and Southeast. Fred Duvall built the switchboard. The service was free, and the ranchers maintained the lines. Their biggest damage came from lightning strikes.

By the 1940's the lines were down to two, north along the Adon Road and down to Bishop's south of Rozet.

Many families within the communities created their own private "barbed wire" phone lines between themselves and their families or closest neighbors. In this way even if they were not on the main lines they could relay news between one another in this manner.

Sources:
"In Rozet it's a Tradition, The Postmaster is a Mrs.," The News Record, Gillette, Wyoming, (_____ 1979), by Ethel Gillette.
"Neighbors," by Mike Rawlings, page 6, The News Record, Gillette, Wyoming, Tuesday, June 2, 1980.

NORTH ROZET
Adon, Cottonwood Valley, Little Iowa, Miller Creek, Well Creek Communities

Adon

The Adon community was located about eighteen miles north of Rozet in the northern portion of Township 52 North, Ranges 69 and 70 West, and the southern portion of Township 53 North, Ranges 69 and 70 West. Adon was named by Arlo Taft. The post office was built on the east side of the Adon Road on land owned by Fred and Ruth Carson. Fred was the postmaster for several years.

Transcribed from Betty Hughes Tilson's manuscript titled: *School Days Trials and Triumphs* She wrote: *It was not known when the Adon Community Hall was first built. For several years it had not been used until (about 1936-37) when a number of local musicians who needed practice decided to hold a dance to see how it went. They cleaned the hardwood floor of the hall and replaced a broken window or two. The group advertised the dance asking attendees to bring a tin can for coffee, their own table service , and a covered dish or two. A good turnout happened. Tom Tilson called the square dances. Perry Wallace, a violinist, and several other men furnished the music, including Charlie Donner, Charley Christianson, Pete Engdahl, George Canoy, and sometimes Ted Norfolk on the drums. The dances and parties were well attended by the community until visitors from surrounding areas began bringing their bottles and causing trouble. The community was forced to end them.*

Families' names who lived in the Adon community were Taft, Norfolk, Christianson, Carson, Hays, Engdahl, Pownall, Hatfield, Donner, Melton, Tomingas, White. Schools that were established when needed were: The Adon School, Christianson School, Pippin School, Norfolk School, Engdahl School, and others. Teachers were sought out to teach their children and bids to furnish the wood and or coal for heat were let.

Cottonwood Valley

The Cottonwood Valley community was located northwest of Little Iowa along the Adon Road and south of Adon. Some of the family names who lived there were: Speegle, Wallace, Mapes, Weaver, Donner, Reed, Gilliland, Jensen, Whisler, Riley, Kuehne.

about 1925
Men, l-r: George Jensen, Frank Kuehne, Frank Heptner, Charlie Woods, unknown,
Harley Ranney, Carl Kuehne
Women: Eunice Ranney, Minnie Woods, Marna Kuehne, Laura Heptner, Esther Kuehne,
Flora Ranney, and Clara Jensen, holding Virgil
Children: Frederick Jensen, David Ernest, Genevieve Ernest, June Woods, Jeanette Heptner, and Harold Woods
(photo from the collections of Leona and Jeanette Heptner)

Little Iowa

The Little Iowa community was located about nine miles northeast of Rozet in Township 51, Range 69. It was named because many of the inhabitants were from Iowa. Some of the family's' names who lived in the Little Iowa community were Jeffers, Hamm, Schrand, Spencer, Ranney, Heptner, Kuehne, Creach, Cook, Weaver, Woods, Thompson, Simpson, Larsen, Semlek, Raudsep.

Two schools were established. The Little Iowa School located north of the Thompson homestead and across the road east from the Little Iowa Cemetery. The Cottonwood/Woods School was located about a mile east of the Heptner homestead on the Woods homestead. The Pleasant Valley, also known as Little Iowa, cemetery is also located within this community.

Miller Creek

The Miller Creek community was located northeast of Little Iowa. Some of the family names who lived there were: Doane, Kohn, Simpson, Toro, Wells.

A Few Neighborhood Kids – about 1928

Back row: Erna Semlek, Leida Smith, Linda Toro, Elsie Sestrap, Elsie Rush, Alma Toro
Front row: Frank Semlek, Johnny Toro, Bill Semlek
(photo courtesy of Diann Larsen Avery, 2017)

Well Creek

The Well Creek community area was located northeast of Rozet and south of Little Iowa. Some of the family names who lived there were: Wells, Johnson, Stewart, George, Shickley, Woolsey, Fischer, Hinds, Spencer, Bailey, Henry.

The Pleasant Valley (aka Little Iowa) CEMETERY

Graves in foreground Riley and Vida Whisler

The Pleasant Valley (sometimes referred to as the Little Iowa) Cemetery is located about nine miles northeast of Rozet on the Gray Road and across the road from Mrs. Wilbur "Bill" (Lucille) Thompson. The history of this cemetery was written by Mrs. Lucille Thompson in 1986 at the request of the Wyoming Historical Society for their Wyoming Cemetery Inventory Project. Her submission is quoted in part as follows:

"In October 1917, a little boy (Vern Woods) met with an accident and was buried near our home on land owned by a Mr. Charles H. Simpson, at that time called the Harris Simpson Cattle Company. A meeting was held, and Mr. Orrin A. Woods, Mr. Sam Weaver, and Mr. Fayette Thompson were either elected or appointed as directors. Mr. Thompson then drew up a plot of the area dividing the 262.4x332 foot area into designated lots, plots, walkways, and driveways. We still have the original plot and the simple little notebook in which Mr. Thompson recorded each burial thereafter. (*Author's Note: An item found in the Little Iowa Vicinity, Gillette News, Friday, February 10, 1919, "At a meeting in the interest of the cemetery association, Mr. F. B. Jeffers was chosen to serve as a trustee with Messrs. O. A. Woods and F. R. Thompson."*)

"The neighbors living in the Pleasant Valley/Little Iowa community began raising money by having box suppers, pie socials, benefit dances and taking donations for fencing materials and a drive-through gate with Pleasant Valley Cemetery across the top. Flowers and trees were planted.

"On August 16, 1918, Mr. Simpson deeded the land to the community known as Little Iowa. This deed was recorded in the Campbell County Court House on August 20, 1928. Its land description is as follows: Commencing at the southeast corner of the North ½ Section 26, Township 51 North, Range 69 West, thence running north 332 feet, thence west 262.4 feet, thence south 332 feet, thence, east 262.4 feet to the place of beginning.

"Since the very beginning of this cemetery the people of this community have kept the fence in repair, the sagebrush grubbed out and the graves respectable. In 1967 there were still eleven graves without any type of marker except for a lilac bush or a handful of iris plants and the recordings made by Mr. Thompson in the burial book. So, we went to the mortuary and ordered markers, expecting to pay for them, but after they were made up, Mr. and Mrs. LeRoy Noecker, owners of the mortuary donated all eleven markers since their funeral home had been in charge of most of the burials here. So all the graves now have either regular head stones or mortuary type markers.

"Each year we hold a clean-up, fix-up picnic and all interested parties donate their work, plants, food and the whole cemetery is cleaned, mowed, fence posts and gate painted, new trees and plants planted, and we all go home with a warm feeling of community spirit and togetherness.

"Wilber (Lucille's husband) is the unofficial volunteer caretaker, mowing the grass and weeds and watering when needed. We have many trees and flowers planted so in 1976 a waterline was run from the Thompson's well to the cemetery. Now we are able to have more flowers, etc.

"There are a few military men buried here and they each have stones and flag stands. New flags are put out each year by the Veterans of Foreign Wars. All the graves are taken care of even though there is not next of kin living in the area. Everything is donated or volunteered, and usually looks really nice, neat, and cared for.

"Also, in our records in the earlier years there was only one date and I am not sure whether it was the date of death or the burial date. I found differences in names and dates between my record book and the gravestone markings. My husband thinks the stones were put up several years after burial and the mason just got the dates reversed."

The compiler for the Wyoming Historical Society made the following note: "When the stones are put in in later years, the family itself may not agree with the dates of birth and death as recorded in the cemetery's burial book."

After Mr. Fayette Thompson's death in 1944 his wife, Mary, kept up the cemetery records. After her passing in 1955 her daughter-in-law, Mrs. Lucille Thompson, began keeping the records and continues doing so today (July 2001).

Throughout the years families of those who are buried in the cemetery have come to clean up the cemetery after the winter and before Memorial Day. Some years there were gatherings of the community on a weekend before Memorial Day for a joint clean-up day. They brought food and at noon would break for a shared picnic lunch.

How the cemetery was named Pleasant Valley: the answer came from an article published in the *News Record*, May 28, 2017, "Life in death, Pleasant Valley Cemetery a legacy of community's past and future," by Kathy Brown. It is quoted in part:

"Families in the area of Gray Road gathered October 12, 1917, to bury 15-year-old Vern Oscar Woods, who was killed on a neighbor's ranch as they were clipping and tending to cattle. That's when the families began to think about where they would lay their loved ones to rest in the sagebrush-covered plains of northeast Wyoming. After Woods was buried in a plot of land donated by rancher Charlie Simpson, the men gathered in a schoolhouse across the road to discuss the idea. Each man there gave a donation to help build a fence and make improvements. In return, they were given plots in their names. They planned to call it Little Iowa Cemetery, to reflect the community called by those who had homesteaded there from that state. But an unexpected deal offered on the price of a cemetery gate—it had been ordered and made but never paid for—forced a name change. It became the Pleasant Valley Cemetery instead."

Wintertime at the Cemetery - 2016
(photo: *The News Record*, Gillette, Wyoming)

250

CAMPBELL COUNTY IOWANS
HOLD PICNIC NEAR ROZET
GATHER ON HARDSCRABBLE CREEK FOR FIRST ANNUAL MEETING
FIFTY-ONE FORMER HAWKEYES ATTEND – PERMANENT
ORGANIZATION FORMED -- TO MEET ANNUALLY

Last Sunday, August 15th, 1920, fifty-one former Iowans gathered on the creek north of Rozet for their annual meeting.

The day was a fine one for a picnic. The weather was warm but the crowd gathered under the cottonwoods on the "Dad" Stuart place and kept comfortable in spite of the heat. People attended from all over the Iowa precinct, and a few from Moorcroft and Gillette. Dinner was served about 1:30pm.

The Hawkeyes enjoyed themselves thoroughly. Nearly everybody knew of somebody who knew somebody else and the day was spent mostly in visiting and talking about friends in the old home state. No games were played. This was the fault of the ladies who fed us so much that not a man in the crowd felt able to run or jump, or climb a tree.

A short impromptu program was held with Dad Stuart in the chair. Those who responded with short talks were Superintendent C. E. Clarke, Theodore Wanerus, Fred Fair and Mrs. Sarah E. Stewart. Miss Lyla Wells gave a reading that was much enjoyed

The business session was then held. Dad Stuart was elected President, Frank Wall, Vice-president, and Carrie M. Wells, Secretary. The meeting was thoroughly enjoyed and everyone promised to come again.

Following are the names of those present and the names of the towns from which they came:

Mrs. Sarah E. Stewart, East Waterloo, Iowa
G. H. Brown, Sioux City, Iowa
Theodore Wanerus, Iowa City, Iowa
Leota Mack, Wyoming
Marie Nelson, North Dakota
Bernard Nelson, North Dakota
Curtis E. Grove, Weston, Iowa

Lora Grove, Weston, Iowa
Mrs. Fred L. Duvall, Waverly, Iowa
Carrie M. Wells, Vincent, Iowa
Miriam M. Stull, Waterloo, Iowa
Mrs. Fred Fair, Glenwood, Iowa.
Mrs. Emma Nelson, Iowa Falls, Iowa
Edith V. Kessinger, Lohrville, Iowa
Mrs. Florence Wall, Iowa Falls, Iowa
Mrs. C. J. Stockdale, Iowa Falls, Iowa
Mrs. George E. Stull, Waterloo, Iowa
Florence Fair, Glenwood, Iowa
Mary Taylor, Glenwood, Iowa
Marcella Fair, Glenwood, Iowa
Helen Duvall, Waverly, Iowa
Mrs. Ray French, Sheridan, Wyoming
Mary Stockdale, Iowa Falls, Iowa
A. F. Shroyer, Maryville, Missouri
C. Ernest Clarke, Oskaloosa, Iowa
Ray French, Sutton, Nebraska
Fred Fair, Glenwood, Iowa
Frank Wall, Iowa Falls, Iowa
Fred Johnson, Oklahoma
Kermit Johnson, Oklahoma
Lyla Wells, Vincent, Iowa
Ruby Kessinger, Lohrville, Iowa
Wynona Shroyer, Wray, Colorado
I. B. "Dad" Stuart, Iowa Falls, Iowa
Maggie M. Nelson, Mahaska, Kans.
Mrs. J. E. Brennan, Keota, Iowa
Ruth Brennan, Rozet, Wyoming
Margaret Brennan, Rozet, Wyoming
Daniel Brennan, Rozet, Wyoming
Richard Brennan, Rozet, Wyoming
Fred Brennan, Rozet, Wyoming
George Vasey, Gillette, Wyoming
C. J. Stockdale, Iowa Falls, Iowa
Ralph A. Wall, Burdette, Iowa
T. B. Ely, Council Bluffs, Iowa
Mr. and Mrs. Frank Heptner, Council Bluffs, Iowa
Mr. and Mrs. H. J. Chassell, Iowa City, Iowa
Mrs. Curtis E. Grove, Weston, Iowa
Lenora Ely, Moorcroft, Wyoming
Mr. and Mrs. W. Harksley, North Aurora, Illinois
Helen Rose Chassell, Gillette, Wyo.

Sources:
(Transcribed from: Gillette News, Gillette, Wyoming, August 20, 1920, page 1, modified to fit all on one page.)

SOUTH ROZET
Dillinger, Piney Creek and Timber Ridge Communities

Dillinger

This Dillinger community was located about fourteen miles southeast of Rozet north of the Belle Fourche River. Like Adon, the families living in these areas usually traveled by horseback or wagon to Moorcroft for supplies and mail. Anyone going would pick up the mail for everyone in the community. The neighbors got together to gather support for a post office to be placed in the community. One finally was approved; it was named Dillinger after Della Dillinger who was appointed postmistress. Some of the family names who lived in the Dillinger/Enterprise area were Dillinger, Brower, Story, Rivenburgh, Whitcomb, Kummerer, Williams, Talley, Fox, Hamill, Wolfe, Baker, Owens, Bishop, Bowden, and Day.

Several schools were established from time to time with the Dillinger School being the longest running school in this area. Schools that were established were: the Dillinger School, the Enterprise School, the OR School, the Shipwheel School, the Baker School.

Piney Creek

The Piney Creek community was located south of Belle Fourche River along Piney Creek. The United States Post Office Department approved a post office, which was located on the property of Raymond and Lucille Thomas. Lucille was appointed postmistress. Some of the family names who lived in the Piney area were: Kottraba, Thomas, and Pickrel.

Timber Creek

The Timber Creek community was located southwest of Rozet in the Rochelle Hills area. A few of the family names who lived there were: Cook, Brunson, Gardner, Greer, Peterson, Preston, Thar, and Wolfe.

PART THREE

Schools

**School Districts
Three, Four, and portions of Five and Twelve**

The first Rozet High School was built on land donated by Claude Lawrence, the father of Russ Lawrence who graduated from Rozet in 1925, land that was part of his original homestead. Later the school was moved across the road where the famous SOUP HOUSE sat on the school section.

(Information provided by Rich Lawrence at the July 1, 1978 reunion.)

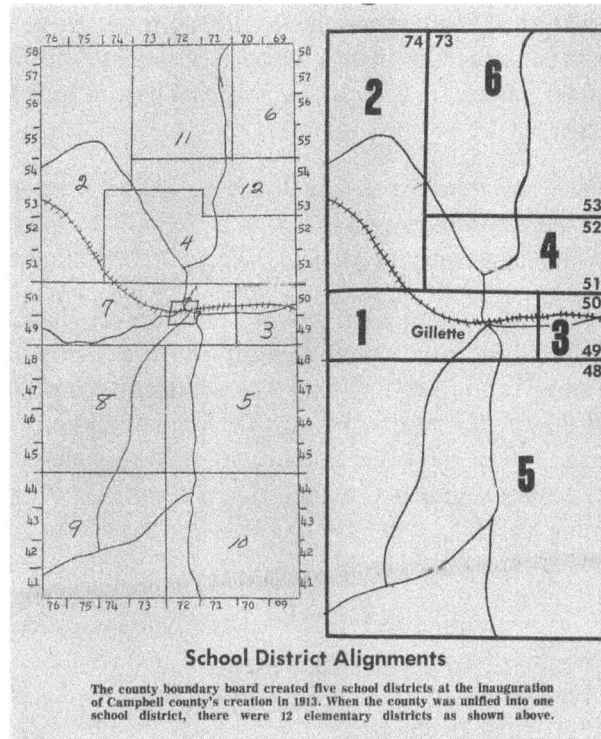

School District Alignments

The county boundary board created five school districts at the inauguration of Campbell county's creation in 1913. When the county was unified into one school district, there were 12 elementary districts as shown above.

County School History Constantly Changes
By Josephine Lucas
The News Record, Gillette, Wyo., Thursday, January 28, 1971, Page 11

The history of the Campbell County school districts was found in this article. Excerpts are quoted here.

Campbell County was created by the legislature in 1911, but the first elected officers did not assume office until January 1913. Therefore, for school history it is necessary to go back to the early history of Crook and Weston counties. Crook county was created in 1875 and was about 100 miles square. It was not organized until 1886 with Sundance chosen as the county seat. In 1890 Weston county was created from slightly less than one half of Crook county with Newcastle named the county seat, so our few early day schools were under the jurisdiction of these two counties. The first record of a school in what is now Campbell County was written by Mae Clevenger Davis, mother of the late Jerry Davis. She wrote that she taught a school held at the Colin Williams ranch on Powder River, about 30 miles north of Arvada, in 1891.

One thing revealed in early school history was the extreme youth of some the teachers. The State Department of Education, realizing the difficulty of securing teachers, compiled examination for those wishing to teach. If passed, they were issued a third-grade certificate and were assigned schools. Thus, many girls just out of the eighth grade started to teach. Due to their irregular schooling many were well over the age of the eighth grader today. A course of study was issued, which was of great help to teachers. It was not unusual for schools to have as many as 25 pupils in all the grades. Difficult as this sounds, these pupils did learn and pass the examinations supervised by the county superintendents. Some teachers taught high school subjects and credits were geared toward a high school diploma.

The first three Campbell county commissioners were W. P. Ricketts, C. A. Moyer and Anthony M. Carey. Josephine Anderson was the first county superintendent, and these four people were the first boundary board. They assumed office in January 1913 and had their first meeting in April of that year, to create the school districts. The accompanying map shows how they were designated. The second map shows how these were altered to reduce the size. None were changed after 1919.

255

In September of 1913 the boundary board enlarged District Four. In 1917 District One was changed, using one for the Gillette area, and creating District Seven from the balance of One. Also, that year District Five was divided into four districts, Five, Eight, Nine, and Ten. The last change was made in 1919 when District Six was divided into Six, Eleven, and Twelve. In 1919 a vote was taken in the county pertaining to forming a county high school district. District Two and Three voted against joining. However, the proposal passed by a vote of 371 to 120 so Campbell county High School became a reality.

Schools were established, and trustees elected by the citizens living within School Districts Three, Four, Five and Twelve. The trustees served as the governing body for the country schools located within a school district. All the school districts within the county were governed by the Superintendent of Campbell County Schools.

Rural or country schools were established in rural areas when, and wherever, the need for them was defined. In the early years local families usually built the school buildings from whatever material existed locally. Basically, they were of a basic design. Usually a small frame building with a closet near the door for the children's outer clothing, overshoes, lunch pails, bridles (if they rode horseback), etc. The school had only one door and at least one wall of windows for light. A blackboard, a wood stove, a table or two, desks for the children, and one for the teacher. A flag stood in the corner. Sometimes a piano was provided by the families that the school served. The Pledge of Allegiance was recited each morning as school began. A flag was also flown outside from a flagpole; it was raised and lowered by the teacher or an older student. There was an outhouse, sometimes two, and a wood/coal shed.

The schools were normally within walking distance for the children who attended. Sometimes horses were ridden, or their parents drove them to school in a horse and buggy/wagon. In area where horses were ridden daily to school by the children a second shed was sometimes built for the horses inside a small corral installed for them next to the school yard. Grain and water were provided by the parents and it was the child's responsibility to ensure their horse had water and grain to eat during school hours. Water was usually carried to school by the children and teacher. Some schools were near water wells and could draw water from them for use during the school day. A water bucket and cups were placed in the front, or back, of the school room, near the door. Also, a wash pan with soap for the children to wash up after eating or playing. Another bucket sometimes was available as a water waste bucket so they could use it to water any plants they may have planted outside in the yard. The maintenance and furnishing of wood or coal for heat were the responsibility of the school district. Some districts placed bids in the newspaper for the hauling the wood or coal, in others, the parents took turns with providing the wood or coal. It was the responsibility of the teacher to see that wood was stocked near the stove ready to make a fire at the beginning of the day. At the end of the day the teacher also was responsible for ensuring the fire in the stove was out to prevent fire. If light was needed during the school day, a kerosene lamp was used. Electricity was still not available in most rural communities during the first half of the 20th century. The teacher was responsible to decorate the interior of the school and for the cleaning the school and the grounds outside.

Grades taught in the rural school could involve all grades one through eight. Prior to the building of a high school in Gillette and in Rozet, some rural schools also taught high school grades. To teach multiple grades required a certain amount of training. Some furnished by the county superintendent, some by experience. For the teacher had to teach classes in each subject for each grade every day. Specialized teaching was not available in those early days. While the teacher worked with one grade level, the students in other levels were busy doing some studying on their own in their own materials. Sometimes the older children helped to teach the younger when the teacher was busy. There was very little homework. All schoolwork was done under the teacher's supervision at school. Excellent work completed at school was sent home for the children to show their parents. There were very few occasions when schoolwork was sent home to be completed. Most of the children had chores to do both morning and night at home. They went to bed early usually right after the families evening meal, and they were up early to do their chores, eat breakfast in time to not be late for school. Not many students made it through all twelve grades due to being needed to work in the fields for the young men and the young women. Sometimes as soon as a young woman finished her eighth grade, she was hired to teach in that, or other, schools as teachers were sometimes hard to find. School programs provided the opportunity for the children and the teacher to show off what they learned during school. Christmas programs were always popular, also valentine and Halloween parties. Thanksgiving was used to learn more about our nation's beginnings and blessings. Most school programs were held in the afternoon. The lack of electricity never seemed to cause a problem; if it was dark the parents brought extra lanterns for light. Most of these country schools also served their community as a place to have a dance, a social event, or a community meeting. Some schoolhouses were designated as polling places during the election processes.

The names of the schools, the teachers who taught them, and the names of the children who attended were identified whenever possible. These names were mostly identified from reading the community news columns for Adon, Cottonwood Valley, Little Iowa, Rozet, Dillinger, Enterprise, Piney, etc., in the early Campbell County newspapers. Sometimes this information was found in feature articles concerning teacher's meetings, school board meetings, the appointments of teachers for the upcoming school terms, etc. Missing names was inevitable, because the names of teachers, their assigned school, and of the children attending were not always published each year. The following sketches on some of the schools within a school district were created from information found in the early newspapers and school programs, annuals, or other items that certain individuals were willing to share with me. To these people who were willing to share their school treasures, we owe a great debt of gratitude.

TEACHING WAS TOUGH

Howard Hobbs of Evansville, Wyoming, who claims it "sure is different in this age of permissiveness, (1990) brought back a list of nine instructions to teachers dated September 1872 that he secured from museum in Mitchell, South Dakota.

The Rules were as follows:

Teachers will fill lamps, clean chimneys and trim wicks each day.

Each teacher will bring a scuttle of coal and a bucket of water for the day's use.

Make your pens carefully. You may whittle nibs for the individual taste of children.

Men teachers may take one evening each week for courting purposes or two evening a week if they go to church regularly.

After ten hours in school, the teacher should spend the remaining time reading the Bible or other good books.

Women teachers who marry or engage in other unseemly conduct will be dismissed.

Any teacher who smokes, uses liquor in any form, frequents a pool or public hall, or gets shaved in a barber shop will give good reason for suspecting his worth, intentions, integrity and honesty.

Every teacher should lay aside from his paycheck a goodly sum for her or his, declining years so that she/he will not become a burden on society. The teacher who performs her/his labors faithfully and without fault for five years will be given an increase of 25 cents a week in her/his pay providing the board of education approves.

(A free handout entitled, "1890-1990 Wyoming Centennial", Courtesy of the Campbell County Rockpile Museum, Gillette, Wyoming) School

District Three
Schools
Before Consolidation (1903-1921)

Bailey School

Teachers:	Ruth King	1919-1920
	Mary Ann Taylor	1920-1921
Children who may have attended:	Loretta Bailey	
	Gladys Bailey	
	Leland Henry	

Best School
(Located five miles west of Rozet on the Harper place.)

Teachers:	Gladys Ashpole	1918-1919
	Gladys Stewart	1919-1920
Children who may have attended:	The William Best Children	
	The _____ Best Children	

Clark School

Teachers:	Bertha Osborn	1917-1918
	Mabel Brower	1919-1920
Children who may have attended:	Freitta (?) Clark	
	Nina (?) Clark	

Duvall School

Teachers:	_____	1917-1918
	_____	1918-1919
	_____	1919-1920
	_____	1920-1921
Children who may have attended:	Margarite Duvall	
	_____	
	_____	
	_____	
	_____	

George School
(Located north of Rozet somewhere along the current South Heptner Road)

Teachers:	Zelia Holman	1916-1917
	Zelia Holman	1917-1918
	Miss Bonnafield	1919-1920
	Jenita Berry	1920-1921
Children who may have attended:	Gwendolyn Fischer	
	Lynn Fischer	
	Carolyn Fischer	

Happy Hollow School

Teachers:	Edith George	1918-1919
	Edith George	1919-1920
	Edith George	1920-1921

Children who may have attended: Margaret, Daniel, Richard and Eileen Brennan
Theresa, Loretta, and Gladys Bailey
Zelma, Ritch, Hannah, Wardie, Lois and
Gladys Weaver
Leland Henry

McClendon School

| Teachers: | Miss Dugan | 1920-1921 |

Shroyer School

Teachers:	Gladys Marquiss	1917-1918
	C. A. Houtchens	1919-1920
	_____	1920-1921

Children who may have attended: Wynona Shroyer
Blanche Shroyer
Donald Shroyer

Timber Creek School

| Teachers: | Miss Ida Dugan | 1921-1922 |

South Rozet School (aka Weckwerth School)

Because of hard winters and distances a school was established in June 1917 for a six weeks term. It was located on the Raven creek Road on the Black Place. The teacher was Emily Clark, sister of A. M. Clark, former Secretary of the State of Wyoming. She drove from her place, which later was a part of the Bob Ewing Ranch, to the school in a one horse buggy.

During the summer of 1918 the school house was moved midway between the Weckwerth and Moran places. Ruth King, a niece of Hite Eddy, was hired as a teacher. She lived in part of the school house. Miss King married Fred Carson and they ranched in the Adon Community for several years.

In 1920, Kathryn Lowery was the teacher and later married Ray Kottraba.

Teachers:	Emily Clark	1917-1918
	Ruth King	1918-1919
	Mrs. Frank Wall	1919-1920
	Kathryn Lowery	1920-1921
Children who may have attended:	The Armstrongs	
	Esther Cain	
	George Dinsmore	
	Vina and Lina Hathaway	
	Lester and Thelma Hoxsie	
	Russell, Marie and George Moon	
	Neta, Gilbert, and Edwin Moran	
	Blanche, Donald and Wynona Shroyer	
	Dorothy, Donald, Walter, and Henry Weckwerth	

(some point between 1917 – 1921)
The year these photos were taken is unknown. The children were not identified on the back of the photo.

Sources:
Photos courtesy of the Campbell Rockpile Museum, Gillette, Wyoming, 2021.
History Scrapbook at the Library at the Rozel Elementary School, Rozet, Wyoming, copies by Ms. Diann Avery, 2021.

Well Creek School

Well Creek School was located on Well Creek five and a half miles northeast of Rozet and one mile from the Johnson homestead. Miss Edith George was the teacher for the first three years.

Teachers:

Edith George	1914-1915
Edith George	1915-1916
Edith George	1916-1917
Zelia Holman	1917-1918
_____	1918-1919
Jenette Berry	1919-1920
_____	1920-1921

Children who attended the 1915-1917 terms:
Loretta and Theresa Bailey
Carolyn, Gwendolyn and Lynn Fischer
Alta and Tommy Garrett
Edna, Myrtle, Ruth, Kermit, Fred, Faye Johnson
Curtis and Gladys Stewart
Wayne Percy
Lyla Wells

Well Creek School – 1916
1st Row: Curtis Stewart, Lynn Fischer, Fred and Kermit Johnson
2nd Row: Loretta Bailey
3rd Row: Lyla Wells, Alta Garrett, Carolyn Fischer
4th Row Myrtle Johnson, Gwendolyn Fischer, Ruth Johnson
Edith George, teacher, Edna Johnson, Theresa Bailey,
Tommy Garrett
(Photo courtesy of the Campbell County Rockpile Museum
  Gillette, Wyoming)

About 1918
Faye Johnson, Carolyn Fischer, _____,
Tommy Garrett, Kermit Johnson, Fred Johnson
(photo provided by Joyce Johnson Ruff)

Sources:
Rockpile Museum, Gillette, Wyoming, 2021.
School History from Library at Rozet/Elementary School, Rozet, Wyoming, copies by Ms. Diann Avery, 2021.

Rozet School

In July 1903, the first school, besides Gillette, was established at Rozet. The school was held in an upstairs room of the Burlington Railroad Section-house. Mrs. Kate Shaughnessy was the person responsible for this school being organized. Five pupils attended, all Shaughnessy's, Claire, Nellie, Mary, Gertrude "Toots", and John. There are three stories indicating the method she used to contact the school authorities: (1) she rode the hand car to Moorcroft, took the stage to Sundance; (2) she rode the train as far as Moorcroft and took the stage to Sundance; or (3) she hired a horse and buggy to make the trip to a school meeting at Carlile, Wyoming, to make a plea for a school at Rozet. She was promised a school, if—there were at least five students, a place to hold school, and desk to be provided by the one seeking the school. Crook County would pay a teacher and furnish the textbooks. Mrs. Shaughnessy found a teacher, provided board and room for the teacher and all other necessary items to furnish a school. It is believed that the salary for the teacher was $37.50 or $40.00 per month. Not a bad deal for a teacher at that time. In following years, the school was moved to various buildings and homesteads.

The school term began in July 1903 and ended in March 1904. Mrs. Shaughnessy furnished the desks. The first teacher was Mary Shaughnessy a niece from Tecumseh, Nebraska.The second teacher was Clara Baker, daughter of Doctor Baker; third teacher was Maggie Brennan, another niece from Gillette. Other succeeding teachers were Bea Lathom of Sundance; May Darlington; Bess Curtis (1906-1907); Constance Green, spring of 1908; and Maude Coffey, the first to teach in Claire's (Shaughnessy) homestead shack.

At this period in the history of our school, there was not a Campbell County. The whole area of what are now Campbell, Crook, and Weston Counties, was then Crook County. Campbell County was organized in 1913 and School District Three was created. District Three was always the smallest school district in Campbell County consisting only four townships. The first dedicated school building (one room) in Rozet was erected in 1917.

The preceding material was gathered by Ruth Whisler from notes kept by the late Nellie Shaughnessy Frey, one of the first pupils, and Ruth Shaughnessy Burke, the youngest of the Shaughnessy family, too young to attend the first school. From these notes Ruth wrote an article for the Rozet School Reunion on July 1, 1978.

Children who may have attended Rozet School prior to 1921 consolidation:

Gladys Bailey	Helen Brennan	Richard Lawrence
Loretta Bailey	Mary Brennan	Russell Lawrence
Dan Brennan	Richard Brennan	Gerald Marquiss
Eileen Brennan	Ruby Kessinger	Quentin Marquiss
Fred Brennan	Pat Lawrence	Galen Miller
Irene Brennan	Paul Lawrence	Keith Miller

List of the Rozet School teachers and their terms 1903-1921

TEACHERS	TERMS
Mary Shaughnessy	1903-1904*
Mary Shaughnessy	1904-1905*
Clara Baker	1905-1906*
Bessie Curtis	1906-1907*
Maggie Brennan	Fall 1907*
Constance Green	Spring 1908
Bea Latham	1908-1909*
May Darlington	1909-1910*
Maude Coffey	1910-1911*
Alma Gielish	1911-1912
Marie Altafer and Doro George	1912-1923
Mrs. O. Hibler and Gladys Marquiss	1913-1924
Vera Eddy and Edith George	1914-1915
Mildred Smith and Emily E. Clark	1915-1916
Bertha Osborne and Ona L. Toland	1916-1917
Ruth King and Ona L. Toland	1917-1918

Frank George served as clerk of the School District Three School Board from 1915 to 1918. Beginning in 1919 Carrie Wells served as clerk for several years.

In August 1919 citizens of District3 voted not to join the newly created Campbell County High School District (25 for, 40 against). The school board elected L. D. Brennan, and Jack Brennan put up a twelve-foot addition to the school to house 9th and 10th grades.

Frank Wall Jessie McPherson Ruth King	1918-1919	First term for high school classes
Mr. Frank Wall Mrs. Florence Wall Jessie McPherson	1919-1920	
Mr. Frank Wall Mrs. Florence Wall, Jessie McPherson	1920-1921	

Late winter and spring of 1921 found serious discussion in the District regarding consolidating the schools in Rozet. In early May consolidation passed by a close vote of 45 to 49. The Rozet School was remodeled and a 20 by 50-foot addition was constructed to handle the increased enrollment. Four bus routes were established (all to be less than nine miles) to convey the pupils to the consolidated school in Rozet. An injunction lawsuit, filed by C.C. Weaver and B. J. Moran, was in circuit court. The injunction was dissolved in mid-July by Judge Ilsley. The July 28, 1921, issue of *Campbell County Record* carried a petition signed by over ninety residents and qualified electors of District Three addressed to the School Board of District Three that the consolidation be abandoned primarily because of the difficulty of transporting the students into Rozet during the winter and spring.

"One Room Schools of Crook County, Wyoming," by R. and K. Mallak, 1985.

District Three
Rozet Consolidated Elementary and High School
Rozet, Wyoming (1921-1958)

© Campbell County Rockpile Museum 2011

Up until 1921, some, but not all, Campbell County rural schools also taught high school courses. In 1919, a vote was taken to form a County High School District with a new high school building to be built in Gillette. It would be open to all students in Campbell County who had completed the eighth grade in the County's rural schools and the Gillette Elementary School. The proposal passed 371 to 120, with School Districts Two and Three voting against it and therefore remained outside the County High School District for forty-five years. After many meetings School District Three decided to consolidate its rural schools and build a consolidated elementary and high school building in Rozet. During this time several men in the school district, including Charles Slattery, obtained a ninety-nine years lease on ten acres on the corner of a school section from the State of Wyoming for a school and gymnasium to be built in Rozet. This would eliminate the rural schools within the district and would involve busing the rural children into Rozet to attend school. All families living in District Three did not accept this idea. After several lawsuits and attempts to stop the consolidation, all rural schools in the district were consolidated into one school at Rozet by a final consolidation vote in March 1921.

The Rozet Consolidated Elementary and High School opened in September 1921 with eight elementary grades and a full four-year high school. The Superintendent was Mr. Frank Wall; the elementary school teachers were Olivia Neville, Laura Spangler and Nellie Boiles/Bales; the high school teachers were Mr. and Mrs. Frank Wall and Miss Hazel Holtz. Seventy-five students were enrolled. Names of some of the children attending elementary and high school classes during that first school term:

Theresa Bailey	Margaret Brennan	Hamilton Davis
Dan Brennan	Ruth Brennan	Mable Dewing
Eileen Brennan	Leslie Burr	Loraine Ditto
Fred Brennan		Helen Duvall
Irene Brennan	Ivan Cain	Jean Duvall
Leo Brennan		
Mary Brennan	Davis Girls	Lois Foley

264

Waldo Foley	Myrtle Johnson	Joe Slattery
Bernice Frey	Ruth Johnson	Donald Shroyr
		Wynona Shroyer
Billy Gardner	Ruby Kessinger	Curtis Stewart
Glen Gardner		Gladys Stewart
John Gardner	Paul Lawrence	
Laine Gardner	Russell Lawrence	Earn Tuller
Mary Gardner		
Alta Garrett	Edyth McClendon	Hannah Weaver
Tessie Garrett	Galen Miller	Leroy Weaver
Tommy Garrett	Keith Miller	Mary Weaver
	George Moon	Richie Weaver
Adolph Hamm	Marie Moon	Wardie Weaver
Bessie Hamm	Russell Moon	Zelma Weaver
Gladys Hamm		Walter Weckwerth
Linn Hathaway	Maggie Nelson	Lyla Wells
Vina Hathaway		Lillie Woods
Lester Hoxsie	Phyllis Owens	
Thelma Hoxsie		
	Doris Riley	
Faye Johnson	Ione Riley	
Fred Johnson		

about 1936

By 1930 the schoolhouse built in 1920-21 had long run out of room for the growing numbers of children attending school. Classes were held in three or more different building in Rozet, the community churches for instance. The gymnasium was unheated. The people of Rozet had long been dissatisfied with the condition of the schoolhouse and the gymnasium. When the Rozet Community Hall burned down, they made plans to rebuild a community hall/gymnasium. It was completed in January 1936. On Saturday night, January 10, 1936, they held a dance with the Syncopators furnishing the music. Over 200 couples attended. The proceeds went towards the Rozet basketball team the Rozet School. When WPA money became available in late 1935 the trustees of the school district began considering building a new schoolhouse also. The families in School District Three voted on January 18, 1936, to bond the district for $5,000.00 to a build a new grade and high school building. The new building would be 60 x 80 feet and would be of the same height as the recently completed gymnasium. It would have half basement containing furnace and lunchrooms with six schoolrooms and a small auditorium above. When looking for building materials for the gymnasium, they found they could build a schoolhouse and a gymnasium at the cost of a gymnasium alone if they used a native stone called "lava rock." Also, the buildings would be fireproof. The Board of Education, Jack Wolfe, Chairman, O'Neal Gray, Treasurer, and Earl Burke, Clerk, with the assistance of F. N. Crossman, the Superintendent of Rozet Schools at that time, contracted Robert Johnson, of Gillette, to build the buildings. The building costs were estimated as $15,000.00. It was built for $10,104.00. Of that total, $6,597.50 was federal funds received through the WPA project. A school district three bond furnished the remaining $3,506.50. There were 21 men employed in the building of the school and gymnasium.

Joe Slattery recalls: "that before the new buildings were built, the basketball team used to dress in a lumber yard building that belonged to the Saunders' Lumber Company. It was located where Coltrane's shop is now (1990). The next place we used as a dressing room was a boxcar that Ashton Whisler was living in (early 1930s) across the highway from the gym. Joe Weaver, Lester Hoxsie, and I used to ride from our homes on horseback to play basketball. Some of those rides were pretty cold. We walked more than we rode. My dad, Charles Slattery, served sixteen years on the school board." (Campbell County the Treasured Years, 1990, page 538, compiled by Campbell County Historical Society)

Vince Thar recalls playing the first basketball game in the new gymnasium in 1935 as he watched two of his grandsons play the final game on in the same gymnasium on January 11, 1983, constructed in Rozet after a fire destroyed the previous one. A new school was also built because the old one was falling apart and was too small. The gymnasium was built ahead of the rest of the school. This led to some complications during the first couple of years. "When I was a sophomore, the school was scattered all over Rozet. Some classes were held in two churches and other buildings in town." Vince Thar added, "Most of the labor used to build the new schoolhouse and a gymnasium came because of post-depression programs. Labor was supplied through the Works Progress Administration (WPA). The government hired people to work for about twenty-six cents an hour. Cinder rocks were gathered from the hills to the west to build it. $17,800 was bonded to build the school. In January 1935 the first basketball game was played in the new gymnasium with Sundance. Rozet nipped Sundance with a score of 27-26. Mr. Thar recalls: "The heating system wasn't installed at that time and I remember it was pretty cold. And they still jumped center after every basket then." Leola Thar, his wife, doesn't remember too much about the first game, but said, "I was probably a cheerleader." ("The First and the Last," Record Sports, *The News Record, Gillette*, Wyoming, February 10, 1983.)

The school was active for the next thirty-six years providing the district's children with a full twelve-year program. Along with an avid following of fans the Rozet High School basketball team played games at all schools in the northeast Wyoming area. The gymnasium was also used as a polling place, community dances, and other functions. It was the social gathering place for families living south and north of Rozet for many years. There was always a Saturday night dance scheduled a couple of times a month or more. Many a marriage was begun at those dances.

The high school graduating class of 1958 was the last class to graduate from Rozet High School. The class members were Joyce Johnson, Sue Slattery, and Carol Fittro. After that year all the high school students in the district were bused to Campbell County High School in Gillette, Wyoming. The elementary grades, one through eight, continued to be taught at the school.

Sources:
Photos: from the collections of Irene Heptner Whisler, Leona and Jeanette Heptner.
1939 Rozet School Annual, page 8.
"Spotted Horse and Rozet will Share Money (WPA)," The News Record, Gillette, Wyoming, August 10, 1935.
"Apply for Rozet School as Project," page 1, The News Record, Gillette, Wyoming, November 1, 1935,
"Local Officials Receive Word of More Projects," page 1, The News Record, Gillette, Wyoming as corrected by November 7, 1935.
"County Projects Gaining Headway," page 1, The News Record, Gillette, Wyoming, November 22, 1935.
"Notice of School District (3) Bond Election," The News Record, Gillette, Wyoming, December 21, 1935.
"Rozet Hall to Open Tonight ," page 1, The News Record, Gillette, Wyoming, Saturday, January 10, 1936.
"Rozet People Vote Bonds," page 1, The News Record, Gillette, Wyoming, January 21, 1936.
"Notice of Sale of School District Bonds," The News Record, Gillette, Wyoming, February 18, 1936.

SCHOOL BUS ROUTES AND DRIVERS

With the consolidation of the schools within School District Three in 1921 the transportation of children became priority. The school board scheduled bus routes to homes throughout the community with school age children. Bids were let by the school board for three school bus routes that first year, an east route, south route, and north route. Teams and covered wagons first transported the children. The wagon had a sheep wagon stove in it and a door at both ends. The children would thaw their sandwiches on top of the stove; sometimes they even toasted them when they desired a "hot" sandwich. There were benches along the sides of the "bus" for the children to sit on. They used teams and wagons for the first five or six years that the school was in operation until 1928 when Model T trucks began being used instead.

Bus drivers for the first school term of 1921-1922 were: Joe McClendon, Clifford Zimmerschied, and Charlie Slattery. For the school term of 1922-1923 Charles Wells and Slim Whisler drove the northeast and Well Creek routes; I. L. Harmon and Adolph Hamm drove the north routes up the Adon Road; and Joe McClendon, Charles Slattery, Clifford Zimmerschied, Jim Duvall, Lee Ridenour, Bill Lubkin, Bob Peterson, Winslow Garrett drove the south and southeast routes with Billy Gardner, Ed Burr and Jo-Jo McClendon driving the south route down the Bishop Road. (*Gillette News*, July 27, 1922; Rozet.)

Bus Drivers from Fall 1921 Through Spring 1958

1921 – 1922	Joe McClendon	South Route
	Clifford Zimmerschied	
	Charlie Slattery	
1922 – 1923	Charles Wells/Slim Whisler	Northeast Route
	I. L. Harmon/Adolph Hamm	North Route
	R. D. Peterson	South Route and southeast routes
	Joe McClendon	
	Charles Slattery	
	Clifford Zimmerschied	
	Jim Duvall	
	Lee Ridenour	
	Bill Lubkin	
	Winslow Garrett	
	Billy Gardner	South Route down the Bishop Road
	Ed Burr	
	Jo-Jo McClendon	
1924 – 1925	Jim Duvall	Southeast Route
1925 – 1926	Jim Duvall	Southeast Route
1926 – 1927	Jim Duvall	Southeast Route
1927 – 1928	Doris Riley	South Route
	Note: Fall 1928 first year motorized buses were used.	
1928 – 1929	Carroll "Toad" Duvall	Southeast Route
	Slim Whisler	Northeast Rout
1929 – 1931	(Drivers unknown)	
1931 – 1932	Mrs. Lila Weaver	Southwest Route
	Stanley Stewart	Northeast Route
	James D. Duvall	Southeast Route
1932 – 1933	Lyla Wells Weaver	Southwest Route
	James D. Duvall	Southeast Route
	Stanley Stewart	Northeast Route

Bus Drivers from Fall 1921 Through Spring 1958 (continued)

1933 – 1934	James D. Duvall	22 /South East Route
	_____	14 /South Route
	_____	15 /South West Route
	_____	22 /North East Route
	_____	12 /North West Route
		85 Children Bused
1934 – 1935	James D. Duvall	22 /South East Route
	Clarence Walker	14 /South Route
	Floyd E. Cook	15 /South West Route
	Frank R. Stewart	22 /North East Route
	Ira VanOrsdale	12 /North West Route
		85 Children Bused
1935 – 1936	C. A. Walker	Southeast Route
	Roy Hoxsie	South Route
	Floyd E. Cook	Southwest Route
	Frank R. Stewart	Northeast Route
	Ira VanOrsdale	North Route
1936 – 1941	(Drivers unidentified)	
1940 – 1958	C. L. Brunson	Southwest Route
	_____	Northeast Route

All 4 school busses for 1929

The first school term when motorized busses were used.

Darleen beside Oscar Heptner's School Bus - 1941

ROZET CONSOLIDATED AND HIGH SCHOOLS

Photos from the collections of Carroll D. "Slim" Whisler.

| | | TEACHERS | |
TERM	SUPERINTENDENT	GRADE SCHOOL	HIGH SCHOOL
1921-1922	Mr. Frank Wall	Olivia Neville Laura Spangler Nellie Boiles/Bales	Frank Wall Florence Wall Hazel Holtz
1922-1923	Mr. Frank Wall	Sylvia Helmer Edith George Olivia Neville	Frank Wall Hazel Holtz Mr. Anderson
1923-1924	Mr. A. J. Boosinger	Fay Morris Boosinger Sylvia Helmer Bertha Miller	A. J. Boosinger Miss Chapp
1924-1925	Mr. Charles Foley	Bertha Miller Anne Morrow Nellie Boiles/Bales	Charles Foley Blanche Foley Belle Walker Emma Holland
1925-1926	Mr. Charles Foley	Belle Walker Mrs. Huston-Kirshner Miss Shay	Charles Foley Emma Holland Mrs. G. W. Beatty
1926-1927	Mr. Wagner	Alma Day Evalene Hester Ann Brennan	Mr. Wagner Belle Walker Anne Cameron
1927-1928	Mr. Wagner	Alma Day Miss Steinberg	Mr. Wagner Anne Cameron Evalene Hester
1928-1929	Mr. Wagner	Alma Day Marge Malsbury	Mr. Wagner Anne Cameron Evalene Hester
1929-1930	Mr. Ernest Reed	Alma Day	Ernest Reed Harold Bricker Marge Malsbury
1930-1931	Mr. Ernest Reed	Mrs. E. Reed Irene Brennan Vina Hathaway	Ernest Reed Harold Bricker Marge Malsbury
1931-1932	Mrs. Eliz. Brandt	Marie Dorsett Leah Peterson Neta Moran	Elizabeth Brandt Evalene Eddy Harold Bricker
1932–1933	Mrs. Eliz. Brandt	Mrs. Marie Dorsett Leah Peterson Neta Moran	Elizabeth Brandt Glenn Birchard Harold Bricker
1933-1934	Mrs. Eliz. Brandt	Mrs. Marie Dorsett Agnes Hawk Neta C. Moran	Elizabeth Brandt Glenn Birchard Harold Bricker
1934-1935	Mrs. Eliz. Brandt	Mrs. Marie Dorsett Agnes Hawk Charles Alexander	Elizabeth Brandt Rosa Bradasich Nerbert Crossman
1935-1936	Nerb Crossman	Mrs. Marie Dorsett Opal Cook Agnes Hawk	Nerbert Crossman Arlene Finch
1936-1937	Nerb Crossman	Lora Dora Berry Agnes Hawk Dain E. Holden	Nerbert Crossman Rose Bradasich

| | | TEACHERS | |
TERM	SUPERINTENDENT	GRADE SCHOOL	HIGH SCHOOL
1937-1938	Nerb Crossman	Lora Davis Berry Marguerite Duvall Gladys Weaver	Nerbert Crossman Rose Bradasich
1938-1939	Nerb Crossman	Leona Heptner Cecelia Closson Gladys Weaver	Nerbert Crossman Rosa Bradasich Doris Miric
1939-1940	Nerb Crossman	Leona Heptner Cecelia Closson Gladys Weaver	Nerbert Crossman Rosa Bradasich
1940-1941	Nerb Crossman	Leona Heptner Bernice Ross Gladys Weaver	Nerbert Crossman Eldora Hanson
1941-1942	Nerb Crossman	Leona Heptner LaVerne New Gladys Weaver	Nerbert Crossman Jen Southworth
1942-1943	Nerb Crossman	Leona Heptner Shirley Preston Gladys Weaver	Nerbert Crossman Doris Mirich
1943-1944	Nerb Crossman	Leona Heptner Katie Riesland Gladys Weaver	Nerbert Crossman Doris Mirich
1944-1945	Nerb Crossman	Ruth B. Whisler Katie Riesland Gladys Weaver	Nerbert Crossman Sylvia Williams
1945-1946	Richard Dumbrill	Leona Heptner Katie Riesland Leora Hubbard	Richard Dumbrill Neta Brennan Ramona Taft
1946-1947	Richard Dumbrill	Flora Rivola Katie Riesland Keith Ware	Richard Dumbrill Mrs. R. Dumbrill Dora Davis Berry
1947-1948	Mr. Hugh Artist	Flora Rivola Neta Brennan Jeanette Heptner	Hugh Artist N. D. Morgan Olive Egglestone Willis Bone
1948-1949	Mr R. U. Johnson	Flora Rivola Dorothy Addison Jasper	Mrs. Gladys Landers Lora Davis Berry Willis Bone
1949-1950	Mr. Mike Coleman	Margaret Carr Neta Brennan Dorothy Addison	Mike Coleman Mattie Coleman
1950-1951	Mr. Meridith Weston	Dorothy Jasper Margaret Carr Harlan Stanley	Dorothy Weston Dorothy. Weston Paul Zimmerman
1951-1952	Mr. Meridith Weston	Harlan Stanley Margaret Carr Dorothy Jasper	Meridith Weston Paul Zimmerman
1952-1953	N. D. Morgan	Mrs. Anna B. Stevens Mrs. Marian T Haveman John G. Nichols	Walter Dobbs Mrs. Eastman Virginia O'Neill Elmer P. Haveman

		TEACHERS	
TERM	SUPERINTENDENT	GRADE SCHOOL	HIGH SCHOOL
1953-1954	Mr. George Sprague	Alma Brennan Ruth B. Whisler Marlys Petersen	Anastasia Sprague Eugene "Buddy" Self
1954-1955	Mr. George H. Sprague	Alma Brennan Ruth B. Whisler Marlys Petersen	Anastasia Sprague Marlys Peterson Eugene "Buddy" Self
1955-1956	Mr. John Homewood	Ruth B. Whisler Alma Brennan Roger Wilson, Jr.	John Homewood Sylvia Martin James Norman
1956-1957	Mr. John Homewood	Alma Brennan (1-6) Roger Wilson, Jr.	John Homewood Sylvia Martin James Norman
1957-1958	Mrs. Leland Landers	Alma Brennan (1-5) (Junior High not filled)	Gladys Landers Charles Martin

At the District Three Annual School Meeting held July 2, 1958, it was voted to send all elementary and high school students to Moorcroft. A second meeting was held July 23, 1958, where it was voted to send only the high school students to Moorcroft. Vincent Thar, F. M. Brennan, and Louis Ewing brought a lawsuit to have the July 2nd meeting declared to be the official meeting. In early October District Judge G. A. Layman ruled that the July 23rd meeting was the official meeting. School started a month later with the elementary grades in Rozet and the high school students bused to Moorcroft in compliance with the second meeting.

Photo Gallery of Classes Through the Years

(photos from the collections of Irene Heptner Whisler, Leona and Jeanette Heptner
and Leola Kottraba Thar courtesy of her daughter Shellie Thar Clark)

Rozet Consolidated & High School
1924

1924 Girls Basketball Team, Rozet High School
Back: Coach Foley
3rd Row: Vina Hathaway, Lena Hathaway, Wynona Schoyer, Lois Foley
2nd Row: Lynnett Hoyt, Ruby Kessinger, Mary Brennan, Mary Gardner
1st Row: Nita Moran, Marie Moon, Irene Heptner

272

1927-1928 Faculty
Mr. Wagner, Alma Day, Anne Cameron, Ann Brennan, Evalene Hester

Sophomore Class – 1927-1928
Dick Brennan, Joe Slattery, Ione Riley, Leona Heptner, Dorothy Whisler,
Laine Gardner, Thelma Hoxsie, Eugene Heptner, Eileen Brennan, Oscar Heptner

Junior Class – 1927-1928
Faye Johnson, Gilbert Moran, Lottie Weaver, George Moon, Doris Riley

273

Senior Class – 1927-1928
Mary Brennan, Russ Moon, Mary Gardner, Hamilton Davis, Irene Heptner

1928
Dick Brennan, Hamilton Davis, Coach Garrett, Oscar Heptner
Russ Moon, Gilbert Moran, Eugene Heptner

1936-1937 Girls High School Basketball Team
Standing: Jean Smith, Evelyn Brennan, Mary Jane Hoxsie, Fern Ridenour, Alpha June Dorset, Marjorie Stok
Kneeling: Evelyn Burr, Marlys Stewart, Katherine Ridenour, Yvonne Smith, Leola Kottraba

1938-1939 Faculty
Cecelia Closson, Gladys Weaver, 6, 7, and 8 grades, Mr. Nerb Crossman, Superintendent,
Rosa Bradasich, 3, 4, 5 Grades, Leona Heptner, 1-2 Grades
Missing: Doris Mirich

1938-1939 High School Basketball Team
Standing: Coach Crossman, Merle Duvall, David Bryant, Leonard Whisler, Vince Thar,
John Talley, James Bryant, Wayne Burr
Kneeling: Jess Jessen, Clyde Edwards, Earl Johnson

(Quoted from the 1938-1939 Rozet High School Annual)
F. N. CROSMAN, Basketball Coach

"When he came to Rozet five years ago, Coach Crossman found a group of inexperienced basketball players. His first three years were spent in teaching them the fundamentals of basketball. During this time, he saw his team defeated many more times than he saw them win. But with unceasing and tireless efforts he worked on to develop a good team. In the last two years, he has been rewarded for his work by seeing his team in the winning ranks. By building up a winning team from "nothing" Coach Crossman has acquired the reputation of being one of Northeastern Wyoming's best coaches."

Source: *Rozet School Yearbook 1939, Rozet, Wyoming, courtesy of Judy Whisler Kehn)*

1938-1939 High School Cheerleaders
Corrine Stewart, Leola Kottraba, Rosa Johnson, Donna Stewart

1940 – 1941, Grades 1 and 2
Back Row: David Riesland (?), Darrell Heptner, Jerry Prazma, Curtis Burr
Front Row: Edna Thompson, Nadine Duvall, Elsie Olsen, Leona Heptner

1940 – 1941, Rozet High School
4th Row: Nyle Bryant, Donna Stewart, Dottie Grey, Corrine Stewart, Helen Robb, Richard Gray
3rd Row: Elvira Halverson, Calvin Tholson, Wayne Burr, Sylvia Riley, Lee Truman,
Phyllis Reel, Mary Thar, Kenneth Duvall, Sylvia Williams, Clara Mae Edwards
2nd Row: Mr. Crossman, Evelyn Whisler, Evelyn Talley, Jess Jessen, Earle Johnson,
Charles Kottraba, Rodney Reel, David Bryant, Jean Reel, Miss Eldora Hansen
1st Row: James Bryant, Ferris Cook, Clyde Edwards, Ida Blakeman,
Willa Kottraba, Phil Frey, Dean Whisler, Leola Kottraba

277

1941 – 1942, Grades 6, 7, and 8
Top Row: John Tholson, Bobby Olson, _____ Harris?, Jimmy Thompson, Charlie Edwards
Middle Row: Gertrude Jessen, Crystal Jessen, John Wolfe, Ruth Ridenour, Judy Frey,
Billy Nelson, Leland Kottraba, Gladys Weaver
Front Row: Shirley Ware, Jerry Ridenour, Tommy Harris, Sam Wolfe, Helen Kottraba,
Doris Stewart, Darleen Heptner, Hazel Kottraba, _____

1941-1942, High School
Top Row: Dottie Mobley, Junior Harrod, Dale Donner, Alvin Gray, Pauline Ridenour, Clifford Burr, Nyle Bryant, Dorothy Donner,
Ken Duvall, Irene Harris, Ida Rose Blakeman, Francis Osborne
Middle: Mrs. Southworth, Elvira Halverson, Leslie Burr, Wayne Burr, Ferris Cook, Sylvia Riley, Calvin Tholson,
Rodey Reel, Evelyn Talley, Earl Johnson, James Bryant, Evelyn Whisler, Jan Reel, Mr. Crossman
Front Row: Phil Frey, Richard Gray, Charles Kottraba, Corrine Stewart, Mary Thar,
Donna Stewart, Phyllis Reel, Clyde Stewart

278

1942 – 1943, Grades 1 and 2
Back Row: Leona Heptner, Donnie Whisler, Johnny Duvall, Lorna Whisler, Dorothy Grey
Front Row: Shirley Heptner, Emma Brunson, Betty Grey, Janice Day, Nadine Brennan

1943 - 1944 High School
Back Row: Mr. Crossman, Kenneth Duvall, Evelyn Whisler, Elvira Halverson, Clifford Burr, Alvin Gray, Clyde Stewart,
Neal Riesland, Irene Harris, Eurith Whisler, Doris Mirich
Front Row: Judy Frey, Gertrude Jessen, Bonnie Jean Neilson, Christel Jessen, Carl Johnson,
Tommy Harris, John Tholson, Jimmy Thompson, John Wolfe, Phil Whisler

1944-1945, Grades 1, 2. 3
Back Row: Johnny Duvall, Damon Reel, Sally Whisler, Charles Skroch, Bobby Donner, Nadine Brennan.
Jackie Fittro, Phyllis Johnson
Front Row: Teacher Ruth Whisler, Joan Whisler, Patty Wells, Nancy Whisler, Carol Potter,
Rosie Ridenour, Jack Parker, Winifred Brunson

1945-1946, Grades 1, 2, and 3
Top Row: Leona Heptner, Wilma Thar
Middle Row: Damon Reel, Louis Hoxsie, Rosa Ridenour, Joanna Uhl, Jimmy Brennan
Front Row: Winifred Brunson, Nancy Whisler, Jerry Brennan, Carol Potter, _____

1945-1946, Grades 7 and 8
3rd Row: David Riesland, John Dumbrill, Darrell Heptner, Jerry Prazma
2nd Row: Leora Hubbard, Harold Ridenour, Donald Harris, Verlin Duvall, Phyllis Petersen
1st Row: Joann Wolff, Patty Brennan, Mary Lu Brennan, Betty Ruff, Nadine Duvall

1947-1948, Faculty
Back Row: N. D. Morgan, Superintendent, Hugh Artist, Bill Bone
Front Row: Flora Rivola, Nita Brennan, Jeanette Heptner

1947 – 1948 Grades 1, 2, and 3
Standing: Denny Brennan, Joyce Johnson, Joanna Uhl, Wilma Thar
Sitting: Shirley Potter, Sue Slattery, Virginia Whisler, Mrs. Rivola,
Verna Anne Edwards, Louise Hoxsie, Ethel Baker
Kneeling: Caroline Slattery and Norma Jean Duvall

1947 – 1948, Grades 4, 5, and 6
Back Row: Neta Brennan, Jimmy Eldredge, Jimmy Brennan, Damon Reel, Larry Brennan, Johnny Duvall
Middle Row: Phyllis Johnson, Ethel Baker, Ruth Potter, Nancy Whisler, Nadine Brennan, Rosa Ridenour, Sally Whisler
First Row: Joan Whisler, Jerry Brennan, Winfred Brunson, Damon Reel

282

1947 – 1948, Grades 7 and 8
Back Row: Norma Preston, Edna Thompson, Darrell Heptner, Arlene Bryant, Jeanette Heptner
Front Row: Hugh Baker, Emma Brunson, Shirley Heptner, Ruth Potter, John Baker

1949 – 1950, Grades 7 - 8
Back Row: Dorothy Jasper, Arnold Moon, Jimmy Eldredge, Larry Brennan, Sally Whisler,
Lorna Whisler, Nadine Brennan, Rosa Ridenour, Jeanne Mathison, Johnny Duvall, Bill Norman
Front Row: Jimmy Brennan, Deloris Whisler, Ann Watt, Anna Baker, Joyce Johnson,
Bea Phillips, Donnie Whisler, Dan Watt, Frank Carr, John Watt

283

GRADUATES
FROM THE 8TH GRADE AND HIGH SCHOOL
at
ROZET CONSOLIDATED AND HIGH SCHOOL

YEAR	EIGHTH GRADE	HIGH SCHOOL (See Note 1)
1922	Beryl Day Dan Brennan Neta Moran LeRoy Weaver	Gladys Stewart Quinn
1923	Tommy Garrett Mildred Hamm Kermit Johnson	Leo Brennan Margaret Brennan Lawrence Ruth Brennan Carr
1924	Mary Brennan Mary Gardner Glen Gardner Wayne Garrett Lina Hathaway Vina Hathaway Galen Miller Doris Riley Wynona Shroyer	Irene Brennan Scott Ruth Bell Johnson Whisler Mary Weaver Nelson Crabill Lyla Wells Weaver
1925	Lois Foley Eugene Heptner Faye Johnson Paul Lawrence Keith Miller George Moon Gilbert Moran Doris Rose Lottie Weaver	Fred Brennan Ruby Kessinger Pomrenke Russell Lawrence Lillian Woods Mathews
1926	Eileen Brennan Ivan Cain Laine Gardner Waldo Foley Leona Heptner Oscar Heptner Thelma Hoxsie Joseph Slattery Ione Riley Dorothy Whisler	Dan Brennan Marie Moon Williams Neta Moran Brennan LeRoy Weaver
1927	Helen Brennan Billy Gardner Edwin Moran Joe Weaver	None
1928	Cleo Cook Helen Duval Leon Gray Lester Hoxsie Marvel Riley	Mary Brennan Carr Hamilton Davis Mary Gardner Schlattmann Irene Heptner Whisler
1929	Bernice Frey	Faye Johnson Wolfe George Moon Gilbert Moran Doris Riley Goodykoontz

YEAR	EIGHTH GRADE	HIGH SCHOOL
1930	Mildred Burr Ruth Shafer John Thar	Eileen Brennan Hiles Laine Gardner Clark Leona Heptner Ione Riley Schlattmann Joseph B. Slattery Thelma Hoxsie
1931	Verne Robert Bartz Marguerite Duvall Babe Gardner Elizabeth Thar Eva Thomas	Helen Brennan Elliot Bill Gardner Edwin Moran Joe Weaver
1932	Marjorie Burke Mae DeRidder Ethel Hoxsie Mary Stewart Fern Thomas Vadyn Thomas	Cleo Cook Hellman Helen Duvall Gilson Leon Gray Lester Hoxsie Marvel Riley Schlattmann
1933	Mary Jane Hoxsie Oliver DeRidder Ralph Shafer Rex Stewart Francis Thar	Bernice Frey Day
1934		Mildred Burr Mooney Ruth Shafer Moon John Thar
1935	Betty Brown Merle Duvall Richard Shafer Max Smith Vincent Thar	Marguerite Duvall Kummerfeld Verna Lubkin Thaine Riley Elizabeth Thar Hagar Tony Thompson
1936		Jeff Thompson Marlys Stewart Peterson
1937		Mary Jane Hoxsie Fonner Francis Thar
1938		Melvin Edwards Louis Frey Katheryn Ridenour Moran Rex Stewart Kenneth Thomas Keith Ware Warren Williams
1939		Jean Duvall Frey Merle Duvall Rosalee Johnson Thompson Edward Poll Vince Thar Leonard Whisler
1940		Irene Edwards Hladky Wilber Lairmore Elaine Stewart Nedeau John Talley Leon Williams

YEAR	EIGHTH GRADE	HIGH SCHOOL
1941		David Bryant
		Clyde Edwards
		Jess Jessen
		Leola Kottraba Thar
		Willa Kottraba Irwin
		Sylvia Williams Crosby
1942		James Bryant
		Wayne Burr
		Ferris Cook
		Dorothy Donner Brown
		Dorothy Gray Mobley
		Earl Johnson
		Calvin Tholson
		Rodney Reel
		Pauline Ridenour Welsh
		Sylvia Riley Spangler
		Evelyn Talley Walsh
1943		Clara M. Edwards VanBuskirk
		Philip Frey
		Richard Gray
		Charles Kottraba
		Corinne Stewart Lone
		Donna Stewart Johnson
1944		Nyle Bryant
		Kenneth Duvall
		Elvera Halverson Thar
		Neal Riesland
		Evelyn Whisler Donner
1945		Clifford Burr
		Alvin Gray
		Clyde Stewart
		Eurith Whisler Romel
1946		Robert Macy
		Phillip Whisler
		John Wolfe
1947		Evelyn Donner Evans
		Bonnie Neilson Switzer
		John Tholson
		Marge M. Whisler
1948		Clifford Baker
		Jack Greer
		Hazel Kottraba Riesland
		Richard Preston
		Jerry Ridenour
		Ruby Ruff Williams Cox
		Shirley Ware Eisele
		Sam Wolfe
1949	Larry Brennan	Charlie Edwards
	Nadine Brennan	Wayne Goerke
	John Duvall	Charleen Felde Gray
	Arnold Moon	Deloris Lyons Kennister
	Billy Norman	Billy Nelson

YEAR	EIGHTH GRADE	HIGH SCHOOL
1949 continued	Beatrice Phillips John Watt Donald J. Whisler Lorna J. Whisler Sally E. Whisler	Robert Prazma Robert "Bucky" Williams
1950		Irene Baker Moser Patty Brennan Zimmerman Verlin Duvall Harold Ridenour Beatrice Phillips Donald L. Whisler
1951		Nadine Duvall Taylor Jerry Prazma
1952		Edna Jane Thompson Comer
1953		John Baker Rodney Addison Larry Brennan Emma Brunson Rogers Arlene Bryant Hing Shirley Heptner Prazma
1954	Denny Brennan Verna Mae Edwards Joyce Johnson Wilma Thar Joan Uhl Virginia Whisler	Nadine Brennan Gaskill John Duvall Donald Whisler Sally Whisler Mellinger
1955	David Bray Norma Duvall Marvin Johnson Jackie Peterson Larry Ruff Caroline Slattery Becky Thar Merle "Buster" Whisler	Anna Baker Rodgers Jimmy Brennan Phyllis Johnson Record Delores Whisler McGillis
1956		Jerry Brennan Winifred Brunson Marion Ruff Joe Slattery, Jr. Jack Svalina Barbara "Bobbie" Whisler
1957		Verna Edwards Martin
1958		Carol Fittro Wakefield Joyce Johnson Ruff Sue Slattery Zimmerschied

Note 1: Names of High School graduates copied from the first Rozet High School Reunion Program, July 1, 1978.

ROZET SCHOOL BOARD OF EDUCATION
TRUSTEES
(1921 – 1958)

SCHOOL TERM	BOARD MEMBERS	OFFICE HELD
1921 – 1922	Charles Slattery	President/Director
	Carrie Wells	Secretary/Clerk
	Charles V. Clark	Treasurer
1922 – 1923	Mrs. Bertha Miller	President/Director
	Carrie Wells	Secretary/Clerk
	Charles V. Clark	Treasurer
1923 - 1924	Mrs. Bertha Miller	President/Director
	Charles J. Slattery	Secretary/Clerk
	Claude Lawrence	Treasurer
1924 - 1925	Mrs. Bertha Miller	President/Director
	Charles J. Slattery	Secretary/Clerk
	Claude Lawrence	Treasurer
1925 - 1926	Mrs. Bertha Miller	President/Director
	Charles J. Slattery	Secretary/Clerk
	Claude Lawrence	Treasurer
1926 - 1927	Bert J. Moran	President/Director
	Lawrence. D. Brennan	Secretary/Clerk
	Samuel K. Weaver	Treasurer
1927 - 1928	Bert J. Moran	President/Director
	Lawrence. D. Brennan	Secretary/Clerk
	Samuel K. Weaver	Treasurer
1928 - 1929	Bert J. Moran	President/Director
	Lawrence D. Brennan	Secretary/Clerk
	Frank Stewart	Treasurer
1929 - 1930	Bert J. Moran	President/Director
	Lawrence D. Brennan	Secretary/Clerk
	Frank Stewart	Treasurer
1930 – 1931	_____	President/Director
	O'Neal Gray	Secretary/Clerk
	_____	Treasurer
1931 – 1932	Frank Stewart	President/Director
	O'Neal Gray	Secretary/Clerk
	E. L. Hoxsie	Treasurer
1932 – 1933	Frank Stewart	President/Director
	O'Neal Gray	Secretary/Clerk
	E. L. Hoxsie	Treasurer
	Earl F. Burke	Secretary/Clerk
	A. C. Douglas	Treasurer
1933 – 1934	E. L. Hoxsie	President/Director
1934 - 1935	John Wolfe	President/Director
	Earl F. Burke	Secretary/Clerk
	O'Neal Gray	Treasurer
1935 - 1936	John E. Wolfe	President/Director
	Earl F. Burke	Secretary/Clerk
	O'Neal Gray	Treasurer

288

SCHOOL TERM	BOARD MEMBERS	OFFICE HELD
1936 – 1937	_____	President/Director
	_____	Secretary/Clerk
	_____	Treasurer
1937 – 1938	_____	President/Director
	_____	Secretary/Clerk
	_____	Treasurer
1938 – 1939	Charles J. Slattery	President/Director
	Mrs. Mary Nelson	Secretary/Clerk
	Charles Peterson	Treasurer
1939 – 1940	Charles J. Slattery	President/Director
	Mrs. Mary Nelson	Secretary/Clerk
	Charles Peterson	Treasurer
1940 – 1941	_____	President/Director
	_____	Secretary/Clerk
	_____	Treasurer
1941 – 1942	_____	President/Director
	_____	Secretary/Clerk
	_____	Treasurer
1942 – 1943	Charles Peterson	President/Director
	Fred Brennan	Secretary/Clerk
	Mrs. Mary Nelson	Treasurer
1943 – 1944	_____	President/Director
	_____	Secretary/Clerk
	_____	Treasurer
1944 – 1945	_____	President/Director
	_____	Secretary/Clerk
	_____	Treasurer
1945 – 1946	_____	President/Director
	_____	Treasurer
1946 – 1947	_____	President/Director
	_____	Secretary/Clerk
	_____	Treasurer
1947 – 1948	Louis M. Ewing	President/Director
	Vincent Thar	Secretary/Clerk
	Kermit Johnson	Treasurer
1948 – 1949	_____	President/Director
	_____	Secretary/Clerk
	_____	Treasurer
1949 – 1950	Louis M. Ewing	President/Director
	Kermit Johnson	Secretary/Clerk
	Vincent Thar	Treasurer
1950 – 1951	Joseph Slattery	President/Director
	Kermit Johnson	Secretary/Clerk
	Vincent Thar	Treasurer
1951 – 1952	_____	President/Director
	_____	Secretary/Clerk
	_____	Treasurer
1952 – 1953	Joseph Slattery	President/Director
	Jack Mobley	Secretary/Clerk
	Vincent R. Thar	Treasurer

SCHOOL TERM	BOARD MEMBERS	OFFICE HELD
1953 – 1954	_____	President/Director
	_____	Secretary/Clerk
	_____	Treasurer
1954 – 1955	Joseph Slattery	President/Director
	Esther Harrod	Secretary/Clerk
	Vincent R. Thar	Treasurer
1955 – 1956	_____	President/Director
	_____	Secretary/Clerk
	_____	Treasurer
1956 – 1957	_____	President/Director
	_____	Secretary/Clerk
	_____	Treasurer
1957 – 1958	_____	President/Director
	_____	Secretary/Clerk
	_____	Treasurer

District Four Schools
Cottonwood Valley, Little Iowa, Miller Creek Areas North of Rozet

(photos from the collections of Irene Heptner Whisler, Leona and Jeanette Heptner)

Norman Grams who is researching Campbell County rural schools for the Campbell County Historical Society sent me the following: "District Four was created in 1923 (Campbell County was created by the legislature in 1911, but was considered unorganized until elected officials in November took office in January 1913 when Campbell County was organized and began functioning as a county. Before this the northern part of what became Campbell County was probably in District Eleven of Crook County. The boundaries of District Four were changed in 1919 when District Six was broken up and District 11 and Twelve were created out of parts of District Six. A small part of District Six and District Two were then put in District Four.

"School houses were not always in the same location. My father (Lewis E. Grams) attended Little Rawhide in District Four and once told me that the school was in a different location each of the eight years he attended (always in the same neighborhood). He believed the school was moved so that it was always halfway between the two farthest families with children attending that year. Schools opened and closed as the need for a school in that vicinity changed. School houses were used not only for school, but as polling places on election day, Sunday School, and church services, literacies, dances, etc."

The Cottonwood School (later years aka Woods School)

The Cottonwood School was established in 1915. It is located about nine miles northeast of Rozet in what was then known as the "Little Iowa" community. It was placed on the Woods homestead about one mile east of the Heptner homestead. Its first teacher was Miss Edna Stewart, who had just completed the eighth grade. The Board of Education members were Fred E. Marvel as Clerk, Floy B. Jeffers as Treasurer, and Tim Gupton as the secretary in 1919. These members very likely served on the board for several years. In the 1930s the school was renamed the Woods School.

Cottonwood School -- 1917-1918
Teacher: Edith George
Back row: Eugene Heptner, Alberta Woods, Gladys Hamm,
    Lyle Woods, Jack Hamm standing behind Adolph
    Hamm
Middle row: Bessie Hamm, Mildred Hamm, Lillie Woods,
    Irene Heptner
Front row: Dorothy Hamm, Leona Heptner, Winnie Hamm,
    Oscar Heptner

The Cottonwood School (1919-1920)
Teacher: Mark G. Richmond

School Board:	Fred D. Marvel	Clerk
	Floy B. Jeffers	Treasurer
	Tim Gupton	Secretary

Teachers:	Edna Stewart	1915 - 1916
	Edith George	1916 - 1917
	Edith George	1917 - 1918
	Ida Thompson	1918 - 1919
	Mark Richmond	1919 - 1920
	Florence Fair	1920 - 1921
	Florence Fair	1921 - 1922
	Anne Noble	1922 - 1923
	Mary Weaver Nelson	1923 - 1924
	Susie DeVore	1924 - 1925
	_____	1925 - 1926
	_____	1926 - 1927
	Alma Day	1927 - 1928
	Inez Stee	1928 – 1929
	Inez Stee	1929 – 1930
	Dorothy Sutherland	1930 – 1931
	Mrs. Latham	1931 – 1932
	Alma Toro	1932 – 1933
	Bertha Jane Anderson	1933 – 1934
	Helen Duvall	1934 – 1935
	_____	1935 – 1936
	Leona Heptner	1936 – 1937
	Leona Heptner	1937 – 1938
	Arlene Carson	1938 – 1939
	Arlene Carson	1939 - 1940

Children who may have attended:

	Blanche Earnest
David Earnest	Genevieve Earnest
Adolph Hamm	Bessie Hamm
Gladys Hamm	Mildred Hamm
Winnie Hamm	Darleen Heptner
Eugene Heptner	Irene Heptner
Jeanette Heptner	Leona Heptner
Oscar Heptner	Betty Matthews
Donny McCune	Lester McCune
Ione Riley	Sylvia Riley
Ellen Whisler	Evelyn Whisle
Pauline Whisler	Bertha Woods
Gerald Woods	Lillie Woods

The school was closed at the end of the 1937-1938 term as there were only two students attending, Darleen Heptner, daughter of Oscar and Dorothy Heptner, and Betty Matthews, daughter of Lillie Woods and Manuel Mathews. Most of the original homestead families were gone. The children who remained in the community were now either attending grade and high school at Rozet or Campbell County High School in Gillette.

Cottonwood Valley School (aka Wallace School)

The Cottonwood Valley School was established about 1917. It was located about two miles south of the Perry Wallace homestead along the Adon Road.

Teachers:

Ida Thompson	1917 - 1918
_____	19__ - 19__
Joe Drake	1927 - 1928
Leona Heptner	1931 – 1932
_____	1932 – 1933
_____	1933 – 1934
_____	19__ - 19__
Ruth B. Whisler	1963 - 1964

Children who may have attended:

Lee Wallace	Ruth Wallace
Leone Donner	Ted Wallace
Melvin Donner	June Donner
Dorothy Donner	Evelyn Donner
Gertrude "Gertie" Hartzell	Orie Gilliland

Spring Picnic 1934
Back Row: Lee Wallace, Leona Heptner, Gladys Weaver
Front Row: June and Leone Donner, Ted Wallace, Dean Whisler,
Alvina Weaver, Mary Hanslip (Leonard Whisler missing)

Deer Creek School

The Deer Creek School was located about a mile southwest of the Roy and Gladys Gilliland place (formerly the Rueben Reed homestead) and about a mile west of the Adon Road.

Teachers:

Ernest Weese	1927 - 1928
Irene Heptner	1928 - 1930
Gladys Weaver	1931 – 1932
Leona Heptner	1932 – 1933
Leona Heptner	1933 - 1934
Carl Carson	1934 – 1935
Carl O. Carlson	1936 – 1938
Joe DeBarthe	1938 - 1940

Children who may have attended:

Dean Whisler	Leonard Whisler
Johnny Weaver	Elvina Weaver
Francis Reed	Mary Hanslip
Jack Reed	Doris Riley
Virgil Jensen	Ione Riley

Little Iowa School

The Little Iowa School was established in 1913 by Miriam (Stull) Wells' aunt, Mrs. May Stewart Doane. First as a summer school held in her house for fourteen students. Mrs. Doane had moved out of her house to live in a tent during the summer. A school meeting was called and with the aid of the children's parents and neighbors, native lumber was hauled, and they built a schoolhouse across the road north of the Fayette Thompson homestead. The Pleasant Valley Cemetery is across the road west of the schoolhouse.

Teachers:	Mrs. May Stewart Doane	1913 – 1914
	_____	1914 – 1915
	_____	1915 – 1916
	_____	1916 - 1917
	Miss _____ Loftin	1917 - 1918

Children who may have attended:		Mariam Stull
	_____	Doris Riley
	Ione Riley	Richard Thompson
	Wilbur Thompson	

About 1919
Names of students are unknown (Miriam Stull would be a student at this time)
(Photos provided by Diann Larsen Avery; the photo was given to Diann's mother by Vern Jeffers a son of Mr. Floy Jeffers)

Trailer School

The Trailer School was located about 14 miles northeast of Rozet. It was first located near the ranch buildings of Jack Simpson (formerly the Kohns ranch); then it was moved down to the mailboxes along the road where the Miller Creek (now Gray Road) forks and turns northeast to Perry's (the old Hans Raudsep ranch) and the Semlek's. Then in the summer of 1958 it was moved a ½ mile north of the Pleasant Valley Cemetery. It was closed after the 1961-1962 school year.

1959
Hilda Ann and Kay Rene Simpson, Selma Raudsep, teacher
Ann and Diann Larsen

Teachers:	1942 - 1943	(Unknown)
	1943 - 1944	Freida Gall
	1944 - 1951	Vione Lane (seven years)
	1951 - 1952	Josephine Magnusson
	1952 - 1953	Mary Cook
	1953 - 1954	(Unknown)
	1954 - 1955	Pearl Yates
	1955 - 1956	(Unknown)
	1956 - 1962	Selma Raudsep (six years

Source:
Photo: courtesy of Diann Larsen Avery, April 19, 2017.
Information provided by Kay Rene (Simpson) Jones to Diann Larsen Avery, August 14, 2017.

Whisler School

The Whisler School was opened in 1943 when Lorna Whisler, daughter of Carroll "Slim" and Irene Whisler (who lived along the Adon Road), and Donnie and Delores Whisler, children of David and Marge Whisler (who lived across the road east from the Heptners) were ready for the first and second grade. The previous year Lorna's and Donnie's parents drove them to and from school at Rozet because there were not enough school age children available to set up a schoolhouse; three were required to warrant placing a rural school in their area. The school was located about halfway between Laura Heptner's farm and the Slim Whisler farm in the northwest quarter of Section 31, Township 51 West, Range 69 West.

Teachers:	Jeanette Heptner	1943 – 1944
	Jeanette Heptner	1944 – 1945
	Jeanette Heptner	1945 – 1946
	Eurith Whisler	1946 – 1947
	Bonnie Jean Nielson	1947 – 1948
	Selma Raudsep	1948 – 1949
Children who attended:		
	Lorna Whisler	1948 –1949
	Olive Whisler	1948 –1949
	Donnie Whisler	1948 –1949
	Delores Whisler	1948 –1949
	Barbara Whisler	1948 –1949
	Loren Simpson	1948 –1949

During the school's last term, Loren Simpson, Selma Raudsep's nephew, attended school in the first grade. There was no school available for him where he lived with his parents. Loren lived with his aunt in her trailer house parked near by the school. He was a son of Jack and Hilda (Raudsep) Simpson. For the 1948–1949 school term a teacher was not found to teach. So, the school was disbanded and the Whisler children were, once again, driven to school at Rozet for that term. Donnie, Delores and Barbara Whisler continued attending school in Rozet; all three were graduates of Rozet High School. Lorna and Olive entered school in Gillette beginning the 1949-1950 school term. Lorna entered Campbell County High School and Olive entered the fifth grade at the Gillette Grade School. Both are Campbell County High School graduates.

Source:
Personal files of Lorna J. Whisler.

1945-46
Lorna Whisler, Olive Whisler, Donnie Whisler, Bobbie Whisler, Deloris Whisler, Jeanette Heptner, teacher

1947-1948
Bobbie Whisler, Lorna Whisler, Bonnie Nielson, teacher, Olive Whisler, Deloris Whisler, Donnie Whisler

1948-1949
Loren Simpson, Barbara Whisler, Olive Whisler, Lorna Whisler,
Deloris Whisler, Donnie Whisler
Teacher Selma Raudsep standing in back

District Five Schools
South of Rozet, Dillinger, and Timber Creek Areas

Baker School

Beavers School

Brower School

Dillinger School

The Dillinger School was established about 1917/18 when the parents of the community decided that a school was needed. They built a small log schoolhouse. Later a frame building was built. It not only served as a school house, but also as a community center for church services, dances, school programs, and many other numerous community functions.

Teachers:		
	_____	1917 - 1918
	Olivia Neville	1918 - 1919
	_____	1919 - 1920
	Jacob Dillinger	1920 - 1921
	_____	1921 - 1922
	Albert Hermeling	1922 - 1923
	Ted G. Berg	1923 - 1924
	Miss ___ Johnson	1924 - 1925
	Eva Bricker	1925 - 1926
	Margaret Dillinger	1926 - 1927

Children who may have attended:

Inez Dillinger	Earl Dillinger
Robert Dillinger	Bill Dillinger
Margaret Dillinger	Jay Dillinger
Jimmy Bishop	John Bill Bishop
Marian Thomas	Gale Thomas
Carol Thomas	Kenneth Thomas
Robert Bratton	Mildred Thomas
Jack Preston	Robert Counce
Lulu Schlattmann	Harvey Schlattmann
Vernet Smith	Raymond Schlattmann
Leon Williams	James Smith
Robert Bratton	Sylvia Williams
Eugenia Patterson	Amy Patterson
Verna Fox	Pat Patterson
Phyllis Owens	Glen Fox
Merrill Owens	Catherine Owens
James Patterson	I. A. Pickrel

Enterprise School

Ferguson School

Four Horse School

Fox School

OR School

It was located 12 miles south of the Enterprise School on the south side of the Belle Fourche River.

Teacher: Mary Gardner (1927?)

Children who may have attended:

Warren Williams	Leon Williams
Gale Thomas	Marion Thomas
Herman Moore	

When the OR School was closed the children were taken to the Dillinger school to continue their rural education.

Piney School

It was located 12 miles south of the Enterprise School on the south side of the Belle Fourche River.

When the Piney School closed the children were taken to the Dillinger school for their schooling.

Teacher: Betty Hughes 1933-1934

Children who may have attended

	Lewis Preston
Kenneth Thomas	Shirley Preston
Carol Thomas	Calvin Tholson

Owens School

It was located 12 miles south of the Enterprise School on the south side of the Belle Fourche River.

Shipwheel School

Was located 12 miles south of the Enterprise School on the south side of the Belle Fourche River.

District Twelve Schools
North of Rozet Adon Area

Adon School

Teachers:
Noreen Hopkins	_____ - _____
Anna Reinsch	1919 – 1920
Mrs. A. C. Carson	1920 – 1921
---????	
LeNora Ely	1931 – 1932
Noreen Carlson	1934 – 1935

Christianson School

Teachers:
Emily Clark	1922 – 1923
Frances Rodman	1934 – 1935
(no teacher)	1935 – 1936 (Note: see *below)
Tom Tilson	1936 – 1937
Tom Tilson	1937 – 1938
Betty Hughes Tilson	1938 – 1939

Children who may have attended:

Dorothy Donner	Bud Christianson
Dale Donner	Ted Christianson
Evelyn Donner	Roy Christianson
Ivan Hatfield	Leone Donner
Margaret Hatfield	June Donner
Donna Tomingas	Melvin Donner

(Note: *Children went to the Engdahl School that year)

Culvin School

Desert School

Engdahl School

Teachers:
Betty Tilson	1935 – 1936
Glenis Wilkerson	1936 – 1937
Betty Hughes Tilson	1937-1938
Betty Hughes Tilson	1938-1939

Children who may have attended:

Margaret and Ivan Hatfield	Richard, Elaine, Mildred Engdahl
Jack and Douglas Pownell	Carmen Melton
	Bud, Ted and Roy Christianson (attended in 1936-37 because the Christianson School was closed that school year)

Norfolk School

Pippin School

PART FOUR

ACKNOWLEDGEMENTS

BIBLIOGRAPHY

APPENDIX

1928 Plat Maps with List of Owners

NAME INDEX

ACKNOWLEDGEMENTS

The author wishes to advise her readers that the names of the homestead families presented in this book were gleaned from reading the microfilmed newspapers of early Crook and Campbell County, Wyoming, (1892-1945). The microfilms were read in the Rockbridge County Regional Library in Lexington, Virginia, via inter-library loan with the Campbell County Public Library in Gillette, Wyoming. The readings took place between 1999 through 2004. Most of the family and individual names were collected when they appeared in the local news items for Rozet, Adon, and other communities, plus whenever they appeared elsewhere in the newspapers. I am quite sure I have missed names. I collected their history from such items as birth and marriage announcements, obituaries, probate announcements, legal notices (land), and tax records. Later their stories were flushed out with genealogical documentation from digitized public records found on *Ancestry.com*, such as: federal and state censuses, land records, birth, death, marriage and military records. I tend not to rely on family trees except in rare cases when I found one that was very well documented.

Anyone researching their family's genealogy and history should use this book ONLY as a tool to locate the original primary and secondary sources for your ancestors. An excellent reference book for documenting genealogical primary and secondary sources is Evidence! Citation & Analysis for the Family Historian, by Elizabeth Shown Mills, (1997).

Also, the author would like to thank the staff at the Rockbridge County Regional Library, Lexington, Virginia, for their assistance and kindnesses provided to me while I was reading these microfilms in their local genealogy room. I also would like to thank the Campbell County Public Library, Gillette, Wyoming, for their helpfulness when I started this "little project" that begun in the late 1960s when I was trying to identify the names of the neighbors who homesteaded near my two sets of grandparents, Frank and Laura Heptner in the Little Iowa/Pleasant Valley neighborhood and Riley and Vida Whisler in the Well Creek and Cottonwood Valley/Adon Road areas.

I will be forever grateful for the encouragement and assistance I received from many folks. Here are a few:

To Mrs. Dee Whisler McGillis who graciously searched for obituaries at the library of Rozet citizens who died during 1960-2011. With her assistance I was able to identify family structures of most of the early homesteaders.

To Mrs. Leola Thar, the longest serving postmistress at the Rozet Post Office, for her information regarding the history of Rozet, particularly the post office and Rozet Consolidated Elementary School and High School.

To Diann and Matt Avery who spent an extraordinary amount of time running down records (especially the Township Plat Records at the Campbell County Assessors Office), drew maps, copied and/or took pictures that helped to fill in a local or family history.

To the members of the Campbell County Wyoming Historical Society and Penny Schroder at the Campbell County Rockpile Museum, in Gillette, Wyoming. They provided invaluable assistance and pointed me toward other resources. Other individuals who provided information on several families include Judy Kehn, Janice Day Stratman, Phil Frey, Margarite Duvall, Nadine Duvall Taylor, Elsie Spielman Sicks, Dorothy Slattery, Cindy Stewart, Sandy Stewart Holyoak, and Matthew and Diann (Larsen) Avery. And posthumously, the many historical photographs and items I inherited from my parents Slim and Irene Whisler, and my aunts Leona and Jeanette Heptner.

And lastly, to Terry Flaherty, my editor and my friend, there are no words. THANK YOU!

Lorna J. Whisler
2022

BIBLOGRAPHY

Newspapers:

Campbell County Record	(June 27, 1918 – April 1925)	microfilmed
The Gillette News	(November 1, 1912 – April 25, 1925)	microfilmed
The News Record	(April 25, 1925 – 1949)	microfilmed
The News Record	(1950 – present); individual issues, articles/clippings saved by the author	

Published:

Campbell County, The Treasured Years, 1990, compiled by the Campbell County Historical Society.

"History of Campbell County," by Senior English Class, Campbell County High School, 1954.

"Crook County Pioneers," compiled by the Crook County Historical Society.

"Campbell County Profiles," by Leora Hubbard, 1985.

Only a Cow Country, by Dick Nelson, copyright 1951 by Mae M. Nelson.

Wyoming Pageant, by Virginia Cole Trenholm and Maurine Carley, Prairie Publishing Company, Casper, Wyoming, 1946.

"Wyoming 1916! Here We Come," by Margaret Dillinger Bowden, 2002.

The Way it Was, by Earl Dillinger, published by Asuwil Graphic Company, 1980.

Wyoming Frontier State, by Velma Linford, The Old West Publishing Co, Denver, CO, 1947.

History of Wyoming, Second Edition, by T. R. Larsen.

Wyoming's Teachers, by S. Houston, Cultural Resource Specialist, Wyoming State Archives 1997-1999.

"One Room Rural Schools of Crook County," by Crook County Retired Teachers, Crook County, Wyoming 1985

"Burnett Writes Interesting Story of Early Texas Trail," by Edward Burnett, *The News Record*, Gillette, Wyoming, July 20, 1935.

"Wyoming Place Names," by Mae Urbanek, 1988.

"Burlington Route, A History of the Burlington Lines," by Richard C. Overton, 1965.

The Banditti of the Plains, or the Cattlemen's Invasion of Wyoming in 1892, by A. S. Mercer, copyright 1954 by The University of Oklahoma Press.

The War on Powder River, pages 187, by Helena Huntington Smith, published 1966.

Atlas of Westward Expansion, by Alan Wexler and Molly Braun, copyright by Alan Wexler, 1995

Atlas of Historical County Boundaries, Copyright 2003, The Newberry Library, Chicago, Illinois.

Assorted Rozet School Yearbooks

www.ancestry.com **assorted public records, i.e.:**

- U.S. Federal Census Schedules 1880, 1900, 1910, 1920, 1930, 1940 for Crook, Weston and Campbell counties, Wyoming
- Bureau of Land Management Patents Index
- U.S. Land Records, Bureau of Land Management
- Birth Records
- Death Records
- Immigration Records
- Marriage Records
- Military Records
- Social Security Death Index
- U.S. Find A Grave Index

APPENDIX

1928 Plat Maps with List of Owners

1928 Plat Maps
of
Patented Homesteads and Owners
Rozet, Campbell County, Wyoming

N

T52N R70W (Sections: 19-36) Adon	

T51N R70W Cottonwood Valley	**T51N R69W** Little Iowa

W   To Gillette

T50N R70W	**T50N R69W** Rozet

To Moorcroft   E

T49N R70W Timber Creek	**T49N R69W**

T48N R69W Belle Fourche River Dillinger

S

Plat Maps created by Lorna J. Whislet, Diann and Matt Avery from the Township Plat Book at the Campbell County Assessors Office, Gillette, Wyoming - 2021.
Maps were created using Word software with Courier New/11 and Lucinda Handwriting/8 fonts. Maps are not to scale.

(Source: Campbell County Assessors Office, Gillette, Wyoming.)

List of Owners
Township 53 North, Range 70 West (T53N R70W)

	Names	**Section(s)**
1.		
2.	Booton, Victor E.	3, 4
3.	Bunnell, W. G.	7, 18
4.	Carter, Florence Jackson	13
5.	Carson, J. W. and A.V.	34, 35
6.	**Christiansen, C. K.**	22, 26, 27
7.	**Donner, Charlie**	34, 35
8.	Donegon, Esperance	12
9.	**Empire Sheep Co.**	1, 2
10.	Fishelson, Samuel	31, 32
11.	**Harris Simpson Co.**	2, 3, 4, 5, 6, 7, 8, 9, 17, 18, 21, 22, 23, 26, 31, 32, 35
12.	Hart, Martin, Est.	2
13.	Hatfield, Elmer	29, 30
14.	Hatfield, Ralph W.	26, 27
15.	**Hatfield, Louis H.**	21, 22, 28
16.	Herndon, Albert G.	4, 9
17.	Moorcroft Sheep Co.	1
18.	Norfolk, Wm. H.	5, 6
9.	Norfolk, James	10, 15
20.	**Pownell, E. L.**	14
21.	Simpson, Robert B.	3, 4, 9, 10
22.	Simpson, Iva	15
23.	Thompson, Fred L.	15, 22, 23, 26
24.	**Tomingas, John**	22, 28, 33, 34
25.	Tullar, Frank A.	25
26.	Tullar, Glen S.	24
27.	Umland, Charles	11
28.	Wilson, Victor S.	19, 20
29.	Wynkoop, Nancy J.	17, 20, 21
30.		

S State Land

Owns land in other townships:

2.	Booton, Victor E.	T54N R70W
3.	Bunnell, W. G.	T53N R71W
9.	Empire Sheep Co.	T53N R69W
11.	Harris Simpson Co.	T53N R69W, T53N R71W
12.	Hart, Martin, Est.	T54N R70W
17.	Moorcroft Sheep Co,	T53N R69W, T54N R69W, T54N R70W
18.	Norfolk, William H.	T54N R70W

Names in **bold** have brief bios elsewhere in this book.

Township 53 North, Range 70 West, School District 12

18 | William H. Norfolk | 11 | 16 | 2 | Victor E. Booton | 11 | 12 | Martin Hart Est. | 9

21 | 11 | Albert | Empire | 17

6 | 5 | 4 | 3 | 2 | 1

Herndon | Harris | Sheep

Harris | Simpson | Company

Robert B. | Company

Simpson | Simpson

Company

19 | 27 | 8

Charles | Esperance

7 | 8 | 9 | 10 | 11 | 12

3 | W. G. Bunnell | 16 A. Herndon | 21 | Umland | Donegan

James

11 | 22 | 20 | 4

Harris | Norfolk | Florence

11 | 18 | Simpson | School | 15 | E. L. 14 | 13

S | S | 29 | 17 Co. | 16 | 23 | Jackson

Section | Pownall

S | S | Nancy J. | Carter

28 | Wynkoop | 11 | 26

Harris | Fred

15 | Simpson | Glen S.

19 | 20 | 21 | 22 | L. 23 | 24

Victor S. | 6 | 15 | Co. | Thompson | Tullar

Wilson | Louis H. | C. K.

13 | Hatfield | Christensen | 11 | 25

Elmer | Frank A.

30 | 29 | 28 | 27 | 23 | 26 | 25

24 | 14

Hatfield | John | Ralph Hatfield | Tullar

10 | Tomingas | 7

Charlie | 11

5 | Donner | School

31 | Samuel 32 | 33 | 34 | 35 | 36

J. W. & A. C.

Fishelson | 5 | Section

Carson

1928
Rozet, Campbell County, Wyoming

(Source: *Campbell County Assessors Office, Gillette, Wyoming.*)

311

List of Owners
Township 53 North, Range 69 West (T53N R69W)

	Names	Section(s)
1.	Anderson, Edwin	1
2.	Dickenson, Henry Elmer	4, 8, 9, 10, 11, 14
3.	Dickinson, Henry	10, 11, 14, 15, 24, 25, 26
4.	**Empire Sheep Company**	**14, 21, 26, 32**
5.	**Engdahl, Merl S.**	30, 31
6.	Fine, Martha Payne	4, 5
7.	**Harris Simpson Company**	28, 19, 30, 31, 32
8.	Huffaker, J. W.	29, 31, 32
9.	Investors Mtg. Co.	19, 30
10.	Jacobsen, Nelson	21, 22, 27, 28
11.	Jacobsen, Thomas B.	24, 25
12.	Johnson, Ernest	1, 2
13.	Kimsey, Pearl, Mrs.	13
14.	Lowery, Constance D.	3, 5, 6
15.	Moorcroft Sheep Company	5, 6, 8, 9, 28, 29
16.	Smothers, Hugh L.	25, 26, 32
17.	Stewart, George M., Jr.	20
18.	Svalina, Pete	11, 13, 14
19.	Wagner, Frank	6, 7, 8
20.	Wright and Cates	19, 20

S State Land

Owns land in other townships:

4.	Empire Sheep Company	T53N R70W
6.	Fine, Martha Payne	T54N R69W
7.	Harris Simpson Company	T52N R70W, T51N R71W
12.	Johnson, Ernest	T54N R69W
15.	Moorcroft Sheep Company	T53N R70W, T54N R69W, T54N R70

Names in **bold** have brief bios elsewhere in this book.

Township 53 North, Range 69 West, School District 12

1928
Rozet, Campbell County, Wyoming.

(Source: *Campbell County Assessors Office, Gillette, Wyoming.*)

List of Owners
Township 52 North, Range 70 West (T52N R70W)

	Names	Section(s)
1.	Allison, Vadail	10
2.	American Livestock Co.	30
3.	Carson, J. W. and A. C.	2, 3
4.	Carson, Ruth E,	1
5.	Carson, A. C.	1, 2, 11, 12
6.	Carson J. W.	1, 15, 19
7.	Chassell, Louise V.	8, 9, 10
8.	Cook, John H.	14, 20, 29
9.	Galliday, I. S.	22
10.	Hays, Anna L	10, 11, 24
11.	**Hays, Henry K.**	4, 5, 6, 7, 8, 10, 11, 14, 15, 23, 24
12.	Haynes, Ernest	25, 35
13.	Kaslo, Ellen	10, 15
14.	Litke, Henry	2, 3, 26
15.	Logan, J. O.	10
16.	May, Albert E.	24, 25
17.	Norfolk, Anna L., Est.	25, 26
18.	Norfolk, Maud	12
19.	Norfolk, Jno. B	1, 8, 9, 10, 12, 13, 17
20.	O'Hanlan, J. I.	11, 13, 14, 24
21.	Pollok, Daisy S.	20, 21
22.	**Reed, Reuben W.**	31
23.	Reinsch, A. C.	2, 3
24.	Schroeder, Bertha	27, 34, 35
25.	Wallace, Otis, Est.	34, 35
26.	**White, Clifford**	18
27.	White, H. Morton	27, 28, 31, 32, 33
28.	Whitehouse, C. B.	21, 28
29.	Wright, William R.	32, 33
30.		

S State Land

Owns land in other townships:

2.	American Livestock Co.	T51N R69W, T51N R70W
		T51N R71W, T52N R71W
4.	Carson, Ruth E.	T52N R69W
12.	Haynes, Ernest	T51N R70W
18.	Norfolk, Maud	T52N R69W
21.	Pollok, Daisy S.	T52N R72W
25.	Wallace, Otis, Est.	T51N R70W
26.	White, Clifford	T52N R71W
29.	Wright, William R.	T51N R70W

Names in **bold** have brief bios elsewhere in this book.

Township 52 North, Range 70 West, School District 12

		11			11			3		5	4	19	S	19
								J. W. & A. C.					S	
								23			6		S	
6	5		4		3	Carson	2		1		
								A. E.		S	
Henry K.					A. C.	Carson			
Hays					Reinsch			S	

		19			1	10		18	S	
			John B. Norfolk		Vadail					
		7			Allison	Anna L.		S	S
7	8	9		10	11	12	
			Louise V.	15	Hays	20	Maud	S	18
			Chassell				Norfolk	S	
			13	11					
				Henry K.				
26			19	6	Ellen			S	
				Kaylo	Hays	J. I.		
18	17	School	J. W. 15	8	14	O'Hanlan	13	S
		16	11		John H.		19
		Section	Hays		Cook	
			Carson			

		21	9	11		10
		Daisy S.		Henry K.	
6		Pollok		Hays	
19	20	21	22	23	24
	6		I. S.	14	Hays
	8	Galliday	Henry	16
John H. Cook	28	Litke	
	C. B.	24	17
	Bertha	Anna L. Norfolk
2	White	Schroeder	Est.
30	29	28	27	26	25
Am.	house	27	12
Livestock			Ernest
Co.	H. Morton White	Haynes

	27		12
	22	Ernest	School
31	32	33	34	35	36
	H. Morton White	25 O.	Haynes	Section
		Wallace	
	29 Wm. R.	Est	
	Wright	

1928
Rozet, Campbell County, Wyoming.

(Source: *Campbell County Assessors Office, Gillette, Wyoming.*)

List of Owners
Township 52 North, Range 69 West (T52N R69W)

	Names	Section(s)
1.	Ayers, Anna and Wm. Hartzell	19
2.	Bronson, Chester H.	28, 29, 32, 33
3.	Carson, D. O.	31
4.	Carson, Ruth E.	17, 20
5.	**Donner, George O.**	28, 33
6.	Hannum, Mabel	35
7.	**Harris Simpson Co.**	1, 5, 6, 9, 10, 11, 12, 14, 15, 22, 23, 24, 31, 33, 34
8.	Loftin, Gretch	21, 28, 33, 34
9.	Loftin Sisters	31
10.	Norfolk, Maude	7, 18
11.	Norfolk, Jno. B.	6, 7
12.	Poole, Bertha	32
13.	Simms, Gertrude	19, 30
14.	--	
15.	Stephenson, Ella, Mrs.	19, 20
16.	Sutherland, Alice O.	2, 3, 4, 9, 10
17.	**Toro, John**	25
18.	Waite, Minnie	19, 20, 28, 29
19.	Waite, Frank, L.	7, 18
20.	Wells, Frank E.	19, 20, 29, 30
21.		
22.		
23.		
24.		
25.		

S State Land

Owns land in other townships:

3.	Carson, D. O.	T51N R69W, T51N R70W
4.	Carson, Ruth E.	T52N R70W
5.	Donner, George O.	T51N R69W, T51N R70W
6.	Hannum, Mabel	T51N R69W
7.	Harris Simpson Company	T51N R69W
9.	Loftin Sisters	T51N R69W
11.	Norfolk, Jno. B.	T51N R70W
17.	Toro, John	T51N R69W

Names in **bold** have brief bios elsewhere in this book.

Township 52 North, Range 69 West, School District 12

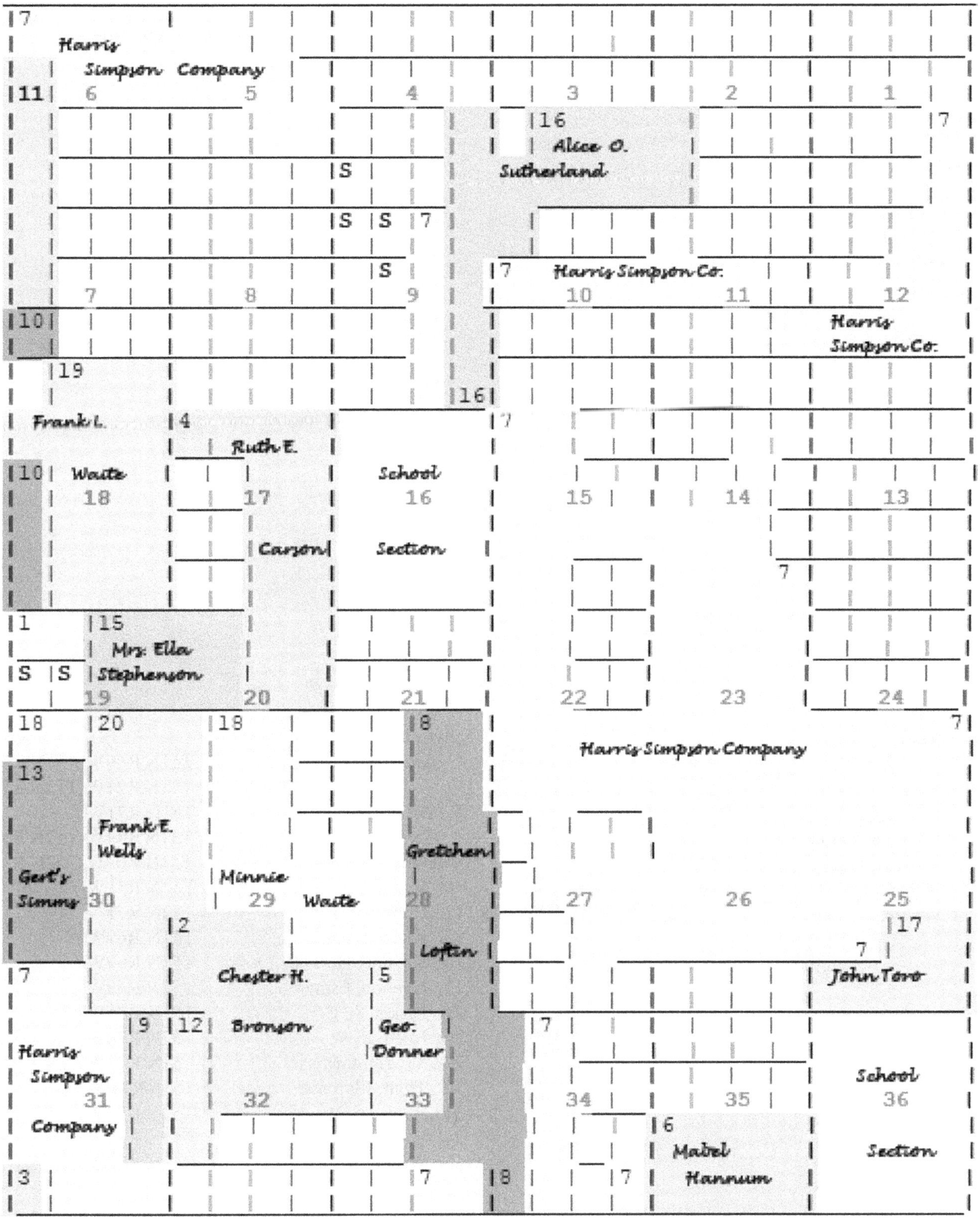

Harris Simpson Company

11 6 5 4 3 2 1

7

16 Alice O. Sutherland

S

S S 7

S

7 8 9 10 11 12

7 Harris Simpson Co.

10

Harris Simpson Co.

19

16

7

Frank L. 4

Ruth E.

10 Waite 18 17 School 16 15 14 13

Carson Section

7

1 15

Mrs. Ella Stephenson

S S 19 20 21 22 23 24

18 20 18 8 7

Harris Simpson Company

13

Frank E. Wells

Gretchen

Gert's Simms 30 Minnie 29 Waite 28 27 26 25

2 17

Loftin 7

Chester H. 5 John Toro

9 12 Bronson Geo. 7 Donner

Harris Simpson 31 32 33 34 35 School 36

Company 6

Mabel Section

3 7 8 7 Hannum

1928
Rozet, Campbell County, Wyoming.

(Source: *Campbell County Assessors Office, Gillette, Wyoming.*)

317

List of Owners
Township 51 North, Range 70 West (T51N R70W)

	Names	Section(s)		Names	Section(s)
1					
2.	American Stock Co.	20, 28, 29, 30, 31, 32, 33			
3.	Anderson, Johanna	32			
4.	Bailey, Mary	20, 29			
5.	Britt, N. E.	19			
6.	**Burr, Andrew A.**	23, 24			
7.	Carson, D. O.	1			
8.	Donner, George O.	12			
9.	Gillespie, J. D., Est.	13			
10.	Haynes, Ernest	2			
11.	Hopkins, H. C.	18			
12.	**Jensen, George**	26			
13.	**Kuehne, Frank**	13, 24			
14.	**Kuehne, William**	23, 24, 25			
15.	**Kuehne Brothers**	12, 13			
16.	**Kuehne, Herman**	12, 35			
17.	**Kuehne, Esther**	24			
18.	**Mapes, Herschel C.**	14, 15, 22, 23			
19.	Means, Edith, Mrs.	9, 10, 15			
20.	**Melton, L. A.**	22, 23, 27			
21.	Murdy, Susan K.	20, 28, 30, 32, 33			
22.	**McCurdy, G. O.**	21, 22, 27, 28			
23.	Niemcyk, Clara D.	5, 6, 8, 9			
24.	Parker, A. C.	30, 31			
25.	Rayn, O. T., Mrs.	20, 21			
26.	**Reed, R. W.**	13, 14			
27.	Iliff, Ray, Est.	17			
28.	**Riley, Leslie B.**	26			
29.	Sewright, Muriel	7, 8, 18			
30.	Trent, Florence	6			
31.	Wallace, Otis, Est.	2, 3			
32.	**Wallace, Thomas P.**	2, 11			
33.	**Weaver, Henry C.**	15, 21, 22			
34.	Weber, Sarah A.	19, 30			
35.	Wright, William R.	3, 4, 5, 8, 9, 10, 11, 14, 17, 18			
—	Whisler, Riley (deceased)	35			

Owns land in other townships:

	Names	Section(s)
1.	American Livestock Co.	T51N R69W, T51N R71W T52N R71W, T52N R70W
5.	Britt, N. E.	T51N R71W
7.	Carson, D. O.	T51N R69W, T52N R69W
8.	Donner, George O.	T51N R69W, T52N R69W
10.	Haynes, Ernest	T52N R51W
11.	Hopkins, H. E.	T51N R71
13.	Kuehne, Frank	T51N R69W
16.	Kuehne, Herman	T51N R69W
17.	Kuehne, Esther G.	T51N R69W
24.	Parker, A. C.	T51N R71W
26.	Reed, R, W.	T52N R70W
29.	Sewright, Muriel	T51N R71W
30.	Trent, Florence	T51n R71W
31.	Wallace, Otis, Est.	T52N R70W
34.	Weber, Sarah A.	T51N R71
35.	Wright, William R.	T52N R70W

Names in **bold** have brief bios elsewhere in this book.

Township 51 North, Range 70 West, School District 4

William R. Wright

30

6

23

5

4

Otis
Wallace, Est.

3

32 10 E.
Haynes

7

D. O. Carson

1

2

Thomas Perry
Wallace

8

w

William R. Wright

Clara

29

7

Niemeyk

8

9

19

10

George O. Donner

11

12

16

S S

Muriel SeWright

35

Mrs. Edith
Means

William R.
Wright

15

S S

H.
Kuehne

S S

26

9

William R. Wright

27

17

School

16

Section

33

S S

35

18

15

R. W. Reed

14

J. D.
Gillespie
Est.

13

11
H. C.
Hopkins

18

Ray Iliff
Est.

Herschel C.
Mapes

Henry

K.
Bros

13
Frank

5
N. E.
Britt

19

2 4

Am

L.

25

Mrs. O. T. Rayn

21

Weaver

22

20

22 L. A.
Melton

6
Andrew
Burr

Kuehne

17

34
Sarah A.
Webber

24

Mary

Co.

21

Susan
Murdy

2

20

G. O. McCurdy

24

Esther
Kuehne

12 28

L. B.
George
Jensen

Riley

S S

S S

Bailey

29

28

27

26

25

William
Kuehne

American

2

21
Susan
2 Murdy

16
Herman
Kuehne (40)

School

Livestock

31
Company

2

32

3 Johanna
Anderson

33

34

35
(Riley
Whisler
deceased

36
Section

1928
Rozet, Campbell County, Wyoming.

(Source: *Campbell County Assessors Office, Gillette, Wyoming.*)

List of Owners
Township 51 North, Range 69 West (T51N R69W)

	Names	Section(s)		Names	Section(s)
1.	Allison, J. A.	18, 19	31.	Scott, Henrietta	13
2.	American Livestock Co.	5, 6	32.	Shinn, Willis E.	13, 24
3.	Carson, D. O.	5, 6, 7, 8, 9	33.	Simpson, Charles	13, 14
4.	**Doane, May**	27, 35	34.	Stewart, Sarah E.	27, 34, 35
5.	**Donner, George O.**	8	35.	Stull, George E.	26, 27, 34
6.	Durst, C. L., Mrs.	3, 4, 5, 9, 10	36.	Stull, Alice E.	26
7.	Fisher, J. C.	32	37.	Thompson, Fayette R.	23, 25
8.	Gillespie, J. D., Est.	18	38.	Toro, John	24, 25
9.	Glover, Guy	21	39.	VanIngen, Bertha	14, 15
10.	Graves, William	10, 15	40.	Weaver S. K.	32
11.	**Grunke, Paul**	33, 34	41.	Woods, Orrin A.	22, 27
12.	**Hamm, F. L.**	20, 21, 28	42.	Woods, Roy B.	22, 27, 28, 33, 34
13.	Hannum, Mabel	2	43.	Woods, Charlie	29
14.	Harris Simpson & Co.	3, 4, 6, 9, 10, 11, 12, 13, 14, 23, 24	44.	Woolsey, D. D.	31
			45.		
15.	**Heptner, Frank H., Est.**	19, 30, 31, 32			
16.	High, Willis	11, 14, 15			
17.	**Jeffers, Floyd B.**	35			
18.	Jennings, R. O., Mrs.	22, 23			
19.	Keller, Henry	12			
20.	**Kuehne, Frank**	8, 9, 17, 18, 19, 20			
21.	**Kuehne, Herman**	7, 18, 30			
22.	Kuehne, Esther G.	19			
23.	Kurtz, G. H.	4, 5, 6			
24.	Langord, Nels A.	7, 18			
25.	Loftin Sisters	1, 2, 11, 12			
26.	**Ranney, Harley C.**	21, 28			
27.	**Raudsep, Hans**	12			
28.	Richards, Elsie A.	23, 24, 25, 26, 28			
29.	**Semlek, Alex**	1			
30.	**Schrand, Ben**	29			

S State Land

Owns land in other townships:

2.	American Livestock Co.	T51N R70W, T51N R71W, T52N R71W
3.	Carson, D. O.	T51N R70W, T52N R69W
5.	Donner, George O.	T51N R70W, T52N R69W
8.	Gillespie, J. D., Est.	T51N R70W
13.	Hannum, Mabel	T52N R69W
14.	Harris Simpson Co.	T52N R69W
20.	Kuehne, Frank	T51N R70W
21.	Kuehne, Herman	T51N R70W
22.	Kuehne, Esther G.	T51N R70W
25.	Loften Sisters	T53N R69W
38.	Toro, John	T52N R69W

Names in **bold** have brief bios elsewhere in this book.

Township 51 North, Range 69 West, School District 4

G. H. Kurtz

Harris Simpson

S S S S

Mrs. C. L. Durst

& Co: 13

Alex Semlek

Geo. Donner

S S S

Sisters Loften

D. O. Carson

S S S

Harris Simpson & Co.

Henry Keller

Herman Kuehne

N. A. Frank

William Graves

16

Charles Simpson

Frank Kuehne

Lang-ford

Kuehne

School Section

Willis High

Harris Simpson

Esther Kuehne

Frank Kuehne

Guy Glover

Orrin A. Woods

F. A. T.

Elsie A. Richards

F. L. Hamm

Roy

Harley Ranney

Woods

May Doane

John Toro

Frank H. Hepther Est.

Charlie Woods

Ben Schrand

Roy

George Stull

Fayette A. Thompson

S. K. Weaver

Elsie A. Richards

Woods

Floyd B. Jeffers

School Section

D. D. Woolsey

J. C. Fischer

Paul Grunke

Sarah E. Stewart

May Doane

1928
Rozet, Campbell County, Wyoming.

(Source: *Campbell County Assessors Office, Gillette, Wyoming.*)

List of Owners
Township 50 North, Range 70 West (T50N R70W)

	Names	Section(s)
1.	American Livestock	6, 19, 22, 23, 26, 27
2.	Anderson, Joanna	5, 6
3.	Baumfalk, Dick	30, 31
4.	Best, Charles	32, 33
5.	Best, William	29, 30
6.	Clark, Emily E.	27, 28, 33
7.	Ditto, Chester S.	7, 18
8.	**Fortin, Gertrude**	18, 19
9.	**Garrett, Thomas B.**	4, 5, 8, 9
10.	Graham, W. E.	25, 26, 28, 29, 32, 33, 34, 35
11.	**Halverson, Jake**	29, 34, 38
12.	Harper, George W.	29, 30
13.	Harris Simpson Co.	13
14.	**Hinds, Charley**	1
15.	Jones, N. B.	25
16.	Kelly, Ben N.	31
17.	Kendall, Roy	26, 27
18.	---	
19.	Lincoln Land Co.	19
20.	Lueptow, Frank	26, 35
21.	**Marquiss, Nora**	24
22.	Norris, Arthur C.	30
23.	McGlothlan, Hattie J.	14, 23
24.	**Nelson, Sara**	11, 12, 13, 23, 23, 26
25.	**Nelson, Oscar L.**	11
26.	Nelson. Pearl R.	9, 10
27.	Nelson, Francis Lee	21, 22
28.	Peterson, Harley	33, 34
29.	**Shaughnessy, Katherine**	17, 20, 21
30.	**Spencer, George, Mrs.**	1, 12
31.	Toland, J. E.	35
32.	Towne, G. C.	8, 17, 19, 20
33.	Turner, Linnie E.	4, 8, 9
34.	Turner, John L.	5, 6, 7,
35.	Wall, Ralph	24, 25
36.	**Wall, Frank**	8, 9, 14, 15 29
37.	Ward, Frank F.	29, 32
38.	Weese, Frank	7, 18
39	Weese, Dewey	7

* Rozet Site
S State Land

Owns land in other townships:

	Names	Section(s)
1.	American Livestock Co.	T50N R69W
10.	Graham, W. E.	T49N R70W, T49N R69W T50N R69W
13.	Harris Simpson Co.	T50N R69W
16.	Kelly, Ben N.	T49N R70W
20.	Lueptow, Frank	T49N R69W, T50N R69W
24.	Nelson, Sarah	T50N R69W
28.	Peterson, Harley	T49N R70W
30.	Spencer, George, Mrs.	T50N R69W
37.	Ward, Frank F.	T49N R70W

Names in **bold** have brief bios elsewhere in this book.

Township 50 North, Range 70 West, School District 3

The map shows land plots with the following names and numbers:

1	2									30	14
Am. Live-stock 6	Johanna Anderson 9	5	4	3	2					Charley Hinds 1	

- Am. Live-stock 6
- Johanna Anderson
- 34
- Thomas B. Garrett
- Mrs. George Spencer
- John L. Turner
- 33
- Pearl R. Nelson
- 26
- 25
- Oscar L. Nelson
- 38 F. Weese 7
- Linnie E. Turner 8
- 9
- 10
- 11
- 12
- 39 S S 32 36
- Frank Wall
- 24
- 7
- 29
- 36
- 8
- C. S. Ditto 18
- G. C. Towne 7
- School Section 16
- 15 Frank Wall
- 14 Sarah Nelson
- 13
- 23
- 13
- Gertrude Fortin
- 27
- 21 N. Marquis
- 29
- Francis Lee Nelson
- 19
- 20
- 21
- 22
- 23
- 24
- 19
- 8
- McGlothlan 35
- 1 American Livestock
- S S S S S S S S 1
- Ralph Wall
- 22 5 2
- 10 6
- American Livestock
- 15 N. B. Jones
- George W. Harper
- William Best
- 17
- 30
- 29
- 28
- 27
- 26
- 25
- 3
- 11
- 10
- 10
- W. E. Graham
- Emily E Clark
- Roy Kendall
- W. E. Graham
- Dick Baumfalk
- 37
- S S
- 20
- *
- S 10
- W. E. Graham
- F.
- 16 31
- Frank E. Ward 4 2
- 10 Charles Best 33
- 11 S 11 34
- S S Lueptow 35
- 31. J. E. Toland
- School 36 Section
- Ben N. Kelly
- Jake Halverson
- 28
- 28

1928
Rozet, Campbell County, Wyoming.

(Source: Campbell County Assessors Office, Gillette, Wyoming.)

List of Owners
Township 50 North, Range 69 West (T50N R69W)

	Names	Section(s)		Names	Section(s)
1.	American Livestock	9	46.	Reka, Charles C.	33, 34
2.	**Brennan, John E.**	28, 29, 32, 33	47.	Schuler, John	7, 18
3.	**Brennan, L. D.**	20, 21, 29, 32	48.	**Shafer, C. J.**	1
4.	Chalfant, Guy E.	4, 5, 8, 9	49.	**Shickley, M. B.**	9
5.	Church, Ralph E.	25, 26	50.	**Stewart, Stanley V.**	2, 11, 12
6.	**Clark, D. W.**	34, 35	51.	**Stewart, Frank R.**	2, 3, 10, 11
7.	Clark, C. V.	34	52.	**Stewart, Sarah E., Est.**	2, 3
8.	**Doane, May S.**	2	53.	**Stewart, G. M.**	11, 13, 14
9.	**Doane, W. L., Est.**	1, 2	54.	Stok, Alois	24, 25
10.	**Duvall, James D.**	35	55.	**Stull, George E.**	2, 3
11.	Eddy, Frank L.	7, 17, 18	56.	Thorne, Clara M.	4
12.	**Eddy, U. H.**	32	57.	**Spencer, George, Mrs.**	6, 7
13.	Elly, Robert P. S.	25	58.	Wadsworth, Abbie M., Est.	12, 13, 14
14.	Fair, Fred	17, 18, 19, 20	59.	Wakeman, E. E.	20, 29, 30
15.	**Fischer, John C.**	4, 5, 8	60.	**Weaver, Clay C.**	28, 33
16.	**French, Ernest**	8, 17	61.	**Wells, Charles**	3, 10, 15
17.	**French, Ray**	7	62.	**Wells, Carrie**	10, 15, 20, 21, 22
18.	**Frey, T. A.**	30	63.	**Woolsey, D. D.**	6
19.	**George, Edith B.**	17, 20			
20.	**George, Frank**	8			
21.	Graham, W. E.	31, 33			
22.	**Gray, O'Neal**	13, 14, 23, 24, 25			
23.	Grimm, Mary Abigail	17			
24.	**Grunke, Paul**	4			
25.	Haynes, Ernest	3			
26.	**Halverson, Anna**	26, 27			
27.	Harty, Patrick, Est.	34, 35			
28.	Harris Simpson, Co.	25			
29.	**Hinds, Charley**	6, 7, 8			
30.	Hipple, Leroy	26, 27			
31.	Jacobs, John	21, 22, 27, 28			
32.	Jennings, R. O.	9			
33.	Jensen, Peter	14, 22, 23, 26			
34.	**Johnson, Tom, Est.**	15			
35.	Kent, M. B.	35			
36.	**Kuehne, Herman**	14, 19, 23, 29. 30			
37.	Kummerfeld, Hans	1, 12			
38.	**Lawrence, Claude**	25, 26, 31			
39	Levander, John	32, 33			
40.	Lueptow, Frank	33			
41.	**Marquiss, H. M., Est.**	18, 19			
42.	Miller, Bertha A.	31, 32			
43.	McKee, C. H.	19, 20			
44.	**Nelson, Sarah**	18			
45.	Nemec, Frank S.	23, 24			

Owns land in other townships:

1.	American Livestock Co.	T50N R70W
6.	Clark, D. W.	T49N R69W
7.	Clark, C. V.	T49N R69W
10.	Duvall, James D.	T49N R69W
12.	Eddy, U. H.	T49N R69W
21.	Graham, W. E.	T50N R70W
26.	Halverson, Anna	T49N R69W
28.	Harris Simpson	T50N R70W
29.	Hinds, Charley	T50N R70W
33.	Jensen, Peter	T49N R70W
35.	Kent, M. C.	T49N R69W
38.	Lawrence, Claude	T48N R70W
42.	Miller, Bertha A.	T49N R69W
43.	McKee, C. H.	T49N R69W
44.	Nelson, Sarah	T50N R70W
46.	Reka, Charles C.	T49N R69W
57.	Spencer, George, Mrs.	T50N R70W

S State Land

Names in **bold** have brief bios elsewhere in this book.

Township 50 North, Range 69 West, School District 3

1928
Rozet, Campbell County, Wyoming.

(Source: *Campbell County Assessors Office, Gillette, Wyoming.*)

List of Owners
Township 49 North, Range 70 West (T49N R70W)

	Names	Section(s)			Names	Section(s)
1.	Beard, Albert E.	27		40.	Smith, E. R.	7
2.	Best, Charles	4		41.	Smith, Sophia M.	19
3.	**Burr, Andrew A.**	15, 21, 22		42.	Spaeth, E. P.	2, 9, 7,18, 33 34, 35
4.	**Cain, Nelson E.**	34		43.	Steininger, Eugene	29, 30
5.	**Cook, Floyd E.**	7, 8, 17, 18		44.	**Thar, Henry**	25
6.	Czpanski, Ralph	12, 15		45.	**Toland, Ona L.**	2, 11
7.	Devine, Mary	17, 18		46.	Tritseh, Anna	1
8.	Ditto, Daisy D.	14, 23, 24, 26		47.	Ward, Frank F.	5
9.	Ditto, Andy M.	14, 22, 23, 26		48.	Weirmuller, Albert	1, 12
10.	Drumm, Harley P.	31		49.	Williams, Louis	24
11.	Graham, W. E.	1		50.	Williams, C. J.	23, 24, 25, 26
12.	**Halverson, Jake**	1, 2, 11, 13		51.	**Williams, Anna**	25
13.	**Halverson, Eric**	3		52.	Young, Opal B.	34
14.	Hathaway, R. V.	12, 27		53.	Young, Dell F.	35
15.	Hiles, Erwin W.	24		54.	Darrison, Earl	26, 35
16.	Hoke, A. J.	3, 4, 5, 6, 18, 28, 29		55.		
17.	Hoke, Jessie Brownlee	4, 5, 28, 29		56.		
18.	Horseman, B. T. and J. W. Peck	30		57.		
19.	Jensen, Peter	3		58.		
20.	Kelly, Claude	6, 7		59.		
21.	Kelly, J. C. and Claude	6		60.		
22.	Kelly, Ben N.	6				
23.	Kinneman, E. L.	7				
24.	**Lawrence, Claude**	15				
25.	Manitowoc Mtg. Hld. Co,	10				
26.	Marshall, Clifford Dale	8				
27.	Mock, William O.	28, 29				
28.	**Moran, Bert**	10, 11, 12, 13, 14				
29.	McCloud, E. J.	29, 30				
30.	Olsen, Daisy B.	19				
31.	Peterson, R. D.	2, 3, 10, 11				
32.	Peterson, Charles A.	4, 5, 8, 17, 19, 20				
33.	Peterson, Harley	3				
34.	Philips, Grover O.	4, 9				
35.	Schmidt, William P.	30, 32				
36.	Sherer, Robert N.	10, 14, 15				
37.	Shuart, Margaret	22, 23				
38.	Shuett, John W.	9				
39	Siebers, Olga	20, 21				

Owns land in other townships:

11.	Graham. W. E.	T49N R69W
		T50N R70W, T50N R69W
12.	Halverson, Jake	T49N R69W
19.	Jensen, Peter	T50N R69W
22.	Kelly, Ben N.	T50N R70W
24.	Lawrence, Claude	T50N R69W
28.	Moran, Bert	T49N R69W
31.	Peterson, R. D.	T49N R71W
33.	Peterson, Harley	T50N R70W
44.	Thar, Henry	T49N R69W

Names in **bold** have brief bios elsewhere in this book.

Township 49 North, Range 70 West, School District 3

22 B. Kelly |47| Frank Ward |2| 17 |33 |13 |45 Ono L. Toland |46 Anna Tritsch |11

21 J.C. Kelly |20|16 Hoke |32 5 |16 Jesse Hoke |16 A. Hoke |H.P. 3 |31 2 |12 Jake Halverson |48 1

Claude Kelly |5 Charley Peterson |26 |34 Grover O. |25 Peterson |16|19 R.D. | Albert Weirmuller |14

40|23 7 |42 |8 |9 E.P. Spaeth Chas. Peterson |38 |28 10 |11 36 Bert |28 12 Moran S 6 S

7 Floyd E. Cook |18 |16 17 School 16 Section |32 |24 Robert Sherar 15 Moran 8 Ralph Cyfanski S 14 13 |12 S S

42 Charley Peterson 41 Sophia 19 |20 |39 21 Andrew A. Burr 22 Andy M. Ditto 23 |9 |49|15 Erwin Hiles 24

30 Daisy Olsen |Smith Olga Siebers |37 Margaret Shuast |8 Ditto 8 |50 Louis Williams

18 B.T. Horseman |29 E.J. McCloud 30 |43 Eugene Steininger |16 |42 29 |17 27 William O. Mock 28 A.J. Hoke |1 |14 27 R.V. Hathway |9 A. Ditto |54 Earl Darrison 26 C.J. Wm's |51 Anna Williams |44 25 Henry Thar

10 Hawley P. Drumm 31 |35 Wm. P. Schmidt 32 33 |4 Nelson Cain |52 34 |42 Spaeth 35 School 36 Section

42 |53

1928
Rozet, Campbell County, Wyoming.

(Source: Campbell County Assessors Office, Gillette, Wyoming.)

327

List of Owners
Township 49 North, Range 69 West (T49N R69W)

	Names	Section(s)
1.	**Brennan, Matt., Est.**	17, 18
2.	**Burr, E. E.**	6
3.	**Cain, Nelson E.**	2, 3, 10, 11
4.	**Cain, Leslie W.**	14, 15
5.	**Clark, D. W.**	2, 3
6.	Clark, C. V.	3
7.	**Duvall, James D.**	1, 2, 11, 12
8.	**Duvall, Fred L.**	14, 15, 22
9.	Ealey, Gordon W.	11, 12, 14
10.	**Eddy, Philo B.**	5, 8
11.	**Eddy, U. H. Est.**	5
12.	Edwards, Fannie	12
13.	Evans, E. E.	1
14.	**Gardner, W. A.**	28, 29, 32, 33
15.	Graham, W. E.	4, 6, 18, 21, 28,
16.	Gripp, Lucy R.	20
17.	**Halverson, Anna**	17, 20, 21, 22
18.	**Halverson, Jake**	7, 18
19.	Hathaway, R. V.	6, 7
20.	Hauber, Frank	19
21.	Haszard, Herman H.	18, 19
22.	Hoffman, Bernard	11, 14, 15
23.	Horn. Frank	1, 12
24.	House Frances B., Mrs.	22, 23
25.	Hoxsie, Lemuel	13, 14
26.	**Hoxsie, Edward L.**	15, 21, 22
27.	Jones, Sam	6
28.	Kent, M. B.	1, 2
29.	**Lubkin, W. J.**	9, 10, 15
30.	Lueptow, Frank	4, 8, 9
31.	Melvin, Wilbur	28, 30, 31
32.	Meyers, F. W.	17
33.	Miller, Bertha A.	6
34.	**Moran, Bert**	7
35.	**McClendon, Ella J.**	12, 19, 20
36.	**McDermott, William P.**	27, 28, 33, 34
37.	McDermott, J. S.	32
38.	McDonald, Angus, Est.	2, 3
39	McKee, C. H.	22, 23, 26, 27
40.	Lapham, Amelia	3, 10
41.	Peterson, R. D.	2, 3, 4, 5, 8
42.	Reka, Charles C.	3, 4, 9, 10
43.	**Ridenour, Leo O.**	8, 9, 17
44.	**Riley, L. B.**	9, 10

	Names	Section(s)
45.	Schlattman, William, Est.	25, 33, 34
46.	Shaulis, Eugene	13, 24
47.	Shiflett, Eleanor	35
48.	Shroyer, Ada F.	20, 28, 29
49.	**Slattery Sarah**	27
50.	**Slattery, Charles J.**	13, 23, 24, 25, 26
51.	Smith, John H.	33
52.	Stamps, Luther	26, 27, 34
53.	Stevenson, Mabel	13
54.	**Talley, Mae**	32
55.	**Thar, Henry**	30
56.	Thar, Mary A.	31
57.	Vasey, William J.	7, 8, 17, 18
58.	Weeks, Lela May	34, 35
59.	Williams, Ida T.	26, 35
60.	**Wolf, John C.**	22, 23, 27

S State Land

s

Owns land in other townships:

3.	Cain, Nelson E.	T49N R70W
5.	Clark, D. W.	T50N R69W
6.	Clark, C. V.	T50N R68W
7.	Duvall, James D.	T50N R69W
11.	Eddy, U. H., Est.	T50N R69W
15.	Graham, W. E.	
17.	Halverson, Anna	T50N R69W
18.	Halverson, Jake	T49N R70W
19.	Hathaway, R. V.	T49N R70W
28.	Kent, M. V., Est.	T50N R69W
30.	Lueptow, Frank	T50N R69W
		T50N R70W
33.	Miller, Bertha A.	T50N R69W
34.	Moran, Bert	T49N R70W
41.	Peterson, R. D.	T49N R70W
42.	Reka, Charles C.	T50N R69W

Names in **bold** have brief bios elsewhere in this book.

Township 49 North, Range 69 West, School District 3

| 15 | 33 | 10 | 11 | | 41 | | 15 | 42 | | | 6 | 5 D.W. | | 7 | 28 | | | 23 | |
| Graham | | | U.H. | | | | | Graham | | | | Clark | | M. B. Kent | | | | | |

2 · 27 S. · 6 Jones · Philo · 5 · · 4 · · 38 · 3 Angus · 2 · · 13 · 1

E. E. · Eddy · R. D. · 30 · Chas. · McDonald · James D. · Frank

Burr · 19 Eddy · Peter-son · Reka · 40 · 3 Nelson · Duvall · 12

R. V. Hathaway · Frank Lueptow · Amelia · Cain · Horn

34 · 30 · 44 Lapham · 22

7 · 8 · 9 · 10 Bernard · 11 · 12

S · 57 W. J. Vasey · 43 · L. B. Riley · Hoffman Gordon Ealey

S · 18 · 57 · Leo Ridenour · 29 W. J. Lubkin

Jake Halverson · Vasey · 32 · 26 · 4 · 25 · 53

15 · 1 · F. W. · School · Leslie B. · Lemuel Hoxie · 46

18 · Daisy · 17 · 16 · 15 · 14 · 13

W. E. Graham · B'nan · Meyers · Section · 8 Fred · Cain · 50

21 Herman H. Hazard · 35 · 17 · Duvall · Eugene Shaulis

Ella J. McClendon · Anna Halverson · 26 Edward Hoxie · 24 Mrs. F. B. House · 60

19 · 20 · 21 · 17 · 22 · 23 · 24

20 Frank Hauber · 16 Lucy Gripp · 48 · John C. Wolff

15 · 60 · 39

55 Henry Thar · 31 · W. E. Graham · John Wolff · C. H. McKee · Charles Slattery · 45

30 · Wilbur · 29 Ada F. Shroyer · 28 · 49 Sarah 27 Slattery · 26 · 25

Melvin · 14 William Gardner · 52 Luther Stamps · 59 · Schlatt-man

56 · 31 · 37 · 36 William · 36 · Ida 47 · School

Mary A. · J. S. · 54 · 45 McDermott · Williams · 36 Section

31 · 32 · 33 · 34 · 35 E. Shiflett

Thar · McDer-mott · Mae Talley · 51 · W. W. Schlattman · Stamps

John H. Smith · Est · 58 Lela May Weeks

1928
Rozet, Campbell County, Wyoming.

(Source: *Campbell County Assessors Office, Gillette, Wyoming.*)

329

List of Owners
Township 49 North, Range 69 West (T49N R69W)

Names	Section(s)
1.	
2. **Bishop, W. O.**	31, 32
3. Brower, Thomas S., Est.	4, 9, 10
4. Day, Alval E.	27
5. Day, Willard F.	19, 20
6. Day, Cecil	19
7. DeKay, F. A./Goodykoontz	10, 15
8. **Dillinger, Jacob**	34, 35
9. Foster, Stewart S.	20, 21
10. **Garrett, Winslow J.**	8
11. **Hamill, J. N.**	4, 5, 8, 9
12. Hamm, Martin	21, 22
13. Hungerford, Mary V.	3, 4, 5
14. Idlewild Realty Co.	27, 28, 33
15. **Kottraba, Raymond**	29
16. Morgan, L. W.	12
17. Mott, Freddie R.	10
18. Myrrha, Hans	23, 26
19. Owens, Irvine R.	17
20. Owens, Thomas W.	17, 20
21. Patterson, John F.	29, 30, 32
22. **Pickrell, Ralph**	34
23. Pickrell, Lottie	26, 33, 34
24. Reel, Valerie E.	13, 24
25. Reel, Cecelia, M.	12, 13
26. **Rivenberg, Elizabeth W.**	15 22, 23, 27
27. Schlattman, Wm., Est.	1, 2, 11, 12, 13, 24
28. **Schnitger, Rex G.**	1, 12
29. **Scott, C. S.**	28, 29
30. Seeley, Carl	30, 31
31. Showley, Otis E.	33
32. Smith, John H.	4
33. Smith, Albert P.	23, 26
34. Sowada, Marie	25
35. Stamps, Luther	3
36. Steen, William	2, 3, 10, 11
37. Sover, Hazel P.	26, 27, 34
38. **Story, Marjorie B.**	1, 11, 12, 13, 14, 22, 23, 24, 25, 27, 33
39. Jewett, Mark L.	2, 3, 10

Names	Section(s)
40. Sweeten, Taylor, Est.	31, 32
41. Talley, May	5
42. Taylor, Frank M.	14, 23
43. Thomas, Raymond	7, 18
44. Thomas, Elmer	7, 8
45. Waisner, C. M.	25
46. Wilcox and Mateer	18
47. Williams, William J.	5, 6
48. Wyoming Farm Loan	35

S State Land

Owns land in other townships:

2.	Bishop, W. O.	T48N R71W, T48N R70W T47N R71W, T47N R70W, T47N R69W, T46N R70W, T46N R69W
4.	Day, Alval O.	T47N R69W
8.	Dillinger, Jacob	T47N R69W
22.	Pickrell, Ralph	T47N R69W
30.	Seeley, Carl.	T48N R70W
31.	Showley, Otis E.	T47N R69W
38.	Story, Marjorie B.	T47N R69W
40.	Sweeten, Taylor, Est.	T47N R69W, 47NR70W
43.	Thomas, Raymond	T48N R70W, T47NR70W
44.	Thomas, Elmer	T48N R70W

Names in **bold** have brief bios elsewhere in this book.

Township 48 North, Range 69 West, School District 5

1928
Rozet, Campbell County, Wyoming.

(Source: *Campbell County Assessors Office, Gillette, Wyoming.*)

331

How to Read Township Records

Townships are subdivided into SECTIONS. Each township is six miles by six miles, one township contains 36 square miles, each square mile forms a section. These are identified with a number based on their position.

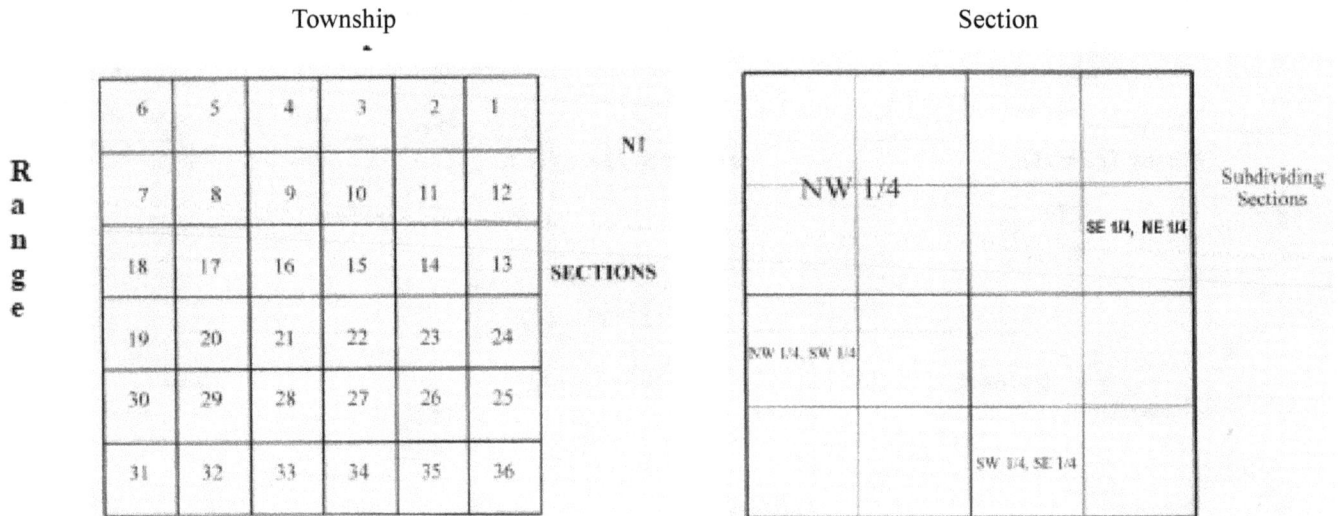

Township

6	5	4	3	2	1
7	8	9	10	11	12
18	17	16	15	14	13
19	20	21	22	23	24
30	29	28	27	26	25
31	32	33	34	35	36

R a n g e

SECTIONS

Section

Subdividing Sections

NW 1/4   SE 1/4, NE 1/4   NW 1/4, SW 1/4   SW 1/4, SE 1/4

Each section is further divided into quarters (see NW ¼ above). These quarters are the northeast, northwest, southeast, and southwest quarters. Each of these usually contain 160 acres.

These quarters are then further divided into smaller quarters, which are usually 40 acres (see SW ¼, SE ¼ above).

In recording land records the smallest quarter is given first, followed by the largest quarter, then the section, and then the township and range. For example, the NE 1/4, SW 1/4, sec. 30. T. 5 S., R. 7 E. This is read as the northeast quarter of the southwest quarter of section thirty, township five south, range seven east.

NAME INDEX

Note: Check *Appendix, 1928 Plat Maps with List of Owners*, even-numbered pages, 310 through 330, for names not appearing in this index.

Burke, Willis, 97
Burns, Mildred, 142
Burr, Alwyn E., 173
Burr, Andrew, 85, 117, 213, 173, 318, 326
Burr, Charles Edward, 173
Burr, Clifford Garrett, 173, 278, 279, 286
Burr, Curtis J., 173
Burr, Darlene (Roberts), 173
Burr, Edrie Jean (Harle), 173
Burr, Edward Eckdahl *Ed*, 173, 213, 267, 328
Burr, Elsie Josephine. *See* Germann, Elsie Josephine (Burr)
Burr, Evelyn Verle. *See* Fisher, Evelyn Verle (Burr)
Burr, Florence Eileen (Eads), 173
Burr, Hilda (Eckdahl), 173
Burr, Kenneth W., 173
Burr, Leslie Alwyn. *See* Herbage, Leslie Alwyn (Burr)
Burr, Marguerite (Lowrey), 173, 213
Burr, Mary Lou (Ellis), 173
Burr, Mildred Alvera. *See* Mooney, Mildred Alvera (Burr)
Burr, Pauline Alberta. *See* Green, Pauline Alberta (Burr)
Burr, Tessie, 173, 213, 264
Burr, Tessie P. (Garrett), 117, 173
Burr, Walter, 173, 213
Burr, Wayne Dean, 173, 213, 276-278, 286
Burrell, _____, 119
Byron, Bradford William, 51

C

Cady, James H., 105
Cady, Watson, 105
Cain, Edna Mae, 109
Cain, Esther Sarah, 109, 260
Cain, Frances (Thompson), 86, 109
Cain, Glen Norval, 109
Cain, Goldie Mae (Duvall), 143
Cain, Hazel Ethel, 109
Cain, Helen Francis, 109
Cain, Irean/Irene. *See* Hoxsie, Irean/Irene (Cain)
Cain, Ivan, 109, 143, 144, 265, 284
Cain, Leslie, 85, 109, 110, 328
Cain, Margaret Anne, 110
Cain, Nelson, 86, 109, 110, 326, 328
Cain, Pauline Edna, 110
Cain, Phyllis Irene, 110
Cain, Robert Leslie, 110
Cain, William A., 144
Camp, Lon Cain, 198
Campbell, Sabella Mae (Norton), 78, 79
Carlson, Carl O., 140, 293
Carlson, Roy Wilber, 93
Carr, Earl F., 45
Carr, Leo A., 45
Carr, Myron, 45
Castle, Marian. *See* Wright, Marian (Castle)
Chace, Kenneth L., 126
Chaddock, Matilda Ann. *See* Duvall, Matilda Ann (Chaddock)
Chamberlain, Joseph, 124
Chamberlain, Louisa (Nash), 124
Chapman, Emma Elvira. *See* White, Emma Elvira (Chapman)
Charlton, Edith V., 47
Christensen, C., 122, 310
Christensen, Howard Thobro, 121

Christensen, Marie. *See* Jessen, Marie (Christensen)
Christianson, Allen H. *Chub*, 113
Christianson, Alvin Clifford, 113
Christianson, Arthur Forest, 113
Christianson, Bertha Margaret, 113
Christianson, Charles, 113, 213, 247
Christianson, Donald Wyoming *Bud*, 113
Christianson, Helen Agnes, 113
Christianson, Jennie (Pearson), 113, 213
Christianson, Kharstan Karl *Charley*, 113
Christianson, Roy, 113, 300
Church, Karle R., 119
Civilian Conservation Corps (CCC), 186, 190, 193
Clark, Alonzo Monroe, 52, 62, 84, 260
Clark, Beatrice Sarah, 143
Clark, Catherine (Slade) Duvall, 143, 147, 186, 193, 221, 222, 225, 244
Clark, Charles V., 143, 288
Clark, Daniel W., 143, 144, 147, 221, 222, 324, 328
Clark, Donald Curtis, 62
Clark, Ellen M., 143
Clark, Emily E., 62, 260, 263, 300
Clark, Emmett, 116
Clark, Florence, 62
Clark, Franklin and Mary, 143
Clark, Grandma, 144
Clark, Julia Edna, 143
Clark, Kent, 42
Clark, Lillian Verna, 149
Clark, Lucy Myra (Smith), 62
Clark, Lulu, 143
Clark, Melvin, 86
Clark, Phoebe. *See* Whitcomb, Ansel and Phoebe (Clark)
Clark, Vernon N., 143
Cline, Matilda Jane. *See* Hamm, Matilda Jane Tillie (Cline)
Cokayne, Mary. *See* Marquiss, Mary (Cokayne)
Coker, Rebecca. *See* Luton, David and Rebecca (Coker)
Coltrin, Oscar Charles, 120
Cook, Blanche Elsie. *See* Moran, Blanche Elsie (Cook)
Cook, Carrie Cecil, 68
Cook, Cleo, 145, 284
Cook, Clifford, 68
Cook, Ferris Edwin, 145, 178, 222, 277, 278, 286
Cook, Floyd, 68, 145, 222, 268, 326
Cook, Gilbert Ray *Gib*, 145, 222
Cook, Grace, 68
Cook, Guy Elmo, 222
Cook, Hazel Irene, 145
Cook, James A., 68
Cook, Jeana Louise (Davis), 222
Cook, John Wesley, 68
Cook, Maude Eleanor, 68
Cook, May Olivia, 145
Cook, Myrtle Agnes (Allen), 68, 145, 222
Cook, Pauline Louise (Whisler), 104, 145, 178, 180, 186, 195, 197, 222, 292
Cook, Philip John, 68
Cook, Ray (Raoul), 68
Cook, Sophia Kit (Groce), 68, 145, 162
Cook, Susan, 68
Cook, Yvonne (Schwab), 222
Cook, Winifred, 68, 145, 162
Cooper, Emma Iola (Brunson), 203, 279, 283

Copple, LaVonne Lula, 124
Cornell, Eugene R., 124
Cornwell, Alice Rae, 242
Cornwell, Ella A. (White), 242
Cornwell, Forest William, 242
Cornwell, Mrs., 242
Cornwell, Rev. Ray, 241-243
Cornwell, Rosy Etha (Hink), 242
Cornwell, William Albert, 242
Correll, Emma. *See* Toland, Emma (Correll)
Cottonwood School (*photo*), 291
Coventry, Mary Christina. *See* Mapes, Mary Christina (Coventry), 159
Cox, Dean, 224
Cox, Jim, 176
Crabill, Gordon LeRoy, 59, 158
Crabill, Mary Estella (Weaver) Nelson, 57, 59, 141, 158, 265, 284, 292
Crandall, Adell. *See* Whisler, Adell (Crandall)
Crayne, Cecil Raymond, 133
Creach, Florence May (Brode), 114
Creach, Ida Mae (Keim), 114
Creach, Jack Mills, 114
Creach, James, 114
Creach, Juanita Elsie, 114
Creach, Lafayette Mills, 114
Creach, Lorraine, 114
Creach, May, 114
Creagin, Mary. *See* Moran, Mary (Creagin)
Crosby, Herschel S., 142
Cullivan, Charles, 213
Culver, Maggie E., 118
Cummings, Douglas Oscar Riley *Doug*, 221, 242
Cummings, Ellen Joan (Whisler), 178, 180, 221
Cummings, Inese Lilija (Verzemnieks), 221
Cummings, Jeffrey Lee, 221
Cummings, Jesse Lee, 212, 221
Cummings, Lee, 178, 221
Cummings, Myrtle, 213
Cummings, Nancy Cates. *See* Slattery, Nancy Cates (Cummings)
Cummings, Sara Lu (Schuster), 221
Cunningham, Benjamin M., 124
Cunningham, Jean E., 69
Cunningham, Savilla. *See* Torbert, Savilla (Cunningham)
Curtis, Frances Lucy, 55
Curtis, Harvey J., 99
Cuthbert, Floyd Arthur, 131
Czapla, Herma Greer, 101
Czapla, Theodore W., 100

D

Dales, Imogene Laverne, 141
Daly, John, 50
Dambman, Elizabeth. *See* Shafer, Elizabeth (Dambman)
Damrow, Ella Louise. *See* McClendon, Ella Louise (Damrow)
Damrow, Fred and Minnie, 48
Daniel, Margaret Anne (Brennan), 46
Daniel, Richard Lawrence, 46
Darlington, Clinton, 121
Darlington, Etna G., 116
Darlington, Glen, 121
Daugherty, Madge, 94
David, Jeana Louise, 222

Davidson, Martha. *See* Slattery, Martha (Davidson)
Davis, Frank Gifford, 68
Davis, John R., 213
Davis, P. A., 213
Dawson, Mattie E. *See* Wells, Mattie E. (Dawson)
Day, Alma, 46, 195, 269, 273, 292
Day, Charlie, 33, 195, 217
Day, Jennie, 195
Day, Mildred Maurine. *See* Whisler, Mildred Maurine (Day)
DeLand, Niles, 109
Delorme, Decedent. *See* Stull, Decedent Dell (Delorme)
Dewey, Elmer, 180
Dewey, Helen. *See* Ridenour, Helen (Dewey)
DeWitt, Deloris, 130
DeWolf, Ruth Gauthier. *See* Talley, Ruth (DeWolf) Gauthier
Dickey, Doris, 141
Dilgard, Vera Faye, 70
Dillinger Family, 218, 252
Dillinger, Clarence Earl, 129
Dillinger, Della, 159, 252
Dillinger, Edwin N., 206
Dillinger, Inez, 129, 298
Dillinger, Jacob, 129, 298, 330
Dillinger, Jay, 129, 298
Dillinger, Margaret, 129, 298
Dillinger, Robert Lee, 129
Dillinger, Shirley A. (Wells), 206
Dillinger, William Raymond, 129
Doane, May Stewart, 64
Doane, Annie (Stewart), 63, 69
Doane, Leonard Nelson, 69
Doane, Mary Elizabeth, 69
Doane, May S., 69, 206, 320, 324
Doane, Warren, 63, 69, 324
Dobbs, Avis. *See* Prazma, Avis (Dobbs)
Donner Family, 131, 247
Donner, Alice Mae Bloomer, 130
Donner, Bob, 130, 280
Donner, Charlie, 130, 131, 213, 225, 247, 310
Donner, Dale, 130, 278, 300
Donner, Daryle Milton, 130
Donner, Dora, 130, 213, 225
Donner, Dorothy, 130, 286
Donner, Emma (Jenks), 130, 131
Donner, Evelyn Lillie (Whisler) Evans, 104, 130, 178, 186, 197, 221, 225, 277, 279, 286, 292
Donner, Gary Harold, 130
Donner, George, 130, 131, 316, 320
Donner, Harvey Melvin, 225
Donner, Iris June, 131
Donner, John Anseley *Jack*, 130
Donner, Joyce Deane, 130
Donner, June, 167, 293, 300
Donner, Leone Avis, 131, 167, 293, 300
Donner, Loren, 131
Donner, Mary Elizabeth (Pierce), 130
Donner, Melvin Harvey, 130, 178, 211, 213, 225, 300
Donner, Merle (Greathouse), 131
Donner, Mildred Ione, 131
Donner, Vida Fern. *See* McCollam, Vida Fern (Donner)
Donner, Virgil, 131
Donner, Walter, 131
Dowdy, Helen Louise (McCurdy), 160

Dowdy, James Howard, 160
Doyle, Christy, Jr., 166
Drake, Walline. *See* Johnson, Walline (Drake)
Dressback, B. M, 55
Dressback, Ella, 55
Drumm, Hawley D., 85
Dunlap, Frank J., 66
Dunphy, Ellen. *See* Slade, Ellen (Dunphy)
Duvall, Andrew, 144
Duvall, Carroll Weaver, 146
Duvall, Carroll William *Toad*, 144, 147, 178, 221, 267
Duvall, Catherine (Slade), 146, 178
Duvall, Elsie (Weaver), 141, 146, 147, 213, 222, 244
Duvall, Fred, 95, 115, 240, 246, 328
Duvall, Goldie Mae, 144
Duvall, Goldie Mae. *See* Cain, Goldie Mae (Duvall)
Duvall, Helen, 115, 251, 265, 292
Duvall, James Dewey, 141, 144, 146, 244, 267, 268, 324, 328
Duvall, Jean, 115, 265
Duvall, Jephthah Powell, 115
Duvall, Jim, 146, 147, 213, 217, 222
Duvall, John *Johnny*, 242, 279, 280, 282, 283, 287
Duvall, Jorna Jean, 242
Duvall, Kathryn Marguerite, 146
Duvall, Kenneth Richard, 146, 213, 277-279, 286
Duvall, Letha (Gaffney), 115
Duvall, Matilda Ann (Chaddock), 115
Duvall, Merle, 146, 211, 213, 276, 285
Duvall, Nadine Louise. *See* Taylor, Nadine Loise (Duvall)
Duvall, Norma Jean, 146, 282, 287
Duvall, Richard, 144, 146, 178
Duvall, Verlin, 146, 242, 281, 287
Duvall, Vida. *See* Whisler, Pearl Vida (Duvall)
Dygert, Wayne, 126

E

Eads, Florence Eileen. *See* Burr, Florence Eileen (Eads)
Earnest, Blanche, 122, 292
Earnest, Clarence, 122
Earnest, David, 122, 292
Earnest, Genevieve, 122, 292
Earnest, Lois, 122
Eastwood, Violet, 148
Eaton, Cordelia. *See* Spencer, Cordelia (Eaton)
Ebben, Nellie. *See* Weaver, Nellie (Ebben)
Eckdahl, Hilda. *See* Burr, Hilda (Eckdahl)
Eddy, Dolly, 70
Eddy, Emma, 70
Eddy, Evalene Marie (Hester), 70, 71, 269, 273
Eddy, Forest, 70
Eddy, Jennie, 70
Eddy, Josie, 70
Eddy, Mary, 70
Eddy, Minnie, 70
Eddy, Myrtle, 70
Eddy, Philo Bell, 70, 71, 241, 328
Eddy, Rollin, 70
Eddy, Ulysses Height *Hite*, 70, 90, 241, 260, 324, 328
Eddy, Vera G. *See* Speegle, Vera G. (Eddy)

Edminson, Barbara Joy. *See* Heptner, Barbara Joy (Edminson)
Edwards, Anna L. (Ketcham), 201
Edwards, Bernadine May (Heckathorn), 201
Edwards, Charles Leo *Charley*, 201, 278
Edwards, Clara M. *See* VanBuskirk, Clara May (Edwards) Homers
Edwards, Clyde, 201, 213, 276, 277, 286
Edwards, Daphne, 201, 213, 243
Edwards, Henry M. *Deafy*, 201, 213
Edwards, Irene Isabelle. *See* Hladkey, Irene Isabelle (Edwards)
Edwards, Melvin, 201, 213, 285
Edwards, Myrtle Marie, 201
Edwards, Nancy Josephine (Southern), 201
Edwards, Verna Mae. *See* Martin, Verna Mae (Edwards)
Egloff, Sophia Danilewicz. *See* Tholson, Sophia (Egloff) Danilewicz
Eisele, Effie. *See* Ruff, Effie (Eisele)
Eisele, John, 224
Eisele, Rosa Garrison, 224
Eisele, Shirley Ann (Ware), 185, 286
Eisele, William, 185
Elder, Alice Mae (Prazma), 184
Elder, Clarence W., 184
Elder, Lottie Augusta (Weaver), 158
Elder, Max E., 158
Elliott, Harry Robert, 45
Ellis, Mary Lou. *See* Burr, Mary Lou (Ellis)
Ely, Lucinda J., 49
Emerson, George, 123
Emerson, Margaret (Finlayson), 123
Emerson, Sarah Elizabeth. *See* Reed, Sarah Elizabeth (Emerson)
Emperor, Edith Mildred *Billee*, 45
Empire Sheep Company, 6, 9, 16, 38, 310, 312
Engdahl, Bertha Mildred, 132
Engdahl, Dorothy Elaine, 132
Engdahl, Everett, 132
Engdahl, Ioris. *See* Baker, Ioris May (Winland)
Engdahl, James Richard, 132
Engdahl, Leota Viola (Huffaker), 132, 213
Engdahl, Merle, 132, 213, 220, 312
Engdahl, Sanford and Esther, 132
Ensign, George H., 63, 69
Ensign, May S., 69
Ensign, Stewart Ellery, 69
Erickson, Fred, 49
Eskew, Betty Rae, 126
Eskew, Emma Elva. *See* Thomas, Emma Elva (Eskew) Day
Evans, Aileen Mary, 132
Evans, Bernard, 130
Evans, Charles Edgar, 55
Evans, Cloma Hazel, 130
Evans, Evelyn (Donner), 179, 180, 286, 293, 300
Evans, Marie Lucille (Jeffers), 55, 56
Ewing, Lynette, 223

F

Fair, Florence, 133, 251, 292
Faris, Cheri Rae (Simpson), 199
Farmer, Ida, 84
Faught, Shorty, 165
Fear, Anna M. (Brittendall), 151
Fear, Gladys. *See* Ridenour, Gladys (Fear)
Fear, William E., 151

337

343

Wallace, John, 140
Wallace, Lee, 167, 211, 293
Wallace, Ollie May (Vincent), 140, 215
Wallace, Otis, 140, 215
Wallace, Perry, 140, 215, 217, 247
Wallace, Ted, 140, 167, 293
Wallace, Thomas Perry, 140, 318
Walsh, John E., 155
Walsh, Phyllis Evelyn (Talley) Bechtold, 155
Wandler, Ann (Slattery), 97
Wandler, Earl Joseph, 97
Wandler, Richard, 97
Ward, Loretta Bailey. *See* Weaver, Loretta
    Bailey (Ward)
Ward, Ruby Harper. *See* Weaver, Ruby
    Harper (Ward)
Ware, Bonnie Eileen, 185
Ware, Emma, 185, 215
Ware, Fred, 91, 185, 215
Ware, Harriet A. (Powers), 185
Ware, Henry E., 185
Ware, Keith, 185, 211, 270, 285
Ware, Merle Jean, 185
Ware, Patricia Ann (Mohan), 185
Ware, Shirley Ann. *See* Eisele, Shirley Ann
    (Ware)
Wassil, Alvina, 77
Wataznauer, Anna, 116
Weatherby, Sarah. *See* Schofield, Sarah
    (Weatherby)
Weaver, Allen Lynn, 158
Weaver, Alvina C. *See* Sunderland, Alvina
    C. (Weaver)
Weaver, Arthur, 167, 190, 215
Weaver, Charles Barrett, 141
Weaver, Clair Bud, 141
Weaver, Clarence, 141, 167
Weaver, Clay, 324
Weaver, Cora, 141
Weaver, Craig Ritchie, 141
Weaver, Dorothy (McCurdy), 160
Weaver, Elsie, 141, 144, 146, 167
Weaver, Faye (Johnson), 158
Weaver, Foster, 160
Weaver, Gladys Lavonne, 141
Weaver, Hannah, 141, 265
Weaver, Hattie, 59, 72, 215
Weaver, Hattie Jeannette (Black), 158
Weaver, Hattie Josephine. *See* Bryant,
    Hattie Joseph (Weaver)
Weaver, Henry, 167, 318
Weaver, John, 167, 293
Weaver, Joseph, 86, 158, 215, 266, 284, 285
Weaver, LeRoy, 158, 265, 284
Weaver, Lois, 141, 259
Weaver, Loretta Bailey (Ward), 167
Weaver, Lottie Augusta. *See* Elder, Lottie
    Augusta (Weaver)
Weaver, Marguerite and Clay, 146
Weaver, Mary Estella. *See* Crabill, Mary
    Estella (Weaver) Nelson
Weaver, Miles, 141, 215
Weaver, Mina Margarette, 141
Weaver, Minnie, 167
Weaver, Nellie (Ebben), 167
Weaver, Nyle, 105, 158
Weaver, Rich, Mrs., 79
Weaver, Ruby Harper (Ward), 167
Weaver, Sam, 59, 72, 158, 215, 230, 249, 288
Weaver, Solomon, 167
Weaver, Thelma Ellen (Hoxsie), 158
Weaver, William Price, 141
Weaver, Zelma, 141, 259, 265

Webb, Bertha. *See* Thomas, Bertha (Webb)
Webb, James W., 126
Webb, Lucy Jane, 126
Webster, Elizabeth. *See* Moore, Elizabeth
    (Webster)
Weckwerth, Alvina (Rinka), 65
Weckwerth, Charles Henry, 65
Weckwerth, Claire, 44, 45, 65
Weckwerth, Donald, 65, 260
Weckwerth, Dorothy, 65, 260
Weckwerth, Geraldine Louise, 65
Weckwerth, John F., 65
Weckwerth, Mary Louise (Verboncoeur), 65
Weckwerth, Walter, 10, 45, 65, 260, 265
Weenig, Ron, 110
Weese, Delbert, 126, 156
Welch, Alta Pauline (Ridenour), 151
Welch, Bruce Baker, 151
Welch, Lucille M. *See* Hurd, Lucille M.
    (Welch)
Wells, Addie, 78
Wells, Albert, 206
Wells, Benjamin and Calista, 78
Wells, Carrie, 53, 67, 78, 79, 239, 241, 251,
    288, 324
Wells, Cecil Thurston, 206
Wells, Charles, 67, 78, 79, 267, 324
Wells, Edith Mae, 80
Wells, Elizabeth, 78, 80
Wells, Elmer Levi, 206
Wells, Erastus, 53, 67, 78, 80
Wells, Fern Izora, 80
Wells, George, 67, 78, 80
Wells, Gertrude, 78
Wells, Ida, 72, 80, 217, 245
Wells, James Dwaine, 206
Wells, Jesse Bell, 53, 67, 78, 79
Wells, John, 206
Wells, Lorinda A. (Shafer), 53, 78, 80
Wells, Lyla, 141, 251, 261, 265
Wells, Marjorie (Stull), 206
Wells, Mattie E. (Dawson), 206
Wells, Merle Albert, 206
Wells, Rita (Reynolds), 206
Wells, Sabella Mae (Norton) Campbell, 78
Wells, Shirley A. *See* Dillinger, Shirley A.
    (Wells)
Wells, Viola, 78
Wenzel, Kate. *See* Fischer, Kate (Wenzel)
West, Annie May. *See* Lowrey, Annie May
    (West)
Westover, C. A., 83
Wheeler, Elta, 73
Whipple, Sid, 15
Whisler Family, 197, 247
Whisler, Adell (Crandall), 178
Whisler, Alberta, 104, 195, 196, 197
Whisler, Alfred Ashton, 180
Whisler, Allan, 196, 197
Whisler, Arlou Leona, 193, 194, 197, 244
Whisler, Ashton Alfred *Ton*, 104, 136, 178,
    179, 180, 186, 190, 193, 195-197, 217,
    223, 244
Whisler, Barbara, 202, 242, 287, 296, 297
Whisler, Carroll Duvall *Slim*, 102, 178-180,
    186, 189, 190, 191, 193, 194, 197,
    217-219, 223, 226, 231, 244, 267, 296
Whisler, Catherine Margaret *Kitty*, (Wolff),
    164, 178
Whisler, Charles, 104, 195, 196
Whisler, David, 179, 180, 197, 202, 217, 296
Whisler, David and Marge, 104, 136
Whisler, David Leonard, 223

Whisler, David Riley, 144, 178, 202, 221, 222,
    226
Whisler, Dean, 104, 135, 167, 178, 186,
    193-195, 197, 212, 216, 219, 223, 226,
    277, 293
Whisler, Deana May. *See* Orona, Deana
    May (Whisler)
Whisler, Deloris Rose. *See* McGillis,
    Deloris Rose *Dee* (Whisler)
Whisler, Diane (Smallwood), 195
Whisler, Dianne (Brodie), 195
Whisler, Donald Lewis, 202
Whisler, Dorothy Catherine. *See* Heptner,
    Dorothy Catherine (Whisler)
Whisler, Elizabeth Ruth *Betty Ruth*, 223
Whisler, Ellen Joan. *See* Cummings, Ellen
    Joan (Whisler)
Whisler, Elmer, 104, 105, 178, 179, 180,
    183, 195
Whisler, Eurith Arlene. *See* Romel, Eurith
    Arlene (Whisler)
Whisler, Evelyn Lillie. *See* Donner, Evelyn
    Lillie (Whisler) Evans
Whisler, Gary Alfred, 195, 196
Whisler, Helen May (Kottraba), 178, 219, 226
Whisler, Henry, 178
Whisler, Irene Lydia (Heptner), 54, 81, 104,
    178, 193, 194, 197, 219, 223, 284, 296
Whisler, Jenise Cathleen (Wallace), 223
Whisler, Jess Willard, 178
Whisler, Jill Suzanne (Soltesz), 195
Whisler, Joan Barbara. *See* Miller, Joan
    Barbara (Whisler) Kuntz
Whisler, Joanne, 143
Whisler, Joella Anne (Robinson), 195
Whisler, Joseph, 178, 179
Whisler, Josephine, 178, 179
Whisler, Joyce (Norris), 183
Whisler, Judith Ann *Judy*, 223
Whisler, Katherine (Wolff), 223
Whisler, Kathy (McManamen), 195
Whisler, Kevin Lee, 223
Whisler, Laura May, 178
Whisler, Leonard, 104, 167, 179, 180, 186,
    193-195, 212, 223, 226, 276, 285, 293
Whisler, Leonard Pershing, 164, 178, 216,
    223
Whisler, Linda Kay (Lynch) 223
Whisler, Lorna Jean, 159, 174, 193, 194, 242,
    279, 283, 287, 296, 297
Whisler, Lynette (Ewing), 223
Whisler, Marge, 197, 286, 296
Whisler, Margorie Adelle (Mayden), 178, 202
Whisler, Mary Jean (Woods) Brownlee, 178,
    223
Whisler, Mary Pauline *Polly*. *See* Miller,
    Mary Pauline *Polly*
Whisler, Merle Robert *Buster*, 195, 287
Whisler, Mildred Maurine (Day), 104, 178,
    196, 197, 217, 223, 244
Whisler, Nancy Kay. *See* Wolff, Nancy Kay
    (Whisler) Hallman
Whisler, Olive Carroll, 193, 194, 296
Whisler, Patricia (Fitzgerald), 202
Whisler, Pauline Louise. *See* Cook, Pauline
    Louise (Whisler)
Whisler, Pearl, 197, 244
Whisler, Pearl Margaret, 193, 194
Whisler, Pearl Vida (Duvall), 143, 178, 179,
    186, 193, 202, 216, 221-223, 225, 226,
    249
Whisler, Philip Raymond *Phil*, 104, 143,
    183, 195, 244, 279, 286

Whisler, Riley, 50, 178, 179, 186, 193, 216, 223, 225, 241, 249
Whisler, Ross Jennings, 178
Whisler, Rusty Dean, 226
Whisler, Ruth Bell (Johnson), 178, 183, 187, 195, 262, 270, 271, 280, 284, 293
Whisler, Sally Ella. *See* Mellinger, Sally Ella (Whisler)
Whisler School (*photo*), 296
Whisler, Steven Raymond, 195
Whisler, Tina Michele (Knapp), 226
Whisler, Vida (Duvall). *See* Whisler, Pearl Vida (Duvall)
Whisler, Virginia Phyllis. *See* Bolton, Virginia Phyllis (Whisler)
Whitcher, Nellie M., 22
Whitcomb Family, 18, 252
Whitcomb Ranch, 107, 155
Whitcomb, Ansel and Phoebe (Clark), 18
Whitcomb, Elias, 7, 13-15, 17, 18, 24, 38, 171
Whitcomb, Elizabeth. *See* Rivenburgh, Elizabeth (Whitcomb)
Whitcomb, Harold Miller *Little Whit*, 18, 24
Whitcomb, Ida Marie, 18
Whitcomb, Ida Marie. *See* Schnitger, Ida Marie (Whitcomb)
Whitcomb, Katherine (Shaw), 18
Whitcomb, Katya, 18
Whitcomb, Lily May. *See* Hume, Lily May (Whitcomb)
White, Anna Mae *Ann*, 74
White, Cassias M. *C. M.*, 182
White, Clifford, 28, 34, 182, 314
White, Ella A. *See* Cornwall, Ella A. (White)
White, Emma Elvira (Chapman), 182
White, H. Morton, 182
White, Howard, 182
White, Mary G. (Shaughnessy) Thompson, 28, 34, 182, 215, 263
White, Nellie, 182
Whitney, Eli, 123
Whitney, Harriet Emeline. *See* Reed, Harriet Emeline (Whitney)
Whitten, F. M., Ranch, 83
Winland, Clifford R., 220
Winland, Ioris May. *See* Baker, Ioris May (Winland)
Wilke, Louise Beverly. *See* Ridenour, Louise Beverly (Wilke)
Williams, Anna, 66, 216, 326
Williams, Augustus, 66
Williams, Carrie Agnes, 66
Williams, Charles James, 66, 216
Williams, Clara. *See* Riley, Clara (Williams)
Williams, Dora Louise, 66
Williams, Etta Frances, 118
Williams, Harry Adolph, 131
Williams, Henry K., 118, 142
Williams, Irene, 142, 216
Williams, James Leon, 142, 216
Williams, Kenneth Warren, 142, 216
Williams, Louis Happy, 66
Williams, Mary Emma (Lyons) Hamill, 118, 142, 156
Williams, Robert E. *Buck*, 142, 224, 237, 287

Williams, Sylvia Irene, 142
Williams, William James *Billy*, 117, 118, 142, 216
Wilson, Amelia June. *See* Lyons Amelia June (Wilson)
Wilson, John Alfred, 120
Wilson, Leslie T., 166
Wilson, Veva June (Pownall) Doyle, 166
Winland, Vivian E. (Wright), 220
Winn, Lois K., 224
Winter of 1949, 194, 204, 218, 219
Wolfe, Catherine E. Kit (Boyle), 107
Wolfe, Harold, 124
Wolfe, John Eligh *Jack*, 85, 107, 181, 266, 288
Wolfe, John Eligh, Jr., 107, 279, 286
Wolfe, Leslie, 105
Wolfe, Samuel Edward *Sam*, 107, 224, 278
Wolfe, Samuel E., 107
Wolfe, Sarah (Thompson), 107
Wolff, Albert, 94
Wolff, Anna C., 94
Wolff, Catherine Loretta (O'Hara), 94, 164, 216
Wolff, Catherine Margaret *Kitty*. *See* Whisler, Catherine Margaret *Kitty* (Wolff)
Wolff, Donald, 164, 216
Wolff, Dorothy (Felde), 164
Wolff, Edward, 94, 195
Wolff, George, 94
Wolff, Gertrude Ann, 164
Wolff, Harry Lee, 164
Wolff, Hazel (Handran), 164
Wolff, Helen (Schreiner), 94
Wolff, Henry, 94, 164, 216
Wolff, James, 164, 216
Wolff, Joanne Ellen. *See* Brent, Joanne Ellen (Wolff)
Wolff, John, 94, 328
Wolff, Katherine. *See* Whisler, Katherine (Wolff)
Wolff, Louis, 164, 216
Wolff, Louisa (Boehm), 94
Wolff, Loveretta (Boccia), 164
Wolff, Martha Joan (Groves), 164
Wolff, Mary Elizabeth. *See* Shippy, Mary Elizabeth (Wolff)
Wolff, Nancy Kay (Whisler) Hallman, 165, 195, 196, 280, 282
Wolff, Peter, 94
Wolff, Phyllis (Badger), 164
Wolff, Raymond Richard, 164
Wolff, Ruth Agnes. *See* Handran, Ruth Agnes (Wolff)
Wolff, Ruth Marie (Japp), 164
Wolff, Thomas, 164, 216
Wolff, Vincent Henry, 164
Wolff, William Edward, 164
Wondercheck, Joe, 223
Woods, Ben, 98
Woods, Bertha, 99, 291, 292
Woods, Charley, 108, 247
Woods, Clarence, 108

Woods, Edward R. and Mary F., 108
Woods, Franklin R., 99
Woods, Gerald, 108, 291, 292
Woods, Harold, 108, 247
Woods, James, 99
Woods, June, 108, 247
Woods, Lillian, 108, 265, 291, 292
Woods, Lyle Alfred, 99, 133
Woods, Mable Ethel, 99
Woods, Mary (Jungkunz), 98, 99
Woods, Mary Frances (Schmitt), 223
Woods, Mary Jean. *See* Whisler, Mary Jean (Woods) Brownlee
Woods, Maurice Gaylord *Jack*, 223
Woods, Minnie, 108, 247
Woods, Orrin, 98, 99, 249
Woods, Roy, 85, 98, 99, 127, 128
Woods, Ruth JoAnna, 99
Woods, Vern, 99, 128, 249, 250
Woods, Viola, 108
Woolsey, D. D., Mrs., 53
Woolsey, Delos, 67
Woolsey, Durward. D. *Delos*, 67, 78, 324
Woolsey, Genevieve Lorinda. *Jenny*, 67
Woolsey, Gertrude, 67, 79
Wright, Henry H., 181
Wright, James Otis, 73
Wright, Marian (Castle), 114
Wright, Verene Vista, 43
Wright, Vivian E. *See* Winland, Vivian E. (Wright)
Wright, W. R., 50
Wright, Wilma Jean (Lubkin), 181, 328

Y

Young, Fredericka (Reinert), 102
Young, Jacob, 102
Young, JoAnn. *See* Tholson, JoAnn (Young)
Young, Laura Margarete, 102

Z

Zhung, Kate, 221
Zimmerschied, Jack, 97
Zimmerschied, Susan Marie (Slattery), 97

About the Author

Lorna J. Whisler

A love of history, especially local and family histories, propelled Lorna in the early 1970s, before internet, to begin researching the history of her paternal and maternal grandparents who homesteaded in the Rozet, Wyoming, area in 1913 and 1922. Several of her vacations were spent in courthouse basements, libraries, and cemeteries in Colorado, Indiana, Iowa, Nebraska, Virginia, Wyoming, and Nova Scotia, Canada. She never intended putting the data into a book until she received inquiries from several of her cousin's children about their grandparents and great grandparents, and then the possibility of compiling a book for them came to fruition. Her first book is *The Heptner Sisters, Wyoming Schoolteachers*, published by Turas Publishing in 2018.

Retired from U. S. Civil Service, Lorna now lives in Natural Bridge, Virginia.

Both of these books can be ordered from Turas Publishing on its website:

www.turaspublishing.com/product/the-heptner-sisters/
www.turaspublishing.com/product/the-homestead-families/

They can also be ordered from:

Campbell County Historical Society
at the
Campbell County Rockpile Museum
900 W 2nd Street
Gillette, WY 82716

(307) 682-5723

www.campbellcountywy.gov/2169/Rockpile-Museum

347

Rozet, Campbell County, Wyoming

Rozet is an unincorporated community in Campbell County, Wyoming, United States.

Founded in the 1890s, it was likely named for local populations of wild roses.

www.ingramcontent.com/pod-product-compliance
Lightning Source LLC
Chambersburg PA
CBHW062017090426
42811CB00005B/881

9 780999 822157